THE
Oxford Book of American Verse

Chosen and with an Introduction by

F. O. Matthiessen

New York
Oxford University Press

Selections from works by the following poets were made possible by the kind permission of their respective publishers:

CONRAD AIKEN: *Turns and Movies,* copyright 1916 (renewed 1944) by Conrad Aiken; *Priapus and the Pool,* copyright 1922 by Conrad Aiken; *Preludes from Memnon,* copyright 1930, 1931 by Conrad Aiken; *Brownstone Eclogues,* copyright 1942 by Conrad Aiken; reprinted by permission of Brandt & Brandt.

W. H. AUDEN: *Collected Poems,* copyright 1933, 1941 by W. H. Auden; reprinted by permission of Random House, Inc., and Faber and Faber Limited, London.

HOWARD BAKER: *A Letter from the Country,* copyright 1941 by Howard Baker; reprinted by permission of New Directions.

STEPHEN VINCENT BENÉT: *Selected Works,* copyright 1925, 1927, 1935, 1940 by Stephen Vincent Benét; reprinted by permission of Brandt & Brandt.

JOHN PEALE BISHOP: *Collected Poems,* copyright 1933, 1941, 1948 by Charles Scribner's Sons.

HART CRANE: *Collected Poems,* copyright 1933 by Liveright, Inc.

E. E. CUMMINGS: *Collected Poems,* copyright 1923, 1925, 1931, 1935, 1938 by E. E. Cummings; copyright 1926 by Boni & Liveright. *50 Poems,* copyright 1939, 1940 by E. E. Cummings. *1 x 1,* copyright 1944 by E. E. Cummings. Reprinted by permission of Brandt & Brandt.

EMILY DICKINSON: *The Single Hound,* copyright 1914 by Martha Dickinson Bianchi; *Further Poems,* copyright 1929 by Martha Dickinson Bianchi; *Unpublished Poems,* copyright 1937 by Martha Dickinson Bianchi; *Third Series,* copyright 1924 by Little, Brown & Company; all published by Little, Brown & Company. *Bolts of Melody: New Poems of Emily Dickinson,* edited by Mabel Todd Loomis and Millicent Todd Bingham, copyright 1945 by Millicent Todd Bingham; *Ancestors' Brocades* by Millicent Todd Bingham and Emily Dickinson, copyright 1945 by Millicent Todd Bingham; published by Harper & Brothers.

HILDA DOOLITTLE: *Collected Poems of H. D.,* copyright 1925 by Boni and Liveright, Inc.; reprinted by permission of Liveright Publishing Corporation.

T. S. ELIOT: *Collected Poems, 1909-1935,* copyright 1936 by Harcourt, Brace and Company, Inc.; *Four Quartets,* copyright 1943 by T. S. Eliot; reprinted by permission of Harcourt, Brace and Company, and Faber and Faber, Limited, London.

ROBERT FROST: *Complete Poems of Robert Frost,* copyright 1930, 1939, 1949 by Henry Holt and Company, Inc., copyright 1936, 1942 by Robert Frost; reprinted by permission of Henry Holt and Company and Jonathan Cape Limited, London.

v

TO THE MEMORY
OF
THEODORE SPENCER
1902-1949

INTRODUCTION

THERE are so many different ways of making an-
thologies that any anthologist had better begin by stating
the rules of the game as he accepts them. A generation ago
the usual practice was to include as many poets as possible,
represented by two or three poems apiece. That served to
introduce you to all the talents, but had the same confusing
effect as a party that is too big. So my first rule has been:
fewer poets, with more space for each. This means that I
have included only those with a fairly substantial body of
work from which to choose. We have lost thereby several
delicately accomplished lyric poets whose continuing life is
in a few anthology pieces. But we have gained the ability
to see through the shrubbery to the trees, to get a sustained
impression of every figure.

The second rule accepted here is to include nothing on
merely historical grounds, and the third is similar, to in-
clude nothing that the anthologist does not really like, no
matter what its reputation with others. These rules recog-
nize that there are differing reasons for liking a canto from
'The Hasty Pudding' and a canto from Ezra Pound. They
grant that the pleasure of savoring and comparing different
periods is one of the rewards of a lively interest in cultural
history. They merely insist that it is not a sufficient reason
to reprint Lowell's 'Commemoration Ode' for the Civil
War dead solely because it once passed for poetry in Cam-
bridge.

Rule four is: not too many sonnets. They may seem to provide the easiest and neatest way of filling your pages, but they will kill one another. Yet if you limit them rigorously enough to hear what you have, you will find that there have been some unexpected masters and innovators in this form. You will also have gained another of the pleasures for which an anthology is designed—that of comparing different poets on the same ground. Longfellow, like other diffuse talents in other languages, achieved through the restrictions of octave and sestet his nearest approach to concentration. It is less often recalled that one of Poe's latest and most human expressions was the sonnet, 'To My Mother.' Jones Very found its demands exactly right for his severe meditations, and so occasionally did Trumbull Stickney for his more graceful yet no less classically controlled spirit. Robinson used the sonnet to help him formulate the leading aims of his thought and art just before the revolt of the Imagists against outworn patterns drove this form out of fashion for most experimenters. But a traditionalist like Elinor Wylie could still learn, at the very end of her life, how to release her deeper personal emotion through its strictness. By comparison the once far more popular sonnets of Edna Millay seem never to have quite digested Keats. If the last two names appear to lead to the generalization that women in our day have turned to the conventional sonnet more naturally than men, nothing could be more deceptive. The most rebellious of all modern experimenters, E. E. Cummings, has discovered the sonnet's singleness to be an occasionally appropriate channel both for his love and for his satire. The greatest American master of the sonnet, Frost, has used it sparingly, with so many quietly bold innovations that you are hardly aware what his form is until he is finished.

INTRODUCTION

The excursion upon which this last rule led us is hardly anything to what we might fall into through the next one. For rule five runs counter to all Golden Treasuries by holding that, whenever practicable, a poet should be represented by poems of some length. One of the effects of anthologies upon popular taste has been to overemphasize the lyric at the expense of all other genres, to the point of establishing in unreflective minds the notion that the short lyric is the chief surviving poetic form.

The longest poems included here are 'Song of Myself,' 'Snow-Bound,' and 'The Comedian as the Letter C.' These three can begin to indicate what various things long poems may be. Whitman's is essentially a lyrical autobiography, Stevens' is a symbolic meditation upon the relation between art and reality, and only Whittier's is mainly narrative. Many American poets, among them Longfellow and Robinson, Jeffers and Stephen Benét and MacLeish, have written book-length narrative poems, which are necessarily out of the question in an anthology. But mere length is of course deceptive. 'The Waste Land' is less than half as long as 'The Courtship of Miles Standish.' The best of Frost's longer poems are usually not much over a hundred lines, and score by the compactness of their drama.

Length is obviously no criterion of quality. Many readers will prefer Robinson's brief, more intensely dramatic portraits to his discursive psychological studies. Faced with the longest modern poem, Pound's still unfinished 'Cantos,' one may question whether it will ever be more than a series of brilliant fragments. Yet the power to compose works of diverse lengths is one of the signs of mastery of one's craft. Lindsay's occasional ability to sustain a theme has saved a few of his poems from the undisciplined diffusion that overwhelmed the bulk of his production.

INTRODUCTION

The gravity and weight of Eliot's later poems depend upon his experienced control over the long formal meditation.

The sixth and last rule is: no excerpts. This does not apply to loosely joined works like Crane's 'The Bridge' or Sandburg's 'The People, Yes,' from which wholly separable sections may be given in their entirety. But it means not to make anything pass for a whole which is really a part. This has been the hardest rule to live up to, and I regretted it most in dealing with Freneau. Some passages in 'The Beauties of Santa Cruz' and more in 'The House of Night' possess a richness of exotic color and, more particularly, a heightening of macabre terror not to be equaled before Poe. But both these poems are very uneven and run to several hundred lines, so the best I can do is to quote a couple of stanzas from the latter, in the hope that they will lead the reader to search out the other scattered excellences in Freneau's text:

> O'er a dark field I held my dubious way
> Where Jack-a-lanthorn walk'd his lonely round,
> Beneath my feet substantial darkness lay,
> And screams were heard from the distempered ground.
>
> Nor look'd I back, till to a far off wood
> Trembling with fear, my weary feet had sped—
> Dark was the night, but at the inchanted dome
> I saw the infernal windows flaming red.

In the end I was led to break this last rule three times. It was a shock to discover that 'A Fable for Critics' is considerably longer than forty poems by Frost. The passages of lively commentary upon some of Lowell's fellow authors, by which it still circulates, have frequently been detached, and, as is not the case with Freneau's poems, constitute distinct units. It seemed worth making an exception in order to include Lowell at his informal best. Then a comparable situation faced me in Melville's 'Clarel.' That vast 'Poem and Pilgrimage in the Holy Land,' as it is subtitled, is out of print and largely unread. But it contains, here and there, some of Melville's most searching thought upon the dangers threatening American society. These passages, once again, are not dependent upon their meandering context, and they give a unique facet of Melville's rugged verse.

My last violation may be least defensible. In this case I have given only the concluding portion of one of Pound's 'Pisan Cantos.' But the lyric meditation beginning,

> What thou lovest well remains,
> the rest is dross,

rises clear and entire above the latter fragments that Pound has shored against his ruins. These lines, from one of the latest volumes to be published before this anthology was made, are some of the most remarkable in the entire course of American poetry. They show Pound at last reaching a fusion between his great technical gift and a content worthy of his skills. They demonstrate that out of the aberration of his Fascist politics, he has at last experienced suffering and learned humility. They are lines to be borne in mind as we move into the second half of our menaced century.

II

The space allotted to the various poets is not always proportional to their relative importance. The two great pivotal figures in our nineteenth century, Poe and Whitman, present opposite problems. After his early imitations of Byron and Tom Moore, Poe wrote somewhat less than fifty pieces of verse altogether. Selection involves little more than the elimination of several casual occasional poems and of one or two notorious stunts like 'The Bells,' which no adult reader can now face without pain. The viable body of Poe's work, the work from which France would date the beginning of modern poetry, amounts to barely thirty pages.

On the other hand, Whitman's place in American poetry is one of amplitude both of form and of feeling. The decision to include 'Song of Myself' did not spring from a belief that it is his best poem as a whole. But it is his first and most ambitious affirmation, the seed-bed of all his future development. It embraces virtually all his essential moods, and in many passages, both realistic and rhapsodic, it is not to be surpassed elsewhere in his work. Yet it was equally necessary to represent all the subsequent stages of his progression, particularly since his use of the over-all title, 'Leaves of Grass,' for all his collections, has tended to obscure these stages for the general reader. In any author so voluminous, several of the long poems had to be sacrificed, but no main phase has been neglected, from 'Children of Adam' and 'Calamus' through 'Drum Taps' to 'Whispers of Heavenly Death' and 'Sands at Seventy.'

Behind Whitman stands Emerson. As Whitman expressed his debt to Emerson's essay calling for a poet equal to our American possibilities: 'I was simmering, simmering, simmering; Emerson brought me to a boil.' Emerson's fertility is further attested by the fact that his pure eloquence enkindled Emily Dickinson. 'The little tippler leaning against the sun' drew one source of her inspiration directly from his symbolical 'Bacchus.' She, incidentally, can be represented by the greatest number of poems because these scarcely take up a quarter of the pages required for an adequate suggestion of Whitman. Since her books were all published after her death, and her editors have allowed into print all the casual fragments she jotted on the backs of envelopes, it has seemed important to winnow out here only her most finished pieces. We may thus perceive her art at its best.

Emily Dickinson and Emerson both looked back to the seventeenth century. If they could have read Edward Taylor's 'Sacramental Meditation' on the scriptural text, 'My blood is drink indeed,' they would certainly have claimed him for an ancestor. But Taylor, who was the minister in the frontier village of Westfield, Massachusetts, did not print his poems, and it was not until the discovery of his manuscripts in the Yale library in the late nineteen-thirties that we could begin to realize that we had had in America a metaphysical poet in the same sense that George Herbert was a metaphysical. This gives a deeper American tap-root to the revival by Eliot and others of that strain of poetry in our day. Taylor was also like our modern poets in making an astonishing use of bold colloquialisms.

But Anne Bradstreet still remains our first American poet, 'The Tenth Muse, lately sprung up in America,' as her 1650 title page described her. Anne Bradstreet and Edward Taylor were both born in England—though they came to Massachusetts Bay in their youth—and this raises the question of what is meant by 'American' poets. I take it to mean poets whose lives have been deeply shaped by American experience. They must have written in our language, since primitive Indian poetry belongs to an utterly different civilization, and, like the foreign-language verse of our various immigrant groups, can reach us only diluted by translation.

The question arises again in the twentieth century. One of the most hopeful counterforces to blind tension between nations is the increasingly international character of modern art. Since the death of Yeats, Eliot now stands as the leading poet in England, but one came from Ireland and the other from America. And no matter how foreign to most American lives Eliot's Anglo-Catholicism may be, it is still inescapably interwoven with the Puritanism that drove the first American Eliot from East Coker to Cape Ann. Even the latest of his poems included here, 'The Dry Salvages,' is filled with images of the New England coast and of 'the big river,' the Mississippi near which he was born. If Eliot can never stop being an American poet, Auden hardly becomes one until his arrival in this country in the year before the outbreak of the Second World War. But from then on, as he writes about the problems of being a refugee and an exile, and makes his tributes to Melville and Henry James, he belongs to his adopted country as well as to Europe.

That florid title page of Anne Bradstreet's may also be prophetic of another problem in American art. Her ambitious inflated excursions in the manner of Du Bartas are now unreadable, whereas a few simple lyrics about her husband and her children and the burning of her house have something of the homely functionalism of early New England pewter. A problem besetting American writers even before that chimera, the great American novel, was the great American epic. The Connecticut Wits turned out epics wholesale in the heroic days of the early republic, but it is significant that the one among them with the most claim to survival as a poet is Joel Barlow, who, in a fit of homesickness in a Savoyard inn, forgot the pretensions of his 'Columbiad,' and poured forth the humorous realism of his mock-heroic tribute to hasty pudding.

Many other Americans in the seventeenth and eighteenth

centuries wrote verse. For all of them it was a by-product, subordinate to the compelling demands of colonial existence. The cultural historian can learn a great deal about our life from the Puritan tributes to the dead, etched with the same spare grimness as their tombstones, or from the ballads and jingles in the almanacs, or from the impromptu songs and satires that accompanied every stage of the Revolution. But none of their authors had the time or talent to develop into poets. This is not to forget that a volume as long as this one could be devoted to the folk songs that have given expression to so many phases of American development: songs of occupations, in Whitman's sense of the word, from the sailors and mountaineers and lumberjacks, from the riverboat and railroad men, down to the songs about John Henry and Joe Hill and the union workers of yesterday and tomorrow. (Such volumes have, of course, already been collected, by Carl Sandburg, and by John and Alan Lomax.)

The first American to think of himself as a professional poet was Philip Freneau. But his active career as a Jeffersonian radical was spent in journalistic satire. You can relive the major issues of that day in his couplets, which make up in healthy anger what they lack in polish and elegance. But to turn from his eighteenth-century raillery with its stock devices to his sheaf of lyrics is to understand why he came to feel that his real gift had been almost destroyed by an unpropitious time and place. Born almost twenty years before Wordsworth, Freneau possessed, in addition to the more lurid Gothic qualities that we have noted, a sensibility to nature that was also his own.

With the nineteenth century we are among the once familiar household names. What the anthologist needed here was something like the painter's varnish bottle to freshen faded surfaces. The problem was to avoid dulling Bryant's fine sonorous dignity by giving too many examples of his massive but largely unvaried vision of nature. Though no one now is likely to accept Matthew Arnold's estimate of 'To a Waterfowl' as 'the most perfect brief poem in the language,' Bryant was unrivaled—except by Cooper—in conveying the grandeur of American forests and prairies.

With Longfellow my one aim was to smash the plaster bust of his dead reputation, to eliminate the hackneyed inflated one-time favorites, and to demonstrate that from the vast flow of his production there may still be salvaged many shorter pieces which display, especially on the themes of the sea and the night, a quickening imagination and a mastery of delicate versification. His gift for telling a story still enchants far more children than subsequently admit it. But instead of reprinting 'Paul Revere's Ride' or 'The Wreck of the Hesperus' or any of those others which have become part of our American legend, it seemed better to recall his abundance by introducing two of the less familiar 'Tales of a Wayside Inn,' particularly since both could illustrate his often forgotten light humor.

Throughout my representation of this period I have tried to wring the neck of the kind of rhetoric that overflowed into poetry from the oratory of the day, and that was fulsome even there. Holmes, Whittier, and Lowell were the worst offenders. But to those who have been elaborately bored by the forensic periods of 'The Chambered Nautilus,' it may come as a delight to find, in 'Contentment,' Holmes the ripely sophisticated wit, with his mocking acceptance of his desire to build 'more stately mansions' on the water side of Beacon Street. 'Snow-Bound,' though marred by some heavy moralizing, is our most thoroughly realized piece of early regionalism, and preserves with loving detail the essence of a self-contained way of life that the motor highway and the radio have now carried us beyond. Whittier knew the grimmer side of his idyllic picture, as can be clearly seen in the prelude to his companion-piece, 'Among the Hills.' He was as close to the working man as any of our poets have been, and his folk-ballads have an authentic ring. Lowell too, though the air has by now leaked out of his pumped-up lyrics and odes, possessed a knack in some of 'The Biglow Papers' for catching the locutions of common life.

Jones Very was as little familiar to his contemporaries as he is to us. But while Emerson and the other transcendentalists were soaring away from all orthodoxy, Very wrote strictly devotional poems of such firmness in spirit and execution that their place is not to be denied. The place of Thoreau or of Melville is somewhat different. It is hard to be sure whether, without the steadily accruing interest in their prose, either would still be known as a poet. Neither released anything like as much music in his verse as in his best prose. This odd fact must be partly attributable to their feeling unable to draw upon an established poetic tradition in the way they could have in any European country. But both had so much energy of mind that their serious content can occasionally override the bumpiness of the verse. And Thoreau's poems in particular, with what he called his 'Puritan toughness,' round out our central debt to the seventeenth century.

Where I have departed farthest from the judgments of a generation ago is in the case of Lanier. He is still sometimes mentioned as one of our two chief poets of the last half of the nineteenth century, the successor to Poe as Emily Dickinson is the successor to Emerson. But to my ear his dubious analogies between music and poetry in 'The Symphony' serve only to muddy both. The ambitious social thought in his 'Psalm of the West' now seems vague and loosely phrased, and I find him sustainingly moving only in 'The Marshes of Glynn,' and in some of his simpler statements of the desperate problem involved in being a poet in the ravaged post-war South. By contrast, Henry Timrod's few war poems, which state the Southern cause with deep conviction, endure with a classic hardness. I am encouraged in the belief that Timrod is the best Southern poet of his time by knowing that it is also held by the leading Southern poets of our time, Ransom and Tate.

III

The beginning of the twentieth century is marked by the significant contrast between Moody and Robinson. Moody deliberately strove for the grand manner of Milton, in the sense that a traditionalist like Arnold had also striven for it. If Moody had lived longer, he might have worked towards a more colloquial style; but this was the aim of his contemporary, Robinson, from the start. Robinson's main subject was dramatic character, but he was more directly akin to Hardy than to Browning—though still deeply imbued with some of the transcendental values of Emerson. In 'The Man against the Sky,' he made one of the few sustained efforts by an American poet to produce a serious philosophical poem.

With Robinson we have entered the area of sharp contemporary debate. Some readers will think that there is too much Robinson in this volume—but they will not be the same readers who think there is too much Stevens. The most notable fact about American literature in the twentieth century, at least as seen at the halfway mark, is the number and variety of our poets. In the last forty years in particular we have produced for the first time a body of poetry comparable to that of any European country during the same interval. Since the same principle of selection obtains as in the earlier part of the volume, this has meant keeping my choices down to the leading figures in each school. My most recent choices will inevitably appear my most arbitrary; and I am well aware that those included could be easily doubled with other poets of fine quality.

But one of the assistances in making an anthology at the middle of our century is that much of 'the new poetry' is no longer new, and many of its reputations are already established. A fascinating cultural phenomenon is the way in which artists generally appear in fairly compact generations. This has been strikingly true of American poets. Half a dozen years between 1803 and 1809 saw the birth of Emerson, Longfellow, Whittier, Holmes, and Poe. The second wave of our mid-nineteenth-century renaissance was carried forward by young men who were just growing up when Emerson was publishing his first essays. Thoreau and Lowell, Whitman and Melville, all born between 1817 and 1819, were all deeply affected by the ideas first enunciated in 'Nature' and 'The American Scholar.' They were young enough to have reached their full maturity in the decade before the Civil War.

How unpropitious the violently expanding post-war era was for poetry could hardly be witnessed more forcibly than by the bare fact that from the half century that separates the births of Whitman and Robinson only three poets were able to create work comparable to that of poets from our earlier and later history. Of these three, Timrod died of tuberculosis brought on by malnutrition in the Civil War; Lanier, who was finally to die of the same disease, said: 'With us of the younger generation in the South since the war, pretty much the whole of life has been merely not dying'; and Emily Dickinson could survive only by withdrawal into her Amherst room.

Just why the years that inaugurated the Gilded Age should have given birth not only to Robinson and Moody and Masters but also to the pioneer figures in our naturalistic fiction, Norris and Stephen Crane and Dreiser, has not yet been adequately explained. But from then on our poetic generations occurred with extraordinary frequency and volume. From the middle and late 'seventies came Stickney, Amy Lowell, Frost, Sandburg, Lindsay, and Stevens. From the middle and late 'eighties came Williams, Elinor Wylie, Pound, H.D., Marianne Moore, Jeffers, Eliot, Ransom, and Aiken. Those born in the 'nineties could already begin to share in that harvest, and during the years just before and just after the First World War there were probably more poets among American undergraduates than at any other time. That was when John Peale Bishop was at Princeton, Edna Millay at Vassar, MacLeish and Phelps Putnam and Stephen Benét at Yale, when Cummings joined the already long line of Harvard poets, and when Tate became a student of Ransom's at Vanderbilt. The one enormously and violently gifted poet of that decade was Hart Crane, whose random and spasmodic education did not include college at all.

After Crane's birth in the final year of the nineteenth century comes a lapse. Crane, more fully than anyone else, gave expression to the restless contradictions of the nineteen-twenties, but the writers of our more socially conscious 'thirties turned primarily to the novel and the theater, and we had no generation of poets comparable to that of Auden in England. In fact, in the twentieth century so far, the only years that have surely given birth to a considerable number of poets are 1913-1917. This was ironically to mean that Delmore Schwartz, Karl Shapiro, Randall Jarrell, and Robert Lowell, born under the shadow of one war, were to publish their first books just before or during the next one.

Of our living poets of greatest distinction all but a handful are now over fifty, and many are well beyond that. We are therefore in a position to view the main contours of a range of accomplished work. In my selections from the lesser known figures I have consequently been guided by my belief that you can gain your first impression of a new poet most satisfactorily through one of his longer poems, since the act of creating it will have involved more of his mind and art. Bishop, who mastered his craft in the period of the later Yeats and the earlier Eliot, was at his best in his elegy for Scott Fitzgerald; and Putnam, an odd but authentic descendant of Emerson's Bacchus, was at his best in the romantic ballad in which he reincarnated Pan in New England. Robert Penn Warren, who began writing just after Eliot had recovered Donne and Marvell as central sources for our poetry, might have been represented by a series of complexly intellectual poems, but his 'Ballad of Billie Potts' is a bolder attempt to reunite what Yeats called 'the poetry of the coteries' and 'the poetry of the folk.' The kind of poetry represented by Howard Baker's 'Ode to the Sea' stands apart from that of most other modern schools. Strongly influenced by Robert Bridges, this ode is the best example so far of the renewal of the classical poetry for which Baker's fellow Californian, Yvor Winters, has been arguing. Two of our most recent poets, Shapiro and Robert Lowell, may be fruitfully compared through their long elegies, 'For a Dead Soldier' and 'The Quaker Graveyard in Nantucket.'

Some of the juxtapositions made by listing our poets in their generations bear out further the immensely various directions modern art has taken. Crane and Tate were born in the same year, as were Lindsay and Stevens, and Stickney and Amy Lowell. The nearly forgotten Stickney, who spent much of his life in France, is our closest approximation to the *fin de siècle* mood, the mood of Verlaine. A decade after Stickney had died of a brain tumor, Amy Lowell was to wake up to the possibilities of being the energetic spokesman for 'the new poetry.' She threw overboard her nineteenth-century kinsman along with the rest of the Victorians, and was heard to say with gusto: 'I'm the only member of my family who is worth a damn.' It is more than likely that her hearty appetite for younger talents would have revised that statement in favor of her cousin Robert, who was only eight years old when she died.

Imagism, the school to which her efforts gave wider popular advertisement than has been accorded to any subsequent group, created very few lasting works. H.D.'s poems were its only pure products, and they disclose the limitations in its aims. Pound seceded when the movement became what he dubbed 'Amygism,' and Williams was later to say that 'Imagism failed because it lost structural necessity.' Marianne Moore, when she and Hilda Doolittle were undergraduates at Bryn Mawr, went on poetic walks with Williams and Pound, then students of medicine and romance languages at the University of Pennsylvania. Sharing in that generation's devotion to 'objectivism,' she proceeded to develop one of the most lightly subtle techniques in the whole range of modern poetry.

INTRODUCTION

The most obvious way to group our poets is by regions. In our earlier history the great majority wrote in New England, but the twentieth century has brought to expression many other sections of the country. While Robinson and Frost still spoke for 'north of Boston,' Masters, Sandburg, and Lindsay were appearing as a distinct Middle Western group. And the creative awakening of the South, in fiction and criticism no less than in poetry, has been the most notable new feature in our culture since 1920. The 'Fugitive' group from Nashville, in its closely shared view of the meaning of Southern history, has been our most integrated school in the French sense.

But divisions by places of origin are often superficial in our time of uprooted lives. The two leading poets from St. Louis, Eliot and Marianne Moore, have long made their homes in London and Brooklyn. And Jeffers and Eliot, born only a year apart, are separated by something wider than the distance between Pittsburgh and St. Louis, wider even than that between the California and the England to which they have migrated. They are as far apart as Spengler and St. John of the Cross, and find a meeting point only in their equally somber convictions of modern decay.

IV

Looking through the volume as a whole, I trust that my distaste for certain brands of nineteenth-century rhetoric has not caused me to underemphasize our poets' concern with public speech. Our first example here is 'Advice to a Raven in Russia,' Barlow's powerful denunciation of Napoleon's reckless campaign. Emerson's 'Concord Hymn' is as rigorously simple a success in the difficult art of memorial verse as is Timrod's 'Ode' to be sung at the Charleston

INTRODUCTION

cemetery. Although I greatly prefer what Whitman called his method of lyric 'indirection' to his other moods of frontal assault upon 'Democracy, ma femme,' there is no question that he reached his full maturity in 'Drum Taps.' Here his passion for man and his passion for his country were fused, and as he said: 'It delivers my ambition of the task that has haunted me, namely, to express in a poem (& in the way I like, which is not at all by directly stating it) the pending action of this Time & Land we swim in, with all their large conflicting fluctuations of despair and hope.' His chief tribute to Lincoln, 'When Lilacs Last in the Dooryard Bloom'd,' is our most deeply compassionate poem.

Most of the abolitionist verse seems in comparison merely self-righteous. But when Whittier forgot the superiority of Massachusetts to Virginia, and concentrated on an enemy nearer home, such as Daniel Webster, or on the sufferings of the slaves, his verses still resound with something of their original force. Lowell was at his most vigorous in 'The Biglow Papers' denouncing the Mexican War, just as Moody was to be in his denunciation of our equally unwarranted imperialism at the time of the Spanish-American War.

Our twentieth-century poets have also dealt with public issues, to a greater degree than critics have usually recognized. The title of Tate's 'Ode to the Confederate Dead' was deliberately ironic, since the poem's theme is that the modern individual is so cut off from nature and society that he cannot participate in a traditional ceremony. Yet Lindsay's poems for Altgeld and Bryan are filled with the most generous social faiths of their day, and Sandburg's 'The People, Yes,' drawing on his background of socialism, affirms the major aspirations made current by the New Deal. Jeffers and Cummings have written bitterly of both the great wars they have lived through, and MacLeish and Benét, following the lead of the younger Auden, devoted many of their poems after the mid-'thirties to the rising menace of Fascism. Jarrell and Shapiro both served in the last war. But the one dedicated himself to themes of death and loss, and the other's elegy, gravely discerning and sympathetic, reveals an intense awareness of limitations in our national character. In 'The Conscientious Objector' Shapiro also showed his understanding of the reasons that made Robert Lowell choose to go to prison. The most enduring poetry of our recent victorious wars seems to have sprung out of suffering rather than out of triumph.

Any cataloguing of poetry in relation to political events is bound to be inadequate. How inadequate we may judge by realizing that such a catalogue would miss almost entirely the subject matter of, for example, Poe and Emily Dickinson, Frost and Eliot and Stevens. A more inclusive approach would bear in mind that, in the broadest terms, most of our later poets could be described as descendants of Whitman or as descendants of Poe.

The Whitman tradition has been continuously alive ever since Robinson's poem, just after Whitman's death, in tribute to his large powers. Even Pound could grant: 'It was you that broke the new wood.' Sandburg in particular has inherited Whitman's form, though we can see now that Whitman's influence extends far beyond the mere question of free verse. It is bound up with a vision of American promise, with an immersion in the stuff of our common life. In the latter respect poets as different as Williams and Cummings have found Whitman a natural ally. Lindsay responded to much of Whitman's vision, while Masters dwelt on some of the harsher facts that Whitman passed by. It was unfortunate that the 'Ode to Walt Whitman,' writ-

ten by Lindsay's successor Stephen Benét during the worst
days of the depression, was so sprawlingly diffuse. By that
time Jeffers was making a deliberate denial of Whitman's
promise of the West. He contemplated our society 'at the
continent's end,' and sensed only the soft poisons seeping
up the coast from Hollywood.

Crane made the major effort of our day to span the
world of Whitman and our own. He wanted to celebrate
again the splendors and the brute force of Manhattan. But
his vision broke, and destroyed him. As a result a spokesman
for the next generation, Shapiro, could feel that 'When
Whitman had the nation on his brain, He served us ill,'
that his exhortations to America were too generalized and
too cloudy to be of use. Yet Jarrell and Lowell, indebted
at first to Ransom and Tate, have now begun in their criti-
cism to dwell on the need for a broader American tradition,
and to praise Williams for re-establishing in his long poem,
'Paterson,' a poetry that uses, as Whitman's did, every ordi-
nary fact at hand.

The influence of Poe has been more indirect. For, in one
of the oddest turns of literary history, Poe has been as-
similated into American poetry largely through what has
been made of him in France. Eliot's early debts to La-
forgue and Baudelaire were profound, and Valéry, who
continued to insist upon the supreme importance of Poe,
stands behind Tate's 'Ode.' But in retrospect the poet who
seems to have gained most from the Symbolists is Stevens,
who has spoken of his debt to 'the lightness, the grace, the
sound and the color of the French.' Stevens is in the
school of Poe only in the general sense that both conceive
of the poet primarily as craftsman, whereas Whitman and
his closest followers conceive of the poet as inspired seer.
The lines are, of course, often being crossed. Despite his

desire to inherit Whitman's confidence, Crane was a *poète maudit* whose tortured consciousness was much nearer to that of Poe and Rimbaud. The New York of Delmore Schwartz is akin to the *fourmillante cité* of 'Les Fleurs du Mal,' as is the London of 'The Waste Land,' and the Boston of 'Prufrock' and of the 'Brownstone Eclogues' of Aiken.

The devotion to craftsmanship has been shared by Marianne Moore and Ransom and others who would hardly be thought to belong in the Poe tradition. Yet Poe was the first American to dwell upon the principles of art with the kind of strictness that many writers in our chaotic society have again found necessary. Art itself has become a central theme for poets, and in a more obsessive way than when Whitman drafted his loose sketches of the American bard, or when Emerson and Poe symbolized their conceptions of the poetical character in 'Saadi' and 'Israfel.' Pound's most living *personae* are scarcely men and women in Browning's sense, but ingenious 'masks of the actor' which enabled him to assume an iridescent and challenging diversity of guises and attitudes of style, whether of Guido Cavalcanti or Rihaku or Propertius.

Stevens has proved much steadier than Pound, and has become now for many younger poets one of the most encouraging examples in their uncertain trade. Through a life of already more than seventy years he has resisted all the fierce pressures that have distracted or ruined so many of our artists. With a surprisingly mounting fecundity as he has grown older, he has continued to convey, in ever fresh images of elegance and gusto, his conviction of the immense role played by the imagination. The contrast with his immediate contemporary Lindsay suggests again the variety that awaits the reader of our modern poetry, and the futility of attempting any simple generalizations about it.

Lindsay's aims were much broader; he longed, like Whitman, to speak to the people. And in his readings in auditoriums throughout the country he came much closer to doing it than Whitman ever did. But though he made exciting use of jazz rhythms and the cadences of revival hymns, Lindsay's vision of America was far less solidly based, much more sentimental than Whitman's. With the first harsh shock of the depression, the discrepancy between his ideal and the actual struck Lindsay as hard as it did Crane, and neither could bear life longer. In contrast Stevens may seem the withdrawn aristocratic dandy, but he too has known that 'a violent order is disorder.' And as he has meditated on the other arts of music and painting, on the meaning of Picasso's transformation of reality, he has declared that the imagination is in a sense an escape, but an escape to our proper domain. He holds that the poet's role is 'to help people to lead their lives' by making them epicures, since the poet loves 'the world he contemplates and thereby enriches.'

When the history of American poetry in our time comes to be written, its central figures will probably be Frost and Eliot. They again enforce a whole series of contrasts. Frost does not fit conveniently into either the Whitman tradition or the Poe tradition. The title of his first book, *A Boy's Will*, comes from Longfellow, but his closest ancestor is the more authentic regionalist, Whittier. Twenty-five years old by the turn of the century, Frost still belongs to the older America. He is the poet of the country, of man in nature, as Eliot is the poet of the city, of man in the metropolitan desert. Frost is also the poet of individualism, in the Emersonian tradition, whereas Eliot, in the darker vein of

Hawthorne, has been more aware of the weaknesses of individualism, of the need for the individual to find completion in something larger than himself. Frost has voiced a naturalistic faith, which has not always escaped complacence, and Eliot's return to orthodoxy has never quite surmounted the somber weariness of doubt. Neither has been at his best when he has tried to handle immediate political issues, the one suggesting the tactics of a woodchuck, the other those of a broken Coriolanus.

They have in common only what both would consider the leading obligation of the poet: what Frost has called 'the renewal of words' and what Eliot has described as an unflagging devotion to the purity of the language, a devotion to its continuity and yet to its continued modification into a more resilient and more capacious instrument for our ever changing needs. This primary concern with language raises the question so often asked us now by Europeans, whether we have yet developed an American style. Our writers have been preoccupied with the question ever since we declared our national existence. Frost has summed up our peculiar problem:

> The land was ours before we were the land's.
> She was our land more than a hundred years
> Before we were her people. She was ours
> In Massachusetts, in Virginia,
> But we were England's, still colonials,
> Possessing what we still were unpossessed by,
> Possessed by what we now no more possessed.

A wide strange continent could not be assimilated by an act of will. It was not until the time of Freneau and Bryant that our poets could stop thinking about nightingales and begin to hear the whippoorwill in the elm. Emerson was the first American to articulate an organic theory of language and art, opening with the functional proposition that 'Words are signs of natural facts.' He longed to possess the vulgar eloquence of the streets, to emulate Dante in throwing the whole weight of his body into every act of speech. His theory outran his ability to practice it, and only the far earthier Whitman could begin to bridge the gap. Even Whitman, in his sometimes too laborious effort to absorb all of his surroundings and to encompass all of his thoughts, wrote what Emerson had to regard as 'a remarkable mixture of the *Bhagvat-Geeta* and the *New York Herald*.' At the same time Lowell was taking the doubtful risk of writing poetry in dialect. But he believed that 'the Yankee lingo' could at least allow his lines to escape 'that faint perfume of musk which Mr. Tennyson has left behind him,' even if it limited him to gathering 'no better flowers . . . than goldenrod and hardhack.'

The problem has continued to face us. Emily Dickinson, with a more immediate relish for nature than the graver Emerson, owned a language capable of filling to overflowing her tiny quatrains. But when Robinson wanted to range more widely, he was led to experiment with the involved locutions of the psychological novelists. Sandburg may have had a more direct knowledge than Whitman of some of the occupations, but his speech has been far less lyric without having gained the essential exactness. And Cummings' occasional efforts to emulate the tough guy's lingo usually fail to be more than nervous stunts. The Southern regionalists' awareness of the life-sustaining continuity between past and present is best exemplified in the language of Ransom, which is at once colloquial and archaic, homely and witty.

Both Frost and Eliot based their metrics on a comparable desire to bring conversational tones into poetry. Certain critics have observed that poets of other periods have had other desires, Poe and Longfellow no less than Milton. Eliot, looking back now, believes the poetry of the twentieth century to be best characterized by its 'search for a proper modern colloquial idiom.' The generation of Auden in particular has voiced its debt to Eliot for his part in opening new doors and making once again available for poetry what the late nineteenth century had lacked—fresh material from everyday life. But now that 'the common word' has been repossessed, Eliot in his later work has been calling attention to the other partner, 'the formal word,' since only through their union of opposites may we have 'the complete consort dancing together.' After any period of iconoclastic breaking through old forms, there is a 'tendency to return to set, and even elaborate patterns.' This belief of Eliot's would seem borne out not only by his own 'Quartets,' but by Stevens' variations upon a theme in 'The Man with a Blue Guitar,' by Tate's 'Winter Mask,' by Auden's oratorio and Lowell's elegy.

We may not have had an American style in poetry as the French, for example, measure such things. We have lacked until very lately a formed critical tradition in anything like the European sense. But we have produced by now a body of poetry of absorbing quality. If this poetry reveals violent contrasts and unresolved conflicts, it corresponds thereby to American life.

F. O. MATTHIESSEN

Boston, Massachusetts
March 1950

CONTENTS

CONTENTS

CONTENTS

CONTENTS

EDGAR ALLAN POE, 1809-49

JONES VERY, 1813-80

CONTENTS

CONTENTS

CONTENTS

CONTENTS

CONTENTS

CONTENTS

xliv

CONTENTS

CONTENTS

CONTENTS

CONTENTS

CONTENTS

CONTENTS

1

CONTENTS

CONTENTS

CONTENTS

STEPHEN VINCENT BENÉT, 1898-1943

CONTENTS

CONTENTS

CONTENTS

ANNE BRADSTREET

c. 1612-1672

1   *The Prologue*

To sing of Wars, of Captains, and of Kings,
Of Cities founded, Common-wealths begun,
For my mean pen are too superiour things:
Or how they all or each their dates have run,
Let Poets and Historians set these forth,
My obscure Lines shall not so dim their worth.

But when my wondring eyes and envious heart
Great *Bartas'* sugar'd lines do but read o're,
Fool I do grudge the Muses did not part
'Twixt him and me that overfluent store;
A *Bartas* can do what a *Bartas* will,
But simple I according to my skill.

From school-boyes' tongues no rhet'rick we expect,
Nor yet a sweet Consort from broken strings,
Nor perfect beauty where's a main defect:
My foolish, broken, blemish'd Muse so sings
And this to mend, alas, no Art is able,
'Cause nature made it so irreparable.

Nor can I, like that fluent sweet tongu'd Greek
Who lisp'd at first, in future times speak plain;

ANNE BRADSTREET

By Art he gladly found what he did seek—
A full requital of his striving pain.
Art can do much, but this maxime's most sure:
A weak or wounded brain admits no cure.

I am obnoxious to each carping tongue
Who says my hand a needle better fits,
A Poet's pen all scorn I should thus wrong,
For such despite they cast on Female wits:
If what I do prove well, it won't advance,
They'l say it's stoln, or else it was by chance.

But sure the Antique Greeks were far more mild,
Else of our Sexe why feigned they those Nine,
And Poesy made *Calliope's* own Child?
So 'mongst the rest they placed the Arts Divine.
But this weak knot they will full soon untie—
The Greeks did nought but play the fools and lye.

Let Greeks be Greeks, and women what they are,
Men have precedency and still excell.
It is but vain unjustly to wage warre,
Men can do best, and women know it well.
Preheminence in all and each is yours—
Yet grant some small acknowledgement of ours.

And oh ye high flown quills that soar the Skies,
And ever with your prey still catch your praise,
If e're you daigne these lowly lines your eyes,
Give Thyme or Parsley wreath, I ask no bayes.
This mean and unrefined ore of mine
Will make your glistring gold but more to shine.

2   *The Author to her Book*

THOU ill-form'd offspring of my feeble brain,
Who after birth didst by my side remain
Till snatcht from thence by friends less wise than true
Who thee abroad expos'd to publick view,
Made thee in raggs, halting to th'press to trudge
Where errors were not lessened (all may judge)
At thy return my blushing was not small,
My rambling brat (in print) should mother call.
I cast thee by as one unfit for light,
Thy Visage was so irksome in my sight;
Yet being mine own, at length affection would
Thy blemishes amend, if so I could:
I wash'd thy face, but more defects I saw,
And rubbing off a spot, still made a flaw.
I stretcht thy joints to make thee even feet,
Yet still thou run'st more hobling than is meet;
In better dress to trim thee was my mind,
But nought save home-spun Cloth i'th'house I find.
In this array 'mongst Vulgars mayst thou roam,
In Criticks hands beware thou dost not come,
And take thy way where yet thou art not known.
If for thy Father askt, say, thou hadst none:
And for thy Mother, she alas is poor,
Which caus'd her thus to send thee out of door.

ANNE BRADSTREET

3

The Flesh and the Spirit

IN secret place where once I stood
Close by the Banks of *Lacrim* flood,
I heard two sisters reason on
Things that are past, and things to come.
One Flesh was call'd, who had her eye
On worldly wealth and vanity;
The other Spirit, who did rear
Her thoughts unto a higher sphere:
Sister, quoth Flesh, what liv'st thou on—
Nothing but Meditation?
Doth Contemplation feed thee so
Regardlessly to let earth goe?
Can Speculation satisfy
Notion without Reality?
Dost dream of things beyond the Moon
And dost thou hope to dwell there soon?
Hast treasures there laid up in store
That all in th' world thou count'st but poor?
Art fancy sick, or turn'd a Sot
To catch at shadowes which are not?
Come, come, Ile shew unto thy sence
Industry hath its recompence.
What canst desire, but thou maist see
True substance in variety?
Dost honour like? Acquire the same,
As some to their immortal fame:
And trophyes to thy name erect
Which wearing time shall ne're deject.
For riches dost thou long full sore?

Behold enough of precious store.
Earth hath more silver, pearls and gold,
Than eyes can see, or hands can hold.
Affect'st thou pleasure? Take thy fill,
Earth hath enough of what you will.
Then let not goe what thou maist find
For things unknown, only in mind.

Spirit:

Be still thou unregenerate part,
Disturb no more my setled heart,
For I have vow'd (and so will doe)
Thee as a foe still to pursue.
And combate with thee will and must
Untill I see thee laid in th' dust.
Sisters we are, yea, twins we be,
Yet deadly feud 'twixt thee and me;
For from one father are we not,
Thou by old Adam wast begot,
But my arise is from above,
Whence my dear Father I do love.
Thou speak'st me fair, but hat'st me sore,
Thy flatt'ring shews Ile trust no more.
How oft thy slave hast thou me made
When I believ'd what thou hast said,
And never had more cause of woe
Than when I did what thou bad'st doe.
Ile stop mine ears at these thy charms,
And count them for my deadly harms.
Thy sinfull pleasures I doe hate,
Thy riches are to me no bait,
Thine honours doe nor will I love,
For my ambition lyes above.
My greatest honour it shall be

When I am victor over thee,
And triumph shall, with laurel head,
When thou my Captive shalt be led.
How I do live thou need'st not scoff,
For I have meat thou know'st not of:
The hidden Manna I doe eat,
The word of life it is my meat.
My thoughts do yield me more content
Than can thy hours in pleasure spent.
Nor are they shadows which I catch,
Nor fancies vain at which I snatch,
But reach at things that are so high,
Beyond thy dull Capacity.
Eternal substance I do see,
With which inriched I would be;
Mine Eye doth pierce the heavens, and see
What is Invisible to thee.
My garments are not silk nor gold,
Nor such like trash which Earth doth hold,
But Royal Robes I shall have on,
More glorious than the glistring Sun;
My Crown not Diamonds, Pearls, and Gold,
But such as Angels heads infold.
The City where I hope to dwell,
There's none on Earth can parallel:
The stately Walls both high and strong,
Are made of pretious Jasper stone;
The Gates of Pearl, both rich and clear,
And Angels are for Porters there;
The Streets thereof transparent gold,
Such as no Eye did e're behold;
A Chrystal River there doth run,
Which doth proceed from the Lamb's Throne.

Of Life there are the waters sure,
Which shall remain for ever pure;
Nor Sun, nor Moon, they have no need,
For glory doth from God proceed;
No Candle there, nor yet Torch light,
For there shall be no darksome night.
From sickness and infirmity
For evermore they shall be free,
Nor withering age shall e're come there,
But beauty shall be bright and clear.
This City pure is not for thee,
For things unclean there shall not be.
If I of Heaven may have my fill,
Take thou the world, and all that will.

4   *To my Dear and Loving Husband*

IF ever two were one, then surely we.
If ever man were lov'd by wife, then thee.
If ever wife was happy in a man,
Compare with me, ye women, if you can.
I prize thy love more than whole Mines of gold,
Or all the riches that the East doth hold.
My love is such that Rivers cannot quench,
Nor ought but love from thee give recompence.
Thy love is such I can no way repay;
The heavens reward thee manifold I pray.
Then while we live, in love lets so persever,
That when we live no more, we may live ever.

5 *A Letter to her Husband, absent upon Publick Employment*

As loving Hind that (Hartless) wants her Deer,
Scuds through the woods and fern with harkning ear,
Perplext, in every bush & nook doth pry
Her dearest Deer might answer ear or eye:
So doth my anxious soul, which now doth miss
A dearer Dear (far dearer Heart) than this,
Still wait with doubts, & hopes, and failing eye,
His voice to hear or person to discry.
Or as the pensive Dove doth all alone
On withered bough most uncouthly bemoan
The absence of her Love and loving Mate,
Whose loss hath made her so unfortunate:
Ev'n thus doe I, with many a deep sad groan,
Bewail my turtle true, who now is gone,
His presence and his safe return still woo
With thousand dolefull sighs & mournfull Coo.
Or as the loving Mullet, that true Fish,
Her fellow lost, nor joy nor life doth wish,
But lanches on that shore, there for to dye
Where she her captive husband doth espy.
Mine being gone, I lead a joyless life,
I have a loving fere, yet seem no wife:
But worst of all, to him can't steer my course,
I here, he there, alas, both kept by force.
Return my Dear, my joy, my only Love,
Unto thy Hinde, thy Mullet and thy Dove,
Who neither joyes in pasture, house nor streams;
The substance gone, O me, these are but dreams.

Together at one Tree, oh let us brouze,
And like two Turtles roost within one house,
And like the Mullets in one River glide,
Let's still remain but one, till death divide.

> *Thy loving Love and Dearest Dear,*
> *At home, abroad, and every where,*
>
> *A.B.*

6   *Upon the Burning of our House*
              JULY 10TH, 1666

I N silent night when rest I took,
For sorrow near I did not look,
I waken'd was with thundring noise
And piteous shreiks of dreadfull voice.
That fearfull sound of 'Fire!' and 'Fire!'
Let no man know is my Desire.

I, starting up, the light did spye,
And to my God my heart did cry
To strengthen me in my Distresse,
And not to leave me succourlesse.
Then coming out, beheld apace
The flame consume my dwelling place.

And when I could no longer look,
I blest his Name that gave and took,
That layd my goods now in the dust:
Yea so it was, and so 'twas just.
It was his own: it was not mine;
Far be it that I should repine.

He might of All justly bereft,
But yet sufficient for us left.
When by the Ruines oft I past,
My sorrowing eyes aside did cast,
And here and there the places spye
Where oft I sate, and long did lye.

Here stood that Trunk, and there that chest;
There lay that store I counted best:
My pleasant things in ashes lye,
And them behold no more shall I.
Under thy roof no guest shall sitt,
Nor at thy Table eat a bitt.

No pleasant tale shall e'er be told,
Nor things recounted done of old.
No Candle e'er shall shine in Thee,
Nor bridegroom's voice e'er heard shall bee.
In silence ever shalt thou lye;
Adeiu, Adeiu; All's vanity.

Then streight I 'gan my heart to chide:
And did thy wealth on earth abide?
Didst fix thy hope on mouldring dust,
The arm of flesh didst make thy trust?
Raise up thy thoughts above the skye,
That dunghill mists away may flie.

Thou hast an house on high erect,
Fram'd by that mighty Architect,
With glory richly furnished,
Stands permanent though this bee fled.

ANNE BRADSTREET

It's purchaséd, and paid for, too,
By Him who hath enough to doe.

A Prise so vast as is unknown,
Yet, by his Gift, is made thine own.
There's wealth enough, I need no more;
Farewell my Pelf, farewell my Store.
The world no longer let me Love,
My Hope and Treasure lyes Above.

EDWARD TAYLOR

c. 1645-1729

7   *The Preface*

INFINITY, when all things it beheld,
In Nothing, and of Nothing all did build,
Upon what Base was fixt the Lath, wherein
He turn'd this Globe, and riggalld it so trim?
Who blew the Bellows of his Furnace Vast?
Or held the Mould wherein the world was Cast?
Who laid its Corner Stone? Or whose Command?
Where stand the Pillars upon which it stands?
Who Lac'de and Fillitted the earth so fine,
With Rivers like Green Ribbons Smaragdine?
Who made the Sea's its Selvedge, and it locks
Like a Quilt Ball within a Silver Box?
Who Spread its Canopy? Or Curtains Spun?
Who in this Bowling Alley bowld the Sun?

Who made it always when it rises set:
To go at once both down, and up to get?
Who th' Curtain rods made for this Tapistry?
Who hung the twinckling Lanthorns in the Sky?
Who? who did this? or who is he? Why, know
It's Onely Might Almighty this did doe.
His hand hath made this noble worke which Stands
His Glorious Handywork not made by hands.
Who spake all things from nothing; and with ease
Can speake all things to nothing, if he please.
Whose Little finger at his pleasure Can
Out mete ten thousand worlds with halfe a Span:
Whose Might Almighty can by half a looks
Root up the rocks and rock the hills by th' roots.
Can take this mighty World up in his hande,
And shake it like a Squitchen or a Wand.
Whose single Frown will make the Heavens shake
Like as an aspen leafe the Winde makes quake.
Oh! what a might is this! Whose single frown
Doth shake the world as it would shake it down?
Which All from Nothing fet, from Nothing, All:
Hath All on Nothing set, lets Nothing fall.
Gave All to nothing Man indeed, whereby
Through nothing man all might him Glorify.
In Nothing is imbosst the brightest Gem
More pretious than all pretiousness in them.
But Nothing man did throw down all by sin:
And darkened that lightsom Gem in him,
  That now his Brightest Diamond is grown
  Darker by far than any Coalpit Stone.

8   ## *The Joy of Church Fellowship*
rightly attended

I N Heaven soaring up, I dropt an Eare
  On Earth: and oh! sweet Melody!
And listening, found it was the Saints who were
  Encoacht for Heaven that sang for Joy.
  For in Christs Coach they sweetly sing,
  As they to Glory ride therein.

Oh! joyous hearts! Enfir'de with holy Flame!
  Is speech thus tasseled with praise?
Will not your inward fire of Joy contain,
  That it in open flames doth blaze?
  For in Christs Coach Saints sweetly sing,
  As they to Glory ride therein.

And if a string do slip by Chance, they soon
  Do screw it up again: whereby
They set it in a more melodious Tune
  And a Diviner Harmony.
  For in Christs Coach they sweetly sing,
  As they to Glory ride therein.

In all their Acts, publick and private, nay,
  And secret too, they praise impart.
But in their Acts Divine, and Worship, they
  With Hymns do offer up their Heart.
  Thus in Christs Coach they sweetly sing,
  As they to Glory ride therein.

Some few not in; and some whose Time and Place
   Block up this Coaches way, do goe
As Travellers afoot: and so do trace
   The Road that gives them right thereto;
   While in this Coach these sweetly sing,
   As they to Glory ride therein.

9   *An Address to the Soul Occasioned*
              by a Rain

Y E Flippering Soule,
   Why dost between the Nippers dwell?
Not stay, nor goe. Not yea, nor yet Controle.
   Doth this doe well?
      Rise journy'ng when the skies fall weeping Showers,
      Not o're nor under th' Clouds and Cloudy Powers.

Not yea, nor noe:
   On tiptoes thus? Why sit on thorns?
Resolve the matter: Stay thyselfe or goe:
   Ben't both wayes born.
      Wager thyselfe against thy surplic'de see,
      And win thy Coate, or let thy Coate win thee.

Is this th' Effect
   To leaven thus my Spirits all?
To make my heart a Crabtree Cask direct?
   A Verjuc'te Hall?
      As Bottle Ale, whose Spirits prison'd must
      When jogg'd, the bung with Violence doth burst?

Shall I be made
   A sparkling Wildfire Shop,
Where my dull Spirits at the Fireball trade
   Do frisk and hop?
         And while the Hammer doth the Anvill pay,
         The fire ball matter sparkles ev'ry way.

One sorry fret,
   An anvill Sparke, rose higher,
And in thy Temple falling, almost set
   The house on fire.
         Such fireballs dropping in the Temple Flame
         Burns up the building: Lord, forbid the same.

10   *Upon a Spider Catching a Fly*

   THOU sorrow, venom Elfe:
      Is this thy play,
   To spin a web out of thyselfe
      To Catch a Fly?
         For why?

   I saw a pettish wasp
      Fall foule therein:
   Whom yet thy whorle pins did not hasp
      Lest he should fling
         His sting.

   But as afraid, remote
      Didst stand hereat,

And with thy little fingers stroke
  And gently tap
    His back.

Thus gently him didst treate
  Lest he should pet,
And in a froppish, aspish heate
  Should greatly fret
    Thy net.

Whereas the silly Fly,
  Caught by its leg,
Thou by the throate took'st hastily,
  And 'hinde the head
    Bite Dead.

This goes to pot, that not
  Nature doth call.
Strive not above what strength hath got,
  Lest in the brawle
    Thou fall.

This Fray seems thus to us:
  Hells Spider gets
His intrails spun to whip Cords thus,
  And wove to nets,
    And sets.

To tangle Adams race
  In's stratagems
To their Destructions, Spoil'd, made base
  By venom things,
    Damn'd Sins.

But mighty, Gracious Lord,
   Communicate
Thy Grace to breake the Cord; afford
   Us Glorys Gate
      And State.

We'll Nightingaile sing like,
   When pearcht on high
In Glories Cage, thy glory, bright:
   Yea, thankfully,
      For joy.

11 *Huswifery*

MAKE me, O Lord, thy Spinning Wheele compleat;
   Thy Holy Worde my Distaff make for mee.
Make mine Affections thy Swift Flyers neate,
   And make my Soule thy holy Spoole to bee.
   My Conversation make to be thy Reele,
   And reele the yarn thereon spun of thy Wheele.

Make me thy Loome then, knit therein this Twine:
   And make thy Holy Spirit, Lord, winde quills:
Then weave the Web thyselfe. The yarn is fine.
   Thine Ordinances make my Fulling Mills.
   Then dy the same in Heavenly Colours Choice,
   All pinkt with Varnish't Flowers of Paradise.

Then cloath therewith mine Understanding, Will,
   Affections, Judgment, Conscience, Memory;

My Words and Actions, that their shine may fill
My wayes with glory and thee glorify.
Then mine apparell shall display before yee
That I am Cloathd in Holy robes for glory.

12   *The Reflexion*

CANTICLES II: I: I am the rose of Sharon.

LORD, art thou at the Table Head above
Meat, Med'cine, Sweetness, sparkling Beautys, to
Enamour Souls with Flaming Flakes of Love,
And not my Trencher, nor my Cup o'reflow?
Ben't I a bidden guest? Oh! sweat mine Eye:
O'reflow with Teares: Oh! draw thy fountains dry.

Shall I not smell thy sweet, oh! Sharons Rose?
Shall not mine Eye salute thy Beauty? Why?
Shall thy sweet leaves their Beautious sweets upclose?
As halfe ashamde my sight should on them ly?
Woe's me! For this my sighs shall be in grain,
Offer'd on Sorrows Altar for the same.

Had not my Soule's, thy Conduit, Pipes stopt bin
With mud, what Ravishment would'st thou Convay?
Let Graces Golden Spade dig till the Spring
Of tears arise, and cleare this filth away.
Lord, let thy Spirit raise my sighings till
These Pipes my soule do with thy sweetness fill.

20

EDWARD TAYLOR

Earth once was Paradise of Heaven below,
  Till inkefac'd sin had it with poyson stockt;
And Chast this Paradise away into
  Heav'ns upmost Loft, and it in Glory Lockt.
  But thou, sweet Lord, hast with thy golden Key
  Unlockt the Doore, and made a golden day.

Once at thy Feast, I saw thee Pearle-like stand
  'Tween Heaven and Earth, where Heavens Bright glory
      all
In streams fell on thee, as a floodgate and
  Like Sun Beams through thee on the World to Fall.
  Oh! Sugar sweet then! My Deare sweet Lord, I see
  Saints Heaven-lost Happiness restor'd by thee.

Shall Heaven and Earth's bright Glory all up lie,
  Like Sun Beams bundled in the sun in thee?
Dost thou sit Rose at Table Head, where I
  Do sit, and Carv'st no morsell sweet for mee?
  So much before, so little now! Sprindge, Lord,
  Thy Rosie Leaves, and me their Glee afford.

Shall not thy Rose my Garden fresh perfume?
  Shall not thy Beauty my dull Heart assaile?
Shall not thy golden gleams run through this gloom?
  Shall my black Velvet Mask thy fair Face Vaile?
  Pass o're my Faults: shine forth, bright sun; arise!
  Enthrone thy Rosy-selfe within mine Eyes.

Sacramental Meditations

VI

<small>CANTICLES II: I:</small> I am . . . the lily of the valleys.

AM I thy gold? Or Purse, Lord, for thy Wealth;
    Whether in mine or mint refinde for thee?
Ime counted so, but count me o're thyselfe,
    Lest gold washt face, and brass in Heart I bee.
    I Feare my Touchstone touches when I try
    Mee, and my Counted Gold too overly.

Am I new minted by thy Stamp indeed?
    Mine Eyes are dim; I cannot clearly see.
Be thou my Spectacles that I may read
    Thine Image and Inscription stampt on mee.
    If thy bright Image do upon me stand,
    I am a Golden Angell in thy hand.

Lord, make my Soule thy Plate: thine Image bright
    Within the Circle of the same enfoile.
And on its brims in golden Letters write
    Thy Superscription in an Holy style.
    Then I shall be thy Money, thou my Hord:
    Let me thy Angell bee, bee thou my Lord.

VIII

<small>JOHN VI: 51:</small> I am the living bread.

I KENNING through Astronomy Divine
    The Worlds bright Battlement, wherein I spy

EDWARD TAYLOR

A Golden Path my Pensill cannot line
   From that bright Throne unto my Threshold ly.
   And while my puzzled thoughts about it pore,
   I find the Bread of Life in't at my doore.

When that this Bird of Paradise put in
   This Wicker Cage (my Corps) to tweedle praise
Had peckt the Fruite forbid: and so did fling
   Away its Food, and lost its golden dayes,
   It fell into Celestiall Famine sore,
   And never could attain a morsell more.

Alas! alas! Poore Bird, what wilt thou doe?
   This Creatures field no food for Souls e're gave:
And if thou knock at Angells dores, they show
   An Empty Barrell: they no soul bread have.
   Alas! Poore Bird, the Worlds White Loafe is done,
   And cannot yield thee here the smallest Crumb.

In this sad state, Gods Tender Bowells run
   Out streams of Grace: And he to end all strife,
The Purest Wheate in Heaven, his deare-dear Son
   Grinds, and kneads up into this Bread of Life:
   Which Bread of Life from Heaven down came and
      stands
   Disht in thy Table up by Angells Hands.

Did God mould up this Bread in Heaven, and bake,
   Which from his Table came, and to thine goeth?
Doth he bespeake thee thus: This Soule Bread take;
   Come, Eate thy fill of this, thy Gods White Loafe?
   Its Food too fine for Angells; yet come, take
   And Eate thy fill! Its Heavens Sugar Cake.

What Grace is this knead in this Loafe? This thing
  Souls are but petty things it to admire.
Yee Angells, help: This fill would to the brim
  Heav'ns whelm'd-down Chrystall meele Bowle, yea and
      higher.
  This Bread of Life dropt in thy mouth doth Cry:
  Eate, Eate me, Soul, and thou shalt never dy.

X

JOHN VI: 55: For my flesh is meat indeed, and my blood
is drink indeed.

STUPENDIOUS Love! All Saints Astonishment!
  Bright Angells are black Motes in this Suns Light.
Heav'ns canopy, the Pantile to Gods tent,
  Can't cover't neither with its breadth nor height.
Its Glory doth all Glory else outrun,
  Beams of bright Glory to't are motes i'th'sun.

My Soule had caught an Ague, and like Hell
  Her thirst did burn: she to each spring did fly,
But this bright blazing Love did spring a Well
  Of Aqua-Vitae in the Deity,
  Which on the top of Heav'ns high Hill out burst
  And down came running thence t'allay my thirst.

But how it came, amazeth all communion.
  Gods onely Son doth hug Humanity
Into his very person. By which Union
  His Humane Veans its golden gutters ly.

And rather than my Soule should dy by thirst,
These Golden Pipes, to give me drink, did burst.

This Liquour brew'd, thy sparkling Art Divine,
  Lord, in thy Chrystall Vessells did up tun,
(Thine Ordinances) which all Earth o're shine,
  Set in thy rich Wine Cellars out to run.
  Lord, make thy Butlar draw, and fill with speed
  My Beaker full: for this is drink indeed.

Whole Buts of this blesst Nectar shining stand
  Lockt up with Saph'rine Taps, whose splendid Flame
Too bright do shine for brightest Angells hands
  To touch, my Lord. Do thou untap the same.
  Oh! make thy Chrystall Buts of Red Wine bleed
  Into my Chrystall Glass this Drink-Indeed.

How shall I praise thee then? My blottings jar
  And wrack my Rhymes to pieces in thy praise.
Thou breath'st thy Vean still in my Porringer,
  To lay my thirst, and fainting spirits raise.
  Thou makest Glory's chiefest Grape to bleed
  Into my cup: And this is Drink-Indeed.

Nay, though I make no pay for this Red Wine,
  And scarce do say I thank ye for't; strange thing!
Yet were thy silver skies my Beer bowle fine,
  I finde my Lord would fill it to the brim.
  Then make my life, Lord, to thy praise proceed
  For thy rich blood, which is my Drink-Indeed.

XXXVIII

1 JOHN II: 1: And if any man sin, we have an advocate with the Father.

OH! What a thing is Man? Lord, Who am I?
That thou shouldst give him Law (Oh! golden Line)
To regulate his Thoughts, Words, Life thereby:
    And judge him wilt thereby too in thy time.
    A Court of Justice thou in heaven holdst,
    To try his Case while he's here housd on mould.

How do thy Angells lay before thine eye
    My Deeds both White and Black I dayly doe?
How doth thy Court thou Pannellst there them try?
    But flesh complains. What right for this? let's know!
    For right or wrong, I can't appeare unto't.
    And shall a sentence Pass on such a suite?

Soft; blemish not this golden Bench, or place.
    Here is no Bribe, nor Colourings to hide,
Nor Pettifogger to befog the Case;
    But Justice hath her Glory here well tri'de:
    Her spotless Law all spotted Cases tends;
    Without Respect or Disrespect them ends.

God's Judge himselfe, and Christ Atturny is;
    The Holy Ghost Regesterer is founde.
Angells the sergeants are, all Creatures kiss
    The booke, and doe as Evidence abounde.
    All Cases pass according to pure Law,
    And in the sentence is no Fret nor flaw.

What saith, my soule? Here all thy Deeds are tri'de.
　　Is Christ thy Advocate to pleade thy Cause?
Art thou his Client? Such shall never slide.
　　He never lost his Case: he pleads such Laws
　　As Carry do the same, nor doth refuse
　　The Vilest sinners Case that doth him Choose.

This is his Honour, not Dishonour: nay,
　　No Habeas-Corpus 'gainst his Clients came;
For all their Fines his Purse doth make down pay.
　　He Non-Suites Satan's suite or Casts the same.
　　He'll plead thy Case, and not accept a Fee.
　　He'll plead Sub Forma Pauperis for thee.

My Case is bad. Lord, be my Advocate.
　　My sin is red: I'me under Gods Arrest.
Thou hast the Hit of Pleading; plead my state.
　　Although it's bad, thy Plea will make it best.
　　If thou wilt plead my Case before the King,
　　I'le Waggon Loads of Love and Glory bring.

XL

I JOHN II: 21: And he is the propitiation for our sins;
and not for ours only, but also for the sins of the whole
world.

STILL I complain; I am complaining still.
　　O woe is me! Was ever Heart like mine?
A Sty of Filth, a Trough of Washing-Swill,
　　A Dunghill Pit, a Puddle of mere Slime,
　　A Nest of Vipers, Hive of Hornets-stings,
　　A Bag of Poyson, Civit-Box of Sins.

Was ever Heart like mine? So bad? black? vile?
  Is any Divell blacker? Or can Hell
Produce its match? It is the very soile
  Where Satan reads his charms and sets his spell;
  His Bowling Ally where he sheeres his fleece
  At Nine Pins, Nine Holes, Morrice, Fox and Geese.

His Palace Garden where his courtiers walke;
  His Jewells cabbinet. Here his caball
Do sham it and truss up their Privie talk
  In Fardells of Consults and bundles all.
  His shambles and his Butchers stalls herein.
  It is the Fuddling Schoole of every sin.

Was ever Heart like mine? Pride, Passion fell,
  Ath'ism, Blasphemy pot, pipe it, dance,
Play Barlybreaks, and at last couple in Hell:
  At Cudgells, Kit-Cat, Cards and Dice here prance:
  At Noddy, Ruff-and-Trump, Jink, Post and Pare,
  Put, One-and-thirty, and such other ware.

Grace shuffled is away; Patience oft sticks
  Too soon, or draws itselfe out, and's out put.
Faith's over-trumpt, and oft doth lose her tricks.
  Repentance's chalkt up Noddy, and out shut.
  They Post and Pare off Grace thus, and its shine.
  Alas! alas! was ever Heart like mine?

Sometimes methinks the serpents head I mall:
  Now all is still: my spirits do recreute.
But ere my Harpe can tune sweet praise, they fall
  On me afresh and tare me at my Root.
  They bite like Badgers now: nay worse, although
  I tooke them toothless sculls, rot long agoe.

EDWARD TAYLOR

My Reason now's more than my sense, I feele
  I have more sight than sense: Which seems to bee
A Rod of sunbeams t'whip mee for my steele.
  My Spirits spiritless and dull in mee
  For my dead prayerless Prayers: the Spirits winde
  Scarce blows my mill about. I little grinde.

Was ever Heart like mine? My Lord, declare
  I know not what to do: What shall I doe?
I wonder, split I don't upon Despare.
  Its grace's wonder that I wrack not so.
  I faintly shun't, although I see this case
  Would say my sin is greater than thy grace.

Hope's Day-peep down hence through this chinck, Christs
    name,
  Propitiation is for sins. Lord, take
It so for mine. Thus quench thy burning flame
  In that clear stream that from his side forth brake.
  I can no comfort take while thus I see
  Hells cursed Imps thus jetting strut in mee.

Lord, take thy sword: these Anakims destroy;
  Then soake my soule in Zions Bucking-tub
With Holy Soap, and Nitre, and rich Lye.
  From all Defilement me cleanse, wash, and rub.
  Then wrince, and wring mee out till th'water fall
  As pure as in the Well: not foule at all.

And let thy Sun shine on my Head out cleare.
  And bathe my Heart within its radient beams:

Thy Christ make my Propitiation Deare:
   Thy Praise shall from my Heart breake forth in streams.
   This reeching Vertue of Christs blood will quench
   Thy Wrath, slay Sin, and in thy Love mee bench.

LVI

JOHN XV: 24: **If I had not done among them the works
which none other man did, they had not had sin: but
now have they both seen and hated both me and my
Father.**

SHOULD I with silver tooles delve through the Hill
   Of Cordilera for rich thoughts, that I
My Lord, might weave with an angelick skill
   A Damask Web of Velvet Verse, thereby
   To deck thy Works up, all my Web would run
   To rags and jags: so snick-snarld to the thrum.

Thine are so rich: within, without refin'd:
   No worke like thine. No Fruits so sweete that grow
On th' trees of righteousness of Angell kinde,
   And Saints, whose limbs reev'd with them bow down
      low.
   Should I search ore the Nutmeg Gardens shine,
   Its fruits in flourish are but skegs to thine.

The Clove, when in its White-green'd blossoms shoots,
   Some Call the pleasantst scent the World doth show,
None Eye e're saw, nor nose e're smelt such Fruits,
   My Lord, as thine, Thou Tree of Life in'ts blow.
   Thou Rose of Sharon, Vallies Lilly true,
   Thy Fruits most sweet and glorious ever grew.

EDWARD TAYLOR

Thou art a Tree of Perfect nature trim,
  Whose golden lining is of perfect Grace,
Perfum'de with Deity unto the brim,
  Whose fruits, of the perfection, grow, of Grace.
  Thy Buds, thy Blossoms, and thy fruits adorne
  Thyselfe and Works, more shining than the morn.

Art, natures Ape, hath many brave things done:
  As th' Pyramids, the Lake of Meris vast,
The Pensile Orchards built in Babylon,
  Psammitich's Labyrinth, (arts Cramping task)
  Archimedes his Engins made for war,
  Romes Golden House, Titus his Theater.

The Clock of Strasburgh, Dresdens Table-sight,
  Regsamonts Fly of Steele about that flew,
Turrian's Wooden Sparrows in a flight,
  And th' Artificiall man Aquinas slew,
  Mark Scaliota's Lock and Key and Chain
  Drawn by a Flea, in our Queen Betties reign.

Might but my pen in natures Inventory
  Its progress make, 't might make such things to jump,
All which are but Inventions Vents or glory:
  Wits Wantonings, and Fancies frollicks plump:
  Within whose maws lies buried Times, and Treasures,
  Embalmed up in thick dawbd sinfull pleasures.

Nature doth better work than Art, yet thine
  Out vie both works of nature and of Art.
Natures Perfection and the perfect shine
  Of Grace attend thy deed in ev'ry part.
  A Thought, a Word, and Worke of thine, will kill
  Sin, Satan, and the Curse: and Law fulfill.

EDWARD TAYLOR

Thou art the Tree of Life in Paradise,
  Whose lively branches are with Clusters hung
Of Lovely fruits, and Flowers more sweet than spice.
  Bende down to us, and doe outshine the sun.
  Delightfull unto God, doe man rejoyce
  The pleasant'st fruits in all Gods Paradise.

Lord, feed mine eyes then with thy Doings rare,
  And fat my heart with these ripe fruites thou bear'st;
Adorn my Life well with thy works; make faire
  My Person with apparrell thou prepar'st.
  My Boughs shall loaded bee with fruits that spring
  Up from thy Works, while to thy praise I sing.

PHILIP FRENEAU

1752-1832

14   *To an Author*

Y OUR leaves bound up compact and fair
In neat array at length prepare
To pass their hour on learning's stage,
To meet the surly critic's rage;
The statesman's slight, the smatterer's sneer—
Were these, indeed, your only fear,
You might be tranquil and resigned:
What most should touch your fluttering mind
Is that, few critics will be found
To sift your works, and deal the wound.

Thus, when one fleeting year is past
On some bye-shelf your book is cast—
Another comes, with something new,
And drives you fairly out of view:
With some to praise, but more to blame,
The mind returns to—whence it came;
And some alive, who scarce could read
Will publish satires on the dead.

Thrice happy Dryden, who could meet
Some rival bard in every street!
When all were bent on writing well
It was some credit to excel:—

Thrice happy Dryden, who could find
A Milbourne for his sport designed—
And Pope, who saw the harmless rage
Of Dennis bursting o'er his page
Might justly spurn the critic's aim,
Who only helped to swell his fame.

On these bleak climes by Fortune thrown,
Where rigid Reason reigns alone,
Where lovely Fancy has no sway,
Nor magic forms about us play—
Nor nature takes her summer hue
Tell me, what has the muse to do?—

An age employed in edging steel
Can no poetic raptures feel;
No solitude's attracting power,
No leisure of the noon day hour,
No shaded stream, no quiet grove
Can this fantastic century move;

The muse of love in no request—
Go—try your fortune with the rest,
One of the nine you should engage,
To meet the follies of the age:—

On one, we fear, your choice must fall—
The least engaging of them all—
Her visage stern—an angry style—
A clouded brow—malicious smile—
A mind on murdered victims placed—
She, only she, can please the taste!

t.5   *Stanzas*
*Occasioned by the Ruins of a Country Inn, unroofed and
blown down in a storm*

WHERE now these mingled ruins lie
    A temple once to Bacchus rose,
Beneath whose roof, aspiring high,
    Full many a guest forgot his woes:

No more this dome, by tempests torn,
    Affords a social safe retreat;
But ravens here, with eye forlorn,
    And clustering bats henceforth will meet.

The Priestess of this ruined shrine,
    Unable to survive the stroke,
Presents no more the ruddy wine,
    Her glasses gone, her china broke.

The friendly Host, whose social hand
   Accosted strangers at the door,
Has left at length his wonted stand,
   And greets the weary guest no more.

Old creeping Time, that brings decay,
   Might yet have spared these mouldering walls,
Alike beneath whose potent sway
   A temple or a tavern falls.

Is this the place where mirth and joy,
   Coy nymphs and sprightly lads were found?
Indeed! no more the nymphs are coy,
   No more the flowing bowls go round.

Is this the place where festive song
   Deceived the wintry hours away?
No more the swains the tune prolong,
   No more the maidens join the lay:

Is this the place where Nancy slept
   In downy beds of blue and green?—
Dame Nature here no vigils kept,
   No cold unfeeling guards were seen.

'Tis gone!—and Nancy tempts no more,
   Deep, unrelenting silence reigns;
Of all that pleased, that charmed before,
   The tottering chimney scarce remains!

Ye tyrant winds, whose ruffian blast
   Through doors and windows blew too strong,
And all the roof to ruin cast,
   The roof that sheltered us so long.

Your wrath appeased, I pray be kind
   If Mopsus should the dome renew;
That we again may quaff his wine,
   Again collect our jovial crew.

16   *The Wild Honey Suckle*

FAIR flower, that dost so comely grow,
Hid in this silent, dull retreat,
Untouched thy honied blossoms blow,
Unseen thy little branches greet:
     No roving foot shall crush thee here,
     No busy hand provoke a tear.

By Nature's self in white arrayed,
She bade thee shun the vulgar eye,
And planted here the guardian shade,
And sent soft waters murmuring by;
     Thus quietly thy summer goes,
     Thy days declining to repose.

Smit with those charms, that must decay,
I grieve to see your future doom;
They died—nor were those flowers more gay,
The flowers that did in Eden bloom;
     Unpitying frosts, and Autumn's power
     Shall leave no vestige of this flower.

From morning suns and evening dews
At first thy little being came:
If nothing once, you nothing lose,

For when you die you are the same;
    The space between, is but an hour,
    The frail duration of a flower.

17   *The Indian Student*

OR, FORCE OF NATURE

FROM Susquehanna's farthest springs
Where savage tribes pursue their game,
(His blanket tied with yellow strings,)
A shepherd of the forest came.

Not long before, a wandering priest
Expressed his wish, with visage sad—
'Ah, why (he cried) in Satan's waste,
'Ah, why detain so fine a lad?

'In white-man's land there stands a town
'Where learning may be purchased low—
'Exchange his blanket for a gown,
'And let the lad to college go.'—

From long debate the council rose,
And viewing Shalum's tricks with joy
To Cambridge Hall, o'er wastes of snows,
They sent the copper-coloured boy.

One generous chief a bow supplied,
This gave a shaft, and that a skin;
The feathers, in vermillion dyed,
Himself did from a turkey win:

37

Thus dressed so gay, he took his way
O'er barren hills, alone, alone!
His guide a star, he wandered far,
His pillow every night a stone.

At last he came, with foot so lame,
Where learned men talk heathen Greek,
And Hebrew lore is gabbled o'er,
To please the Muses,—twice a week.

Awhile he writ, awhile he read,
Awhile he conned their grammar rules—
(An Indian savage so well bred
Great credit promised to the schools.)

Some thought he would in law excel,
Some said in physic he would shine;
And one that knew him, passing well,
Beheld, in him, a sound Divine.

But those of more discerning eye
Even then could other prospects show,
And saw him lay his Virgil by
To wander with his dearer bow.

The tedious hours of study spent,
The heavy-moulded lecture done,
He to the woods a hunting went,
Through lonely wastes he walked, he run.

No mystic wonders fired his mind;
He sought to gain no learned degree,
But only sense enough to find
The squirrel in the hollow tree.

PHILIP FRENEAU

The shady bank, the purling stream,
The woody wild his heart possessed,
The dewy lawn, his morning dream
In fancy's gayest colours dressed.

'And why (he cried) did I forsake
'My native wood for gloomy walls;
'The silver stream, the limpid lake
'For musty books and college halls.

'A little could my wants supply—
'Can wealth and honour give me more;
'Or, will the sylvan god deny
'The humble treat he gave before?

'Let seraphs gain the bright abode,
'And heaven's sublimest mansions see—
'I only bow to Nature's God—
'The land of shades will do for me.

'These dreadful secrets of the sky
'Alarm my soul with chilling fear—
'Do planets in their orbits fly,
'And is the earth, indeed, a sphere?

'Let planets still their course pursue,
'And comets to the centre run —
'In Him my faithful friend I view,
'The image of my God—the Sun.

'Where Nature's ancient forests grow,
'And mingled laurel never fades,
'My heart is fixed;—and I must go
'To die among my native shades.'

He spoke, and to the western springs,
(His gown discharged, his money spent,
His blanket tied with yellow strings,)
The shepherd of the forest went.

The Indian Burying Ground

I N spite of all the learned have said,
    I still my old opinion keep;
The posture, that we give the dead,
    Points out the soul's eternal sleep.

Not so the ancients of these lands—
    The Indian, when from life released,
Again is seated with his friends,
    And shares again the joyous feast.

His imaged birds, and painted bowl,
    And venison, for a journey dressed,
Bespeak the nature of the soul,
    Activity, that knows no rest.

His bow, for action ready bent,
    And arrows, with a head of stone,
Can only mean that life is spent,
    And not the old ideas gone.

Thou, stranger, that shalt come this way,
    No fraud upon the dead commit—
Observe the swelling turf, and say
    They do not lie, but here they sit.

Here still a lofty rock remains,
  On which the curious eye may trace
(Now wasted, half, by wearing rains)
  The fancies of a ruder race.

Here still an aged elm aspires,
  Beneath whose far-projecting shade
(And which the shepherd still admires)
  The children of the forest played!

There oft a restless Indian queen
  (Pale Shebah, with her braided hair)
And many a barbarous form is seen
  To chide the man that lingers there.

By midnight moons, o'er moistening dews;
  In habit for the chase arrayed,
The hunter still the deer pursues,
  The hunter and the deer, a shade!

And long shall timorous fancy see
  The painted chief, and pointed spear,
And Reason's self shall bow the knee
  To shadows and delusions here.

JOEL BARLOW

1754-1812

19　　　　*The Hasty Pudding*

CANTO I.

YE Alps audacious, thro' the Heavens that rise,
To cramp the day and hide me from the skies;

41

Ye Gallic flags, that o'er their heights unfurl'd,
Bear death to kings, and freedom to the world,
I sing not you. A softer theme I chuse,
A virgin theme, unconscious of the Muse,
But fruitful, rich, well suited to inspire
The purest frenzy of poetic fire.

   Despise it not, ye Bards to terror steel'd,
Who hurl'd your thunders round the epic field;
Nor ye who strain your midnight throats to sing
Joys that the vineyard and the still-house bring;
Or on some distant fair your notes employ,
And speak of raptures that you ne'er enjoy.
I sing the sweets I know, the charms I feel,
My morning incense, and my evening meal,
The sweets of Hasty-Pudding. Come, dear bowl,
Glide o'er my palate, and inspire my soul.
The milk beside thee, smoking from the kine,
Its substance mingled, married in with thine,
Shall cool and temper thy superior heat,
And save the pains of blowing while I eat.

   Oh! could the smooth, the emblematic song
Flow like thy genial juices o'er my tongue,
Could those mild morsels in my numbers chime,
And, as they roll in substance, roll in rhyme,
No more thy aukward unpoetic name
Should shun the Muse, or prejudice thy fame;
But rising grateful to th' accustom'd ear,
All Bards should catch it, and all realms revere!

   Assist me first with pious toil to trace
Thro' wrecks of time thy lineage and thy race;

JOEL BARLOW

Declare what lovely squaw, in days of yore,
(Ere great Columbus sought thy native shore)
First gave thee to the world; her works of fame
Have liv'd indeed, but liv'd without a name.
Some tawny Ceres, goddess of her days,
First learn'd with stones to crack the well-dry'd maize,
Thro' the rough sieve to shake the golden show'r,
In boiling water stir the yellow flour:
The yellow flour, bestrew'd and stir'd with haste,
Swells in the flood and thickens to a paste,
Then puffs and wallops, rises to the brim,
Drinks the dry knobs that on the surface swim:
The knobs at last the busy ladle breaks,
And the whole mass its true consistence takes.

Could but her sacred name, unknown so long,
Rise like her labors, to the song of song,
To her, to them, I'd consecrate my lays,
And blow her pudding with the breath of praise.
If 'twas Oella, whom I sang before,
I here ascribe her one great virtue more.
Not thro' the rich Peruvian realms alone
The fame of Sol's sweet daughter should be known,
But o'er the world's wide climes should live secure,
Far as his rays extend, as long as they endure.

Dear Hasty-Pudding, what unpromis'd joy
Expands my heart, to meet thee in Savoy!
Doom'd o'er the world thro' devious paths to roam,
Each clime my country, and each house my home,
My soul is sooth'd, my cares have found an end,
I greet my long-lost, unforgotten friend.

43

For thee thro' Paris, that corrupted town,
How long in vain I wandered up and down,
Where shameless Bacchus, with his drenching hoard
Cold from his cave usurps the morning board.
London is lost in smoke and steep'd in tea;
No Yankee there can lisp the name of thee;
The uncouth word, a libel on the town,
Would call a proclamation from the crown.
For climes oblique, that fear the sun's full rays,
Chill'd in their fogs, exclude the generous maize;
A grain whose rich luxurient growth requires
Short gentle showers, and bright etherial fires.

But here tho' distant from our native shore,
With mutual glee we meet and laugh once more,
The same! I know thee by that yellow face,
That strong complexion of true Indian race,
Which time can never change, nor soil impair,
Nor Alpine snows, nor Turkey's morbid air;
For endless years, thro' every mild domain,
Where grows the maize, there thou art sure to reign.

But man, more fickle, the bold licence claims,
In different realms to give thee different names.
Thee the soft nations round the warm Levant
Polanta call, the French of course *Polante;*
Ev'n in thy native regions, how I blush
To hear the Pennsylvanians call thee *Mush!*
On Hudson's banks, while men of Belgic spawn
Insult and eat thee by the name *Suppawn.*
All spurious appellations, void of truth:
I've better known thee from my earliest youth,
Thy name is *Hasty-Pudding!* thus our sires

JOEL BARLOW

Were wont to greet thee fuming from their fires;
And while they argu'd in thy just defence
With logic clear, they thus explain'd the sense:—
'In *haste* the boiling cauldron o'er the blaze,
'Receives and cooks the ready-powder'd maize;
'In *haste* 'tis serv'd, and then in equal *haste*,
'With cooling milk, we make the sweet repast.
'No carving to be done, no knife to grate
'The tender ear, and wound the stony plate;
'But the smooth spoon, just fitted to the lip,
'And taught with art the yielding mass to dip,
'By frequent journies to the bowl well stor'd,
'Performs the hasty honors of the board.'
Such is thy name, significant and clear,
A name, a sound to every Yankey dear,
But most to me, whose heart and palate chaste
Preserve my pure hereditary taste.

There are who strive to stamp with disrepute
The luscious food, because it feeds the brute;
In tropes of high-strain'd wit, while gaudy prigs
Compare thy nursling man to pamper'd pigs;
With sovereign scorn I treat the vulgar jest,
Nor fear to share thy bounties with the beast.
What though the generous cow gives me to quaff
The milk nutritious; am I then a calf?
Or can the genius of the noisy swine,
Tho' nurs'd on pudding, thence lay claim to mine?
Sure the sweet song, I fashion to thy praise,
Runs more melodious than the notes they raise.

My song resounding in its grateful glee,
No merit claims; I praise myself in thee.

My father lov'd thee thro' his length of days:
For thee his fields were shaded o'er with maize;
From thee what health, what vigour he possest,
Ten sturdy freemen from his loins attest:
Thy constellation rul'd my natal morn,
And all my bones were made of Indian corn.
Delicious grain! whatever form it take,
To roast or boil, to smother or to bake,
In every dish 'tis welcome still to me,
But most, my Hasty-Pudding, most in thee.

Let the green Succatash with thee contend,
Let beans and corn their sweetest juices blend,
Let butter drench them in its yellow tide,
And a long slice of bacon grace their side;
Not all the plate, how fam'd soe'er it be,
Can please my palate like a bowl of thee.

Some talk of Hoe-cake, fair Virginia's pride,
Rich Johnny-cake this mouth has often tri'd;
Both please me well, their virtues much the same;
Alike their fabric, as allied their fame,
Except in dear New-England, where the last
Receives a dash of pumpkin in the paste,
To give it sweetness and improve the taste.
But place them all before me, smoking hot,
The big round dumpling rolling from the pot;
The pudding of the bag, whose quivering breast,
With suet lin'd leads on the Yankey feast;
The Charlotte brown, within whose crusty sides
A belly soft the pulpy apple hides;
The yellow bread, whose face like amber glows,
And all of Indian that the bake-pan knows—

You tempt me not—my fav'rite greets my eyes,
To that lov'd bowl my spoon by instinct flies.

20 *Advice to a Raven in Russia*
December, 1812

BLACK fool, why winter here? These frozen skies,
Worn by your wings and deafen'd by your cries,
Should warn you hence, where milder suns invite,
And day alternates with his mother night.
    You fear perhaps your food will fail you there,
Your human carnage, that delicious fare
That lured you hither, following still your friend,
The great Napoleon, to the world's bleak end.
You fear, because the southern climes pour'd forth
Their clustering nations to infest the north,
Bavarians, Austrians, those who Drink the Po
And those who skirt the Tuscan seas below,
With all Germania, Neustria, Belgia, Gaul,
Doom'd here to wade through slaughter to their fall,
You fear he left behind no wars, to feed
His feather'd canibals and nurse the breed.
    Fear not, my screamer, call your greedy train,
Sweep over Europe, hurry back to Spain,
You'll find his legions there; the valliant crew
Please best their master when they toil for you.
Abundant there they spread the country o'er
And taint the breeze with every nation's gore,
Iberian, Lusian, British widely strown,
But still more wide and copious flows their own.
    Go where you will; Calabria, Malta, Greece,

Egypt and Syria still his fame increase,
Domingo's fatten'd isle and India's plains
Glow deep with purple drawn from Gallic veins.
No Raven's wing can stretch the flight so far
As the torn bandrols of Napoleon's war.
Choose then your climate, fix your best abode,
He'll make you deserts and he'll bring you blood.

How could you fear a dearth? have not mankind,
Though slain by millions, millions left behind?
Has not CONSCRIPTION still the power to wield
Her annual falchion o'er the human field?
A faithful harvester; or if a man
Escape that gleaner, shall he scape the BAN?
The triple BAN, that like the hound of hell
Gripes with three jowls, to hold his victim well.

Fear nothing then, hatch fast your ravenous brood,
Teach them to cry to Bonaparte for food;
They'll be like you, of all his suppliant train,
The only class that never cries in vain.
For see what mutual benefits you lend!
(The surest way to fix the mutual friend)
While on his slaughter'd troops your tribes are fed,
You cleanse his camp and carry off his dead.
Imperial Scavenger! but now you know
Your work is vain amid these hills of snow.
His tentless troops are marbled through with frost
And change to crystal when the breath is lost.
Mere trunks of ice, though limb'd like human frames
And lately warm'd with life's endearing flames,
They cannot taint the air, the world impest,
Nor can you tear one fiber from their breast.
No! from their visual sockets, as they lie,
With beak and claws you cannot pluck an eye.

The frozen orb, preserving still its form,
Defies your talons as it braves the storm,
But stands and stares to God, as if to know
In what curst hands he leaves his world below.
    Fly then, or starve; though all the dreadful road
From Minsk to Moskow with their bodies strow'd
May count some myriads, yet they can't suffice
To feed you more beneath these dreary skies.
Go back, and winter in the wilds of Spain;
Feast there awhile, and in the next campaign
Rejoin your master; for you'll find him then,
With his new million of the race of men,
Clothed in his thunders, all his flags unfurl'd,
Raging and storming o'er the prostrate world.
    War after war his hungry soul requires,
State after State shall sink beneath his fires,
Yet other Spains in victim smoke shall rise
And other Moskows suffocate the skies,
Each land lie reeking with its people's slain
And not a stream run bloodless to the main.
Till men resume their souls, and dare to shed
Earth's total vengeance on the monster's head,
Hurl from his blood-built throne this king of woes,
Dash him to dust, and let the world repose.

WILLIAM CULLEN BRYANT

1794-1878

21   *Thanatopsis*

To him who in the love of Nature holds
Communion with her visible forms, she speaks

A various language; for his gayer hours
She has a voice of gladness, and a smile
And eloquence of beauty, and she glides
Into his darker musings, with a mild
And healing sympathy, that steals away
Their sharpness, ere he is aware. When thoughts
Of the last bitter hour come like a blight
Over thy spirit, and sad images
Of the stern agony, and shroud, and pall,
And breathless darkness, and the narrow house,
Make thee to shudder, and grow sick at heart;—
Go forth, under the open sky, and list
To Nature's teachings, while from all around—
Earth and her waters, and the depths of air—
Comes a still voice—Yet a few days, and thee
The all-beholding sun shall see no more
In all his course; nor yet in the cold ground,
Where thy pale form was laid, with many tears,
Nor in the embrace of ocean, shall exist
Thy image. Earth, that nourished thee, shall claim
Thy growth, to be resolved to earth again,
And, lost each human trace, surrendering up
Thine individual being, shalt thou go
To mix for ever with the elements,
To be a brother to the insensible rock
And to the sluggish clod, which the rude swain
Turns with his share, and treads upon. The oak
Shall send his roots abroad, and pierce thy mould.

Yet not to thine eternal resting-place
Shalt thou retire alone, nor couldst thou wish
Couch more magnificent. Thou shalt lie down
With patriarchs of the infant world—with kings,

The powerful of the earth—the wise, the good,
Fair forms, and hoary seers of ages past,
All in one mighty sepulchre. The hills
Rock-ribbed and ancient as the sun,—the vales
Stretching in pensive quietness between;
The venerable woods—rivers that move
In majesty, and the complaining brooks
That make the meadows green; and, poured round all,
Old Ocean's gray and melancholy waste,—
Are but the solemn decorations all
Of the great tomb of man. The golden sun,
The planets, all the infinite host of heaven,
Are shining on the sad abodes of death,
Through the still lapse of ages. All that tread
The globe are but a handful to the tribes
That slumber in its bosom.—Take the wings
Of morning, pierce the Barcan wilderness,
Or lose thyself in the continuous woods
Where rolls the Oregon, and hears no sound,
Save his own dashings—yet the dead are there:
And millions in those solitudes, since first
The flight of years began, have laid them down
In their last sleep—the dead reign there alone.
So shalt thou rest, and what if thou withdraw
In silence from the living, and no friend
Take note of thy departure? All that breathe
Will share thy destiny. The gay will laugh
When thou art gone, the solemn brood of care
Plod on, and each one as before will chase
His favorite phantom; yet all these shall leave
Their mirth and their employments, and shall come
And make their bed with thee. As the long train
Of ages glide away, the sons of men,

The youth in life's green spring, and he who goes
In the full strength of years, matron and maid,
The speechless babe, and the gray-headed man—
Shall one by one be gathered to thy side,
By those, who in their turn shall follow them.

So live, that when thy summons comes to join
The innumerable caravan, which moves
To that mysterious realm, where each shall take
His chamber in the silent halls of death,
Thou go not, like the quarry-slave at night,
Scourged to his dungeon, but, sustained and soothed
By an unfaltering trust, approach thy grave,
Like one who wraps the drapery of his couch
About him, and lies down to pleasant dreams.

22 *Inscription for the Entrance to a Wood*

STRANGER, if thou hast learned a truth which
    needs
No school of long experience, that the world
Is full of guilt and misery, and hast seen
Enough of all its sorrows, crimes, and cares,
To tire thee of it, enter this wild wood
And view the haunts of Nature. The calm shade
Shall bring a kindred calm, and the sweet breeze
That makes the green leaves dance, shall waft a balm
To thy sick heart. Thou wilt find nothing here
Of all that pained thee in the haunts of men,
And made thee loathe thy life. The primal curse
Fell, it is true, upon the unsinning earth,

But not in vengeance. God hath yoked to guilt
Her pale tormentor, misery. Hence, these shades
Are still the abodes of gladness; the thick roof
Of green and stirring branches is alive
And musical with birds, that sing and sport
In wantonness of spirit; while below
The squirrel, with raised paws and form erect,
Chirps merrily. Throngs of insects in the shade
Try their thin wings and dance in the warm beam
That waked them into life. Even the green trees
Partake the deep contentment; as they bend
To the soft winds, the sun from the blue sky
Looks in and sheds a blessing on the scene.
Scarce less the cleft-born wild-flower seems to enjoy
Existence, than the wingèd plunderer
That sucks its sweets. The mossy rocks themselves,
And the old and ponderous trunks of prostrate trees
That lead from knoll to knoll a causey rude
Or bridge the sunken brook, and their dark roots,
With all their earth upon them, twisting high,
Breathe fixed tranquillity. The rivulet
Sends forth glad sounds, and tripping o'er its bed
Of pebbly sands, or leaping down the rocks,
Seems, with continuous laughter, to rejoice
In its own being. Softly tread the marge,
Lest from her midway perch thou scare the wren
That dips her bill in water. The cool wind,
That stirs the stream in play, shall come to thee,
Like one that loves thee nor will let thee pass
Ungreeted, and shall give its light embrace.

23 *To a Waterfowl*

WHITHER, midst falling dew,
While glow the heavens with the last steps of day
Far, through their rosy depths, dost thou pursue
   Thy solitary way?

   Vainly the fowler's eye
Might mark thy distant flight to do thee wrong
As, darkly seen against the crimson sky,
   Thy figure floats along.

   Seek'st thou the plashy brink
Of weedy lake, or marge of river wide,
Or where the rocking billows rise and sink
   On the chafed ocean-side?

   There is a Power whose care
Teaches thy way along that pathless coast—
The desert and illimitable air—
   Lone wandering, but not lost.

   All day thy wings have fanned,
At that far height, the cold, thin atmosphere,
Yet stoop not, weary, to the welcome land,
   Though the dark night is near.

   And soon that toil shall end;
Soon shalt thou find a summer home, and rest,
And scream among thy fellows; reeds shall bend,
   Soon, o'er thy sheltered nest.

54

Thou'rt gone, the abyss of heaven
Hath swallowed up thy form; yet, on my heart
Deeply has sunk the lesson thou hast given,
    And shall not soon depart.

He who, from zone to zone,
Guides through the boundless sky thy certain flight,
In the long way that I must tread alone,
    Will lead my steps aright.

24   *Green River*

WHEN breezes are soft and skies are fair,
I steal an hour from study and care,
And hie me away to the woodland scene,
Where wanders the stream with waters of green,
As if the bright fringe of herbs on its brink
Had given their stain to the waves they drink;
And they, whose meadows it murmurs through,
Have named the stream from its own fair hue.

Yet pure its waters—its shallows are bright
With colored pebbles and sparkles of light,
And clear the depths where its eddies play,
And dimples deepen and whirl away,
And the plane-tree's speckled arms o'ershoot
The swifter current that mines its root,
Through whose shifting leaves, as you walk the hill,
The quivering glimmer of sun and rill
With a sudden flash on the eye is thrown,
Like the ray that streams from the diamond-stone.

Oh, loveliest there the spring days come,
With blossoms, and birds, and wild-bees' hum;
The flowers of summer are fairest there,
And freshest the breath of the summer air;
And sweetest the golden autumn day
In silence and sunshine glides away.

Yet, fair as thou art, thou shunnest to glide,
Beautiful stream! by the village side;
But windest away from haunts of men,
To quiet valley and shaded glen;
And forest, and meadow, and slope of hill,
Around thee, are lonely, lovely, and still,
Lonely—save when, by thy rippling tides,
From thicket to thicket the angler glides;
Or the simpler comes, with basket and book,
For herbs of power on thy banks to look;
Or haply, some idle dreamer, like me,
To wander, and muse, and gaze on thee,
Still—save the chirp of birds that feed
On the river cherry and seedy reed,
And thy own wild music gushing out
With mellow murmur of fairy shout,
From dawn to the blush of another day,
Like traveller singing along his way.

That fairy music I never hear,
Nor gaze on those waters so green and clear,
And mark them winding away from sight,
Darkened with shade or flashing with light,
While o'er them the vine to its thicket clings,
And the zephyr stoops to freshen his wings,
But I wish that fate had left me free

To wander these quiet haunts with thee,
Till the eating cares of earth should depart,
And the peace of the scene pass into my heart;
And I envy thy stream, as it glides along
Through its beautiful banks in a trance of song.

Though forced to drudge for the dregs of men,
And scrawl strange words with the barbarous pen,
And mingle among the jostling crowd,
Where the sons of strife are subtle and loud—
I often come to this quiet place,
To breathe the airs that ruffle thy face,
And gaze upon thee in silent dream,
For in thy lonely and lovely stream
An image of that calm life appears
That won my heart in my greener years.

25   *A Winter Piece*

THE time has been that these wild solitudes,
Yet beautiful as wild, were trod by me
Oftener than now; and when the ills of life
Had chafed my spirit—when the unsteady pulse
Beat with strange flutterings—I would wander forth
And seek the woods. The sunshine on my path
Was to me as a friend. The swelling hills,
The quiet dells retiring far between,
With gentle invitation to explore
Their windings, were a calm society
That talked with me and soothed me. Then the chant
Of birds, and chime of brooks, and soft caress

Of the fresh sylvan air, made me forget
The thoughts that broke my peace, and I began
To gather simples by the fountain's brink,
And lose myself in day-dreams. While I stood
In Nature's loneliness, I was with one
With whom I early grew familiar, one
Who never had a frown for me, whose voice
Never rebuked me for the hours I stole
From cares I loved not, but of which the world
Deems highest, to converse with her. When shrieked
The bleak November winds, and smote the woods,
And the brown fields were herbless, and the shades,
That met above the merry rivulet,
Were spoiled, I sought, I loved them still; they seemed
Like old companions in adversity.
Still there was beauty in my walks; the brook,
Bordered with sparkling frost-work, was as gay
As with its fringe of summer flowers. Afar,
The village with its spires, the path of streams
And dim receding valleys, hid before
By interposing trees, lay visible
Through the bare grove, and my familiar haunts
Seemed new to me. Nor was I slow to come
Among them, when the clouds, from their still skirts,
Had shaken down on earth the feathery snow,
And all was white. The pure keen air abroad,
Albeit it breathed no scent of herb, nor heard
Love-call of bird nor merry hum of bee,
Was not the air of death. Bright mosses crept
Over the spotted trunks, and the close buds,
That lay along the boughs, instinct with life,
Patient, and waiting the soft breath of Spring,
Feared not the piercing spirit of the North.

WILLIAM CULLEN BRYANT

The snow-bird twittered on the beechen bough,
And 'neath the hemlock, whose thick branches bent
Beneath its bright cold burden, and kept dry
A circle, on the earth, of withered leaves,
The partridge found a shelter. Through the snow
The rabbit sprang away. The lighter track
Of fox, and the raccoon's broad path, were there,
Crossing each other. From his hollow tree
The squirrel was abroad, gathering the nuts
Just fallen, that asked the winter cold and sway
Of winter blast, to shake them from their hold.

But Winter has yet brighter scenes——he boasts
Splendors beyond what gorgeous Summer knows;
Or Autumn with his many fruits, and woods
All flushed with many hues. Come when the rains
Have glazed the snow and clothed the trees with ice,
While the slant sun of February pours
Into the bowers a flood of light. Approach!
The incrusted surface shall upbear thy steps,
And the broad arching portals of the grove
Welcome thy entering. Look! the massy trunks
Are cased in the pure crystal; each light spray,
Nodding and tinkling in the breath of heaven,
Is studded with its trembling water-drops,
That glimmer with an amethystine light.
But round the parent-stem the long low boughs
Bend, in a glittering ring, and arbors hide
The glassy floor. Oh! you might deem the spot
The spacious cavern of some virgin mine,
Deep in the womb of earth——where the gems grow,
And diamonds put forth radiant rods and bud
With amethyst and topaz——and the place

Lit up, most royally, with the pure beam
That dwells in them. Or haply the vast hall
Of fairy palace, that outlasts the night,
And fades not in the glory of the sun;—
Where crystal columns send forth slender shafts
And crossing arches; and fantastic aisles
Wind from the sight in brightness, and are lost
Among the crowded pillars. Raise thine eye;
Thou seest no cavern roof, no palace vault;
There the blue sky and the white drifting cloud
Look in. Again the wildered fancy dreams
Of spouting fountains, frozen as they rose,
And fixed, with all their branching jets, in air,
And all their sluices sealed. All, all is light;
Light without shade. But all shall pass away
With the next sun. From numberless vast trunks
Loosened, the crashing ice shall make a sound
Like the far roar of rivers, and the eve
Shall close o'er the brown woods as it was wont.

And it is pleasant, when the noisy streams
Are just set free, and milder suns melt off
The plashy snow, save only the firm drift
In the deep glen or the close shade of pines—
'Tis pleasant to behold the wreaths of smoke
Roll up among the maples of the hill,
Where the shrill sound of youthful voices wakes
The shriller echo, as the clear pure lymph,
That from the wounded trees, in twinkling drops,
Falls, mid the golden brightness of the morn,
Is gathered in with brimming pails, and oft,
Wielded by sturdy hands, the stroke of axe
Makes the woods ring. Along the quiet air,

Come and float calmly off the soft light clouds,
Such as you see in summer, and the winds
Scarce stir the branches. Lodged in sunny cleft,
Where the cold breezes come not, blooms alone
The little wind-flower, whose just opened eye
Is blue as the spring heaven it gazes at—
Startling the loiterer in the naked groves
With unexpected beauty, for the time
Of blossoms and green leaves is yet afar.
And ere it comes, the encountering winds shall oft
Muster their wrath again, and rapid clouds
Shade heaven, and bounding on the frozen earth
Shall fall their volleyed stores, rounded like hail
And white like snow, and the loud North again
Shall buffet the vexed forest in his rage.

26 *The Prairies*

THESE are the gardens of the Desert, these
The unshorn fields, boundless and beautiful,
For which the speech of England has no name—
The Prairies. I behold them for the first,
And my heart swells, while the dilated sight
Takes in the encircling vastness. Lo! they stretch,
In airy undulations, far away,
As if the ocean, in his gentlest swell,
Stood still, with all his rounded billows fixed,
And motionless forever.—Motionless?—
No—they are all unchained again. The clouds
Sweep over with their shadows, and, beneath,
The surface rolls and fluctuates to the eye;

Dark hollows seem to glide along and chase
The sunny ridges. Breezes of the South!
Who toss the golden and the flame-like flowers,
And pass the prairie-hawk that, poised on high,
Flaps his broad wings, yet moves not—ye have played
Among the palms of Mexico and vines
Of Texas, and have crisped the limpid brooks
That from the fountains of Sonora glide
Into the calm Pacific—have ye fanned
A nobler or a lovelier scene than this?
Man hath no power in all this glorious work:
The hand that built the firmament hath heaved
And smoothed these verdant swells, and sown their slopes
With herbage, planted them with island groves,
And hedged them round with forests. Fitting floor
For this magnificent temple of the sky—
With flowers whose glory and whose multitude
Rival the constellations! The great heavens
Seem to stoop down upon the scene in love,—
A nearer vault, and of a tenderer blue,
Than that which bends above our eastern hills.

As o'er the verdant waste I guide my steed,
Among the high rank grass that sweeps his sides
The hollow beating of his footstep seems
A sacrilegious sound. I think of those
Upon whose rest he tramples. Are they here—
The dead of other days?—and did the dust
Of these fair solitudes once stir with life
And burn with passion? Let the mighty mounds
That overlook the rivers, or that rise
In the dim forest crowded with old oaks,
Answer. A race, that long has passed away,

Built them;—a disciplined and populous race
Heaped, with long toil, the earth, while yet the Greek
Was hewing the Pentelicus to forms
Of symmetry, and rearing on its rock
The glittering Parthenon. These ample fields
Nourished their harvests, here their herds were fed,
When haply by their stalls the bison lowed,
And bowed his manèd shoulder to the yoke.
All day this desert murmured with their toils,
Till twilight blushed, and lovers walked, and wooed
In a forgotten language, and old tunes,
From instruments of unremembered form,
Gave the soft winds a voice. The red man came—
The roaming hunter tribes, warlike and fierce,
And the mound-builders vanished from the earth.
The solitude of centuries untold
Has settled where they dwelt. The prairie-wolf
Hunts in their meadows, and his fresh-dug den
Yawns by my path. The gopher mines the ground
Where stood their swarming cities. All is gone;
All—save the piles of earth that hold their bones,
The platforms where they worshipped unknown gods,
The barriers which they builded from the soil
To keep the foe at bay—till o'er the walls
The wild beleaguerers broke, and, one by one,
The strongholds of the plain were forced, and heaped
With corpses. The brown vultures of the wood
Flocked to those vast uncovered sepulchres,
And sat unscared and silent at their feast.
Haply some solitary fugitive,
Lurking in marsh and forest, till the sense
Of desolation and of fear became
Bitterer than death, yielded himself to die.

Man's better nature triumphed then. Kind words
Welcomed and soothed him; the rude conquerors
Seated the captive with their chiefs; he chose
A bride among their maidens, and at length
Seemed to forget—yet ne'er forgot—the wife
Of his first love, and her sweet little ones,
Butchered, amid their shrieks, with all his race.

Thus change the forms of being. Thus arise
Races of living things, glorious in strength,
And perish, as the quickening breath of God
Fills them, or is withdrawn. The red man, too,
Has left the blooming wilds he ranged so long,
And, nearer to the Rocky Mountains, sought
A wilder hunting-ground. The beaver builds
No longer by these streams, but far away,
On waters whose blue surface ne'er gave back
The white man's face—among Missouri's springs,
And pools whose issues swell the Oregon—
He rears his little Venice. In these plains
The bison feeds no more. Twice twenty leagues
Beyond remotest smoke of hunter's camp,
Roams the majestic brute, in herds that shake
The earth with thundering steps—yet here I meet
His ancient footprints stamped beside the pool.

Still this great solitude is quick with life.
Myriads of insects, gaudy as the flowers
They flutter over, gentle quadrupeds,
And birds, that scarce have learned the fear of man,
Are here, and sliding reptiles of the ground,
Startlingly beautiful. The graceful deer
Bounds to the wood at my approach. The bee,

WILLIAM CULLEN BRYANT

A more adventurous colonist than man,
With whom he came across the eastern deep,
Fills the savannas with his murmurings,
And hides his sweets, as in the golden age,
Within the hollow oak. I listen long
To his domestic hum, and think I hear
The sound of that advancing multitude
Which soon shall fill these deserts. From the ground
Comes up the laugh of children, the soft voice
Of maidens, and the sweet and solemn hymn
Of Sabbath worshippers. The low of herds
Blends with the rustling of the heavy grain
Over the dark brown furrows. All at once
A fresher wind sweeps by, and breaks my dream,
And I am in the wilderness alone.

RALPH WALDO EMERSON

1803-1882

27   *A Letter*

D EAR brother, would you know the life,
Please God, that I would lead?
On the first wheels that quit this weary town
Over yon western bridges I would ride
And with a cheerful benison forsake
Each street and spire and roof, incontinent.
Then would I seek where God might guide my steps,
Deep in a woodland tract, a sunny farm,

RALPH WALDO EMERSON

Amid the mountain counties, Hants, Franklin, Berks,
Where down the rock ravine a river roars,
Even from a brook, and where old woods
Not tamed and cleared cumber the ground
With their centennial wrecks.
Find me a slope where I can feel the sun
And mark the rising of the early stars.
There will I bring my books,—my household gods,
The reliquaries of my dead saint, and dwell
In the sweet odor of her memory.
Then in the uncouth solitude unlock
My stock of art, plant dials in the grass,
Hang in the air a bright thermometer
And aim a telescope at the inviolate sun.

CHARDON STREET, BOSTON, 1831.

28   *The Rhodora:*

ON BEING ASKED, WHENCE IS THE FLOWER?

I N May, when sea-winds pierced our solitudes,
I found the fresh Rhodora in the woods,
Spreading its leafless blooms in a damp nook,
To please the desert and the sluggish brook.
The purple petals, fallen in the pool,
Made the black water with their beauty gay;
Here might the red-bird come his plumes to cool,
And court the flower that cheapens his array.
Rhodora! if the sages ask thee why
This charm is wasted on the earth and sky,
Tell them, dear, that if eyes were made for seeing,

66

Then Beauty is its own excuse for being:
Why thou wert there, O rival of the rose!
I never thought to ask, I never knew:
But, in my simple ignorance, suppose
The self-same Power that brought me there brought you.

29   *The Humble-Bee*

Burly, dozing humble-bee,
Where thou art is clime for me.
Let them sail for Porto Rique,
Far-off heats through seas to seek;
I will follow thee alone,
Thou animated torrid-zone!
Zigzag steerer, desert cheerer,
Let me chase thy waving lines;
Keep me nearer, me thy hearer,
Singing over shrubs and vines.

Insect lover of the sun,
Joy of thy dominion!
Sailor of the atmosphere;
Swimmer through the waves of air;
Voyager of light and noon;
Epicurean of June;
Wait, I prithee, till I come
Within earshot of thy hum,—
All without is martyrdom.

When the south wind, in May days,
With a net of shining haze

Silvers the horizon wall,
And with softness touching all,
Tints the human countenance
With a color of romance,
And infusing subtle heats,
Turns the sod to violets,
Thou, in sunny solitudes,
Rover of the underwoods,
The green silence dost displace
With thy mellow, breezy bass.

Hot midsummer's petted crone,
Sweet to me thy drowsy tone
Tells of countless sunny hours,
Long days, and solid banks of flowers;
Of gulfs of sweetness without bound
In Indian wildernesses found;
Of Syrian peace, immortal leisure,
Firmest cheer, and bird-like pleasure.

Aught unsavory or unclean
Hath my insect never seen;
But violets and bilberry bells,
Maple-sap and daffodels,
Grass with green flag half-mast high,
Succory to match the sky,
Columbine with horn of honey,
Scented fern, and agrimony,
Clover, catchfly, adder's-tongue
And brier-roses, dwelt among;
All beside was unknown waste,
All was picture as he passed.

Wiser far than human seer,
Yellow-breeched philosopher!
Seeing only what is fair,
Sipping only what is sweet,
Thou dost mock at fate and care,
Leave the chaff, and take the wheat.
When the fierce northwestern blast
Cools sea and land so far and fast,
Thou already slumberest deep;
Woe and want thou canst outsleep;
Want and woe, which torture us,
Thy sleep makes ridiculous.

30   *Concord Hymn*

Sung at the completion of the Battle Monument,
July 4, 1837

By the rude bridge that arched the flood,
  Their flag to April's breeze unfurled,
Here once the embattled farmers stood
  And fired the shot heard round the world.

The foe long since in silence slept;
  Alike the conqueror silent sleeps;
And Time the ruined bridge has swept
  Down the dark stream which seaward creeps.

On this green bank, by this soft stream,
  We set to-day a votive stone;
That memory may their deed redeem,
  When, like our sires, our sons are gone.

Spirit, that made those heroes dare
   To die, and leave their children free,
Bid Time and Nature gently spare
   The shaft we raise to them and thee.

31   *Each and All*

LITTLE thinks, in the field, yon red-cloaked clown
Of thee from the hill-top looking down;
The heifer that lows in the upland farm,
Far-heard, lows not thine ear to charm;
The sexton, tolling his bell at noon,
Deems not that great Napoleon
Stops his horse, and lists with delight,
Whilst his files sweep round yon Alpine height;
Nor knowest thou what argument
Thy life to thy neighbor's creed has lent.
All are needed by each one;
Nothing is fair or good alone.
I thought the sparrow's note from heaven,
Singing at dawn on the alder bough;
I brought him home, in his nest, at even;
He sings the song, but it cheers not now,
For I did not bring home the river and sky;—
He sang to my ear,—they sang to my eye.
The delicate shells lay on the shore;
The bubbles of the latest wave
Fresh pearls to their enamel gave,
And the bellowing of the savage sea
Greeted their safe escape to me.
I wiped away the weeds and foam,

RALPH WALDO EMERSON

I fetched my sea-born treasures home;
But the poor, unsightly, noisome things
Had left their beauty on the shore
With the sun and the sand and the wild uproar.
The lover watched his graceful maid,
As 'mid the virgin train she strayed,
Nor knew her beauty's best attire
Was woven still by the snow-white choir.
At last she came to his hermitage,
Like the bird from the woodlands to the cage;—
The gay enchantment was undone,
A gentle wife, but fairy none.
Then I said, 'I covet truth;
Beauty is unripe childhood's cheat;
I leave it behind with the games of youth:'—
As I spoke, beneath my feet
The ground-pine curled its pretty wreath,
Running over the club-moss burrs;
I inhaled the violet's breath;
Around me stood the oaks and firs;
Pine-cones and acorns lay on the ground;
Over me soared the eternal sky,
Full of light and of deity;
Again I say, again I heard,
The rolling river, the morning bird;—
Beauty through my senses stole;
I yielded myself to the perfect whole.

The Problem

I LIKE a church; I like a cowl;
I love a prophet of the soul;
And on my heart monastic aisles
Fall like sweet strains, or pensive smiles;
Yet not for all his faith can see
Would I that cowlèd churchman be.

Why should the vest on him allure,
Which I could not on me endure?

Not from a vain or shallow thought
His awful Jove young Phidias brought;
Never from lips of cunning fell
The thrilling Delphic oracle;
Out from the heart of nature rolled
The burdens of the Bible old;
The litanies of nations came,
Like the volcano's tongue of flame,
Up from the burning core below,—
The canticles of love and woe:
The hand that rounded Peter's dome
And groined the aisles of Christian Rome
Wrought in a sad sincerity;
Himself from God he could not free;
He builded better than he knew;—
The conscious stone to beauty grew.

Know'st thou what wove yon woodbird's nest
Of leaves, and feathers from her breast?

Or how the fish outbuilt her shell,
Painting with morn each annual cell?
Or how the sacred pine-tree adds
To her old leaves new myriads?
Such and so grew these holy piles,
Whilst love and terror laid the tiles.
Earth proudly wears the Parthenon,
As the best gem upon her zone,
And Morning opes with haste her lids
To gaze upon the Pyramids;
O'er England's abbeys bends the sky,
As on its friends, with kindred eye;
For out of Thought's interior sphere
These wonders rose to upper air;
And Nature gladly gave them place,
Adopted them into her race,
And granted them an equal date
With Andes and with Ararat.

These temples grew as grows the grass;
Art might obey, but not surpass.
The passive Master lent his hand
To the vast soul that o'er him planned;
And the same power that reared the shrine
Bestrode the tribes that knelt within.
Ever the fiery Pentecost
Girds with one flame the countless host,
Trances the heart through chanting choirs,
And through the priest the mind inspires.
The word unto the prophet spoken
Was writ on tables yet unbroken;
The word by seers or sibyls told,
In groves of oak, or fanes of gold,

Still floats upon the morning wind,
Still whispers to the willing mind.
One accent of the Holy Ghost
The heedless world hath never lost.
I know what say the fathers wise,—
The Book itself before me lies,
Old *Chrysostom*, best Augustine,
And he who blent both in his line,
The younger *Golden Lips* or mines,
Taylor, the Shakspeare of divines.
His words are music in my ear.
I see his cowlèd portrait dear;
And yet, for all his faith could see,
I would not the good bishop be.

33 *Uriel*

IT fell in the ancient periods
    Which the brooding soul surveys,
Or ever the wild Time coined itself
    Into calendar months and days.

This was the lapse of Uriel,
Which in Paradise befell.
Once, among the Pleiads walking,
Seyd overheard the young gods talking;
And the treason, too long pent,
To his ears was evident.
The young deities discussed
Laws of form, and metre just,
Orb, quintessence, and sunbeams,

What subsisteth, and what seems.
One, with low tones that decide,
And doubt and reverend use defied,
With a look that solved the sphere,
And stirred the devils everywhere,
Gave his sentiment divine
Against the being of a line.
'Line in nature is not found;
Unit and universe are round;
In vain produced, all rays return;
Evil will bless, and ice will burn.'
As Uriel spoke with piercing eye,
A shudder ran around the sky;
The stern old war-gods shook their heads,
The seraphs frowned from myrtle-beds;
Seemed to the holy festival
The rash word boded ill to all;
The balance-beam of Fate was bent;
The bounds of good and ill were rent;
Strong Hades could not keep his own,
But all slid to confusion.

A sad self-knowledge, withering, fell
On the beauty of Uriel;
In heaven once eminent, the god
Withdrew, that hour, into his cloud;
Whether doomed to long gyration
In the sea of generation,
Or by knowledge grown too bright
To hit the nerve of feebler sight.
Straightway, a forgetting wind
Stole over the celestial kind,
And their lips the secret kept,

If in ashes the fire-seed slept.
But now and then, truth-speaking things
Shamed the angels' veiling wings;
And, shrilling from the solar course,
Or from fruit of chemic force,
Procession of a soul in matter,
Or the speeding change of water,
Or out of the good of evil born,
Came Uriel's voice of cherub scorn,
And a blush tinged the upper sky,
And the gods shook, they knew not why.

34 *Woodnotes*

I

WHEN the pine tosses its cones
To the song of its waterfall tones,
Who speeds to the woodland walks?
To birds and trees who talks?
Cæsar of his leafy Rome,
There the poet is at home.
He goes to the river-side,—
Not hook nor line hath he;
He stands in the meadows wide,—
Nor gun nor scythe to see.
Sure some god his eye enchants:
What he knows nobody wants.
In the wood he travels glad,
Without better fortune had,
Melancholy without bad.

RALPH WALDO EMERSON

Knowledge this man prizes best
Seems fantastic to the rest:
Pondering shadows, colors, clouds,
Grass-buds and caterpillar-shrouds,
Boughs on which the wild bees settle,
Tints that spot the violet's petal,
Why Nature loves the number five,
And why the star-form she repeats:
Lover of all things alive,
Wonderer at all he meets,
Wonderer chiefly at himself,
Who can tell him what he is?
Or how meet in human elf
Coming and past eternities?

2

And such I knew, a forest seer,
A minstrel of the natural year,
Foreteller of the vernal ides,
Wise harbinger of spheres and tides,
A lover true, who knew by heart
Each joy the mountain dales impart;
It seemed that Nature could not raise
A plant in any secret place,
In quaking bog, on snowy hill,
Beneath the grass that shades the rill,
Under the snow, between the rocks,
In damp fields known to bird and fox.
But he would come in the very hour
It opened in its virgin bower,
As if a sunbeam showed the place,
And tell its long-descended race.

It seemed as if the breezes brought him,
It seemed as if the sparrows taught him;
As if by secret sight he knew
Where, in far fields, the orchis grew.
Many haps fall in the field
Seldom seen by wishful eyes,
But all her shows did Nature yield,
To please and win this pilgrim wise.
He saw the partridge drum in the woods;
He heard the woodcock's evening hymn;
He found the tawny thrushes' broods;
And the shy hawk did wait for him;
What others did at distance hear,
And guessed within the thicket's gloom,
Was shown to this philosopher,
And at his bidding seemed to come.

3

In unploughed Maine he sought the lumberers' gang
Where from a hundred lakes young rivers sprang;
He trode the unplanted forest floor, whereon
The all-seeing sun for ages hath not shone;
Where feeds the moose, and walks the surly bear,
And up the tall mast runs the woodpecker.
He saw beneath dim aisles, in odorous beds,
The slight Linnæa hang its twin-born heads,
And blessed the monument of the man of flowers,
Which breathes his sweet fame through the northern
    bowers.
He heard, when in the grove, at intervals,
With sudden roar the aged pine-tree falls,—
One crash, the death-hymn of the perfect tree,

Declares the close of its green century.
Low lies the plant to whose creation went
Sweet influence from every element;
Whose living towers the years conspired to build,
Whose giddy top the morning loved to gild.
Through these green tents, by eldest Nature dressed,
He roamed, content alike with man and beast.
Where darkness found him he lay glad at night;
There the red morning touched him with its light.
Three moons his great heart him a hermit made,
So long he roved at will the boundless shade.
The timid it concerns to ask their way,
And fear what foe in caves and swamps can stray,
To make no step until the event is known,
And ills to come as evils past bemoan.
Not so the wise; no coward watch he keeps
To spy what danger on his pathway creeps;
Go where he will, the wise man is at home,
His hearth the earth,—his hall the azure dome;
Where his clear spirit leads him, there's his road
By God's own light illumined and foreshowed.

4

'T was one of the charmèd days
When the genius of God doth flow;
The wind may alter twenty ways,
A tempest cannot blow;
It may blow north, it still is warm;
Or south, it still is clear;
Or east, it smells like a clover-farm;
Or west, no thunder fear.
The musing peasant, lowly great,

Beside the forest water sate;
The rope-like pine-roots crosswise grown
Composed the network of his throne;
The wide lake, edged with sand and grass,
Was burnished to a floor of glass,
Painted with shadows green and proud
Of the tree and of the cloud.
He was the heart of all the scene;
On him the sun looked more serene;
To hill and cloud his face was known,—
It seemed the likeness of their own;
They knew by secret sympathy
The public child of earth and sky.
'You ask,' he said, 'what guide
Me through trackless thickets led,
Through thick-stemmed woodlands rough and wide.
I found the water's bed.
The watercourses were my guide;
I travelled grateful by their side,
Or through their channel dry;
They led me through the thicket damp,
Through brake and fern, the beavers' camp,
Through beds of granite cut my road,
And their resistless friendship showed.
The falling waters led me,
The foodful waters fed me,
And brought me to the lowest land,
Unerring to the ocean sand.
The moss upon the forest bark
Was pole-star when the night was dark;
The purple berries in the wood
Supplied me necessary food;
For Nature ever faithful is

To such as trust her faithfulness.
When the forest shall mislead me,
When the night and morning lie,
When sea and land refuse to feed me,
'T will be time enough to die;
Then will yet my mother yield
A pillow in her greenest field,
Nor the June flowers scorn to cover
The clay of their departed lover.'

35 *The Snow-Storm*

ANNOUNCED by all the trumpets of the sky,
Arrives the snow, and, driving o'er the fields,
Seems nowhere to alight: the whited air
Hides hills and woods, the river, and the heaven,
And veils the farm-house at the garden's end.
The sled and traveller stopped, the courier's feet
Delayed, all friends shut out, the housemates sit
Around the radiant fireplace, enclosed
In a tumultuous privacy of storm.

Come see the north wind's masonry.
Out of an unseen quarry evermore
Furnished with tile, the fierce artificer
Curves his white bastions with projected roof
Round every windward stake, or tree, or door.
Speeding, the myriad-handed, his wild work
So fanciful, so savage, nought cares he
For number or proportion. Mockingly,
On coop or kennel he hangs Parian wreaths;

A swan-like form invests the hidden thorn;
Fills up the farmer's lane from wall to wall,
Maugre the farmer's sighs; and at the gate
A tapering turret overtops the work.
And when his hours are numbered, and the world
Is all his own, retiring, as he were not,
Leaves, when the sun appears, astonished Art
To mimic in slow structures, stone by stone,
Built in an age, the mad wind's night-work,
The frolic architecture of the snow.

36   *The Sphinx*

THE Sphinx is drowsy,
    Her wings are furled:
Her ear is heavy,
    She broods on the world.
'Who'll tell me my secret,
    The ages have kept? —
I awaited the seer
    While they slumbered and slept:—

'The fate of the man-child,
    The meaning of man;
Known fruit of the unknown;
    Dædalian plan;
Out of sleeping a waking,
    Out of waking a sleep;
Life death overtaking;
    Deep underneath deep?

'Erect as a sunbeam,
   Upspringeth the palm;
The elephant browses,
   Undaunted and calm;
In beautiful motion
   The thrush plies his wings;
Kind leaves of his covert,
   Your silence he sings.

'The waves, unashamèd,
   In difference sweet,
Play glad with the breezes,
   Old playfellows meet;
The journeying atoms,
   Primordial wholes,
Firmly draw, firmly drive,
   By their animate poles.

'Sea, earth, air, sound, silence,
   Plant, quadruped, bird,
By one music enchanted,
   One deity stirred,—
Each the other adorning,
   Accompany still;
Night veileth the morning,
   The vapor the hill.

'The babe by its mother
   Lies bathèd in joy;
Glide its hours uncounted,—
   The sun is its toy;
Shines the peace of all being,
   Without cloud, in its eyes;

And the sum of the world
  In soft miniature lies.

'But man crouches and blushes,
  Absconds and conceals;
He creepeth and peepeth,
  He palters and steals;
Infirm, melancholy,
  Jealous glancing around,
An oaf, an accomplice,
  He poisons the ground.

'Out spoke the great mother,
  Beholding his fear;—
At the sound of her accents
  Cold shuddered the sphere:—
"Who has drugged my boy's cup?
  Who has mixed my boy's bread?
Who, with sadness and madness,
  Has turned my child's head?"'

I heard a poet answer
  Aloud and cheerfully,
'Say on, sweet Sphinx! thy dirges
  Are pleasant songs to me.
Deep love lieth under
  These pictures of time;
They fade in the light of
  Their meaning sublime.

'The fiend that man harries
  Is love of the Best;

Yawns the pit of the Dragon,
    Lit by rays from the Blest.
The Lethe of Nature
    Can't trance him again,
Whose soul sees the perfect,
    Which his eyes seek in vain.

'To vision profounder,
    Man's spirit must dive;
His aye-rolling orb
    At no goal will arrive;
The heavens that now draw him
    With sweetness untold,
Once found,—for new heavens
    He spurneth the old.

'Pride ruined the angels,
    Their shame them restores;
Lurks the joy that is sweetest
    In stings of remorse.
Have I a lover
    Who is noble and free?—
I would he were nobler
    Than to love me.

'Eterne alternation
    Now follows, now flies;
And under pain, pleasure,—
    Under pleasure, pain lies.
Love works at the centre,
    Heart-heaving alway;
Forth speed the strong pulses
    To the borders of day.

'Dull Sphinx, Jove keep thy five wits;
    Thy sight is growing blear;
Rue, myrrh and cummin for the Sphinx,
    Her muddy eyes to clear!'
The old Sphinx bit her thick lip,—
    Said, 'Who taught thee me to name?
I am thy spirit, yoke-fellow;
    Of thine eye I am eyebeam.

'Thou art the unanswered question;
    Couldst see thy proper eye,
Alway it asketh, asketh;
    And each answer is a lie.
So take thy quest through nature,
    It through thousand natures ply;
Ask on, thou clothed eternity;
    Time is the false reply.'

Uprose the merry Sphinx,
    And crouched no more in stone;
She melted into purple cloud,
    She silvered in the moon;
She spired into a yellow flame;
    She flowered in blossoms red;
She flowed into a foaming wave:
    She stood Monadnoc's head.

Thorough a thousand voices
    Spoke the universal dame;
'Who telleth one of my meanings
    Is master of all I am.'

37   *Saadi*

TREES in groves,
Kine in droves,
In ocean sport the scaly herds,
Wedge-like cleave the air the birds,
To northern lakes fly wind-borne ducks
Browse the mountain sheep in flocks,
Men consort in camp and town,
But the poet dwells alone.

God, who gave to him the lyre,
Of all mortals the desire,
For all breathing men's behoof,
Straitly charged him, 'Sit aloof;'
Annexed a warning, poets say,
To the bright premium,—
Ever, when twain together play,
Shall the harp be dumb.

Many may come,
But one shall sing;
Two touch the string,
The harp is dumb.
Though there come a million,
Wise Saadi dwells alone.

Yet Saadi loved the race of men,—
No churl, immured in cave or den;
In bower and hall
He wants them all,

Nor can dispense
With Persia for his audience;
They must give ear,
Grow red with joy and white with fear;
But he has no companion;
Come ten, or come a million,
Good Saadi dwells alone.

Be thou ware where Saadi dwells;
Wisdom of the gods is he,—
Entertain it reverently.
Gladly round that golden lamp
Sylvan deities encamp,
And simple maids and noble youth
Are welcome to the man of truth.
Most welcome they who need him most,
They feed the spring which they exhaust;
For greater need
Draws better deed:
But, critic, spare thy vanity,
Nor show thy pompous parts,
To vex with odious subtlety
The cheerer of men's hearts.

Sad-eyed Fakirs swiftly say
Endless dirges to decay,
Never in the blaze of light
Lose the shudder of midnight;
Pale at overflowing noon
Hear wolves barking at the moon;
In the bower of dalliance sweet
Hear the far Avenger's feet:
And shake before those awful Powers,

RALPH WALDO EMERSON

Who in their pride forgive not ours.
Thus the sad-eyed Fakirs preach:
'Bard, when thee would Allah teach,
And lift thee to his holy mount,
He sends thee from his bitter fount
Wormwood,—saying, "Go thy ways;
Drink not the Malaga of praise,
But do the deed thy fellows hate,
And compromise thy peaceful state;
Smite the white breasts which thee fed,
Stuff sharp thorns beneath the head
Of them thou shouldst have comforted;
For out of woe and out of crime
Draws the heart a lore sublime." '
And yet it seemeth not to me
That the high gods love tragedy;
For Saadi sat in the sun,
And thanks was his contrition;
For haircloth and for bloody whips,
Had active hands and smiling lips;
And yet his runes he rightly read,
And to his folk his message sped.
Sunshine in his heart transferred
Lighted each transparent word,
And well could honoring Persia learn
What Saadi wished to say;
For Saadi's nightly stars did burn
Brighter than Jami's day.

Whispered the Muse in Saadi's cot:
'O gentle Saadi, listen not,
Tempted by thy praise of wit,
Or by thirst and appetite

For the talents not thine own,
To sons of contradiction.
Never, son of eastern morning,
Follow falsehood, follow scorning.
Denounce who will, who will deny,
And pile the hills to scale the sky;
Let theist, atheist, pantheist,
Define and wrangle how they list,
Fierce conserver, fierce destroyer,—
But thou, joy-giver and enjoyer,
Unknowing war, unknowing crime,
Gentle Saadi, mind thy rhyme;
Heed not what the brawlers say,
Heed thou only Saadi's lay.

'Let the great world bustle on
With war and trade, with camp and town;
A thousand men shall dig and eat;
At forge and furnace thousands sweat;
And thousands sail the purple sea,
And give or take the stroke of war,
Or crowd the market and bazaar;
Oft shall war end, and peace return,
And cities rise where cities burn,
Ere one man my hill shall climb,
Who can turn the golden rhyme.
Let them manage how they may,
Heed thou only Saadi's lay.
Seek the living among the dead,—
Man in man is imprisonèd;
Barefooted Dervish is not poor,
If fate unlock his bosom's door,
So that what his eye hath seen

His tongue can paint as bright, as keen;
And what his tender heart hath felt
With equal fire thy heart shalt melt.
For, whom the Muses smile upon,
And touch with soft persuasion,
His words like a storm-wind can bring
Terror and beauty on their wing;
In his every syllable
Lurketh Nature veritable;
And though he speak in midnight dark,—
In heaven no star, on earth no spark,—
Yet before the listener's eye
Swims the world in ecstasy,
The forest waves, the morning breaks,
The pastures sleep, ripple the lakes,
Leaves twinkle, flowers like persons be,
And life pulsates in rock or tree.
Saadi, so far thy words shall reach:
Suns rise and set in Saadi's speech!'

And thus to Saadi said the Muse:
'Eat thou the bread which men refuse;
Flee from the goods which from thee flee;
Seek nothing,—Fortune seeketh thee.
Nor mount, nor dive; all good things keep
The midway of the eternal deep.
Wish not to fill the isles with eyes
To fetch thee birds of paradise:
On thine orchard's edge belong
All the brags of plume and song;
Wise Ali's sunbright sayings pass
For proverbs in the market-place:
Through mountains bored by regal art,

Toil whistles as he drives his cart.
Nor scour the seas, nor sift mankind,
A poet or a friend to find:
Behold, he watches at the door!
Behold his shadow on the floor!
Open innumerable doors
The heaven where unveiled Allah pours
The flood of truth, the flood of good,
The Seraph's and the Cherub's food.
Those doors are men: the Pariah hind
Admits thee to the perfect Mind.
Seek not beyond thy cottage wall
Redeemers that can yield thee all:
While thou sittest at thy door
On the desert's yellow floor,
Listening to the gray-haired crones,
Foolish gossips, ancient drones,
Saadi, see! they rise in stature
To the height of mighty Nature,
And the secret stands revealed
Fraudulent Time in vain concealed,—
That blessed gods in servile masks
Plied for thee thy household tasks.'

38   *Hamatreya*

BULKELEY, Hunt, Willard, Hosmer, Meriam, Flint,
Possessed the land which rendered to their toil
Hay, corn, roots, hemp, flax, apples, wool and wood.
Each of these landlords walked amidst his farm,
Saying, ' 'T is mine, my children's and my name's.

RALPH WALDO EMERSON

How sweet the west wind sounds in my own trees!
How graceful climb those shadows on my hill!
I fancy these pure waters and the flags
Know me, as does my dog: we sympathize;
And, I affirm, my actions smack of the soil.'

Where are these men? Asleep beneath their grounds:
And strangers, fond as they, their furrows plough.
Earth laughs in flowers, to see her boastful boys
Earth-proud, proud of the earth which is not theirs;
Who steer the plough, but cannot steer their feet
Clear of the grave.
They added ridge to valley, brook to pond,
And sighed for all that bounded their domain;
'This suits me for a pasture; that's my park;
We must have clay, lime, gravel, granite-ledge,
And misty lowland, where to go for peat.
The land is well,—lies fairly to the south.
'T is good, when you have crossed the sea and back,
To find the sitfast acres where you left them.'
Ah! the hot owner sees not Death, who adds
Him to his land, a lump of mould the more.
Hear what the Earth says:—

EARTH-SONG

'Mine and yours;
Mine, not yours.
Earth endures;
Stars abide—
Shine down in the old sea;
Old are the shores;
But where are old men?

I who have seen much,
Such have I never seen.

'The lawyer's deed
Ran sure,
In tail,
To them, and to their heirs
Who shall succeed,
Without fail,
Forevermore.

'Here is the land,
Shaggy with wood,
With its old valley,
Mound and flood.
But the heritors? —
Fled like the flood's foam.
The lawyer, and the laws,
And the kingdom,
Clean swept herefrom.

'They called me theirs,
Who so controlled me;
Yet every one
Wished to stay, and is gone,
How am I theirs,
If they cannot hold me,
But I hold them?'

When I heard the Earth-song
I was no longer brave;
My avarice cooled
Like lust in the chill of the grave.

Forerunners

LONG I followed happy guides,
I could never reach their sides;
Their step is forth, and, ere the day
Breaks up their leaguer, and away.
Keen my sense, my heart was young,
Right good-will my sinews strung,
But no speed of mine avails
To hunt upon their shining trails.
On and away, their hasting feet
Make the morning proud and sweet;
Flowers they strew,—I catch the scent;
Or tone of silver instrument
Leaves on the wind melodious trace;
Yet I could never see their face.
On eastern hills I see their smokes,
Mixed with mist by distant lochs.
I met many travellers
Who the road had surely kept;
They saw not my fine revellers,—
These had crossed them while they slept.
Some had heard their fair report,
In the country or the court.
Fleetest couriers alive
Never yet could once arrive,
As they went or they returned,
At the house where these sojourned.
Sometimes their strong speed they slacken,
Though they are not overtaken;
In sleep their jubilant troop is near,—

I tuneful voices overhear;
It may be in wood or waste,—
At unawares 't is come and past.
Their near camp my spirit knows
By signs gracious as rainbows.
I thenceforward and long after
Listen for their harp-like laughter,
And carry in my heart, for days,
Peace that hallows rudest ways.

40   *Bacchus*

BRING me wine, but wine which never grew
In the belly of the grape,
Or grew on vine whose tap-roots, reaching through
Under the Andes to the Cape,
Suffer no savor of the earth to scape.

Let its grapes the morn salute
From a nocturnal root,
Which feels the acrid juice
Of Styx and Erebus;
And turns the woe of Night,
By its own craft, to a more rich delight.

We buy ashes for bread;
We buy diluted wine;
Give me of the true,—
Whose ample leaves and tendrils curled
Among the silver hills of heaven
Draw everlasting dew;

RALPH WALDO EMERSON

Wine of wine,
Blood of the world,
Form of forms, and mould of statures,
That I intoxicated,
And by the draught assimilated,
May float at pleasure through all natures;
The bird-language rightly spell,
And that which roses say so well.

Wine that is shed
Like the torrents of the sun
Up the horizon walls,
Or like the Atlantic streams, which run
When the South Sea calls.

Water and bread,
Food which needs no transmuting,
Rainbow-flowering, wisdom-fruiting,
Wine which is already man,
Food which teach and reason can.

Wine which Music is,—
Music and wine are one,—
That I, drinking this,
Shall hear far Chaos talk with me;
Kings unborn shall walk with me;
And the poor grass shall plot and plan
What it will do when it is man.
Quickened so, will I unlock
Every crypt of every rock.

I thank the joyful juice
For all I know;—

Winds of remembering
Of the ancient being blow,
And seeming-solid walls of use
Open and flow.

Pour, Bacchus! the remembering wine;
Retrieve the loss of me and mine!
Vine for vine be antidote,
And the grape requite the lote!
Haste to cure the old despair,—
Reason in Nature's lotus drenched,
The memory of ages quenched;
Give them again to shine;
Let wine repair what this undid;
And where the infection slid,
A dazzling memory revive;
Refresh the faded tints,
Recut the aged prints,
And write my old adventures with the pen
Which on the first day drew,
Upon the tablets blue,
The dancing Pleiads and eternal men.

41   *Merlin*

THY trivial harp will never please
Or fill my craving ear;
Its chords should ring as blows the breeze,
Free, peremptory, clear.
No jingling serenader's art,
Nor tinkle of piano strings,
Can make the wild blood start

In its mystic springs.
The kingly bard
Must smite the chords rudely and hard,
As with hammer or with mace;
That they may render back
Artful thunder, which conveys
Secrets of the solar track,
Sparks of the supersolar blaze.
Merlin's blows are strokes of fate,
Chiming with the forest tone,
When boughs buffet boughs in the wood;
Chiming with the gasp and moan
Of the ice-imprisoned flood;
With the pulse of manly hearts;
With the voice of orators;
With the din of city arts;
With the cannonade of wars;
With the marches of the brave;
And prayers of might from martyrs' cave.

Great is the art,
Great be the manners, of the bard.
He shall not his brain encumber
With the coil of rhythm and number;
But, leaving rule and pale forethought,
He shall aye climb
For his rhyme.
'Pass in, pass in,' the angels say,
'In to the upper doors,
Nor count compartments of the floors,
But mount to paradise
By the stairway of surprise.'

Blameless master of the games,
King of sport that never shames,
He shall daily joy dispense
Hid in song's sweet influence.
Forms more cheerly live and go,
What time the subtle mind
Sings aloud the tune whereto
Their pulses beat,
And march their feet,
And their members are combined.

By Sybarites beguiled,
He shall no task decline;
Merlin's mighty line
Extremes of nature reconciled,—
Bereaved a tyrant of his will,
And made the lion mild.
Songs can the tempest still,
Scattered on the stormy air,
Mould the year to fair increase,
And bring in poetic peace.

He shall not seek to weave,
In weak, unhappy times,
Efficacious rhymes;
Wait his returning strength.
Bird that from the nadir's floor
To the zenith's top can soar,—
The soaring orbit of the muse exceeds that
        journey's length.
Nor profane affect to hit
Or compass that, by meddling wit,

Which only the propitious mind
Publishes when 't is inclined.
There are open hours
When the God's will sallies free,
And the dull idiot might see
The flowing fortunes of a thousand years;—
Sudden, at unawares,
Self-moved, fly-to the doors,
Nor sword of angels could reveal
What they conceal.

42 *Merops*

WHAT care I, so they stand the same,—
  Things of the heavenly mind,—
How long the power to give them name
  Tarries yet behind?

Thus far to-day your favors reach,
  O fair, appeasing presences!
Ye taught my lips a single speech,
  And a thousand silences.

Space grants beyond his fated road
  No inch to the god of day;
And copious language still bestowed
  One word, no more, to say.

43 *Ode*

Inscribed to W. H. Channing

THOUGH loath to grieve
The evil time's sole patriot,
I cannot leave
My honied thought
For the priest's cant,
Or statesman's rant.

If I refuse
My study for their politique,
Which at the best is trick,
The angry Muse
Puts confusion in my brain.

But who is he that prates
Of the culture of mankind,
Of better arts and life?
Go, blindworm, go,
Behold the famous States
Harrying Mexico
With rifle and with knife!

Or who, with accent bolder,
Dare praise the freedom-loving mountaineer?
I found by thee, O rushing Contoocook!
And in thy valleys, Agiochook!
The jackals of the negro-holder.

The God who made New Hampshire
Taunted the lofty land

With little men;—
Small bat and wren
House in the oak:—
If earth-fire cleave
The upheaved land, and bury the folk,
The southern crocodile would grieve.
Virtue palters; Right is hence;
Freedom praised, but hid;
Funeral eloquence
Rattles the coffin-lid.

What boots thy zeal,
O glowing friend,
That would indignant rend
The northland from the south?
Wherefore? to what good end?
Boston Bay and Bunker Hill
Would serve things still;—
Things are of the snake.

The horseman serves the horse,
The neatherd serves the neat,
The merchant serves the purse,
The eater serves his meat;
'T is the day of the chattel,
Web to weave, and corn to grind;
Things are in the saddle,
And ride mankind.

There are two laws discrete,
Not reconciled,—
Law for man, and law for thing;
The last builds town and fleet,

But it runs wild,
And doth the man unking.

'T is fit the forest fall,
The steep be graded,
The mountain tunnelled,
The sand shaded,
The orchard planted,
The glebe tilled,
The prairie granted,
The steamer built.

Let man serve law for man;
Live for friendship, live for love,
For truth's and harmony's behoof;
The state may follow how it can,
As Olympus follows Jove.

Yet do not I implore
The wrinkled shopman to my sounding woods,
Nor bid the unwilling senator
Ask votes of thrushes in the solitudes.
Every one to his chosen work;—
Foolish hands may mix and mar;
Wise and sure the issues are.
Round they roll till dark is light,
Sex to sex, and even to odd;—
The over-god
Who marries Right to Might,
Who peoples, unpeoples,—
He who exterminates
Races by stronger races,
Black by white faces,—

Knows to bring honey
Out of the lion;
Grafts gentlest scion
On pirate and Turk.

The Cossack eats Poland,
Like stolen fruit;
Her last noble is ruined,
Her last poet mute:
Straight, into double band
The victors divide;
Half for freedom strike and stand;—
The astonished Muse finds thousands at her side.

44   *Give All to Love*

GIVE all to love;
Obey thy heart;
Friends, kindred, days,
Estate, good-fame,
Plans, credit and the Muse,—
Nothing refuse.

'T is a brave master;
Let it have scope:
Follow it utterly,
Hope beyond hope:
High and more high
It dives into noon,
With wing unspent,
Untold intent;

But it is a god,
Knows its own path
And the outlets of the sky.

It was never for the mean;
It requireth courage stout.
Souls above doubt,
Valor unbending,
It will reward,—
They shall return
More than they were,
And ever ascending.

Leave all for love;
Yet, hear me, yet,
One word more thy heart behoved,
One pulse more of firm endeavor,—
Keep thee to-day,
To-morrow, forever,
Free as an Arab
Of thy beloved.

Cling with life to the maid;
But when the surprise,
First vague shadow of surmise
Flits across her bosom young,
Of a joy apart from thee,
Free be she, fancy-free;
Nor thou detain her vesture's hem,
Nor the palest rose she flung
From her summer diadem.

Though thou loved her as thyself,
As a self of purer clay,

Though her parting dims the day,
Stealing grace from all alive;
Heartily know,
When half-gods go,
The gods arrive.

45 *Days*

Daughters of Time, the hypocritic Days,
Muffled and dumb like barefoot dervishes,
And marching single in an endless file,
Bring diadems and fagots in their hands.
To each they offer gifts after his will,
Bread, kingdoms, stars, and sky that holds them all.
I, in my pleached garden, watched the pomp,
Forgot my morning wishes, hastily
Took a few herbs and apples, and the Day
Turned and departed silent. I, too late,
Under her solemn fillet saw the scorn.

46 *Brahma*

If the red slayer think he slays,
  Or if the slain think he is slain,
They know not well the subtle ways
  I keep, and pass, and turn again.

Far or forgot to me is near;
  Shadow and sunlight are the same;

The vanished gods to me appear;
   And one to me are shame and fame.

They reckon ill who leave me out;
   When me they fly, I am the wings;
I am the doubter and the doubt,
   And I the hymn the Brahmin sings.

The strong gods pine for my abode,
   And pine in vain the sacred Seven;
But thou, meek lover of the good!
   Find me, and turn thy back on heaven.

47   *Seashore*

I HEARD or seemed to hear the chiding Sea
Say, Pilgrim, why so late and slow to come?
Am I not always here, thy summer home?
Is not my voice thy music, morn and eve?
My breath thy healthful climate in the heats,
My touch thy antidote, my bay thy bath?
Was ever building like my terraces?
Was ever couch magnificent as mine?
Lie on the warm rock-ledges, and there learn
A little hut suffices like a town.
I make your sculptured architecture vain,
Vain beside mine. I drive my wedges home,
And carve the coastwise mountain into caves.
Lo! here is Rome and Nineveh and Thebes,
Karnak and Pyramid and Giant's Stairs
Half piled or prostrate: and my newest slab
Older than all thy race.

RALPH WALDO EMERSON

Behold the Sea,
The opaline, the plentiful and strong,
Yet beautiful as is the rose in June,
Fresh as the trickling rainbow of July;
Sea full of food, the nourisher of kinds,
Purger of earth, and medicine of men;
Creating a sweet climate by my breath,
Washing out harms and griefs from memory,
And, in my mathematic ebb and flow,
Giving a hint of that which changes not.
Rich are the sea-gods:—who gives gifts but they?
They grope the sea for pearls, but more than pearls:
They pluck Force thence, and give it to the wise.
For every wave is wealth to Dædalus,
Wealth to the cunning artist who can work
This matchless strength. Where shall he find, O waves!
A load your Atlas shoulders cannot lift?

I with my hammer pounding evermore
The rocky coast, smite Andes into dust,
Strewing my bed, and, in another age,
Rebuild a continent of better men.
Then I unbar the doors: my paths lead out
The exodus of nations: I disperse
Men to all shores that front the hoary main.

I too have arts and sorceries;
Illusion dwells forever with the wave.
I know what spells are laid. Leave me to deal
With credulous and imaginative man;
For, though he scoop my water in his palm,
A few rods off he deems it gems and clouds.
Planting strange fruits and sunshine on the shore,

I make some coast alluring, some lone isle,
To distant men, who must go there, or die.

48   *Two Rivers*

THY summer voice, Musketaquit,
Repeats the music of the rain;
But sweeter rivers pulsing flit
Through thee, as thou through Concord **Plain.**

Thou in thy narrow banks art pent:
The stream I love unbounded goes
Through flood and sea and firmament;
Through light, through life, it forward flows.

I see the inundation sweet,
I hear the spending of the stream
Through years, through men, through Nature fleet,
Through love and thought, through power and dream.

Musketaquit, a goblin strong,
Of shard and flint makes jewels gay;
They lose their grief who hear his song,
And where he winds is the day of day.

So forth and brighter fares my stream,—
Who drink it shall not thirst again;
No darkness stains its equal gleam,
And ages drop in it like rain.

49

Quatrains

ORATOR

He who has no hands
Perforce must use his tongue;
Foxes are so cunning
Because they are not strong.

POET

To clothe the fiery thought
In simple words succeeds,
For still the craft of genius is
To mask a king in weeds.

GARDENER

True Brahmin, in the morning meadows wet,
Expound the Vedas of the violet,
Or, hid in vines, peeping through many a loop,
See the plum redden, and the beurré stoop.

50

Terminus

It is time to be old,
To take in sail:—
The god of bounds,
Who sets to seas a shore,
Came to me in his fatal rounds,
And said: 'No more!
No farther shoot
Thy broad ambitious branches, and thy root.

Fancy departs: no more invent;
Contract thy firmament
To compass of a tent.
There's not enough for this and that,
Make thy option which of two;
Economize the failing river,
Not the less revere the Giver,
Leave the many and hold the few.
Timely wise accept the terms,
Soften the fall with wary foot;
A little while
Still plan and smile,
And,—fault of novel germs,—
Mature the unfallen fruit.
Curse, if thou wilt, thy sires,
Bad husbands of their fires,
Who, when they gave thee breath,
Failed to bequeath
The needful sinew stark as once,
The Baresark marrow to thy bones,
But left a legacy of ebbing veins,
Inconstant heat and nerveless reins,—
Amid the Muses, left thee deaf and dumb,
Amid the gladiators, halt and numb.'

As the bird trims her to the gale,
I trim myself to the storm of time,
I man the rudder, reef the sail,
Obey the voice at eve obeyed at prime:
'Lowly faithful, banish fear,
Right onward drive unharmed;
The port, well worth the cruise, is near,
And every wave is charmed.'

51 *Hymn to the Night*

Ασπασίη, τρίλλιστος

I HEARD the trailing garments of the Night
  Sweep through her marble halls!
I saw her sable skirts all fringed with light
  From the celestial walls!

I felt her presence, by its spell of might,
  Stoop o'er me from above;
The calm, majestic presence of the Night,
  As of the one I love.

I heard the sounds of sorrow and delight,
  The manifold, soft chimes,
That fill the haunted chambers of the Night,
  Like some old poet's rhymes.

From the cool cisterns of the midnight air
  My spirit drank repose;
The fountain of perpetual peace flows there,—
  From those deep cisterns flows.

O holy Night! from thee I learn to bear
  What man has borne before!
Thou layest thy finger on the lips of Care,
  And they complain no more.

Peace! Peace! Orestes-like I breathe this prayer!
    Descend with broad-winged flight,
The welcome, the thrice-prayed for, the most fair,
    The best-beloved Night!

52   *The Day Is Done*

THE day is done, and the darkness
    Falls from the wings of Night,
As a feather is wafted downward
    From an eagle in his flight.

I see the lights of the village
    Gleam through the rain and the mist,
And a feeling of sadness comes o'er me
    That my soul cannot resist:

A feeling of sadness and longing,
    That is not akin to pain,
And resembles sorrow only
    As the mist resembles the rain.

Come, read to me some poem,
    Some simple and heartfelt lay,
That shall soothe this restless feeling,
    And banish the thoughts of day.

Not from the grand old masters,
    Not from the bards sublime,
Whose distant footsteps echo
    Through the corridors of Time.

For, like strains of martial music,
   Their mighty thoughts suggest
Life's endless toil and endeavor;
   And to-night I long for rest.

Read from some humbler poet,
   Whose songs gushed from his heart,
As showers from the clouds of summer,
   Or tears from the eyelids start;

Who, through long days of labor,
   And nights devoid of ease,
Still heard in his soul the music
   Of wonderful melodies.

Such songs have power to quiet
   The restless pulse of care,
And come like the benediction
   That follows after prayer.

Then read from the treasured volume
   The poem of thy choice,
And lend to the rhyme of the poet
   The beauty of thy voice.

And the night shall be filled with music,
   And the cares, that infest the day,
Shall fold their tents, like the Arabs,
   And as silently steal away.

53   *Seaweed*

WHEN descends on the Atlantic
     The gigantic
Storm-wind of the equinox,
Landward in his wrath he scourges
     The toiling surges,
Laden with seaweed from the rocks:

From Bermuda's reefs; from edges
     Of sunken ledges,
In some far-off, bright Azore;
From Bahama, and the dashing,
     Silver-flashing
Surges of San Salvador;

From the tumbling surf, that buries
     The Orkneyan skerries,
Answering the hoarse Hebrides;
And from wrecks of ships, and drifting
     Spars, uplifting
On the desolate, rainy seas;—

Ever drifting, drifting, drifting
     On the shifting
Currents of the restless main;
Till in sheltered coves, and reaches
     Of sandy beaches,
All have found repose again.

So when storms of wild emotion
     Strike the ocean

Of the poet's soul, erelong
From each cave and rocky fastness,
    In its vastness,
Floats some fragment of a song:

From the far-off isles enchanted,
    Heaven has planted
With the golden fruit of Truth;
From the flashing surf, whose vision
    Gleams Elysian
In the tropic clime of Youth;

From the strong Will, and the Endeavor
    That forever
Wrestle with the tides of Fate;
From the wreck of Hopes far-scattered,
    Tempest-shattered,
Floating waste and desolate;—

Ever drifting, drifting, drifting
    On the shifting
Currents of the restless heart;
Till at length in books recorded,
    They, like hoarded
Household words, no more depart.

54   *Curfew*

I

SOLEMNLY, mournfully,
    Dealing its dole,
The Curfew Bell
    Is beginning to toll.

Cover the embers,
    And put out the light;
Toil comes with the morning,
    And rest with the night.

Dark grow the windows,
    And quenched is the fire;
Sound fades into silence,—
    All footsteps retire.

No voice in the chambers,
    No sound in the hall!
Sleep and oblivion
    Reign over all!

II

The book is completed,
    And closed, like the day;
And the hand that has written it
    Lays it away.

Dim grow its fancies;
    Forgotten they lie;
Like coals in the ashes,
    They darken and die.

Song sinks into silence,
    The story is told,
The windows are darkened,
    The hearth-stone is cold.

Darker and darker
    The black shadows fall;
Sleep and oblivion
    Reign over all.

55   *The Fire of Drift-Wood*
Devereux Farm, near Marblehead

WE sat within the farm-house old,
    Whose windows, looking o'er the bay,
Gave to the sea-breeze damp and cold
    An easy entrance, night and day.

Not far away we saw the port,
    The strange, old-fashioned, silent town,
The lighthouse, the dismantled fort,
    The wooden houses, quaint and brown.

We sat and talked until the night,
    Descending, filled the little room;
Our faces faded from the sight,
    Our voices only broke the gloom.

We spake of many a vanished scene,
    Of what we once had thought and said,
Of what had been, and might have been,
    And who was changed, and who was dead;

And all that fills the hearts of friends,
    When first they feel, with secret pain,
Their lives henceforth have separate ends,
    And never can be one again;

The first slight swerving of the heart,
    That words are powerless to express,

And leave it still unsaid in part,
  Or say it in too great excess.

The very tones in which we spake
  Had something strange, I could but mark;
The leaves of memory seemed to make
  A mournful rustling in the dark.

Oft died the words upon our lips,
  As suddenly, from out the fire
Built of the wreck of stranded ships,
  The flames would leap and then expire.

And, as their splendor flashed and failed,
  We thought of wrecks upon the main,
Of ships dismasted, that were hailed
  And sent no answer back again.

The windows, rattling in their frames,
  The ocean, roaring up the beach,
The gusty blast, the bickering flames,
  All mingled vaguely in our speech;

Until they made themselves a part
  Of fancies floating through the brain,
The long-lost ventures of the heart,
  That send no answers back again.

O flames that glowed! O hearts that yearned!
  They were indeed too much akin,
The drift-wood fire without that burned,
  The thoughts that burned and glowed within.

56   *The Jewish Cemetery at Newport*

How strange it seems! These Hebrews in their graves,
   Close by the street of this fair seaport town,
Silent beside the never-silent waves,
   At rest in all this moving up and down!

The trees are white with dust, that o'er their sleep
   Wave their broad curtains in the southwind's breath,
While underneath these leafy tents they keep
   The long, mysterious Exodus of Death.

And these sepulchral stones, so old and brown,
   That pave with level flags their burial-place,
Seem like the tablets of the Law, thrown down
   And broken by Moses at the mountain's base.

The very names recorded here are strange,
   Of foreign accent, and of different climes;
Alvares and Rivera interchange
   With Abraham and Jacob of old times.

'Blessed be God, for he created Death!'
   The mourners said, 'and Death is rest and peace';
Then added, in the certainty of faith,
   'And giveth Life that nevermore shall cease.'

Closed are the portals of their Synagogue,
   No Psalms of David now the silence break,
No Rabbi reads the ancient Decalogue
   In the grand dialect the Prophets spake.

Gone are the living, but the dead remain,
   And not neglected; for a hand unseen,
Scattering its bounty, like a summer rain,
   Still keeps their graves and their remembrance green.

How came they here? What burst of Christian hate,
   What persecution, merciless and blind,
Drove o'er the sea—that desert desolate—
   These Ishmaels and Hagars of mankind?

They lived in narrow streets and lanes obscure,
   Ghetto and Judenstrass, in mirk and mire;
Taught in the school of patience to endure
   The life of anguish and the death of fire.

All their lives long, with the unleavened bread
   And bitter herbs of exile and its fears,
The wasting famine of the heart they fed,
   And slaked its thirst with marah of their tears.

Anathema maranatha! was the cry
   That rang from town to town, from street to street:
At every gate the accursed Mordecai
   Was mocked and jeered, and spurned by Christian feet.

Pride and humiliation hand in hand
   Walked with them through the world where'er they
       went;
Trampled and beaten were they as the sand,
   And yet unshaken as the continent.

For in the background figures vague and vast
   Of patriarchs and of prophets rose sublime,

And all the great traditions of the Past
  They saw reflected in the coming time.

And thus forever with reverted look
  The mystic volume of the world they read,
Spelling it backward, like a Hebrew book,
  Till life became a Legend of the Dead.

But ah! what once has been shall be no more!
  The groaning earth in travail and in pain
Brings forth its races, but does not restore,
  And the dead nations never rise again.

57 *My Lost Youth*

OFTEN I think of the beautiful town
  That is seated by the sea;
Often in thought go up and down
The pleasant streets of that dear old town,
  And my youth comes back to me.
    And a verse of a Lapland song
    Is haunting my memory still:
    'A boy's will is the wind's will,
And the thoughts of youth are long, long thoughts.'

I can see the shadowy lines of its trees,
  And catch, in sudden gleams,
The sheen of the far-surrounding seas,
And islands that were the Hesperides
  Of all my boyish dreams.
    And the burden of that old song,

It murmurs and whispers still:
'A boy's will is the wind's will,
And the thoughts of youth are long, long thoughts.'

I remember the black wharves and the slips,
And the sea-tides tossing free;
And Spanish sailors with bearded lips,
And the beauty and mystery of the ships,
And the magic of the sea.
And the voice of that wayward song
Is singing and saying still:
'A boy's will is the wind's will,
And the thoughts of youth are long, long thoughts.'

I remember the bulwarks by the shore,
And the fort upon the hill;
The sunrise gun, with its hollow roar,
The drum-beat repeated o'er and o'er,
And the bugle wild and shrill.
And the music of that old song
Throbs in my memory still:
'A boy's will is the wind's will,
And the thoughts of youth are long, long thoughts.'

I remember the sea-fight far away,
How it thundered o'er the tide!
And the dead captains, as they lay
In their graves, o'erlooking the tranquil bay
Where they in battle died.
And the sound of that mournful song
Goes through me with a thrill:
'A boy's will is the wind's will,
And the thoughts of youth are long, long thoughts.'

I can see the breezy dome of groves,
   The shadows of Deering's Woods;
And the friendships old and the early loves
Come back with a Sabbath sound, as of doves
   In quiet neighborhoods.
     And the verse of that sweet old song,
     It flutters and murmurs still:
     'A boy's will is the wind's will,
And the thoughts of youth are long, long thoughts.'

I remember the gleams and glooms that dart
   Across the school-boy's brain;
The song and the silence in the heart,
That in part are prophecies, and in part
   Are longings wild and vain.
     And the voice of that fitful song
     Sings on, and is never still:
     'A boy's will is the wind's will,
And the thoughts of youth are long, long thoughts.'

There are things of which I may not speak;
   There are dreams that cannot die;
There are thoughts that make the strong heart weak,
And bring a pallor into the cheek,
   And a mist before the eye.
     And the words of that fatal song
     Come over me like a chill:
     'A boy's will is the wind's will,
And the thoughts of youth are long, long thoughts.'

Strange to me now are the forms I meet
   When I visit the dear old town;
But the native air is pure and sweet,
And the trees that o'ershadow each well-known street,

As they balance up and down,
　　Are singing the beautiful song,
　　Are sighing and whispering still:
　　'A boy's will is the wind's will,
And the thoughts of youth are long, long thoughts.'

And Deering's Woods are fresh and fair,
　　And with joy that is almost pain
My heart goes back to wander there,
And among the dreams of the days that were,
　　I find my lost youth again.
　　　　And the strange and beautiful song,
　　　　The groves are repeating it still:
　　　　'A boy's will is the wind's will,
And the thoughts of youth are long, long thoughts.'

58　　*The Birds of Killingworth*

IT was the season, when through all the land
　　The merle and mavis build, and building sing
Those lovely lyrics, written by His hand,
　　Whom Saxon Cædmon calls the Blitheheart King;
When on the boughs the purple buds expand,
　　The banners of the vanguard of the Spring,
And rivulets, rejoicing, rush and leap,
And wave their fluttering signals from the steep.

The robin and the bluebird, piping loud,
　　Filled all the blossoming orchards with their glee;
The sparrows chirped as if they still were proud
　　Their race in Holy Writ should mentioned be;

126

And hungry crows, assembled in a crowd,
  Clamored their piteous prayer incessantly,
Knowing who hears the ravens cry, and said:
'Give us, O Lord, this day, our daily bread!'

Across the Sound the birds of passage sailed,
  Speaking some unknown language strange and sweet
Of tropic isle remote, and passing hailed
  The village with the cheers of all their fleet;
Or quarrelling together, laughed and railed
  Like foreign sailors, landed in the street
Of seaport town, and with outlandish noise
Of oaths and gibberish frightening girls and boys.

Thus came the jocund Spring in Killingworth,
  In fabulous days, some hundred years ago;
And thrifty farmers, as they tilled the earth,
  Heard with alarm the cawing of the crow,
That mingled with the universal mirth,
  Cassandra-like, prognosticating woe;
They shook their heads, and doomed with dreadful words
To swift destruction the whole race of birds.

And a town-meeting was convened straightway
  To set a price upon the guilty heads
Of these marauders, who, in lieu of pay,
  Levied black-mail upon the garden beds
And cornfields, and beheld without dismay
  The awful scarecrow, with his fluttering shreds;
The skeleton that waited at their feast,
Whereby their sinful pleasure was increased.

Then from his house, a temple painted white,
  With fluted columns, and a roof of red,

The Squire came forth, august and splendid sight!
   Slowly descending, with majestic tread,
Three flights of steps, nor looking left nor right,
   Down the long street he walked, as one who said,
'A town that boasts inhabitants like me
Can have no lack of good society!'

The Parson, too, appeared, a man austere,
   The instinct of whose nature was to kill;
The wrath of God he preached from year to year,
   And read, with fervor, Edwards on the Will;
His favorite pastime was to slay the deer
   In Summer on some Adirondac hill;
E'en now, while walking down the rural lane,
He lopped the wayside lilies with his cane.

From the Academy, whose belfry crowned
   The hill of Science with its vane of brass,
Came the Preceptor, gazing idly round,
   Now at the clouds, and now at the green grass,
And all absorbed in reveries profound
   Of fair Almira in the upper class,
Who was, as in a sonnet he had said,
As pure as water, and as good as bread.

And next the Deacon issued from his door,
   In his voluminous neck-cloth, white as snow;
A suit of sable bombazine he wore;
   His form was ponderous, and his step was slow;
There never was so wise a man before;
   He seemed the incarnate 'Well, I told you so!'
And to perpetuate his great renown
There was a street named after him in town.

These came together in the new town-hall,
  With sundry farmers from the region round.
The Squire presided, dignified and tall,
  His air impressive and his reasoning sound;
Ill fared it with the birds, both great and small;
  Hardly a friend in all that crowd they found,
But enemies enough, who every one
Charged them with all the crimes beneath the sun.

When they had ended, from his place apart
  Rose the Preceptor, to redress the wrong,
And, trembling like a steed before the start,
  Looked round bewildered on the expectant throng;
Then thought of fair Almira, and took heart
  To speak out what was in him, clear and strong,
Alike regardless of their smile or frown,
And quite determined not to be laughed down.

'Plato, anticipating the Reviewers,
  From his Republic banished without pity
The Poets; in this little town of yours,
  You put to death, by means of a Committee,
The ballad-singers and the Troubadours,
  The street-musicians of the heavenly city,
The birds, who make sweet music for us all
In our dark hours, as David did for Saul.

'The thrush that carols at the dawn of day
  From the green steeples of the piny wood;
The oriole in the elm; the noisy jay,
  Jargoning like a foreigner at his food;
The bluebird balanced on some topmost spray,
  Flooding with melody the neighborhood;

Linnet and meadow-lark, and all the throng
That dwell in nests, and have the gift of song.

'You slay them all! and wherefore? for the gain
 Of a scant handful more or less of wheat,
Or rye, or barley, or some other grain,
 Scratched up at random by industrious feet,
Searching for worm or weevil after rain!
 Or a few cherries, that are not so sweet
As are the songs these uninvited guests
Sing at their feast with comfortable breasts.

'Do you ne'er think what wondrous beings these?
 Do you ne'er think who made them, and who taught
The dialect they speak, where melodies
 Alone are the interpreters of thought?
Whose household words are songs in many keys,
 Sweeter than instrument of man e'er caught!
Whose habitations in the tree-tops even
Are half-way houses on the road to heaven!

'Think, every morning when the sun peeps through
 The dim, leaf-latticed windows of the grove,
How jubilant the happy birds renew
 Their old, melodious madrigals of love!
And when you think of this, remember too
 'Tis always morning somewhere, and above
The awakening continents, from shore to shore,
Somewhere the birds are singing evermore.

'Think of your woods and orchards without birds!
 Of empty nests that cling to boughs and beams
As in an idiot's brain remembered words
 Hang empty 'mid the cobwebs of his dreams!

Will bleat of flocks or bellowing of herds
  Make up for the lost music, when your teams
Drag home the stingy harvest, and no more
The feathered gleaners follow to your door?

'What! would you rather see the incessant stir
  Of insects in the windrows of the hay,
And hear the locust and the grasshopper
  Their melancholy hurdy-gurdies play?
Is this more pleasant to you than the whir
  Of meadow-lark, and her sweet roundelay,
Or twitter of little field-fares, as you take
Your nooning in the shade of bush and brake?

'You call them thieves and pillagers; but know,
  They are the wingèd wardens of your farms,
Who from the cornfields drive the insidious foe,
  And from your harvests keep a hundred harms;
Even the blackest of them all, the crow,
  Renders good service as your man-at-arms,
Crushing the beetle in his coat of mail,
And crying havoc on the slug and snail.

'How can I teach your children gentleness,
  And mercy to the weak, and reverence
For Life, which, in its weakness or excess,
  Is still a gleam of God's omnipotence,
Or Death, which, seeming darkness, is no less
  The selfsame light, although averted hence,
When by your laws, your actions, and your speech,
You contradict the very things I teach?'

With this he closed; and through the audience went
  A murmur, like the rustle of dead leaves;

The farmers laughed and nodded, and some bent
  Their yellow heads together like their sheaves;
Men have no faith in fine-spun sentiment
  Who put their trust in bullocks and in beeves.
The birds were doomed; and, as the record shows,
A bounty offered for the heads of crows.

There was another audience out of reach,
  Who had no voice nor vote in making laws,
But in the papers read his little speech,
  And crowned his modest temples with applause;
They made him conscious, each one more than each,
  He still was victor, vanquished in their cause.
Sweetest of all the applause he won from thee,
O fair Almira at the Academy!

And so the dreadful massacre began;
  O'er fields and orchards, and o'er woodland crests,
The ceaseless fusillade of terror ran.
  Dead fell the birds, with blood-stains on their breasts,
Or wounded crept away from sight of man,
  While the young died of famine in their nests;
A slaughter to be told in groans, not words,
The very St. Bartholomew of Birds!

The Summer came, and all the birds were dead;
  The days were like hot coals; the very ground
Was burned to ashes; in the orchards fed
  Myriads of caterpillars, and around
The cultivated fields and garden beds
  Hosts of devouring insects crawled, and found
No foe to check their march, till they had made
The land a desert without leaf or shade.

Devoured by worms, like Herod, was the town,
  Because, like Herod, it had ruthlessly
Slaughtered the Innocents. From the trees spun down
  The canker-worms upon the passers-by,
Upon each woman's bonnet, shawl, and gown,
  Who shook them off with just a little cry;
They were the terror of each favorite walk,
The endless theme of all the village talk.

The farmers grew impatient, but a few
  Confessed their error, and would not complain,
For after all, the best thing one can do
  When it is raining, is to let it rain.
Then they repealed the law, although they knew
  It would not call the dead to life again;
As school-boys, finding their mistake too late,
Draw a wet sponge across the accusing slate.

That year in Killingworth the Autumn came
  Without the light of his majestic look,
The wonder of the falling tongues of flame,
  The illumined pages of his Doom's-Day book.
A few lost leaves blushed crimson with their shame,
  And drowned themselves despairing in the brook,
While the wild wind went moaning everywhere,
Lamenting the dead children of the air!

But the next Spring a stranger sight was seen,
  A sight that never yet by bard was sung,
As great a wonder as it would have been
  If some dumb animal had found a tongue!
A wagon, overarched with evergreen,
  Upon whose boughs were wicker cages hung,

All full of singing birds, came down the street,
Filling the air with music wild and sweet.

From all the country round these birds were brought,
　By order of the town, with anxious quest,
And, loosened from their wicker prisons, sought
　In woods and fields the places they loved best,
Singing loud canticles, which many thought
　Were satires to the authorities addressed,
While others, listening in green lanes, averred
Such lovely music never had been heard!

But blither still and louder carolled they
　Upon the morrow, for they seemed to know
It was the fair Almira's wedding-day,
　And everywhere, around, above, below,
When the Preceptor bore his bride away,
　Their songs burst forth in joyous overflow,
And a new heaven bent over a new earth
Amid the sunny farms of Killingworth.

59　　　　　*Divina Commedia*

I

OFT have I seen at some cathedral door
　A laborer, pausing in the dust and heat,
　Lay down his burden, and with reverent feet
　Enter, and cross himself, and on the floor
Kneel to repeat his paternoster o'er;
　Far off the noises of the world retreat;
　The loud vociferations of the street
　Become an undistinguishable roar.

HENRY WADSWORTH LONGFELLOW

So, as I enter here from day to day,
   And leave my burden at this minster gate,
   Kneeling in prayer, and not ashamed to pray,
The tumult of the time disconsolate
   To inarticulate murmurs dies away,
   While the eternal ages watch and wait.

II

How strange the sculptures that adorn these towers!
   This crowd of statues, in whose folded sleeves
   Birds build their nests; while canopied with leaves
   Parvis and portal bloom like trellised bowers,
And the vast minster seems a cross of flowers!
   But fiends and dragons on the gargoyled eaves
   Watch the dead Christ between the living thieves,
   And, underneath, the traitor Judas lowers!
Ah! from what agonies of heart and brain,
   What exultations trampling on despair,
   What tenderness, what tears, what hate of wrong,
What passionate outcry of a soul in pain,
   Uprose this poem of the earth and air,
   This mediæval miracle of song!

III

I enter, and I see thee in the gloom
   Of the long aisles, O poet saturnine!
   And strive to make my steps keep pace with thine.
   The air is filled with some unknown perfume;
The congregation of the dead make room
   For thee to pass; the votive tapers shine;
   Like rooks that haunt Ravenna's groves of pine
   The hovering echoes fly from tomb to tomb.

From the confessionals I hear arise
  Rehearsals of forgotten tragedies,
  And lamentations from the crypts below;
And then a voice celestial that begins
  With the pathetic words, 'Although your sins
  As scarlet be,' and ends with 'as the snow.'

IV

With snow-white veil and garments as of flame,
  She stands before thee, who so long ago
  Filled thy young heart with passion and the woe
  From which thy song and all its splendors came;
And while with stern rebuke she speaks thy name,
  The ice about thy heart melts as the snow
  On mountain heights, and in swift overflow
  Comes gushing from thy lips in sobs of shame.
Thou makest full confession; and a gleam,
  As of the dawn on some dark forest cast,
  Seems on thy lifted forehead to increase;
Lethe and Eunoë—the remembered dream
  And the forgotten sorrow—bring at last
  That perfect pardon which is perfect peace.

V

I lift mine eyes, and all the windows blaze
  With forms of Saints and holy men who died,
  Here martyred and hereafter glorified;
  And the great Rose upon its leaves displays
Christ's Triumph, and the angelic roundelays,
  With splendor upon splendor multiplied;
  And Beatrice again at Dante's side
  No more rebukes, but smiles her words of praise.

And then the organ sounds, and unseen choirs
  Sing the old Latin hymns of peace and love
  And benedictions of the Holy Ghost;
And the melodious bells among the spires
  O'er all the house-tops and through heaven above
  Proclaim the elevation of the Host!

VI

O star of morning and of liberty!
  O bringer of the light, whose splendor shines
  Above the darkness of the Apennines,
  Forerunner of the day that is to be!
The voices of the city and the sea,
  The voices of the mountains and the pines,
  Repeat thy song, till the familiar lines
  Are footpaths for the thought of Italy!
Thy flame is blown abroad from all the heights,
  Through all the nations, and a sound is heard,
  As of a mighty wind, and men devout,
Strangers of Rome, and the new proselytes,
  In their own language hear thy wondrous word,
  And many are amazed and many doubt.

60   *The Monk of Casal-Maggiore*

ONCE on a time, some centuries ago,
  In the hot sunshine two Franciscan friars
Wended their weary way, with footsteps slow,
  Back to their convent, whose white walls and spires
Gleamed on the hillside like a patch of snow;
  Covered with dust they were, and torn by briers,

And bore like sumpter-mules upon their backs
The badge of poverty, their beggar's sacks.

The first was Brother Anthony, a spare
    And silent man, with pallid cheeks and thin,
Much given to vigils, penance, fasting, prayer,
    Solemn and gray, and worn with discipline,
As if his body but white ashes were,
    Heaped on the living coals that glowed within;
A simple monk, like many of his day,
Whose instinct was to listen and obey.

A different man was Brother Timothy,
    Of larger mould and of a coarser paste;
A rubicund and stalwart monk was he,
    Broad in the shoulders, broader in the waist,
Who often filled the dull refectory
    With noise by which the convent was disgraced,
But to the mass-book gave but little heed,
By reason he had never learned to read.

Now, as they passed the outskirts of a wood,
    They saw, with mingled pleasure and surprise,
Fast tethered to a tree an ass, that stood
    Lazily winking his large, limpid eyes.
The farmer Gilbert, of that neighborhood,
    His owner was, who, looking for supplies
Of fagots, deeper in the wood had strayed,
Leaving his beast to ponder in the shade.

As soon as Brother Timothy espied
    The patient animal, he said: 'Goodlack!

Thus for our needs doth Providence provide;
  We'll lay our wallets on the creature's back.'
This being done, he leisurely untied
  From head and neck the halter of the jack,
And put it round his own, and to the tree
Stood tethered fast as if the ass were he.

And, bursting forth into a merry laugh,
  He cried to Brother Anthony: 'Away!
And drive the ass before you with your staff;
  And when you reach the convent you may say
You left me at a farm, half tired and half
  Ill with a fever, for a night and day,
And that the farmer lent this ass to bear
Our wallets, that are heavy with good fare.'

Now Brother Anthony, who knew the pranks
  Of Brother Timothy, would not persuade
Or reason with him on his quirks and cranks,
  But, being obedient, silently obeyed;
And, smiting with his staff the ass's flanks,
  Drove him before him over hill and glade,
Safe with his provend to the convent gate,
Leaving poor Brother Timothy to his fate.

Then Gilbert, laden with fagots for his fire,
  Forth issued from the wood, and stood aghast
To see the ponderous body of the friar
  Standing where he had left his donkey last.
Trembling he stood, and dared not venture nigher,
  But stared, and gaped, and crossed himself full fast;
For, being credulous and of little wit,
He thought it was some demon from the pit.

While speechless and bewildered thus he gazed,
    And dropped his load of fagots on the ground,
Quoth Brother Timothy: 'Be not amazed
    That where you left a donkey should be found
A poor Franciscan friar, half-starved and crazed,
    Standing demure and with a halter bound;
But set me free, and hear the piteous story
Of Brother Timothy of Casal-Maggiore.

'I am a sinful man, although you see
    I wear the consecrated cowl and cape;
You never owned an ass, but you owned me,
    Changed and transformed from my own natural shape
All for the deadly sin of gluttony,
    From which I could not otherwise escape,
Than by this penance, dieting on grass,
And being worked and beaten as an ass.

'Think of the ignominy I endured;
    Think of the miserable life I led,
The toil and blows to which I was inured,
    My wretched lodging in a windy shed,
My scanty fare so grudgingly procured,
    The damp and musty straw that formed my bed!
But, having done this penance for my sins,
My life as man and monk again begins.'

The simple Gilbert, hearing words like these,
    Was conscience-stricken, and fell down apace
Before the friar upon his bended knees,
    And with a suppliant voice implored his grace;
And the good monk, now very much at ease,
    Granted him pardon with a smiling face,

Nor could refuse to be that night his guest,
It being late, and he in need of rest.

Upon a hillside, where the olive thrives,
   With figures painted on its whitewashed walls,
The cottage stood; and near the humming hives
   Made murmurs as of far-off waterfalls;
A place where those who love secluded lives
   Might live content, and, free from noise and brawls,
Like Claudian's Old Man of Verona here
Measure by fruits the slow-revolving year.

And, coming to this cottage of content,
   They found his children, and the buxom wench
His wife, Dame Cicely, and his father, bent
   With years and labor, seated on a bench,
Repeating over some obscure event
   In the old wars of Milanese and French;
All welcomed the Franciscan, with a sense
Of sacred awe and humble reverence.

When Gilbert told them what had come to pass,
   How beyond question, cavil, or surmise,
Good Brother Timothy had been their ass,
   You should have seen the wonder in their eyes;
You should have heard them cry 'Alas! alas!'
   Have heard their lamentations and their sighs!
For all believed the story, and began
To see a saint in this afflicted man.

Forthwith there was prepared a grand repast,
   To satisfy the craving of the friar

After so rigid and prolonged a fast;
　　The bustling housewife stirred the kitchen fire;
Then her two barn-yard fowls, her best and last,
　　Were put to death, at her express desire,
And served up with a salad in a bowl,
And flasks of country wine to crown the whole.

It would not be believed should I repeat
　　How hungry Brother Timothy appeared;
It was a pleasure but to see him eat,
　　His white teeth flashing through his russet beard,
His face aglow and flushed with wine and meat,
　　His roguish eyes that rolled and laughed and leered!
Lord! how he drank the blood-red country wine
As if the village vintage were divine!

And all the while he talked without surcease,
　　And told his merry tales with jovial glee
That never flagged, but rather did increase,
　　And laughed aloud as if insane were he,
And wagged his red beard, matted like a fleece,
　　And cast such glances at Dame Cicely
That Gilbert now grew angry with his guest,
And thus in words his rising wrath expressed.

'Good father,' said he, 'easily we see
　　How needful in some persons, and how right,
Mortification of the flesh may be.
　　The indulgence you have given it tonight,
After long penance, clearly proves to me
　　Your strength against temptation is but slight,
And shows the dreadful peril you are in
Of a relapse into your deadly sin.

'To-morrow morning, with the rising sun,
    Go back unto your convent, nor refrain
From fasting and from scourging, for you run
    Great danger to become an ass again,
Since monkish flesh and asinine are one;
    Therefore be wise, nor longer here remain,
Unless you wish the scourge should be applied
By other hands, that will not spare your hide.'

When this the monk had heard, his color fled
    And then returned, like lightning in the air,
Till he was all one blush from foot to head,
    And even the bald spot in his russet hair
Turned from its usual pallor to bright red!
    The old man was asleep upon his chair.
Then all retired, and sank into the deep
And helpless imbecility of sleep.

They slept until the dawn of day drew near,
    Till the cock should have crowed, but did not crow,
For they had slain the shining chanticleer
    And eaten him for supper, as you know.
The monk was up betimes and of good cheer,
    And, having breakfasted, made haste to go,
As if he heard the distant matin bell,
And had but little time to say farewell.

Fresh was the morning as the breath of kine;
    Odors of herbs commingled with the sweet
Balsamic exhalations of the pine;
    A haze was in the air presaging heat;
Uprose the sun above the Apennine,
    And all the misty valleys at its feet

Were full of the delirious song of birds,
Voices of men, and bells, and low of herds.

All this to Brother Timothy was naught;
   He did not care for scenery, nor here
His busy fancy found the thing it sought;
   But when he saw the convent walls appear,
And smoke from kitchen chimneys upward caught
   And whirled aloft into the atmosphere,
He quickened his slow footsteps, like a beast
That scents the stable a league off at least.

And as he entered through the convent gate
   He saw there in the court the ass, who stood
Twirling his ears about, and seemed to wait,
   Just as he found him waiting in the wood;
And told the Prior that, to alleviate
   The daily labors of the brotherhood,
The owner, being a man of means and thrift,
Bestowed him on the convent as a gift.

And thereupon the Prior for many days
   Revolved this serious matter in his mind,
And turned it over many different ways,
   Hoping that some safe issue he might find;
But stood in fear of what the world would say,
   If he accepted presents of this kind,
Employing beasts of burden for the packs
That lazy monks should carry on their backs.

Then, to avoid all scandal of the sort,
   And stop the mouth of cavil, he decreed
That he would cut the tedious matter short,
   And sell the ass with all convenient speed,

Thus saving the expense of his support,
   And hoarding something for a time of need.
So he despatched him to the neighboring Fair,
And freed himself from cumber and from care.

It happened now by chance, as some might say,
   Others perhaps would call it destiny,
Gilbert was at the Fair; and heard a bray,
   And nearer came, and saw that it was he,
And whispered in his ear, 'Ah, lackaday!
   Good father, the rebellious flesh, I see,
Has changed you back into an ass again,
And all my admonitions were in vain.'

The ass, who felt this breathing in his ear,
   Did not turn round to look, but shook his head,
As if he were not pleased these words to hear,
   And contradicted all that had been said.
And this made Gilbert cry in voice more clear
   'I know you well; your hair is russet-red;
Do not deny it; for you are the same
Franciscan friar, and Timothy by name.'

The ass, though now the secret had come out,
   Was obstinate, and shook his head again;
Until a crowd was gathered round about
   To hear this dialogue between the twain;
And raised their voices in a noisy shout
   When Gilbert tried to make the matter plain,
And flouted him and mocked him all day long
With laughter and with jibes and scraps of song.

'If this be Brother Timothy,' they cried,
   'Buy him, and feed him on the tenderest grass;

Thou canst not do too much for one so tried
   As to be twice transformed into an ass.'
So simple Gilbert bought him, and untied
   His halter, and o'er mountain and morass
He led him homeward, talking as he went
Of good behavior and a mind content.

The children saw them coming, and advanced,
   Shouting with joy, and hung about his neck,—
Not Gilbert's but the ass's,—round him danced,
   And wove green garlands wherewithal to deck
His sacred person; for again it chanced
   Their childish feelings, without rein or check,
Could not discriminate in any way
A donkey from a friar of Orders Gray.

'O Brother Timothy,' the children said,
   'You have come back to us just as before;
We were afraid, and thought that you were dead,
   And we should never see you any more.'
And then they kissed the white star on his head,
   That like a birth-mark or a badge he wore,
And patted him upon the neck and face,
And said a thousand things with childish grace.

Thenceforward and forever he was known
   As Brother Timothy, and led alway
A life of luxury, till he had grown
   Ungrateful, being stuffed with corn and hay,
And very vicious. Then in angry tone,
   Rousing himself, poor Gilbert said one day,
'When simple kindness is misunderstood
A little flagellation may do good.'

His many vices need not here be told;
  Among them was a habit that he had
Of flinging up his heels at young and old,
  Breaking his halter, running off like mad
O'er pasture-lands and meadow, wood and wold,
  And other misdemeanors quite as bad;
But worst of all was breaking from his shed
At night, and ravaging the cabbage-bed.

So Brother Timothy went back once more
  To his old life of labor and distress;
Was beaten worse than he had been before;
  And now, instead of comfort and caress,
Came labors manifold and trials sore;
  And as his toils increased his food grew less,
Until at last the great consoler, Death,
Ended his many sufferings with his breath.

Great was the lamentation when he died;
  And mainly that he died impenitent;
Dame Cicely bewailed, the children cried,
  The old man still remembered the event
In the French war, and Gilbert magnified
  His many virtues, as he came and went,
And said: 'Heaven pardon Brother Timothy,
And keep us from the sin of gluttony.'

61   *Chaucer*

AN old man in a lodge within a park;
  The chamber walls depicted all around

With portraitures of huntsman, hawk, and hound,
And the hurt deer. He listeneth to the lark,
Whose song comes with the sunshine through the dark
Of painted glass in leaden lattice bound;
He listeneth and he laugheth at the sound,
Then writeth in a book like any clerk.
He is the poet of the dawn, who wrote
The Canterbury Tales, and his old age
Made beautiful with song; and as I read
I hear the crowing cock, I hear the note
Of lark and linnet, and from every page
Rise odors of ploughed field or flowery mead.

62   *The Tide Rises, The Tide Falls*

THE tide rises, the tide falls,
The twilight darkens, the curlew calls;
Along the sea-sands damp and brown
The traveller hastens toward the town,
    And the tide rises, the tide falls.

Darkness settles on roofs and walls,
But the sea, the sea in the darkness calls;
The little waves, with their soft, white hands,
Efface the footprints in the sands,
    And the tide rises, the tide falls.

The morning breaks; the steeds in their stalls
Stamp and neigh, as the hostler calls;
The day returns, but nevermore
Returns the traveller to the shore,
    And the tide rises, the tide falls.

63   *The Cross of Snow*

IN the long, sleepless watches of the night,
   A gentle face—the face of one long dead—
   Looks at me from the wall, where round its head
   The night-lamp casts a halo of pale light.
Here in this room she died; and soul more white
   Never through martyrdom of fire was led
   To its repose; nor can in books be read
   The legend of a life more benedight.
There is a mountain in the distant West
   That, sun-defying, in its deep ravines
   Displays a cross of snow upon its side.
Such is the cross I wear upon my breast
   These eighteen years, through all the changing scenes
   And seasons, changeless since the day she died.

64   *The Bells of San Blas*

WHAT say the Bells of San Blas
To the ships that southward pass
   From the harbor of Mazatlan?
To them it is nothing more
Than the sound of surf on the shore,—
   Nothing more to master or man.

But to me, a dreamer of dreams,
To whom what is and what seems
   Are often one and the same,—

The Bells of San Blas to me
Have a strange, wild melody,
    And are something more than a name.

For bells are the voice of the church;
They have tones that touch and search
    The hearts of young and old;
One sound to all, yet each
Lends a meaning to their speech,
    And the meaning is manifold.

They are a voice of the Past,
Of an age that is fading fast,
    Of a power austere and grand;
When the flag of Spain unfurled
Its folds o'er this western world,
    And the Priest was lord of the land.

The chapel that once looked down
On the little seaport town
    Has crumbled into the dust;
And on oaken beams below
The bells swing to and fro,
    And are green with mould and rust.

'Is, then, the old faith dead,'
They say, 'and in its stead
    Is some new faith proclaimed,
That we are forced to remain
Naked to sun and rain,
    Unsheltered and ashamed?

'Once in our tower aloof
We rang over wall and roof
    Our warnings and our complaints;
And round about us there
The white doves filled the air,
    Like the white souls of the saints.

'The saints! Ah, have they grown
Forgetful of their own?
    Are they asleep, or dead,
That open to the sky
Their ruined Missions lie,
    No longer tenanted?

'Oh, bring us back once more
The vanished days of yore,
    When the world with faith was filled;
Bring back the fervid zeal,
The hearts of fire and steel,
    The hands that believe and build.

'Then from our tower again
We will send over land and main
    Our voices of command,
Like exiled kings who return
To their thrones, and the people learn
    That the Priest is lord of the land!'

O Bells of San Blas, in vain
Ye call back the Past again!
    The Past is deaf to your prayer;
Out of the shadows of night
The world rolls into light;
    It is daybreak everywhere.

JOHN GREENLEAF WHITTIER

1807-1892

65   *Proem*

I LOVE the old melodious lays
Which softly melt the ages through,
 The songs of Spenser's golden days,
 Arcadian Sidney's silvery phrase,
Sprinkling our noon of time with freshest morning dew.

Yet, vainly in my quiet hours
To breathe their marvellous notes I try;
 I feel them, as the leaves and flowers
 In silence feel the dewy showers,
And drink with glad, still lips the blessing of the sky.

The rigor of a frozen clime,
The harshness of an untaught ear,
 The jarring words of one whose rhyme
 Beat often Labor's hurried time,
Or Duty's rugged march through storm and strife, are here.

Of mystic beauty, dreamy grace,
No rounded art the lack supplies;
 Unskilled the subtle lines to trace,
 Or softer shades of Nature's face,
I view her common forms with unanointed eyes.

Nor mine the seer-like power to show
The secrets of the heart and mind;
To drop the plummet-line below
Our common world of joy and woe,
A more intense despair or brighter hope to find.

Yet here at least an earnest sense
Of human right and weal is shown;
A hate of tyranny intense,
And hearty in its vehemence,
As if my brother's pain and sorrow were my own.

O Freedom! if to me belong
Nor mighty Milton's gift divine,
Nor Marvell's wit and graceful song,
Still with a love as deep and strong
As theirs, I lay, like them, my best gifts on thy shrine.

AMESBURY, 11*th mo.*, 1847.

66   *Songs of Labor*

DEDICATION

I WOULD the gift I offer here
Might graces from thy favor take,
And, seen through Friendship's atmosphere,
On softened lines and coloring, wear
The unaccustomed light of beauty, for thy sake.

Few leaves of Fancy's spring remain:
But what I have I give to thee,

The o'er-sunned bloom of summer's plain,
And paler flowers, the latter rain
Calls from the westering slope of life's autumnal lea.

Above the fallen groves of green,
   Where youth's enchanted forest stood,
Dry root and mossëd trunk between,
A sober after-growth is seen,
As springs the pine where falls the gay-leafed maple wood!

Yet birds will sing, and breezes play
   Their leaf-harps in the sombre tree;
And through the bleak and wintry day
It keeps its steady green alway,—
So, even my after-thoughts may have a charm for thee.

Art's perfect forms no moral need,
   And beauty is its own excuse;
But for the dull and flowerless weed
Some healing virtue still must plead,
And the rough ore must find its honors in its use.

So haply these, my simple lays
   Of homely toil, may serve to show
The orchard bloom and tasselled maize
That skirt and gladden duty's ways,
The unsung beauty hid life's common things below.

Haply from them the toiler, bent
   Above his forge or plough, may gain
A manlier spirit of content,
And feel that life is wisest spent
Where the strong working hand makes strong the working
     brain.

The doom which to the guilty pair
   Without the walls of Eden came,
Transforming sinless ease to care
And rugged toil, no more shall bear
The burden of old crime, or mark of primal shame.

A blessing now, a curse no more;
   Since He, whose name we breathe with awe,
The coarse mechanic vesture wore,
A poor man toiling with the poor,
In labor, as in prayer, fulfilling the same law.

67   *Ichabod*

So fallen! so lost! the light withdrawn
   Which once he wore!
The glory from his gray hairs gone
   Forevermore!

Revile him not, the Tempter hath
   A snare for all;
And pitying tears, not scorn and wrath,
   Befit his fall!

Oh, dumb be passion's stormy rage,
   When he who might
Have lighted up and led his age,
   Falls back in night.

Scorn! would the angels laugh, to mark
   A bright soul driven,

Fiend-goaded, down the endless dark,
　　From hope and heaven!

Let not the land once proud of him
　　Insult him now,
Nor brand with deeper shame his dim,
　　Dishonored brow.

But let its humbled sons, instead,
　　From sea to lake,
A long lament, as for the dead,
　　In sadness make.

Of all we loved and honored, naught
　　Save power remains:
A fallen angel's pride of thought,
　　Still strong in chains.

All else is gone; from those great eyes
　　The soul has fled:
When faith is lost, when honor dies,
　　The man is dead!

Then, pay the reverence of old days
　　To his dead fame;
Walk backward, with averted gaze,
　　And hide the shame!

68　　*Song of Slaves in the Desert*

WHERE are we going? where are we going,
　　Where are we going, Rubee?
Lord of peoples, lord of lands,
Look across these shining sands,

JOHN GREENLEAF WHITTIER

Through the furnace of the noon,
Through the white light of the moon.
Strong the Ghiblee wind is blowing,
Strange and large the world is growing!
Speak and tell us where we are going,
   Where are we going, Rubee?

Bornou land was rich and good,
Wells of water, fields of food,
Dourra fields, and bloom of bean,
And the palm-tree cool and green:
Bornou land we see no longer,
Here we thirst and here we hunger,
Here the Moor-man smites in anger:
   Where are we going, Rubee?

When we went from Bornou land,
We were like the leaves and sand,
We were many, we are few;
Life has one, and death has two:
Whitened bones our path are showing,
Thou All-seeing, thou All-knowing!
Hear us, tell us, where are we going,
   Where are we going, Rubee?

Moons of marches from our eyes
Bornou land behind us lies;
Stranger round us day by day
Bends the desert circle gray;
Wild the waves of sand are flowing,
Hot the winds above them blowing,—
Lord of all things! where are we going?
   Where are we going, Rubee?

We are weak, but Thou art strong;
Short our lives, but Thine is long;
We are blind, but Thou hast eyes;
We are fools, but Thou art wise!
Thou, our morrow's pathway knowing
Through the strange world round us growing,
Hear us, tell us where are we going,
     Where are we going, Rubee?

69   *Skipper Ireson's Ride*

Of all the rides since the birth of time,
Told in story or sung in rhyme,—
On Apuleius's Golden Ass,
Or one-eyed Calender's horse of brass,
Witch astride of a human back,
Islam's prophet on Al-Borák,—
The strangest ride that ever was sped
Was Ireson's, out from Marblehead!
     Old Floyd Ireson, for his hard heart,
     Tarred and feathered and carried in a cart
          By the women of Marblehead!

Body of turkey, head of owl,
Wings a-droop like a rained-on fowl,
Feathered and ruffled in every part,
Skipper Ireson stood in the cart.
Scores of women, old and young,
Strong of muscle, and glib of tongue,
Pushed and pulled up the rocky lane,
Shouting and singing the shrill refrain:

> 'Here's Flud Oirson, fur his horrd horrt,
>   Torr'd an' futherr'd an' corr'd in a corrt
>   By the women o' Morble'ead!'

Wrinkled scolds with hands on hips,
Girls in bloom of cheek and lips,
Wild-eyed, free-limbed, such as chase
Bacchus round some antique vase,
Brief of skirt, with ankles bare,
Loose of kerchief and loose of hair,
With conch-shells blowing and fish-horns' twang,
Over and over the Mænads sang:
  'Here's Flud Oirson, fur his horrd horrt,
    Torr'd an' futherr'd an' corr'd in a corrt
      By the women o' Morble'ead!'

Small pity for him!—He sailed away
From a leaking ship in Chaleur Bay,—
Sailed away from a sinking wreck,
With his own town's-people on her deck!
'Lay by! lay by!' they called to him.
Back he answered, 'Sink or swim!
Brag of your catch of fish again!'
And off he sailed through the fog and rain!
  Old Floyd Ireson, for his hard heart,
    Tarred and feathered and carried in a cart
      By the women of Marblehead!

Fathoms deep in dark Chaleur
That wreck shall lie forevermore.
Mother and sister, wife and maid,
Looked from the rocks of Marblehead
Over the moaning and rainy sea,—
Looked for the coming that might not be!

What did the winds and the sea-birds say
Of the cruel captain who sailed away? —
   Old Floyd Ireson, for his hard heart,
   Tarred and feathered and carried in a cart
   By the women of Marblehead!

Through the street, on either side,
Up flew windows, doors swung wide;
Sharp-tongued spinsters, old wives gray,
Treble lent the fish-horn's bray.
Sea-worn grandsires, cripple-bound,
Hulks of old sailors, run aground,
Shook head, and fist, and hat, and cane,
And cracked with curses the hoarse refrain:
   'Here's Flud Oirson, fur his horrd horrt,
   Torr'd an' futherr'd an' corr'd in a corrt
   By the women o' Morble'ead!'

Sweetly along the Salem road
Bloom of orchard and lilac showed.
Little the wicked skipper knew
Of the fields so green and the sky so blue.
Riding there in his sorry trim,
Like an Indian idol glum and grim,
Scarcely he seemed the sound to hear
Of voices shouting, far and near:
   'Here's Flud Oirson, fur his horrd horrt,
   Torr'd an' futherr'd an' corr'd in a corrt
   By the women o' Morble'ead!'

'Hear me, neighbors!' at last he cried, —
'What to me is this noisy ride?
What is the shame that clothes the skin
To the nameless horror that lives within?

Waking or sleeping, I see a wreck,
And hear a cry from a reeling deck!
Hate me and curse me,—I only dread
The hand of God and the face of the dead!'
  Said old Floyd Ireson, for his hard heart,
    Tarred and feathered and carried in a cart
    By the women of Marblehead!

Then the wife of the skipper lost at sea
Said, 'God has touched him! why should we!'
Said an old wife mourning her only son,
'Cut the rogue's tether and let him run!'
So with soft relentings and rude excuse,
Half scorn, half pity, they cut him loose,
And gave him a cloak to hide him in,
And left him alone with his shame and sin.
  Poor Floyd Ireson, for his hard heart,
    Tarred and feathered and carried in a cart
    By the women of Marblehead!

70   *Snow-Bound*

A Winter Idyl

THE sun that brief December day
Rose cheerless over hills of gray,
And, darkly circled, gave at noon
A sadder light than waning moon.
Slow tracing down the thickening sky
Its mute and ominous prophecy,

A portent seeming less than threat,
It sank from sight before it set.
A chill no coat, however stout,
Of homespun stuff could quite shut out,
A hard, dull bitterness of cold,
That checked, mid-vein, the circling race
Of life-blood in the sharpened face,
The coming of the snow-storm told.
The wind blew east; we heard the roar
Of Ocean on his wintry shore,
And felt the strong pulse throbbing there
Beat with low rhythm our inland air.

Meanwhile we did our nightly chores,—
Brought in the wood from out of doors,
Littered the stalls, and from the mows
Raked down the herd's-grass for the cows;
Heard the horse whinnying for his corn;
And, sharply clashing horn on horn,
Impatient down the stanchion rows
The cattle shake their walnut bows;
While, peering from his early perch
Upon the scaffold's pole of birch,
The cock his crested helmet bent
And down his querulous challenge sent.

Unwarmed by any sunset light
The gray day darkened into night,
A night made hoary with the swarm
And whirl-dance of the blinding storm,
As zigzag, wavering to and fro,
Crossed and recrossed the wingèd snow:

And ere the early bedtime came
The white drift piled the window-frame,
And through the glass the clothes-line posts
Looked in like tall and sheeted ghosts.

So all night long the storm roared on:
The morning broke without a sun;
In tiny spherule traced with lines
Of Nature's geometric signs,
In starry flake, and pellicle,
All day the hoary meteor fell;
And, when the second morning shone,
We looked upon a world unknown,
On nothing we could call our own.
Around the glistening wonder bent
The blue walls of the firmament,
No cloud above, no earth below,—
A universe of sky and snow!
The old familiar sights of ours
Took marvellous shapes; strange domes and towers
Rose up where sty or corn-crib stood,
Or garden-wall, or belt of wood;
A smooth white mound the brush-pile showed,
A fenceless drift what once was road;
The bridle-post an old man sat
With loose-flung coat and high cocked hat;
The well-curb had a Chinese roof,
And even the long sweep, high aloof,
In its slant splendor, seemed to tell
Of Pisa's leaning miracle.

A prompt, decisive man, no breath
Our father wasted: 'Boys, a path!'

Well pleased, (for when did farmer boy
Count such a summons less than joy?)
Our buskins on our feet we drew;
With mittened hands, and caps drawn low,
To guard our necks and ears from snow,
We cut the solid whiteness through.
And, where the drift was deepest, made
A tunnel walled and overlaid
With dazzling crystal: we had read
Of rare Aladdin's wondrous cave,
And to our own his name we gave,
With many a wish the luck were ours
To test his lamp's supernal powers.
We reached the barn with merry din,
And roused the prisoned brutes within.
The old horse thrust his long head out,
And grave with wonder gazed about;
The cock his lusty greeting said,
And forth his speckled harem led;
The oxen lashed their tails, and hooked,
And mild reproach of hunger looked;
The hornëd patriarch of the sheep,
Like Egypt's Amun roused from sleep,
Shook his sage head with gesture mute,
And emphasized with stamp of foot.

All day the gusty north-wind bore
The loosening drift its breath before;
Low circling round its southern zone,
The sun through dazzling snow-mist shone.
No church-bell lent its Christian tone
To the savage air, no social smoke
Curled over woods of snow-hung oak.

A solitude made more intense
By dreary-voicëd elements,
The shrieking of the mindless wind,
The moaning tree-boughs swaying blind,
And on the glass the unmeaning beat
Of ghostly finger-tips of sleet.
Beyond the circle of our hearth
No welcome sound of toil or mirth
Unbound the spell, and testified
Of human life and thought outside.
We minded that the sharpest ear
The buried brooklet could not hear,
The music of whose liquid lip
Had been to us companionship,
And, in our lonely life, had grown
To have an almost human tone.

As night drew on, and, from the crest
Of wooded knolls that ridged the west,
The sun, a snow-blown traveller, sank
From sight beneath the smothering bank,
We piled, with care, our nightly stack
Of wood against the chimney-back,—
The oaken log, green, huge, and thick,
And on its top the stout back-stick;
The knotty forestick laid apart,
And filled between with curious art
The ragged brush; then, hovering near,
We watched the first red blaze appear,
Heard the sharp crackle, caught the gleam
On whitewashed wall and sagging beam,
Until the old, rude-furnished room
Burst, flower-like, into rosy bloom;

While radiant with a mimic flame
Outside the sparkling drift became,
And through the bare-boughed lilac-tree
Our own warm hearth seemed blazing free.
The crane and pendent trammels showed,
The Turks' heads on the andirons glowed;
While childish fancy, prompt to tell
The meaning of the miracle,
Whispered the old rhyme: '*Under the tree,
When fire outdoors burns merrily,
There the witches are making tea.*'

The moon above the eastern wood
Shone at its full; the hill-range stood
Transfigured in the silver flood,
Its blown snows flashing cold and keen,
Dead white, save where some sharp ravine
Took shadow, or the sombre green
Of hemlocks turned to pitchy black
Against the whiteness at their back.
For such a world and such a night
Most fitting that unwarming light,
Which only seemed where'er it fell
To make the coldness visible.

Shut in from all the world without,
We sat the clean-winged hearth about,
Content to let the north-wind roar
In baffled rage at pane and door,
While the red logs before us beat
The frost-line back with tropic heat;
And ever, when a louder blast
Shook beam and rafter as it passed,

The merrier up its roaring draught
The great throat of the chimney laughed;
The house-dog on his paws outspread
Laid to the fire his drowsy head,
The cat's dark silhouette on the wall
A couchant tiger's seemed to fall;
And, for the winter fireside meet,
Between the andirons' straddling feet,
The mug of cider simmered slow,
The apples sputtered in a row,
And, close at hand, the basket stood
With nuts from brown October's wood.

What matter how the night behaved?
What matter how the north-wind raved?
Blow high, blow low, not all its snow
Could quench our hearth-fire's ruddy glow.
O Time and Change!—with hair as gray
As was my sire's that winter day,
How strange it seems, with so much gone
Of life and love, to still live on!
Ah, brother! only I and thou
Are left of all that circle now,—
The dear home faces whereupon
That fitful firelight paled and shone.
Henceforward, listen as we will,
The voices of that hearth are still;
Look where we may, the wide earth o'er,
Those lighted faces smile no more.
We tread the paths their feet have worn,
    We sit beneath their orchard trees,
    We hear, like them, the hum of bees
And rustle of the bladed corn;

We turn the pages that they read,
  Their written words we linger o'er,
But in the sun they cast no shade,
No voice is heard, no sign is made,
  No step is on the conscious floor!
Yet Love will dream, and Faith will trust,
(Since He who knows our need is just,)
That somehow, somewhere, meet we must.
Alas for him who never sees
The stars shine through his cypress-trees!
Who, hopeless, lays his dead away,
Nor looks to see the breaking day
Across the mournful marbles play!
Who hath not learned, in hours of faith,
  The truth to flesh and sense unknown,
That Life is ever lord of Death,
  And Love can never lose its own!

We sped the time with stories old,
Wrought puzzles out, and riddles told,
Or stammered from our school-book lore
'The Chief of Gambia's golden shore.'
How often since, when all the land
Was clay in Slavery's shaping hand,
As if a far-blown trumpet stirred
The languorous sin-sick air, I heard:
'Does not the voice of reason cry,
  Claim the first right which Nature gave,
From the red scourge of bondage fly,
  Nor deign to live a burdened slave!'
Our father rode again his ride
On Memphremagog's wooded side;
Sat down again to moose and samp

In trapper's hut and Indian camp;
Lived o'er the old idyllic ease
Beneath St. François' hemlock-trees;
Again for him the moonlight shone
On Norman cap and bodiced zone;
Again he heard the violin play
Which led the village dance away.
And mingled in its merry whirl
The grandam and the laughing girl.
Or, nearer home, our steps he led
Where Salisbury's level marshes spread

   Mile-wide as flies the laden bee;
Where merry mowers, hale and strong,
Swept, scythe on scythe, their swaths along

   The low green prairies of the sea.
We shared the fishing off Boar's Head,

   And round the rocky Isles of Shoals

   The hake-broil on the drift-wood coals
The chowder on the sand-beach made,
Dipped by the hungry, steaming hot,
With spoons of clam-shell from the pot.
We heard the tales of witchcraft old,
And dream and sign and marvel told
To sleepy listeners as they lay
Stretched idly on the salted hay,
Adrift along the winding shores,
When favoring breezes deigned to blow
The square sail of the gundelow
And idle lay the useless oars.

Our mother, while she turned her wheel
Or run the new-knit stocking-heel,

Told how the Indian hordes came down
At midnight on Cocheco town,
And how her own great-uncle bore
His cruel scalp-mark to fourscore.
Recalling, in her fitting phrase,
   So rich and picturesque and free,
   (The common unrhymed poetry
Of simple life and country ways,)
The story of her early days,—
She made us welcome to her home;
Old hearths grew wide to give us room;
We stole with her a frightened look
At the gray wizard's conjuring-book,
The fame whereof went far and wide
Through all the simple country side;
We heard the hawks at twilight play,
The boat-horn on Piscataqua,
The loon's weird laughter far away;
We fished her little trout-brook, knew
What flowers in wood and meadow grew,
What sunny hillsides autumn-brown
She climbed to shake the ripe nuts down,
Saw where in sheltered cove and bay
The ducks' black squadron anchored lay,
And heard the wild-geese calling loud
Beneath the gray November cloud.

Then, haply, with a look more grave,
And soberer tone, some tale she gave
From painful Sewel's ancient tome,
Beloved in every Quaker home,
Of faith fire-winged by martyrdom,
Or Chalkley's Journal, old and quaint,—

JOHN GREENLEAF WHITTIER

Gentlest of skippers, rare sea-saint!—
Who, when the dreary calms prevailed,
And water-butt and bread-cask failed,
And cruel, hungry eyes pursued
His portly presence mad for food,
With dark hints muttered under breath
Of casting lots for life or death,
Offered, if Heaven withheld supplies,
To be himself the sacrifice.
Then, suddenly, as if to save
The good man from his living grave,
A ripple on the water grew,
A school of porpoise flashed in view.
'Take, eat,' he said, 'and be content;
These fishes in my stead are sent
By Him who gave the tangled ram
To spare the child of Abraham.'

Our uncle, innocent of books,
Was rich in lore of fields and brooks,
The ancient teachers never dumb
Of Nature's unhoused lyceum.
In moons and tides and weather wise,
He read the clouds as prophecies,
And foul or fair could well divine,
By many an occult hint and sign,
Holding the cunning-warded keys
To all the woodcraft mysteries;
Himself to Nature's heart so near
That all her voices in his ear
Of beast or bird had meanings clear,
Like Apollonius of old,
Who knew the tales the sparrows told,

Or Hermes, who interpreted
What the sage cranes of Nilus said;
A simple, guileless, childlike man,
Content to live where life began;
Strong only on his native grounds,
The little world of sights and sounds
Whose girdle was the parish bounds,
Whereof his fondly partial pride
The common features magnified,
As Surrey hills to mountains grew
In White of Selborne's loving view,—
He told how teal and loon he shot,
And how the eagle's eggs he got,
The feats on pond and river done,
The prodigies of rod and gun;
Till, warming with the tales he told,
Forgotten was the outside cold,
The bitter wind unheeded blew,
From ripening corn the pigeons flew,
The partridge drummed i' the wood, the mink
Went fishing down the river-brink.
In fields with bean or clover gay,
The woodchuck, like a hermit gray,
   Peered from the doorway of his cell;
The muskrat plied the mason's trade,
And tier by tier his mud-walls laid;
And from the shagbark overhead
   The grizzled squirrel dropped his shell.

Next, the dear aunt, whose smile of cheer
And voice in dreams I see and hear,—
The sweetest woman ever Fate
Perverse denied a household mate,

JOHN GREENLEAF WHITTIER

Who, lonely, homeless, not the less
Found peace in love's unselfishness,
And welcome wheresoe'er she went,
A calm and gracious element,
Whose presence seemed the sweet income
And womanly atmosphere of home,—
Called up her girlhood memories,
The huskings and the apple-bees,
The sleigh-rides and the summer sails,
Weaving through all the poor details
And homespun warp of circumstance
A golden woof-thread of romance.
For well she kept her genial mood
And simple faith of maidenhood;
Before her still a cloud-land lay,
The mirage loomed across her way;
The morning dew, that dries so soon
With others, glistened at her noon;
Through years of toil and soil and care,
From glossy tress to thin gray hair,
All unprofaned she held apart
The virgin fancies of the heart.
Be shame to him of woman born
Who hath for such but thought of scorn.

There, too, our elder sister plied
Her evening task the stand beside;
A full, rich nature, free to trust,
Truthful and almost sternly just,
Impulsive, earnest, prompt to act,
And make her generous thought a fact,
Keeping with many a light disguise
The secret of self-sacrifice.

O heart sore-tried! thou hast the best
That Heaven itself could give thee,—rest,
Rest from all bitter thoughts and things!
  How many a poor one's blessing went
  With thee beneath the low green tent
Whose curtain never outward swings!

As one who held herself a part
Of all she saw, and let her heart
  Against the household bosom lean,
Upon the motley-braided mat
Our youngest and our dearest sat,
Lifting her large, sweet, asking eyes,
  Now bathed in the unfading green
And holy peace of Paradise.
Oh, looking from some heavenly hill,
  Or from the shade of saintly palms,
  Or silver reach of river calms,
Do those large eyes behold me still?
With me one little year ago:—
The chill weight of the winter snow
  For months upon her grave has lain;
And now, when summer south-winds blow
  And brier and harebell bloom again,
I tread the pleasant paths we trod,
I see the violet-sprinkled sod
Whereon she leaned, too frail and weak
The hillside flowers she loved to seek,
Yet following me where'er I went
With dark eyes full of love's content.
The birds are glad; the brier-rose fills
The air with sweetness; all the hills

Stretch green to June's unclouded sky;
But still I wait with ear and eye
For something gone which should be nigh,
A loss in all familiar things,
In flower that blooms, and bird that sings.
And yet, dear heart! remembering thee,
 Am I not richer than of old?
Safe in thy immortality,
  What change can reach the wealth I hold?
  What chance can mar the pearl and gold
Thy love hath left in trust with me?
And while in life's late afternoon,
  Where cool and long the shadows grow,
I walk to meet the night that soon
  Shall shape and shadow overflow,
I cannot feel that thou art far,
Since near at need the angels are;
And when the sunset gates unbar,
  Shall I not see thee waiting stand,
And, white against the evening star,
  The welcome of thy beckoning hand?

Brisk wielder of the birch and rule,
The master of the district school
Held at the fire his favored place,
Its warm glow lit a laughing face
Fresh-hued and fair, where scarce appeared
The uncertain prophecy of beard.
He teased the mitten-blinded cat,
Played cross-pins on my uncle's hat,
Sang songs, and told us what befalls
In classic Dartmouth's college halls.

175

Born the wild Northern hills among,
From whence his yeoman father wrung
By patient toil subsistence scant,
Not competence and yet not want,
He early gained the power to pay
His cheerful, self-reliant way;
Could doff at ease his scholar's gown
To peddle wares from town to town;
Or through the long vacation's reach
In lonely lowland districts teach,
Where all the droll experience found
At stranger hearths in boarding round,
The moonlit skater's keen delight,
The sleigh-drive through the frosty night,
The rustic party, with its rough
Accompaniment of blind-man's-buff,
And whirling-plate, and forfeits paid,
His winter task a pastime made.
Happy the snow-locked homes wherein
He tuned his merry violin,
Or played the athlete in the barn,
Or held the good dame's winding-yarn,
Or mirth-provoking versions told
Of classic legends rare and old,
Wherein the scenes of Greece and Rome
Had all the commonplace of home,
And little seemed at best the odds
'Twixt Yankee pedlers and old gods;
Where Pindus-born Arachthus took
The guise of any grist-mill brook,
And dread Olympus at his will
Became a huckleberry hill.

A careless boy that night he seemed;
   But at his desk he had the look
And air of one who wisely schemed,
   And hostage from the future took
   In trainëd thought and lore of book.
Large-brained, clear-eyed, of such as he
Shall Freedom's young apostles be,
Who, following in War's bloody trail,
Shall every lingering wrong assail;
All chains from limb and spirit strike,
Uplift the black and white alike;
Scatter before their swift advance
The darkness and the ignorance,
.The pride, the lust, the squalid sloth,
Which nurtured Treason's monstrous growth,
Made murder pastime, and the hell
Of prison-torture possible;
The cruel lie of caste refute,
Old forms remould, and substitute
For Slavery's lash the freeman's will,
For blind routine, wise-handed skill;
A school-house plant on every hill,
Stretching in radiate nerve-lines thence
The quick wires of intelligence;
Till North and South together brought
Shall own the same electric thought,
In peace a common flag salute,
And, side by side in labor's free
And unresentful rivalry,
Harvest the fields wherein they fought.

Another guest that winter night
Flashed back from lustrous eyes the light.

Unmarked by time, and yet not young,
The honeyed music of her tongue
And words of meekness scarcely told
A nature passionate and bold,
Strong, self-concentred, spurning guide,
Its milder features dwarfed beside
Her unbent will's majestic pride.
She sat among us, at the best,
A not unfeared, half-welcome guest,
Rebuking with her cultured phrase
Our homeliness of words and ways.
A certain pard-like, treacherous grace
Swayed the lithe limbs and drooped the lash,
Lent the white teeth their dazzling flash;
And under low brows, black with night,
Rayed out at times a dangerous light;
The sharp heat-lightnings of her face
Presaging ill to him whom Fate
Condemned to share her love or hate.
A woman tropical, intense
In thought and act, in soul and sense,
She blended in a like degree
The vixen and the devotee,
Revealing with each freak or feint

    The temper of Petruchio's Kate,
The raptures of Siena's saint.
Her tapering hand and rounded wrist
Had facile power to form a fist;
The warm, dark languish of her eyes
Was never safe from wrath's surprise.
Brows saintly calm and lips devout
Knew every change of scowl and pout;

And the sweet voice had notes more high
And shrill for social battle-cry.

Since then what old cathedral town
Has missed her pilgrim staff and gown,
What convent-gate has held its lock
Against the challenge of her knock!
Through Smyrna's plague-hushed thoroughfares,
Up sea-set Malta's rocky stairs,
Gray olive slopes of hills that hem
Thy tombs and shrines, Jerusalem,
Or startling on her desert throne
The crazy Queen of Lebanon
With claims fantastic as her own,
Her tireless feet have held their way;
And still, unrestful, bowed, and gray,
She watches under Eastern skies,
    With hope each day renewed and fresh,
    The Lord's quick coming in the flesh,
Whereof she dreams and prophesies!

Where'er her troubled path may be,
    The Lord's sweet pity with her go!
The outward wayward life we see,
    The hidden springs we may not know.
Nor is it given us to discern
    What threads the fatal sisters spun,
    Through what ancestral years has run
The sorrow with the woman born,
What forged her cruel chain of moods,
What set her feet in solitudes,
    And held the love within her mute,

179

What mingled madness in the blood,
  A life-long discord and annoy,
  Water of tears with oil of joy,
And hid within the folded bud
  Perversities of flower and fruit.
It is not ours to separate
The tangled skein of will and fate,
To show what metes and bounds should stand
Upon the soul's debatable land,
And between choice and Providence
Divide the circle of events;
But He who knows our frame is just,
Merciful and compassionate,
And full of sweet assurances
And hope for all the language is,
That He remembereth we are dust!

At last the great logs, crumbling low,
Sent out a dull and duller glow,
The bull's-eye watch that hung in view,
Ticking its weary circuit through,
Pointed with mutely warning sign
Its black hand to the hour of nine.
That sign the pleasant circle broke:
My uncle ceased his pipe to smoke,
Knocked from its bowl the refuse gray,
And laid it tenderly away;
Then roused himself to safely cover
The dull red brands with ashes over.
And while, with care, our mother laid
The work aside, her steps she stayed
One moment, seeking to express
Her grateful sense of happiness

For food and shelter, warmth and health,
And love's contentment more than wealth,
With simple wishes (not the weak,
Vain prayers which no fulfilment seek,
But such as warm the generous heart,
O'er prompt to do with Heaven its part)
That none might lack, that bitter night,
For bread and clothing, warmth and light.

Within our beds awhile we heard
The wind that round the gables roared,
With now and then a ruder shock,
Which made our very bedsteads rock.
We heard the loosened clapboards tost,
The board-nails snapping in the frost;
And on us, through the unplastered wall,
Felt the light sifted snow-flakes fall.
But sleep stole on, as sleep will do
When hearts are light and life is new;
Faint and more faint the murmurs grew,
Till in the summer-land of dreams
They softened to the sound of streams,
Low stir of leaves, and dip of oars,
And lapsing waves on quiet shores.

Next morn we wakened with the shout
Of merry voices high and clear;
And saw the teamsters drawing near
To break the drifted highways out.
Down the long hillside treading slow
We saw the half-buried oxen go,
Shaking the snow from heads uptost,
Their straining nostrils white with frost.

Before our door the straggling train
Drew up, an added team to gain.
The elders threshed their hands a-cold,
   Passed, with the cider-mug, their jokes
   From lip to lip; the younger folks
Down the loose snow-banks, wrestling, rolled,
Then toiled again the cavalcade
   O'er windy hill, through clogged ravine,
   And woodland paths that wound between
Low drooping pine-boughs winter-weighed.
From every barn a team afoot,
At every house a new recruit,
Where, drawn by Nature's subtlest law,
Haply the watchful young men saw
Sweet doorway pictures of the curls
And curious eyes of merry girls,
Lifting their hands in mock defence
Against the snow-ball's compliments,
And reading in each missive tost
The charm with Eden never lost.

We heard once more the sleigh-bells' sound;
   And, following where the teamsters led,
The wise old Doctor went his round,
Just pausing at our door to say,
In the brief autocratic way
Of one who, prompt at Duty's call,
Was free to urge her claim on all,
   That some poor neighbor sick abed
At night our mother's aid would need.
For, one in generous thought and deed,
   What mattered in the sufferer's sight
   The Quaker matron's inward light,

The Doctor's mail of Calvin's creed?
All hearts confess the saints elect
  Who, twain in faith, in love agree,
And melt not in an acid sect
  The Christian pearl of charity!

So days went on: a week had passed
Since the great world was heard from last.
The Almanac we studied o'er,
Read and reread our little store
Of books and pamphlets, scarce a score;
One harmless novel, mostly hid
From younger eyes, a book forbid,
And poetry, (or good or bad,
A single book was all we had,)
Where Ellwood's meek, drab-skirted Muse,
  A stranger to the heathen Nine,
  Sang, with a somewhat nasal whine,
The wars of David and the Jews.
At last the floundering carrier bore
The village paper to our door.
Lo! broadening outward as we read,
To warmer zones the horizon spread
In panoramic length unrolled
We saw the marvels that it told.
Before us passed the painted Creeks,
  And daft McGregor on his raids
  In Costa Rica's everglades.
And up Taygetos winding slow
Rode Ypsilanti's Mainote Greeks,
A Turk's head at each saddle-bow!
Welcome to us its week-old news,

Its corner for the rustic Muse,
    Its monthly gauge of snow and rain,
Its record, mingling in a breath
The wedding bell and dirge of death:
Jest, anecdote, and love-lorn tale,
The latest culprit sent to jail;
Its hue and cry of stolen and lost,
Its vendue sales and goods at cost,

    And traffic calling loud for gain.
We felt the stir of hall and street,
The pulse of life that round us beat;
The chill embargo of the snow
Was melted in the genial glow;
Wide swung again our ice-locked door,
And all the world was ours once more!

Clasp, Angel of the backward look
    And folded wings of ashen gray
    And voice of echoes far away,
The brazen covers of thy book;
The weird palimpsest old and vast,
Wherein thou hid'st the spectral past;
Where, closely mingling, pale and glow
The characters of joy and woe;
The monographs of outlived years,
Or smile-illumed or dim with tears,

    Green hills of life that slope to death,
And haunts of home, whose vistaed trees
Shade off to mournful cypresses

    With the white amaranths underneath.
Even while I look, I can but heed

    The restless sands' incessant fall,
Importunate hours that hours succeed,

Each clamorous with its own sharp need,
  And duty keeping pace with all.
Shut down and clasp the heavy lids;
I hear again the voice that bids
  The dreamer leave his dream midway
For larger hopes and graver fears:
Life greatens in these later years,
The century's aloe flowers to-day!

Yet, haply, in some lull of life,
Some Truce of God which breaks its strife,
The worldling's eyes shall gather dew,
  Dreaming in throngful city ways
Of winter joys his boyhood knew;
And dear and early friends—the few
Who yet remain—shall pause to view
  These Flemish pictures of old days;
Sit with me by the homestead hearth,
And stretch the hands of memory forth
  To warm them at the wood-fire's blaze!
And thanks untraced to lips unknown
Shall greet me like the odors blown
From unseen meadows newly mown,
Or lilies floating in some pond,
Wood-fringed, the wayside gaze beyond;
The traveller owns the grateful sense
Of sweetness near, he knows not whence,
And, pausing, takes with forehead bare
The benediction of the air.

71 *Among the Hills*

PRELUDE

ALONG the roadside, like the flowers of gold
That tawny Incas for their gardens wrought,
Heavy with sunshine droops the golden-rod,
And the red pennons of the cardinal-flowers
Hang motionless upon their upright staves.
The sky is hot and hazy, and the wind,
Wing-weary with its long flight from the south,
Unfelt; yet, closely scanned, yon maple leaf
With faintest motion, as one stirs in dreams,
Confesses it. The locust by the wall
Stabs the noon-silence with his sharp alarm.
A single hay-cart down the dusty road
Creaks slowly, with its driver fast asleep
On the load's top. Against the neighboring hill,
Huddled along the stone wall's shady side,
The sheep show white, as if a snowdrift still
Defied the dog-star. Through the open door
A drowsy smell of flowers—gray heliotrope,
And white sweet clover, and shy mignonette—
Comes faintly in, and silent chorus lends
To the pervading symphony of peace.

No time is this for hands long over-worn
To task their strength: and (unto Him be praise
Who giveth quietness!) the stress and strain
Of years that did the work of centuries
Have ceased, and we can draw our breath once more
Freely and full. So, as yon harvesters

Make glad their nooning underneath the elms
With tale and riddle and old snatch of song,
I lay aside grave themes, and idly turn
The leaves of memory's sketch-book, dreaming o'er
Old summer pictures of the quiet hills,
And human life, as quiet, at their feet.

And yet not idly all. A farmer's son,
Proud of field-lore and harvest craft, and feeling
All their fine possibilities, how rich
And restful even poverty and toil
Become when beauty, harmony, and love
Sit at their humble hearth as angels sat
At evening in the patriarch's tent, when man
Makes labor noble, and his farmer's frock
The symbol of a Christian chivalry
Tender and just and generous to her
Who clothes with grace all duty; still, I know
Too well the picture has another side,—
How wearily the grind of toil goes on
Where love is wanting, how the eye and ear
And heart are starved amidst the plenitude
Of nature, and how hard and colorless
Is life without an atmosphere. I look
Across the lapse of half a century,
And call to mind old homesteads, where no flower
Told that the spring had come, but evil weeds,
Nightshade and rough-leaved burdock in the place
Of the sweet doorway greeting of the rose
And honeysuckle, where the house walls seemed
Blistering in sun, without a tree or vine
To cast the tremulous shadow of its leaves
Across the curtainless windows, from whose panes

Fluttered the signal rags of shiftlessness.
Within, the cluttered kitchen floor, unwashed
(Broom-clean I think they called it); the best room
Stifling with cellar-damp, shut from the air
In hot midsummer, bookless, pictureless
Save the inevitable sampler hung
Over the fireplace, or a mourning piece,
A green-haired woman, peony-cheeked, beneath
Impossible willows; the wide-throated hearth
Bristling with faded pine-boughs half concealing
The piled-up rubbish at the chimney's back;
And, in sad keeping with all things about them,
Shrill, querulous women, sour and sullen men,
Untidy, loveless, old before their time,
With scarce a human interest save their own
Monotonous round of small economies,
Or the poor scandal of the neighborhood;
Blind to the beauty everywhere revealed,
Treading the May-flowers with regardless feet;
For them the song-sparrow and the bobolink
Sang not, nor winds made music in the leaves;
For them in vain October's holocaust
Burned, gold and crimson, over all the hills,
The sacramental mystery of the woods.
Church-goers, fearful of the unseen Powers,
But grumbling over pulpit-tax and pew-rent,
Saving, as shrewd economists, their souls
And winter pork with the least possible outlay
Of salt and sanctity; in daily life
Showing as little actual comprehension
Of Christian charity and love and duty,
As if the Sermon on the Mount had been
Outdated like a last year's almanac:

Rich in broad woodlands and in half-tilled fields,
And yet so pinched and bare and comfortless,
The veriest straggler limping on his rounds,
The sun and air his sole inheritance,
Laughed at a poverty that paid its taxes,
And hugged his rags in self-complacency!

Not such should be the homesteads of a land
Where whoso wisely wills and acts may dwell
As king and lawgiver, in broad-acred state,
With beauty, art, taste, culture, books, to make
His hour of leisure richer than a life
Of fourscore to the barons of old time,
Our yeoman should be equal to his home
Set in the fair, green valleys, purple walled,
A man to match his mountains, not to creep
Dwarfed and abased below them. I would fain
In this light way (of which I needs must own
With the knife-grinder of whom Canning sings,
'Story, God bless you! I have none to tell you!')
Invite the eye to see and heart to feel
The beauty and the joy within their reach,—
Home, and home loves, and the beatitudes
Of nature free to all. Haply in years
That wait to take the places of our own,
Heard where some breezy balcony looks down
On happy homes, or where the lake in the moon
Sleeps dreaming of the mountains, fair as Ruth,
In the old Hebrew pastoral, at the feet
Of Boaz, even this simple lay of mine
May seem the burden of a prophecy,
Finding its late fulfilment in a change
Slow as the oak's growth, lifting manhood up

Through broader culture, finer manners, love,
And reverence, to the level of the hills.

O Golden Age, whose light is of the dawn,
And not of sunset, forward, not behind,
Flood the new heavens and earth, and with thee bring
All the old virtues, whatsoever things
Are pure and honest and of good repute,
But add thereto whatever bard has sung
Or seer has told of when in trance and dream
They saw the Happy Isles of prophecy!
Let Justice hold her scale, and Truth divide
Between the right and wrong; but give the heart
The freedom of its fair inheritance;
Let the poor prisoner, cramped and starved so long,
At Nature's table feast his ear and eye
With joy and wonder; let all harmonies
Of sound, form, color, motion, wait upon
The princely guest, whether in soft attire
Of leisure clad, or the coarse frock of toil,
And, lending life to the dead form of faith,
Give human nature reverence for the sake
Of One who bore it, making it divine
With the ineffable tenderness of God;
Let common need, the brotherhood of prayer,
The heirship of an unknown destiny,
The unsolved mystery round about us, make
A man more precious than the gold of Ophir.
Sacred, inviolate, unto whom all things
Should minister, as outward types and signs
Of the eternal beauty which fulfils
The one great purpose of creation, Love,
The sole necessity of Earth and Heaven!

OLIVER WENDELL HOLMES

1809-1894

Contentment

'Man wants but little here below'

LITTLE I ask; my wants are few;
   I only wish a hut of stone,
(A *very plain* brown stone will do,)
   That I may call my own;—
And close at hand is such a one,
In yonder street that fronts the sun.

Plain food is quite enough for me;
   Three courses are as good as ten;—
If Nature can subsist on three,
   Thank Heaven for three. Amen!
I always thought cold victual nice;—
My *choice* would be vanilla-ice.

I care not much for gold or land;—
   Give me a mortgage here and there,—
Some good bank-stock, some note of hand,
   Or trifling railroad share,—
I only ask that Fortune send
A *little* more than I shall spend.

Honors are silly toys, I know,
   And titles are but empty names;

I would, *perhaps*, be Plenipo,—
   But only near St. James;
I'm very sure I should not care
To fill our Gubernator's chair.

Jewels are baubles; 't is a sin
   To care for such unfruitful things;—
One good-sized diamond in a pin,—
   Some, *not so large*, in rings,—
A ruby, and a pearl, or so,
Will do for me;—I laugh at show.

My dame should dress in cheap attire;
   (Good, heavy silks are never dear;)—
I own perhaps I *might* desire
   Some shawls of true Cashmere,—
Some marrowy crapes of China silk,
Like wrinkled skins on scalded milk.

I would not have the horse I drive
   So fast that folks must stop and stare;
An easy gait—two, forty-five—
   Suits me; I do not care;—
Perhaps, for just a *single spurt*,
Some seconds less would do no hurt.

Of pictures, I should like to own
   Titians and Raphaels three or four,—
I love so much their style and tone,
   One Turner, and no more,
(A landscape,—foreground golden dirt,—
The sunshine painted with a squirt.)

Of books but few,—some fifty score
  For daily use, and bound for wear;
The rest upon an upper floor;—
  Some *little* luxury *there*
Of red morocco's gilded gleam
And vellum rich as country cream.

Busts, cameos, gems,—such things as these,
  Which others often show for pride,
I value for their power to please,
  And selfish churls deride;—
One Stradivarius, I confess,
Two Meerschaums, I would fain possess.

Wealth's wasteful tricks I will not learn,
  Nor ape the glittering upstart fool;—
Shall not carved tables serve my turn,
  But *all* must be of buhl?
Give grasping pomp its double share,—
I ask but *one* recumbent chair.

Thus humble let me live and die,
  Nor long for Midas' golden touch;
If Heaven more generous gifts deny,
  I shall not miss them *much*,—
Too grateful for the blessing lent
Of simple tastes and mind content!

73 *The Deacon's Masterpiece*
or, The Wonderful 'One-Hoss Shay'

A LOGICAL STORY

Have you heard of the wonderful one-hoss shay,
That was built in such a logical way
It ran a hundred years to a day,
And then, of a sudden, it—ah, but stay,
I'll tell you what happened without delay,
Scaring the parson into fits,
Frightening people out of their wits,—
Have you ever heard of that, I say?

Seventeen hundred and fifty-five.
Georgius Secundus was then alive,—
Snuffy old drone from the German hive.
That was the year when Lisbon-town
Saw the earth open and gulp her down,
And Braddock's army was done so brown,
Left without a scalp to its crown.
It was on the terrible Earthquake-day
That the Deacon finished the one-hoss shay.

Now in building of chaises, I tell you what,
There is always *somewhere* a weakest spot,—
In hub, tire, felloe, in spring or thill,
In panel, or crossbar, or floor, or sill,
In screw, bolt, thoroughbrace,—lurking still,
Find it somewhere you must and will,—
Above or below, or within or without,—
And that's the reason, beyond a doubt,
That a chaise *breaks down*, but doesn't *wear out*.

But the Deacon swore (as Deacons do,
With an 'I dew vum,' or an 'I tell *yeou*')
He would build one shay to beat the taown
'n' the keounty 'n' all the kentry raoun';
It should be so built that it *couldn*' break daown:
'Fur,' said the Deacon, ' 't 's mighty plain
Thut the weakes' place mus' stan' the strain;
'n' the way t' fix it, uz I maintain,
  Is only jest
T' make that place uz strong uz the rest.'

So the Deacon inquired of the village folk
Where he could find the strongest oak,
That couldn't be split nor bent nor broke,—
That was for spokes and floor and sills;
He sent for lancewood to make the thills;
The crossbars were ash, from the straightest trees,
The panels of white-wood, that cuts like cheese,
But lasts like iron for things like these;
The hubs of logs from the 'Settler's ellum,'—
Last of its timber,—they couldn't sell 'em,
Never an axe had seen their chips,
And the wedges flew from between their lips,
Their blunt ends frizzled like celery-tips;
Step and prop-iron, bolt and screw,
Spring, tire, axle, and linchpin too,
Steel of the finest, bright and blue;
Thoroughbrace bison-skin, thick and wide;
Boot, top, dasher, from tough old hide
Found in the pit when the tanner died.
That was the way he 'put her through.'
'There!' said the Deacon, 'naow she'll dew!'

Do! I tell you, I rather guess
She was a wonder, and nothing less!
Colts grew horses, beards turned gray,
Deacon and deaconess dropped away,
Children and grandchildren—where were they?
But there stood the stout old one-hoss shay
As fresh as on Lisbon-earthquake-day!

EIGHTEEN HUNDRED;—it came and found
The Deacon's masterpiece strong and sound.
Eighteen hundred increased by ten;—
'Hahnsum kerridge' they called it then.
Eighteen hundred and twenty came;—
Running as usual; much the same.
Thirty and forty at last arrive,
And then come fifty, and FIFTY-FIVE.

Little of all we value here
Wakes on the morn of its hundredth year
Without both feeling and looking queer.
In fact, there's nothing that keeps its youth,
So far as I know, but a tree and truth.
(This is a moral that runs at large;
Take it.—You're welcome.—No extra charge.)

FIRST OF NOVEMBER,—the Earthquake-day,—
There are traces of age in the one-hoss shay,
A general flavor of mild decay,
But nothing local, as one may say.
There couldn't be,—for the Deacon's art
Had made it so like in every part
That there wasn't a chance for one to start.
For the wheels were just as strong as the thills,
And the floor was just as strong as the sills,

And the panels just as strong as the floor,
And the whipple-tree neither less nor more,
And the back-crossbar as strong as the fore,
And spring and axle and hub *encore*.
And yet, *as a whole*, it is past a doubt
In another hour it will be *worn out!*

First of November, 'Fifty-five!
This morning the parson takes a drive.
Now, small boys, get out of the way!
Here comes the wonderful one-hoss shay,
Drawn by a rat-tailed, ewe-necked bay.
'Huddup!' said the parson.—Off went they.
The parson was working his Sunday's text,—
Had got to *fifthly*, and stopped perplexed
At what the—Moses—was coming next.
All at once the horse stood still,
Close by the meet'n'-house on the hill.
First a shiver, and then a thrill,
Then something decidedly like a spill,—
And the parson was sitting upon a rock,
At half past nine by the meet'n'-house clock,—
Just the hour of the Earthquake shock!
What do you think the parson found,
When he got up and stared around?
The poor old chaise in a heap or mound,
As if it had been to the mill and ground!
You see, of course, if you're not a dunce,
How it went to pieces all at once,—
All at once, and nothing first,—
Just as bubbles do when they burst.

End of the wonderful one-hoss shay.
Logic is logic. That's all I say.

EDGAR ALLAN POE

1809-1849

74   *Dreams*

OH! that my young life were a lasting dream!
My spirit not awak'ning till the beam
Of an Eternity should bring the morrow.
Yes! tho' that long dream were of hopeless sorrow,
'T were better than the cold reality
Of waking life, to him whose heart must be,
And hath been still, upon the lovely earth,
A chaos of deep passion, from his birth.
But should it be—that dream eternally
Continuing—as dreams have been to me
In my young boyhood—should it thus be giv'n,
'T were folly still to hope for higher Heav'n.
For I have revell'd, when the sun was bright
I' the summer sky, in dreams of living light
And loveliness,—have left my very heart
In climes of mine imagining, apart
From mine own home, with beings that have been
Of mine own thought—what more could I have seen?
'T was once—and only once—and the wild hour
From my remembrance shall not pass—some pow'r
Or spell had bound me—'t was the chilly wind
Came o'er me in the night, and left behind
Its image on my spirit—or the moon
Shone on my slumbers in her lofty noon
Too coldly—or the stars—howe'er it was,
That dream was as that night-wind—let it pass.

I *have been* happy, tho' but in a dream.
I have been happy—and I love the theme:
Dreams! in their vivid coloring of life,
As in that fleeting, shadowy, misty strife
Of semblance with reality which brings
To the delirious eye, more lovely things
Of Paradise and Love—and all our own!
Than young Hope in his sunniest hour hath known.

75   *A Dream within a Dream*

TAKE this kiss upon the brow!
And, in parting from you now,
Thus much let me avow:
You are not wrong, who deem
That my days have been a dream;
Yet if Hope has flown away
In a night, or in a day,
In a vision, or in none,
Is it therefore the less *gone?*
All that we see or seem
Is but a dream within a dream.

I stand amid the roar
Of a surf-tormented shore,
And I hold within my hand
Grains of the golden sand—
How few! yet how they creep
Through my fingers to the deep,
While I weep—while I weep!

O God! can I not grasp
Them with a tighter clasp?
O God! can I not save
One from the pitiless wave?
Is *all* that we see or seem
But a dream within a dream?

76 'The Happiest Day, The Happiest Hour'

THE happiest day, the happiest hour
My sear'd and blighted heart hath known,
The highest hope of pride and power,
I feel hath flown.

Of power! said I? yes! such I ween;
But they have vanish'd long, alas!
The visions of my youth have been—
But let them pass.

And, pride, what have I now with thee?
Another brow may ev'n inherit
The venom thou hast pour'd on me—
Be still, my spirit!

The happiest day, the happiest hour
Mine eyes shall see, have ever seen,
The brightest glance of pride and power,
I feel—have been:

But were that hope of pride and power
Now offer'd, with the pain
Ev'n *then* I felt—that brightest hour
I would not live again:

For on its wing was dark alloy,
    And as it flutter'd, fell
An essence—powerful to destroy
    A soul that knew it well.

77   *Sonnet—To Science*

SCIENCE! true daughter of Old Time thou art!
    Who alterest all things with thy peering eyes.
Why preyest thou thus upon the poet's heart,
    Vulture, whose wings are dull realities?
How should he love thee? or how deem thee wise,
    Who wouldst not leave him in his wandering
To seek for treasure in the jewelled skies,
    Albeit he soared with an undaunted wing?
Hast thou not dragged Diana from her car,
    And driven the Hamadryad from the wood
To seek a shelter in some happier star?
    Hast thou not torn the Naiad from her flood,
The Elfin from the green grass, and from me
The summer dream beneath the tamarind tree?

78   *Song from 'Al Aaraaf'*

'NEATH blue-bell or streamer—
    Or tufted wild spray
That keeps from the dreamer
    The moonbeam away—

Bright beings! that ponder,
  With half closing eyes,
On the stars which your wonder
  Hath drawn from the skies,
Till they glance thro' the shade, and
  Come down to your brow
Like—eyes of the maiden
  Who calls on you now—
Arise! from your dreaming
  In violet bowers,
To duty beseeming
  These star-litten hours —
And shake from your tresses,
  Encumber'd with dew,
The breath of those kisses
  That cumber them too
(O, how, without you, Love!
  Could angels be blest?)—
Those kisses of true love
  That lull'd ye to rest!
Up!—shake from your wing
  Each hindering thing:
The dew of the night—
  It would weigh down your flight;
And true love caresses—
  O! leave them apart:
They are light on the tresses,
  But lead on the heart.

Ligeia! Ligeia!
  My beautiful one!
Whose harshest idea
  Will to melody run,

O! is it thy will
    On the breezes to toss?
Or, capriciously still,
    Like the lone Albatross,
Incumbent on night
    (As she on the air)
To keep watch with delight
    On the harmony there?

Ligeia! wherever
    Thy image may be,
No magic shall sever
    Thy music from thee.
Thou hast bound many eyes
    In a dreamy sleep—
But the strains still arise
    Which *thy* vigilance keep:
The sound of the rain
    Which leaps down to the flower,
And dances again
    In the rhythm of the shower—
The murmur that springs
    From the growing of grass
Are the music of things—
    But are modell'd, alas!—
Away, then, my dearest,
    O! hie thee away
To springs that lie clearest
    Beneath the moon-ray—
To lone lake that smiles,
    In its dream of deep rest,
At the many star-isles
    That enjewel its breast—

Where wild flowers, creeping,
    Have mingled their shade,
On its margin is sleeping
    Full many a maid—
Some have left the cool glade, and
    Have slept with the bee—
Arouse them, my maiden,
    On moorland and lea—
Go! breathe on their slumber,
    All softly in ear,
The musical number
    They slumber'd to hear—
For what can awaken
    An angel so soon,
Whose sleep hath been taken
    Beneath the cold moon,
As the spell which no slumber
    Of witchery may test,
The rhythmical number
    Which lull'd him to rest?

79   *Romance*

Romance, who loves to nod and sing,
With drowsy head and folded wing,
Among the green leaves as they shake
Far down within some shadowy lake,
To me a painted paroquet
Hath been—a most familiar bird—

Taught me my alphabet to say,
To lisp my very earliest word,
While in the wild wood I did lie,
A child—with a most knowing eye.

Of late, eternal Condor years
So shake the very Heaven on high
With tumult as they thunder by,
I have no time for idle cares
Through gazing on the unquiet sky.
And when an hour with calmer wings
Its down upon my spirit flings—
That little time with lyre and rhyme
To while away—forbidden things!
My heart would feel to be a crime
Unless it trembled with the strings.

80   *To Helen*

Helen, thy beauty is to me
    Like those Nicéan barks of yore,
That gently, o'er a perfumed sea,
    The weary, way-worn wanderer bore
    To his own native shore.

On desperate seas long wont to roam,
    Thy hyacinth hair, thy classic face,
Thy Naiad airs have brought me home
    To the glory that was Greece
And the grandeur that was Rome.

Lo! in yon brilliant window-niche
　How statue-like I see thee stand,
　The agate lamp within thy hand!
Ah, Psyche, from the regions which
　Are Holy Land!

　　　　　　　Israfel

*And the angel Israfel, whose heart-strings are a lute,
and who has the sweetest voice of all God's creatures.*
　　　　　　　　　　　　　　　—KORAN.

In Heaven a spirit doth dwell
　'Whose heart-strings are a lute';
None sing so wildly well
As the angel Israfel,
And the giddy stars (so legends tell),
Ceasing their hymns, attend the spell
　Of his voice, all mute.

Tottering above
　In her highest noon,
　The enamoured moon
Blushes with love,
　While, to listen, the red levin
　(With the rapid Pleiads, even,
　Which were seven,)
　Pauses in Heaven.

And they say (the starry choir
　And the other listening things)

EDGAR ALLAN POE

That Israfeli's fire
Is owing to that lyre
    By which he sits and sings—
The trembling living wire
    Of those unusual strings.

But the skies that angel trod,
    Where deep thoughts are a duty,
Where Love's a grown-up God,
    Where the Houri glances are
Imbued with all the beauty
    Which we worship in a star.

Therefore, thou art not wrong,
    Israfeli, who despisest
An unimpassioned song;
To thee the laurels belong,
    Best bard, because the wisest!
Merrily live, and long!

The ecstasies above
    With thy burning measures suit—
Thy grief, thy joy, thy hate, thy love,
    With the fervour of thy lute—
    Well may the stars be mute!

Yes, Heaven is thine; but this
    Is a world of sweets and sours,
    Our flowers are merely—flowers,
And the shadow of thy perfect bliss
    Is the sunshine of ours.

If I could dwell
Where Israfel
   Hath dwelt, and he where I,
He might not sing so wildly well
   A mortal melody,
While a bolder note than this might swell
   From my lyre within the sky.

82   *The City in the Sea*

Lo! Death has reared himself a throne
In a strange city lying alone
Far down within the dim West,
Where the good and the bad and the worst and the best
Have gone to their eternal rest.
There shrines and palaces and towers
(Time-eaten towers that tremble not!)
Resemble nothing that is ours.
Around, by lifting winds forgot,
Resignedly beneath the sky
The melancholy waters lie.

No rays from the holy heaven come down
On the long night-time of that town;
But light from out the lurid sea
Streams up the turrets silently—
Gleams up the pinnacles far and free—
Up domes—up spires—up kingly halls—

Up fanes—up Babylon-like walls—
Up shadowy long-forgotten bowers

Of sculptured ivy and stone flowers—
Up many and many a marvellous shrine
Whose wreathéd friezes intertwine
The viol, the violet, and the vine.

Resignedly beneath the sky
The melancholy waters lie.
So blend the turrets and shadows there
That all seem pendulous in air,
While from a proud tower in the town
Death looks gigantically down.

There open fanes and gaping graves
Yawn level with the luminous waves;
But not the riches there that lie
In each idol's diamond eye—
Not the gaily-jewelled dead
Tempt the waters from their bed;
For no ripples curl, alas!
Along that wilderness of glass—
No swellings tell that winds may be
Upon some far-off happier sea—
No heavings hint that winds have been
On seas less hideously serene.

But lo, a stir is in the air!
The wave—there is a movement there!
As if the towers had thrust aside,
In slightly sinking, the dull tide—
As if their tops had feebly given
A void within the filmy Heaven.
The waves have now a redder glow—
The hours are breathing faint and low—

And when, amid no earthly moans,
Down, down that town shall settle hence,
Hell, rising from a thousand thrones,
Shall do it reverence.

83   *The Sleeper*

A T midnight, in the month of June,
I stand beneath the mystic moon.
An opiate vapor, dewy, dim,
Exhales from out her golden rim,
And softly dripping, drop by drop,
Upon the quiet mountain top,
Steals drowsily and musically
Into the universal valley.
The rosemary nods upon the grave;
The lily lolls upon the wave;
Wrapping the fog about its breast,
The ruin moulders into rest;
Looking like Lethe, see! the lake
A conscious slumber seems to take,
And would not, for the world, awake.
All Beauty sleeps!—and lo! where lies
Irene, with her Destinies!

Oh, lady bright! can it be right—
This window open to the night?
The wanton airs, from the tree-top,
Laughingly through the lattice drop—
The bodiless airs, a wizard rout,
Flit through thy chamber in and out,

And wave the curtain canopy
So fitfully—so fearfully—
Above the closed and fringéd lid
'Neath which thy slumb'ring soul lies hid,
That, o'er the floor and down the wall,
Like ghosts the shadows rise and fall!
Oh, lady dear, hast thou no fear?
Why and what art thou dreaming here?
Sure thou art come o'er far-off seas,
A wonder to these garden trees!
Strange is thy pallor! strange thy dress!
Strange, above all, thy length of tress,
And this all solemn silentness!

The lady sleeps! Oh, may her sleep,
Which is enduring, so be deep!
Heaven have her in its sacred keep!
This chamber changed for one more holy,
This bed for one more melancholy,
I pray to God that she may lie
Forever with unopened eye,
While the pale sheeted ghosts go by!

My love, she sleeps! Oh, may her sleep,
As it is lasting, so be deep!
Soft may the worms about her creep!
Far in the forest, dim and old,
For her may some tall vault unfold—
Some vault that oft hath flung its black
And wingéd pannels fluttering back,
Triumphant, o'er the crested palls
Of her grand family funerals—

Some sepulchre, remote, alone,
Against whose portal she hath thrown,
In childhood, many an idle stone—
Some tomb from out whose sounding door
She ne'er shall force an echo more,
Thrilling to think, poor child of sin!
It was the dead who groaned within.

84   *To One in Paradise*

THOU wast that all to me, love,
  For which my soul did pine—
A green isle in the sea, love,
  A fountain and a shrine,
All wreathed with fairy fruits and flowers,
  And all the flowers were mine.

Ah, dream too bright to last!
  Ah, starry Hope! that didst arise
But to be overcast!
  A voice from out the Future cries,
'On! on!'—but o'er the Past
  (Dim gulf!) my spirit hovering lies
Mute, motionless, aghast!

For, alas! alas! with me
  The light of Life is o'er!
No more—no more—no more—
  (Such language holds the solemn sea
To the sands upon the shore)
  Shall bloom the thunder-blasted tree,
Or the stricken eagle soar!

And all my days are trances,
　And all my nightly dreams
Are where thy grey eye glances,
　And where thy footstep gleams—
In what ethereal dances,
　By what eternal streams.

85　　　　　*The Haunted Palace*

IN the greenest of our valleys
　By good angels tenanted,
Once a fair and stately palace—
　Radiant palace—reared its head.
In the monarch Thought's dominion,
　It stood there!
Never seraph spread a pinion
　Over fabric half so fair!

Banners yellow, glorious, golden,
　On its roof did float and flow
(This—all this—was in the olden
　Time long ago),
And every gentle air that dallied,
　In that sweet day,
Along the rampart plumed and pallid,
　A wingéd odor went away.

Wanderers in that happy valley,
　Through two luminous windows, saw
Spirits moving musically,
　To a lute's well-tunéd law,

Round about a throne where, sitting,
   Porphyrogene!
In state his glory well befitting,
   The ruler of the realm was seen.

And all with pearl and ruby glowing
   Was the fair palace door,
Through which came flowing, flowing, flowing,
   And sparkling evermore,
A troop of Echoes, whose sweet duty
   Was but to sing,
In voices of surpassing beauty,
   The wit and wisdom of their king.

But evil things, in robes of sorrow,
   Assailed the monarch's high estate.
(Ah, let us mourn!—for never morrow
   Shall dawn upon him, desolate!)
And round about his home the glory
   That blushed and bloomed,
Is but a dim-remembered story
   Of the old time entombed.

And travellers, now, within that valley,
   Through the red-litten windows see
Vast forms that move fantastically
   To a discordant melody,
While, like a ghastly rapid river,
   Through the pale door
A hideous throng rush out forever,
   And laugh—but smile no more.

86　　　　　　　*Dream-Land*

Bʏ a route obscure and lonely,
Haunted by ill angels only,
Where an Eidolon, named Nɪɢʜᴛ,
On a black throne reigns upright,
I have reached these lands but newly
From an ultimate dim Thule—
From a wild weird clime that lieth, sublime,
Out of Sᴘᴀᴄᴇ—out of Tɪᴍᴇ.

Bottomless vales and boundless floods,
And chasms, and caves, and Titan woods,
With forms that no man can discover
For the tears that drip all over;
Mountains toppling evermore
Into seas without a shore;
Seas that restlessly aspire,
Surging, unto skies of fire;
Lakes that endlessly outspread
Their lone waters, lone and dead,—
Their still waters, still and chilly
With the snows of the lolling lily.

By the lakes that thus outspread
Their lone waters, lone and dead,—
Their sad waters, sad and chilly
With the snows of the lolling lily,—
By the mountains—near the river
Murmuring lowly, murmuring ever,—

By the grey woods,—by the swamp
Where the toad and the newt encamp,—
By the dismal tarns and pools
   Where dwell the Ghouls,—
By each spot the most unholy—
In each nook most melancholy,—
There the traveller meets, aghast,
Sheeted Memories of the Past—
Shrouded forms that start and sigh
As they pass the wanderer by—
White-robed forms of friends long given,
In agony, to the Earth—and Heaven.

For the heart whose woes are legion
'T is a peaceful, soothing region—
For the spirit that walks in shadow
'T is—oh, 't is an Eldorado!
But the traveller, travelling through it,
May not—dare not openly view it;
Never its mysteries are exposed
To the weak human eye unclosed;
So wills its King, who hath forbid
The uplifting of the fringéd lid;
And thus the sad Soul that here passes
Beholds it but through darkened glasses.

By a route obscure and lonely,
Haunted by ill angels only,
Where an Eidolon, named Night,
On a black throne reigns upright,
I have wandered home but newly
From this ultimate dim Thule.

EDGAR ALLAN POE

87

The Raven

ONCE upon a midnight dreary, while I pondered, weak
   and weary,
Over many a quaint and curious volume of forgotten lore—
While I nodded, nearly napping, suddenly there came a
   tapping,
As of some one gently rapping, rapping at my chamber
   door.
' 'T is some visitor,' I muttered, 'tapping at my chamber
   door—
         Only this and nothing more.'

Ah, distinctly I remember it was in the bleak December;
And each separate dying ember wrought its ghost upon the
   floor.
Eagerly I wished the morrow;—vainly I had sought to
   borrow
From my books surcease of sorrow—sorrow for the lost
   Lenore—
For the rare and radiant maiden whom the angels name
   Lenore—
         Nameless *here* for evermore.

And the silken, sad, uncertain rustling of each purple
   curtain
Thrilled me—filled me with fantastic terrors never felt
   before;
So that now, to still the beating of my heart, I stood
   repeating,

'T is some visitor entreating entrance at my chamber
door—
Some late visitor entreating entrance at my chamber
door;—
This it is and nothing more.'

Presently my soul grew stronger; hesitating then no longer,
'Sir,' said I, 'or Madam, truly your forgiveness I implore;
But the fact is I was napping, and so gently you came
rapping,
And so faintly you came tapping, tapping at my chamber
door,
That I scarce was sure I heard you'—here I opened wide
the door;—
Darkness there and nothing more.

Deep into that darkness peering, long I stood there
wondering, fearing,
Doubting, dreaming dreams no mortal ever dared to dream
before;
But the silence was unbroken, and the stillness gave no
token,
And the only word there spoken was the whispered word,
'Lenore?'
This I whispered, and an echo murmured back the word,
'Lenore!'
Merely this and nothing more.

Back into the chamber turning, all my soul within me
burning,
Soon again I heard a tapping somewhat louder than before.
'Surely,' said I, 'surely that is something at my window
lattice;

Let me see, then, what thereat is, and this mystery
    explore—
Let my heart be still a moment and this mystery explore;—
            'T is the wind and nothing more!'

Open here I flung the shutter, when, with many a flirt and
    flutter,
In there stepped a stately Raven of the saintly days of yore;
Not the least obeisance made he; not a minute stopped or
    stayed he;
But, with mien of lord or lady, perched above my chamber
    door—
Perched upon a bust of Pallas just above my chamber
    door—
            Perched, and sat, and nothing more.

Then this ebony bird beguiling my sad fancy into smiling,
By the grave and stern decorum of the countenance it wore,
'Though thy crest be shorn and shaven, thou,' I said, 'art
    sure no craven,
Ghastly grim and ancient Raven wandering from the
    Nightly shore—
Tell me what thy lordly name is on the Night's Plutonian
    shore!'
            Quoth the Raven, 'Nevermore.'

Much I marvelled this ungainly fowl to hear discourse so
    plainly,
Though its answer little meaning—little relevancy bore;
For we cannot help agreeing that no living human being
Ever yet was blessed with seeing bird above his chamber
    door—

Bird or beast upon the sculptured bust above his chamber
    door,
        With such name as 'Nevermore.'

But the Raven, sitting lonely on the placid bust, spoke only
That one word, as if his soul in that one word he did
    outpour.
Nothing farther then he uttered—not a feather then he
    fluttered—
Till I scarcely more than muttered, 'Other friends have
    flown before—
On the morrow *he* will leave me, as my Hopes have flown
    before.'
        Then the bird said, 'Nevermore.'

Startled at the stillness broken by reply so aptly spoken,
'Doubtless,' said I, 'what it utters is its only stock and
    store
Caught from some unhappy master whom unmerciful
    Disaster
Followed fast and followed faster till his songs one burden
    bore—
Till the dirges of his Hope that melancholy burden bore
        Of "Never—nevermore." '

But the Raven still beguiling my sad fancy into smiling,
Straight I wheeled a cushioned seat in front of bird and
    bust and door;
Then, upon the velvet sinking, I betook myself to linking
Fancy unto fancy, thinking what this ominous bird of
    yore—
What this grim, ungainly, ghastly, gaunt, and ominous
    bird of yore
        Meant in croaking 'Nevermore.'

This I sat engaged in guessing, but no syllable expressing
To the fowl whose fiery eyes now burned into my bosom's
    core;
This and more I sat divining, with my head at ease re-
    clining
On the cushion's velvet lining that the lamp-light gloated
    o'er,
But whose velvet-violet lining with the lamp-light gloating
    o'er,
        She shall press, ah, nevermore!

Then, methought, the air grew denser, perfumed from an
    unseen censer
Swung by seraphim whose foot-falls tinkled on the tufted
    floor.
'Wretch,' I cried, 'thy God hath lent thee—by these angels
    he hath sent thee
Respite—respite and nepenthe from thy memories of
    Lenore;
Quaff, oh, quaff this kind nepenthe and forget this lost
    Lenore!'
        Quoth the Raven, 'Nevermore.'

'Prophet!' said I, 'thing of evil!—prophet still, if bird or
    devil!—
Whether Tempter sent, or whether tempest tossed thee
    here ashore,
Desolate yet all undaunted, on this desert land enchanted—
On this home by Horror haunted—tell me truly, I im-
    plore—
Is there—*is* there balm in Gilead?—tell me—tell me, I
    implore!'
        Quoth the Raven, 'Nevermore.'

'Prophet!' said I, 'thing of evil!—prophet still, if bird
or devil!
By that Heaven that bends above us—by that God we both
adore—
Tell this soul with sorrow laden if, within the distant
Aidenn,
It shall clasp a sainted maiden whom the angels name
Lenore—
Clasp a rare and radiant maiden whom the angels name
Lenore.'
      Quoth the Raven, 'Nevermore.'

'Be that word our sign of parting, bird or fiend!' I shrieked,
upstarting—
'Get thee back into the tempest and the Night's Plutonian
shore!
Leave no black plume as a token of that lie thy soul hath
spoken!
Leave my loneliness unbroken!—quit the bust above my
door!
Take thy beak from out my heart, and take thy form from
off my door!'
      Quoth the Raven, 'Nevermore.'

And the Raven, never flitting, still is sitting, *still* is sitting
On the pallid bust of Pallas just above my chamber door;
And his eyes have all the seeming of a demon's that is
dreaming,
And the lamp-light o'er him streaming throws his shadow
on the floor;
And my soul from out that shadow that lies floating on the
floor
      Shall be lifted—nevermore!

88

Ulalume—A Ballad

THE skies they were ashen and sober;
    The leaves they were crispéd and sere—
    The leaves they were withering and sere:
It was night, in the lonesome October
    Of my most immemorial year:
It was hard by the dim lake of Auber,
    In the misty mid region of Weir—
It was down by the dank tarn of Auber,
    In the ghoul-haunted woodland of Weir.

Here once, through an alley Titanic,
    Of cypress, I roamed with my Soul—
    Of cypress, with Psyche, my Soul.
These were days when my heart was volcanic
    As the scoriac rivers that roll—
    As the lavas that restlessly roll
Their sulphurous currents down Yaanek
    In the ultimate climes of the Pole—
That groan as they roll down Mount Yaanek
    In the realms of the Boreal Pole.

Our talk had been serious and sober,
    But our thoughts they were palsied and sere—
    Our memories were treacherous and sere;
For we knew not the month was October,
    And we marked not the night of the year
    (Ah, night of all nights in the year!)—
We noted not the dim lake of Auber
    (Though once we had journeyed down here)—
We remembered not the dank tarn of Auber,
    Nor the ghoul-haunted woodland of Weir.

And now, as the night was senescent
    And star-dials pointed to morn—
    As the star-dials hinted of morn—
At the end of our path a liquescent
    And nebulous lustre was born,
Out of which a miraculous crescent
    Arose with a duplicate horn—
Astarte's bediamonded crescent
    Distinct with its duplicate horn.

And I said: 'She is warmer than Dian;
    She rolls through an ether of sighs—
    She revels in a region of sighs.
She has seen that the tears are not dry on
    These cheeks, where the worm never dies,
And has come past the stars of the Lion,
    To point us the path to the skies—
    To the Lethean peace of the skies—
Come up, in despite of the Lion,
    To shine on us with her bright eyes—
Come up through the lair of the Lion,
    With love in her luminous eyes.'

But Psyche, uplifting her finger,
    Said: 'Sadly this star I mistrust—
    Her pallor I strangely mistrust:
Ah, hasten!—ah, let us not linger:
    Ah, fly!—let us fly!—for we must.'
In terror she spoke, letting sink her
    Wings till they trailed in the dust—
In agony sobbed, letting sink her
    Plumes till they trailed in the dust—
    Till they sorrowfully trailed in the dust.

I replied: 'This is nothing but dreaming:
    Let us on by this tremulous light!
    Let us bathe in this crystalline light!
Its Sibyllic splendor is beaming
    With Hope and in Beauty to-night:—
    See!—it flickers up the sky through the night!
Ah, we safely may trust to its gleaming,
    And be sure it will lead us aright—
We surely may trust to a gleaming,
    That cannot but guide us aright,
    Since it flickers up to Heaven through the night.'

Thus I pacified Psyche and kissed her,
    And tempted her out of her gloom—
    And conquered her scruples and gloom;
And we passed to the end of the vista,
    But were stopped by the door of a tomb—
    By the door of a legended tomb;
And I said: 'What is written, sweet sister,
    On the door of this legended tomb?'
    She replied: 'Ulalume—Ulalume!—
    'T is the vault of thy lost Ulalume!'

Then my heart it grew ashen and sober
    As the leaves that were crispéd and sere—
    As the leaves that were withering and sere;
And I cried: 'It was surely October
    On *this* very night of last year
    That I journeyed—I journeyed down here!—
    That I brought a dread burden down here—
    On this night of all nights in the year,
    Ah, what demon hath tempted me here?

Well I know, now, this dim lake of Auber—
    This misty mid region of Weir—
Well I know, now, this dank tarn of Auber,
    This ghoul-haunted woodland of Weir.'

Said we, then—the two, then: 'Ah, can it
    Have been that the woodlandish ghouls—
    The pitiful, the merciful ghouls—
To bar up our way and to ban it
    From the secret that lies in these wolds—
    From the thing that lies hidden in these wolds—
Have drawn up the spectre of a planet
    From the limbo of lunary souls—
This sinfully scintillant planet
    From the Hell of the planetary souls?'

89   *Eldorado*

GAILY bedight,
    A gallant knight,
In sunshine and in shadow,
    Had journeyed long,
    Singing a song,
In search of Eldorado.

    But he grew old—
    This knight so bold—
And o'er his heart a shadow
    Fell as he found
    No spot of ground
That looked like Eldorado.

And, as his strength
  Failed him at length,
He met a pilgrim shadow—
  'Shadow,' said he,
  'Where can it be—
This land of Eldorado?'

  'Over the Mountains
  Of the Moon,
Down the Valley of the Shadow,
  Ride, boldly ride,'
  The shade replied,—
'If you seek for Eldorado!'

90   *For Annie*

THANK Heaven! the crisis,
  The danger, is past,
And the lingering illness
  Is over at last—
And the fever called 'Living'
  Is conquered at last.

Sadly, I know
  I am shorn of my strength,
And no muscle I move
  As I lie at full length—
But no matter!—I feel
  I am better at length.

And I rest so composedly,
　Now, in my bed,
That any beholder
　Might fancy me dead—
Might start at beholding me,
　Thinking me dead.

The moaning and groaning,
　The sighing and sobbing,
Are quieted now,
　With that horrible throbbing
At heart:—ah, that horrible,
　Horrible throbbing!

The sickness—the nausea—
　The pitiless pain—
Have ceased, with the fever
　That maddened my brain—
With the fever called 'Living'
　That burned in my brain.

And oh! of all tortures
　That torture the worst
Has abated—the terrible
　Torture of thirst
For the naphthaline river
　Of Passion accurst:—
I have drank of a water
　That quenches all thirst:—

Of a water that flows,
　With a lullaby sound,
From a spring but a very **few**
　Feet under ground—

From a cavern not very far
   Down under ground.

And ah! let it never
   Be foolishly said
That my room it is gloomy
   And narrow my bed;
For man never slept
   In a different bed—
And, to *sleep*, you must slumber
   In just such a bed.

My tantalized spirit
   Here blandly reposes,
Forgetting, or never
   Regretting, its roses—
Its old agitations
   Of myrtles and roses:

For now, while so quietly
   Lying, it fancies
A holier odor
   About it, of pansies—
A rosemary odor,
   Commingled with pansies—
With rue and the beautiful
   Puritan pansies.

And so it lies happily,
   Bathing in many
A dream of the truth
   And the beauty of Annie—
Drowned in a bath
   Of the tresses of Annie.

She tenderly kissed me,
   She fondly caressed,
And then I fell gently
   To sleep on her breast—
Deeply to sleep
   From the heaven of her breast.

When the light was extinguished,
   She covered me warm,
And she prayed to the angels
   To keep me from harm—
To the queen of the angels
   To shield me from harm.

And I lie so composedly,
   Now, in my bed
(Knowing her love),
   That you fancy me dead—
And I rest so contentedly,
   Now, in my bed
(With her love at my breast),
   That you fancy me dead—
That you shudder to look at me,
   Thinking me dead:—

But my heart it is brighter
   Than all of the many
Stars in the sky,
   For it sparkles with Annie—
It glows with the light
   Of the love of my Annie—
With the thought of the light
   Of the eyes of my Annie.

91 *To My Mother*

BECAUSE I feel that, in the Heavens above,
   The angels, whispering to one another,
Can find, among their burning terms of love,
   None so devotional as that of 'Mother,'
Therefore by that dear name I long have called you—
   You who are more than mother unto me,
And fill my heart of hearts, where Death installed you
   In setting my Virginia's spirit free.
My mother—my own mother, who died early,
   Was but the mother of myself; but you
Are mother to the one I loved so dearly,
   And thus are dearer than the mother I knew
By that infinity with which my wife
   Was dearer to my soul than its soul-life.

92 *Annabel Lee*

IT was many and many a year ago,
    In a kingdom by the sea,
That a maiden there lived whom you may know
    By the name of Annabel Lee;—
And this maiden she lived with no other thought
    Than to love and be loved by me.

She was a child and *I* was a child,
    In this kingdom by the sea,

But we loved with a love that was more than love—
    I and my Annabel Lee—
With a love that the wingéd seraphs of Heaven
    Coveted her and me.

And this was the reason that, long ago,
    In this kingdom by the sea,
A wind blew out of a cloud by night
    Chilling my Annabel Lee;
So that her highborn kinsmen came
    And bore her away from me,
To shut her up in a sepulchre
    In this kingdom by the sea.

The angels, not half so happy in Heaven,
    Went envying her and me:—
Yes! that was the reason (as all men know,
    In this kingdom by the sea)
That the wind came out of the cloud, chilling
    And killing my Annabel Lee.

But our love it was stronger by far than the love
    Of those who were older than we—
    Of many far wiser than we—
And neither the angels in Heaven above
    Nor the demons down under the sea,
Can ever dissever my soul from the soul
    Of the beautiful Annabel Lee:—

For the moon never beams without bringing me dreams
    Of the beautiful Annabel Lee;
And the stars never rise but I see the bright eyes
    Of the beautiful Annabel Lee;

And so, all the night-tide, I lie down by the side
Of my darling, my darling, my life and my bride,
 In her sepulchre there by the sea—
 In her tomb by the side of the sea.

JONES VERY

1813-1880

93   *In Him We Live*

FATHER! I bless thy name that I do live,
And in each motion am made rich with Thee,
That when a glance is all that I can give,
It is a kingdom's wealth, if I but see;
This stately body cannot move, save I
Will to its nobleness my little bring;
My voice its measured cadence will not try,
Save I with every note consent to sing;
I cannot raise my hands to hurt or bless,
But I with every action must conspire
To show me there how little I possess,
And yet that little more than I desire;
May each new act my new allegiance prove,
Till in thy perfect love I ever live and move.

94   *The Earth*

I WOULD lie low—the ground on which men tread—
Swept by thy Spirit like the wind of heaven;

An earth, where gushing springs and corn for bread
By me at every season should be given;
Yet not the water or the bread that now
Supplies their tables with its daily food,
But they should gather fruit from every bough,
Such as Thou givest me, and call it good;
And water from the stream of life should flow,
By every dwelling that thy love has built,
Whose taste the ransomed of thy Son shall know,
Whose robes are washed from every stain of guilt;
And men would own it was thy hand that blest,
And from my bosom find a surer rest.

95   *The Garden*

I SAW the spot where our first parents dwelt;
And yet it wore to me no face of change,
For while amid its fields and groves, I felt
As if I had not sinned, nor thought it strange;
My eye seemed but a part of every sight,
My ear heard music in each sound that rose;
Each sense forever found a new delight,
Such as the spirit's vision only knows;
Each act some new and ever-varying joy
Did by my Father's love for me prepare;
To dress the spot my ever fresh employ,
And in the glorious whole with Him to share;
No more without the flaming gate to stray,
No more for sin's dark stain the debt of death to pay.

96   *The Latter Rain*

THE latter rain,—it falls in anxious haste
Upon the sun-dried fields and branches bare,
Loosening with searching drops the rigid waste,
As if it would each root's lost strength repair;
But not a blade grows green as in the spring,
No swelling twig puts forth its thickening leaves;
The robins only mid the harvests sing,
Pecking the grain that scatters from the sheaves:
The rain falls still,—the fruit all ripened drops,
It pierces chestnut burr and walnut shell,
The furrowed fields disclose the yellow crops,
Each bursting pod of talents used can tell,
And all that once received the early rain
Declare to man it was not sent in vain.

97   *The Dead*

I SEE them,—crowd on crowd they walk the earth,
Dry leafless trees no autumn wind laid bare;
And in their nakedness find cause for mirth,
And all unclad would winter's rudeness dare;
No sap doth through their clattering branches flow,
Whence springing leaves and blossoms bright appear;
Their hearts the living God have ceased to know
Who gives the spring-time to th' expectant year.
They mimic life, as if from Him to steal
His glow of health to paint the livid cheek;

They borrow words for thoughts they cannot feel,
That with a seeming heart their tongue may speak;
And in their show of life more dead they live
Than those that to the earth with many tears they give.

98   *The Cottage*

THE house my earthly parent left
My heavenly parent still throws down,
For 't is of air and sun bereft,
Nor stars its roof with beauty crown.

He gave it me, yet gave it not
As one whose gifts are wise and good;
'T was but a poor and clay-built cot,
And for a time the storms withstood.

But lengthening years and frequent rain
O'ercame its strength: it tottered, fell,
And left me homeless here again,—
And where to go I could not tell.

But soon the light and open air
Received me as a wandering child,
And I soon thought their house more fair,
And all my grief their love beguiled.

Mine was the grove, the pleasant field
Where dwelt the flowers I daily trod;
And there beside them, too, I kneeled
And called their friend, my Father, God.

99 *The Prayer*

WILT Thou not visit me?
The plant beside me feels thy gentle dew,
  And every blade of grass I see
From thy deep earth its quickening moisture drew.

  Wilt Thou not visit me?
Thy morning calls on me with cheering tone;
  And every hill and tree
Lend but one voice,—the voice of Thee alone.

  Come, for I need thy love,
More than the flower the dew or grass the rain;
  Come, gently as thy holy dove;
And let me in thy sight rejoice to live again.

  I will not hide from them
When thy storms come, though fierce may be their wrath,
  But bow with leafy stem,
And strengthened follow on thy chosen path.

  Yes, Thou wilt visit me:
Nor plant nor tree thine eye delights so well,
  As, when from sin set free,
My spirit loves with thine in peace to dwell.

100 *The Hand and Foot*

THE hand and foot that stir not, they shall find
Sooner than all the rightful place to go:

Now in their motion free as roving wind,
Though first no snail so limited and slow;
I mark them full of labor all the day,
Each active motion made in perfect rest;
They cannot from their path mistaken stray,
Though 't is not theirs, yet in it they are blest;
The bird has not their hidden track found out,
The cunning fox though full of art he be;
It is the way unseen, the certain route,
Where ever bound, yet thou art ever free;
The path of Him, whose perfect law of love
Bids spheres and atoms in just order move.

101   *Yourself*

'TIS to yourself I speak; you cannot know
Him whom I call in speaking such a one,
For you beneath the earth lie buried low,
Which he alone as living walks upon:
You may at times have heard him speak to you,
And often wished perchance that you were he;
And I must ever wish that it were true,
For then you could hold fellowship with me:
But now you hear us talk as strangers, met
Above the room wherein you lie abed;
A word perhaps loud spoken you may get,
Or hear our feet when heavily they tread;
But he who speaks, or him who's spoken to,
Must both remain as strangers still to you.

238

102   *The Strangers*

Each care-worn face is but a book
    To tell of houses bought or sold;
Or filled with words that mankind took
    From those who lived and spoke of old.

I see none whom I know, for they
    See other things than him they meet;
And though they stop me by the way,
    'T is still some other one to greet.

There are no words that reach my ear
    Those speak who tell of other things
Than what they mean for me to hear,
    For in their speech the counter rings.

I would be where each word is true,
    Each eye sees what it looks upon;
For here my eye has seen but few,
    Who in each act that act have done.

103   *The Lament of the Flowers*

I looked to find Spring's early flowers,
    In spots where they were wont to bloom;
But they had perished in their bowers;
    The haunts they loved had proved their tomb!

The alder, and the laurel green,
   Which sheltered them, had shared their fate;
And but the blackened ground was seen,
   Where hid their swelling buds of late.

From the bewildered, homeless bird,
   Whose half-built nest the flame destroys,
A low complaint of wrong I heard,
   Against the thoughtless, ruthless boys.

Sadly I heard its notes complain,
   And ask the young its haunts to spare;
Prophetic seemed the sorrowing strain,
   Sung o'er its home, but late so fair!

'No more with hues like ocean shell
   The delicate wind-flower here shall blow;
The spot that loved its form so well
   Shall ne'er again its beauty know.

'Or, if it bloom, like some pale ghost
   'T will haunt the black and shadeless dell,
Where once it bloomed a numerous host,
   Of its once pleasant bowers to tell.

'And coming years no more shall find
   The laurel green upon the hills;
The frequent fire leaves naught behind,
   But e'en the very roots it kills.

'No more upon the turnpike's side
   The rose shall shed its sweet perfume;
The traveler's joy, the summer's pride,
   Will share with them a common doom.

'No more shall these returning fling
   Round childhood's home a heavenly charm,
With song of bird in early spring,
   To glad the heart and save from harm.'

HENRY DAVID THOREAU

1817-1862

104   *Sic Vita*

I AM a parcel of vain strivings tied
   By a chance bond together,
Dangling this way and that, their links
   Were made so loose and wide,
      Methinks,
    For milder weather.

A bunch of violets without their roots,
   And sorrel intermixed,
Encircled by a wisp of straw
   Once coiled about their shoots,
     The law
    By which I'm fixed.

A nosegay which Time clutched from out
   Those fair Elysian fields,
With weeds and broken stems, in haste,
   Doth make the rabble rout
     That waste
    The day he yields.

And here I bloom for a short hour unseen,
    Drinking my juices up,
  With no root in the land
    To keep my branches green,
        But stand
    In a bare cup.

Some tender buds were left upon my stem
    In mimicry of life,
  But ah! the children will not know,
    Till time has withered them,
        The woe
    With which they're rife.

But now I see I was not plucked for naught,
    And after in life's vase
  Of glass set while I might survive,
    But by a kind hand brought
        Alive
    To a strange place.

That stock thus thinned will soon redeem its hours,
    And by another year,
  Such as God knows, with freer air,
    More fruits and fairer flowers
        Will bear,
    While I droop here.

105   *Winter Memories*

WITHIN the circuit of this plodding life
There enter moments of an azure hue,

HENRY DAVID THOREAU

Untarnished fair as is the violet
Or anemone, when the spring strews them
By some meandering rivulet, which make
The best philosophy untrue that aims
But to console man for his grievances.
I have remembered when the winter came,
High in my chamber in the frosty nights,
When in the still light of the cheerful moon,
On every twig and rail and jutting spout,
The icy spears were adding to their length
Against the arrows of the coming sun,
How in the shimmering noon of summer past
Some unrecorded beam slanted across
The upland pastures where the Johnswort grew;
Or heard, amid the verdure of my mind,
The bee's long smothered hum, on the blue flag
Loitering amidst the mead; or busy rill,
Which now through all its course stands still and dumb
Its own memorial,—purling at its play
Along the slopes, and through the meadows next,
Until its youthful sound was hushed at last
In the staid current of the lowland stream;
Or seen the furrows shine but late upturned,
And where the fieldfare followed in the rear,
When all the fields around lay bound and hoar
Beneath a thick integument of snow.
So by God's cheap economy made rich
To go upon my winter's task again.

106 *To the Maiden in the East*

Low in the eastern sky
Is set thy glancing eye;
And though its gracious light
Ne'er riseth to my sight,
Yet every star that climbs
Above the gnarled limbs
   Of yonder hill,
Conveys thy gentle will.

Believe I knew thy thought,
And that the zephyrs brought
Thy kindest wishes through,
As mine they bear to you,
That some attentive cloud
Did pause amid the crowd
   Over my head,
While gentle things were said.

Believe the thrushes sung,
And that the flower-bells rung,
That herbs exhaled their scent,
And beasts knew what was meant,
The trees a welcome waved,
And lakes their margins laved,
   When thy free mind
To my retreat did wind.

It was a summer eve,
The air did gently heave

While yet a low-hung cloud
Thy eastern skies did shroud;
The lightning's silent gleam,
Startling my drowsy dream,
  Seemed like the flash
Under thy dark eyelash.

Still will I strive to be
As if thou wert with me;
Whatever path I take,
It shall be for thy sake,
Of gentle slope and wide,
As thou wert by my side,
  Without a root
To trip thy gentle foot.

I'll walk with gentle pace,
And choose the smoothest place,
And careful dip the oar,
And shun the winding shore,
And gently steer my boat
Where water-lilies float,
  And cardinal flowers
Stand in their sylvan bowers.

107   *Smoke*

LIGHT-WINGED Smoke, Icarian bird,
Melting thy pinions in thy upward flight,
Lark without song, and messenger of dawn,
Circling above the hamlets as thy nest;

Or else, departing dream, and shadowy form
Of midnight vision, gathering up thy skirts;
By night star-veiling, and by day
Darkening the light and blotting out the sun;
Go thou my incense upward from this hearth,
And ask the gods to pardon this clear flame.

108   *Mist*

Low-anchored cloud,
Newfoundland air,
Fountain-head and source of rivers,
Dew-cloth, dream drapery,
And napkin spread by fays;
Drifting meadow of the air,
Where bloom the daisied banks and violets,
And in whose fenny labyrinth
The bittern booms and heron wades;
Spirit of lakes and seas and rivers,
Bear only perfumes and the scent
Of healing herbs to just men's fields!

109   *Inspiration*

Whate'er we leave to God, God does,
    And blesses us;
The work we choose should be our own,
    God lets alone.

HENRY DAVID THOREAU

If with light head erect I sing,
  Though all the muses lend their force,
From my poor love of anything,
  The verse is weak and shallow as its source.

But if with bended neck I grope,
  Listening behind me for my wit,
With faith superior to hope,
  More anxious to keep back than forward it,

Making my soul accomplice there
  Unto the flame my heart hath lit,
Then will the verse forever wear,—
  Time cannot bend the line which God hath writ.

Always the general show of things
  Floats in review before my mind,
And such true love and reverence brings,
  That sometimes I forget that I am blind.

But now there comes unsought, unseen,
  Some clear, divine electuary,
And I who had but sensual been,
  Grow sensible, and as God is, am wary.

I hearing get who had but ears,
  And sight, who had but eyes before,
I moments live who lived but years,
  And truth discern who knew but learning's lore.

I hear beyond the range of sound,
  I see beyond the range of sight,
New earths and skies and seas around,
  And in my day the sun doth pale his light.

A clear and ancient harmony
    Pierces my soul through all its din,
As through its utmost melody,—
    Farther behind than they—farther within.

More swift its bolt than lightning is,
    Its voice than thunder is more loud,
It doth expand my privacies
    To all, and leave me single in the crowd.

It speaks with such authority,
    With so serene and lofty tone,
That idle Time runs gadding by,
    And leaves me with Eternity alone.

Then chiefly is my natal hour,
    And only then my prime of life,
Of manhood's strength it is the flower,
    'Tis peace's end and war's beginning strife.

'T 'hath come in summer's broadest noon,
    By a grey wall or some chance place,
Unseasoned time, insulted June,
    And vexed the day with its presuming face.

Such fragrance round my couch it makes,
    More rich than are Arabian drugs,
That my soul scents its life and wakes
    The body up beneath its perfumed rugs.

Such is the Muse—the heavenly maid,
    The star that guides our mortal course,
Which shows where life's true kernel's laid,
    Its wheat's fine flower, and its undying force.

HENRY DAVID THOREAU

She with one breath attunes the spheres,
    And also my poor human heart,
With one impulse propels the years
    Around, and gives my throbbing pulse its start.

I will not doubt forever more,
    Nor falter from a steadfast faith,
For though the system be turned o'er,
    God takes not back the word which once he saith.

I will then trust the love untold
    Which not my worth nor want has bought,
Which wooed me young and woos me old,
    And to this evening hath me brought.

My memory I'll educate
    To know the one historic truth,
Remembering to the latest date
    The only true and sole immortal youth.

Be but thy inspiration given,
    No matter through what danger sought,
I'll fathom hell or climb to heaven,
    And yet esteem that cheap which love has bought.

    Fame cannot tempt the bard
        Who's famous with his God,
    Nor laurel him reward
        Who hath his Maker's nod.

JAMES RUSSELL LOWELL

1819-1891

110   From *A Fable for Critics*

EMERSON

THERE comes Emerson first, whose rich words, every one,
Are like gold nails in temples to hang trophies on,
Whose prose is grand verse, while his verse, the Lord knows,
Is some of it pr— No, 'tis not even prose;
I'm speaking of metres; some poems have welled
From those rare depths of soul that have ne'er been excelled;
They're not epics, but that doesn't matter a pin,
In creating, the only hard thing's to begin;
A grass-blade's no easier to make than an oak;
If you've once found the way, you've achieved the grand stroke;
In the worst of his poems are mines of rich matter,
But thrown in a heap with a crash and a clatter;
Now it is not one thing nor another alone
Makes a poem, but rather the general tone,
The something pervading, uniting the whole,
The before unconceived, unconceivable soul,
So that just in removing this trifle or that, you
Take away, as it were, a chief limb of the statue;
Roots, wood, bark, and leaves singly perfect may be,
But, clapt hodge-podge together, they don't make a tree.

JAMES RUSSELL LOWELL

But, to come back to Emerson (whom, by the way,
I believe we left waiting),—his is, we may say,
A Greek head on right Yankee shoulders, whose range
Has Olympus for one pole, for t'other the Exchange;
He seems, to my thinking (although I'm afraid
The comparison must, long ere this, have been made),
A Plotinus-Montaigne, where the Egyptian's gold mist
And the Gascon's shrewd wit cheek-by-jowl coexist;
All admire, and yet scarcely six converts he's got
To I don't (nor they either) exactly know what;
For though he builds glorious temples, 't is odd
He leaves never a doorway to get in a god.
'T is refreshing to old-fashioned people like me
To meet such a primitive Pagan as he,
In whose mind all creation is duly respected
As parts of himself—just a little projected;
And who's willing to worship the stars and the sun,
A convert to—nothing but Emerson.
So perfect a balance there is in his head,
That he talks of things sometimes as if they were dead;
Life, nature, love, God, and affairs of that sort,
He looks at as merely ideas; in short,
As if they were fossils stuck round in a cabinet,
Of such vast extent that our earth's a mere dab in it;
Composed just as he is inclined to conjecture her,
Namely, one part pure earth, ninety-nine parts pure
    lecturer;
You are filled with delight at his clear demonstration,
Each figure, word, gesture, just fits the occasion,
With the quiet precision of science he'll sort 'em,
But you can't help suspecting the whole a *post mor-
    tem*.

There are persons, mole-blind to the soul's make and
    style,
Who insist on a likeness 'twixt him and Carlyle;
To compare him with Plato would be vastly fairer,
Carlyle's the more burly, but E. is the rarer;
He sees fewer objects, but clearlier, truelier,
If C.'s as original, E.'s more peculiar;
That he's more of a man you might say of the one,
Of the other he's more of an Emerson;
C.'s the Titan, as shaggy of mind as of limb,—
E. the clear-eyed Olympian, rapid and slim;
The one's two thirds Norseman, the other half Greek,
Where the one's most abounding, the other's to seek;
C.'s generals require to be seen in the mass,—
E.'s specialties gain if enlarged by the glass;
C. gives nature and God his own fits of the blues,
And rims common-sense things with mystical hues,—
E. sits in a mystery calm and intense,
And looks coolly around him with sharp common-sense;
C. shows you how every-day matters unite
With the dim transdiurnal recesses of night,—
While E., in a plain, preternatural way,
Makes mysteries matters of mere every day;
C. draws all his characters quite *à la* Fuseli,—
Not sketching their bundles of muscles and thews illy,
He paints with a brush so untamed and profuse,
They seem nothing but bundles of muscles and thews;
E. is rather like Flaxman, lines strait and severe,
And a colorless outline, but full, round, and clear;—
To the men he thinks worthy he frankly accords
The design of a white marble statue in words.
C. labors to get at the centre, and then
Take a reckoning from there of his actions and men;

E. calmly assumes the said centre as granted,
And, given himself, has whatever is wanted.

He has imitators in scores, who omit
No part of the man but his wisdom and wit,—
Who go carefully o'er the sky-blue of his brain,
And when he has skimmed it once, skim it again;
If at all they resemble him, you may be sure it is
Because their shoals mirror his mists and obscurities,
As a mud-puddle seems deep as heaven for a minute,
While a cloud that floats o'er is reflected within it.

WHITTIER

THERE is Whittier, whose swelling and vehement
  heart
Strains the strait-breasted drab of the Quaker apart,
And reveals the live Man, still supreme and erect,
Underneath the bemummying wrappers of sect;
There was ne'er a man born who had more of the swing
Of the true lyric bard and all that kind of thing;
And his failures arise (though he seem not to know it)
From the very same cause that has made him a poet,—
A fervor of mind which knows no separation
'Twixt simple excitement and pure inspiration,
As my Pythoness erst sometimes erred from not knowing
If 't were I or mere wind through her tripod was blowing;
Let his mind once get head in its favorite direction
And the torrent of verse bursts the dams of reflection,
While, borne with the rush of the metre along,
The poet may chance to go right or go wrong,
Content with the whirl and delirium of song;

Then his grammar's not always correct, nor his rhymes,
And he's prone to repeat his own lyrics sometimes,
Not his best, though, for those are struck off at white-heats
When the heart in his breast like a trip-hammer beats,
And can ne'er be repeated again any more
Than they could have been carefully plotted before:
Like old what's-his-name there at the battle of Hastings
(Who, however, gave more than mere rhythmical bastings),
Our Quaker leads off metaphorical fights
For reform and whatever they call human rights,
Both singing and striking in front of the war,
And hitting his foes with the mallet of Thor;
Anne haec, one exclaims, on beholding his knocks,
Vestis filii tui, O leather-clad Fox?
Can that be thy son, in the battle's mid din,
Preaching brotherly love and then driving it in
To the brain of the tough old Goliath of sin,
With the smoothest of pebbles from Castaly's spring
Impressed on his hard moral sense with a sling?

All honor and praise to the right-hearted bard
Who was true to The Voice when such service was hard,
Who himself was so free he dared sing for the slave
When to look but a protest in silence was brave;
All honor and praise to the women and men
Who spoke out for the dumb and the down-trodden then!

HAWTHORNE

THERE is Hawthorne, with genius so shrinking and
rare
That you hardly at first see the strength that is there;

JAMES RUSSELL LOWELL

A frame so robust, with a nature so sweet,
So earnest, so graceful, so lithe and so fleet,
Is worth a descent from Olympus to meet;
'T is as if a rough oak that for ages had stood,
With his gnarled bony branches like ribs of the wood,
Should bloom, after cycles of struggle and scathe,
With a single anemone trembly and rathe;
His strength is so tender, his wildness so meek,
That a suitable parallel sets one to seek,—
He's a John Bunyan Fouqué, a Puritan Tieck;
When Nature was shaping him, clay was not granted
For making so full-sized a man as she wanted,
So, to fill out her model, a little she spared
From some finer-grained stuff for a woman prepared,
And she could not have hit a more excellent plan
For making him fully and perfectly man.

COOPER

Here's Cooper, who's written six volumes to show
He's as good as a lord: well, let's grant that he's so;
If a person prefer that description of praise,
Why, a coronet's certainly cheaper than bays;
But he need take no pains to convince us he's not
(As his enemies say) the American Scott.
Choose any twelve men, and let C. read aloud
That one of his novels of which he's most proud,
And I'd lay any bet that, without ever quitting
Their box, they'd be all, to a man, for acquitting.
He has drawn you one character, though, that is new,
One wildflower he's plucked that is wet with the dew

JAMES RUSSELL LOWELL

Of this fresh Western world, and, the thing not to mince,
He has done naught but copy it ill ever since;
His Indians, with proper respect be it said,
Are just Natty Bumppo, daubed over with red,
And his very Long Toms are the same useful Nat,
Rigged up in duck pants and a sou'wester hat
(Though once in a Coffin, a good chance was found
To have slipped the old fellow away underground).
All his other men-figures are clothes upon sticks,
The *dernière chemise* of a man in a fix
(As a captain besieged, when his garrison's small,
Sets up caps upon poles to be seen o'er the wall);
And the women he draws from one model don't vary,
All sappy as maples and flat as a prairie.
When a character's wanted, he goes to the task
As a cooper would do in composing a cask;
He picks out the staves, of their qualities heedful,
Just hoops them together as tight as is needful,
And, if the best fortune should crown the attempt, he
Has made at the most something wooden and empty.

Don't suppose I would underrate Cooper's abilities;
If I thought you'd do that, I should feel very ill at ease;
The men who have given to *one* character life
And objective existence are not very rife;
You may number them all, both prose-writers and singers,
Without overrunning the bounds of your fingers,
And Natty won't go to oblivion quicker
Than Adams the parson or Primrose the vicar.

There is one thing in Cooper I like, too, and that is
That on manners he lectures his countrymen gratis;

Not precisely so either, because, for a rarity,
He is paid for his tickets in unpopularity.
Now he may overcharge his American pictures,
But you'll grant there's a good deal of truth in his
    strictures;
And I honor the man who is willing to sink
Half his present repute for the freedom to think,
And, when he has thought, be his cause strong or weak,
Will risk t'other half for the freedom to speak,
Caring naught for what vengeance the mob has in store,
Let that mob be the upper ten thousand or lower.

There are truths you Americans need to be told,
And it never'll refute them to swagger and scold;
John Bull, looking o'er the Atlantic, in choler
At your aptness for trade, says you worship the dollar;
But to scorn such eye-dollar-try's what very few do,
And John goes to that church as often as you do.
No matter what John says, don't try to outcrow him,
'T is enough to go quietly on and outgrow him;
Like most fathers, Bull hates to see Number One
Displacing himself in the mind of his son,
And detests the same faults in himself he'd neglected
When he sees them again in his child's glass reflected;
To love one another you're too like by half;
If he is a bull, you're a pretty stout calf,
And tear your own pasture for naught but to show
What a nice pair of horns you're beginning to grow.

There are one or two things I should just like to hint,
For you don't often get the truth told you in print;
The most of you (this is what strikes all beholders)
Have a mental and physical stoop in the shoulders;

Though you ought to be free as the winds and the waves,
You've the gait and the manners of runaway slaves;
Though you brag of your New World, you don't half
    believe in it;
And as much of the Old as is possible weave in it;
Your goddess of freedom, a tight, buxom girl,
With lips like a cherry and teeth like a pearl,
With eyes bold as Herë's, and hair floating free,
And full of the sun as the spray of the sea,
Who can sing at a husking or romp at a shearing,
Who can trip through the forests alone without fearing,
Who can drive home the cows with a song through the
    grass,
Keeps glancing aside into Europe's cracked glass,
Hides her red hands in gloves, pinches up her lithe waist,
And makes herself wretched with transmarine taste;
She loses her fresh country charm when she takes
Any mirror except her own rivers and lakes.

    You steal Englishmen's books and think Englishmen's
      thought,
With their salt on her tail your wild eagle is caught;
Your literature suits its each whisper and motion
To what will be thought of it over the ocean;
The cast clothes of Europe your statemanship tries
And mumbles again the old blarneys and lies;—
Forget Europe wholly, your veins throb with blood,
To which the dull current in hers is but mud:
Let her sneer, let her say your experiment fails,
In her voice there's a tremble e'en now while she rails,
And your shore will soon be in the nature of things
Covered thick with gilt drift-wood of cast-away kings,

JAMES RUSSELL LOWELL

Where alone, as it were in a Longfellow's Waif,
Her fugitive pieces will find themselves safe.
O my friends, thank your god, if you have one, that he
'Twixt the Old World and you set the gulf of a sea;
Be strong-backed, brown-handed, upright as your pines,
By the scale of a hemisphere shape your designs,
Be true to yourselves and this new nineteenth age,
As a statue by Powers, or a picture by Page,
Plough, sail, forge, build, carve, paint, make all over new,
To your own New-World instincts contrive to be true,
Keep your ears open wide to the Future's first call,
Be whatever you will, but yourselves first of all,
Stand fronting the dawn on Toil's heaven-scaling peaks,
And become my new race of more practical Greeks.—
Hem! your likeness at present, I shudder to tell o't,
Is that you have your slaves, and the Greek had his helot.

POE AND LONGFELLOW

THERE comes Poe, with his raven, like Barnaby
   Rudge,
Three fifths of him genius and two fifths sheer fudge,
Who talks like a book of iambs and pentameters,
In a way to make people of common sense damn metres,
Who has written some things quite the best of their kind,
But the heart somehow seems all squeezed out by the mind,
Who— But hey-day! What's this? Messieurs Mathews and
      Poe,
You mustn't fling mud-balls at Longfellow so,
Does it make a man worse that his character's such
As to make his friends love him (as you think) too much?

Why, there is not a bard at this moment alive
More willing than he that his fellows should thrive;
While you are abusing him thus, even now
He would help either one of you out of a slough;
You may say that he's smooth and all that till you're hoarse,
But remember that elegance also is force;
After polishing granite as much as you will,
The heart keeps its tough old persistency still;
Deduct all you can, *that* still keeps you at bay;
Why, he'll live till men weary of Collins and Gray.
I'm not over-fond of Greek metres in English,
To me rhyme's a gain, so it be not too jinglish,
And your modern hexameter verses are no more
Like Greek ones than sleek Mr. Pope is like Homer;
As the roar of the sea to the coo of a pigeon is,
So, compared to your moderns, sounds old Melesigenes;
I may be too partial, the reason, perhaps, o't is
That I've heard the old blind man recite his own rhapso-
      dies,
And my ear with that music impregnate may be,
Like the poor exiled shell with the soul of the sea,
Or as one can't bear Strauss when his nature is cloven
To its deeps within deeps by the stroke of Beethoven;
But, set that aside, and 'tis truth that I speak,
Had Theocritus written in English, not Greek,
I believe that his exquisite sense would scarce change a line
In that rare, tender, virgin-like pastoral Evangeline.
That's not ancient nor modern, its place is apart
Where time has no sway, in the realm of pure Art,
'T is a shrine of retreat from Earth's hubbub and strife
As quiet and chaste as the author's own life.

JAMES RUSSELL LOWELL

LOWELL

THERE is Lowell, who's striving Parnassus to climb
With a whole bale of *isms* tied together with rhyme,
He might get on alone, spite of brambles and boulders,
But he can't with that bundle he has on his shoulders,
The top of the hill he will ne'er come nigh reaching
Till he learns the distinction 'twixt singing and preaching;
His lyre has some chords that would ring pretty well,
But he'd rather by half make a drum of the shell,
And rattle away till he's old as Methusalem,
At the head of a march to the last new Jerusalem.

III   *The Biglow Papers*

No. I

A Letter

FROM MR. EZEKIEL BIGLOW OF JAALAM TO THE HON.
JOSEPH T. BUCKINGHAM, EDITOR OF THE BOSTON
COURIER, INCLOSING A POEM OF HIS SON, MR. HOSEA
BIGLOW

JAYLEM, june 1846.

MISTER EDDYTER:—Our Hosea wuz down to Booton
last week, and he see a cruetin Sarjunt a struttin round as
popler as a hen with 1 chicking, with 2 fellers a drummin
and fifin arter him like all nater. the sarjunt he thout Hosea
hedn't gut his i teeth cut cos he looked a kindo's though
he'd jest com down, so he cal'lated to hook him in, but
Hosy woodn't take none o' his sarse for all he hed much as

20 Rŏoster's tales stuck onto his hat and eenamost enuf
brass a bobbin up and down on his shoulders and figureed
onto his coat and trousis, let alone wut nater hed sot in his
featers, to make a 6 pounder out on.

wal, Hosea he com home considerabal riled, and arter
I'd gone to bed I heern Him a thrashin round like a short-
tailed Bull in fli-time. The old Woman ses she to me ses
she, Zekle, ses she, our Hosee's gut the chollery or suthin
anuther ses she, don't you Bee skeered, ses I, he's oney
amakin pottery ses i, he's ollers on hand at that ere busynes
like Da & martin, and shure enuf, cum mornin, Hosy he
cum down stares full chizzle, hare on eend and cote tales
flyin, and sot rite of to go reed his varses to Parson Wilbur
bein he haint aney grate shows o' book larnin himself,
bimeby he cum back and sed the parson wuz dreffle tickled
with 'em as i hoop you will Be, and said they wuz True
grit.

Hosea ses taint hardly fair to call 'em hisn now, cos the
parson kind o' slicked off sum o' the last varses, but he told
Hosee he didn't want tu put his ore in to tetch to the Rest
on 'em, bein they wuz verry well As thay wuz, and then
Hosy ses he sed suthin a nuther about Simplex Mundishes
or sum sech feller, but I guess Hosea kind o' didn't hear
him, for I never hearn o' nobody o' that name in this
villadge, and I've lived here man and boy 76 year cum
next tater diggin, and thair aint no wheres a kitting spryer
'n I be.

If you print 'em I wish you'd jest let folks know who
hosy's father is, cos my ant Keziah used to say it's nater to
be curus ses she, she aint livin though and he's a likely kind
o' lad.

EZEKIEL BIGLOW.

JAMES RUSSELL LOWELL

Thrash away, you'll *hev* to rattle
　　On them kittle-drums o' yourn,—
'Taint a knowin' kind o' cattle
　　Thet is ketched with mouldy corn;
Put in stiff, you fifer feller,
　　Let folks see how spry you be,—
Guess you'll toot till you are yeller
　　'Fore you git ahold o' me!

Thet air flag's a leetle rotten,
　　Hope it aint your Sunday's best;—
Fact! it takes a sight o' cotton
　　To stuff out a soger's chest:
Sence we farmers hev to pay fer't,
　　Ef you must wear humps like these,
S'posin' you should try salt hay fer 't,
　　It would du ez slick ez grease.

'Twouldn't suit them Southun fellers,
　　They're a dreffle graspin' set,
We must ollers blow the bellers
　　Wen they want their irons het;
May be it's all right ez preachin',
　　But *my* narves it kind o' grates,
Wen I see the overreachin'
　　O' them nigger-drivin' States.

Them thet rule us, them slave-traders,
　　Haint they cut a thunderin' swarth
(Helped by Yankee renegaders),
　　Thru the vartu o' the North!
We begin to think it's nater
　　To take sarse an' not be riled;—

Who'd expect to see a tater
   All on eend at bein' biled?

Ez fer war, I call it murder,—
   There you hev it plain an' flat;
I don't want to go no furder
   Than my Testyment fer that;
God hez sed so plump an' fairly,
   It's ez long ez it is broad,
An' you've gut to git up airly
   Ef you want to take in God.

'Taint your eppyletts an' feathers
   Make the thing a grain more right;
'Taint afollerin' your bell-wethers
   Will excuse ye in His sight;
Ef you take a sword an' dror it,
   An' go stick a feller thru,
Guv'ment aint to answer for it,
   God'll send the bill to you.

Wut's the use o' meetin'-goin'
   Every Sabbath, wet or dry,
Ef it's right to go amowin'
   Feller-men like oats an' rye?
I dunno but wut it's pooty
   Trainin' round in bobtail coats,—
But it's curus Christian dooty
   This 'ere cuttin' folks's throats.

They may talk o' Freedom's airy
   Tell they're pupple in the face,—
It's a grand gret cemetary
   Fer the barthrights of our race;

They jest want this Californy
   So's to lug new slave-states in
To abuse ye, an' to scorn ye,
   An' to plunder ye like sin.

Aint it cute to see a Yankee
   Take sech everlastin' pains,
All to get the Devil's thankee
   Helpin' on 'em weld their chains?
Wy, it's jest ez clear ez figgers,
   Clear ez one an' one make two,
Chaps that make black slaves o' niggers
   Want to make wite slaves o' you.

Tell ye jest the eend I've come to
   Arter cipherin' plaguy smart,
An' it makes a handy sum, tu,
   Any gump could larn by heart;
Laborin' man an' laborin' woman
   Hev one glory an' one shame.
Ev'y thin' thet's done inhuman
   Injers all on 'em the same.

'Taint by turnin' out to hack folks
   You're agoin' to git your right,
Nor by lookin' down on black folks
   Coz you're put upon by wite;
Slavery aint o' nary color,
   'Taint the hide thet makes it wus,
All it keers fer in a feller
   'S jest to make him fill its pus.

Want to tackle *me* in, du ye?
   I expect you'll hev to wait;

Wen cold lead puts daylight thru ye
    You'll begin to kal'late;
S'pose the crows wun't fall to pickin'
    All the carkiss from your bones,
Coz you helped to give a lickin'
    To them poor half-Spanish drones?

Jest go home an' ask our Nancy
    Wether I'd be sech a goose
Ez to jine ye,—guess you'd fancy
    The etarnal bung wuz loose!
She wants me fer home consumption,
    Let alone the hay 's to mow,—
Ef you're arter folks o' gumption,
    You've a darned long row to hoe.

Take them editors thet's crowin'
    Like a cockerel three months old,—
Don't ketch any on 'em goin',
    Though they *be* so blasted bold;
Aint they a prime lot o' fellers?
    'Fore they think on't guess they'll sprout
(Like a peach thet's got the yellers),
    With the meanness bustin' out.

Wal, go 'long to help 'em stealin'
    Bigger pens to cram with slaves,
Help the men thet's ollers dealin'
    Insults on your fathers' graves;
Help the strong to grind the feeble,
    Help the many agin the few,
Help the men thet call your people
    Witewashed slaves an' peddlin' crew!

JAMES RUSSELL LOWELL

Massachusetts, God forgive her,
  She's akneelin' with the rest,
She, thet ough' to ha' clung ferever
  In her grand old eagle-nest;
She thet ough' to stand so fearless
  W'ile the wracks are round her hurled,
Holdin' up a beacon peerless
  To the oppressed of all the world!

Ha'n't they sold your colored seamen?
  Ha'n't they made your env'ys w'iz?
Wut'll make ye act like freemen?
  Wut'll git your dander riz?
Come, I'll tell ye wut I'm thinkin'
  Is our dooty in this fix,
They'd ha' done't ez quick ez winkin'
  In the days o' seventy-six.

Clang the bells in every steeple,
  Call all true men to disown
The tradoocers of our people,
  The enslavers o' their own;
Let our dear old Bay State proudly
  Put the trumpet to her mouth,
Let her ring this messidge loudly
  In the ears of all the South:—

'I'll return ye good fer evil
  Much ez we frail mortils can
But I wun't go help the Devil
  Makin' man the cus o' man;
Call me coward, call me traiter,
  Jest ez suits your mean idees,—

Here I stand a tyrant-hater,
    An' the friend o' God an' Peace!'

Ef I'd *my* way I hed ruther
    We should go to work an' part,
They take one way, we take t' other,
    Guess it wouldn't break my heart;
Man hed ough' to put asunder
    Them thet God has noways jined;
An' I shouldn't gretly wonder
    Ef there's thousands o' my mind.

No. II

A Letter

FROM MR. HOSEA BIGLOW TO THE HON. J. T. BUCKINGHAM,
EDITOR OF THE BOSTON COURIER, COVERING A LETTER
FROM MR. B. SAWIN, PRIVATE IN THE MASSACHUSETTS
REGIMENT

MISTER BUCKINUM, the follerin Billet was writ hum by
a Yung feller of our town that was cussed fool enuff to goe
atrottin inter Miss Chiff arter a Drum and fife. it ain't
Nater for a feller to let on that he's sick o' any bizness that
He went intu off his own free will and a Cord, but I rather
cal'late he's middlin tired o' voluntearin By this Time.
I bleeve u may put dependunts on his statemence. For I
never heered nothin bad on him let Alone his havin what
Parson Wilbur cals a *pong shong* for cocktales, and he ses it
wuz a soshiashun of idees sot him agoin arter the Crootin
Sargient cos he wore a cocktale onto his hat.

his Folks gin the letter to me and i shew it to parson
Wilbur and he ses it oughter Bee printed. send It to mister
Buckinum, ses he, i don't ollers agree with him, ses he, but
by Time, ses he, I *du* like a feller that aint a Feared.

I have intusspussed a Few refleckshuns hear and thair.
We're kind o' prest with Hayin.

Ewers respecfly

HOSEA BIGLOW.

THIS kind o' sogerin' aint a mite like our October trainin',
A chap could clear right out from there ef't only looked
    like rainin',
An' th' Cunnles, tu, could kiver up their shappoes with
    bandanners,
An' send the insines skootin' to the barroom with their
    banners
(Fear o' gittin' on 'em spotted), an' a feller could cry
    quarter
Ef he fired away his ramrod arter tu much rum an' water.
Recollect wut fun we hed, you 'n' I an' Ezry Hollis,
Up there to Waltham plain last fall, along o' the Corn-
    wallis?
This sort o' thing aint *jest* like thet,—I wish thet I wuz
    furder,—
Nimepunce a day fer killin' folks comes kind o' low fer
    murder,
(Wy I've worked out to slarterin' some fer Deacon Cephas
    Billins,
An' in the hardest times there wuz I ollers tetched ten
    shillins,)
There's sutthin' gits into my throat thet makes it hard to
    swaller,
It comes so nateral to think about a hempen collar;

It's glory,—but, in spite o' all my tryin' to git callous,
I feel a kind o' in a cart, aridin' to the gallus.
But wen it comes to *bein'* killed,—I tell ye I felt streaked
The fust time 't ever I found out wy baggonets wuz peaked;
Here's how it wuz: I started out to go to a fandango,
The sentinul he ups an' sez, 'Thet's furder 'an you can go.'
'None o' your sarse,' sez I; sez he, 'Stan' back!' 'Aint you
    a buster?'
Sez I, 'I'm up to all thet air, I guess I've ben to muster;
I know wy sentinuls air sot; you aint agoin' to eat us;
Caleb haint no monopoly to court the seenoreetas;
My folks to hum air full ez good ez his'n be, by golly!'
An' so ez I wuz goin' by, not thinkin' wut would folly,
The everlastin' cus he stuck his one-pronged pitchfork
    in me
An' made a hole right thru my close ez ef I wuz an in'my.

Wal, it beats all how big I felt hoorawin' in ole Funnel
Wen Mister Bolles he gin the sword to our Leftenant
    Cunnle,
(It's Mister Secondary Bolles,[1] thet writ the prize peace
    essay;
Thet's wy he didn't list himself along o' us, I dessay,)
An' Rantoul, tu, talked pooty loud, but don't put *his* foot
    in it,
Coz human life's so sacred thet he's principled agin it,—
Though I myself can't rightly see it's any wus achokin'
    on 'em,
Than puttin' bullets thru their lights, or with a bagnet
    pokin' on 'em;

[1] the ignerant creeter means Sekketary; but he ollers stuck
to his books like cobbler's wax to an ilestone.—H. B.

How dreffle slick he reeled it off (like Blitz at our lyceum
Ahaulin' ribbins from his chops so quick you skeercely see
   'em),
About the Anglo-Saxon race (an' saxons would be handy
To du the buryin' down here upon the Rio Grandy),
About our patriotic pas an' our star-spangled banner,
Our country's bird alookin' on an' singin' out hosanner,
An' how he (Mister B. himself) wuz happy fer
   Ameriky,—
I felt, ez sister Patience sez, a leetle mite histericky.
I felt, I swon, ez though it wuz a dreffle kind o' privilege
Atrampin' round thru Boston streets among the gutter's
   drivelage;
I act'lly thought it wuz a treat to hear a little drummin',
An' it did bonyfidy millanyum wuz acomin'
Wen all on us got suits (darned like them wore in the state
   prison)
An' every feller felt ez though all Mexico wuz hisn.

This 'ere's about the meanest place a skunk could wal
   diskiver
(Saltillo's Mexican, I b'lieve, fer wut we call Salt-river);
The sort o' trash a feller gits to eat doos beat all nater,
I'd give a year's pay fer a smell o' one good blue-nose tater;
The country here thet Mister Bolles declared to be so
   charmin'
Throughout is swarmin' with the most alarmin' kind o'
   varmin.
He talked about delishis froots, but then it wuz a wopper
   all,
The holl on 't 's mud an' prickly pears, with here and there
   a chapparal;

You see a feller peekin' out, an', fust you know, a lariat
Is round your throat an' you a copse, 'fore you can say,
    'Wut air ye at?'
You never see sech darned gret bugs (it may not be
    irrelevant
To say I've seen a *scarabœus pilularius* [1] big ez a year old
    elephant),
The rigiment come up one day in time to stop a red bug
From runnin' off with Cunnie Wright,—'t wuz jest a
    common *cimex lectularius.*

One night I started up on eend an' thought I wuz to hum
    agin,
I heern a horn, thinks I it's Sol the fisherman hez come
    agin,
His bellowses is sound enough,—ez I'm a livin' creeter,
I felt a thing go thru my leg,—'twuz nothin' more'n a
    skeeter!
Then there's the yaller fever, tu, they call it here el
    vomito,—
(Come, thet wun't du, you landcrab there, I tell ye to le'
    go my toe!
My gracious! it's a scorpion thet's took a shine to play
    with't,
I darsn't skeer the tarnal thing fer fear he'd run away
    with't.)
Afore I come away from hum I hed a strong persuasion
Thet Mexicans worn't human beans,—an ourang outang
    nation,

[1] it wuz 'tumblebug' as he Writ it, but the parson put the
Latten instid. i sed tother maid better meeter, but he said tha
was eddykated peepl to Boston and tha wouldn't stan' it no
how. idnow as tha *wood* and idnow *as* tha wood.—H. B.

A sort o' folks a chap could kill an' never dream on't arter,
No more'n a feller'd dream o' pigs thet he hed hed to
      slarter;
I'd an idee thet they were built arter the darkie fashion all,
An' kickin' colored folks about, you know, 's a kind o'
      national;
But wen I jined I worn't so wise ez thet air queen o' Sheby,
Fer, come to look at 'em, they ain't much diff'rent from
      wut we be,
An' here we air ascrougin' 'em out o' thir own dominions,
Ashelterin' 'em, ez Caleb sez, under our eagle's pinions,
Wich means to take a feller up jest by the slack o' 's
      trowsis
An' walk him Spanish clean right out o' all his homes an'
      houses;
Wal, it doos seem a curus way, but then hooraw fer
      Jackson!
It must be right, fer Caleb sez it's reg'lar Anglo-saxon.

The Mex'cans don't fight fair, they say, they piz'n all the
      water,
An' du amazin' lots o' things thet isn't wut they ough' to;
Bein' they haint no lead, they make their bullets out o'
      copper
An' shoot the darned things at us, tu, wich Caleb sez aint
      proper;
He sez they'd ough' to stan' right up an' let us pop 'em
      fairly
(Guess wen he ketches 'em at thet he'll hev to get up
      airly),
Thet our nation's bigger'n theirn an' so its rights air bigger,
An' thet it's all to make 'em free thet we air pullin' trigger,
Thet Anglo Saxondom's idee's abreakin' 'em to pieces,

An' thet idee's thet every man doos jest wut he damn
    pleases;
Ef I don't make his meanin' clear, perhaps in some respex
    I can,
I know thet 'every man' don't mean a nigger or a Mexican;
An' there's another thing I know, an' thet is, ef these
    creeturs,
Thet stick an Anglosaxon mask onto State-prison feeturs,
They'd let the daylight into me to pay me fer desartin!
I don't approve o' tellin' tales, but jest to you I may state
Our ossifers aint wut they wuz afore they left the Bay-
    state;
Then it wuz 'Mister Sawin, sir, you're middlin' well now,
    be ye?
Step up an' take a nipper, sir; I'm dreffle glad to see ye';
But now it's 'Ware 's my eppylet? here, Sawin, step an'
    fetch it!
An' mind your eye, be thund'rin' spry, or, damn ye, you
    shall ketch it!'
Wal, ez the Doctor sez, some pork will bile so, but by
    mighty,
Ef I hed some on 'em to hum, I'd give 'em linkum vity,
I'd play the rogue's march on their hides an' other music
    follerin'—
But I must close my letter here, fer one on 'em 's
    ahollerin',
These Anglosaxon ossifers,—wal, taint no use ajawin',
I'm safe enlisted fer the war,
      Yourn,

                BIRDOFREDUM SAWIN.

WALT WHITMAN

1819-1892

112 *One's-Self I Sing*

ONE'S-SELF I sing, a simple separate person,
Yet utter the word Democratic, the word En-Masse.

Of physiology from top to toe I sing,
Not physiognomy alone nor brain alone is worthy for the
     Muse, I say the Form complete is worthier far,
The Female equally with the Male I sing.

Of Life immense in passion, pulse, and power,
Cheerful, for freest action form'd under the laws divine,
The Modern Man I sing.

113 *Beginning My Studies*

BEGINNING my studies the first step pleas'd me so
     much,
The mere fact consciousness, these forms, the power of
     motion,
The least insect or animal, the senses, eyesight, love,
The first step I say awed me and pleas'd me so much,
I have hardly gone and hardly wish'd to go any farther,
But stop and loiter all the time to sing it in ecstatic songs.

114   *Shut Not Your Doors*

Shut not your doors to me proud libraries,
For that which was lacking on all your well-fill'd shelves,
    yet needed most, I bring,
Forth from the war emerging, a book I have made,
The words of my book nothing, the drift of it every thing,
A book separate, not link'd with the rest nor felt by the
    intellect,
But you ye untold latencies will thrill to every page.

115   *There Was a Child Went Forth*

There was a child went forth every day,
And the first object he look'd upon, that object he became,
And that object became part of him for the day or a
    certain part of the day,
Or for many years or stretching cycles of years.

The early lilacs became part of this child,
And grass and white and red morning-glories, and white
    and red clover, and the song of the phœbe-bird,
And the Third-month lambs and the sow's pink-faint litter,
    and the mare's foal and the cow's calf,
And the noisy brood of the barnyard or by the mire of the
    pond-side,
And the fish suspending themselves so curiously below
    there, and the beautiful curious liquid,
And the water-plants with their graceful flat heads, all
    became part of him.

The field-sprouts of Fourth-month and Fifth-month be-
 came part of him,
Winter-grain sprouts and those of the light-yellow corn,
 and the esculent roots of the garden,
And the apple-trees cover'd with blossoms and the fruit
 afterward, and wood-berries, and the commonest
 weeds by the road,
And the old drunkard staggering home from the outhouse
 of the tavern whence he had lately risen,
And the schoolmistress that pass'd on her way to the school,
And the friendly boys that pass'd, and the quarrelsome
 boys,
And the tidy and fresh-cheek'd girls, and the barefoot
 negro boy and girl,
And all the changes of city and country wherever he went.

His own parents, he that had father'd him and she that had
 conceiv'd him in her womb and birth'd him,
They gave this child more of themselves than that,
They gave him afterward every day, they became part of
 him.

The mother at home quietly placing the dishes on the
 supper-table,
The mother with mild words, clean her cap and gown, a
 wholesome odor falling off her person and clothes as
 she walks by,
The father, strong, self-sufficient, manly, mean, anger'd,
 unjust,
The blow, the quick loud word, the tight bargain, the
 crafty lure,
The family usages, the language, the company, the furni-
 ture, the yearning and swelling heart,

277

Affection that will not be gainsay'd, the sense of what is
 real, the thought if after all it should prove unreal,

The doubts of day-time and the doubts of night-time, the
 curious whether and how,

Whether that which appears so is so, or is it all flashes and
 specks?

Men and women crowding fast in the streets, if they are
 not flashes and specks what are they?

The streets themselves and the façades of houses, and goods
 in the windows,

Vehicles, teams, the heavy-plank'd wharves, the huge cross-
 ing at the ferries,

The village on the highland seen from afar at sunset, the
 river between,

Shadows, aureola and mist, the light falling on roofs and
 gables of white or brown two miles off,

The schooner near by sleepily dropping down the tide, the
 little boat slack-tow'd astern,

The hurrying tumbling waves, quick-broken crests, slap-
 ping,

The strata of color'd clouds, the long bar of maroon-tint
 away solitary by itself, the spread of purity it lies
 motionless in,

The horizon's edge, the flying sea-crow, the fragrance of
 salt marsh and shore mud,

These became part of that child who went forth every day,
 and who now goes, and will always go forth every
 day.

116

Song of Myself

1

I CELEBRATE myself, and sing myself,
And what I assume you shall assume,
For every atom belonging to me as good belongs to you.

I loafe and invite my soul,
I lean and loafe at my ease observing a spear of summer
    grass.

My tongue, every atom of my blood, form'd from this soil,
    this air,
Born here of parents born here from parents the same, and
    their parents the same,
I, now thirty-seven years old in perfect health begin,
Hoping to cease not till death.

Creeds and schools in abeyance,
Retiring back a while sufficed at what they are, but never
    forgotten,
I harbor for good or bad, I permit to speak at every hazard,
Nature without check with original energy.

2

Houses and rooms are full of perfumes, the shelves are
    crowded with perfumes,
I breathe the fragrance myself and know it and like it,
The distillation would intoxicate me also, but I shall not
    let it.

The atmosphere is not a perfume, it has no taste of the
    distillation, it is odorless,
It is for my mouth forever, I am in love with it,
I will go to the bank by the wood and become undisguised
    and naked,
I am mad for it to be in contact with me.

The smoke of my own breath,
Echoes, ripples, buzz'd whispers, love-root, silk-thread,
    crotch and vine,
My respiration and inspiration, the beating of my heart,
    the passing of blood and air through my lungs,
The sniff of green leaves and dry leaves, and of the shore
    and dark-color'd sea-rocks, and hay in the barn,
The sound of the belch'd words of my voice loos'd to the
    eddies of the wind,
A few light kisses, a few embraces, a reaching around of
    arms,
The play of shine and shade on the trees as the supple
    boughs wag,
The delight alone or in the rush of the streets, or along the
    fields and hill-sides,
The feeling of health, the full-noon trill, the song of me
    rising from bed and meeting the sun.

Have you reckon'd a thousand acres much? have you reck-
    on'd the earth much?
Have you practis'd so long to learn to read?
Have you felt so proud to get at the meaning of poems?

Stop this day and night with me and you shall possess the
    origin of all poems,
You shall possess the good of the earth and sun, (there are
    millions of suns left,)

You shall no longer take things at second or third hand,
    nor look through the eyes of the dead, nor feed on
    the spectres in books,
You shall not look through my eyes either, nor take things
    from me,
You shall listen to all sides and filter them from your self.

3

I have heard what the talkers were talking, the talk of the
    beginning and the end,
But I do not talk of the beginning or the end.

There was never any more inception than there is now,
Nor any more youth or age than there is now,
And will never be any more perfection than there is now,
Nor any more heaven or hell than there is now.

Urge and urge and urge,
Always the procreant urge of the world.
Out of the dimness opposite equals advance, always sub-
    stance and increase, always sex,
Always a knit of identity, always distinction, always a
    breed of life.

To elaborate is no avail, learn'd and unlearn'd feel that
    it is so.

Sure as the most certain sure, plumb in the uprights, well
    entretied, braced in the beams,
Stout as a horse, affectionate, haughty, electrical,
I and this mystery here we stand.

Clear and sweet is my soul, and clear and sweet is all that
    is not my soul.

Lack one lacks both, and the unseen is proved by the seen,
Till that becomes unseen and receives proof in its turn.

Showing the best and dividing it from the worst age vexes
    age,
Knowing the perfect fitness and equanimity of things,
    while they discuss I am silent, and go bathe and
    admire myself.
Welcome is every organ and attribute of me, and of any
    man hearty and clean,
Not an inch nor a particle of an inch is vile, and none
    shall be less familiar than the rest.

I am satisfied—I see, dance, laugh, sing;
As the hugging and loving bed-fellow sleeps at my side
    through the night, and withdraws at the peep of the
    day with stealthy tread,
Leaving me baskets cover'd with white towels swelling the
    house with their plenty,
Shall I postpone my acceptation and realization and scream
    at my eyes,
That they turn from gazing after and down the road,
And forthwith cipher and show me to a cent,
Exactly the value of one and exactly the value of two, and
    which is ahead?

4

Trippers and askers surround me,
People I meet, the effect upon me of my early life or the
    ward and city I live in, or the nation,
The latest dates, discoveries, inventions, societies, authors
    old and new,

My dinner, dress, associates, looks, compliments, dues,
The real or fancied indifference of some man or woman
I love,
The sickness of one of my folks or of myself, or ill-doing
or loss or lack of money, or depressions or exaltations,
Battles, the horrors of fratricidal war, the fever of doubt-
ful news, the fitful events;
These come to me days and nights and go from me again,
But they are not the Me myself.
Apart from the pulling and hauling stands what I am,
Stands amused, complacent, compassionating, idle, unitary,
Looks down, is erect, or bends an arm on an impalpable
certain rest,
Looking with side-curved head curious what will come
next,
Both in and out of the game and watching and wondering
at it.

Backward I see in my own days where I sweated through
fog with linguists and contenders,
I have no mockings or arguments, I witness and wait.

5

I believe in you my soul, the other I am must not abase
itself to you,
And you must not be abased to the other.

Loafe with me on the grass, loose the stop from your throat,
Not words, not music or rhyme I want, not custom or
lecture, not even the best,

Only the lull I like, the hum of your valvèd voice.

I mind how once we lay such a transparent summer morn-
ing,

How you settled your head athwart my hips and gently
turn'd over upon me,

And parted the shirt from my bosom-bone, and plunged
your tongue to my bare-stript heart,

And reach'd till you felt my beard, and reach'd till you
held my feet.

Swiftly arose and spread around me the peace and knowl-
edge that pass all the argument of the earth,

And I know that the hand of God is the promise of my
own,

And I know that the spirit of God is the brother of my
own,

And that all the men ever born are also my brothers, and
the women my sisters and lovers,

And that a kelson of the creation is love,

And limitless are leaves stiff or drooping in the fields,

And brown ants in the little wells beneath them,

And mossy scabs of the worm fence, heap'd stones, elder,
mullein and poke-weed.

6

A child said *What is the grass?* fetching it to me with full
hands,

How could I answer the child? I do not know what it is
any more than he.

I guess it must be the flag of my disposition, out of hopeful
green stuff woven.

Or I guess it is the handkerchief of the Lord,

A scented gift and remembrancer designedly dropt,
Bearing the owner's name someway in the corners, that we
    may see and remark, and say *Whose?*

Or I guess the grass is itself a child, the produced babe of
    the vegetation.

Or I guess it is a uniform hieroglyphic,
And it means, Sprouting alike in broad zones and narrow
    zones,
Growing among black folks as among white,
Kanuck, Tuckahoe, Congressman, Cuff, I give them the
    same, I receive them the same.

And now it seems to me the beautiful uncut hair of graves.

Tenderly will I use you curling grass,
It may be you transpire from the breasts of young men,
It may be if I had known them I would have loved them,
It may be you are from old people, or from offspring
    taken soon out of their mothers' laps,
And here you are the mothers' laps.

This grass is very dark to be from the white heads of old
    mothers,
Darker than the colourless beards of old men,
Dark to come from under the faint red roofs of mouths.

O I perceive after all so many uttering tongues,
And I perceive they do not come from the roofs of mouths
    for nothing.

I wish I could translate the hints about the dead young
    men and women,
And the hints about old men and mothers, and the off-
    spring taken soon out of their laps.

What do you think has become of the young and old men?
And what do you think has become of the women and
    children?

They are alive and well somewhere,
The smallest sprout shows there is really no death,
And if ever there was it led forward life, and does not
    wait at the end to arrest it,
And ceas'd the moment life appear'd.

All goes onward and outward, nothing collapses,
And to die is different from what any one supposed, and
    luckier.

7

Has any one supposed it lucky to be born?
I hasten to inform him or her it is just as lucky to die,
    and I know it.

I pass death with the dying and birth with the new-wash'd
    babe, and am not contain'd between my hat and boots,
And peruse manifold objects, no two alike and every one
    good,
The earth good and the stars good, and their adjuncts all
    good.

I am not an earth nor an adjunct of an earth,
I am the mate and companion of people, all just as im-
    mortal and fathomless as myself,
(They do not know how immortal, but I know.)

Every kind for itself and its own, for me mine male and
female,
For me those that have been boys and that love women,
For me the man that is proud and feels how it stings to be
slighted,
For me the sweet-heart and the old maid, for me mothers
and the mothers of mothers,
For me lips that have smiled, eyes that have shed tears,
For me children and the begetters of children.

Undrape! you are not guilty to me, nor stale nor discarded,
I see through the broadcloth and gingham whether or no,
And am around, tenacious, acquisitive, tireless, and cannot
be shaken away.

8

The little one sleeps in its cradle,
I lift the gauze and look a long time, and silently brush
away flies with my hand.

The youngster and the red-faced girl turn aside up the
bushy hill,
I peeringly view them from the top.

The suicide sprawls on the bloody floor of the bedroom,
I witness the corpse with its dabbled hair, I note where the
pistol has fallen.

The blab of the pave, tires of carts, sluff of boot-soles, talk
of the promenaders,
The heavy omnibus, the driver with his interrogating
thumb, the clank of the shod horses on the granite
floor,
The snow-sleighs, clinking, shouted jokes, pelts of snow-
balls,

The hurrahs for popular favorites, the fury of rous'd
 mobs,
The flap of the curtain'd litter, a sick man inside borne
 to the hospital,
The meeting of enemies, the sudden oath, the blows and
 fall,
The excited crowd, the policeman with his star quickly
 working his passage to the centre of the crowd,
The impassive stones that receive and return so many
 echoes,
What groans of over-fed or half-starv'd who fall sunstruck
 or in fits,
What exclamations of women taken suddenly who hurry
 home and give birth to babes,
What living and buried speech is always vibrating here,
 what howls restrain'd by decorum,
Arrests of criminals, slights, adulterous offers made, accept-
 ances, rejections with convex lips,
I mind them or the show or resonance of them—I come
 and I depart.

9

The big doors of the country barn stand open and ready,
The dried grass of the harvest-time loads the slow-drawn
 wagon,
The clear light plays on the brown gray and green inter-
 tinged,
The armfuls are pack'd to the sagging mow.

I am there, I help, I came stretch'd atop of the load,
I felt its soft jolts, one leg reclined on the other,
I jump from the cross-beams and seize the clover and
 timothy,
And roll head over heels and tangle my hair full of wisps.

10

Alone far in the wilds and mountains I hunt,
Wandering amazed at my own lightness and glee,
In the late afternoon choosing a safe spot to pass the night,
Kindling a fire and broiling the fresh-kill'd game,
Falling asleep on the gather'd leaves with my dog and gun
   by my side.

The Yankee clipper is under her sky-sails, she cuts the
   sparkle and scud,
My eyes settle the land, I bend at her prow or shout joy-
   ously from the deck.

The boatmen and clam-diggers arose early and stopt for
   me,
I tuck'd my trowser-ends in my boots and went and had a
   good time;
You should have been with us that day round the chowder-
   kettle.

I saw the marriage of the trapper in the open air in the far
   west, the bride was a red girl,
Her father and his friends sat near cross-legged and
   dumbly smoking, they had moccasins to their feet and
   large thick blankets hanging from their shoulders,
On a bank lounged the trapper, he was drest mostly in
   skins, his luxuriant beard and curls protected his neck,
   he held his bride by the hand,
She had long eyelashes, her head was bare, her coarse
   straight locks descended upon her voluptuous limbs
   and reach'd to her feet.

The runaway slave came to my house and stopt outside,
I heard his motions crackling the twigs of the woodpile,
Through the swung half-door of the kitchen I saw him
limpsy and weak,
And went where he sat on a log and led him in and
assured him,
And brought water and fill'd a tub for his sweated body and
bruis'd feet,
And gave him a room that enter'd from my own, and gave
him some coarse clean clothes,
And remember perfectly well his revolving eyes and his
awkwardness,
And remember putting plasters on the galls of his neck and
ankles;
He staid with me a week before he was recuperated and
pass'd north,
I had him sit next me at table, my fire-lock lean'd in the
corner.

11

Twenty-eight young men bathe by the shore,
Twenty-eight young men and all so friendly;
Twenty-eight years of womanly life and all so lonesome.

She owns the fine house by the rise of the bank,
She hides handsome and richly drest aft the blinds of the
window.
Which of the young men does she like the best?
Ah the homeliest of them is beautiful to her.

Where are you off to, lady? for I see you,
You splash in the water there, yet stay stock still in your
room.

Dancing and laughing along the beach came the twenty-
ninth bather,
The rest did not see her, but she saw them and loved them.

The beards of the young men glisten'd with wet, it ran
from their long hair,
Little streams pass'd all over their bodies.

An unseen hand also pass'd over their bodies,
It descended tremblingly from their temples and ribs.

The young men float on their backs, their white bellies
bulge to the sun, they do not ask who seizes fast to
them,
They do not know who puffs and declines with pendant
and bending arch,
They do not think whom they souse with spray.

12

The butcher-boy puts off his killing-clothes, or sharpens
his knife at the stall in the market,
I loiter enjoying his repartee and his shuffle and break-
down.

Blacksmiths with grimed and hairy chests environ the anvil,
Each has his main-sledge, they are all out, there is a great
heat in the fire.

From the cinder-strew'd threshold I follow their move-
ments,
The lithe sheer of their waists plays even with their mas-
sive arms,
Overhand the hammers swing, overhand so slow, overhand
so sure,
They do not hasten, each man hits in his place.

13

The negro holds firmly the reins of his four horses, the
    block swags underneath on its tied-over chain,
The negro that drives the long dray of the stone-yard,
    steady and tall he stands pois'd on one leg on the
    string-piece,
His blue shirt exposes his ample neck and breast and loosens
    over his hip-band,
His glance is calm and commanding, he tosses the slouch
    of his hat away from his forehead,
The sun falls on his crispy hair and mustache, falls on the
    black of his polish'd and perfect limbs.

I behold the picturesque giant and love him, and I do not
    stop there,
I go with the team also.

In me the caresser of life wherever moving, backward as
    well as forward sluing,
To niches aside and junior bending, not a person or object
    missing,
Absorbing all to myself and for this song.

Oxen that rattle the yoke and chain or halt in the leafy
    shade, what is that you express in your eyes?
It seems to me more than all the print I have read in my
    life.

My tread scares the wood-drake and wood-duck on my
    distant and day-long ramble,
They rise together, they slowly circle around.

I believe in those wing'd purposes,
And acknowledge red, yellow, white, playing within me,
And consider green and violet and the tufted crown in-
tentional,
And do not call the tortoise unworthy because she is not
something else,
And the jay in the woods never studied the gamut, yet
trills pretty well to me,
And the look of the bay mare shames silliness out of me.

14

The wild gander leads his flock through the cool night,
Ya-honk he says, and sounds it down to me like an invita-
tion,
The pert may suppose it meaningless, but I listening close,
Find its purpose and place up there toward the wintry sky.

The sharp-hoof'd moose of the north, the cat on the house-
sill, the chickadee, the prairie-dog,
The litter of the grunting sow as they tug at her teats,
The brood of the turkey-hen and she with her half-spread
wings,
I see in them and myself the same old law.

The press of my foot to the earth springs a hundred affec-
tions,
They scorn the best I can do to relate them.

I am enamour'd of growing out-doors,
Of men that live among cattle or taste of the ocean or
woods,
Of the builders and steerers of ships and the wielders of
axes and mauls, and the drivers of horses,
I can eat and sleep with them week in and week out.

What is commonest, cheapest, nearest, easiest, is Me,
Me going in for my chances, spending for vast returns,
Adorning myself to bestow myself on the first that will
    take me,
Not asking the sky to come down to my good will,
Scattering it freely forever.

15

The pure contralto sings in the organ loft,
The carpenter dresses his plank, the tongue of his fore-
    plane whistles its wild ascending lisp,
The married and unmarried children ride home to their
    Thanksgiving dinner,
The pilot seizes the king-pin, he heaves down with a strong
    arm,
The mate stands braced in the whale-boat, lance and
    harpoon are ready,
The duck-shooter walks by silent and cautious stretches,
The deacons are ordain'd with cross'd hands at the altar,
The spinning-girl retreats and advances to the hum of the
    big wheel,
The farmer stops by the bars as he walks on a First-day
    loafe and looks at the oats and rye,
The lunatic is carried at last to the asylum a confirm'd case,
(He will never sleep any more as he did in the cot in his
    mother's bedroom;)
The jour printer with gray head and gaunt jaws works at
    his case,
He turns his quid of tobacco while his eyes blurr with the
    manuscript;
The malform'd limbs are tied to the surgeon's table,
What is removed drops horribly in a pail;

The quadroon girl is sold at the auction-stand, the drunk-
    ard nods by the bar-room stove,

The machinist rolls up his sleeves, the policeman travels
    his beat, the gate-keeper marks who pass,

The young fellow drives the express-wagon, (I love him,
    though I do not know him;)

The half-breed straps on his light boots to compete in the
    race,

The western turkey-shooting draws old and young, some
    lean on their rifles, some sit on logs,

Out from the crowd steps the marksman, takes his posi-
    tion, levels his piece;

The groups of newly-come immigrants cover the wharf or
    levee,

As the woolly-pates hoe in the sugar-field, the overseer
    views them from his saddle,

The bugle calls in the ball-room, the gentlemen run for
    their partners, the dancers bow to each other,

The youth lies awake in the cedar-roof'd garret and harks
    to the musical rain,

The Wolverine sets traps on the creek that helps fill the
    Huron,

The squaw wrapt in her yellow-hemm'd cloth is offering
    moccasins and bead-bags for sale,

The connoisseur peers along the exhibition-gallery with
    half-shut eyes bent sideways,

As the deck-hands make fast the steamboat the plank is
    thrown for the shore-going passengers,

The young sister holds out the skein while the elder sister
    winds it off in a ball, and stops now and then for
    the knots,

The one-year wife is recovering and happy having a week
    ago borne her first child,

The clean-hair'd Yankee girl works with her sewing-machine or in the factory or mill,

The paving-man leans on his two-handed rammer, the reporter's lead flies swiftly over the note-book, the sign-painter is lettering with blue and gold,

The canal boy trots on the tow-path, the book-keeper counts at his desk, the shoemaker waxes his thread,

The conductor beats time for the band and all the performers follow him,

The child is baptized, the convert is making his first professions,

The regatta is spread on the bay, the race is begun, (how the white sails sparkle!)

The drover watching his drove sings out to them that would stray,

The pedler sweats with his pack on his back, (the purchaser higgling about the odd cent;)

The bride unrumples her white dress, the minute-hand of the clock moves slowly,

The opium-eater reclines with rigid head and just-open'd lips,

The prostitute draggles her shawl, her bonnet bobs on her tipsy and pimpled neck,

The crowd laugh at her blackguard oaths, the men jeer and wink to each other,

(Miserable! I do not laugh at your oaths nor jeer you;)

The President holding a cabinet council is surrounded by the great Secretaries,

On the piazza walk three matrons stately and friendly with twined arms,

The crew of the fish-smack pack repeated layers of halibut in the hold,

The Missourian crosses the plains toting his wares and his
    cattle,

As the fare-collector goes through the train he gives no-
    tice by the jingling of loose change,

The floor-men are laying the floor, the tinners are tinning
    the roof, the masons are calling for mortar,

In single file each shouldering his hod pass onward the
    laborers;

Seasons pursuing each other the indescribable crowd is
    gather'd, it is the fourth of Seventh-month, (what
    salutes of cannon and small arms!)

Seasons pursuing each other the plougher ploughs, the
    mower mows, and the winter-grain falls in the
    ground;

Off on the lakes the pike-fisher watches and waits by the
    hole in the frozen surface,

The stumps stand thick round the clearing, the squatter
    strikes deep with his axe,

Flatboatmen make fast towards dusk near the cotton-wood
    or pecan-trees,

Coon-seekers go through the regions of the Red river or
    through those drain'd by the Tennessee, or through
    those of the Arkansas,

Torches shine in the dark that hangs on the Chattahooche
    or Altamahaw,

Patriarchs sit at supper with sons and grandsons and great-
    grandsons around them,

In walls of adobie, in canvas tents, rest hunters and trappers
    after their day's sport,

The city sleeps and the country sleeps,

The living sleep for their time, the dead sleep for their
    time,

The old husband sleeps by his wife and the young husband
  sleeps by his wife;
And these tend inward to me, and I tend outward to them,
And such as it is to be of these more or less I am,
And of these one and all I weave the song of myself.

16

I am of old and young, of the foolish as much as the wise,
Regardless of others, ever regardful of others,
Maternal as well as paternal, a child as well as a man,
Stuff'd with the stuff that is coarse and stuff'd with the
  stuff that is fine,
One of the Nation of many nations, the smallest the same
  and the largest the same,
A Southerner soon as a Northerner, a planter nonchalant
  and hospitable down by the Oconee I live,
A Yankee bound my own way ready for trade, my joints
  the limberest joints on earth and the sternest joints
  on earth,
A Kentuckian walking the vale of the Elkhorn in my deer-
  skin leggings, a Louisianian or Georgian,
A boatman over lakes or bays or along coasts, a Hoosier,
  Badger, Buck-eye;
At home on Kanadian snow-shoes or up in the bush, or
  with fishermen off Newfoundland,
At home in the fleet of ice-boats, sailing with the rest and
  tacking,
At home on the hills of Vermont or in the woods of Maine,
  or the Texan ranch,
Comrade of Californians, comrade of free North-Western-
  ers, (loving their big proportions,)

Comrade of raftsmen and coalmen, comrade of all who
    shake hands and welcome to drink and meat,
A learner with the simplest, a teacher of the thought-
    fullest,
A novice beginning yet experient of myriads of seasons,
Of every hue and caste am I, of every rank and religion,
A farmer, mechanic, artist, gentleman, sailor, quaker,
Prisoner, fancy-man, rowdy, lawyer, physician, priest.

I resist any thing better than my own diversity,
Breathe the air but leave plenty after me,
And am not stuck up, and am in my place.

(The moth and the fish-eggs are in their place,
The bright suns I see and the dark suns I cannot see are
    in their place,
The palpable is in its place and the impalpable is in its
    place.)

17

These are really the thoughts of all men in all ages and
    lands, they are not original with me,
If they are not yours as much as mine they are nothing,
    or next to nothing,
If they are not the riddle and the untying of the riddle
    they are nothing,
If they are not just as close as they are distant they are
    nothing.

This is the grass that grows wherever the land is and the
    water is,
This the common air that bathes the globe.

18

With music strong I come, with my cornets and my drums,
I play not marches for accepted victors only, I play marches
for conquer'd and slain persons.

Have you heard that it was good to gain the day?
I also say it is good to fall, battles are lost in the same
spirit in which they are won.

I beat and pound for the dead,
I blow through my embouchures my loudest and gayest for
them.

Vivas to those who have fail'd!
And to those whose war-vessels sank in the sea!
And to those themselves who sank in the sea!
And to all generals that lost engagements, and all over-
come heroes!
And the numberless unknown heroes equal to the greatest
heroes known!

19

This is the meal equally set, this the meat for natural
hunger,
It is for the wicked just the same as the righteous, I make
appointments with all,
I will not have a single person slighted or left away,
The kept-woman, sponger, thief, are hereby invited,
The heavy-lipp'd slave is invited, the venerealee is invited;
There shall be no difference between them and the rest.

This is the press of a bashful hand, this the float and odor
    of hair,
This the touch of my lips to yours, this the murmur of
    yearning,
This the far-off depth and height reflecting my own face,
This the thoughtful merge of myself, and the outlet again.

Do you guess I have some intricate purpose?
Well I have, for the Fourth-month showers have, and the
    mica on the side of a rock has.

Do you take it I would astonish?
Does the daylight astonish? does the early redstart twitter-
    ing through the woods?
Do I astonish more than they?

This hour I tell things in confidence,
I might not tell everybody, but I will tell you.

20

Who goes there? hankering, gross, mystical, nude;
How is it I extract strength from the beef I eat?

What is a man anyhow? what am I? what are you?

All I mark as my own you shall offset it with your own,
Else it were time lost listening to me.

I do not snivel that snivel the world over,
That months are vacuums and the ground but wallow and
    filth.

Whimpering and truckling fold with powders for invalids,
    conformity goes to the fourth-remov'd,
I wear my hat as I please indoors or out.

Why should I pray? why should I venerate and be cere-
monious?

Having pried through the strata, analyzed to a hair,
counsel'd with doctors and calculated close,
I find no sweeter fat than sticks to my own bones.

In all people I see myself, none more and not one a
barley-corn less,
And the good or bad I say of myself I say of them.

I know I am solid and sound,
To me the converging objects of the universe perpetually
flow,
All are written to me, and I must get what the writing
means.

I know I am deathless,
I know this orbit of mine cannot be swept by a carpenter's
compass,
I know I shall not pass like a child's carlacue cut with a
burnt stick at night.

I know I am august,
I do not trouble my spirit to vindicate itself or be under-
stood,
I see that the elementary laws never apologize,
(I reckon I behave no prouder than the level I plant my
house by, after all.)

I exist as I am, that is enough,
If no other in the world be aware I sit content,
And if each and all be aware I sit content.

One world is aware and by far the largest to me, and that
    is myself,
And whether I come to my own to-day or in ten thousand
    or ten million years,
I can cheerfully take it now, or with equal cheerfulness I
    can wait.

My foothold is tenon'd and mortis'd in granite,
I laugh at what you call dissolution,
And I know the amplitude of time.

21

I am the poet of the Body and I am the poet of the Soul,
The pleasures of heaven are with me and the pains of hell
    are with me,
The first I graft and increase upon myself, the latter I
    translate into a new tongue.

I am the poet of the woman the same as the man,
And I say it is as great to be a woman as to be a man,
And I say there is nothing greater than the mother of men.

I chant the chant of dilation or pride,
We have had ducking and deprecating about enough,
I show that size is only development.

Have you outstript the rest? are you the President?
It is a trifle, they will more than arrive there every one,
    and still pass on.

I am he that walks with the tender and growing night,
I call to the earth and sea half-held by the night.

Press close bare-bosom'd night—press close magnetic nour-
    ishing night!
Night of south winds—night of the large few stars!
Still nodding night—mad naked summer night.

Smile O voluptuous cool-breath'd earth!
Earth of the slumbering and liquid trees!
Earth of departed sunset—earth of the mountains misty-
    topt!
Earth of the vitreous pour of the full moon just tinged
    with blue!
Earth of shine and dark mottling the tide of the river!
Earth of the limpid gray of clouds brighter and clearer
    for my sake!
Far-swooping elbow'd earth—rich apple-blossom'd earth!
Smile, for your lover comes.

Prodigal, you have given me love—therefore I to you
    give love!
O unspeakable passionate love.

22

You sea! I resign myself to you also—I guess what you
    mean,
I behold from the beach your crooked inviting fingers,
I believe you refuse to go back without feeling of me,
We must have a turn together, I undress, hurry me out of
    sight of the land,
Cushion me soft, rock me in billowy drowse,
Dash me with amorous wet, I can repay you.

Sea of stretch'd ground-swells,
Sea breathing broad and convulsive breaths,

Sea of the brine of life and of unshovell'd yet always-
    ready graves,
Howler and scooper of storms, capricious and dainty sea,
I am integral with you, I too am of one phase and of all
    phases.

Partaker of influx and efflux, I, extoller of hate and con-
    ciliation,
Extoller of amies and those that sleep in each others' arms.

I am he attesting sympathy,
(Shall I make my list of things in the house and skip the
    house that supports them?)

I am not the poet of goodness only, I do not decline to be
    the poet of wickedness also.

What blurt is this about virtue and about vice?
Evil propels me and reform of evil propels me, I stand
    indifferent,
My gait is no fault-finder's or rejecter's gait,
I moisten the roots of all that has grown.

Did you fear some scrofula out of the unflagging preg-
    nancy?
Did you guess the celestial laws are yet to be work'd over
    and rectified?

I find one side a balance and the antipodal side a balance,
Soft doctrine as steady help as stable doctrine,
Thoughts and deeds of the present our rouse and early
    start.

This minute that comes to me over the past decillions,
There is no better than it and now.

What behaved well in the past or behaves well to-day is
not such a wonder,
The wonder is always and always how there can be a mean
man or an infidel.

23

Endless unfolding of words of ages!
And mine a word of the modern, the word En-Masse.

A word of the faith that never balks,
Here or henceforward it is all the same to me, I accept
Time absolutely.

It alone is without flaw, it alone rounds and completes
all,
That mystic baffling wonder alone completes all.

I accept Reality and dare not question it,
Materialism first and last imbuing.

Hurrah for positive science! long live exact demonstration!
Fetch stonecrop mixt with cedar and branches of lilac,
This is the lexicographer, this the chemist, this made a
grammar of the old cartouches,
These mariners put the ship through dangerous unknown
seas,
This is the geologist, this works with the scalpel, and this
is a mathematician.

Gentlemen, to you the first honors always!
Your facts are useful, and yet they are not my dwelling,
I but enter by them to an area of my dwelling.

Less the reminders of properties told my words,
And more the reminders they of life untold, and of free-
     dom and extrication,
And make short account of neuters and geldings, and favor
     men and women fully equipt,
And beat the gong of revolt, and stop with fugitives and
     them that plot and conspire.

24

Walt Whitman, a kosmos, of Manhattan the son,
Turbulent, fleshy, sensual, eating, drinking and breeding,
No sentimentalist, no stander above men and women or
     apart from them,
No more modest than immodest.

Unscrew the locks from the doors!
Unscrew the doors themselves from their jambs!

Whoever degrades another degrades me,
And whatever is done or said returns at last to me.

Through me the afflatus surging and surging, through me
     the current and index.

I speak the pass-word primeval, I give the sign of democ-
     racy,
By God! I will accept nothing which all cannot have their
     counterpart of on the same terms.

Through me many long dumb voices,
Voices of the interminable generation of prisoners and
    slaves,
Voices of the diseas'd and despairing and of thieves and
    dwarfs,
Voices of cycles of preparation and accretion,
And of the threads that connect the stars, and of wombs
    and of the father-stuff,
And of the rights of them the others are down upon,
Of the deform'd, trivial, flat, foolish, despised,
Fog in the air, beetles rolling balls of dung.

Through me forbidden voices,
Voices of sexes and lusts, voices veil'd and I remove the
    veil,
Voices indecent by me clarified and transfigur'd.

I do not press my fingers across my mouth,
I keep as delicate around the bowels as around the head
    and heart,
Copulation is no more rank to me than death is.

I believe in the flesh and the appetites,
Seeing, hearing, feeling, are miracles, and each part and
    tag of me is a miracle.

Divine am I inside and out, and I make holy whatever I
    touch or am touch'd from,
The scent of these arm-pits aroma finer than prayer,
This head more than churches, bibles, and all the creeds.

If I worship one thing more than another it shall be the
    spread of my own body, or any part of it,
Translucent mould of me it shall be you!

Shaded ledges and rests it shall be you!
Firm masculine colter it shall be you!
Whatever goes to the tilth of me it shall be you!
You my rich blood! your milky stream pale strippings of
    my life!
Breast that presses against other breasts it shall be you!
My brain it shall be your occult convolutions!
Root of wash'd sweet-flag! timorous pond-snipe! nest of
    guarded duplicate eggs! it shall be you!
Mix'd tussled hay of head, beard, brawn, it shall be you!
Trickling sap of maple, fibre of manly wheat, it shall be
    you!
Sun so generous it shall be you!
Vapors lighting and shading my face it shall be you!
You sweaty brooks and dews it shall be you!
Winds whose soft-tickling genitals rub against me it shall
    be you!
Broad muscular fields, branches of live oak, loving lounger
    in my winding paths, it shall be you!
Hands I have taken, face I have kiss'd, mortal I have ever
    touch'd, it shall be you.

I dote on myself, there is that lot of me and all so luscious,
Each moment and whatever happens thrills me with joy,
I cannot tell how my ankles bend, nor whence the cause
    of my faintest wish,
Nor the cause of the friendship I emit, nor the cause of
    the friendship I take again.

That I walk up my stoop, I pause to consider if it really
    be,
A morning-glory at my window satisfies me more than the
    metaphysics of books.

To behold the day-break!

The little light fades the immense and diaphanous shadows,

The air tastes good to my palate.

Hefts of the moving world at innocent gambols silently rising, freshly exuding,

Scooting obliquely high and low.

Something I cannot see puts upward libidinous prongs,

Seas of bright juice suffuse heaven.

The earth by the sky staid with, the daily close of their junction,

The heav'd challenge from the east that moment over my head,

The mocking taunt, See then whether you shall be master!

25

Dazzling and tremendous how quick the sun-rise would kill me,

If I could not now and always send sun-rise out of me.

We also ascend dazzling and tremendous as the sun,

We found our own O my soul in the calm and cool of the day-break.

My voice goes after what my eyes cannot reach,

With the twirl of my tongue I encompass worlds and volumes of worlds.

Speech is the twin of my vision, it is unequal to measure itself,

It provokes me forever, it says sarcastically,

Walt you contain enough, why don't you let it out then?

Come now I will not be tantalized you conceive too much
    of articulation,
Do you not know O speech how the buds beneath you are
    folded?
Waiting in gloom, protected by frost,
The dirt receding before my prophetical screams,
I underlying causes to balance them at last,
My knowledge my live parts, it keeping tally with the
    meaning of all things,
Happiness, (which whoever hears me let him or her set out
    in search of this day.)

My final merit I refuse you, I refuse putting from me
    what I really am,
Encompass worlds, but never try to encompass me,
I crowd your sleekest and best by simply looking toward
    you.

Writing and talk do not prove me,
I carry the plenum of proof and every thing else in my
    face,
With the hush of my lips I wholly confound the skeptic.

26

Now I will do nothing but listen,
To accrue what I hear into this song, to let sounds con-
    tribute toward it.

I hear bravuras of birds, bustle of growing wheat, gossip
    of flames, clack of sticks cooking my meals,
I hear the sound I love, the sound of the human voice,
I hear all sounds running together, combined, fused or
    following,

Sounds of the city and sounds out of the city, sounds of
    the day and night,

Talkative young ones to those that like them, the loud
    laugh of work-people at their meals,

The angry base of disjointed friendship, the faint tones
    of the sick,

The judge with hands tight to the desk, his pallid lips
    pronouncing a death-sentence,

The heav'e'yo of stevedores unlading ships by the wharves,
    the refrain of the anchor-lifters,

The ring of alarm-bells, the cry of fire, the whirr of swift-
    streaking engines and hose-carts with premonitory
    tinkles and color'd lights,

The steam-whistle, the solid roll of the train of approach-
    ing cars,

The slow march play'd at the head of the association
    marching two and two,

(They go to guard some corpse, the flag-tops are draped
    with black muslin.)

I hear the violoncello, ('tis the young man's heart's com-
    plaint,)

I hear the key'd cornet, it glides quickly in through my
    ears,

It shakes mad-sweet pangs through my belly and breast.

I hear the chorus, it is a grand opera,
Ah this indeed is music—this suits me.

A tenor large and fresh as the creation fills me,
The orbic flex of his mouth is pouring and filling me full.

I hear the train'd soprano (what work with hers is this?)
The orchestra whirls me wider than Uranus flies,

It wrenches such ardors from me I did not know I pos-
    sess'd them,
It sails me, I dab with bare feet, they are lick'd by the
    indolent waves,
I am cut by bitter and angry hail, I lose my breath,
Steep'd amid honey'd morphine, my windpipe throttled
    in fakes of death,
At length let up again to feel the puzzle of puzzles,
And that we call Being.

27

To be in any form, what is that?
(Round and round we go, all of us, and ever come back
    thither,)
If nothing lay more develop'd the quahaug in its callous
    shell were enough.

Mine is no callous shell,
I have instant conductors all over me whether I pass or
    stop,
They seize every object and lead it harmlessly through
    me.

I merely stir, press, feel with my fingers, and am happy,
To touch my person to some one else's is about as much as
    I can stand.

28

Is this then a touch? quivering me to a new identity,
Flames and ether making a rush for my veins,
Treacherous tip of me reaching and crowding to help
    them,

My flesh and blood playing out lightning to strike what is
    hardly different from myself,
On all sides prurient provokers stiffening my limbs,
Straining the udder of my heart for its withheld drip,
Behaving licentious toward me, taking no denial,
Depriving me of my best as for a purpose,
Unbuttoning my clothes, holding me by the bare waist,
Deluding my confusion with the calm of the sunlight and
    pasture-fields,
Immodestly sliding the fellow-senses away,
They bribed to swap off with touch and go and graze at
    the edges of me,
No consideration, no regard for my draining strength or
    my anger,
Fetching the rest of the herd around to enjoy them a
    while,
Then all uniting to stand on a headland and worry me.

The sentries desert every other part of me,
They have left me helpless to a red marauder,
They all come to the headland to witness and assist against
    me.

I am given up by traitors,
I talk wildly, I have lost my wits, I and nobody else am
    the greatest traitor,
I went myself first to the headland, my own hands carried
    me there.

You villain touch! what are you doing? my breath is tight
    in its throat,
Unclench your floodgates, you are too much for me.

29

Blind loving wrestling touch, sheath'd hooded sharp-
    tooth'd touch!
Did it make you ache so, leaving me?

Parting track'd by arriving, perpetual payment of per-
    petual loan,
Rich showering rain, and recompense richer afterward.

Sprouts take and accumulate, stand by the curb prolific and
    vital,
Landscapes projected masculine, full-sized and golden.

30

All truths wait in all things,
They neither hasten their own delivery nor resist it,
They do not need the obstetric forceps of the surgeon,
The insignificant is as big to me as any,
(What is less or more than a touch?)

Logic and sermons never convince,
The damp of the night drives deeper into my soul.

(Only what proves itself to every man and woman is so,
Only what nobody denies is so.)

A minute and a drop of me settle my brain,
I believe the soggy clods shall become lovers and lamps,
And a compend of compends is the meat of a man or
    woman,
And a summit and flower there is the feeling they have for
    each other,

And they are to branch boundlessly out of that lesson until
it becomes omnific,
And until one and all shall delight us, and we them.

31

I believe a leaf of grass is no less than the journey-work
of the stars,
And the pismire is equally perfect, and a grain of sand,
and the egg of the wren,
And the tree-toad is a chef-d'œuvre for the highest,
And the running blackberry would adorn the parlors of
heaven,
And the narrowest hinge in my hand puts to scorn all
machinery,
And the cow crunching with depress'd head surpasses any
statue,
And a mouse is miracle enough to stagger sextillions of
infidels.

I find I incorporate gneiss, coal, long-threaded moss, fruits,
grains, esculent roots,
And am stucco'd with quadrupeds and birds all over,
And have distanced what is behind me for good reasons,
But call any thing back again when I desire it.

In vain the speeding or shyness,
In vain the plutonic rocks send their old heat against my
approach,
In vain the mastodon retreats beneath its own powder'd
bones,
In vain objects stand leagues off and assume manifold
shapes,

In vain the ocean setting in hollows and the great mon-
    sters lying low,
In vain the buzzard houses herself with the sky,
In vain the snake slides through the creepers and logs,
In vain the elk takes to the inner passes of the woods,
In vain the razor-bill'd auk sails far north to Labrador,
I follow quickly, I ascend to the nest in the fissure of the
    cliff.

32

I think I could turn and live with animals, they're so
    placid and self-contain'd,
I stand and look at them long and long.

They do not sweat and whine about their condition,
They do not lie awake in the dark and weep for their
    sins,
They do not make me sick discussing their duty to God,
Not one is dissatisfied, not one is demented with the mania
    of owning things,
Not one kneels to another, nor to his kind that lived thou-
    sands of years ago,
Not one is respectable or unhappy over the whole earth.

So they show their relations to me and I accept them,
They bring me tokens of myself, they evince them plainly
    in their possession.

I wonder where they get those tokens,
Did I pass that way huge times ago and negligently drop
    them?

Myself moving forward then and now and forever,
Gathering and showing more always and with velocity,

Infinite and omnigenous, and the like of these among
  them,
Not too exclusive toward the reachers of my remem-
  brancers,
Picking out here one that I love, and now go with him
  on brotherly terms.

A gigantic beauty of a stallion, fresh and responsive to my
  caresses,
Head high in the forehead, wide between the ears,
Limbs glossy and supple, tail dusting the ground,
Eyes full of sparkling wickedness, ears finely cut, flexibly
  moving.

His nostrils dilate as my heels embrace him,
His well-built limbs tremble with pleasure as we race
  around and return.
I but use you a minute, then I resign you, stallion,
Why do I need your paces when I myself out-gallop them?
Even as I stand or sit passing faster than you.

33

Space and Time! now I see it is true, what I guess'd at,
What I guess'd when I loaf'd on the grass,
What I guess'd while I lay alone in my bed,
And again as I walk'd the beach under the paling stars of
  the morning.

My ties and ballasts leave me, my elbows rest in sea-gaps,
I skirt sierras, my palms cover continents,
I am afoot with my vision.

By the city's quadrangular houses—in log huts, camping
    with lumbermen,

Along the ruts of the turnpike, along the dry gulch and
    rivulet bed,

Weeding my onion-patch or hoeing rows of carrots and
    parsnips, crossing savannas, trailing in forests,

Prospecting, gold-digging, girdling the trees of a new pur-
    chase,

Scorch'd ankle-deep by the hot sand, hauling my boat
    down the shallow river,

Where the panther walks to and fro on a limb overhead,
    where the buck turns furiously at the hunter,

Where the rattlesnake suns his flabby length on a rock,
    where the otter is feeding on fish,

Where the alligator in his tough pimples sleeps by the
    bayou,

Where the black bear is searching for roots or honey, where
    the beaver pats the mud with his paddle-shaped tail;

Over the growing sugar, over the yellow-flower'd cotton
    plant, over the rice in its low moist field,

Over the sharp-peak'd farm house, with its scallop'd scum
    and slender shoots from the gutters,

Over the western persimmon, over the long-leav'd corn,
    over the delicate blue-flower flax,

Over the white and brown buckwheat, a hummer and
    buzzer there with the rest,

Over the dusky green of the rye as it ripples and shades in
    the breeze;

Scaling mountains, pulling myself cautiously up, holding
    on by low scragged limbs,

Walking the path worn in the grass and beat through the
    leaves of the brush,

Where the quail is whistling betwixt the woods and the
wheat-lot,

Where the bat flies in the Seventh-month eve, where the
great gold-bug drops through the dark,

Where the brook puts out of the roots of the old tree and
flows to the meadow,

Where cattle stand and shake away flies with the tremulous
shuddering of their hides,

Where the cheese-cloth hangs in the kitchen, where and-
irons straddle the hearth-slab, where cobwebs fall in
festoons from the rafters;

Where trip-hammers crash, where the press is whirling its
cylinders,

Where the human heart beats with terrible throes under its
ribs,

Where the pear-shaped balloon is floating aloft, (floating in
it myself and looking composedly down,)

Where the life-car is drawn on the slip-noose, where the
heat hatches pale-green eggs in the dented sand,

Where the she-whale swims with her calf and never for-
sakes it,

Where the steam-ship trails hind-ways its long pennant of
smoke,

Where the fin of the shark cuts like a black chip out of the
water,

Where the half-burn'd brig is riding on unknown currents,

Where shells grow to her slimy deck, where the dead are
corrupting below;

Where the dense-starr'd flag is borne at the head of the
regiments,

Approaching Manhattan up by the long-stretching island,

Under Niagara, the cataract falling like a veil over my
countenance,

Upon a door-step, upon the horse-block of hard wood out-
  side,

Upon the race-course, or enjoying picnics or jigs or a good
  game of base-ball,

At he-festivals, with blackguard gibes, ironical license, bull-
  dances, drinking, laughter,

At the cider-mill tasting the sweets of the brown mash,
  sucking the juice through a straw,

At apple-peelings wanting kisses for all the red fruit I find,

At musters, beach-parties, friendly bees, huskings, house-
  raisings;

Where the mocking-bird sounds his delicious gurgles,
  cackles, screams, weeps,

Where the hay-rick stands in the barn-yard, where the dry-
  stalks are scatter'd, where the brood-cow waits in the
  hovel,

Where the bull advances to do his masculine work, where
  the stud to the mare, where the cock is treading the
  hen,

Where the heifers browse, where geese nip their food with
  short jerks,

Where sun-down shadows lengthen over the limitless and
  lonesome prairie,

Where herds of buffalo make a crawling spread of the
  square miles far and near,

Where the humming-bird shimmers, where the neck of the
  long-lived swan is curving and winding,

Where the laughing-gull scoots by the shore, where she
  laughs her near-human laugh,

Where bee-hives range on a gray bench in the garden half
  hid by the high weeds,

Where band-neck'd partridges roost in a ring on the ground
  with their heads out,

Where burial coaches enter the arch'd gates of a cemetery,
Where winter wolves bark amid wastes of snow and icicled
    trees,
Where the yellow-crown'd heron comes to the edge of the
    marsh at night and feeds upon small crabs,
Where the splash of swimmers and divers cools the warm
    noon,
Where the katy-did works her chromatic reed on the
    walnut-tree over the wall,
Through patches of citrons and cucumbers with silver-
    wired leaves,
Through the salt-lick or orange glade, or under conical firs,
Through the gymnasium, through the curtain'd saloon,
    through the office or public hall;
Pleas'd with the native and pleas'd with the foreign, pleas'd
    with the new and old,
Pleas'd with the homely woman as well as the handsome,
Pleas'd with the quakeress as she puts off her bonnet and
    talks melodiously,
Pleas'd with the tune of the choir of the whitewash'd
    church,
Pleas'd with the earnest words of the sweating Methodist
    preacher, impress'd seriously at the camp-meeting;
Looking in at the shop-windows of Broadway the whole
    forenoon, flatting the flesh of my nose on the thick
    plate glass,
Wandering the same afternoon with my face turn'd up to
    the clouds, or down a lane or along the beach,
My right and left arms round the sides of two friends, and
    I in the middle;
Coming home with the silent and dark-cheek'd bush-boy,
    (behind me he rides at the drape of the day,)

Far from the settlements studying the print of animals'
    feet, or the moccasin print,
By the cot in the hospital reaching lemonade to a feverish
    patient,
Nigh the coffin'd corpse when all is still, examining with a
    candle;
Voyaging to every port to dicker and adventure,
Hurrying with the modern crowd as eager and fickle as any,
Hot toward one I hate, ready in my madness to knife him,
Solitary at midnight in my back yard, my thoughts gone
    from me a long while,
Walking the old hills of Judæa with the beautiful gentle
    God by my side,
Speeding through space, speeding through heaven and the
    stars,
Speeding amid the seven satellites and the broad ring, and
    the diameter of eighty thousand miles,
Speeding with tail'd meteors, throwing fire-balls like the
    rest,
Carrying the crescent child that carries its own full mother
    in its belly,
Storming, enjoying, planning, loving, cautioning,
Backing and filling, appearing and disappearing,
I tread day and night such roads.

I visit the orchards of spheres and look at the product,
And look at quintillions ripen'd and look at quintillions
    green.

I fly those flights of a fluid and swallowing soul,
My course runs below the soundings of plummets.

I help myself to material and immaterial,
No guard can shut me off, no law prevent me.

I anchor my ship for a little while only,
My messengers continually cruise away or bring their
returns to me.

I go hunting polar furs and the seal, leaping chasms with a
pike-pointed staff, clinging to topples of brittle and
blue.

I ascend to the foretruck,
I take my place late at night in the crow's-nest,
We sail the arctic sea, it is plenty light enough,
Through the clear atmosphere I stretch around on the
wonderful beauty,
The enormous masses of ice pass me and I pass them, the
scenery is plain in all directions,
The white-topt mountains show in the distance, I fling out
my fancies toward them,
We are approaching some great battle-field in which we are
soon to be engaged,
We pass the colossal outposts of the encampment, we pass
with still feet and caution,
Or we are entering by the suburbs some vast and ruin'd city,
The blocks and fallen architecture more than all the living
cities of the globe.

I am a free companion, I bivouac by invading watchfires,
I turn the bridegroom out of bed and stay with the bride
myself,
I tighten her all night to my thighs and lips.

My voice is the wife's voice, the screech by the rail of the
stairs,
They fetch my man's body up dripping and drown'd.

I understand the large hearts of heroes,
The courage of present times and all times,
How the skipper saw the crowded and rudderless wreck of
the steamship, and Death chasing it up and down the
storm,
How he knuckled tight and gave not back an inch, and was
faithful of days and faithful of nights,
And chalk'd in large letters on a board, *Be of good cheer,
we will not desert you;*
How he follow'd with them and tack'd with them three
days and would not give it up,
How he saved the drifting company at last,
How the lank loose-gown'd women look'd when boated
from the side of their prepared graves,
How the silent old-faced infants and the lifted sick, and
the sharp-lipp'd unshaved men;
All this I swallow, it tastes good, I like it well, it becomes
mine,
I am the man, I suffer'd, I was there.

The disdain and calmness of martyrs,
The mother of old, condemn'd for a witch, burnt with dry
wood, her children gazing on,
The hounded slave that flags in the race, leans by the
fence, blowing, cover'd with sweat,
The twinges that sting like needles his legs and neck, the
murderous buckshot and the bullets,
All these I feel or am.

I am the hounded slave, I wince at the bite of the dogs,
Hell and despair are upon me, crack and again crack the
marksmen,

I clutch the rails of the fence, my gore dribs, thinn'd with
the ooze of my skin,
I fall on the weeds and stones,
The riders spur their unwilling horses, haul close,
Taunt my dizzy ears and beat me violently over the head
with whip-stocks.

Agonies are one of my changes of garments,
I do not ask the wounded person how he feels, I myself
become the wounded person,
My hurts turn livid upon me as I lean on a cane and
observe.

I am the mash'd fireman with breast-bone broken,
Tumbling walls buried me in their debris,
Heat and smoke I inspired, I heard the yelling shouts of
my comrades,
I heard the distant click of their picks and shovels,
They have clear'd the beams away, they tenderly lift me
forth.

I lie in the night air in my red shirt, the pervading hush
is for my sake,
Painless after all I lie exhausted but not so unhappy,
White and beautiful are the faces around me, the heads are
bared of their fire-caps,
The kneeling crowd fades with the light of the torches.

Distant and dead resuscitate,
They show as the dial or move as the hands of me, I am
the clock myself.

I am an old artillerist, I tell of my fort's bombardment,
I am there again.

Again the long roll of the drummers,
Again the attacking cannon, mortars,
Again to my listening ears the cannon responsive.

I take part, I see and hear the whole,
The cries, curses, roar, the plaudits for well-aim'd shots,
The ambulanza slowly passing trailing its red drip,
Workmen searching after damages, making indispensable
    repairs,
The fall of grenades through the rent roof, the fan-shaped
    explosion,
The whizz of limbs, heads, stone, wood, iron, high in the
    air.

Again gurgles the mouth of my dying general, he furiously
    waves with his hand,
He gasps through the clot *Mind not me—mind—the en-*
    trenchments.

34

Now I tell what I knew in Texas in my early youth,
(I tell not the fall of Alamo,
Not one escaped to tell the fall of Alamo,
The hundred and fifty are dumb yet at Alamo,)
Tis the tale of the murder in cold blood of four hundred
    and twelve young men.

Retreating they had form'd in a hollow square with their
    baggage for breastworks,
Nine hundred lives out of the surrounding enemy's, nine
    times their number, was the price they took in ad-
    vance,

Their colonel was wounded and their ammunition gone,
They treated for an honorable capitulation, receiv'd writing
and seal, gave up their arms and march'd back prison-
ers of war.

They were the glory of the race of rangers,
Matchless with horse, rifle, song, supper, courtship,
Large, turbulent, generous, handsome, proud, and affec-
tionate,
Bearded, sunburnt, drest in the free costume of hunters,
Not a single one over thirty years of age.

The second First-day morning they were brought out in
squads and massacred, it was beautiful early summer,
The work commenced about five o'clock and was over by
eight.

None obey'd the command to kneel,
Some made a mad and helpless rush, some stood stark and
straight,
A few fell at once, shot in the temple or heart, the living
and dead lay together,
The maim'd and mangled dug in the dirt, the new-comers
saw them there,
Some half-kill'd attempted to crawl away,
These were despatch'd with bayonets or batter'd with the
blunts of muskets.
A youth not seventeen years old seiz'd his assassin till two
more came to release him,
The three were all torn and cover'd with the boy's blood.

At eleven o'clock began the burning of the bodies;
That is the tale of the murder of the four hundred and
twelve young men.

35

Would you hear of an old-time sea-fight?

Would you learn who won by the light of the moon and
stars?

List to the yarn, as my grandmother's father the sailor told
it to me.

Our foe was no skulk in his ship I tell you, (said he,)

His was the surly English pluck, and there is no tougher or
truer, and never was, and never will be;

Along the lower'd eve he came horribly raking us.

We closed with him, the yards entangled, the cannon
touch'd,

My captain lash'd fast with his own hands.

We had receiv'd some eighteen pound shots under the
water,

On our lower-gun-deck two large pieces had burst at the
first fire, killing all around and blowing up overhead.

Fighting at sun-down, fighting at dark,

Ten o'clock at night, the full moon well up, our leaks on
the gain, and five feet of water reported,

The master-at-arms loosing the prisoners confined in the
after-hold to give them a chance for themselves.

The transit to and from the magazine is now stopt by the
sentinels,

They see so many strange faces they do not know whom to
trust.

Our frigate takes fire,
The other asks if we demand quarter?
If our colors are struck and the fighting done?

Now I laugh content, for I hear the voice of my little
    captain,
We have not struck, he composedly cries, *we have just
    begun our part of the fighting.*

Only three guns are in use,
One is directed by the captain himself against the enemy's
    main-mast,
Two well serv'd with grape and canister silence his mus-
    ketry and clear his decks.

The tops alone second the fire of this little battery, espe-
    cially the main-top,
They hold out bravely during the whole of the action.

Not a moment's cease,
The leaks gain fast on the pumps, the fire eats toward the
    powder-magazine.

One of the pumps has been shot away, it is generally
    thought we are sinking.

Serene stands the little captain,
He is not hurried, his voice is neither high nor low,
His eyes give more light to us than our battle-lanterns.

Toward twelve there in the beams of the moon they sur-
    render to us.

36

Stretch'd and still lies the midnight,

Two great hulls motionless on the breast of the darkness,

Our vessel riddled and slowly sinking, preparations to pass
to the one we have conquer'd,

The captain on the quarter-deck coldly giving his orders
through a countenance white as a sheet,

Near by the corpse of the child that serv'd in the cabin,

The dead face of an old salt with long white hair and care-
fully curl'd whiskers,

The flames spite of all that can be done flickering aloft and
below,

The husky voices of the two or three officers yet fit for
duty,

Formless stacks of bodies and bodies by themselves, dabs of
flesh upon the masts and spars,

Cut of cordage, dangle of rigging, slight shock of the
soothe of waves,

Black and impassive guns, litter of powder-parcels, strong
scent,

A few large stars overhead, silent and mournful shining,

Delicate sniffs of sea-breeze, smells of sedgy grass and fields
by the shore, death-messages given in charge to sur-
vivors,

The hiss of the surgeon's knife, the gnawing teeth of his
saw,

Wheeze, cluck, swash of falling blood, short wild scream,
and long, dull, tapering groan,

These so, these irretrievable.

37

You laggards there on guard! look to your arms!

In at the conquer'd doors they crowd! I am possess'd!

Embody all presences outlaw'd or suffering,
See myself in prison shaped like another man,
And feel the dull unintermitted pain,
For me the keepers of convicts shoulder their carbines and
keep watch,
It is I let out in the morning and barr'd at night.

Not a mutineer walks handcuff'd to jail but I am hand-
cuff'd to him and walk by his side,
(I am less the jolly one there, and more the silent one with
sweat on my twitching lips.)

Not a youngster is taken for larceny but I go up too, and
am tried and sentenced.

Not a cholera patient lies at the last gasp but I also lie at
the last gasp,
My face is ash-color'd, my sinews gnarl, away from me
people retreat.

Askers embody themselves in me and I am embodied in
them,
I project my hat, sit shame-faced, and beg.

38

Enough! enough! enough!
Somehow I have been stunn'd. Stand back!
Give me a little time beyond my cuff'd head, slumbers,
dreams, gaping,
I discover myself on the verge of a usual mistake.

That I could forget the mockers and insults!
That I could forget the trickling tears and the blows of the
    bludgeons and hammers!
That I could look with a separate look on my own crucifix-
    ion and bloody crowning!

I remember now,
I resume the overstaid fraction,
The grave of rock multiplies what has been confided to it,
    or to any graves,
Corpses rise, gashes heal, fastenings roll from me.

I troop forth replenish'd with supreme power, one of an
    average unending procession,
Inland and sea-coast we go, and pass all boundary lines,
Our swift ordinances on their way over the whole earth,
The blossoms we wear in our hats the growth of thousands
    of years.

Eleves, I salute you! come forward!
Continue your annotations, continue your questionings.

39

The friendly and flowing savage, who is he?
Is he waiting for civilization, or past it and mastering it?

Is he some Southwesterner rais'd out-doors? is he Kana-
    dian?
Is he from the Mississippi country? Iowa, Oregon, Cali-
    fornia?
The mountains? prairie-life, bush-life? or sailor from the
    sea?

Wherever he goes men and women accept and desire him,
They desire he should like them, touch them, speak to
them, stay with them.

Behavior lawless as snow-flakes, words simple as grass, un-
comb'd head, laughter, and naivetè,
Slow-stepping feet, common features, common modes and
emanations,
They descend in new forms from the tips of his fingers,
They are wafted with the odor of his body or breath, they
fly out of the glance of his eyes.

40

Flaunt of the sunshine I need not your bask—lie over!
You light surfaces only, I force surfaces and depths also.

Earth! you seem to look for something at my hands,
Say, old top-knot, what do you want?

Man or woman, I might tell how I like you, but cannot,
And might tell what it is in me and what it is in you, but
cannot,
And might tell that pining I have, that pulse of my nights
and days.

Behold, I do not give lectures or a little charity,
When I give I give myself.

You there, impotent, loose in the knees,
Open your scarf'd chops till I blow grit within you,
Spread your palms and lift the flaps of your pockets,
I am not to be denied, I compel, I have stores plenty and
to spare,
And any thing I have I bestow.

I do not ask who you are, that is not important to me,
You can do nothing and be nothing but what I will infold
you.

To cotton-field drudge or cleaner of privies I lean,
On his right cheek I put the family kiss,
And in my soul I swear I never will deny him.

On women fit for conception I start bigger and nimbler
babes,
(This day I am jetting the stuff of far more arrogant re-
publics.)

To any one dying, thither I speed and twist the knob of the
door,
Turn the bed-clothes toward the foot of the bed,
Let the physician and the priest go home.

I seize the descending man and raise him with resistless
will,
O despairer, here is my neck,
By God, you shall not go down! hang your whole weight
upon me.

I dilate you with tremendous breath, I buoy you up,
Every room of the house do I fill with an arm'd force
Lovers of me, bafflers of graves.

Sleep—I and they keep guard all night,
Not doubt, not disease shall dare to lay finger upon you,
I have embraced you, and henceforth possess you to myself,
And when you rise in the morning you will find what I tell
you is so.

I am he bringing help for the sick as they pant on their
backs,
And for strong upright men I bring yet more needed help.

I heard what was said of the universe,
Heard it and heard it of several thousand years;
It is middling well as far as it goes—but is that all?

Magnifying and applying come I,
Outbidding at the start the old cautious hucksters,
Taking myself the exact dimensions of Jehovah,
Lithographing Kronos, Zeus his son, and Hercules his
grandson,
Buying drafts of Osiris, Isis, Belus, Brahma, Buddha,
In my portfolio placing Manito loose, Allah on a leaf, the
crucifix engraved,
With Odin and the hideous-faced Mexitli and every idol
and image,
Taking them all for what they are worth and not a cent
more,
Admitting they were alive and did the work of their days,
(They bore mites as for unfledg'd birds who have now to
rise and fly and sing for themselves,)
Accepting the rough deific sketches to fill out better in
myself, bestowing them freely on each man and
woman I see,
Discovering as much or more in a framer framing a house,
Putting higher claims for him there with his roll'd-up
sleeves driving the mallet and chisel,

Not objecting to special revelations, considering a curl of
    smoke or a hair on the back of my hand just as curious
    as any revelation,
Lads ahold of fire-engines and hook-and-ladder ropes no
    less to me than the gods of the antique wars,
Minding their voices peal through the crash of destruction,
Their brawny limbs passing safe over charr'd laths, their
    white foreheads whole and unhurt out of the flames;
By the mechanic's wife with her babe at her nipple inter-
    ceding for every person born,
Three scythes at harvest whizzing in a row from three
    lusty angels with shirts bagg'd out at their waists,
The snag-tooth'd hostler with red hair redeeming sins past
    and to come,
Selling all he possesses, traveling on foot to fee lawyers for
    his brother and sit by him while he is tried for
    forgery;
What was strewn in the amplest strewing the square rod
    about me, and not filling the square rod then,
The bull and the bug never worshipp'd half enough,
Dung and dirt more admirable than was dream'd,
The supernatural of no account, myself waiting my time to
    be one of the supremes,
The day getting ready for me when I shall do as much
    good as the best, and be as prodigious;
By my life-lumps! becoming already a creator,
Putting myself here and now to the ambush'd womb of the
    shadows.

42

A call in the midst of the crowd,
My own voice, orotund sweeping and final.

Come my children,

Come my boys and girls, my women, household and intimates,

Now the performer launches his nerve, he has pass'd his prelude on the reeds within.

Easily written loose-finger'd chords—I feel the thrum of your climax and close.

My head slues round on my neck,

Music rolls, but not from the organ,

Folks are around me, but they are no household of mine.

Ever the hard unsunk ground,

Ever the eaters and drinkers, ever the upward and downward sun, ever the air and the ceaseless tides,

Ever myself and my neighbors, refreshing, wicked, real,

Ever the old inexplicable query, ever that thorn'd thumb, that breath of itches and thirsts,

Ever the vexer's *hoot! hoot!* till we find where the sly one hides and bring him forth,

Ever love, ever the sobbing liquid of life,

Ever the bandage under the chin, ever the trestles of death.

Here and there with dimes on the eyes walking,

To feed the greed of the belly the brains liberally spooning,

Tickets buying, taking, selling, but in to the feast never once going,

Many sweating, ploughing, thrashing, and then the chaff for payment receiving,

A few idly owning, and they the wheat continually claiming.

WALT WHITMAN

This is the city and I am one of the citizens,
Whatever interests the rest interests me, politics, wars, markets, newspapers, schools,
The mayor and councils, banks, tariffs, steamships, factories, stocks, stores, real estate and personal estate.

The little plentiful manikins skipping around in collars and tail'd coats,
I am aware who they are, (they are positively not worms or fleas,)
I acknowledge the duplicates of myself, the weakest and shallowest is deathless with me,
What I do and say the same waits for them,
Every thought that flounders in me the same flounders in them.

I know perfectly well my own egotism,
Know my omnivorous lines and must not write any less,
And would fetch you whoever you are flush with myself.

Not words of routine this song of mine,
But abruptly to question, to leap beyond yet nearer bring;
This printed and bound book—but the printer and the printing-office boy?
The well-taken photographs—but your wife or friend close and solid in your arms?
The black ship mail'd with iron, her mighty guns in her turrets—but the pluck of the captain and engineers?
In the houses the dishes and fare and furniture—but the host and hostess, and the look out of their eyes?
The sky up there—yet here or next door, or across the way?
The saints and sages in history—but you yourself?

Sermons, creeds, theology—but the fathomless human brain,
And what is reason? and what is love? and what is life?

43

I do not despise you priests, all time, the world over,
My faith is the greatest of faiths and the least of faiths,
Enclosing worship ancient and modern and all between ancient and modern,
Believing I shall come again upon the earth after five thousand years,
Waiting responses from oracles, honoring the gods, saluting the sun,
Making a fetich of the first rock or stump, powowing with sticks in the circle of obis,
Helping the llama or brahmin as he trims the lamps of the idols,
Dancing yet through the streets in a phallic procession, rapt and austere in the woods a gymnosophist,
Drinking mead from the skull-cup, to Shastas and Vedas admirant, minding the Koran,
Walking the teokallis, spotted with gore from the stone and knife, beating the serpent-skin drum,
Accepting the Gospels, accepting him that was crucified, knowing assuredly that he is divine,
To the mass kneeling or the puritan's prayer rising, or sitting patiently in a pew,
Ranting and frothing in my insane crisis, or waiting dead-like till my spirit arouses me,
Looking forth on pavement and land, or outside of pavement and land,
Belonging to the winders of the circuit of circuits.

One of that centripetal and centrifugal gang I turn and
talk like a man leaving charges before a journey.

Down-hearted doubters dull and excluded,
Frivolous, sullen, moping, angry, affected, dishearten'd,
atheistical,
I know every one of you, I know the sea of torment, doubt,
despair and unbelief.

How the flukes splash!
How they contort rapid as lightning, with spasms and
spouts of blood!

Be at peace bloody flukes of doubters and sullen mopers,
I take my place among you as much as among any,
The past is the push of you, me, all, precisely the same,
And what is yet untried and afterward is for you, me, all
precisely the same.

I do not know what is untried and afterward,
But I know it will in its turn prove sufficient, and cannot
fail.

Each who passes is consider'd, each who stops is consider'd,
not a single one can it fail.

It cannot fail the young man who died and was buried,
Nor the young woman who died and was put by his side,
Nor the little child that peep'd in at the door, and then
drew back and was never seen again,
Nor the old man who has lived without purpose, and feels
it with bitterness worse than gall,

Nor him in the poor house tubercled by rum and the bad
 disorder,
Nor the numberless slaughter'd and wreck'd, nor the brutish
 koboo call'd the ordure of humanity,
Nor the sacs merely floating with open mouths for food to
 slip in,
Nor any thing in the earth, or down in the oldest graves of
 the earth,
Nor any thing in the myriads of spheres, nor the myriads
 of myriads that inhabit them,
Nor the present, nor the least wisp that is known.

44
It is time to explain myself—let us stand up.

What is known I strip away,
I launch all men and women forward with me into the
 Unknown.

The clock indicates the moment—but what does eternity
 indicate?

We have thus far exhausted trillions of winters and
 summers,
There are trillions ahead, and trillions ahead of them.

Births have brought us richness and variety,
And other births will bring us richness and variety.

I do not call one greater and one smaller,
That which fills its period and place is equal to any.

Were mankind murderous or jealous upon you, my brother,
    my sister?
I am sorry for you, they are not murderous or jealous upon
    me,
All has been gentle with me, I keep no account with lamen-
    tation,
(What have I to do with lamentation?)
I am an acme of things accomplish'd, and I an encloser of
    things to be.

My feet strike an apex of the apices of the stairs,
On every step bunches of ages, and larger bunches between
    the steps,
All below duly travel'd, and still I mount and mount.

Rise after rise bow the phantoms behind me,
Afar down I see the huge first Nothing, I know I was even
    there,
I waited unseen and always, and slept through the lethargic
    mist,
And took my time, and took no hurt from the fetid carbon.

Long I was hugg'd close—long and long.

Immense have been the preparations for me,
Faithful and friendly the arms that have help'd me.

Cycles ferried my cradle, rowing and rowing like cheerful
    boatmen,
For room to me stars kept aside in their own rings,
They sent influences to look after what was to hold me.

Before I was born out of my mother generations guided me,
My embryo has never been torpid, nothing could overlay it.

For it the nebula cohered to an orb,
The long slow strata piled to rest it on,
Vast vegetables gave it sustenance,
Monstrous sauroids transported it in their mouths and de-
    posited it with care

All forces have been steadily employ'd to complete and
    delight me,
Now on this spot I stand with my robust soul.

45

O span of youth! ever-push'd elasticity!
O manhood, balanced, florid and full.

My lovers suffocate me,
Crowding my lips, thick in the pores of my skin,
Jostling me through streets and public halls, coming naked
    to me at night,
Crying by day *Ahoy!* from the rocks of the river, swinging
    and chirping over my head,
Calling my name from flower-beds, vines, tangled under-
    brush,
Lighting on every moment of my life,
Bussing my body with soft balsamic busses,
Noiselessly passing handfuls out of their hearts and giving
    them to be mine.

Old age superbly rising! O welcome, ineffable grace of
    dying days!

Every condition promulges not only itself, it promulges
    what grows after and out of itself,
And the dark hush promulges as much as any.

WALT WHITMAN

I open my scuttle at night and see the far-sprinkled systems,
And all I see multiplied as high as I can cipher edge but
the rim of the farther systems.

Wider and wider they spread, expanding, always expand-
ing,
Outward and outward and forever outward.

My sun has his sun and round him obediently wheels,
He joins with his partners a group of superior circuit,
And greater sets follow, making specks of the greatest inside
them.

There is no stoppage and never can be stoppage,
If I, you, and the worlds, and all beneath or upon their
surfaces, were this moment reduced back to a pallid
float, it would not avail in the long run,
We should surely bring up again where we now stand,
And surely go as much farther, and then farther and
farther.

A few quadrillions of eras, a few octillions of cubic leagues,
do not hazard the span or make it impatient,
They are but parts, any thing is but a part.

See ever so far, there is limitless space outside of that,
Count ever so much, there is limitless time around that.

My rendezvous is appointed, it is certain,
The Lord will be there and wait till I come on perfect
terms,
The great Camerado, the lover true for whom I pine will
be there.

46

I know I have the best of time and space, and was never
    measured and never will be measured.

I tramp a perpetual journey, (come listen all!)
My signs are a rain-proof coat, good shoes, and a staff cut
    from the woods,
No friend of mine takes his ease in my chair,
I have no chair, no church, no philosophy,
I lead no man to a dinner-table, library, exchange,
But each man and each woman of you I lead upon a knoll,
My left hand hooking you round the waist,
My right hand pointing to landscapes of continents and
    the public road.

Not I, not any one else can travel that road for you,
You must travel it for yourself.

It is not far, it is within reach,
Perhaps you have been on it since you were born and did
    not know,
Perhaps it is everywhere on water and on land.

Shoulder your duds dear son, and I will mine, and let us
    hasten forth,
Wonderful cities and free nations we shall fetch as we go.

If you tire, give me both burdens, and rest the chuff of
    your hand on my hip,
And in due time you shall repay the same service to me,
For after we start we never lie by again.

This day before dawn I ascended a hill and look'd at the
crowded heaven,

And I said to my spirit *When we become the enfolders of
those orbs, and the pleasure and knowledge of every
thing in them, shall we be fill'd and satisfied then?*

And my spirit said *No, we but level that lift to pass and
continue beyond.*

You are also asking me questions and I hear you,

I answer that I cannot answer, you must find out for
yourself.

Sit a while dear son,

Here are biscuits to eat and here is milk to drink,

But as soon as you sleep and renew yourself in sweet
clothes, I kiss you with a good-by kiss and open the
gate for your egress hence.

Long enough have you dream'd contemptible dreams,

Now I wash the gum from your eyes,

You must habit yourself to the dazzle of the light and of
every moment of your life.

Long have you timidly waded holding a plank by the shore,

Now I will you to be a bold swimmer,

To jump off in the midst of the sea, rise again, nod to me,
shout, and laughingly dash with your hair.

47

I am the teacher of athletes,

He that by me spreads a wider breast than my own proves
the width of my own,

He most honors my style who learns under it to destroy the
teacher.

The boy I love, the same becomes a man not through
    derived power, but in his own right,
Wicked rather than virtuous out of conformity or fear,
Fond of his sweetheart, relishing well his steak,
Unrequited love or a slight cutting him worse than sharp
    steel cuts,
First-rate to ride, to fight, to hit the bull's eye, to sail a
    skiff, to sing a song or play on the banjo,
Preferring scars and the beard and faces pitted with small-
    pox over all latherers,
And those well-tann'd to those that keep out of the sun.

I teach straying from me, yet who can stray from me?
I follow you whoever you are from the present hour,
My words itch at your ears till you understand them.

I do not say these things for a dollar or to fill up the time
    while I wait for a boat,
(It is you talking just as much as myself, I act as the
    tongue of you,
Tied in your mouth, in mine it begins to be loosen'd.)

I swear I will never again mention love or death inside a
    house,
And I swear I will never translate myself at all, only to
    him or her who privately stays with me in the open
    air.

If you would understand me go to the heights or water-
    shore,
The nearest gnat is an explanation, and a drop or motion
    of waves a key,
The maul, the oar, the hand-saw, second my words.

No shutter'd room or school can commune with me,
But roughs and little children better than they.

The young mechanic is closest to me, he knows me well,
The woodman that takes his axe and jug with him shall
    take me with him all day,
The farm-boy ploughing in the field feels good at the
    sound of my voice,
In vessels that sail my words sail, I go with fishermen and
    seamen and love them.

The soldier camp'd or upon the march is mine,
On the night ere the pending battle many seek me, and I
    do not fail them,
On that solemn night (it may be their last) those that
    know me seek me.

My face rubs to the hunter's face when he lies down alone
    in his blanket,
The driver thinking of me does not mind the jolt of his
    wagon,
The young mother and old mother comprehend me,
The girl and the wife rest the needle a moment and forget
    where they are,
They and all would resume what I have told them.

48

I have said that the soul is not more than the body,
And I have said that the body is not more than the soul,
And nothing, not God, is greater to one than one's self is,
And whoever walks a furlong without sympathy walks to
    his own funeral drest in his shroud,
And I or you pocketless of a dime may purchase the pick
    of the earth,

And to glance with an eye or show a bean in its pod con-
    founds the learning of all times,
And there is no trade or employment but the young man
    following it may become a hero,
And there is no object so soft but it makes a hub for the
    wheel'd universe,
And I say to any man or woman, Let your soul stand cool
    and composed before a million universes.

And I say to mankind, Be not curious about God,
For I who am curious about each am not curious about God,
(No array of terms can say how much I am at peace about
    God and about death.)

I hear and behold God in every object, yet understand God
    not in the least,
Nor do I understand who there can be more wonderful
    than myself.

Why should I wish to see God better than this day?
I see something of God each hour of the twenty-four, and
    each moment then,
In the faces of men and women I see God, and in my own
    face in the glass,
I find letters from God dropt in the street, and every one
    is sign'd by God's name,
And I leave them where they are, for I know that where-
    soe'er I go,
Others will punctually come for ever and ever.

49

And as to you Death, and you bitter hug of mortality, it is
    idle to try to alarm me.

WALT WHITMAN

To his work without flinching the accoucheur comes,
I see the elder-hand pressing receiving supporting,
I recline by the sills of the exquisite flexible doors,
And mark the outlet, and mark the relief and escape.

And as to you Corpse I think you are good manure, but
   that does not offend me,
I smell the white roses sweet-scented and growing,
I reach to the leafy lips, I reach to the polish'd breasts of
   melons.

And as to you Life I reckon you are the leavings of many
   deaths,
(No doubt I have died myself ten thousand times before.)

I hear you whispering there O stars of heaven,
O suns—O grass of graves—O perpetual transfers and
   promotions,
If you do not say any thing how can I say any thing?

Of the turbid pool that lies in the autumn forest,
Of the moon that descends the steeps of the soughing twi-
   light,
Toss, sparkles of day and dusk—toss on the black stems that
   decay in the muck,
Toss to the moaning gibberish of the dry limbs.

I ascend from the moon, I ascend from the night,
I perceive that the ghastly glimmer is noonday sunbeams
   reflected,
And debouch to the steady and central from the offspring
   great or small.

50

There is that in me—I do not know what it is—but I know
    it is in me.

Wrench'd and sweaty—calm and cool then my body be-
    comes,
I sleep—I sleep long.

I do not know it—it is without name—it is a word unsaid
It is not in any dictionary, utterance, symbol.

Something it swings on more than the earth I swing on,
To it the creation is the friend whose embracing awakes
    me.

Perhaps I might tell more. Outlines! I plead for my
    brothers and sisters.

Do you see O my brothers and sisters?
It is not chaos or death—it is form, union, plan—it is
    eternal life—it is Happiness.

51

The past and present wilt—I have fill'd them, emptied
    them,
And proceed to fill my next fold of the future.

Listener up there! what have you to confide to me?
Look in my face while I snuff the sidle of evening,
(Talk honestly, no one else hears you, and I stay only a
    minute longer.)

Do I contradict myself?
Very well then I contradict myself,
(I am large, I contain multitudes.)

I concentrate toward them that are nigh, I wait on the
    door-slab.

Who has done his day's work? who will soonest be through
    with his supper?
Who wishes to walk with me?

Will you speak before I am gone? will you prove already
    too late?

52

The spotted hawk swoops by and accuses me, he complains
    of my gab and my loitering.

I too am not a bit tamed, I too am untranslatable,
I sound my barbaric yawp over the roofs of the world.

The last scud of day holds back for me,
It flings my likeness after the rest and true as any on the
    shadow'd wilds,
It coaxes me to the vapor and the dusk.

I depart as air, I shake my white locks at the runaway sun,
I effuse my flesh in eddies, and drift it in lacy jags.

I bequeath myself to the dirt to grow from the grass I love,
If you want me again look for me under your boot-soles.

You will hardly know who I am or what I mean,
But I shall be good health to you nevertheless,
And filter and fibre your blood.

Failing to fetch me at first keep encouraged,
Missing me one place search another,
I stop somewhere waiting for you.

117

Spontaneous Me

SPONTANEOUS me, Nature,

The loving day, the mounting sun, the friend I am happy with,

The arm of my friend hanging idly over my shoulder,

The hillside whiten'd with blossoms of the mountain ash,

The same late in autumn, the hues of red, yellow, drab, purple, and light and dark green,

The rich coverlet of the grass, animals and birds, the private untrimm'd bank, the primitive apples, the pebblestones,

Beautiful dripping fragments, the negligent list of one after another as I happen to call them to me or think of them,

The real poems, (what we call poems being merely pictures,)

The poems of the privacy of the night, and of men like me,

This poem drooping shy and unseen that I always carry, and that all men carry,

(Know once for all, avow'd on purpose, wherever are men like me, are our lusty lurking masculine poems,)

Love-thoughts, love-juice, love-odor, love-yielding, love-climbers, and the climbing sap,

Arms and hands of love, lips of love, phallic thumb of love, breasts of love, bellies press'd and glued together with love,

Earth of chaste love, life that is only life after love,

The body of my love, the body of the woman I love, the body of the man, the body of the earth,

354

Soft forenoon airs that blow from the south-west,

The hairy wild-bee that murmurs and hankers up and down, that gripes the full-grown lady-flower, curves upon her with amorous firm legs, takes his will of her, and holds himself tremulous and tight till he is satisfied;

The wet of woods through the early hours,

Two sleepers at night lying close together as they sleep, one with an arm slanting down across and below the waist of the other,

The smell of apples, aromas from crush'd sage-plant, mint, birch-bark,

The boy's longings, the glow and pressure as he confides to me what he was dreaming,

The dead leaf whirling its spiral whirl and falling still and content to the ground,

The no-form'd stings that sights, people, objects, sting me with,

The hubb'd sting of myself, stinging me as much as it ever can any one,

The sensitive, orbic, underlapp'd brothers, that only privileged feelers may be intimate where they are,

The curious roamer the hand roaming all over the body, the bashful withdrawing of flesh where the fingers soothingly pause and edge themselves,

The limpid liquid within the young man,

The vex'd corrosion so pensive and so painful,

The torment, the irritable tide that will not be at rest,

The like of the same I feel, the like of the same in others,

The young man that flushes and flushes, and the young woman that flushes and flushes,

The young man that wakes deep at night, the hot hand seeking to repress what would master him,

The mystic amorous night, the strange half-welcome pangs, visions, sweats,

The pulse pounding through palms and trembling encircling fingers, the young man all color'd, red, ashamed, angry;

The souse upon me of my lover the sea, as I lie willing and naked,

The merriment of the twin babies that crawl over the grass in the sun, the mother never turning her vigilant eyes from them,

The walnut-trunk, the walnut-husks, and the ripening or ripen'd long-round walnuts,

The continence of vegetables, birds, animals,

The consequent meanness of me should I skulk or find myself indecent, while birds and animals never once skulk or find themselves indecent,

The great chastity of paternity, to match the great chastity of maternity,

The oath of procreation I have sworn, my Adamic and fresh daughters,

The greed that eats me day and night with hungry gnaw, till I saturate what shall produce boys to fill my place when I am through,

The wholesome relief, repose, content,

And this bunch pluck'd at random from myself,

It has done its work—I toss it carelessly to fall where it may.

118 *Native Moments*

NATIVE moments—when you come upon me—ah you
 are here now,
Give me now libidinous joys only,
Give me the drench of my passions, give me life coarse
 and rank,
To-day I go consort with Nature's darlings, to-night too,
I am for those who believe in loose delights, I share the
 midnight orgies of young men,
I dance with the dancers and drink with the drinkers,
The echoes ring with our indecent calls, I pick out some
 low person for my dearest friend,
He shall be lawless, rude, illiterate, he shall be one con-
 demned by others for deeds done,
I will play a part no longer, why should I exile myself
 from my companions?
O you shunn'd persons, I at least do not shun you,
I come forthwith in your midst, I will be your poet,
I will be more to you than to any of the rest.

119 *Once I Pass'd Through a Populous City*

ONCE I pass'd through a populous city imprinting my
 brain for future use with its shows, architecture,
 customs, traditions,
Yet now of all that city I remember only a woman I
 casually met there who detain'd me for love of me,

Day by day and night by night we were together—all else
　　has long been forgotten by me,
I remember I say only that woman who passionately clung
　　to me,
Again we wander, we love, we separate again,
Again she holds me by the hand, I must not go,
I see her close beside me with silent lips sad and tremulous.

120　　*I Heard You Solemn-Sweet Pipes*
　　　　　of the Organ

I HEARD you solemn-sweet pipes of the organ as last
　　Sunday morn I pass'd the church,
Winds of autumn, as I walk'd the woods at dusk I heard
　　your long-stretch'd sighs up above so mournful,
I heard the perfect Italian tenor singing at the opera, I
　　heard the soprano in the midst of the quartet singing;
Heart of my love! you too I heard murmuring low
　　through one of the wrists around my head,
Heard the pulse of you when all was still ringing little
　　bells last night under my ear.

121　　*As Adam Early in the Morning*

As Adam early in the morning,
Walking forth from the bower refresh'd with sleep,
Behold me where I pass, hear my voice, approach,
Touch me, touch the palm of your hand to my body as I
　　pass,
Be not afraid of my body.

122   *In Paths Untrodden*

IN paths untrodden,
In the growths by margins of pond-waters,
Escaped from the life that exhibits itself,
From all the standards hitherto publish'd, from the plea-
    sures, profits, conformities,
Which too long I was offering to feed my soul,
Clear to me now standards not yet publish'd, clear to me
    that my soul,
That the soul of the man I speak for rejoices in comrades,
Here by myself away from the clank of the world,
Tallying and talk'd to here by tongues aromatic,
No longer abash'd, (for in this secluded spot I can respond
    as I would not dare elsewhere,)
Strong upon me the life that does not exhibit itself, yet
    contains all the rest,
Resolv'd to sing no songs to-day but those of manly attach-
    ment,
Projecting them along that substantial life,
Bequeathing hence types of athletic love,
Afternoon this delicious Ninth-month in my forty-first
    year,
I proceed for all who are or have been young men,
To tell the secret of my nights and days,
To celebrate the need of comrades.

123   *When I Heard at the Close
of the Day*

WHEN I heard at the close of the day how my name
had been receiv'd with plaudits in the capitol, still it
was not a happy night for me that follow'd,

And else when I carous'd, or when my plans were accom-
plish'd, still I was not happy,

But the day when I rose at dawn from the bed of perfect
health, refresh'd, singing, inhaling the ripe breath of
autumn,

When I saw the full moon in the west grow pale and dis-
appear in the morning light,

When I wander'd alone over the beach, and undressing
bathed, laughing with the cool waters, and saw the
sun rise,

And when I thought how my dear friend my lover was on
his way coming, O then I was happy,

O then each breath tasted sweeter, and all that day my food
nourish'd me more, and the beautiful day pass'd well,

And the next came with equal joy, and with the next at
evening came my friend,

And that night while all was still I heard the waters roll
slowly continually up the shores,

I heard the hissing rustle of the liquid and sands as
directed to me whispering to congratulate me,

For the one I love most lay sleeping by me under the same
cover in the cool night,

In the stillness in the autumn moonbeams his face was in-
clined toward me,

And his arm lay lightly around my breast—and that night
I was happy.

124 *I Saw in Louisiana a Live-Oak*
Growing

I SAW in Louisiana a live-oak growing,
All alone stood it and the moss hung down from the
branches,
Without any companion it grew there uttering joyous
leaves of dark green,
And its look, rude, unbending, lusty, made me think of
myself,
But I wonder'd how it could utter joyous leaves standing
alone there without its friend near, for I knew I
could not,
And I broke off a twig with a certain number of leaves
upon it, and twined around it a little moss,
And brought it away, and I have placed it in sight, in my
room,
It is not needed to remind me as of my own dear friends,
(For I believe lately I think of little else than of them,)
Yet it remains to me a curious token, it makes me think of
manly love;
For all that, and though the live-oak glistens there in
Louisiana solitary in a wide flat space,
Uttering joyous leaves all its life without a friend a lover
near,
I know very well I could not.

125   *A Glimpse*

A GLIMPSE through an interstice caught,
Of a crowd of workmen and drivers in a bar-room around
    the stove late of a winter night, and I unremark'd
    seated in a corner,
Of a youth who loves me and whom I love, silently ap-
    proaching and seating himself near, that he may hold
    me by the hand,
A long while amid the noises of coming and going, of
    drinking and oath and smutty jest,
There we two, content, happy in being together, speaking
    little, perhaps not a word.

126   *Earth, My Likeness*

EARTH, my likeness,
Though you look so impassive, ample and spheric there,
I now suspect that is not all;
I now suspect there is something fierce in you eligible to
    burst forth,
For an athlete is enamour'd of me, and I of him,
But toward him there is something fierce and terrible in
    me eligible to burst forth,
I dare not tell it in words, not even in these songs.

127   *Out of the Cradle Endlessly Rocking*

OUT of the cradle endlessly rocking,
Out of the mocking-bird's throat, the musical shuttle,
Out of the Ninth-month midnight,
Over the sterile sands and the fields beyond, where the
    child leaving his bed wander'd alone, bareheaded,
    barefoot,
Down from the shower'd halo,
Up from the mystic play of shadows twining and twisting
    as if they were alive,
Out from the patches of briers and blackberries,
From the memories of the bird that chanted to me,
From your memories sad brother, from the fitful risings
    and fallings I heard,
From under that yellow half-moon late-risen and swollen
    as if with tears,
From those beginning notes of yearning and love there in
    the mist,
From the thousand responses of my heart never to cease,
From the myriad thence-arous'd words,
From the word stronger and more delicious than any,
From such as now they start the scene revisiting,
As a flock, twittering, rising, or overhead passing,
Borne hither, ere all eludes me, hurriedly,
A man, yet by these tears a little boy again,
Throwing myself on the sand, confronting the waves,
I, chanter of pains and joys, uniter of here and hereafter,
Taking all hints to use them, but swiftly leaping beyond
    them,
A reminiscence sing.

Once Paumanok,
When the lilac-scent was in the air and Fifth-month grass
    was growing,
Up this seashore in some briers,
Two feather'd guests from Alabama, two together,
And their nest, and four light-green eggs spotted with
    brown,
And every day the he-bird to and fro near at hand,
And every day the she-bird crouch'd on her nest, silent,
    with bright eyes,
And every day I, a curious boy, never too close, never dis-
    turbing them,
Cautiously peering, absorbing, translating.

Shine! shine! shine!
Pour down your warmth, great sun!
While we bask, we two together.

Two together!
Winds blow south, or winds blow north,
Day come white, or night come black,
Home, or rivers and mountains from home,
Singing all time, minding no time,
While we two keep together.

Till of a sudden,
May-be kill'd, unknown to her mate,
One forenoon the she-bird crouch'd not on the nest,
Nor return'd that afternoon, nor the next,
Nor ever appear'd again.

And thenceforward all summer in the sound of the sea,
And at night under the full of the moon in calmer
    weather,

Over the hoarse surging of the sea,
Or flitting from brier to brier by day,
I saw, I heard at intervals the remaining one, the he-bird,
The solitary guest from Alabama.

Blow! blow! blow!
Blow up sea-winds along Paumanok's shore;
I wait and I wait till you blow my mate to me.

Yes, when the stars glisten'd,
All night long on the prong of a moss-scallop'd stake,
Down almost amid the slapping waves,
Sat the lone singer wonderful causing tears.

He call'd on his mate,
He pour'd forth the meanings which I of all men know.

Yes my brother I know,
The rest might not, but I have treasur'd every note,
For more than once dimly down to the beach gliding,
Silent, avoiding the moonbeams, blending myself with the
	shadows,
Recalling now the obscure shapes, the echoes, the sounds
	and sights after their sorts,
The white arms out in the breakers tirelessly tossing,
I, with bare feet, a child, the wind wafting my hair,
Listen'd long and long.

Listen'd to keep, to sing, now translating the notes,
Following you my brother.

Soothe! soothe! soothe!
Close on its wave soothes the wave behind,

*And again another behind embracing and lapping, every
        one close,*
But my love soothes not me, not me.

Low hangs the moon, it rose late,
It is lagging—O I think it is heavy with love, with love.

O madly the sea pushes upon the land,
With love, with love.

*O night! do I not see my love fluttering out among the
        breakers?*
What is that little black thing I see there in the white?

Loud! loud! loud!
Loud I call to you, my love!
High and clear I shoot my voice over the waves,
Surely you must know who is here, is here,
You must know who I am, my love.

Low-hanging moon!
What is that dusky spot in your brown yellow?
O it is the shape, the shape of my mate!
O moon do not keep her from me any longer.

Land! land! O land!
*Whichever way I turn, O I think you could give me my
        mate back again if you only would,*
For I am almost sure I see her dimly whichever way I look.

O rising stars!
*Perhaps the one I want so much will rise, will rise with
        some of you.*

O throat! O trembling throat!
Sound clearer through the atmosphere!
Pierce the woods, the earth,
Somewhere listening to catch you must be the one I want.

Shake out carols!
Solitary here, the night's carols!
Carols of lonesome love! death's carols!
Carols under that lagging, yellow, waning moon!
O under that moon where she droops almost down into the
        sea!
O reckless despairing carols.

But soft! sink low!
Soft! let me just murmur,
And do you wait a moment you husky-nois'd sea,
For somewhere I believe I heard my mate responding to
        me,
So faint, I must be still, be still to listen,
But not altogether still, for then she might not come im-
        mediately to me.

Hither my love!
Here I am! here!
With this just-sustain'd note I announce myself to you,
This gentle call is for you my love, for you.

Do not be decoy'd elsewhere,
That is the whistle of the wind, it is not my voice,
That is the fluttering, the fluttering of the spray,
Those are the shadows of leaves.

O darkness! O in vain!
O I am very sick and sorrowful.

*O brown halo in the sky near the moon, drooping upon the
        sea!*
O troubled reflection in the sea!
O throat! O throbbing heart!
And I singing uselessly, uselessly all the night.

O past! O happy life! O songs of joy!
In the air, in the woods, over fields,
Loved! loved! loved! loved! loved!
But my mate no more, no more with me!
We two together no more.

The aria sinking,
All else continuing, the stars shining,
The winds blowing, the notes of the bird continuous echo-
        ing,
With angry moans the fierce old mother incessantly moan-
        ing,
On the sands of Paumanok's shore gray and rustling,
The yellow half-moon enlarged, sagging down, drooping,
        the face of the sea almost touching,
The boy ecstatic, with his bare feet the waves, with his
        hair the atmosphere dallying,
The love in the heart long pent, now loose, now at last
        tumultuously bursting,
The aria's meaning, the ears, the soul, swiftly depositing,
The strange tears down the cheeks coursing,
The colloquy there, the trio, each uttering,
The undertone, the savage old mother incessantly crying,
To the boy's soul's questions sullenly timing, some drown'd
        secret hissing,
To the outsetting bard.

Demon or bird! (said the boy's soul,)
Is it indeed toward your mate you sing? or is it really to
    me?
For I, that was a child, my tongue's use sleeping, now I
    have heard you,
Now in a moment I know what I am for, I awake,
And already a thousand singers, a thousand songs, clearer,
    louder and more sorrowful than yours,
A thousand warbling echoes have started to life within me,
    never to die.

O you singer solitary, singing by yourself, projecting
    me,
O solitary me listening, never more shall I cease perpetu-
    ating you,
Never more shall I escape, never more the reverberations,
Never more the cries of unsatisfied love be absent from
    me,
Never again leave me to be the peaceful child I was be-
    fore what there in the night,
By the sea under the yellow and sagging moon,
The messenger there arous'd, the fire, the sweet hell
    within,
The unknown want, the destiny of me.

O give me the clew! (it lurks in the night here some-
    where,)
O if I am to have so much, let me have more!

A word then, (for I will conquer it,)
The word final, superior to all,
Subtle, sent up—what is it?—I listen;

Are you whispering it, and have been all the time, you sea
    waves?
Is that it from your liquid rims and wet sands?

Whereto answering, the sea,
Delaying not, hurrying not,
Whisper'd me through the night, and very plainly before
    daybreak,
Lisp'd to me the low and delicious word death,
And again death, death, death, death,
Hissing melodious, neither like the bird nor like my
    arous'd child's heart,
But edging near as privately for me rustling at my feet,
Creeping thence steadily up to my ears and laving me
    softly all over,
Death, death, death, death, death.

Which I do not forget,
But fuse the song of my dusky demon and brother,
That he sang to me in the moonlight on Paumanok's gray
    beach,
With the thousand responsive songs at random,
My own songs awaked from that hour,
And with them the key, the word up from the waves,
The word of the sweetest song and all songs,
That strong and delicious word which, creeping to my feet,
(Or like some old crone rocking the cradle, swathed in
    sweet garments, bending aside,)
The sea whisper'd me.

128   *A Hand-Mirror*

Hold it up sternly—see this it sends back, (who is
     it? is it you?)
Outside fair costume, within ashes and filth,
No more a flashing eye, no more a sonorous voice or springy
     step,
Now some slave's eye, voice, hands, step,
A drunkard's breath, unwholesome eater's face, venerealee's
     flesh,
Lungs rotting away piecemeal, stomach sour and cankerous,
Joints rheumatic, bowels clogged with abomination,
Blood circulating dark and poisonous streams,
Words babble, hearing and touch callous,
No brain, no heart left, no magnetism of sex;
Such from one look in this looking-glass ere you go hence,
Such a result so soon—and from such a beginning!

129   *When I Heard the Learn'd*
                    Astronomer

When I heard the learn'd astronomer,
When the proofs, the figures, were ranged in columns be-
     fore me,
When I was shown the charts and diagrams, to add, divide,
     and measure them,
When I sitting heard the astronomer where he lectured
     with much applause in the lecture-room,

How soon unaccountable I became tired and sick,
Till rising and gliding out I wander'd off by myself,
In the mystical moist night-air, and from time to time,
Look'd up in perfect silence at the stars.

130   *I Sit and Look Out*

I SIT and look out upon all the sorrows of the world,
    and upon all oppression and shame,
I hear secret convulsive sobs from young men at anguish
    with themselves, remorseful after deeds done,
I see in low life the mother misused by her children, dy-
    ing, neglected, gaunt, desperate,
I see the wife misused by her husband, I see the treacherous
    seducer of young women,
I mark the ranklings of jealousy and unrequited love at-
    tempted to be hid, I see these sights on the earth,
I see the workings of battle, pestilence, tyranny, I see
    martyrs and prisoners,
I observe a famine at sea, I observe the sailors casting lots
    who shall be kill'd to preserve the lives of the rest,
I observe the slights and degradations cast by arrogant per-
    sons upon laborers, the poor, and upon negroes, and
    the like;
All these—all the meanness and agony without end I sit-
    ting look out upon,
See, hear, and am silent.

131   *Cavalry Crossing a Ford*

A LINE in long array where they wind betwixt green
    islands,
They take a serpentine course, their arms flash in the sun—
    hark to the musical clank,
Behold the silvery river, in it the splashing horses loiter-
    ing stop to drink,
Behold the brown-faced men, each group, each person a
    picture, the negligent rest on the saddles,
Some emerge on the opposite bank, others are just entering
    the ford—while,
Scarlet and blue and snowy white,
The guidon flags flutter gayly in the wind.

132   *Bivouac on a Mountain Side*

I SEE before me now a traveling army halting,
Below a fertile valley spread, with barns and the orchards
    of summer,
Behind, the terraced sides of a mountain, abrupt, in places
    rising high,
Broken, with rocks, with clinging cedars, with tall shapes
    dingily seen,
The numerous camp-fires scatter'd near and far, some away
    up on the mountain,
The shadowy forms of men and horses, looming, large-
    sized, flickering,
And over all the sky—the sky! far, far out of reach,
    studded, breaking out, the eternal stars.

373

133   By the Bivouac's Fitful Flame

BY the bivouac's fitful flame,
A procession winding around me, solemn and sweet and
   slow—but first I note,
The tents of the sleeping army, the fields' and woods' dim
   outline,
The darkness lit by spots of kindled fire, the silence,
Like a phantom far or near an occasional figure moving,
The shrubs and trees, (as I lift my eyes they seem to be
   stealthily watching me,)
While wind in procession thoughts, O tender and wondrous
   thoughts,
Of life and death, of home and the past and loved, and
   of those that are far away;
A solemn and slow procession there as I sit on the ground,
By the bivouac's fitful flame.

134   Come Up from the Fields Father

COME up from the fields father, here's a letter from
   our Pete,
And come to the front door mother, here's a letter from
   thy dear son.

Lo, 'tis autumn,
Lo, where the trees, deeper green, yellower and redder,
Cool and sweeten Ohio's villages with leaves fluttering in
   the moderate wind,

374

Where apples ripe in the orchards hang and grapes on the
    trellis'd vines,
(Smell you the smell of the grapes on the vines?
Smell you the buckwheat where the bees were lately buzz-
    ing?)

Above all, lo, the sky so calm, so transparent after the
    rain, and with wondrous clouds,
Below too, all calm, all vital and beautiful, and the farm
    prospers well.

Down in the fields all prospers well,
But now from the fields come father, come at the daugh-
    ter's call,
And come to the entry mother, to the front door come
    right away.

Fast as she can she hurries, something ominous, her steps
    trembling,
She does not tarry to smooth her hair nor adjust her cap.

Open the envelope quickly,
O this is not our son's writing, yet his name is sign'd,
O a strange hand writes for our dear son, O stricken
    mother's soul!
All swims before her eyes, flashes with black, she catches
    the main words only,
Sentences broken, *gunshot wound in the breast, cavalry skir-
    mish, taken to hospital,*
At present low, but will soon be better.

Ah now the single figure to me,
Amid all teeming and wealthy Ohio with all its cities and
    farms,

Sickly white in the face and dull in the head, very faint,
By the jamb of a door leans.

Grieve not so, dear mother, (the just-grown daughter
    speaks through her sobs,
The little sisters huddle around speechless and dismay'd,)
See, dearest mother, the letter says Pete will soon be better.

Alas poor boy, he will never be better, (nor may-be needs
    to be better, that brave and simple soul,)
While they stand at home at the door he is dead already,
The only son is dead.

But the mother needs to be better,
She with thin form presently drest in black,
By day her meals untouch'd, then at night fitfully sleep-
    ing, often waking,
In the midnight waking, weeping, longing with one deep
    longing,
O that she might withdraw unnoticed, silent from life
    escape and withdraw,
To follow, to seek, to be with her dear dead son.

135   *A March in the Ranks Hard-Prest, and the Road Unknown*

A MARCH in the ranks hard-prest, and the road un-
    known,
A route through a heavy wood with muffled steps in the
    darkness,
Our army foil'd with loss severe, and the sullen remnant
    retreating,

Till after midnight glimmer upon us the lights of a dim-
lighted building,
We come to an open space in the woods, and halt by the
dim-lighted building,
'Tis a large old church at the crossing roads, now an im-
promptu hospital,
Entering but for a minute I see a sight beyond all the
pictures and poems ever made,
Shadows of deepest, deepest black, just lit by moving
candles and lamps,
And by one great pitchy torch stationary with wild red
flame and clouds of smoke,
By these, crowds, groups of forms vaguely I see on the
floor, some in the pews laid down,
At my feet more distinctly a soldier, a mere lad, in danger
of bleeding to death, (he is shot in the abdomen,)
I stanch the blood temporarily, (the youngster's face is
white as a lily,)
Then before I depart I sweep my eyes o'er the scene fain
to absorb it all,
Faces, varieties, postures beyond description, most in ob-
scurity, some of them dead,
Surgeons operating, attendants holding lights, the smell of
ether, the odor of blood,
The crowd, O the crowd of the bloody forms, the yard
outside also fill'd,
Some on the bare ground, some on planks or stretchers,
some in the death-spasm sweating,
An occasional scream or cry, the doctor's shouted orders or
calls,
The glisten of the little steel instruments catching the glint
of the torches,

These I resume as I chant, I see again the forms, I smell
the odor,
Then hear outside the orders given, *Fall in, my men,
fall in;*
But first I bend to the dying lad, his eyes open, a half-smile
gives he me,
Then the eyes close, calmly close, and I speed forth to the
darkness,
Resuming, marching, ever in darkness marching, on in the
ranks,
The unknown road still marching.

*136   A Sight in Camp in the Daybreak
Gray and Dim*

A SIGHT in camp in the daybreak gray and dim,
As from my tent I emerge so early sleepless,
As slow I walk in the cool fresh air the path near by the
hospital tent,
Three forms I see on stretchers lying, brought out there
untended lying,
Over each the blanket spread, ample brownish woolen
blanket,
Gray and heavy blanket, folding, covering all.

Curious I halt and silent stand,
Then with light fingers I from the face of the nearest the
first just lift the blanket;
Who are you elderly man so gaunt and grim, with well-
gray'd hair, and flesh all sunken about the eyes?
Who are you my dear comrade?

Then to the second I step—and who are you my child and
    darling?
Who are you sweet boy with cheeks yet blooming?

Then to the third—a face nor child nor old, very calm,
    as of beautiful yellow-white ivory;
Young man I think I know you—I think this face is the
    face of the Christ himself,
Dead and divine and brother of all, and here again he lies.

137   *O Tan-Faced Prairie-Boy*

O TAN-FACED prairie-boy,
Before you came to camp came many a welcome gift,
Praises and presents came and nourishing food, till at last
    among the recruits,
You came, taciturn, with nothing to give—we but look'd
    on each other,
When lo! more than all the gifts of the world you gave me.

138   *As I Lay with My Head in Your
    Lap Camerado*

As I lay with my head in your lap camerado,
The confession I made I resume, what I said to you and
    the open air I resume,
I know I am restless and make others so,
I know my words are weapons full of danger, full of death,

For I confront peace, security, and all the settled laws, to
    unsettle them,
I am more resolute because all have denied me than I could
    ever have been had all accepted me,
I heed not and have never heeded either experience, cau-
    tions, majorities, nor ridicule,
And the threat of what is call'd hell is little or nothing
    to me,
And the lure of what is call'd heaven is little or nothing
    to me;
Dear camerado! I confess I have urged you onward with
    me, and still urge you, without the least idea what is
    our destination,
Or whether we shall be victorious, or utterly quell'd and
    defeated.

139   *Reconciliation*

WORD over all, beautiful as the sky,
Beautiful that war and all its deeds of carnage must in
    time be utterly lost,
That the hands of the sisters Death and Night incessantly
    softly wash again, and ever again, this soil'd world;
For my enemy is dead, a man divine as myself is dead,
I look where he lies white-faced and still in the coffin—
    I draw near,
Bend down and touch lightly with my lips the white face
    in the coffin.

140 *When Lilacs Last in the Dooryard
Bloom'd*

1

WHEN lilacs last in the dooryard bloom'd,
And the great star early droop'd in the western sky in the
    night,
I mourn'd, and yet shall mourn with ever-returning spring.

Ever-returning spring, trinity sure to me you bring,
Lilac blooming perennial and drooping star in the west,
And thought of him I love.

2

O powerful western fallen star!
O shades of night—O moody, tearful night!
O great star disappear'd—O the black murk that hides the
    star!
O cruel hands that hold me powerless—O helpless soul of
    me!
O harsh surrounding cloud that will not free my soul.

3

In the dooryard fronting an old farm-house near the white-
    wash'd palings,
Stands the lilac-bush tall-growing with heart-shaped leaves
    of rich green,
With many a pointed blossom rising delicate, with the per-
    fume strong I love,
With every leaf a miracle—and from this bush in the door-
    yard,

With delicate-color'd blossoms and heart-shaped leaves of
    rich green,
A sprig with its flower I break.

4

In the swamp in secluded recesses,
A shy and hidden bird is warbling a song.

Solitary the thrush,
The hermit withdrawn to himself, avoiding the settle-
    ments,
Sings by himself a song.

Song of the bleeding throat,
Death's outlet song of life, (for well dear brother I know,
If thou wast not granted to sing thou would'st surely die.)

5

Over the breast of the spring, the land, amid cities,
Amid lanes and through old woods, where lately the violets
    peep'd from the ground, spotting the gray debris,
Amid the grass in the fields each side of the lanes, passing
    the endless grass,
Passing the yellow-spear'd wheat, every grain from its
    shroud in the dark-brown fields uprisen,
Passing the apple-tree blows of white and pink in the
    orchards,
Carrying a corpse to where it shall rest in the grave,
Night and day journeys a coffin.

6

Coffin that passes through lanes and streets,
Through day and night with the great cloud darkening the
    land,

With the pomp of the inloop'd flags with the cities draped
in black,
With the show of the States themselves as of crape-veil'd
women standing,
With processions long and winding and the flambeaus of
the night,
With the countless torches lit, with the silent sea of faces
and the unbared heads,
With the waiting depot, the arriving coffin, and the sombre
faces,
With dirges through the night, with the thousand voices
rising strong and solemn,
With all the mournful voices of the dirges pour'd around
the coffin,
The dim-lit churches and the shuddering organs—where
amid these you journey,
With the tolling tolling bells' perpetual clang,
Here, coffin that slowly passes,
I give you my sprig of lilac.

7

(Nor for you, for one alone,
Blossoms and branches green to coffins all I bring,
For fresh as the morning, thus would I chant a song for
you O sane and sacred death.

All over bouquets of roses,
O death, I cover you over with roses and early lilies,
But mostly and now the lilac that blooms the first,
Copious I break, I break the sprigs from the bushes,
With loaded arms I come, pouring for you,
For you and the coffins all of you O death.)

8

O western orb sailing the heaven,
Now I know what you must have meant as a month since I
    walk'd,
As I walk'd in silence the transparent shadowy night,
As I saw you had something to tell as you bent to me night
    after night,
As you drooped from the sky low down as if to my side,
    (while the other stars all look'd on,)
As we wander'd together the solemn night, (for something
    I know not what kept me from sleep,)
As the night advanced, and I saw on the rim of the west how
    full you were of woe,
As I stood on the rising ground in the breeze in the cool
    transparent night,
As I watch'd where you pass'd and was lost in the nether-
    ward black of the night,
As my soul in its trouble dissatisfied sank, as where you sad
    orb,
Concluded, dropt in the night, and was gone.

9

Sing on there in the swamp,
O singer bashful and tender, I hear your notes, I hear your
    call,
I hear, I come presently, I understand you,
But a moment I linger, for the lustrous star has detain'd
    me,
The star my departing comrade holds and detains me.

10

O how shall I warble myself for the dead one there I
    loved?
And how shall I deck my song for the large sweet soul
    that has gone?
And what shall my perfume be for the grave of him I
    love?

Sea-winds blown from east and west,
Blown from the Eastern sea and blown from the Western
    sea, till there on the prairies meeting,
These and with these and the breath of my chant.
I'll perfume the grave of him I love.

11

O what shall I hang on the chamber walls?
And what shall the pictures be that I hang on the walls,
To adorn the burial-house of him I love?

Pictures of growing spring and farms and homes,
With the Fourth-month eve at sundown, and the gray
    smoke lucid and bright,
With floods of the yellow gold of the gorgeous, indolent,
    sinking sun, burning, expanding the air,
With the fresh sweet herbage under foot, and the pale
    green leaves of the trees prolific,
In the distance the flowing glaze, the breast of the river,
    with a wind-dapple here and there,
With ranging hills on the banks, with many a line against
    the sky, and shadows,

And the city at hand with dwellings so dense, and stacks of
    chimneys,
And all the scenes of life and the workshops, and the
    workmen homeward returning.

12

Lo, body and soul—this land,
My own Manhattan with spires, and the sparkling and
    hurrying tides, and the ships,
The varied and ample land, the South and the North in the
    light, Ohio's shores and flashing Missouri,
And ever the far-spreading prairies cover'd with grass and
    corn.

Lo, the most excellent sun so calm and haughty,
The violet and purple morn with just-felt breezes,
The gentle soft-born measureless light,
The miracle spreading bathing all, the fulfill'd noon,
The coming eve delicious, the welcome night and the stars,
Over my cities shining all, enveloping man and land.

13

Sing on, sing on you gray-brown bird,
Sing from the swamps, the recesses, pour your chant from
    the bushes,
Limitless out of the dusk, out of the cedars and pines.

Sing on dearest brother, warble your reedy song,
Loud human song, with voice of uttermost woe.

O liquid and free and tender!
O wild and loose to my soul—O wondrous singer!

You only I hear—yet the star holds me, (but will soon
  depart,)
Yet the lilac with mastering odor holds me.

14

Now while I sat in the day and look'd forth,
In the close of the day with its light and the fields of
  spring, and the farmers preparing their crops,
In the large unconscious scenery of my land with its lakes
  and forests,
In the heavenly aerial beauty, (after the perturb'd winds
  and the storms,)
Under the arching heavens of the afternoon swift passing,
  and the voices of children and women,
The many-moving sea-tides, and I saw the ships how they
  sail'd,
And the summer approaching with richness, and the fields
  all busy with labor,
And the infinite separate houses, how they all went on, each
  with its meals and minutia of daily usages,
And the streets how their throbbings throbb'd, and the
  cities pent—lo, then and there,
Falling upon them all and among them all, enveloping me
  with the rest,
Appear'd the cloud, appear'd the long black trail,
And I knew death, its thought, and the sacred knowledge
  of death.

Then with the knowledge of death as walking one side of
  me,
And the thought of death close-walking the other side of
  me,

And I in the middle as with companions, and as holding
    the hands of companions,
I fled forth to the hiding receiving night that talks not,
Down to the shores of the water, the path by the swamp in
    the dimness,
To the solemn shadowy cedars and ghostly pines so still.

And the singer so shy to the rest receiv'd me,
The gray-brown bird I know receiv'd us comrades three,
And he sang the carol of death, and a verse for him I love.

From deep secluded recesses,
From the fragrant cedars and the ghostly pines so still,
Came the carol of the bird.

And the charm of the carol rapt me,
As I held as if by their hands my comrades in the night,
And the voice of my spirit tallied the song of the bird.

Come lovely and soothing death,
Undulate round the world, serenely arriving, arriving,
In the day, in the night, to all, to each,
Sooner or later delicate death.

Prais'd be the fathomless universe,
For life and joy, and for objects and knowledge curious,
And for love, sweet love—but praise! praise! praise!
For the sure-enwinding arms of cool-enfolding death.

Dark mother always gliding near with soft feet,
Have none chanted for thee a chant of fullest welcome?
Then I chant it for thee, I glorify thee above all,
I bring thee a song that when thou must indeed come, come
*   unfalteringly.*

Approach strong deliveress,
When it is so, when thou hast taken them I joyously sing
    the dead,
Lost in the loving floating ocean of thee,
Laved in the flood of thy bliss O death.

From me to thee glad serenades,
Dances for thee I propose saluting thee, adornments and
    feastings for thee,
And the sights of the open landscape and the high-spread
    sky are fitting,
And life and the fields, and the huge and thoughtful night.

The night in silence under many a star,
The ocean shore and the husky whispering wave whose
    voice I know,
And the soul turning to thee O vast and well-veil'd death,
And the body gratefully nestling close to thee.

Over the tree-tops I float thee a song,
Over the rising and sinking waves, over the myriad fields
    and the prairies wide,
Over the dense-pack'd cities all and the teeming wharves
    and ways,
I float this carol with joy, with joy to thee O death.

15

To the tally of my soul,
Loud and strong kept up the gray-brown bird,
With pure deliberate notes spreading filling the night.

Loud in the pines and cedars dim,
Clear in the freshness moist and the swamp-perfume,
And I with my comrades there in the night.

While my sight that was bound in my eyes unclosed,
As to long panoramas of visions.

And I saw askant the armies,
I saw as in noiseless dreams hundreds of battle-flags,
Borne through the smoke of the battles and pierc'd with
    missiles I saw them,
And carried hither and yon through the smoke, and torn
    and bloody,
And at last but a few shreds left on the staffs, (and all in
    silence,)
And the staffs all splinter'd and broken.

I saw battle-corpses, myriads of them,
And the white skeletons of young men, I saw them,
I saw the debris and debris of all the slain soldiers of the
    war,
But I saw they were not as was thought,
They themselves were fully at rest, they suffer'd not,
The living remain'd and suffer'd, the mother suffer'd,
And the wife and the child and the musing comrade
    suffer'd,
And the armies that remain'd suffer'd.

16

Passing the visions, passing the night,
Passing, unloosing the hold of my comrades' hands,
Passing the song of the hermit bird and the tallying song
    of my soul,
Victorious song, death's outlet song, yet varying ever-
    altering song,
As low and wailing, yet clear the notes, rising and falling,
    flooding the night,

390

Sadly sinking and fainting, as warning and warning, and
    yet again bursting with joy,
Covering the earth and filling the spread of the heaven,
As that powerful psalm in the night I heard from recesses,
Passing, I leave thee lilac with heart-shaped leaves,
I leave thee there in the door-yard, blooming, returning
    with spring.

I cease from my song for thee,
From my gaze on thee in the west, fronting the west, com-
    muning with thee,
O comrade lustrous with silver face in the night.

Yet each to keep and all, retrievements out of the night,
The song, the wondrous chant of the gray-brown bird,
And the tallying chant, the echo arous'd in my soul,
With the lustrous and drooping star with the countenance
    full of woe,
With the holders holding my hand nearing the call of the
    bird,
Comrades mine and I in the midst, and their memory ever
    to keep, for the dead I loved so well,
For the sweetest, wisest soul of all my days and lands—and
    this for his dear sake,
Lilac and star and bird twined with the chant of my soul,
There in the fragrant pines and the cedars dusk and dim.

141   *Aboard at a Ship's Helm*

ABOARD at a ship's helm,
A young steersman steering with care.

Through fog on a sea-coast dolefully ringing,
An ocean-bell—O a warning bell, rock'd by the waves.

O you give good notice indeed, you bell by the sea-reefs
    ringing,
Ringing, ringing, to warn the ship from its wreck-place.

For as on the alert O steersman, you mind the loud admo-
    nition,
The bows turn, the freighted ship tacking speeds away
    under her gray sails,
The beautiful and noble ship with all her precious wealth
    speeds away gayly and safe.

But O the ship, the immortal ship! O ship aboard the ship!
Ship of the body, ship of the soul, voyaging, voyaging,
    voyaging.

142   *On the Beach at Night*

ON the beach at night,
Stands a child with her father,
Watching the east, the autumn sky.

Up through the darkness,
While ravening clouds, the burial clouds, in black masses
    spreading,
Lower sullen and fast athwart and down the sky,
Amid a transparent clear belt of ether yet left in the east,
Ascends large and calm the lord-star Jupiter,
And nigh at hand, only a very little above,
Swim the delicate sisters the Pleiades.

From the beach the child holding the hand of her father,
Those burial clouds that lower victorious soon to devour all,
Watching, silently weeps.

Weep not, child,
Weep not, my darling,
With these kisses let me remove your tears,
The ravening clouds shall not long be victorious,
They shall not long possess the sky, they devour the stars
    only in apparition,
Jupiter shall emerge, be patient, watch again another night,
    the Pleiades shall emerge,
They are immortal, all those stars both silvery and golden
    shall shine out again,
The great stars and the little ones shall shine out again,
    they endure,
The vast immortal suns and the long-enduring pensive
    moons shall again shine.

Then dearest child mournest thou only for Jupiter?
Considerest thou alone the burial of the stars?
Something there is,
(With my lips soothing thee, adding I whisper,
I give thee the first suggestion, the problem and indirec-
    tion,)
Something there is more immortal even than the stars,
(Many the burials, many the days and nights, passing
    away,)
Something that shall endure longer even than lustrous
    Jupiter,
Longer than sun or any revolving satellite,
Or the radiant sisters the Pleiades.

143 *A Noiseless Patient Spider*

A NOISELESS patient spider,
I mark'd where on a little promontory it stood isolated,
Mark'd how to explore the vacant vast surrounding,
It launched forth filament, filament, filament, out of itself,
Ever unreeling them, ever tirelessly speeding them.

And you O my soul where you stand,
Surrounded, detached, in measureless oceans of space,
Ceaselessly musing, venturing, throwing, seeking the
  spheres to connect them,
Till the bridge you will need be form'd, till the ductile
  anchor hold,
Till the gossamer thread you fling catch somewhere, O my
  soul.

144 *The Last Invocation*

AT the last, tenderly,
From the walls of the powerful fortress'd house,
From the clasp of the knitted locks, from the keep of the
  well-closed doors,
Let me be wafted.

Let me glide noiselessly forth;
With the key of softness unlock the locks—with a whisper,
Set ope the doors O soul.

Tenderly—be not impatient,
(Strong is your hold O mortal flesh,
Strong is your hold O love.)

145   *Halcyon Days*

NOT from successful love alone,
Nor wealth, nor honor'd middle age, nor victories of poli-
    tics or war;
But as life wanes, and all the turbulent passions calm,
As gorgeous, vapory, silent hues cover the evening sky,
As softness, fulness, rest, suffuse the frame, like fresher,
    balmier air,
As the days take on a mellower light, and the apple at last
    hangs really finish'd and indolent-ripe on the tree,
Then for the teeming quietest, happiest days of all!
The brooding and blissful halcyon days!

146   *The Dismantled Ship*

IN some unused lagoon, some nameless bay,
On sluggish, lonesome waters, anchor'd near the shore,
An old, dismasted, gray and batter'd ship, disabled, done,
After free voyages to all the seas of earth, haul'd up at last
    and hawser'd tight,
Lies rusting, mouldering.

147   *The Portent*
                (1859)

Hanging from the beam,
    Slowly swaying (such the law),
Gaunt the shadow on your green,
    Shenandoah!
The cut is on the crown
(Lo, John Brown),
And the stabs shall heal no more.

Hidden in the cap
    Is the anguish none can draw;
So your future veils its face,
    Shenandoah!
But the streaming beard is shown
(Weird John Brown),
The meteor of the war.

148   *Misgivings*
                (1860)

When ocean-clouds over inland hills
    Sweep storming in late autumn brown,
And horror the sodden valley fills,
    And the spire falls crashing in the town,

I muse upon my country's ills—
The tempest bursting from the waste of Time
On the world's fairest hope linked with man's foulest
    crime.

Nature's dark side is heeded now—
    (Ah! optimist-cheer disheartened flown)—
A child may read the moody brow
    Of yon black mountain lone.
With shouts the torrents down the gorges go,
And storms are formed behind the storm we feel:
The hemlock shakes in the rafter, the oak in the driving
    keel.

149
                    Shiloh
                A Requiem
            (April, 1862)

SKIMMING lightly, wheeling still,
    The swallows fly low
Over the field in clouded days,
    The forest-field of Shiloh—
Over the field where April rain
Solaced the parched one stretched in pain
Through the pause of night
That followed the Sunday fight
    Around the church of Shiloh—
The church so lone, the log-built one,
That echoed to many a parting groan
      And natural prayer
    Of dying foemen mingled there—

Foemen at morn, but friends at eve—
    Fame or country least their care:
    (What like a bullet can undeceive!)
    But now they lie low,
While over them the swallows skim,
    And all is hushed at Shiloh.

150   From *Clarel*

OF ROME

[The characters here are: Derwent, a facilely optimistic Anglican priest, a mixture of monk and cavalier; and Rolfe, an American whose experience has embraced both action and thought in a way not unlike Melville's own. Derwent is speaking. F. O. M.]

'. . . Rome's guns are spiked; and they'll stay so.
The world is now too civilised
For Rome. Your noble Western soil—
What! *that* be given up for spoil
To—to——'
              'There is an Unforeseen.
Fate never gives a guarantee
That she'll abstain from aught. And men
Get tired at last of being free—
Whether in states—in states or creeds.
For what's the sequel? Verily,
Laws scribbled by law-breakers, creeds
Scrawled by the freethinkers, and deeds
Shameful and shameless. Men get sick
Under that curse of Frederic
The cynical: for punishment

This rebel province I present
To the philosophers. But, how?
Whole nations now philosophise,
And do their own undoing now.—
Who's gained by all the sacrifice
Of Europe's revolutions? who?
The Protestant? the Liberal?
I do not think it—not at all:
Rome and the Atheist have gained:
These two shall fight it out—these two;
Protestantism being retained
For base of operations sly
By Atheism.'

                     . . . 'Oh,
That a New Worlder should talk so!'

    ' 'Tis the New World that mannered me,
Yes, gave me this vile liberty
To reverence naught, not even herself.'

    'How say you? you're the queerest elf!
But here's a thought I still pursue—
A thought I dreamed each thinker knew:
No more can men be what they've been;
All's altered—earth's another scene.'

    'Man's heart is what it used to be.'
'I don't know that.'

               'But Rome does, though:
And hence her stout persistency.
What mean her re-adopted modes
Even in the enemy's abodes?
Their place old emblems reassume.
She bides—content to let but blow
Among the sects that peak and pine,
Incursions of her taking bloom.'

. . . Considerate uncommitted eyes
Charged with things manifold and wise,
Rolfe turned upon good Derwent here;
Then changed: 'Fall back we must. Yon mule
With pannier: Come, in stream we'll cool
The wine ere quaffing.—Muleteer!'

ON MAMMON

[*The speaker here is Ungar, 'a wandering Ishmael
from the West,' a descendant of Maryland Catholics,
an inheritor of the Latin mind, though no longer in
the Church himself.* F. O. M.]

'AS *cruel as a Turk:* Whence came
That proverb old as the crusades ?
From Anglo-Saxons. What are they? . . .
The Anglo-Saxons—lacking grace
To win the love of any race;
Hated by myriads dispossessed
Of rights—the Indians East and West.
These pirates of the sphere! grave looters—
Grave, canting, Mammonite freebooters,
Who in the name of Christ and Trade
(Oh, bucklered forehead of the brass!)
Deflower the world's last sylvan glade! . . .
Respond to this: Old ballads sing
Fair Christian children crucified
By impious Jews; you've heard the thing:
Yes, fable; but there's truth hard by:
How many Hughs of Lincoln, say,
Does Mammon in his mills, to-day,
Crook, if he do not crucify?'

HERMAN MELVILLE

'. . . I pray,' said Rolfe, 'a word';
And turned toward Ungar; 'be adjured,
And tell us if for earth may be
In ripening arts, no guarantee
Of happy sequel.'
        'Arts are tools;
But tools, they say, are to the strong:
Is Satan weak? weak is the Wrong?
No blessed augury overrules:
Your arts advance in faith's decay:
You are but drilling the new Hun
Whose growl even now can some dismay;
Vindictive in his heart of hearts,
He schools him in your mines and marts—
A skilled destroyer.'
        'But, need own
That portent does in no degree
Westward impend, across the sea.'

'Over there? And do ye not forebode?
Against pretences void or weak
The impieties of "Progress" speak.
What say *these*, in effect, to God?
"How profits it? And who art Thou
That we should serve Thee? Of Thy ways
No knowledge we desire; *new* ways
We have found out, and better. Go—
Depart from us; we do erase
Thy sinecure: behold, the sun
Stands still no more in Ajalon:
Depart from us!"—And if He do?

(And that He may, the Scripture says)
Is aught betwixt ye and the hells?
For He, nor in irreverent view,
'Tis He distils that savour true
Which keeps good essences from taint;
Where He is not, corruption dwells,
And man and chaos are without restraint.'

    'Oh, oh, you do but generalise
In void abstractions.'

                  'Hypothesise:
If be a people which began
Without impediment, or let
From any ruling which foreran;
Even striving all things to forget
But this—the excellence of man
Left to himself, his natural bent,
His own devices and intent;
And if, in satire of the heaven,
A world, a new world have been given
For stage whereon to deploy the event;
If such a people be—well, well,
One hears the kettledrums of hell!
Exemplary act awaits its place
In drama of the human race.'

    'Is such act certain?' Rolfe here ran;
'Not much is certain.'

                'God is—man.
The human nature, the divine—
Have both been proved by many a sign.
'Tis no astrologer and star.
The world has now so old become,
Historic memory goes so far
Backward through long defiles of doom;

Whoso consults it honestly
That mind grows prescient in degree;
For man, like God, abides the same
Always, through all variety
Of woven garments to the frame.'

    'Yes, God is God, and men are men,
For ever and for aye. What then? . . .
But leave this: the New World's the theme,
Here, to oppose your dark extreme . . .
Those waste-weirs which the New World yields
To inland freshets—the free vents
Supplied to turbid elements;
The vast reserves—the untried fields;
These long shall keep off and delay
The class-war, rich-and-poor-man fray
Of history. From that alone
Can serious trouble spring. Even that
Itself, this good result may own—
The first firm founding of the state.'

    Here ending, with a watchful air
Inquisitive, Rolfe waited him.
And Ungar:

        'True heart do ye bear
In this discussion? or but trim
To draw my monomania out,
For monomania, past doubt,
Some of ye deem it. Yet I'll on.
Yours seems a reasonable tone;
But in the New World things make haste:
Not only men, the *state* lives fast—
Fast breeds the pregnant eggs and shells,
The slumberous combustibles
Sure to explode. 'Twill come, 'twill come!

One demagogue can trouble much:
How of a hundred thousand such?
And universal suffrage lent
To back them with brute element
Overwhelming? What shall bind these seas
Of rival sharp communities
Unchristianised? Yea, but 'twill come!'
   'What come?'
                'Your Thirty Years (of) War.'
   'Should fortune's favourable star
Avert it?'
         'Fortune? nay, 'tis doom.'
'Then what comes after? spasms but tend
Ever, at last, to quiet.'
          'Know,
Whatever happen in the end,
Be sure 'twill yield to one and all
New confirmation of the fall
Of Adam. Sequel may ensue,
Indeed, whose germs one now may view:
Myriads playing pygmy parts—
Debased into equality:
In glut of all material arts
A civic barbarism may be:
Man disennobled—brutalised
By popular science—atheised
Into a smatterer——'
         'Oh, oh!'
   'Yet knowing all self need to know
In self's base little fallacy;
Dead level or rank commonplace:
An Anglo-Saxon China, see,

May on your vast plains shame the race
In the Dark Ages of Democracy.'

 America!
   In stilled estate,
On him, half-brother and co-mate—
In silence, and with vision dim
Rolfe, Vine, and Clarel gazed on him;
They gazed, nor one of them found heart
To upbraid the crotchet of his smart . . .
Nor dull they were in honest tone
To some misgivings of their own:
They felt how far beyond the scope
Of elder Europe's saddest thought
Might be the New World's sudden brought
In youth to share old age's pains—
To feel the arrest of hope's advance,
And squandered last inheritance;
And cry—'To Terminus build fanes!
Columbus ended earth's romance:
No New World to mankind remains!'

151   *The Maldive Shark*

ABOUT the Shark, phlegmatical one,
Pale sot of the Maldive sea,
The sleek little pilot-fish, azure and slim,
How alert in attendance be.
From his saw-pit of mouth, from his charnel of maw
They have nothing of harm to dread,

But liquidly glide on his ghastly flank
Or before his Gorgonian head;
Or lurk in the port of serrated teeth
In white triple tiers of glittering gates,
And there find a haven when peril's abroad,
An asylum in jaws of the Fates!
They are friends; and friendly they guide him to prey,
Yet never partake of the treat—
Eyes and brains to the dotard lethargic and dull,
Pale ravener of horrible meat.

HENRY TIMROD

1828-1867

152   *Ethnogenesis*

*Written During the Meeting of the First Southern
Congress, at Montgomery, February,* 1861

I

Hath not the morning dawned with added light?
And shall not evening call another star
Out of the infinite regions of the night,
To mark this day in Heaven? At last, we are
A nation among nations; and the world
Shall soon behold in many a distant port
        Another flag unfurled!
Now, come what may, whose favor need we court?
And, under God, whose thunder need we fear?
        Thank Him who placed us here

Beneath so kind a sky—the very sun
Takes part with us; and on our errands run
All breezes of the ocean; dew and rain
Do noiseless battle for us; and the Year,
And all the gentle daughters in her train,
March in our ranks, and in our service wield
      Long spears of golden grain!
A yellow blossom as her fairy shield,
June flings her azure banner to the wind,
  While in the order of their birth
Her sisters pass, and many an ample field
Grows white beneath their steps, till now, behold,
      Its endless sheets unfold
THE SNOW OF SOUTHERN SUMMERS! Let the earth
Rejoice! beneath those fleeces soft and warm
      Our happy land shall sleep
      In a repose as deep
  As if we lay intrenched behind
Whole leagues of Russian ice and Arctic storm!

II

And what if, mad with wrongs themselves have wrought,
      In their own treachery caught,
      By their own fears made bold,
      And leagued with him of old,
Who long since in the limits of the North
Set up his evil throne, and warred with God—
What if, both mad and blinded in their rage,
Our foes should fling us down their mortal gage,
And with a hostile step profane our sod!
We shall not shrink, my brothers, but go forth
To meet them, marshaled by the Lord of Hosts,
And overshadowed by the mighty ghosts

Of Moultrie and of Eutaw—who shall foil
Auxiliars such as these? Nor these alone,
    But every stock and stone
    Shall help us; but the very soil,
And all the generous wealth it gives to toil,
And all for which we love our noble land,
Shall fight beside, and through us; sea and strand,
    The heart of woman, and her hand,
Tree, fruit, and flower, and every influence,
    Gentle, or grave, or grand;
    The winds in our defence
Shall seem to blow; to us the hills shall lend
    Their firmness and their calm;
And in our stiffened sinews we shall blend
    The strength of pine and palm!

III

Nor would we shun the battle-ground,
    Though weak as we are strong;
Call up the clashing elements around,
    And test the right and wrong!
On one side, creeds that dare to teach
What Christ and Paul refrained to preach;
Codes built upon a broken pledge,
And Charity that whets a poniard's edge;
Fair schemes that leave the neighboring poor
To starve and shiver at the schemer's door,
While in the world's most liberal ranks enrolled,
He turns some vast philanthropy to gold;
Religion, taking every mortal form
But that a pure and Christian faith makes warm,
Where not to vile fanatic passion urged,
Or not in vague philosophies submerged,

Repulsive with all Pharisaic leaven,
And making laws to stay the laws of Heaven!
And on the other, scorn of sordid gain,
Unblemished honor, truth without a stain,
Faith, justice, reverence, charitable wealth,
And, for the poor and humble, laws which give.
Not the mean right to buy the right to live,
      But life, and home, and health!
To doubt the end were want of trust in God,
      Who, if he has decreed
    That we must pass a redder sea
Than that which rang to Miriam's holy glee,
      Will surely raise at need
      A Moses with his rod!

IV

But let our fears—if fears we have—be still,
And turn us to the future! Could we climb
Some mighty Alp, and view the coming time,
    The rapturous sight would fill
      Our eyes with happy tears!
Not only for the glories which the years
Shall bring us; not for lands from sea to sea,
And wealth, and power, and peace, though these shall be;
But for the distant peoples we shall bless,
And the hushed murmurs of a world's distress:
For, to give labor to the poor,
      The whole sad planet o'er,
And save from want and crime the humblest door,
Is one among the many ends for which
      God makes us great and rich!
The hour perchance is not yet wholly ripe
When all shall own it, but the type

Whereby we shall be known in every land
Is that vast gulf which lips our Southern strand,
And through the cold, untempered ocean pours
Its genial streams, that far off Arctic shores
May sometimes catch upon the softened breeze
Strange tropic warmth and hints of summer seas.

153 *Charleston*

CALM as that second summer which precedes
  The first fall of the snow,
In the broad sunlight of heroic deeds,
  The City bides the foe.

As yet, behind their ramparts stern and proud,
  Her bolted thunders sleep—
Dark Sumter, like a battlemented cloud,
  Looms o'er the solemn deep.

No Calpe frowns from lofty cliff or scar
  To guard the holy strand;
But Moultrie holds in leash her dogs of war
  Above the level sand.

And down the dunes a thousand guns lie couched,
  Unseen, beside the flood—
Like tigers in some Orient jungle crouched
  That wait and watch for blood.

Meanwhile, through streets still echoing with trade,
  Walk grave and thoughtful men,

Whose hands may one day wield the patriot's blade
   As lightly as the pen.

And maidens, with such eyes as would grow dim
   Over a bleeding hound,
Seem each one to have caught the strength of him
   Whose sword she sadly bound.

Thus girt without and garrisoned at home,
   Day patient following day,
Old Charleston looks from roof, and spire, and dome,
   Across her tranquil bay.

Ships, through a hundred foes, from Saxon lands
   And spicy Indian ports,
Bring Saxon steel and iron to her hands,
   And Summer to her courts.

But still, along yon dim Atlantic line,
   The only hostile smoke
Creeps like a harmless mist above the brine,
   From some frail, floating oak.

Shall the Spring dawn, and she still clad in smiles,
   And with an unscathed brow,
Rest in the strong arms of her palm-crowned isles,
   As fair and free as now?

We know not; in the temple of the Fates
   God has inscribed her doom;
And, all untroubled in her faith, she waits
   The triumph or the tomb.

154   *Ode*

*Sung on the Occasion of Decorating the Graves of
the Confederate Dead, at Magnolia Cemetery,
Charleston, S. C., 1867*

I

SLEEP sweetly in your humble graves,
    Sleep, martyrs of a fallen cause;
Though yet no marble column craves
    The pilgrim here to pause.

II

In seeds of laurel in the earth
    The blossom of your fame is blown,
And somewhere, waiting for its birth,
    The shaft is in the stone!

III

Meanwhile, behalf the tardy years
    Which keep in trust your storied tombs,
Behold! your sisters bring their tears,
    And these memorial blooms.

IV

Small tributes! but your shades will smile
    More proudly on these wreaths to-day,
Than when some cannon-moulded pile
    Shall overlook this bay.

V

Stoop, angels, hither from the skies!
    There is no holier spot of ground
Than where defeated valor lies,
    By mourning beauty crowned!

EMILY DICKINSON

1830-1886

155   '*This is my letter to the world*'

THIS is my letter to the world,
  That never wrote to me,—
The simple news that Nature told,
  With tender majesty.

Her message is committed
  To hands I cannot see;
For love of her, sweet countrymen,
  Judge tenderly of me!

156   '*I dwell in Possibility*'

I DWELL in Possibility
A fairer house than Prose,
More numerous of windows,
Superior of doors.

Of chambers, as the cedars—
Impregnable of eye;
And for an everlasting roof
The gables of the sky.

Of visitors—the fairest—
For occupation—this—
The spreading wide my narrow hands
To gather Paradise.

157   *'Success is counted sweetest'*

SUCCESS is counted sweetest
By those who ne'er succeed.
To comprehend a nectar
Requires sorest need.

Not one of all the purple host
Who took the flag to-day
Can tell the definition,
So clear, of victory,

As he, defeated, dying,
On whose forbidden ear
The distant strains of triumph
Break, agonized and clear.

158   *'The heart asks pleasure first'*

THE heart asks pleasure first,
And then, excuse from pain;
And then, those little anodynes
That deaden suffering;

And then, to go to sleep;
And then, if it should be
The will of its Inquisitor,
The liberty to die.

159 *'Much madness is divinest sense'*

MUCH madness is divinest sense
To a discerning eye;
Much sense the starkest madness.
'T is the majority
In this, as all, prevails.
Assent, and you are sane;
Demur,—you're straightway dangerous,
And handled with a chain.

160 *'I asked no other thing'*

I ASKED no other thing,
No other was denied.
I offered Being for it;
The mighty merchant smiled.

Brazil? He twirled a button,
Without a glance my way:
'But, madam, is there nothing else
That we can show to-day?'

161   *'The soul selects her own society'*

THE soul selects her own society,
Then shuts the door;
On her divine majority
Obtrude no more.

Unmoved, she notes the chariot's pausing
At her low gate;
Unmoved, an emperor is kneeling
Upon her mat.

I've known her from an ample nation
Choose one;
Then close the valves of her attention
Like stone.

162   *'Some things that fly there be'*

SOME things that fly there be,—
Birds, hours, the bumble-bee:
Of these no elegy.

Some things that stay there be,—
Grief, hills, eternity:
Nor this behooveth me.

There are, that resting, rise.
Can I expound the skies?
How still the riddle lies!

163   *'I know some lonely houses off
the road'*

I KNOW some lonely houses off the road
A robber'd like the look of,—
Wooden barred,
And windows hanging low,
Inviting to
A portico,

Where two could creep:
One hand the tools,
The other peep
To make sure all's asleep.
Old-fashioned eyes,
Not easy to surprise!

How orderly the kitchen'd look by night,
With just a clock,—
But they could gag the tick,
And mice won't bark;
And so the walls don't tell,
None will.

A pair of spectacles ajar just stir—
An almanac's aware.
Was it the mat winked,
Or a nervous star?
The moon slides down the stair
To see who's there.

417

There's plunder,—where?
Tankard, or spoon,
Earring, or stone,
A watch, some ancient brooch
To match the grandmamma,
Staid sleeping there.

Day rattles, too,
Stealth's slow;
The sun has got as far
As the third sycamore.
Screams chanticleer,
'Who's there?'

And echoes, trains away,
Sneer—'Where?'
While the old couple, just astir,
Think that the sunrise left the door ajar!

164   *'I taste a liquor never brewed'*

I TASTE a liquor never brewed,
From tankards scooped in pearl;
Not all the vats upon the Rhine
Yield such an alcohol!

Inebriate of air am I,
And debauchee of dew,
Reeling, through endless summer days,
From inns of molten blue.

When landlords turn the drunken bee
Out of the foxglove's door,
When butterflies renounce their drams,
I shall but drink the more!

Till seraphs swing their snowy hats,
And saints to windows run,
To see the little tippler
Leaning against the sun!

165   *'Hope is the thing with feathers'*

HOPE is the thing with feathers
That perches in the soul,
And sings the tune without the words,
And never stops at all,

And sweetest in the gale is heard;
And sore must be the storm
That could abash the little bird
That kept so many warm.

I've heard it in the chillest land,
And on the strangest sea;
Yet, never, in extremity,
It asked a crumb of me.

166 *'The thought beneath so slight a film'*

THE thought beneath so slight a film
Is more distinctly seen,—
As laces just reveal the surge,
Or mists the Apennine.

167 *'I like to see it lap the miles'*

I LIKE to see it lap the miles,
And lick the valleys up,
And stop to feed itself at tanks;
And then, prodigious, step

Around a pile of mountains,
And, supercilious, peer
In shanties by the sides of roads;
And then a quarry pare

To fit its sides, and crawl between,
Complaining all the while
In horrid, hooting stanza;
Then chase itself down hill

And neigh like Boanerges;
Then, punctual as a star,
Stop—docile and omnipotent—
At its own stable door.

168   *'Faith is a fine invention'*

FAITH is a fine invention
For gentlemen who see;
But microscopes are prudent
In an emergency!

169   *'I years had been from home'*

I YEARS had been from home,
And now, before the door
I dared not open, lest a face
I never saw before

Stare vacant into mine
And ask my business there.
My business,—just a life I left,
Was such still dwelling there?

I fumbled at my nerve,
I scanned the windows near;
The silence like an ocean rolled,
And broke against my ear.

I laughed a wooden laugh
That I could fear a door,
Who danger and the dead had faced,
But never quaked before.

I fitted to the latch
My hand, with trembling care,

Lest back the awful door should spring,
And leave me standing there.

I moved my fingers off
As cautiously as glass,
And held my ears, and like a thief
Fled gasping from the house.

170   'The first Day's Night had come'

THE first Day's Night had come—
And, grateful that a thing
So terrible had been endured,
I told my Soul to sing.

She said her strings were snapt,
Her bow to atoms blown;
And so, to mend her, gave me work
Until another morn.

And then a Day as huge
As Yesterday in pairs
Unrolled its horror on my face—
Until it blocked my eyes.

171   'My life closed twice before its close'

MY life closed twice before its close;
It yet remains to see

If Immortality unveil
  A third event to me,

So huge, so hopeless to conceive,
  As these that twice befell.
Parting is all we know of heaven,
  And all we need of hell.

172   *'I felt a cleavage in my mind'*

I FELT a cleavage in my mind
  As if my brain had split;
I tried to match it, seam by seam,
  But could not make them fit.

The thought behind I strove to join
  Unto the thought before,
But sequence ravelled out of reach
  Like balls upon a floor.

173   *'It dropped so low in my regard'*

IT dropped so low in my regard
  I heard it hit the ground,
And go to pieces on the stones
  At bottom of my mind;

Yet blamed the fate that fractured, less
  Than I reviled myself
For entertaining plated wares
  Upon my silver shelf.

EMILY DICKINSON

174   *'The brain is wider than the sky'*

THE brain is wider than the sky,
   For, put them side by side,
The one the other will include
   With ease, and you beside.

The brain is deeper than the sea,
   For, hold them, blue to blue,
The one the other will absorb,
   As sponges, buckets do.

The brain is just the weight of God,
   For, lift them, pound for pound,
And they will differ, if they do,
   As syllable from sound.

175   *'At half-past three a single bird'*

AT half-past three a single bird
Unto a silent sky
Propounded but a single term
Of cautious melody.

At half-past four, experiment
Had subjugated test,
And lo! her silver principle
Supplanted all the rest.

At half-past seven, element
Nor implement was seen,
And place was where the presence was,
Circumference between.

176   *'An altered look about the hills'*

AN altered look about the hills;
A Tyrian light the village fills;
A wider sunrise in the dawn;
A deeper twilight on the lawn;
A print of a vermilion foot;
A purple finger on the slope;
A flippant fly upon the pane;
A spider at his trade again;

An added strut in chanticleer;
A flower expected everywhere;
An axe shrill singing in the woods;
Fern-odors on untravelled roads,—
All this, and more I cannot tell,
A furtive look you know as well,
And Nicodemus' mystery
Receives its annual reply.

177   *'A bird came down the walk'*

A BIRD came down the walk:
He did not know I saw;
He bit an angle-worm in halves
And ate the fellow, raw.

And then he drank a dew
From a convenient grass,
And then hopped sidewise to the wall
To let a beetle pass.

He glanced with rapid eyes
That hurried all abroad,—
They looked like frightened beads, I thought
He stirred his velvet head

Like one in danger; cautious,
I offered him a crumb,
And he unrolled his feathers
And rowed him softer home

Than oars divide the ocean,
Too silver for a seam,
Or butterflies, off banks of noon,
Leap, plashless, as they swim.

178   *'A narrow fellow in the grass'*

A NARROW fellow in the grass
Occasionally rides;
You may have met him,—did you not?
His notice sudden is.

The grass divides as with a comb,
A spotted shaft is seen;
And then it closes at your feet
And opens further on.

He likes a boggy acre,
A floor too cool for corn.
Yet when a child, and barefoot,
I more than once, at morn,

Have passed, I thought, a whip-lash
Unbraiding in the sun,—
When, stooping to secure it,
It wrinkled, and was gone.

Several of nature's people
I know, and they know me;
I feel for them a transport
Of cordiality;

But never met this fellow,
Attended or alone,
Without a tighter breathing,
And zero at the bone.

179   *'There came a wind like a bugle'*

THERE came a wind like a bugle;
It quivered through the grass,
And a green chill upon the heat
So ominous did pass
We barred the windows and the doors
As from an emerald ghost;
The doom's electric moccasin
That very instant passed.

On a strange mob of panting trees,
And fences fled away,
And rivers where the houses ran
The living looked that day.
The bell within the steeple wild
The flying tidings whirled.
How much can come
And much can go,
And yet abide the world!

180   *'Besides the autumn poets sing'*

BESIDES the autumn poets sing,
A few prosaic days
A little this side of the snow
And that side of the haze.

A few incisive mornings,
A few ascetic eves,—
Gone Mr. Bryant's golden-rod,
And Mr. Thomson's sheaves.

Still is the bustle in the brook,
Sealed are the spicy valves;
Mesmeric fingers softly touch
The eyes of many elves.

Perhaps a squirrel may remain,
My sentiments to share.
Grant me, O Lord, a sunny mind,
Thy windy will to bear!

181   *'Presentiment is that long shadow*
on the lawn'

PRESENTIMENT is that long shadow on the lawn
Indicative that suns go down;
The notice to the startled grass
That darkness is about to pass.

182   *'The sky is low, the clouds are mean'*

THE sky is low, the clouds are mean,
A travelling flake of snow
Across a barn or through a rut
Debates if it will go.

A narrow wind complains all day
How some one treated him;
Nature, like us, is sometimes caught
Without her diadem.

183   *'There's a certain slant of light'*

THERE'S a certain slant of light,
On winter afternoons,
That oppresses, like the weight
Of cathedral tunes.

Heavenly hurt it gives us;
We can find no scar,
But internal difference
Where the meanings are.

None may teach it anything,
'T is the seal, despair,—
An imperial affliction
Sent us of the air.

When it comes, the landscape listens,
Shadows hold their breath;
When it goes, 't is like the distance
On the look of death.

184   *'Glass was the street'*

GLASS was the street, in tinsel peril
Tree and traveler stood;
Filled was the air with merry venture,
Hearty with boys the road;

Shot the lithe sleds like shod vibrations
Emphasized and gone—-
It is the past's supreme italic
Makes the present mean.

'A light exists in spring'

A LIGHT exists in spring
　　Not present on the year
At any other period.
　　When March is scarcely here

A color stands abroad
　　On solitary hills
That science cannot overtake,
　　But human nature *feels*.

It waits upon the lawn;
　　It shows the furthest tree
Upon the furthest slope we know;
　　It almost speaks to me.

Then, as horizons step,
　　Or noons report away,
Without the formula of sound,
　　It passes, and we stay:

A quality of loss
　　Affecting our content,
As trade had suddenly encroached
　　Upon a sacrament.

186   *'To make a prairie'*

To make a prairie it takes a clover
    and one bee,—
One clover, and a bee,
And revery.
The revery alone will do
If bees are few.

187   *'There is a morn by men unseen'*

THERE is a morn by men unseen,
Whose maids upon remoter green
Keep their seraphic May,
And all day long, with dance and game
And gambol I may never name,
Employ their holiday.

Here to light measure move the feet
Which walk no more the village street
Nor by the wood are found;
Here are the birds that sought the sun
When last year's distaff idle hung
And summer's brows were bound.

Ne'er saw I such a wondrous scene,
Ne'er such a ring on such a green,
Nor so serene array—
As if the stars some summer night

Should swing their cups of chrysolite
And revel till the day.

Like thee to dance, like thee to sing,
People upon that mystic green,
I ask each new May morn.
I wait thy far, fantastic bells
Announcing me in other dells
Unto the different dawn!

188   *'Elysium is as far as to'*

ELYSIUM is as far as to
The very nearest room,
If in that room a friend await
Felicity or doom.

What fortitude the soul contains,
That it can so endure
The accent of a coming foot,
The opening of a door!

189   *'If you were coming in the fall'*

IF you were coming in the fall,
I'd brush the summer by
With half a smile and half a spurn,
As housewives do a fly.

433

If I could see you in a year,
I'd wind the months in balls,
And put them each in separate drawers,
Until their time befalls.

If only centuries delayed,
I'd count them on my hand,
Subtracting till my fingers dropped
Into Van Diemen's land.

If certain, when this life was out,
That yours and mine should be,
I'd toss it yonder like a rind,
And taste eternity.

But now, all ignorant of the length
Of time's uncertain wing,
It goads me, like the goblin bee,
That will not state its sting.

190   *'I cannot live with you'*

I CANNOT live with you,
It would be life,
And life is over there
Behind the shelf

The sexton keeps the key to,
Putting up
Our life, his porcelain,
Like a cup

Discarded of the housewife,
Quaint or broken;
A newer Sèvres pleases,
Old ones crack.

I could not die with you,
For one must wait
To shut the other's gaze down,—
You could not.

And I, could I stand by
And see you freeze,
Without my right of frost,
Death's privilege?

Nor could I rise with you,
Because your face
Would put out Jesus',
That new grace

Glow plain and foreign
On my homesick eye,
Except that you, than he
Shone closer by.

They'd judge us—how?
For you served Heaven, you know,
Or sought to;
I could not,

Because you saturated sight,
And I had no more eyes
For sordid excellence
As Paradise.

And were you lost, I would be,
Though my name
Rang loudest
On the heavenly fame.

And were you saved,
And I condemned to be
Where you were not,
That self were hell to me.

So we must keep apart,
You there, I here,
With just the door ajar
That oceans are,
And prayer,
And that pale sustenance,
Despair!

191   *'Wild nights! Wild nights!'*

WILD nights! Wild nights!
Were I with thee,
Wild nights should be
Our luxury!

Futile the winds
To a heart in port,—
Done with the compass,
Done with the chart.

Rowing in Eden!
Ah! the sea!
Might I but moor
To-night in thee!

192   *'Safe in their alabaster chambers'*

SAFE in their alabaster chambers,
Untouched by morning and untouched by noon,
Sleep the meek members of the resurrection,
Rafter of satin, and roof of stone.

Light laughs the breeze in her castle of sunshine;
Babbles the bee in a stolid ear;
Pipe the sweet birds in ignorant cadence,—
Ah, what sagacity perished here!

Grand go the years in the crescent above them;
Worlds scoop their arcs, and firmaments row,
Diadems drop and Doges surrender,
Soundless as dots on a disk of snow.

193   *'The last night that she lived'*

THE last night that she lived,
It was a common night,
Except the dying; this to us
Made nature different.

We noticed smallest things,—
Things overlooked before,
By this great light upon our minds
Italicized, as 't were.

That others could exist
While she must finish quite,
A jealousy for her arose
So nearly infinite.

We waited while she passed;
It was a narrow time,
Too jostled were our souls to speak,
At length the notice came.

She mentioned, and forgot;
Then lightly as a reed
Bent to the water, shivered scarce,
Consented, and was dead.

And we, we placed the hair,
And drew the head erect;
And then an awful leisure was,
Our faith to regulate.

194   *'The bustle in a house'*

THE bustle in a house
The morning after death
Is solemnest of industries
Enacted upon earth,—

The sweeping up the heart,
And putting love away
We shall not want to use again
Until eternity.

195 '*Because I could not stop for Death*'

BECAUSE I could not stop for Death,
He kindly stopped for me;
The carriage held but just ourselves
And Immortality.

We slowly drove, he knew no haste,
And I had put away
My labor, and my leisure too,
For his civility.

We passed the school where children played
At wrestling in a ring;
We passed the fields of gazing grain,
We passed the setting sun.

We paused before a house that seemed
A swelling of the ground;
The roof was scarcely visible,
The cornice but a mound.

Since then 't is centuries; but each
Feels shorter than the day
I first surmised the horses' heads
Were toward eternity.

196 *'Ample make this bed'*

AMPLE make this bed.
Make this bed with awe;
In it wait till judgment break
Excellent and fair.

Be its mattress straight,
Be its pillow round;
Let no sunrise' yellow noise
Interrupt this ground.

197 *'I felt a funeral in my brain'*

I FELT a funeral in my brain,
    And mourners, to and fro,
Kept treading, treading, till it seemed
    That sense was breaking through.

And when they all were seated,
    A service like a drum
Kept beating, beating, till I thought
    My mind was going numb.

And then I heard them lift a box,
    And creak across my soul
With those same boots of lead, again.
    Then space began to toll

As all the heavens were a bell,
    And Being but an ear,
And I and silence some strange race,
    Wrecked, solitary, here.

198   *'I heard a fly buzz when I died'*

I HEARD a fly buzz when I died;
The stillness in the room
Was like the stillness in the air
Between the heaves of storm.

The eyes around had wrung them dry,
And breaths were gathering firm
For that last onset, when the king
Be witnessed in the room.

I willed my keepsakes, signed away
What portion of me be
Assignable—and then it was
There interposed a fly,

With blue, uncertain, stumbling buzz,
Between the light and me;
And then the windows failed, and then
I could not see to see.

199   *'Lightly stepped a yellow star'*

LIGHTLY stepped a yellow star
To its lofty place,

Loosed the Moon her silver hat
From her lustral face.
All of evening softly lit
As an astral hall—
'Father,' I observed to Heaven,
'You are punctual.'

200 *'This quiet Dust was Gentlemen and
Ladies'*

THIS quiet Dust was Gentlemen and Ladies,
  And Lads and Girls;
Was laughter and ability and sighing,
  And frocks and curls.

This passive place a Summer's nimble mansion,
  Where Bloom and Bees
Fulfilled their Oriental Circuit,
  Then ceased like these.

201 *'In winter, in my room'*

IN winter, in my room,
I came upon a worm,
Pink, lank, and warm.
But as he was a worm
And worms presume,
Not quite with him at home—
Secured him by a string
To something neighboring,
And went along.

442

A trifle afterward
A thing occurred,
I'd not believe it if I heard—
But state with creeping blood;
A snake, with mottles rare,
Surveyed my chamber floor,
In feature as the worm before,
But ringed with power.
The very string
With which I tied him, too,
When he was mean and new,
That string was there.

I shrank—'How fair you are!'
Propitiation's claw—
'Afraid,' he hissed,
'Of me?'
'No cordiality?'
He fathomed me.
Then, to a rhythm slim
Secreted in his form,
As patterns swim,
Projected him.

That time I flew,
Both eyes his way,
Lest he pursue—
Nor ever ceased to run,
Till, in a distant town,
Towns on from mine—
I sat me down;
This was a dream.

202   *'After a hundred years'*

AFTER a hundred years
Nobody knows the place,—
Agony, that enacted there,
Motionless as peace.

Weeds triumphant ranged,
Strangers strolled and spelled
At the lone orthography
Of the elder dead.

Winds of summer fields
Recollect the way,—
Instinct picking up the key
Dropped by memory.

SIDNEY LANIER

1842-1881

203   *The Raven Days*

OUR hearths are gone out, and our hearts are broken,
     And but the ghosts of homes to us remain,
And ghostly eyes and hollow sighs give token
     From friend to friend of an unspoken pain.

O, Raven Days, dark Raven Days of sorrow,
     Bring to us, in your whetted ivory beaks,

Some sign out of the far land of To-morrow,
  Some strip of sea-green dawn, some orange streaks.

Ye float in dusky files, forever croaking—
  Ye chill our manhood with your dreary shade.
Pale, in the dark, not even God invoking,
  We lie in chains, too weak to be afraid.

O Raven Days, dark Raven Days of sorrow,
  Will ever any warm light come again?
Will ever the lit mountains of To-morrow
  Begin to gleam across the mournful plain?

204   *From the Flats*

W HAT heartache—ne'er a hill!
Inexorable, vapid, vague, and chill
The drear sand-levels drain my spirit low.
With one poor word they tell me all they know;
Whereat their stupid tongues, to tease my pain,
Do drawl it o'er again and o'er again.
They hurt my heart with griefs I cannot name:
    Always the same, the same.

    Nature hath no surprise,
No ambuscade of beauty 'gainst mine eyes
From brake or lurking dell or deep defile;
No humors, frolic forms—this mile, that mile;
No rich reserves or happy-valley hopes
Beyond the bends of roads, the distant slopes.
Her fancy fails, her wild is all run tame:
    Ever the same, the same.

Oh, might I through these tears
But glimpse some hill my Georgia high uprears,
Where white the quartz and pink the pebble shine,
The hickory heavenward strives, the muscadine
Swings o'er the slope, the oak's far-falling shade
Darkens the dogwood in the bottom glade,
And down the hollow from a ferny nook
Bright leaps a living brook!

205   *The Marshes of Glynn*

GLOOMS of the live-oaks, beautiful-braided **and**
woven
With intricate shades of the vines that myriad-cloven
Clamber the forks of the multiform boughs,—
Emerald twilights,—
Virginal shy lights,
Wrought of the leaves to allure to the whisper of vows,
When lovers pace timidly down through the green
colonnades
Of the dim sweet woods, of the dear dark woods,
Of the heavenly woods and glades,
That run to the radiant marginal sand-beach within
The wide sea-marshes of Glynn;—

Beautiful glooms, soft dusks in the noon-day fire,—
Wildwood privacies, closets of lone desire,
Chamber from chamber parted with wavering arras of
leaves,—
Cells for the passionate pleasure of prayer to the soul that
grieves,

Pure with a sense of the passing of saints through the wood,
Cool for the dutiful weighing of ill with good;—

O braided dusks of the oak and woven shades of the vine,
While the riotous noon-day sun of the June-day long did shine,
Ye held me fast in your heart and I held you fast in mine;
But now when the noon is no more, and riot is rest,
And the sun is a-wait at the ponderous gate of the West,
And the slant yellow beam down the wood-aisle doth seem
Like a lane into heaven that leads from a dream,—
Ay, now, when my soul all day hath drunken the soul of the oak,
And my heart is at ease from men, and the wearisome sound of the stroke
Of the scythe of time and the trowel of trade is low,
And belief overmasters doubt, and I know that I know,
And my spirit is grown to a lordly great compass within,
That the length and the breadth and the sweep of the marshes of Glynn
Will work me no fear like the fear they have wrought me of yore
When length was fatigue, and when breadth was but bitterness sore,
And when terror and shrinking and dreary unnamable pain
Drew over me out of the merciless miles of the plain,—
Oh, now, unafraid, I am fain to face
The vast sweet visage of space.

To the edge of the wood I am drawn, I am drawn,
Where the gray beach glimmering runs, as a belt of
the dawn,
For a mete and a mark
To the forest-dark:—
So:
Affable live-oak, leaning low,—
Thus—with your favor—soft, with a reverent hand,
(Not lightly touching your person, Lord of the land!)
Bending your beauty aside, with a step I stand
On the firm-packed sand,
Free
By a world of marsh that borders a world of sea.
Sinuous southward and sinuous northward the shimmer-
ing band
Of the sand-beach fastens the fringe of the marsh to the
folds of the land.
Inward and outward to northward and southward the
beach-lines linger and curl
As a silver-wrought garment that clings to and follows the
firm sweet limbs of a girl.
Vanishing, swerving, evermore curving again into sight,
Softly the sand-beach wavers away to a dim gray loop-
ing of light.
And what if behind me to westward the wall of the
woods stands high?
The world lies east: how ample, the marsh and the sea
and the sky!
A league and a league of marsh-grass, waist-high, broad
in the blade,
Green, and all of a height, and unflecked with a light
or a shade,

Stretch leisurely off, in a pleasant plain,
To the terminal blue of the main.

Oh, what is abroad in the marsh and the terminal sea?
Somehow my soul seems suddenly free
From the weighing of fate and the sad discussion of
sin,
By the length and the breadth and the sweep of the
marshes of Glynn.
Ye marshes, how candid and simple and nothing-withhold-
ing and free
Ye publish yourselves to the sky and offer yourselves to
the sea!
Tolerant plains, that suffer the sea and the rains and the
sun,
Ye spread and span like the catholic man who hath
mightily won
God out of knowledge and good out of infinite pain
And sight out of blindness and purity out of a stain.

As the marsh-hen secretly builds on the watery sod,
Behold I will build me a nest on the greatness of God:
I will fly in the greatness of God as the marsh-hen flies
In the freedom that fills all the space 'twixt the marsh
and the skies:
By so many roots as the marsh-grass sends in the sod
I will heartily lay me a-hold on the greatness of God.
Oh, like to the greatness of God is the greatness within
The range of the marshes, the liberal marshes of Glynn.

And the sea lends large, as the marsh: lo, out of his plenty
the sea
Pours fast: full soon the time of the flood-tide must be:

449

Look how the grace of the sea doth go
About and about through the intricate channels that
flow
Here and there,
Everywhere,
Till his waters have flooded the uttermost creeks and the
low-lying lanes,
And the marsh is meshed with a million veins,
That like as with rosy and silvery essences flow
In the rose-and-silver evening glow.
Farewell, my lord Sun!
The creeks overflow: a thousand rivulets run
'Twixt the roots of the sod; the blades of the marsh-
grass stir;
Passeth a hurrying sound of wings that westward whirr;
Passeth, and all is still; and the currents cease to run;
And the sea and the marsh are one.
How still the plains of the waters be!
The tide is in his ecstasy.
The tide is at his highest height:
And it is night.

And now from the Vast of the Lord will the waters of
sleep
Roll in on the souls of men,
But who will reveal to our waking ken
The forms that swim and the shapes that creep
Under the waters of sleep?
And I would I could know what swimmeth below when
the tide comes in
On the length and the breadth of the marvellous
marshes of Glynn.

206 *A Ballad of Trees and the Master*

INTO the woods my Master went,
  Clean forspent, forspent.
Into the woods my Master came,
  Forspent with love and shame.
But the olives they were not blind to Him,
The little gray leaves were kind to Him:
The thorn-tree had a mind to Him
  When into the woods He came.

Out of the woods my Master went,
  And He was well content.
Out of the woods my Master came,
  Content with death and shame.
When Death and Shame would woo Him last,
From under the trees they drew Him last:
'Twas on a tree they slew Him—last
  When out of the woods He came.

207 *Struggle*

MY Soul is like the oar that momently
  Dies in a desperate stress beneath the wave,
Then glitters out again and sweeps the sea:
  Each second I'm new-born from some new grave.

WILLIAM VAUGHN MOODY

208   *Gloucester Moors*

A MILE behind is Gloucester town
Where the fishing fleets put in,
A mile ahead the land dips down
And the woods and farms begin.
Here, where the moors stretch free
In the high blue afternoon,
Are the marching sun and talking sea,
And the racing winds that wheel and flee
On the flying heels of June.

Jill-o'er-the-ground is purple blue,
Blue is the quaker-maid,
The wild geranium holds its dew
Long in the boulder's shade.
Wax-red hangs the cup
From the huckleberry boughs,
In barberry bells the grey moths sup,
Or where the choke-cherry lifts high up
Sweet bowls for their carouse.

Over the shelf of the sandy cove
Beach-peas blossom late.
By copse and cliff the swallows rove
Each calling to his mate.

WILLIAM VAUGHN MOODY

Seaward the sea-gulls go,
And the land-birds all are here;
That green-gold flash was a vireo,
And yonder flame where the marsh-flags grow
Was a scarlet tanager.

This earth is not the steadfast place
We landsmen build upon;
From deep to deep she varies pace,
And while she comes is gone.
Beneath my feet I feel
Her smooth bulk heave and dip;
With velvet plunge and soft upreel
She swings and steadies to her keel
Like a gallant, gallant ship.

These summer clouds she sets for sail,
The sun is her masthead light,
She tows the moon like a pinnace frail
Where her phosphor wake churns bright.
Now hid, now looming clear,
On the face of the dangerous blue
The star fleets tack and wheel and veer,
But on, but on does the old earth steer
As if her port she knew.

God, dear God! Does she know her port,
Though she goes so far about?
Or blind astray, does she make her sport
To brazen and chance it out?
I watched when her captains passed:
She were better captainless.
Men in the cabin, before the mast,

But some were reckless and some aghast,
And some sat gorged at mess.

By her battened hatch I leaned and caught
Sounds from the noisome hold,—
Cursing and sighing of souls distraught
And cries too sad to be told.
Then I strove to go down and see;
But they said, 'Thou art not of us!'
I turned to those on the deck with me
And cried, 'Give help!' But they said, 'Let be:
Our ship sails faster thus.'

Jill-o'er-the-ground is purple blue,
Blue is the quaker-maid,
The alder-clump where the brook comes through
Breeds cresses in its shade.
To be out of the moiling street
With its swelter and its sin!
Who has given to me this sweet,
And given my brother dust to eat?
And when will his wage come in?

Scattering wide or blown in ranks,
Yellow and white and brown,
Boats and boats from the fishing banks
Come home to Gloucester town.
There is cash to purse and spend,
There are wives to be embraced,
Hearts to borrow and hearts to lend,
And hearts to take and keep to the end,—
O little sails, make haste!

But thou, vast outbound ship of souls,
What harbor town for thee?
What shapes, when thy arriving tolls,
Shall crowd the banks to see?
Shall all the happy shipmates then
Stand singing brotherly?
Or shall a haggard ruthless few
Warp her over and bring her to,
While the many broken souls of men
Fester down in the slaver's pen,
And nothing to say or do?

209   *An Ode in Time of Hesitation*

(After seeing at Boston the statue of Robert Gould Shaw, killed while storming Fort Wagner, July 18, 1863, at the head of the first enlisted negro regiment, the Fifty-fourth Massachusetts.)

I

BEFORE the solemn bronze Saint Gaudens made
To thrill the heedless passer's heart with awe,
And set here in the city's talk and trade
To the good memory of Robert Shaw,
This bright March morn I stand,
And hear the distant spring come up the land;
Knowing that what I hear is not unheard
Of this boy soldier and his negro band,
For all their gaze is fixed so stern ahead,
For all the fatal rhythm of their tread.

The land they died to save from death and shame
Trembles and waits, hearing the spring's great name,
And by her pangs these resolute ghosts are stirred.

II

Through street and mall the tides of people go
Heedless; the trees upon the Common show
No hint of green; but to my listening heart
The still earth doth impart
Assurance of her jubilant emprise,
And it is clear to my long-searching eyes
That love at last has might upon the skies.
The ice is runneled on the little pond;
A telltale patter drips from off the trees;
The air is touched with southland spiceries,
As if but yesterday it tossed the frond
Of pendant mosses where the live-oaks grow
Beyond Virginia and the Carolines,
Or had its will among the fruits and vines
Of aromatic isles asleep beyond
Florida and the Gulf of Mexico.

III

Soon shall the Cape Ann children shout in glee,
Spying the arbutus, spring's dear recluse;
Hill lads at dawn shall hearken the wild goose
Go honking northward over Tennessee;
West from Oswego to Sault Sainte-Marie,
And on to where the Pictured Rocks are hung,
And yonder where, gigantic, wilful, young,
Chicago sitteth at the northwest gates,
With restless violent hands and casual tongue
Moulding her mighty fates,

456

The Lakes shall robe them in ethereal sheen;
And like a larger sea, the vital green
Of springing wheat shall vastly be outflung
Over Dakota and the prairie states.
By desert people immemorial
On Arizona's mesas shall be done
Dim rites unto the thunder and the sun;
Nor shall the primal gods lack sacrifice
More splendid, when the white Sierras call
Unto the Rockies straightway to arise
And dance before the unveiled ark of the year,
Sounding their windy cedars as for shawms,
Unrolling rivers clear
For flutter of broad phylacteries;
While Shasta signals to Alaskan seas
That watch old sluggish glaciers downward creep
To fling their icebergs thundering from the steep,
And Mariposa through the purple calms
Gazes at far Hawaii crowned with palms
Where East and West are met,—
A rich seal on the ocean's bosom set
To say that East and West are twain,
With different loss and gain:
The Lord hath sundered them; let them be sundered yet.

IV

Alas! what sounds are these that come
Sullenly over the Pacific seas,—
Sounds of ignoble battle, striking dumb
The season's half-awakened ecstasies?
Must I be humble, then,
Now when my heart hath need of pride?
Wild love falls on me from these sculptured men;

By loving much the land for which they died
I would be justified.
My spirit was away on pinions wide
To soothe in praise of her its passionate mood
And ease it of its ache of gratitude.
Too sorely heavy is the debt they lay
On me and the companions of my day.
I would remember now
My country's goodliness, make sweet her name.
Alas! what shade art thou
Of sorrow or of blame
Liftest the lyric leafage from her brow,
And pointest a slow finger at her shame?

v

Lies! lies! It cannot be! The wars we wage
Are noble, and our battles still are won
By justice for us, ere we lift the gage.
We have not sold our loftiest heritage.
The proud republic hath not stooped to cheat
And scramble in the market-place of war;
Her forehead weareth yet its solemn star.
Here is her witness: this, her perfect son,
This delicate and proud New England soul
Who leads despisèd men, with just-unshackled feet,
Up the large ways where death and glory meet,
To show all peoples that our shame is done,
That once more we are clean and spirit-whole.

vi

Crouched in the sea fog on the moaning sand
All night he lay, speaking some simple word

458

From hour to hour to the slow minds that heard,
Holding each poor life gently in his hand
And breathing on the base rejected clay
Till each dark face shone mystical and grand
Against the breaking day;
And lo, the shard the potter cast away
Was grown a fiery chalice crystal-fine
Fulfilled of the divine
Great wine of battle wrath by God's ring-finger stirred.
Then upward, where the shadowy bastion loomed
Huge on the mountain in the wet sea light,
Whence now, and now, infernal flowerage bloomed,
Bloomed, burst, and scattered down its deadly seed,—
They swept, and died like freemen on the height,
Like freemen, and like men of noble breed;
And when the battle fell away at night
By hasty and contemptuous hands were thrust
Obscurely in a common grave with him
The fair-haired keeper of their love and trust.
Now limb doth mingle with dissolvèd limb
In nature's busy old democracy
To flush the mountain laurel when she blows
Sweet by the southern sea,
And heart with crumbled heart climbs in the rose:—
The untaught hearts with the high heart that knew
This mountain fortress for no earthly hold
Of temporal quarrel, but the bastion old
Of spiritual wrong,
Built by an unjust nation sheer and strong,
Expugnable but by a nation's rue
And bowing down before that equal shrine
By all men held divine,
Whereof his band and he were the most holy sign.

VII

O bitter, bitter shade!
Wilt thou not put the scorn
And instant tragic question from thine eye?
Do thy dark brows yet crave
That swift and angry stave—
Unmeet for this desirous morn—
That I have striven, striven to evade?
Gazing on him, must I not deem they err
Whose careless lips in street and shop aver
As common tidings, deeds to make his cheek
Flush from the bronze, and his dead throat to speak?
Surely some elder singer would arise,
Whose harp hath leave to threaten and to mourn
Above this people when they go astray.
Is Whitman, the strong spirit, overworn?
Has Whittier put his yearning wrath away?
I will not and I dare not yet believe!
Though furtively the sunlight seems to grieve,
And the spring-laden breeze
Out of the gladdening west is sinister
With sounds of nameless battle overseas;
Though when we turn and question in suspense
If these things be indeed after these ways,
And what things are to follow after these,
Our fluent men of place and consequence
Fumble and fill their mouths with hollow phrase,
Or for the end-all of deep arguments
Intone their dull commercial liturgies—
I dare not yet believe! My ears are shut!
I will not hear the thin satiric praise
And muffled laughter of our enemies,

Bidding us never sheathe our valiant sword
Till we have changed our birthright for a gourd
Of wild pulse stolen from a barbarian's hut;
Showing how wise it is to cast away
The symbols of our spiritual sway,
That so our hands with better ease
May wield the driver's whip and grasp the jailer's keys.

VIII

Was it for this our fathers kept the law?
This crown shall crown their struggle and their ruth?
Are we the eagle nation Milton saw
Mewing its mighty youth,
Soon to possess the mountain winds of truth,
And be a swift familiar of the sun
Where aye before God's face his trumpets run?
Or have we but the talons and the maw,
And for the abject likeness of our heart
Shall some less lordly bird be set apart? —
Some gross-billed wader where the swamps are fat?
Some gorger in the sun? Some prowler with the bat?

IX

Ah no!
We have not fallen so.
We are our fathers' sons: let those who lead us know!
'Twas only yesterday sick Cuba's cry
Came up the tropic wind, 'Now help us, for we die!'
Then Alabama heard,
And rising, pale, to Maine and Idaho
Shouted a burning word.
Proud state with proud impassioned state conferred,

And at the lifting of a hand sprang forth,
East, west, and south, and north,
Beautiful armies. Oh, by the sweet blood and young
Shed on the awful hill slope at San Juan,
By the unforgotten names of eager boys
Who might have tasted girls' love and been stung
With the old mystic joys
And starry griefs, now the spring nights come on,
But that the heart of youth is generous,—
We charge you, ye who lead us,
Breathe on their chivalry no hint of stain!
Turn not their new-world victories to gain!
One least leaf plucked for chaffer from the bays
Of their dear praise,
One jot of their pure conquest put to hire,
The implacable republic will require;
With clamor, in the glare and gaze of noon,
Or subtly, coming as a thief at night,
But surely, very surely, slow or soon
That insult deep we deeply will requite.
Tempt not our weakness, our cupidity!
For save we let the island men go free,
Those baffled and dislaureled ghosts
Will curse us from the lamentable coasts
Where walk the frustrate dead.
The cup of trembling shall be drainèd quite,
Eaten the sour bread of astonishment,
With ashes of the hearth shall be made white
Our hair, and wailing shall be in the tent;
Then on your guiltier head
Shall our intolerable self-disdain
Wreak suddenly its anger and its pain
For manifest in that disastrous light

We shall discern the right
And do it, tardily.—O ye who lead,
Take heed!
Blindness we may forgive, but baseness we will smite.

EDWIN ARLINGTON ROBINSON
1869-1935

210   *The Children of the Night*

FOR those that never know the light,
  The darkness is a sullen thing;
And they, the Children of the Night,
  Seem lost in Fortune's winnowing.

But some are strong and some are weak,—
  And there's the story. House and home
Are shut from countless hearts that seek
  World-refuge that will never come.

And if there be no other life,
  And if there be no other chance
To weigh their sorrow and their strife
  Than in the scales of circumstance,

'T were better, ere the sun go down
  Upon the first day we embark,
In life's imbittered sea to drown,
  Than sail forever in the dark.

But if there be a soul on earth
    So blinded with its own misuse
Of man's revealed, incessant worth,
    Or worn with anguish, that it views

No light but for a mortal eye,
    No rest but of a mortal sleep,
No God but in a prophet's lie,
    No faith for 'honest doubt' to keep;

If there be nothing, good or bad,
    But chaos for a soul to trust,—
God counts it for a soul gone mad,
    And if God be God, He is just.

And if God be God, He is Love;
    And though the Dawn be still so dim,
It shows us we have played enough
    With creeds that make a fiend of Him.

There is one creed, and only one,
    That glorifies God's excellence;
So cherish, that His will be done,
    The common creed of common sense.

It is the crimson, not the gray,
    That charms the twilight of all time;
It is the promise of the day
    That makes the starry sky sublime;

It is the faith within the fear
    That holds us to the life we curse;—
So let us in ourselves revere
    The Self which is the Universe!

Let us, the Children of the Night,
    Put off the cloak that hides the scar!
Let us be Children of the Light,
    And tell the ages what we are!

211   *'Oh for a poet—for a beacon bright'*

OH for a poet—for a beacon bright
To rift this changeless glimmer of dead gray;
To spirit back the Muses, long astray,
And flush Parnassus with a newer light;
To put these little sonnet-men to flight
Who fashion, in a shrewd mechanic way,
Songs without souls, that flicker for a day,
To vanish in irrevocable night.

What does it mean, this barren age of ours?
Here are the men, the women, and the flowers,
The seasons, and the sunset, as before.
What does it mean? Shall there not one arise
To wrench one banner from the western skies,
And mark it with his name forevermore?

212   *Walt Whitman*

THE master-songs are ended, and the man
That sang them is a name. And so is God
A name; and so is love, and life, and death,

465

And everything. But we, who are too blind
To read what we have written, or what faith
Has written for us, do not understand:
We only blink, and wonder.

Last night it was the song that was the man,
But now it is the man that is the song.
We do not hear him very much to-day:
His piercing and eternal cadence rings
Too pure for us—too powerfully pure,
Too lovingly triumphant, and too large;
But there are some that hear him, and they know
That he shall sing to-morrow for all men,
And that all time shall listen.

The master-songs are ended? Rather say
No songs are ended that are ever sung,
And that no names are dead names. When we write
Men's letters on proud marble or on sand,
We write them there forever.

213   *Zola*

Because he puts the compromising chart
Of hell before your eyes, you are afraid;
Because he counts the price that you have paid
For innocence, and counts it from the start,
You loathe him. But he sees the human heart
Of God meanwhile, and in His hand was weighed
Your squeamish and emasculate crusade
Against the grim dominion of his art.

Never until we conquer the uncouth
Connivings of our shamed indifference
(We call it Christian faith) are we to scan
The racked and shrieking hideousness of Truth
To find, in hate's polluted self-defence
Throbbing, the pulse, the divine heart of man.

214 *George Crabbe*

GIVE him the darkest inch your shelf allows,
Hide him in lonely garrets, if you will,—
But his hard, human pulse is throbbing still
With the sure strength that fearless truth endows.
In spite of all fine science disavows,
Of his plain excellence and stubborn skill
There yet remains what fashion cannot kill,
Though years have thinned the laurel from his brows.

Whether or not we read him, we can feel
From time to time the vigor of his name
Against us like a finger for the shame
And emptiness of what our souls reveal
In books that are as altars where we kneel
To consecrate the flicker, not the flame.

215 *Credo*

I CANNOT find my way: there is no star
In all the shrouded heavens anywhere;

And there is not a whisper in the air
Of any living voice but one so far
That I can hear it only as a bar
Of lost, imperial music, played when fair
And angel fingers wove, and unaware,
Dead leaves to garlands where no roses are.

No, there is not a glimmer, nor a call,
For one that welcomes, welcomes when he fears,
The black and awful chaos of the night;
For through it all—above, beyond it all—
I know the far-sent message of the years,
I feel the coming glory of the Light.

216   *John Evereldown*

'WHERE are you going to-night, to-night,—
    Where are you going, John Evereldown?
There's never the sign of a star in sight,
    Nor a lamp that's nearer than Tilbury Town.
Why do you stare as a dead man might?
Where are you pointing away from the light?
And where are you going to-night, to-night,—
    Where are you going, John Evereldown?'

'Right through the forest, where none can see,
    There's where I'm going, to Tilbury Town.
The men are asleep,—or awake, may be,—
    But the women are calling John Evereldown.
Ever and ever they call for me,
And while they call can a man be free?

So right through the forest, where none can see,
   There's where I'm going, to Tilbury Town.'

'But why are you going so late, so late,—
   Why are you going, John Evereldown?
Though the road be smooth and the way be straight,
   There are two long leagues to Tilbury Town.
Come in by the fire, old man, and wait!
Why do you chatter out there by the gate?
And why are you going so late, so late,—
   Why are you going, John Evereldown?'

'I follow the women wherever they call,—
   That's why I'm going to Tilbury Town.
God knows if I pray to be done with it all,
   But God is no friend to John Evereldown.
So the clouds may come and the rain may fall,
The shadows may creep and the dead men crawl,—
But I follow the women wherever they call,
   And that's why I'm going to Tilbury Town.'

217   *Richard Cory*

WHENEVER Richard Cory went down town,
We people on the pavement looked at him:
He was a gentleman from sole to crown,
Clean favored, and imperially slim.

And he was always quietly arrayed,
And he was always human when he talked;

469

But still he fluttered pulses when he said,
'Good-morning,' and he glittered when he walked.

And he was rich—yes, richer than a king—
And admirably schooled in every grace:
In fine, we thought that he was everything
To make us wish that we were in his place.

So on we worked, and waited for the light,
And went without the meat, and cursed the bread;
And Richard Cory, one calm summer night,
Went home and put a bullet through his head.

218 *Charles Carville's Eyes*

A MELANCHOLY face Charles Carville had,
But not so melancholy as it seemed,
When once you knew him, for his mouth redeemed
His insufficient eyes, forever sad:
In them there was no life-glimpse, good or bad,
Nor joy nor passion in them ever gleamed;
His mouth was all of him that ever beamed,
His eyes were sorry, but his mouth was glad.

He never was a fellow that said much,
And half of what he did say was not heard
By many of us: we were out of touch
With all his whims and all his theories
Till he was dead, so those blank eyes of his
Might speak them. Then we heard them, every word.

470

219 *Isaac and Archibald*

(TO MRS. HENRY RICHARDS)

ISAAC and Archibald were two old men.
I knew them, and I may have laughed at them
A little; but I must have honored them
For they were old, and they were good to me.

I do not think of either of them now,
Without remembering, infallibly,
A journey that I made one afternoon
With Isaac to find out what Archibald
Was doing with his oats. It was high time
Those oats were cut, said Isaac; and he feared
That Archibald—well, he could never feel
Quite sure of Archibald. Accordingly
The good old man invited me—that is,
Permitted me—to go along with him;
And I, with a small boy's adhesiveness
To competent old age, got up and went.

I do not know that I cared overmuch
For Archibald's or anybody's oats,
But Archibald was quite another thing,
And Isaac yet another; and the world
Was wide, and there was gladness everywhere.
We walked together down the River Road
With all the warmth and wonder of the land
Around us, and the wayside flash of leaves,—
And Isaac said the day was glorious;

But somewhere at the end of the first mile
I found that I was figuring to find
How long those ancient legs of his would keep
The pace that he had set for them. The sun
Was hot, and I was ready to sweat blood;
But Isaac, for aught I could make of him,
Was cool to his hat-band. So I said then
With a dry gasp of affable despair,
Something about the scorching days we have
In August without knowing it sometimes;
But Isaac said the day was like a dream,
And praised the Lord, and talked about the breeze.
I made a fair confession of the breeze,
And crowded casually on his thought
The nearness of a profitable nook
That I could see. First I was half inclined
To caution him that he was growing old,
But something that was not compassion soon
Made plain the folly of all subterfuge.
Isaac was old, but not so old as that.

So I proposed, without an overture,
That we be seated in the shade a while,
And Isaac made no murmur. Soon the talk
Was turned on Archibald, and I began
To feel some premonitions of a kind
That only childhood knows; for the old man
Had looked at me and clutched me with his eye,
And asked if I had ever noticed things.
I told him that I could not think of them,
And I knew then, by the frown that left his face
Unsatisfied, that I had injured him.
'My good young friend,' he said, 'you cannot feel

What I have seen so long. You have the eyes—
Oh, yes—but you have not the other things:
The sight within that never will deceive,
You do not know—you have no right to know;
The twilight warning of experience,
The singular idea of loneliness,—
These are not yours. But they have long been mine,
And they have shown me now for seven years
That Archibald is changing. It is not
So much that he should come to his last hand,
And leave the game, and go the old way down;
But I have known him in and out so long,
And I have seen so much of good in him
That other men have shared and have not seen,
And I have gone so far through thick and thin,
Through cold and fire with him, that now it brings
To this old heart of mine an ache that you
Have not yet lived enough to know about.
But even unto you, and your boy's faith,
Your freedom, and your untried confidence,
A time will come to find out what it means
To know that you are losing what was yours,
To know that you are being left behind;
And then the long contempt of innocence—
God bless you, boy!—don't think the worse of it
Because an old man chatters in the shade—
Will all be like a story you have read
In childhood and remembered for the pictures.
And when the best friend of your life goes down,
When first you know in him the slackening
That comes, and coming always tells the end,—
Now in a common word that would have passed
Uncaught from any other lips than his,

Now in some trivial act of every day,
Done as he might have done it all along
But for a twinging little difference
That nips you like a squirrel's teeth—oh, yes,
Then you will understand it well enough.
But oftener it comes in other ways;
It comes without your knowing when it comes;
You know that he is changing, and you know
That he is going—just as I know now
That Archibald is going, and that I
Am staying. . . Look at me, my boy,
And when the time shall come for you to see
That I must follow after him, try then
To think of me, to bring me back again,
Just as I was to-day. Think of the place
Where we are sitting now, and think of me—
Think of old Isaac as you knew him then,
When you set out with him in August once
To see old Archibald.'—The words come back
Almost as Isaac must have uttered them,
And there comes with them a dry memory
Of something in my throat that would not move.

If you had asked me then to tell just why
I made so much of Isaac and the things
He said, I should have gone far for an answer;
For I knew it was not sorrow that I felt,
Whatever I may have wished it, or tried then
To make myself believe. My mouth was full
Of words, and they would have been comforting
To Isaac, spite of my twelve years, I think;
But there was not in me the willingness
To speak them out. Therefore I watched the ground;

And I was wondering what made the Lord
Create a thing so nervous as an ant,
When Isaac, with commendable unrest,
Ordained that we should take the road again—
For it was yet three miles to Archibald's,
And one to the first pump. I felt relieved
All over when the old man told me that;
I felt that he had stilled a fear of mine
That those extremities of heat and cold
Which he had long gone through with Archibald
Had made the man impervious to both;
But Isaac had a desert somewhere in him,
And at the pump he thanked God for all things
That He had put on earth for men to drink,
And he drank well,—so well that I proposed
That we go slowly lest I learn too soon
The bitterness of being left behind,
And all those other things. That was a joke
To Isaac, and it pleased him very much;
And that pleased me—for I was twelve years old.

At the end of an hour's walking after that
The cottage of old Archibald appeared.
Little and white and high on a smooth round hill
It stood, with hackmatacks and apple-trees
Before it, and a big barn-roof beyond;
And over the place—trees, houses, fields and all—
Hovered an air of still simplicity
And a fragrance of old summers—the old style
That lives the while it passes. I dare say
That I was lightly conscious of all this
When Isaac, of a sudden, stopped himself,
And for the long first quarter of a minute

Gazed with incredulous eyes, forgetful quite
Of breezes and of me and of all else
Under the scorching sun but a smooth-cut field,
Faint yellow in the distance. I was young,
But there were a few things that I could see,
And this was one of them.—'Well, well!' said he;
And 'Archibald will be surprised, I think,'
Said I. But all my childhood subtlety
Was lost on Isaac, for he strode along
Like something out of Homer—powerful
And awful on the wayside, so I thought.
Also I thought how good it was to be
So near the end of my short-legged endeavor
To keep the pace with Isaac for five miles.

Hardly had we turned in from the main road
When Archibald, with one hand on his back
And the other clutching his huge-headed cane,
Came limping down to meet us.—'Well! well! well!'
Said he; and then he looked at my red face,
All streaked with dust and sweat, and shook my hand,
And said it must have been a right smart walk
That we had had that day from Tilbury Town.—
'Magnificent,' said Isaac; and he told
About the beautiful west wind there was
Which cooled and clarified the atmosphere.
'You must have made it with your legs, I guess,'
Said Archibald; and Isaac humored him
With one of those infrequent smiles of his
Which he kept in reserve, apparently,
For Archibald alone. 'But why,' said he,
'Should Providence have cider in the world
If not for such an afternoon as this?'

476

And Archibald, with a soft light in his eyes,
Replied that if he chose to go down cellar,
There he would find eight barrels—one of which
Was newly tapped, he said, and to his taste
An honor to the fruit. Isaac approved
Most heartily of that, and guided us
Forthwith, as if his venerable feet
Were measuring the turf in his own door-yard,
Straight to the open rollway. Down we went,
Out of the fiery sunshine to the gloom,
Grateful and half sepulchral, where we found
The barrels, like eight potent sentinels,
Close ranged along the wall. From one of them
A bright pine spile stuck out alluringly,
And on the black flat stone, just under it,
Glimmered a late-spilled proof that Archibald
Had spoken from unfeigned experience.
There was a fluted antique water-glass
Close by, and in it, prisoned, or at rest,
There was a cricket, of the brown soft sort
That feeds on darkness. Isaac turned him out,
And touched him with his thumb to make him jump,
And then composedly pulled out the plug
With such a practised hand that scarce a drop
Did even touch his fingers. Then he drank
And smacked his lips with a slow patronage
And looked along the line of barrels there
With a pride that may have been forgetfulness
That they were Archibald's and not his own.
'I never twist a spigot nowadays,'
He said, and raised the glass up to the light,
'But I thank God for orchards.' And that glass
Was filled repeatedly for the same hand

Before I thought it worth while to discern
Again that I was young, and that old age,
With all his woes, had some advantages.

'Now, Archibald,' said Isaac, when we stood
Outside again, 'I have it in my mind
That I shall take a sort of little walk—
To stretch my legs and see what you are doing.
You stay and rest your back and tell the boy
A story: Tell him all about the time
In Stafford's cabin forty years ago,
When four of us were snowed up for ten days
With only one dried haddock. Tell him all
About it, and be wary of your back.
Now I will go along.'—I looked up then
At Archibald, and as I looked I saw
Just how his nostrils widened once or twice
And then grew narrow. I can hear to-day
The way the old man chuckled to himself—
Not wholesomely, not wholly to convince
Another of his mirth,—as I can hear
The lonely sigh that followed.—But at length
He said: 'The orchard now's the place for us;
We may find something like an apple there,
And we shall have the shade, at any rate.'
So there we went and there we laid ourselves
Where the sun could not reach us; and I champed
A dozen of worm-blighted astrakhans
While Archibald said nothing—merely told
The tale of Stafford's cabin, which was good,
Though 'master chilly'—after his own phrase—
Even for a day like that. But other thoughts
Were moving in his mind, imperative,

And writhing to be spoken: I could see
The glimmer of them in a glance or two,
Cautious, or else unconscious, that he gave
Over his shoulder: . . . 'Stafford and the rest—
But that's an old song now, and Archibald
And Isaac are old men. Remember, boy,
That we are old. Whatever we have gained,
Or lost, or thrown away, we are old men.
You look before you and we look behind,
And we are playing life out in the shadow—
But that's not all of it. The sunshine lights
A good road yet before us if we look,
And we are doing that when least we know it;
For both of us are children of the sun,
Like you, and like the weed there at your feet.
The shadow calls us, and it frightens us—
We think; but there's a light behind the stars
And we old fellows who have dared to live,
We see it—and we see the other things,
The other things . . . Yes, I have seen it come
These eight years, and these ten years, and I know
Now that it cannot be for very long
That Isaac will be Isaac. You have seen—
Young as you are, you must have seen the strange
Uncomfortable habit of the man?
He'll take my nerves and tie them in a knot
Sometimes, and that's not Isaac. I know that—
And I know what it is: I get it here
A little, in my knees, and Isaac—here.'
The old man shook his head regretfully
And laid his knuckles three times on his forehead.
'That's what it is: Isaac is not quite right.
You see it, but you don't know what it means:

The thouasnd little differences—no,
You do not know them, and it's well you don't;
You'll know them soon enough—God bless you, boy!—
You'll know them, but not all of them—not all.
So think of them as little as you can:
There's nothing in them for you, or for me—
But I am old and I must think of them;
I'm in the shadow, but I don't forget
The light, my boy,—the light behind the stars.
Remember that: remember that I said it;
And when the time that you think far away
Shall come for you to say it—say it, boy;
Let there be no confusion or distrust
In you, no snarling of a life half lived,
Nor any cursing over broken things
That your complaint has been the ruin of.
Live to see clearly and the light will come
To you, and as you need it.—But there, there,
I'm going it again, as Isaac says,
And I'll stop now before you go to sleep.—
Only be sure that you growl cautiously,
And always where the shadow may not reach you.'

Never shall I forget, long as I live,
The quaint thin crack in Archibald's voice,
The lonely twinkle in his little eyes,
Or the way it made me feel to be with him.
I know I lay and looked for a long time
Down through the orchard and across the road,
Across the river and the sun-scorched hills
That ceased in a blue forest, where the world
Ceased with it. Now and then my fancy caught
A flying glimpse of a good life beyond—

Something of ships and sunlight, streets and singing,
Troy falling, and the ages coming back,
And ages coming forward: Archibald
And Isaac were good fellows in old clothes,
And Agamemnon was a friend of mine;
Ulysses coming home again to shoot
With bows and feathered arrows made another,
And all was as it should be. I was young.

So I lay dreaming of what things I would,
Calm and incorrigibly satisfied
With apples and romance and ignorance,
And the still smoke from Archibald's clay pipe.
There was a stillness over everything,
As if the spirit of heat had laid its hand
Upon the world and hushed it; and I felt
Within the mightiness of the white sun
That smote the land around us and wrought out
A fragrance from the trees, a vital warmth
And fullness for the time that was to come,
And a glory for the world beyond the forest.
The present and the future and the past,
Isaac and Archibald, the burning bush,
The Trojans and the walls of Jericho,
Were beautifully fused; and all went well
Till Archibald began to fret for Isaac
And said it was a master day for sunstroke.
That was enough to make a mummy smile,
I thought; and I remained hilarious,
In face of all precedence and respect,
Till Isaac (who had come to us unheard)
Found he had no tobacco, looked at me
Peculiarly, and asked of Archibald

What ailed the boy to make him chirrup so.
From that he told us what a blessed world
The Lord had given us.—'But, Archibald,'
He added, with a sweet severity
That made me think of peach-skins and goose-flesh,
'I'm half afraid you cut those oats of yours
A day or two before they were well set.'
'They were set well enough,' said Archibald,—
And I remarked the process of his nose
Before the words came out. 'But never mind
Your neighbor's oats: you stay here in the shade
And rest yourself while I go find the cards.
We'll have a little game of seven-up
And let the boy keep count.'—'We'll have the game,
Assuredly,' said Isaac; 'and I think
That I will have a drop of cider, also.'

They marched away together towards the house
And left me to my childish ruminations
Upon the ways of men. I followed them
Down cellar with my fancy, and then left them
For a fairer vision of all things at once
That was anon to be destroyed again
By the sound of voices and of heavy feet—
One of the sounds of life that I remember,
Though I forget so many that rang first
As if they were thrown down to me from Sinai.

So I remember, even to this day,
Just how they sounded, how they placed themselves,
And how the game went on while I made marks
And crossed them out, and meanwhile made some Trojans
Likewise I made Ulysses, after Isaac,

And a little after Flaxman. Archibald
Was injured when he found himself left out,
But he had no heroics, and I said so:
I told him that his white beard was too long
And too straight down to be like things in Homer.
'Quite so,' said Isaac.—'Low,' said Archibald;
And he threw down a deuce with a deep grin
That showed his yellow teeth and made me happy.
So they played on till a bell rang from the door,
And Archibald said, 'Supper.'—After that
The old men smoked while I sat watching them
And wondered with all comfort what might come
To me, and what might never come to me;
And when the time came for the long walk home
With Isaac in the twilight, I could see
The forest and the sunset and the sky-line,
No matter where it was that I was looking:
The flame beyond the boundary, the music,
The foam and the white ships, and two old men
Were things that would not leave me.—And that night
There came to me a dream—a shining one,
With two old angels in it. They had wings,
And they were sitting where a silver light
Suffused them, face to face. The wings of one
Began to palpitate as I approached,
But I was yet unseen when a dry voice
Cried thinly, with unpatronising triumph,
'I've got you, Isaac; high, low, jack, and the game.'

Isaac and Archibald have gone their way
To the silence of the loved and well-forgotten.
I knew them, and I may have laughed at them;
But there's a laughing that has honor in it,

And I have no regret for light words now.
Rather I think sometimes they may have made
Their sport of me;—but they would not do that,
They were too old for that. They were old men,
And I may laugh at them because I knew them.

220 *Clavering*

I SAY no more for Clavering
    Than I should say of him who fails
To bring his wounded vessel home
    When reft of rudder and of sails;

I say no more than I should say
    Of any other one who sees
Too far for guidance of to-day,
    Too near for the eternities.

I think of him as I should think
    Of one who for scant wages played,
And faintly, a flawed instrument
    That fell while it was being made;

I think of him as one who fared,
    Unfaltering and undeceived,
Amid mirages of renown
    And urgings of the unachieved;

I think of him as one who gave
    To Lingard leave to be amused,

484

And listened with a patient grace
    That we, the wise ones, had refused;

I think of metres that he wrote
    For Cubit, the ophidian guest:
'What Lilith, or Dark Lady' . . . Well,
    Time swallows Cubit with the rest.

I think of last words that he said
    One midnight over Calverly:
'Good-by—good man.' He was not good;
    So Clavering was wrong, you see.

I wonder what had come to pass
    Could he have borrowed for a spell
The fiery-frantic indolence
    That made a ghost of Leffingwell;

I wonder if he pitied us
    Who cautioned him till he was gray
To build his house with ours on earth
    And have an end of yesterday;

I wonder what it was we saw
    To make us think that we were strong;
I wonder if he saw too much,
    Or if he looked one way too long.

But when were thoughts or wonderings
    To ferret out the man within?
Why prate of what he seemed to be,
    And all that he might not have been?

He clung to phantoms and to friends,
  And never came to anything.
He left a wreath on Cubit's grave.
  I say no more for Clavering.

221   *Miniver Cheevy*

MINIVER CHEEVY, child of scorn,
  Grew lean while he assailed the seasons;
He wept that he was ever born,
  And he had reasons.

Miniver loved the days of old
  When swords were bright and steeds were prancing;
The vision of a warrior bold
  Would set him dancing.

Miniver sighed for what was not,
  And dreamed, and rested from his labors;
He dreamed of Thebes and Camelot,
  And Priam's neighbors.

Miniver mourned the ripe renown
  (That made so many a name so fragrant;)
He mourned Romance, now on the town,
  And Art, a vagrant.

Miniver loved the Medici,
  Albeit he had never seen one;
He would have sinned incessantly
  Could he have been one.

486

Miniver cursed the commonplace
  And eyed a khaki suit with loathing;
He missed the mediæval grace
  Of iron clothing.

Miniver scorned the gold he sought,
  But sore annoyed was he without it;
Miniver thought, and thought, and thought,
  And thought about it.

Miniver **Cheevy**, born too late,
  Scratched his head and kept on thinking;
Miniver coughed, and called it fate,
  And kept on drinking.

222   *For a Dead Lady*

No more with overflowing light
Shall fill the eyes that now are faded,
Nor shall another's fringe with night
Their woman-hidden world as they did.
No more shall quiver down the days
The flowing wonder of her ways,
Whereof no language may requite
The shifting and the many-shaded.

The grace, divine, definitive,
  Clings only as a faint forestalling;
The laugh that love could not forgive
Is hushed, and answers to no calling;

The forehead and the little ears
Have gone where Saturn keeps the years;
The breast where roses could not live
Has done with rising and with falling.

The beauty, shattered by the laws
That have creation in their keeping,
No longer trembles at applause,
Or over children that are sleeping;
And we who delve in beauty's lore
Know all that we have known before
Of what inexorable cause
Makes Time so vicious in his reaping.

223   *The Gift of God*

Blessed with a joy that only she
Of all alive shall ever know,
She wears a proud humility
For what it was that willed it so,—
That her degree should be so great
Among the favored of the Lord
That she may scarcely bear the weight
Of her bewildering reward.

As one apart, immune, alone,
Or featured for the shining ones,
And like to none that she has known
Of other women's other sons,—
The firm fruition of her need,
He shines anointed; and he blurs

Her vision, till it seems indeed
A sacrilege to call him hers.

She fears a little for so much
Of what is best, and hardly dares
To think of him as one to touch
With aches, indignities, and cares;
She sees him rather at the goal,
Still shining; and her dream foretells
The proper shining of a soul
Where nothing ordinary dwells.

Perchance a canvass of the town
Would find him far from flags and shouts,
And leave him only the renown
Of many smiles and many doubts;
Perchance the crude and common tongue
Would havoc strangely with his worth;
But she, with innocence unwrung,
Would read his name around the earth.

And others, knowing how this youth
Would shine, if love could make him great,
When caught and tortured for the truth
Would only writhe and hesitate;
While she, arranging for his days
What centuries could not fulfill,
Transmutes him with her faith and praise,
And has him shining where she will.

She crowns him with her gratefulness,
And says again that life is good;
And should the gift of God be less
In him than in her motherhood,

His fame, though vague, will not be small,
As upward through her dream he fares,
Half clouded with a crimson fall
Of roses thrown on marble stairs.

224   *Cassandra*

I HEARD one who said: 'Verily,
  What word have I for children here?
Your Dollar is your only Word,
  The wrath of it your only fear.

'You build it altars tall enough
  To make you see, but you are blind;
You cannot leave it long enough
  To look before you or behind.

'When Reason beckons you to pause,
  You laugh and say that you know best;
But what is it you know, you keep
  As dark as ingots in a chest.

'You laugh and answer, "We are young;
  O leave us now, and let us grow."—
Not asking how much more of this
  Will Time endure or Fate bestow.

'Because a few complacent years
  Have made your peril of your pride,
Think you that you are to go on
  Forever pampered and untried?

'What lost eclipse of history,
   What bivouac of the marching stars,
Has given the sign for you to see
   Millenniums and last great wars?

'What unrecorded overthrow
   Of all the world has ever known,
Or ever been, has made itself
   So plain to you, and you alone?

'Your Dollar, Dove and Eagle make
   A Trinity that even you
Rate higher than you rate yourselves;
   It pays, it flatters, and it's new.

'And though your very flesh and blood
   Be what your Eagle eats and drinks,
You'll praise him for the best of birds,
   Not knowing what the Eagle thinks.

'The power is yours, but not the sight;
   You see not upon what you tread;
You have the ages for your guide,
   But not the wisdom to be led.

'Think you to tread forever down
   The merciless old verities?
And are you never to have eyes
   To see the world for what it is?

'Are you to pay for what you have
   With all you are?'—No other word
We caught, but with a laughing crowd
   Moved on. None heeded, and few heard.

Hillcrest

(TO MRS. EDWARD MAC DOWELL)

NO sound of any storm that shakes
Old island walls with older seas
Comes here where now September makes
An island in a sea of trees.

Between the sunlight and the shade
A man may learn till he forgets
The roaring of a world remade,
And all his ruins and regrets;

And if he still remembers here
Poor fights he may have won or lost,—
If he be ridden with the fear
Of what some other fight may cost,—

If, eager to confuse too soon,
What he has known with what may be
He reads a planet out of tune
For cause of his jarred harmony,—

If here he venture to unroll
His index of adagios,
And he be given to console
Humanity with what he knows,—

He may by contemplation learn
A little more than what he knew,

And even see great oaks return
To acorns out of which they grew.

He may, if he but listen well,
Through twilight and the silence here
Be told what there are none may tell
To vanity's impatient ear;

And he may never dare again
Say what awaits him, or be sure
What sunlit labyrinth of pain
He may not enter and endure.

Who knows to-day from yesterday
May learn to count no thing too strange:
Love builds of what Time takes away,
Till Death itself is less than Change.

Who sees enough in his duress
May go as far as dreams have gone;
Who sees a little may do less
Than many who are blind have done;

Who sees unchastened here the soul
Triumphant has no other sight
Than has a child who sees the whole
World radiant with his own delight.

Far journeys and hard wandering
Await him in whose crude surmise
Peace, like a mask, hides everything
That is and has been from his eyes;

And all his wisdom is unfound,
Or like a web that error weaves
On airy looms that have a sound
No louder now than falling leaves.

226   *Eros Turannos*

SHE fears him, and will always ask
    What fated her to choose him;
She meets in his engaging mask
    All reasons to refuse him;
But what she meets and what she fears
Are less than are the downward years,
Drawn slowly to the foamless weirs
    Of age, were she to lose him.

Between a blurred sagacity
    That once had power to sound him,
And Love, that will not let him be
    The Judas that she found him,
Her pride assuages her almost,
As if it were alone the cost.—
He sees that he will not be lost,
    And waits and looks around him.

A sense of ocean and old trees
    Envelops and allures him;
Tradition, touching all he sees,
    Beguiles and reassures him;

494

And all her doubts of what he says
Are dimmed with what she knows of days—
Till even prejudice delays
   And fades, and she secures him.

The falling leaf inaugurates
   The reign of her confusion;
The pounding wave reverberates
   The dirge of her illusion;
And home, where passion lived and died,
Becomes a place where she can hide,
While all the town and harbor side
   Vibrate with her seclusion.

We tell you, tapping on our brows,
   The story as it should be,—
As if the story of a house
   Were told, or ever could be;
We'll have no kindly veil between
Her visions and those we have seen,—
As if we guessed what hers have been,
   Or what they are or would be.

Meanwhile we do no harm; for they
   That with a god have striven,
Not hearing much of what we say,
   Take what the god has given;
Though like waves breaking it may be,
Or like a changed familiar tree,
Or like a stairway to the sea
   Where down the blind are driven.

227   *The Man Against the Sky*

Between me and the sunset, like a dome
Against the glory of a world on fire,
Now burned a sudden hill,
Bleak, round, and high, by flame-lit height made higher,
With nothing on it for the flame to kill
Save one who moved and was alone up there
To loom before the chaos and the glare
As if he were the last god going home
Unto his last desire.

Dark, marvelous, and inscrutable he moved on
Till down the fiery distance he was gone,
Like one of those eternal, remote things
That range across a man's imaginings
When a sure music fills him and he knows
What he may say thereafter to few men,—
The touch of ages having wrought
An echo and a glimpse of what he thought
A phantom or a legend until then;
For whether lighted over ways that save,
Or lured from all repose,
If he go on too far to find a grave,
Mostly alone he goes.

Even he, who stood where I had found him,
On high with fire all round him,
Who moved along the molten west,
And over the round hill's crest
That seemed half ready with him to go down,

Flame-bitten and flame-cleft,
As if there were to be no last thing left
Of a nameless unimaginable town,—
Even he who climbed and vanished may have taken
Down to the perils of a depth not known,
From death defended though by men forsaken,
The bread that every man must eat alone;
He may have walked while others hardly dared
Look on to see him stand where many fell;
And upward out of that, as out of hell,
He may have sung and striven
To mount where more of him shall yet be given,
Bereft of all retreat,
To sevenfold heat,—
As on a day when three in Dura shared
The furnace, and were spared
For glory by that king of Babylon
Who made himself so great that God, who heard,
Covered him with long feathers, like a bird.

Again, he may have gone down easily,
By comfortable altitudes, and found,
As always, underneath him solid ground
Whereon to be sufficient and to stand
Possessed already of the promised land,
Far stretched and fair to see:
A good sight, verily,
And one to make the eyes of her who bore him
Shine glad with hidden tears.
Why question of his ease of who before him,
In one place or another where they left
Their names as far behind them as their bones,
And yet by dint of slaughter toil and theft,

And shrewdly sharpened stones,
Carved hard the way for his ascendency
Through deserts of lost years?
Why trouble him now who sees and hears
No more than what his innocence requires,
And therefore to no other height aspires
Than one at which he neither quails nor tires?
He may do more by seeing what he sees
Than others eager for iniquities;
He may, by seeing all things for the best,
Incite futurity to do the rest.

Or with an even likelihood,
He may have met with atrabilious eyes
The fires of time on equal terms and passed
Indifferently down, until at last
His only kind of grandeur would have been,
Apparently, in being seen.
He may have had for evil or for good
No argument; he may have had no care
For what without himself went anywhere
To failure or to glory, and least of all
For such a stale, flamboyant miracle;
He may have been the prophet of an art
Immovable to old idolatries;
He may have been a player without a part,
Annoyed that even the sun should have the skies
For such a flaming way to advertise;
He may have been a painter sick at heart
With Nature's toiling for a new surprise;
He may have been a cynic, who now, for all
Of anything divine that his effete
Negation may have tasted,

Saw truth in his own image, rather small,
Forbore to fever the ephemeral,
Found any barren height a good retreat
From any swarming street,
And in the sun saw power superbly wasted;
And when the primitive old-fashioned stars
Came out again to shine on joys and wars
More primitive, and all arrayed for doom,
He may have proved a world a sorry thing
In his imagining,
And life a lighted highway to the tomb.

Or, mounting with infirm unsearching tread,
His hopes to chaos led,
He may have stumbled up there from the past,
And with an aching strangeness viewed the last
Abysmal conflagration of his dreams,—
A flame where nothing seems
To burn but flame itself, by nothing fed;
And while it all went out,
Not even the faint anodyne of doubt
May then have eased a painful going down
From pictured heights of power and lost renown,
Revealed at length to his outlived endeavor
Remote and unapproachable forever;
And at his heart there may have gnawed
Sick memories of a dead faith foiled and flawed
And long dishonored by the living death
Assigned alike by chance
To brutes and hierophants;
And anguish fallen on those he loved around him
May once have dealt the last blow to confound him,
And so have left him as death leaves a child,

Who sees it all too near;
And he who knows no young way to forget
May struggle to the tomb unreconciled.
Whatever suns may rise or set
There may be nothing kinder for him here
Than shafts and agonies;
And under these
He may cry out and stay on horribly;
Or, seeing in death too small a thing to fear,
He may go forward like a stoic Roman
Where pangs and terrors in his pathway lie,—
Or, seizing the swift logic of a woman,
Curse God and die.

Or maybe there, like many another one
Who might have stood aloft and looked ahead,
Black-drawn against wild red,
He may have built, unawed by fiery gules
That in him no commotion stirred,
A living reason out of molecules
Why molecules occurred,
And one for smiling when he might have sighed
Had he seen far enough,
And in the same inevitable stuff
Discovered an odd reason too for pride
In being what he must have been by laws
Infrangible and for no kind of cause.
Deterred by no confusion or surprise
He may have seen with his mechanic eyes
A world without a meaning, and had room,
Alone amid magnificence and doom,
To build himself an airy monument
That should, or fail him in his vague intent,

Outlast an accidental universe—
To call it nothing worse—
Or, by the burrowing guile
Of Time disintegrated and effaced,
Like once-remembered mighty trees go down
To ruin, of which by man may now be traced
No part sufficient even to be rotten,
And in the book of things that are forgotten
Is entered as a thing not quite worth while.
He may have been so great
That satraps would have shivered at his frown,
And all he prized alive may rule a state
No larger than a grave that holds a clown;
He may have been a master of his fate,
And of his atoms,—ready as another
In his emergence to exonerate
His father and his mother;
He may have been a captain of a host,
Self-eloquent and ripe for prodigies,
Doomed here to swell by dangerous degrees,
And then give up the ghost.
Nahum's great grasshoppers were such as these,
Sun-scattered and soon lost.

Whatever the dark road he may have taken,
This man who stood on high
And faced alone the sky,
Whatever drove or lured or guided him,—
A vision answering a faith unshaken,
An easy trust assumed of easy trials,
A sick negation born of weak denials,
A crazed abhorrence of an old condition,
A blind attendance on a brief ambition,—

Whatever stayed him or derided him,
His way was even as ours;
And we, with all our wounds and all our powers,
Must each await alone at his own height
Another darkness or another light;
And there, of our poor self dominion reft,
If inference and reason shun
Hell, Heaven, and Oblivion,
May thwarted will (perforce precarious,
But for our conservation better thus)
Have no misgiving left
Of doing yet what here we leave undone?
Or if unto the last of these we cleave,
Believing or protesting we believe
In such an idle and ephemeral
Florescence of the diabolical,—
If, robbed of two fond old enormities,
Our being had no onward auguries,
What then were this great love of ours to say
For launching other lives to voyage again
A little farther into time and pain,
A little faster in a futile chase
For a kingdom and a power and a Race
That would have still in sight
A manifest end of ashes and eternal night?
Is this the music of the toys we shake
So loud,—as if there might be no mistake
Somewhere in our indomitable will?
Are we no greater than the noise we make
Along one blind atomic pilgrimage
Whereon by crass chance billeted we go
Because our brains and bones and cartilage
Will have it so?

If this we say, then let us all be still
About our share in it, and live and die
More quietly thereby.

Where was he going, this man against the sky?
You know not, nor do I.
But this we know, if we know anything:
That we may laugh and fight and sing
And of our transience here make offering
To an orient Word that will not be erased,
Or, save in incommunicable gleams
Too permanent for dreams,
Be found or known.
No tonic and ambitious irritant
Of increase or of want
Has made an otherwise insensate waste
Of ages overthrown
A ruthless, veiled, implacable foretaste
Of other ages that are still to be
Depleted and rewarded variously
Because a few, by fate's economy,
Shall seem to move the world the way it goes;
No soft evangel of equality,
Safe-cradled in a communal repose
That huddles into death and may at last
Be covered well with equatorial snows—
And all for what, the devil only knows—
Will aggregate an inkling to confirm
The credit of a sage or of a worm,
Or tell us why one man in five
Should have a care to stay alive
While in his heart he feels no violence
Laid on his humor and intelligence

When infant Science makes a pleasant face
And waves again that hollow toy, the Race;
No planetary trap where souls are wrought
For nothing but the sake of being caught
And sent again to nothing will attune
Itself to any key of any reason
Why man should hunger through another season
'To find out why 'twere better late than soon
To go away and let the sun and moon
And all the silly stars illuminate
A place for creeping things,
And those that root and trumpet and have wings,
And herd and ruminate,
Or dive and flash and poise in rivers and seas,
Or by their loyal tails in lofty trees
Hang screeching lewd victorious derision
Of man's immortal vision.

Shall we, because Eternity records
Too vast an answer for the time-born words
We spell, whereof so many are dead that once
In our capricious lexicons
Were so alive and final, hear no more
The Word itself, the living word
That none alive has ever heard
Or ever spelt,
And few have ever felt
Without the fears and old surrenderings
And terrors that began
When Death let fall a feather from his wings
And humbled the first man?
Because the weight of our humility,
Wherefrom we gain

A little wisdom and much pain,
Falls here too sore and there too tedious,
Are we in anguish or complacency,
Not looking far enough ahead
To see by what mad couriers we are led
Along the roads of the ridiculous,
To pity ourselves and laugh at faith
And while we curse life bear it?
And if we see the soul's dead end in death,
Are we to fear it?
What folly is here that has not yet a name
Unless we say outright that we are liars?
What have we seen beyond our sunset fires
That lights again the way by which we came?
Why pay we such a price, and one we give
So clamoringly, for each racked empty day
That leads one more last human hope away,
As quiet fiends would lead past our crazed eyes
Our children to an unseen sacrifice?
If after all that we have lived and thought,
All comes to Nought,—
If there be nothing after Now,
And we be nothing anyhow,
And we know that,—why live?
'Twere sure but weaklings' vain distress
To suffer dungeons where so many doors
Will open on the cold eternal shores
That look sheer down
To the dark tideless floods of Nothingness
Where all who know may drown.

Mr. Flood's Party

OLD Eben Flood, climbing alone one night
Over the hill between the town below
And the forsaken upland hermitage
That held as much as he should ever know
On earth again of home, paused warily.
The road was his with not a native near;
And Eben, having leisure, said aloud,
For no man else in Tilbury Town to hear:

'Well, Mr. Flood, we have the harvest moon
Again, and we may not have many more;
The bird is on the wing, the poet says,
And you and I have said it here before.
Drink to the bird.' He raised up to the light
The jug that he had gone so far to fill,
And answered huskily: 'Well, Mr. Flood,
Since you propose it, I believe I will.'

Alone, as if enduring to the end
A valiant armor of scarred hopes outworn,
He stood there in the middle of the road
Like Roland's ghost winding a silent horn.
Below him, in the town among the trees,
Where friends of other days had honored him,
A phantom salutation of the dead
Rang thinly till old Eben's eyes were dim.

Then, as a mother lays her sleeping child
Down tenderly, fearing it may awake,

He set the jug down slowly at his feet
With trembling care, knowing that most things break;
And only when assured that on firm earth
It stood, as the uncertain lives of men
Assuredly did not, he paced away,
And with his hand extended paused again:

'Well, Mr. Flood, we have not met like this
In a long time; and many a change has come
To both of us, I fear, since last it was
We had a drop together. Welcome home!'
Convivially returning with himself,
Again he raised the jug up to the light;
And with an acquiescent quaver said:
'Well, Mr. Flood, if you insist, I might.

'Only a very little, Mr. Flood—
'For auld lang syne. No more, sir; that will do.'
So, for the time, apparently it did,
And Eben evidently thought so too;
For soon amid the silver loneliness
Of night he lifted up his voice and sang,
Secure, with only two moons listening,
Until the whole harmonious landscape rang—

'For auld lang syne.' The weary throat gave out,
The last word wavered, and the song was done.
He raised again the jug regretfully
And shook his head, and was again alone.
There was not much that was ahead of him,
And there was nothing in the town below—
Where strangers would have shut the many doors
That many friends had opened long ago.

229 *Many Are Called*

THE Lord Apollo, who has never died,
Still holds alone his immemorial reign,
Supreme in an impregnable domain
That with his magic he has fortified;
And though melodious multitudes have tried
In ecstasy, in anguish, and in vain,
With invocation sacred and profane
To lure him, even the loudest are outside.

Only at unconjectured intervals,
By will of him on whom no man may gaze,
By word of him whose law no man has read,
A questing light may rift the sullen walls,
To cling where mostly its infrequent rays
Fall golden on the patience of the dead.

230 *The Sheaves*

WHERE long the shadows of the wind had rolled,
Green wheat was yielding to the change assigned,
And as by some vast magic undivined
The world was turning slowly into gold.
Like nothing that was ever bought or sold
It waited there, the body and the mind;
And with a mighty meaning of a kind
That tells the more the more it is not told.

So in a land where all days are not fair,
Fair days went on till on another day
A thousand golden sheaves were lying there,
Shining and still, but not for long to stay—
As if a thousand girls with golden hair
Might rise from where they slept and go away.

231   *New England*

Here where the wind is always north-north-east
And children learn to walk on frozen toes,
Wonder begets an envy of all those
Who boil elsewhere with such a lyric yeast
Of love that you will hear them at a feast
Where demons would appeal for some repose,
Still clamoring where the chalice overflows
And crying wildest who have drunk the least.

Passion is here a soilure of the wits,
We're told, and Love a cross for them to bear;
Joy shivers in the corner where she knits
And Conscience always has the rocking-chair,
Cheerful as when she tortured into fits
The first cat that was ever killed by Care.

1869-1950

232   *The Hill*

WHERE are Elmer, Herman, Bert, Tom and Charley,
The weak of will, the strong of arm, the clown, the boozer,
    the fighter?
All, all, are sleeping on the hill.

One passed in a fever,
One was burned in a mine,
One was killed in a brawl,
One died in a jail,
One fell from a bridge toiling for children and wife—
All, all are sleeping, sleeping, sleeping on the hill.

Where are Ella, Kate, Mag, Lizzie and Edith,
The tender heart, the simple soul, the loud, the proud, the
    happy one?—
All, all, are sleeping on the hill.

One died in shameful child-birth,
One of a thwarted love,
One at the hands of a brute in a brothel,
One of a broken pride, in the search for heart's desire,
One after life in far-away London and Paris
Was brought to her little space by Ella and Kate and
    Mag—
All, all are sleeping, sleeping, sleeping on the hill.

EDGAR LEE MASTERS

Where are Uncle Isaac and Aunt Emily,
And old Towny Kincaid and Sevigne Houghton,
And Major Walker who had talked
With venerable men of the revolution? —
All, all, are sleeping on the hill.

They brought them dead sons from the war,
And daughters whom life had crushed,
And their children fatherless, crying—
All, all are sleeping, sleeping, sleeping on the hill.

Where is Old Fiddler Jones
Who played with life all his ninety years,
Braving the sleet with bared breast,
Drinking, rioting, thinking neither of wife nor kin,
Nor gold, nor love, nor heaven?
Lo! he babbles of the fish-frys of long ago,
Of the horse-races of long ago at Clary's Grove,
Of what Abe Lincoln said
One time at Springfield.

233   *Cassius Hueffer*

THEY have chiseled on my stone the words:
'His life was gentle, and the elements so mixed in him
That nature might stand up and say to all the world,
This was a man.'
Those who knew me smile
As they read this empty rhetoric.

My epitaph should have been:
'Life was not gentle to him,
And the elements so mixed in him
That he made warfare on life,
In the which he was slain.'
While I lived I could not cope with slanderous tongues,
Now that I am dead I must submit to an epitaph
Graven by a fool!

234 *Knowlt Hoheimer*

I WAS the first fruits of the battle of Missionary Ridge.
When I felt the bullet enter my heart
I wished I had staid at home and gone to jail
For stealing the hogs of Curl Trenary,
Instead of running away and joining the army.
Rather a thousand times the county jail
Than to lie under this marble figure with wings,
And this granite pedestal
Bearing the words, 'Pro Patria.'
What do they mean, anyway?

235 *Fiddler Jones*

THE earth keeps some vibration going
There in your heart, and that is you.
And if the people find you can fiddle,
Why, fiddle you must, for all your life.

What do you see, a harvest of clover?
Or a meadow to walk through to the river?
The wind's in the corn; you rub your hands
For beeves hereafter ready for market;
Or else you hear the rustle of skirts
Like the girls when dancing at Little Grove.
To Cooney Potter a pillar of dust
Or whirling leaves meant ruinous drouth;
They looked to me like Red-Head Sammy
Stepping it off, to 'Toor-a-Loor.'
How could I till my forty acres
Not to speak of getting more,
With a medley of horns, bassoons and piccolos
Stirred in my brain by crows and robins
And the creak of a wind-mill—only these?
And I never started to plow in my life
That some one did not stop in the road
And take me away to a dance or picnic.
I ended up with forty acres;
I ended up with a broken fiddle—
And a broken laugh, and a thousand memories,
And not a single regret.

236   *Petit, the Poet*

SEEDS in a dry pod, tick, tick, tick,
Tick, tick, tick, like mites in a quarrel—
Faint iambics that the full breeze wakens—
But the pine tree makes a symphony thereof.
Triolets, villanelles, rondels, rondeaus,
Ballades by the score with the same old thought:

The snows and the roses of yesterday are vanished;
And what is love but a rose that fades?
Life all around me here in the village:
Tragedy, comedy, valor and truth,
Courage, constancy, heroism, failure—
All in the loom, and oh what patterns!
Woodlands, meadows, streams and rivers—
Blind to all of it all my life long.
Triolets, villanelles, rondels, rondeaus,
Seeds in a dry pod, tick, tick, tick,
Tick, tick, tick, what little iambics,
While Homer and Whitman roared in the pines?

Elsa Wertman

137

I WAS a peasant girl from Germany,
Blue-eyed, rosy, happy and strong.
And the first place I worked was at Thomas Greene's.
On a summer's day when she was away
He stole into the kitchen and took me
Right in his arms and kissed me on my throat,
I turning my head. Then neither of us
Seemed to know what happened.
And I cried for what would become of me.
And cried and cried as my secret began to show.
One day Mrs. Greene said she understood,
And would make no trouble for me,
And, being childless, would adopt it.
(He had given her a farm to be still.)
So she hid in the house and sent out rumors,
As if it were going to happen to her.

And all went well and the child was born—They were so
    kind to me.
Later I married Gus Wertman, and years passed.
But—at political rallies when sitters-by thought I was
    crying
At the eloquence of Hamilton Greene—
That was not it.
No! I wanted to say:
That's my son! That's my son!

238   *Hamilton Greene*

I WAS the only child of Frances Harris of Virginia
And Thomas Greene of Kentucky,
Of valiant and honorable blood both.
To them I owe all that I became,
Judge, member of Congress, leader in the State.
From my mother I inherited
Vivacity, fancy, language;
From my father will, judgment, logic.
All honor to them
For what service I was to the people!

239   *Editor Whedon*

To be able to see every side of every question;
To be on every side, to be everything, to be nothing long;
To pervert truth, to ride it for a purpose,
To use great feelings and passions of the human family
For base designs, for cunning ends,

To wear a mask like the Greek actors—
Your eight-page paper—behind which you huddle,
Bawling through the megaphone of big type:
'This is I, the giant.'
Thereby also living the life of a sneak-thief,
Poisoned with the anonymous words
Of your clandestine soul.
To scratch dirt over scandal for money,
And exhume it to the winds for revenge,
Or to sell papers,
Crushing reputations, or bodies, if need be,
To win at any cost, save your own life.
To glory in demoniac power, ditching civilization,
As a paranoiac boy puts a log on the track
And derails the express train.
To be an editor, as I was.
Then to lie here close by the river over the place
Where the sewage flows from the village,
And the empty cans and garbage are dumped,
And abortions are hidden.

240   *Elliott Hawkins*

I LOOKED like Abraham Lincoln.
I was one of you, Spoon River, in all fellowship,
But standing for the rights of property and for order.
A regular church attendant,
Sometimes appearing in your town meetings to warn you
Against the evils of discontent and envy,
And to denounce those who tried to destroy the Union,
And to point to the peril of the Knights of Labor.

My success and my example are inevitable influences
In your young men and in generations to come,
In spite of attacks of newspapers like the *Clarion*;
A regular visitor at Springfield,
When the Legislature was in session,
To prevent raids upon the railroads,
And the men building up the state.
Trusted by them and by you, Spoon River, equally
In spite of the whispers that I was a lobbyist.
Moving quietly through the world, rich and courted.
Dying at last, of course, but lying here
Under a stone with an open book carved upon it
And the words '*Of such is the Kingdom of Heaven.*'
And now, you world-savers, who reaped nothing in life
And in death have neither stones nor epitaphs,
How do you like your silence from mouths stopped
With the dust of my triumphant career?

241   *English Thornton*

HERE! You sons of the men
Who fought with Washington at Valley Forge,
And whipped Black Hawk at Starved Rock,
Arise! Do battle with the descendants of those
Who bought land in the loop when it was waste sand,
And sold blankets and guns to the army of Grant,
And sat in legislatures in the early days,
Taking bribes from the railroads!
Arise! Do battle with the fops and bluffs,
The pretenders and figurantes of the society column,
And the yokel souls whose daughters marry counts;

And the parasites on great ideas,
And the noisy riders of great causes,
And the heirs of ancient thefts.
Arise! And make the city yours,
And the State yours—
You who are sons of the hardy yeomanry of the forties!
By God! If you do not destroy these vermin
My avenging ghost will wipe out
Your city and your state.

242 *Jonathan Houghton*

THERE is the caw of a crow,
And the hesitant song of a thrush.
There is the tinkle of a cowbell far away,
And the voice of a plowman on Shipley's hill.
The forest beyond the orchard is still
With midsummer stillness;
And along the road a wagon chuckles,
Loaded with corn, going to Atterbury.
And an old man sits under a tree asleep,
And an old woman crosses the road,
Coming from the orchard with a bucket of blackberries
And a boy lies in the grass
Near the feet of the old man,
And looks up at the sailing clouds,
And longs, and longs, and longs
For what, he knows not:
For manhood, for life, for the unknown world!
Then thirty years passed,
And the boy returned worn out by life

And found the orchard vanished,
And the forest gone,
And the house made over,
And the roadway filled with dust from automobiles—
And himself desiring The Hill!

243 *Father Malloy*

YOU are over there, Father Malloy,
Where holy ground is, and the cross marks every grave,
Not here with us on the hill—
Us of wavering faith, and clouded vision
And drifting hope, and unforgiven sins.
You were so human, Father Malloy,
Taking a friendly glass sometimes with us,
Siding with us who would rescue Spoon River
From the coldness and the dreariness of village morality.
You were like a traveler who brings a little box of sand
From the wastes about the pyramids
And makes them real and Egypt real.
You were a part of and related to a great past,
And yet you were so close to many of us.
You believed in the joy of life.
You did not seem to be ashamed of the flesh.
You faced life as it is,
And as it changes.
Some of us almost came to you, Father Malloy,
Seeing how your church had divined the heart,
And provided for it,
Through Peter the Flame,
Peter the Rock.

244   *Anne Rutledge*

OUT of me unworthy and unknown
The vibrations of deathless music;
'With malice toward none, with charity for all.'
Out of me the forgiveness of millions toward millions,
And the beneficent face of a nation
Shining with justice and truth.
I am Anne Rutledge who sleep beneath these weeds,
Beloved in life of Abraham Lincoln,
Wedded to him, not through union,
But through separation.
Bloom forever, O Republic,
From the dust of my bosom!

245   *Rutherford McDowell*

THEY brought me ambrotypes
Of the old pioneers to enlarge.
And sometimes one sat for me—
Some one who was in being
When giant hands from the womb of the world
Tore the republic.
What was it in their eyes?—
For I could never fathom
That mystical pathos of drooped eyelids,
And the serene sorrow of their eyes.
It was like a pool of water,
Amid oak trees at the edge of a forest,
Where the leaves fall,
As you hear the crow of a cock

From a far-off farm house, seen near the hills
Where the third generation lives, and the strong men
And the strong women are gone and forgotten.
And these grand-children and great grand-children
Of the pioneers!
Truly did my camera record their faces, too,
With so much of the old strength gone,
And the old faith gone,
And the old mastery of life gone,
And the old courage gone,
Which labors and loves and suffers and sings
Under the sun!

246 *Lucinda Matlock*

I WENT to the dances at Chandlerville,
And played snap-out at Winchester.
One time we changed partners,
Driving home in the moonlight of middle June,
And then I found Davis.
We were married and lived together for seventy years,
Enjoying, working, raising the twelve children,
Eight of whom we lost
Ere I had reached the age of sixty.
I spun, I wove, I kept the house, I nursed the sick,
I made the garden, and for holiday
Rambled over the fields where sang the larks,
And by Spoon River gathering many a shell,
And many a flower and medicinal weed—
Shouting to the wooded hills, singing to the green valleys.
At ninety-six I had lived enough, that is all,

And passed to a sweet repose.
What is this I hear of sorrow and weariness,
Anger, discontent and drooping hopes?
Degenerate sons and daughters,
Life is too strong for you—
It takes life to love Life.

247   *Herman Altman*

DID I follow Truth wherever she led,
And stand against the whole world for a cause,
And uphold the weak against the strong?
If I did I would be remembered among men
As I was known in life among the people,
And as I was hated and loved on earth,
Therefore, build no monument to me,
And carve no bust for me,
Lest, though I become not a demi-god,
The reality of my soul be lost,
So that thieves and liars,
Who were my enemies and destroyed me,
And the children of thieves and liars,
May claim me and affirm before my bust
That they stood with me in the days of my defeat.
Build me no monument
Lest my memory be perverted to the uses
Of lying and oppression.
My lovers and their children must not be dispossessed of
     me;
I would be the untarnished possession forever
Of those for whom I lived.

522

248   *In the Past*

THERE lies a somnolent lake
Under a noiseless sky,
Where never the mornings break
Nor the evenings die.

Mad flakes of colour
Whirl on its even face
Iridescent and streaked with pallour;
And, warding the silent place,

The rocks rise sheer and gray
From the sedgeless brink to the sky
Dull-lit with the light of pale half-day
Thro' a void space and dry.

And the hours lag dead in the air
With a sense of coming eternity
To the heart of the lonely boatman there:
That boatman am I,

I, in my lonely boat,
A waif on the somnolent lake,
Watching the colours creep and float
With the sinuous track of a snake.

Now I lean o'er the side
And lazy shades in the water see,
Lapped in the sweep of a sluggish tide
Crawled in from the living sea;

And next I fix mine eyes,
So long that the heart declines,
On the changeless face of the open skies
Where no star shines;

And now to the rocks I turn,
To the rocks, around
That lie like walls of a circling urn
Wherein lie bound

The waters that feel my powerless strength
And meet my homeless oar
Labouring over their ashen length
Never to find a shore.

But the gleam still skims
At times on the somnolent lake,
And a light there is that swims
With the whirl of a snake;

And tho' dead be the hour i' the air,
And dayless the sky,
The heart is alive of the boatman there:
That boatman am I.

249 *Mnemosyne*

I T'S autumn in the country I remember.

How warm a wind blew here about the ways!
And shadows on the hillside lay to slumber
During the long sun-sweetened summer-days.

It's cold abroad the country I remember.

The swallows veering skimmed the golden grain
At midday with a wing aslant and limber;
And yellow cattle browsed upon the plain.

It's empty down the country I remember.

I had a sister lovely in my sight:
Her hair was dark, her eyes were very sombre;
We sang together in the woods at night.

It's lonely in the country I remember.

The babble of our children fills my ears,
And on our hearth I stare the perished ember
To flames that show all starry thro' my tears.

It's dark about the country I remember.

There are the mountains where I lived. The path
Is slushed with cattle-tracks and fallen timber,
The stumps are twisted by the tempests' wrath.

But that I knew these places are my own,
I'd ask how came such wretchedness to cumber
The earth, and I to people it alone.

It rains across the country I remember.

250 *At Sainte-Marguerite*

THE gray tide flows and flounders in the rocks
Along the crannies up the swollen sand.
Far out the reefs lie naked—dunes and blocks
Low in the watery wind. A shaft of land
Going to sea thins out the western strand.

It rains, and all along and always gulls
Career sea-screaming in and weather-glossed.
It blows here, pushing round the cliff; in lulls
Within the humid stone a motion lost
Ekes out the flurried heart-beat of the coast.

It blows and rains a pale and whirling mist
This summer morning. I that hither came—
Was it to pluck this savage from the schist,
This crazy yellowish bloom without a name,
With leathern blade and tortured wiry frame?

Why here alone, away, the forehead pricked
With dripping salt and fingers damp with brine,
Before the offal and the derelict
And where the hungry sea-wolves howl and whine,
Live human hours? now that the columbine

526

TRUMBULL STICKNEY

Stands somewhere shaded near the fields that fall
Great starry sheaves of the delighted year,
And globing rosy on the garden wall
The peach and apricot and soon the pear
Drip in the teasing hand their sugared tear.

Inland a little way the summer lies.
Inland a little and but yesterday
I saw the weary teams, I heard the cries
Of sicklemen across the fallen hay,
And buried in the sunburned stacks I lay

Tasting the straws and tossing, laughing soft
Into the sky's great eyes of gold and blue
And nodding to the breezy leaves aloft
Over the harvest's mellow residue.
But sudden then—then strangely dark it grew.

How good it is, before the dreary flow
Of cloud and water, here to lie alone
And in this desolation to let go
Down the ravine one with another, down
Across the surf to linger or to drown

The loves that none can give and none receive,
The fearful asking and the small retort,
The life to dream of and the dream to live!
Very much more is nothing than a part,
Nothing at all and darkness in the heart.

I would my manhood now were like the sea.—
Thou at high-tide, when compassing the land
Thou find'st the issue short, questioningly

A moment poised, thy floods then down the strand
Sink without rancour, sink without command,

Sink of themselves in peace without despair,
And turn as still the calm horizon turns,
Till they repose little by little nowhere
And the long light unfathomable burns
Clear from the zenith stars to the sea-ferns.

Thou art thy Priest, thy Victim and thy God.
Thy life is bulwarked with a thread of foam,
And of the sky, the mountains and the sod
Thou askest nothing, evermore at home
In thy own self's perennial masterdom.

251   *Mt. Lykaion*

ALONE on Lykaion since man hath been
Stand on the height two columns, where at rest
Two eagles hewn of gold sit looking East
Forever; and the sun goes up between.
Far down around the mountain's oval green
An order keeps the falling stones abreast.
Below within the chaos last and least
A river like a curl of light is seen.
Beyond the river lies the even sea,
Beyond the sea another ghost of sky,—-
O God, support the sickness of my eye
Lest the far space and long antiquity
Suck out my heart, and on this awful ground
The great wind kill my little shell with sound.

252   *Six O'Clock*

Now burst above the city's cold twilight
The piercing whistles and the tower-clocks:
For day is done. Along the frozen docks
The workmen set their ragged shirts aright.
Thro' factory doors a stream of dingy light
Follows the scrimmage as it quickly flocks
To hut and home among the snow's gray blocks.—
I love you, human labourers. Good-night!
Good-night to all the blackened arms that ache!
Good-night to every sick and sweated brow,
To the poor girl that strength and love forsake,
To the poor boy who can no more! I vow
The victim soon shall shudder at the stake
And fall in blood: we bring him even now.

253   *Dramatic Fragment*

Sir, say no more.
Within me 't is as if
The green and climbing eyesight of a cat
Crawled near my mind's poor birds.

254 *Patterns*

I WALK down the garden paths,
And all the daffodils
Are blowing, and the bright blue squills.
I walk down the patterned garden-paths
In my stiff, brocaded gown.
With my powdered hair and jewelled fan,
I too am a rare
Pattern. As I wander down
The garden paths.

My dress is richly figured,
And the train
Makes a pink and silver stain
On the gravel, and the thrift
Of the borders.
Just a plate of current fashion,
Tripping by in high-heeled, ribboned shoes.
Not a softness anywhere about me,
Only whalebone and brocade.
And I sink on a seat in the shade
Of a lime tree. For my passion
Wars against the stiff brocade.
The daffodils and squills
Flutter in the breeze
As they please.

And I weep;
For the lime-tree is in blossom
And one small flower has dropped upon my bosom.

And the plashing of waterdrops
In the marble fountain
Comes down the garden-paths.
The dripping never stops.
Underneath my stiffened gown
Is the softness of a woman bathing in a marble basin,
A basin in the midst of hedges grown
So thick, she cannot see her lover hiding,
But she guesses he is near,
And the sliding of the water
Seems the stroking of a dear
Hand upon her.
What is Summer in a fine brocaded gown!
I should like to see it lying in a heap upon the ground.
All the pink and silver crumpled up on the ground.

I would be the pink and silver as I ran along the paths,
And he would stumble after,
Bewildered by my laughter.
I should see the sun flashing from his sword-hilt and the
    buckles on his shoes.
I would choose
To lead him in a maze along the patterned paths,
A bright and laughing maze for my heavy-booted lover.
Till he caught me in the shade,
And the buttons of his waistcoat bruised my body as he
    clasped me,
Aching, melting, unafraid.
With the shadows of the leaves and the sundrops,

And the plopping of the waterdrops,
All about us in the open afternoon—
I am very like to swoon
With the weight of this brocade,
For the sun sifts through the shade.

Underneath the fallen blossom
In my bosom,
Is a letter I have hid.
It was brought to me this morning by a rider from the
    Duke.
'Madam, we regret to inform you that Lord Hartwell
Died in action Thursday se'nnight.'
As I read it in the white, morning sunlight,
The letters squirmed like snakes.
'Any answer, Madam,' said my footman.
'No,' I told him.
'See that the messenger takes some refreshment.
No, no answer.'
And I walked into the garden,
Up and down the patterned paths,
In my stiff, correct brocade.
The blue and yellow flowers stood up proudly in the sun,
Each one.
I stood upright too,
Held rigid to the pattern
By the stiffness of my gown.
Up and down I walked,
Up and down.

In a month he would have been my husband.
In a month, here, underneath this lime,
We would have broke the pattern;

He for me, and I for him,
He as Colonel, I as Lady,
On this shady seat.
He had a whim
That sunlight carried blessing.
And I answered, 'It shall be as you have said.'
Now he is dead.

In Summer and in Winter I shall walk
Up and down
The patterned garden-paths
In my stiff, brocaded gown.
The squills and daffodils
Will give place to pillared roses, and to asters, and to snow.
I shall go
Up and down,
In my gown.
Gorgeously arrayed,
Boned and stayed.
And the softness of my body will be guarded from embrace
By each button, hook, and lace.
For the man who should loose me is dead,
Fighting with the Duke in Flanders,
In a pattern called a war.
Christ! What are patterns for?

255   *Meeting-House Hill*

I MUST be mad, or very tired,
When the curve of a blue bay beyond a railroad track
Is shrill and sweet to me like the sudden springing of a
      tune,

And the sight of a white church above thin trees in a city
    square
Amazes my eyes as though it were the Parthenon.
Clear, reticent, superbly final,
With the pillars of its portico refined to a cautious elegance,
It dominates the weak trees,
And the shot of its spire
Is cool, and candid,
Rising into an unresisting sky.
Strange meeting-house

Pausing a moment upon a squalid hill-top.
I watch the spire sweeping the sky,
I am dizzy with the movement of the sky,
I might be watching a mast
With its royals set full
Straining before a two-reef breeze.
I might be sighting a tea-clipper,
Tacking into the blue bay,
Just back from Canton
With her hold full of green and blue porcelain,
And a Chinese coolie leaning over the rail
Gazing at the white spire
With dull, sea-spent eyes.

256   *Lilacs*

LILACS,
False blue,
White,
Purple,

AMY LOWELL

Colour of lilac,
Your great puffs of flowers
Are everywhere in this my New England.
Among your heart-shaped leaves
Orange orioles hop like music-box birds and sing
Their little weak soft songs;
In the crooks of your branches
The bright eyes of song sparrows sitting on spotted eggs
Peer restlessly through the light and shadow
Of all Springs.
Lilacs in dooryards
Holding quiet conversations with an early moon;
Lilacs watching a deserted house
Settling sideways into the grass of an old road;
Lilacs, wind-beaten, staggering under a lopsided shock of
    bloom
Above a cellar dug into a hill.
You are everywhere.
You were everywhere.
You tapped the window when the preacher preached his
    sermon,
And ran along the road beside the boy going to school.
You stood by pasture-bars to give the cows good milking,
You persuaded the housewife that her dish pan was of silver
And her husband an image of pure gold.
You flaunted the fragrance of your blossoms
Through the wide doors of Custom Houses—
You, and sandal-wood, and tea,
Charging the noses of quill-driving clerks
When a ship was in from China.
You called to them: 'Goose-quill men, goose-quill men,
May is a month for flitting,'
Until they writhed on their high stools

And wrote poetry on their letter-sheets behind the propped-
    up ledgers.
Paradoxical New England clerks,
Writing inventories in ledgers, reading the 'Song of
    Solomon' at night,
So many verses before bed-time,
Because it was the Bible.
The dead fed you
Amid the slant stones of graveyards.
Pale ghosts who planted you
Came in the night-time
And let their thin hair blow through your clustered stems.
You are of the green sea,
And of the stone hills which reach a long distance.
You are of elm-shaded streets with little shops where they
    sell kites and marbles,
You are of great parks where everyone walks and nobody is
    at home.
You cover the blind sides of greenhouses
And lean over the top to say a hurry-word through the glass
To your friends, the grapes, inside.

Lilacs,
False blue,
White,
Purple,
Colour of lilac,
You have forgotten your Eastern origin,
The veiled women with eyes like panthers,
The swollen, aggressive turbans of jewelled Pashas.
Now you are a very decent flower,
A reticent flower,
A curiously clear-cut, candid flower,

AMY LOWELL

Standing beside clean doorways,
Friendly to a house-cat and a pair of spectacles,
Making poetry out of a bit of moonlight
And a hundred or two sharp blossoms.

Maine knows you,
Has for years and years;
New Hampshire knows you,
And Massachusetts
And Vermont.
Cape Cod starts you along the beaches to Rhode Island;
Connecticut takes you from a river to the sea.
You are brighter than apples,
Sweeter than tulips,
You are the great flood of our souls
Bursting above the leaf-shapes of our hearts,
You are the smell of all Summers,
The love of wives and children,
The recollection of the gardens of little children,
You are State Houses and Charters
And the familiar treading of the foot to and fro on a road
    it knows.
May is lilac here in New England,
May is a thrush singing 'Sun up!' on a tip-top ash-tree,
May is white clouds behind pine-trees
Puffed out and marching upon a blue sky.
May is a green as no other,
May is much sun through small leaves,
May is soft earth,
And apple-blossoms,
And windows open to a South wind.
May is a full light wind of lilac
From Canada to Narragansett Bay.

Lilacs,
False blue,
White,
Purple,
Colour of lilac.
Heart-leaves of lilac all over New England,
Roots of lilac under all the soil of New England,
Lilac in me because I am New England,
Because my roots are in it,
Because my leaves are of it,
Because my flowers are for it,
Because it is my country
And I speak to it of itself
And sing of it with my own voice
Since certainly it is mine.

ROBERT FROST

b. 1875

257   *The Pasture*

I'M going out to clean the pasture spring;
I'll only stop to rake the leaves away
(And wait to watch the water clear, I may):
I sha'n't be gone long.—You come too.

I'm going out to fetch the little calf
That's standing by the mother. It's so young
It totters when she licks it with her tongue.
I sha'n't be gone long.—You come too.

258

My November Guest

MY sorrow, when she's here with me,
  Thinks these dark days of autumn rain
Are beautiful as days can be;
She loves the bare, the withered tree;
  She walks the sodden pasture lane.

Her pleasure will not let me stay.
  She talks and I am fain to list:
She's glad the birds are gone away,
She's glad her simple worsted grey
  Is silver now with clinging mist.

The desolate, deserted trees,
  The faded earth, the heavy sky,
The beauties she so truly sees,
She thinks I have no eye for these,
  And vexes me for reason why.

Not yesterday I learned to know
  The love of bare November days
Before the coming of the snow,
But it were vain to tell her so,
  And they are better for her praise.

259

Storm Fear

WHEN the wind works against us in the dark,
And pelts with snow
The lower chamber window on the east,

And whispers with a sort of stifled bark,
The beast,
'Come out! Come out!'—
It costs no inward struggle not to go,
Ah, no!
I count our strength,
Two and a child,
Those of us not asleep subdued to mark
How the cold creeps as the fire dies at length,—
How drifts are piled,
Dooryard and road ungraded,
Till even the comforting barn grows far away,
And my heart owns a doubt
Whether 'tis in us to arise with day
And save ourselves unaided.

260 *To the Thawing Wind*

COME with rain, O loud Southwester!
Bring the singer, bring the nester;
Give the buried flower a dream;
Make the settled snow-bank steam;
Find the brown beneath the white;
But whate'er you do to-night,
Bathe my window, make it flow,
Melt it as the ice will go;
Melt the glass and leave the sticks
Like a hermit's crucifix;
Burst into my narrow stall;
Swing the picture on the wall;
Run the rattling pages o'er;

Scatter poems on the floor;
Turn the poet out of door.

261   *The Vantage Point*

IF tired of trees I seek again mankind,
   Well I know where to hie me—in the dawn,
   To a slope where the cattle keep the lawn.
There amid lolling juniper reclined,
Myself unseen, I see in white defined
   Far off the homes of men, and farther still,
   The graves of men on an opposing hill,
Living or dead, whichever are to mind.

And if by noon I have too much of these,
   I have but to turn on my arm, and lo,
   The sun-burned hillside sets my face aglow,
My breathing shakes the bluet like a breeze,
   I smell the earth, I smell the bruisèd plant,
   I look into the crater of the ant.

262   *Mowing*

THERE was never a sound beside the wood but one,
And that was my long scythe whispering to the ground.
What was it it whispered? I knew not well myself;
Perhaps it was something about the heat of the sun,
Something, perhaps, about the lack of sound—
And that was why it whispered and did not speak.

It was no dream of the gift of idle hours,
Or easy gold at the hand of fay or elf:
Anything more than the truth would have seemed too weak
To the earnest love that laid the swale in rows,
Not without feeble-pointed spikes of flowers
(Pale orchises), and scared a bright green snake.
The fact is the sweetest dream that labor knows.
My long scythe whispered and left the hay to make.

263   *The Tuft of Flowers*

I WENT to turn the grass once after one
Who mowed it in the dew before the sun.

The dew was gone that made his blade so keen
Before I came to view the levelled scene.

I looked for him behind an isle of trees;
I listened for his whetstone on the breeze.

But he had gone his way, the grass all mown,
And I must be, as he had been,—alone,

'As all must be,' I said within my heart,
'Whether they work together or apart.'

But as I said it, swift there passed me by
On noiseless wing a bewildered butterfly,

Seeking with memories grown dim o'er night
Some resting flower of yesterday's delight.

And once I marked his flight go round and round,
As where some flower lay withering on the ground

And then he flew as far as eye could see,
And then on tremulous wing came back to me.

I thought of questions that have no reply,
And would have turned to toss the grass to dry;

But he turned first, and led my eye to look
At a tall tuft of flowers beside a brook,

A leaping tongue of bloom the scythe had spared
Beside a reedy brook the scythe had bared

I left my place to know them by their name,
Finding them butterfly weed when I came.

The mower in the dew had loved them thus,
By leaving them to flourish, not for us,

Nor yet to draw one thought of ours to him,
But from sheer morning gladness at the brim.

The butterfly and I had lit upon,
Nevertheless, a message from the dawn,

That made me hear the wakening birds around,
And hear his long scythe whispering to the ground,

And feel a spirit kindred to my own;
So that henceforth I worked no more alone;

But glad with him, I worked as with his aid,
And weary, sought at noon with him the shade;

And dreaming, as it were, held brotherly speech
With one whose thought I had not hoped to reach.

'Men work together,' I told him from the heart,
'Whether they work together or apart.'

264 *The Demiurge's Laugh*

ABOUT SCIENCE

IT was far in the sameness of the wood;
    I was running with joy on the Demon's trail,
Though I knew what I hunted was no true god.
    It was just as the light was beginning to fail
That I suddenly heard—all I needed to hear:
It has lasted me many and many a year.

The sound was behind me instead of before,
    A sleepy sound, but mocking half,
As of one who utterly couldn't care.
    The Demon arose from his wallow to laugh,
Brushing the dirt from his eye as he went;
And well I knew what the Demon meant.

I shall not forget how his laugh rang out.
    I felt as a fool to have been so caught,
And checked my steps to make pretence
    It was something among the leaves I sought

(Though doubtful whether he stayed to see).
Thereafter I sat me against a tree.

265   *Pan With Us*

PAN came out of the woods one day,—
His skin and his hair and his eyes were gray,
The gray of the moss of walls were they,—
    And stood in the sun and looked his fill
    At wooded valley and wooded hill.

He stood in the zephyr, pipes in hand,
On a height of naked pasture land;
In all the country he did command
    He saw no smoke and he saw no roof.
    That was well! and he stamped a hoof.

His heart knew peace, for none came here
To this lean feeding save once a year
Someone to salt the half-wild steer,
    Or homespun children with clicking pails
    Who see so little they tell no tales.

He tossed his pipes, too hard to teach
A new-world song, far out of reach,
For a sylvan sign that the blue jay's screech
    And the whimper of hawks beside the sun
    Were music enough for him, for one.

Times were changed from what they were:
Such pipes kept less of power to stir

The fruited bough of the juniper
   And the fragile bluets clustered there
Than the merest aimless breath of air.

They were pipes of pagan mirth,
And the world had found new terms of worth.
He laid him down on the sun-burned earth
   And ravelled a flower and looked away—
   Play? Play?—What should he play?

266   *Reluctance*

OUT through the fields and the woods
   And over the walls I have wended;
I have climbed the hills of view
   And looked at the world, and descended;
I have come by the highway home,
   And lo, it is ended.

The leaves are all dead on the ground,
   Save those that the oak is keeping
To ravel them one by one
   And let them go scraping and creeping
Out over the crusted snow,
   When others are sleeping.

And the dead leaves lie huddled and still,
   No longer blown hither and thither;
The last lone aster is gone;
   The flowers of the witch-hazel wither;
The heart is still aching to seek,
   But the feet question 'Whither?'

Ah, when to the heart of man
 Was it ever less than a treason
To go with the drift of things,
 To yield with a grace to reason,
And bow and accept the end
 Of a love or a season?

267   *Mending Wall*

SOMETHING there is that doesn't love a wall,
That sends the frozen-ground-swell under it,
And spills the upper boulders in the sun;
And makes gaps even two can pass abreast.
The work of hunters is another thing:
I have come after them and made repair
Where they have left not one stone on a stone,
But they would have the rabbit out of hiding,
To please the yelping dogs. The gaps I mean,
No one has seen them made or heard them made,
But at spring mending-time we find them there.
I let my neighbour know beyond the hill;
And on a day we meet to walk the line
And set the wall between us once again.
We keep the wall between us as we go.
To each the boulders that have fallen to each.
And some are loaves and some so nearly balls
We have to use a spell to make them balance:
'Stay where you are until our backs are turned!'
We wear our fingers rough with handling them.
Oh, just another kind of out-door game,
One on a side. It comes to little more:

There where it is we do not need the wall:
He is all pine and I am apple orchard.
My apple trees will never get across
And eat the cones under his pines, I tell him.
He only says, 'Good fences make good neighbours.'
Spring is the mischief in me, and I wonder
If I could put a notion in his head:
'*Why* do they make good neighbours? Isn't it
Where there are cows? But here there are no cows.
Before I built a wall I'd ask to know
What I was walling in or walling out,
And to whom I was like to give offence.
Something there is that doesn't love a wall,
That wants it down.' I could say 'Elves' to him,
But it's not elves exactly, and I'd rather
He said it for himself. I see him there
Bringing a stone grasped firmly by the top
In each hand, like an old-stone savage armed.
He moves in darkness as it seems to me,
Not of woods only and the shade of trees.
He will not go behind his father's saying,
And he likes having thought of it so well
He says again, 'Good fences make good neighbours.'

268   *The Death of the Hired Man*

MARY sat musing on the lamp-flame at the table
Waiting for Warren. When she heard his step,
She ran on tip-toe down the darkened passage
To meet him in the doorway with the news
And put him on his guard. 'Silas is back.'

She pushed him outward with her through the door
And shut it after her. 'Be kind,' she said.
She took the market things from Warren's arms
And set them on the porch, then drew him down
To sit beside her on the wooden steps.

'When was I ever anything but kind to him?
But I'll not have the fellow back,' he said.
'I told him so last haying, didn't I?
"If he left then," I said, "that ended it."
What good is he? Who else will harbour him
At his age for the little he can do?
What help he is there's no depending on.
Off he goes always when I need him most.
"He thinks he ought to earn a little pay,
Enough at least to buy tobacco with,
So he won't have to beg and be beholden."
"All right," I say, "I can't afford to pay
Any fixed wages, though I wish I could."
"Someone else can." "Then someone else will have to."
I shouldn't mind his bettering himself
If that was what it was. You can be certain,
When he begins like that, there's someone at him
Trying to coax him off with pocket-money,—
In haying time, when any help is scarce.
In winter he comes back to us. I'm done.'

'Sh! not so loud: he'll hear you,' Mary said.

'I want him to: he'll have to soon or late.'

'He's worn out. He's asleep beside the stove.
When I came up from Rowe's I found him here,

Huddled against the barn-door fast asleep,
A miserable sight, and frightening, too—
You needn't smile—I didn't recognise him—
I wasn't looking for him—and he's changed.
Wait till you see.'

        'Where did you say he'd been?'

'He didn't say. I dragged him to the house,
And gave him tea and tried to make him smoke.
I tried to make him talk about his travels.
Nothing would do: he just kept nodding off.'

'What did he say? Did he say anything?'

'But little.'

       'Anything? Mary, confess
He said he'd come to ditch the meadow for me.'

'Warren!'

      'But did he? I just want to know.'

'Of course he did. What would you have him say?
Surely you wouldn't grudge the poor old man
Some humble way to save his self-respect.
He added, if you really care to know,
He meant to clear the upper pasture, too.
That sounds like something you have heard before?
Warren, I wish you could have heard the way
He jumbled everything. I stopped to look
Two or three times—he made me feel so queer—
To see if he was talking in his sleep.
He ran on Harold Wilson—you remember—
The boy you had in haying four years since.

He's finished school, and teaching in his college.
Silas declares you'll have to get him back.
He says they two will make a team for work:
Between them they will lay this farm as smooth!
The way he mixed that in with other things.
He thinks young Wilson a likely lad, though daft
On education—you know how they fought
All through July under the blazing sun,
Silas up on the cart to build the load,
Harold along beside to pitch it on.'

'Yes, I took care to keep well out of earshot.'

'Well, those days trouble Silas like a dream.
You wouldn't think they would. How some things linger!
Harold's young college boy's assurance piqued him.
After so many years he still keeps finding
Good arguments he sees he might have used.
I sympathise. I know just how it feels
To think of the right thing to say too late.
Harold's associated in his mind with Latin.
He asked me what I thought of Harold's saying
He studied Latin like the violin
Because he liked it—that an argument!
He said he couldn't make the boy believe
He could find water with a hazel prong—
Which showed how much good school had ever done him.
He wanted to go over that. But most of all
He thinks if he could have another chance
To teach him how to build a load of hay—'

'I know, that's Silas' one accomplishment.
He bundles every forkful in its place,

And tags and numbers it for future reference,
So he can find and easily dislodge it
In the unloading. Silas does that well.
He takes it out in bunches like big birds' nests.
You never see him standing on the hay
He's trying to lift, straining to lift himself.'

'He thinks if he could teach him that, he'd be
Some good perhaps to someone in the world.
He hates to see a boy the fool of books.
Poor Silas, so concerned for other folk,
And nothing to look backward to with pride,
And nothing to look forward to with hope,
So now and never any different.'

Part of a moon was falling down the west,
Dragging the whole sky with it to the hills.
Its light poured softly in her lap. She saw it
And spread her apron to it. She put out her hand
Among the harp-like morning-glory strings,
Taut with the dew from garden bed to eaves,
As if she played unheard some tenderness
That wrought on him beside her in the night.
'Warren,' she said, 'he has come home to die:
You needn't be afraid he'll leave you this time.'

'Home,' he mocked gently.

                              'Yes, what else but home?
It all depends on what you mean by home.
Of course he's nothing to us, any more
Than was the hound that came a stranger to us
Out of the woods, worn out upon the trail.'

'Home is the place where, when you have to go there,
They have to take you in.'

                  'I should have called it
Something you somehow haven't to deserve.'

Warren leaned out and took a step or two,
Picked up a little stick, and brought it back
And broke it in his hand and tossed it by.
'Silas has better claim on us you think
Than on his brother? Thirteen little miles
As the road winds would bring him to his door.
Silas has walked that far no doubt to-day.
Why didn't he go there? His brother's rich,
A somebody—director in the bank.'

'He never told us that.'

               'We know it though.'

'I think his brother ought to help, of course.
I'll see to that if there is need. He ought of right
To take him in, and might be willing to—
He may be better than appearances.
But have some pity on Silas. Do you think
If he had any pride in claiming kin
Or anything he looked for from his brother,
He'd keep so still about him all this time?'

'I wonder what's between them.'

                   'I can tell you.
Silas is what he is—we wouldn't mind him—
But just the kind that kinsfolk can't abide.
He never did a thing so very bad.

He don't know why he isn't quite as good
As anybody. Worthless though he is,
He won't be made ashamed to please his brother.'

'I can't think Si ever hurt anyone.'

'No, but he hurt my heart the way he lay
And rolled his old head on that sharp-edged chair-back.
He wouldn't let me put him on the lounge.
You must go in and see what you can do.
I made the bed up for him there to-night.
You'll be surprised at him—how much he's broken.
His working days are done; I'm sure of it.'

'I'd not be in a hurry to say that.'

'I haven't been. Go, look, see for yourself.
But, Warren, please remember how it is:
He's come to help you ditch the meadow.
He has a plan. You mustn't laugh at him.
He may not speak of it, and then he may.
I'll sit and see if that small sailing cloud
Will hit or miss the moon.'

                It hit the moon.
Then there were three there, making a dim row,
The moon, the little silver cloud, and she.

Warren returned—too soon, it seemed to her,
Slipped to her side, caught up her hand and waited.

'Warren?' she questioned.

                'Dead,' was all he answered.

After Apple-Picking

MY long two-pointed ladder's sticking through a tree
Toward heaven still,
And there's a barrel that I didn't fill
Beside it, and there may be two or three
Apples I didn't pick upon some bough.
But I am done with apple-picking now.
Essence of winter sleep is on the night,
The scent of apples: I am drowsing off.
I cannot rub the strangeness from my sight
I got from looking through a pane of glass
I skimmed this morning from the drinking trough
And held against the world of hoary grass.
It melted, and I let it fall and break.
But I was well
Upon my way to sleep before it fell,
And I could tell
What form my dreaming was about to take.
Magnified apples appear and disappear
Stem end and blossom end,
And every fleck of russet showing clear.
My instep arch not only keeps the ache,
It keeps the pressure of a ladder-round.
I feel the ladder sway as the boughs bend.
And I keep hearing from the cellar bin
The rumbling sound
Of load on load of apples coming in.
For I have had too much
Of apple-picking: I am overtired
Of the great harvest I myself desired.

There were ten thousand thousand fruit to touch,
Cherish in hand, lift down, and not let fall.
For all
That struck the earth,
No matter if not bruised or spiked with stubble,
Went surely to the cider-apple heap
As of no worth.
One ean see what will trouble
This sleep of mine, whatever sleep it is.
Were he not gone,
The woodchuck could say whether it's like his
Long sleep, as I describe its coming on,
Or just some human sleep.

270   *The Road Not Taken*

TWO roads diverged in a yellow wood,
And sorry I could not travel both
And be one traveler, long I stood
And looked down one as far as I could
To where it bent in the undergrowth;

Then took the other, as just as fair,
And having perhaps the better claim,
Because it was grassy and wanted wear;
Though as for that the passing there
Had worn them really about the same,

And both that morning equally lay
In leaves no step had trodden black.
Oh, I kept the first for another day!

Yet knowing how way leads on to way,
I doubted if I should ever come back.

I shall be telling this with a sigh
Somewhere ages and ages hence:
Two roads diverged in a wood, and I—
I took the one less traveled by,
And that has made all the difference.

271   *An Old Man's Winter Night*

ALL out of doors looked darkly in at him
Through the thin frost, almost in separate stars,
That gathers on the pane in empty rooms.
What kept his eyes from giving back the gaze
Was the lamp tilted near them in his hand.
What kept him from remembering what it was
That brought him to that creaking room was age.
He stood with barrels round him—at a loss.
And having scared the cellar under him
In clomping there, he scared it once again
In clomping off;—and scared the outer night,
Which has its sounds, familiar, like the roar
Of trees and crack of branches, common things,
But nothing so like beating on a box.
A light he was to no one but himself
Where now he sat, concerned with he knew what,
A quiet light, and then not even that.
He consigned to the moon, such as she was,
So late-arising, to the broken moon
As better than the sun in any case

For such a charge, his snow upon the roof,
His icicles along the wall to keep;
And slept. The log that shifted with a jolt
Once in the stove, disturbed him and he shifted,
And eased his heavy breathing, but still slept.
One aged man—one man—can't keep a house,
A farm, a countryside, or if he can,
It's thus he does it of a winter night.

272　　　　　*Meeting and Passing*

A S I went down the hill along the wall
There was a gate I had leaned at for the view
And had just turned from when I first saw you
As you came up the hill. We met. But all
We did that day was mingle great and small
Footprints in summer dust as if we drew
The figure of our being less than two
But more than one as yet. Your parasol
Pointed the decimal off with one deep thrust.
And all the time we talked you seemed to see
Something down there to smile at in the dust.
(Oh, it was without prejudice to me!)
Afterward I went past what you had passed
Before we met and you what I had passed.

273　　　　　*The Oven Bird*

T HERE is a singer everyone has heard,
Loud, a mid-summer and a mid-wood bird,

Who makes the solid tree trunks sound again.
He says that leaves are old and that for flowers
Mid-summer is to spring as one to ten.
He says the early petal-fall is past
When pear and cherry bloom went down in showers
On sunny days a moment overcast;
And comes that other fall we name the fall.
He says the highway dust is over all.
The bird would cease and be as other birds
But that he knows in singing not to sing.
The question that he frames in all but words
Is what to make of a diminished thing.

274 *Birches*

WHEN I see birches bend to left and right
Across the lines of straighter darker trees,
I like to think some boy's been swinging them.
But swinging doesn't bend them down to stay.
Ice-storms do that. Often you must have seen them
Loaded with ice a sunny winter morning
After a rain. They click upon themselves
As the breeze rises, and turn many-colored
As the stir cracks and crazes their enamel.
Soon the sun's warmth makes them shed crystal shells
Shattering and avalanching on the snow-crust—
Such heaps of broken glass to sweep away
You'd think the inner dome of heaven had fallen.
They are dragged to the withered bracken by the load,
And they seem not to break; though once they are bowed
So low for long, they never right themselves:

You may see their trunks arching in the woods
Years afterwards, trailing their leaves on the ground
Like girls on hands and knees that throw their hair
Before them over their heads to dry in the sun.
But I was going to say when Truth broke in
With all her matter-of-fact about the ice-storm
I should prefer to have some boy bend them
As he went out and in to fetch the cows—
Some boy too far from town to learn baseball,
Whose only play was what he found himself,
Summer or winter, and could play alone.
One by one he subdued his father's trees
By riding them down over and over again
Until he took the stiffness out of them,
And not one but hung limp, not one was left
For him to conquer. He learned all there was
To learn about not launching out too soon
And so not carrying the tree away
Clear to the ground. He always kept his poise
To the top branches, climbing carefully
With the same pains you use to fill a cup
Up to the brim, and even above the brim.
Then he flung outward, feet first, with a swish,
Kicking his way down through the air to the ground.
So was I once myself a swinger of birches.
And so I dream of going back to be.
It's when I'm weary of considerations,
And life is too much like a pathless wood
Where your face burns and tickles with the cobwebs
Broken across it, and one eye is weeping
From a twig's having lashed across it open.
I'd like to get away from earth awhile
And then come back to it and begin over.

May no fate willfully misunderstand me
And half grant what I wish and snatch me away
Not to return. Earth's the right place for love:
I don't know where it's likely to go better.
I'd like to go by climbing a birch tree,
And climb black branches up a snow-white trunk
Toward heaven, till the tree could bear no more,
But dipped its top and set me down again.
That would be good both going and coming back.
One could do worse than be a swinger of birches.

275   *Putting in the Seed*

YOU come to fetch me from my work to-night
When supper's on the table, and we'll see
If I can leave off burying the white
Soft petals fallen from the apple tree
(Soft petals, yes, but not so barren quite,
Mingled with these, smooth bean and wrinkled pea;)
And go along with you ere you lose sight
Of what you came for and become like me,
Slave to a springtime passion for the earth.
How Love burns through the Putting in the Seed
On through the watching for that early birth
When, just as the soil tarnishes with weed,
The sturdy seedling with arched body comes
Shouldering its way and shedding the earth crumbs.

'Out, Out—'

THE buzz-saw snarled and rattled in the yard
And made dust and dropped stove-length sticks of wood,
Sweet-scented stuff when the breeze drew across it.
And from there those that lifted eyes could count
Five mountain ranges one behind the other
Under the sunset far into Vermont.
And the saw snarled and rattled, snarled and rattled,
As it ran light, or had to bear a load.
And nothing happened: day was all but done.
Call it a day, I wish they might have said
To please the boy by giving him the half hour
That a boy counts so much when saved from work.
His sister stood beside them in her apron
To tell them 'Supper.' At the word, the saw,
As if to prove saws knew what supper meant,
Leaped out at the boy's hand, or seemed to leap—
He must have given the hand. However it was,
Neither refused the meeting. But the hand!
The boy's first outcry was a rueful laugh,
As he swung toward them holding up the hand
Half in appeal, but half as if to keep
The life from spilling. Then the boy saw all—
Since he was old enough to know, big boy
Doing a man's work, though a child at heart—
He saw all spoiled. 'Don't let him cut my hand off—
The doctor, when he comes. Don't let him, sister!'
So. But the hand was gone already.
The doctor put him in the dark of ether.
He lay and puffed his lips out with his breath.
And then—the watcher at his pulse took fright.

No one believed. They listened at his heart.
Little—less—nothing!—and that ended it.
No more to build on there. And they, since they
Were not the one dead, turned to their affairs.

277   *The Sound of the Trees*

I WONDER about the trees.
Why do we wish to bear
Forever the noise of these
More than another noise
So close to our dwelling place?
We suffer them by the day
Till we lose all measure of pace,
And fixity in our joys,
And acquire a listening air.
They are that that talks of going
But never gets away;
And that talks no less for knowing,
As it grows wiser and older,
That now it means to stay.
My feet tug at the floor
And my head sways to my shoulder
Sometimes when I watch trees sway,
From the window or the door.
I shall set forth for somewhere,
I shall make the reckless choice
Some day when they are in voice
And tossing so as to scare
The white clouds over them on.
I shall have less to say,
But I shall be gone.

The Axe-Helve

I'VE known ere now an interfering branch
Of alder catch my lifted axe behind me.
But that was in the woods, to hold my hand
From striking at another alder's roots,
And that was, as I say, an alder branch.
This was a man, Baptiste, who stole one day
Behind me on the snow in my own yard
Where I was working at the chopping-block,
And cutting nothing not cut down already.
He caught my axe expertly on the rise,
When all my strength put forth was in his favor.
Held it a moment where it was, to calm me,
Then took it from me—and I let him take it.
I didn't know him well enough to know
What it was all about. There might be something
He had in mind to say to a bad neighbor
He might prefer to say to him disarmed.
But all he had to tell me in French-English
Was what he thought of—not me, but my axe;
Me only as I took my axe to heart.
It was the bad axe-helve some one had sold me—
'Made on machine,' he said, ploughing the grain
With a thick thumbnail to show how it ran
Across the handle's long drawn serpentine,
Like the two strokes across a dollar sign.
'You give her one good crack, she's snap raght off.
Den where's your hax-ead flying t'rough de hair?'
Admitted; and yet, what was that to him?

'Come on my house and I put you one in
What's las' awhile—good hick'ry what's grow crooked,
De second growt' I cut myself—tough, tough!'

Something to sell? That wasn't how it sounded.

'Den when you say you come? It's cost you nothing.
To-naght?'

As well to-night as any night.

Beyond an over-warmth of kitchen stove
My welcome differed from no other welcome.
Baptiste knew best why I was where I was.
So long as he would leave enough unsaid,
I shouldn't mind his being overjoyed
(If overjoyed he was) at having got me
Where I must judge if what he knew about an axe
That not everybody else knew was to count
For nothing in the measure of a neighbor.
Hard if, though cast away for life with Yankees,
A Frenchman couldn't get his human rating!

Mrs. Baptiste came in and rocked a chair
That had as many motions as the world:
One back and forward, in and out of shadow,
That got her nowhere; one more gradual,
Sideways, that would have run her on the stove
In time, had she not realized her danger
And caught herself up bodily, chair and all,
And set herself back where she started from.
'She ain't spick too much Henglish—dat's too bad.'

I was afraid, in brightening first on me,
Then on Baptiste, as if she understood
What passed between us, she was only feigning.
Baptiste was anxious for her; but no more
Than for himself, so placed he couldn't hope
To keep his bargain of the morning with me
In time to keep me from suspecting him
Of really never having meant to keep it.

Needlessly soon he had his axe-helves out,
A quiverful to choose from, since he wished me
To have the best he had, or had to spare—
Not for me to ask which, when what he took
Had beauties he had to point me out at length
To insure their not being wasted on me.
He liked to have it slender as a whipstock,
Free from the least knot, equal to the strain
Of bending like a sword across the knee.
He showed me that the lines of a good helve
Were native to the grain before the knife
Expressed them, and its curves were no false curves
Put on it from without. And there its strength lay
For the hard work. He chafed its long white body
From end to end with his rough hand shut round it.
He tried it at the eye-hole in the axe-head.
'Hahn, hahn,' he mused, 'don't need much taking down.'
Baptiste knew how to make a short job long
For love of it, and yet not waste time either.

Do you know, what we talked about was knowledge?
Baptiste on his defence about the children
He kept from school, or did his best to keep—
Whatever school and children and our doubts

Of laid-on education had to do
With the curves of his axe-helves and his having
Used these unscrupulously to bring me
To see for once the inside of his house.
Was I desired in friendship, partly as some one
To leave it to, whether the right to hold
Such doubts of education should depend
Upon the education of those who held them?

But now he brushed the shavings from his knee
And stood the axe there on its horse's hoof,
Erect, but not without its waves, as when
The snake stood up for evil in the Garden,—
Top-heavy with a heaviness his short,
Thick hand made light of, steel-blue chin drawn down
And in a little—a French touch in that.
Baptiste drew back and squinted at it, pleased;
'See how she's cock her head!'

279   *Fire and Ice*

Some say the world will end in fire,
Some say in ice.
From what I've tasted of desire
I hold with those who favor fire.
But if it had to perish twice,
I think I know enough of hate
To say that for destruction ice
Is also great
And would suffice.

280   *Dust of Snow*

THE way a crow
Shook down on me
The dust of snow
From a hemlock tree

Has given my heart
A change of mood
And saved some part
Of a day I had rued.

281   *Stopping by Woods on a Snowy
Evening*

WHOSE woods these are I think I know.
His house is in the village though;
He will not see me stopping here
To watch his woods fill up with snow.

My little horse must think it queer
To stop without a farmhouse near
Between the woods and frozen lake
The darkest evening of the year.

He gives his harness bells a shake
To ask if there is some mistake.
The only other sound's the sweep
Of easy wind and downy flake.

The woods are lovely, dark and deep,
But I have promises to keep,
And miles to go before I sleep,
And miles to go before I sleep.

The Onset

ALWAYS the same, when on a fated night
At last the gathered snow lets down as white
As may be in dark woods, and with a song
It shall not make again all winter long
Of hissing on the yet uncovered ground,
I almost stumble looking up and round,
As one who overtaken by the end
Gives up his errand, and lets death descend
Upon him where he is, with nothing done
To evil, no important triumph won,
More than if life had never been begun.

Yet all the precedent is on my side:
I know that winter death has never tried
The earth but it has failed: the snow may heap
In long storms an undrifted four feet deep
As measured against maple, birch and oak,
It cannot check the peeper's silver croak;
And I shall see the snow all go down hill
In water of a slender April rill
That flashes tail through last year's withered brake
And dead weeds, like a disappearing snake.
Nothing will be left white but here a birch,
And there a clump of houses with a church.

To Earthward

LOVE at the lips was touch
As sweet as I could bear;
And once that seemed too much;
I lived on air

That crossed me from sweet things,
The flow of—was it musk
From hidden grapevine springs
Down hill at dusk?

I had the swirl and ache
From sprays of honeysuckle
That when they're gathered shake
Dew on the knuckle.

I craved strong sweets, but those
Seemed strong when I was young;
The petal of the rose
It was that stung.

Now no joy but lacks salt
That is not dashed with pain
And weariness and fault;
I crave the stain

Of tears, the aftermark
Of almost too much love,
The sweet of bitter bark
And burning clove.

When stiff and sore and scarred
I take away my hand
From leaning on it hard
In grass and sand,

The hurt is not enough:
I long for weight and strength
To feel the earth as rough
To all my length.

284   *Not to Keep*

THEY sent him back to her. The letter came
Saying . . . And she could have him. And before
She could be sure there was no hidden ill
Under the formal writing, he was there,
Living. They gave him back to her alive—
How else? They are not known to send the dead—
And not disfigured visibly. His face?
His hands? She had to look, to look and ask,
'What is it, dear?' And she had given all
And still she had all—*they* had—they the lucky!
Wasn't she glad now? Everything seemed won,
And all the rest for them permissible ease.
She had to ask, 'What was it, dear?'

                                    'Enough,
Yet not enough. A bullet through and through,
High in the breast. Nothing but what good care
And medicine and rest, and you a week,
Can cure me of to go again.' The same
Grim giving to do over for them both.

She dared no more than ask him with her eyes
How was it with him for a second trial.
And with his eyes he asked her not to ask.
They had given him back to her, but not to keep.

285   *A Brook in the City*

THE farmhouse lingers, though averse to square
With the new city street it has to wear
A number in. But what about the brook
That held the house as in an elbow-crook?
I ask as one who knew the brook, its strength
And impulse, having dipped a finger length
And made it leap my knuckle, having tossed
A flower to try its currents where they crossed.
The meadow grass could be cemented down
From growing under pavements of a town;
The apple trees be sent to hearth-stone flame.
Is water wood to serve a brook the same?
How else dispose of an immortal force
No longer needed? Staunch it at its source
With cinder loads dumped down? The brook was thrown
Deep in a sewer dungeon under stone
In fetid darkness still to live and run—
And all for nothing it had ever done
Except forget to go in fear perhaps.
No one would know except for ancient maps
That such a brook ran water. But I wonder
If from its being kept forever under
The thoughts may not have risen that so keep
This new-built city from both work and sleep.

*The Need of Being Versed in
Country Things*

THE house had gone to bring again
To the midnight sky a sunset glow.
Now the chimney was all of the house that stood,
Like a pistil after the petals go.

The barn opposed across the way,
That would have joined the house in flame
Had it been the will of the wind, was left
To bear forsaken the place's name.

No more it opened with all one end
For teams that came by the stony road
To drum on the floor with scurrying hoofs
And brush the mow with the summer load.

The birds that came to it through the air
At broken windows flew out and in,
Their murmur more like the sigh we sigh
From too much dwelling on what has been.

Yet for them the lilac renewed its leaf,
And the aged elm, though touched with fire;
And the dry pump flung up an awkward arm;
And the fence post carried a strand of wire.

For them there was really nothing sad.
But though they rejoiced in the nest they kept,
One had to be versed in country things
Not to believe the phoebes wept.

287 *Spring Pools*

THESE pools that, though in forests, still reflect
The total sky almost without defect,
And like the flowers beside them, chill and shiver,
Will like the flowers beside them soon be gone,
And yet not out by any brook or river,
But up by roots to bring dark foliage on.

The trees that have it in their pent-up buds
To darken nature and be summer woods—
Let them think twice before they use their powers
To blot out and drink up and sweep away
These flowery waters and these watery flowers
From snow that melted only yesterday.

288 *Acceptance*

WHEN the spent sun throws up its rays on cloud
And goes down burning into the gulf below,
No voice in nature is heard to cry aloud
At what has happened. Birds, at least, must know
It is the change to darkness in the sky.
Murmuring something quiet in her breast,
One bird begins to close a faded eye;
Or overtaken too far from his nest,
Hurrying low above the grove, some waif
Swoops just in time to his remembered tree

At most he thinks or twitters softly, 'Safe!
Now let the night be dark for all of me.
Let the night be too dark for me to see
Into the future. Let what will be, be.'

289 *Bereft*

WHERE had I heard this wind before
Change like this to a deeper roar?
What would it take my standing there for,
Holding open a restive door,
Looking down hill to a frothy shore?
Summer was past and day was past.
Somber clouds in the west were massed.
Out in the porch's sagging floor,
Leaves got up in a coil and hissed,
Blindly struck at my knee and missed.
Something sinister in the tone
Told me my secret must be known:
Word I was in the house alone
Somehow must have gotten abroad,
Word I was in my life alone,
Word I had no one left but God.

290 *Tree at My Window*

TREE at my window, window tree,
My sash is lowered when night comes on;
But let there never be curtain drawn
Between you and me.

Vague dream-head lifted out of the ground,
And thing next most diffuse to cloud,
Not all your light tongues talking aloud
Could be profound.

But tree, I have seen you taken and tossed,
And if you have seen me when I slept,
You have seen me when I was taken and swept
And all but lost.

That day she put our heads together,
Fate had her imagination about her,
Your head so much concerned with outer,
Mine with inner, weather.

291 *The Lovely Shall Be Choosers*

THE Voice said, 'Hurl her down!'

The Voices, 'How far down?'

'Seven levels of the world.'

'How much time have we?'

'Take twenty years.
She *would* refuse love safe with wealth and honor!
The lovely shall be choosers, shall they?
Then let them choose!'

'Then we shall let her choose?'

'Yes, let her choose.
Take up the task beyond her choosing.'

Invisible hands crowded on her shoulder
In readiness to weigh upon her.
But she stood straight still,
In broad round ear-rings, gold and jet with pearls
And broad round suchlike brooch,
Her cheeks high colored,
Proud and the pride of friends.

The Voice asked, 'You can let her choose?'

'Yes, we can let her and still triumph.'

'Do it by joys, and leave her always blameless.
Be her first joy her wedding,
That though a wedding,
Is yet—well something they know, he and she.
And after that her next joy
That though she grieves, her grief is secret:
Those friends know nothing of her grief to make it
    shameful.
Her third joy that though now they cannot help but know,
They move in pleasure too far off
To think much or much care.
Give her a child at either knee for fourth joy
To tell once and once only, for them never to forget,
How once she walked in brightness,
And make them see it in the winter firelight.
But give her friends for then she dare not tell
For their foregone incredulousness.
And be her next joy this:

577

Her never having deigned to tell them.
Make her among the humblest even
Seem to them less than they are.
Hopeless of being known for what she has been,
Failing of being loved for what she is,
Give her the comfort for her sixth of knowing
She fails from strangeness to a way of life
She came to from too high too late to learn.
Then send some *one* with eyes to see
And wonder at her where she is,
And words to wonder in her hearing how she came there,
But without time to linger for her story.
Be her last joy her heart's going out to this one
So that she almost speaks.
You know them—seven in all.'

'Trust us,' the Voices said.

292 *The Investment*

OVER back where they speak of life as staying
('You couldn't call it living, for it ain't'),
There was an old, old house renewed with paint,
And in it a piano loudly playing.

Out in the ploughed ground in the cold a digger,
Among unearthed potatoes standing still,
Was counting winter dinners, one a hill,
With half an ear to the piano's vigor.

All that piano and new paint back there,
Was it some money suddenly come into?

Or some extravagance young love had been to?
Or old love on an impulse not to care—

Not to sink under being man and wife,
But get some color and music out of life?

293   *The White-tailed Hornet*

THE white-tailed hornet lives in a balloon
That floats against the ceiling of the woodshed.
The exit he comes out at like a bullet
Is like the pupil of a pointed gun.
And having power to change his aim in flight,
He comes out more unerring than a bullet.
Verse could be written on the certainty
With which he penetrates my best defense
Of whirling hands and arms about the head
To stab me in the sneeze-nerve of a nostril.
Such is the instinct of it I allow.
Yet how about the insect certainty
That in the neighborhood of home and children
Is such an execrable judge of motives
As not to recognize in me the exception
I like to think I am in everything—
One who would never hang above a bookcase
His Japanese crepe-paper globe for trophy?
He stung me first and stung me afterward.
He rolled me off the field head over heels,
And would not listen to my explanations.

That's when I went as visitor to his house.
As visitor at my house he is better.

Hawking for flies about the kitchen door,
In at one door perhaps and out another,
Trust him then not to put you in the wrong.
He won't misunderstand your freest movements.
Let him light on your skin unless you mind
So many prickly grappling feet at once.
He's after the domesticated fly
To feed his thumping grubs as big as he is.
Here he is at his best, but even here—
I watched him where he swooped, he pounced, he struck;
But what he found he had was just a nailhead.
He struck a second time. Another nailhead.
'Those are just nailheads. Those are fastened down.'
Then disconcerted and not unannoyed,
He stooped and struck a little huckleberry
The way a player curls around a football.
'Wrong shape, wrong color, and wrong scent,' I said.
The huckleberry rolled him on his head.
At last it was a fly. He shot and missed;
And the fly circled round him in derision.
But for the fly he might have made me think
He had been at his poetry, comparing
Nailhead with fly and fly with huckleberry:
How like a fly, how very like a fly.
But the real fly he missed would never do;
The missed fly made me dangerously skeptic.

Won't this whole instinct matter bear revision?
Won't almost any theory bear revision?
To err is human, not to, animal.
Or so we pay the compliment to instinct,
Only too liberal of our compliment
That really takes away instead of gives.

Our worship, humor, conscientiousness
Went long since to the dogs under the table.
And served us right for having instituted
Downward comparisons. As long on earth
As our comparisons were stoutly upward
With gods and angels, we were men at least,
But little lower than the gods and angels.
But once comparisons were yielded downward,
Once we began to see our images
Reflected in the mud and even dust,
'Twas disillusion upon disillusion.
We were lost piecemeal to the animals,
Like people thrown out to delay the wolves.
Nothing but fallibility was left us,
And this day's work made even that seem doubtful.

294   *Desert Places*

SNOW falling and night falling fast, oh, fast
In a field I looked into going past,
And the ground almost covered smooth in snow,
But a few weeds and stubble showing last.

The woods around it have it—it is theirs.
All animals are smothered in their lairs.
I am too absent-spirited to count;
The loneliness includes me unawares.

And lonely as it is that loneliness
Will be more lonely ere it will be less—
A blanker whiteness of benighted snow
With no expression, nothing to express.

581

They cannot scare me with their empty spaces
Between stars—on stars where no human race is.
I have it in me so much nearer home
To scare myself with my own desert places.

295   *The Subverted Flower*

SHE drew back; he was calm:
'It is this that had the power.'
And he lashed his open palm
With the tender-headed flower.
He smiled for her to smile,
But she was either blind
Or willfully unkind.
He eyed her for a while
For a woman and a puzzle.
He flicked and flung the flower,
And another sort of smile
Caught up like finger tips
The corners of his lips
And cracked his ragged muzzle.
She was standing to the waist
In goldenrod and brake,
Her shining hair displaced.
He stretched her either arm
As if she made it ache
To clasp her—not to harm;
As if he could not spare
To touch her neck and hair.
'If this has come to us
And not to me alone—'

So she thought she heard him say;
Though with every word he spoke
His lips were sucked and blown
And the effort made him choke
Like a tiger at a bone.
She had to lean away.
She dared not stir a foot,
Lest movement should provoke
The demon of pursuit
That slumbers in a brute.
It was then her mother's call
From inside the garden wall
Made her steal a look of fear
To see if he could hear
And would pounce to end it all
Before her mother came.
She looked and saw the shame:
A hand hung like a paw,
An arm worked like a saw
As if to be persuasive,
An ingratiating laugh
That cut the snout in half,
An eye become evasive.
A girl could only see
That a flower had marred a man,
But what she could not see
Was that the flower might be
Other than base and fetid:
That the flower had done but part,
And what the flower began
Her own too meager heart
Had terribly completed.
She looked and saw the worst.

And the dog or what it was,
Obeying bestial laws,
A coward save at night,
Turned from the place and ran.
She heard him stumble first
And use his hands in flight.
She heard him bark outright.
And oh, for one so young
The bitter words she spit
Like some tenacious bit
That will not leave the tongue.
She plucked her lips for it,
And still the horror clung.
Her mother wiped the foam
From her chin, picked up her comb
And drew her backward home.

296 *The Gift Outright*

THE land was ours before we were the land's.
She was our land more than a hundred years
Before we were her people. She was ours
In Massachusetts, in Virginia,
But we were England's, still colonials,
Possessing what we still were unpossessed by,
Possessed by what we now no more possessed.
Something we were withholding made us weak
Until we found out that it was ourselves
We were withholding from our land of living,
And forthwith found salvation in surrender.
Such as we were we gave ourselves outright

(The deed of gift was many deeds of war)
To the land vaguely realizing westward,
But still unstoried, artless, unenhanced,
Such as she was, such as she would become.

CARL SANDBURG

b. 1878

297   *Chicago*

Hog Butcher for the World,
Tool maker, Stacker of Wheat,
Player with Railroads and the Nation's Freight
    Handler;
Stormy, husky, brawling,
City of the Big Shoulders:

They tell me you are wicked and I believe them, for I
    have seen your painted women under the gas lamps
    luring the farm boys.
And they tell me you are crooked and I answer: Yes, it
    is true I have seen the gunman kill and go free to
    kill again.
And they tell me you are brutal and my reply is: On the
    faces of women and children I have seen the marks
    of wanton hunger.
And having answered so I turn once more to those who
    sneer at this my city, and I give them back the sneer
    and say to them:

Come and show me another city with lifted head singing
so proud to be alive and coarse and strong and cun-
ning.

Flinging magnetic curses amid the toil of piling job on
job, here is a tall bold slugger set vivid against the
little soft cities;

Fierce as a dog with tongue lapping for action, cunning
as a savage pitted against the wilderness,

  Bareheaded,

  Shoveling,

  Wrecking,

  Planning,

  Building, breaking, rebuilding,

Under the smoke, dust all over his mouth, laughing with
white teeth,

Under the terrible burden of destiny laughing as a young
man laughs,

Laughing even as an ignorant fighter laughs who has
never lost a battle,

Bragging and laughing that under his wrist is the pulse,
and under his ribs the heart of the people,

    Laughing!

Laughing the stormy, husky, brawling laughter of Youth,
half-naked, sweating, proud to be Hog Butcher, Tool
Maker, Stacker of Wheat, Player with Railroads and
Freight Handler to the Nation.

298   *Fish Crier*

I KNOW a Jew fish crier down on Maxwell Street with
a voice like a north wind blowing over corn stubble
in January.

He dangles herring before prospective customers evinc-
ing a joy identical with that of Pavlowa dancing.
His face is that of a man terribly glad to be selling fish,
terribly glad that God made fish, and customers to
whom he may call his wares from a pushcart.

299   *Happiness*

I ASKED professors who teach the meaning of life to
tell me what is happiness.
And I went to famous executives who boss the work of
thousands of men.
They all shook their heads and gave me a smile as though
I was trying to fool with them.
And then one Sunday afternoon I wandered out along the
Desplaines river
And I saw a crowd of Hungarians under the trees with
their women and children and a keg of beer and an
accordion.

300   *Population Drifts*

NEW-MOWN hay smell and wind of the plain made
her a woman whose ribs had the power of the hills in
them and her hands were tough for work and there
was passion for life in her womb.
She and her man crossed the ocean and the years that
marked their faces saw them haggling with landlords
and grocers while six children played on the stones
and prowled in the garbage cans.

One child coughed its lungs away, two more have adenoids and can neither talk nor run like their mother, one is in jail, two have jobs in a box factory
And as they fold the pasteboard, they wonder what the wishing is and the wistful glory in them that flutters faintly when the glimmer of spring comes on the air or the green of summer turns brown:
They do not know it is the new-mown hay smell calling and the wind of the plain praying for them to come back and take hold of life again with tough hands and with passion.

301   *Limited*

I AM riding on a limited express, one of the crack trains of the nation.
Hurtling across the prairie into blue haze and dark air go fifteen all-steel coaches holding a thousand people.
(All the coaches shall be scrap and rust and all the men and women laughing in the diners and sleepers shall pass to ashes.)
I ask a man in the smoker where he is going and he answers: 'Omaha.'

302   *Ice Handler*

I KNOW an ice handler who wears a flannel shirt with pearl buttons the size of a dollar,
And he lugs a hundred-pound hunk into a saloon icebox, helps himself to cold ham and rye bread,

Tells the bartender it's hotter than yesterday and will be
    hotter yet to-morrow, by Jesus,

And is on his way with his head in the air and a hard
    pair of fists.

He spends a dollar or so every Saturday night on a two
    hundred pound woman who washes dishes in the
    Hotel Morrison.

He remembers when the union was organized he broke
    the noses of two scabs and loosened the nuts so the
    wheels came off six different wagons one morning,
    and he came around and watched the ice melt in the
    street.

All he was sorry for was one of the scabs bit him on the
    knuckles of the right hand so they bled when he
    came around to the saloon to tell the boys about it.

303   *I Am the People, the Mob*

I AM the people—the mob—the crowd—the mass.

Do you know that all the great work of the world is done
    through me?

I am the workingman, the inventor, the maker of the
    world's food and clothes.

I am the audience that witnesses history. The Napoleons
    come from me and the Lincolns. They die. And then
    I send forth more Napoleons and Lincolns.

I am the seed ground. I am a prairie that will stand for
    much plowing. Terrible storms pass over me. I for-
    get. The best of me is sucked out and wasted. I for-
    get. Everything but Death comes to me and makes
    me work and give up what I have. And I forget.

Sometimes I growl, shake myself and spatter a few red
  drops for history to remember. Then—I forget.
When I, the People, learn to remember, when I, the
  People, use the lessons of yesterday and no longer
  forget who robbed me last year, who played me for
  a fool—then there will be no speaker in all the world
  say the name: 'The People,' with any fleck of a sneer
  in his voice or any far-off smile of derision.
The mob—the crowd—the mass—will arrive then.

304   Psalm of Those Who Go Forth
before Daylight

THE policeman buys shoes slow and careful; the team-
  ster buys gloves slow and careful; they take care of
  their feet and hands; they live on their feet and
  hands.

The milkman never argues; he works alone and no one
  speaks to him; the city is asleep when he is on the
  job; he puts a bottle on six hundred porches and
  calls it a day's work; he climbs two hundred wooden
  stairways; two horses are company for him; he never
  argues.

The rolling-mill men and the sheet-steel men are brothers
  of cinders; they empty cinders out of their shoes
  after the day's work; they ask their wives to fix burnt
  holes in the knees of their trousers; their necks and
  ears are covered with a smut; they scour their necks
  and ears; they are brothers of cinders.

305 *Grass*

PILE the bodies high at Austerlitz and Waterloo.
Shovel them under and let me work—
　　　　　I am the grass; I cover all.

And pile them high at Gettysburg
And pile them high at Ypres and Verdun.
Shovel them under and let me work.
Two years, ten years, and passengers ask the conductor:
　　　　　What place is this?
　　　　　Where are we now?

　　　　　I am the grass.
　　　　　Let me work.

306 *Broken-Face Gargoyles*

ALL I can give you is broken-face gargoyles.
It is too early to sing and dance at funerals,
Though I can whisper to you I am looking for an under-
　　　taker humming a lullaby and throwing his feet in a
　　　swift and mystic buck-and-wing, now you see it and
　　　now you don't.

Fish to swim a pool in your garden flashing a speckled
　　　silver,
A basket of wine-saps filling your room with flame-dark
　　　for your eyes and the tang of valley orchards for
　　　your nose,

Such a beautiful pail of fish, such a beautiful peck of
apples, I cannot bring you now.
It is too early and I am not footloose yet.

I shall come in the night when I come with a hammer
and saw.
I shall come near your window, where you look out when
your eyes open in the morning,
And there I shall slam together bird-houses and bird-baths
for wing-loose wrens and hummers to live in, birds
with yellow wing tips to blur and buzz soft all sum-
mer,
So I shall make little fool homes with doors, always open
doors for all and each to run away when they want
to.
I shall come just like that even though now it is early
and I am not yet footloose,
Even though I am still looking for an undertaker with
a raw, wind-bitten face and a dance in his feet.
I make a date with you (put it down) for six o'clock in
the evening a thousand years from now.

All I can give you now is broken-face gargoyles.
All I can give you now is a double gorilla head with two
fish mouths and four eagle eyes hooked on a street
wall, spouting water and looking two ways to the
ends of the street for the new people, the young
strangers, coming, coming, always coming.

It is early.
I shall yet be footloose.

Ossawatomie

I DON'T know how he came,
shambling, dark, and strong.

He stood in the city and told men:
My people are fools, my people are young and strong,
    my people must learn, my people are terrible workers
    and fighters.
Always he kept on asking: Where did that blood come
    from?

    They said: You for the fool killer,
                you for the booby hatch
                and a necktie party.

    They hauled him into jail.
    They sneered at him and spit on him,
    And he wrecked their jails,
    Singing, 'God damn your jails,'
    And when he was most in jail
    Crummy among the crazy in the dark
    Then he was most of all out of jail
    Shambling, dark, and strong,
Always asking: Where did that blood come from?

    They laid hands on him
    And the fool killers had a laugh
    And the necktie party was a go, by God.
    They laid hands on him and he was a goner.
        They hammered him to pieces and he stood up.
    They buried him and he walked out of the grave, by God,
        Asking again: Where did that blood come from?

308   *Threes*

I WAS a boy when I heard three red words
a thousand Frenchmen died in the streets
for: Liberty, Equality, Fraternity—I asked
why men die for words.

I was older; men with mustaches, sideburns,
lilacs, told me the high golden words are:
Mother, Home, and Heaven—other older men with
face decorations said: God, Duty, Immortality
—they sang these threes slow from deep lungs.

Years ticked off their say-so on the great clocks
of doom and damnation, soup and nuts: meteors flashed
their say-so: and out of great Russia came three
dusky syllables workmen took guns and went out to die
for: Bread, Peace, Land.

And I met a marine of the U.S.A., a leatherneck with
a girl on his knee for a memory in ports circling the
earth and he said: Tell me how to say three things
and I always get by—gimme a plate of ham and eggs—
how much?—and—do you love me, kid?

309   '*Who shall speak for the people?*'

WHO shall speak for the people?
who has the answers?
where is the sure interpreter?
who knows what to say?

Who can write the music jazz-classical
    smokestacks-geraniums hyacinths-biscuits
    now whispering easy
    now boom doom crashing angular
    now tough monotonous tom tom
Who has enough split-seconds and slow sea-tides?

The ships of the sea and the mists of
    night and the sheen of old battle-
    fields and the moon on the city rub-
    bish dumps belong to the people.
The crops this year, last and next year,
    and the winds and frosts in many
    orchards and tomato gardens, are
    listed in the people's acquaintance.
Horses and wagons, trucks and tractors,
    from the shouting cities to the sleep-
    ing prairies, from worn pavements
    to mountain mule paths, the people
    have strange possessions.
The plow and the hammer, the knife and
    the shovel, the planting hoe and the
    reaping sickle, everywhere these are
    the people's possessions by right of
    use.
Their handles are smoothed to the grain
    of the wood by the enclosing
    thumbs and fingers of familiar
    hands,
Maintenance-of-way men in a Tennessee
    gang singing, 'If I die a railroad
    man put a pick and shovel at my

head and my feet and a nine-pound
hammer in my hand,'

Larry, the Kansas section boss, on his
dying bed asking for one last look at
the old hand-car,

His men saying in the coffin on his chest
he should by rights have the spike
maul, the gauge and the old claw-bar.

The early morning in the fields, the
brown thrush warbling and the imi-
tations of the catbird, the neverend-
ing combat with pest and destroyer,
the chores of feeding and watching,
seedtime and harvest,

The clocking of the months toward a
birthing day, the newly dropped
calves and the finished steers loaded
in stock-cars for market, the gamble
on what we'll get tomorrow for
what we put in today—

These are belongings of the people, dusty
with the dust of earth, merciless as
sudden hog cholera, hopeful as a
rainwashed hill of moonlit pines.

310   *'The man in the street is fed'*

T HE man in the street is fed
with lies in peace, gas in war,
and he may live now

just around the corner from you
trying to sell
the only thing he has to sell,
the power of his hand and brain
to labor for wages, for pay,
for cash of the realm.
And there are no takers, he can't connect.
Maybe he says, 'Some pretty good men are on the street.'
Maybe he says, 'I'm just a palooka . . . all washed up.'
Maybe he's a wild kid ready for his first stickup.
Maybe he's bummed a thousand miles and has a diploma.
Maybe he can take whatever the police can hand him,
Too many of him saying in their own wild way,
'The worst they can give you is lead in the guts.'
Whatever the wild kids want to do they'll do
And whoever gives them ideas, faiths, slogans,
Whoever touches the bottom flares of them,
Connects with something prouder than all deaths
For they can live on hard corn and like it.
They are the original sons of the wild jackass
Crowned and clothed with what the Unknown Soldier had
If he went to his fate in a pride over all deaths.
Give them a cause and they are a living dynamite.
They are the game fighters who will die fighting.

Here and there a man in the street
is young, hard as nails,
cold with questions he asks
from his burning insides.

Bred in a motorized world of trial and error
He measures by millionths of an inch,
Knows ball bearings from spiral gearings,
Chain transmission, heat treatment of steel,

Speeds and feeds of automatic screw machines,
Having handled electric tools
With pistol grip and trigger switch.
Yet he can't connect and he can name thousands
Like himself idle amid plants also idle.
He studies the matter of what is justice
And revises himself on money, comfort, good name.
He doesn't know what he wants
And says when he gets it he'll know it.
He asks, 'Why is this what it is?'
He asks, 'Who is paying for this propaganda?'
He asks, 'Who owns the earth and why?'
Here and there a wife or sweetheart sees with him
The pity of being sold down the river in a smoke
Of confusions taken from the mouths of the dead
And spoken as though those dead are alive now
And would say now what they said then.

'Let him go as far as he likes,' says one lawyer who sits on
    several heavy directorates.
'What do we care? Is he any of our business? If he knew
    how he could manage.
'There are exceptional cases but where there is poverty you
    will generally find they were improvident and lack-
    ing in thrift and industry.
'The system of free competition we now have has made
    America the greatest and richest country on the face
    of the globe.
'You will seek in vain for any land where so large a num-
    ber of people have had so many of the good things
    of life.
'The malcontents who stir up class feeling and engender

class hatred are the foremost enemies of our republic
and its constitutional government.'
And so on and so on in further confusions taken from the
mouths of the dead and spoken as though those dead
are alive now and would say now what they said
then.

Like the form of a seen and unheard prowler,
Like a slow and cruel violence,
is the known unspoken menace:
Do what we tell you or go hungry;
listen to us or you don't eat.

He walks and walks and walks
and wonders why the hell he built the road.

Once I built a railroad
. . . now . . .
brother, can you spare a dime?

To his dry well a man carried
all the water he could carry,
primed the pump, drew out the water,
and now
he has all the water he can carry.

We asked the cyclone
to go around our barn
but it didn't hear us.

'The people will live on'

T HE people will live on.
The learning and blundering people will live on.
They will be tricked and sold and again sold
And go back to the nourishing earth for rootholds,
The people so peculiar in renewal and comeback,
You can't laugh off their capacity to take it.
The mammoth rests between his cyclonic dramas.

The people so often sleepy, weary, enigmatic,
is a vast huddle with many units saying:
'I earn my living.
I make enough to get by
and it takes all my time.
If I had more time
I could do more for myself
and maybe for others.
I could read and study
and talk things over
and find out about things.
It takes time.
I wish I had the time.'

The people is a tragic and comic two-face:
hero and hoodlum: phantom and gorilla twist-
ing to moan with a gargoyle mouth: 'They
buy me and sell me . . . it's a game . . .
sometime I'll break loose . . .'

Once having marched
Over the margins of animal necessity,

Over the grim line of sheer subsistence
    Then man came
To the deeper rituals of his bones,
To the lights lighter than any bones,
To the time for thinking things over,
To the dance, the song, the story,
Or the hours given over to dreaming,
    Once having so marched.

Between the finite limitations of the five senses
and the endless yearnings of man for the beyond
the people hold to the humdrum bidding of work and food
while reaching out when it comes their way
for lights beyond the prison of the five senses,
for keepsakes lasting beyond any hunger or death.
    This reaching is alive.
The panderers and liars have violated and smutted it.
    Yet this reaching is alive yet
    for lights and keepsakes.

      The people know the salt of the sea
      and the strength of the winds
      lashing the corners of the earth.
      The people take the earth
      as a tomb of rest and a cradle of hope.
      Who else speaks for the Family of Man?
      They are in tune and step
      with constellations of universal law.

      The people is a polychrome,
      a spectrum and a prism
      held in a moving monolith,
      a console organ of changing themes,

a clavilux of color poems
wherein the sea offers fog
and the fog moves off in rain
and the labrador sunset shortens
to a nocturne of clear stars
serene over the shot spray
of northern lights.

The steel mill sky is alive.
The fire breaks white and zigzag
shot on a gun-metal gloaming.
Man is a long time coming.
Man will yet win.
Brother may yet line up with brother:

This old anvil laughs at many broken hammers.
There are men who can't be bought.
The fireborn are at home in fire.
The stars make no noise.
You can't hinder the wind from blowing.
Time is a great teacher.
Who can live without hope?

In the darkness with a great bundle of grief
the people march.
In the night, and overhead a shovel of stars for
keeps, the people march:
'Where to? what next?'

VACHEL LINDSAY

1879-1931

312   General William Booth Enters into Heaven

(*To be sung to the tune of 'The Blood of the Lamb' with indicated instrument*)

I

(*Bass drum beaten loudly.*)
Booth led boldly with his big bass drum—
(Are you washed in the blood of the Lamb?)
The Saints smiled gravely and they said: 'He's come.'
(Are you washed in the blood of the Lamb?)
Walking lepers followed, rank on rank,
Lurching bravos from the ditches dank,
Drabs from the alleyways and drug fiends pale—
Minds still passion-ridden, soul-powers frail:—
Vermin-eaten saints with moldy breath,
Unwashed legions with the ways of Death—
(Are you washed in the blood of the Lamb?)

(*Banjos.*)
Every slum had sent its half-a-score
The round world over, (Booth had groaned for more.)
Every banner that the wide world flies
Bloomed with glory and transcendent dyes.
Big-voiced lasses made their banjos bang,
Tranced, fanatical they shrieked and sang:—
'Are you washed in the blood of the Lamb?'
Hallelujah! It was queer to see

Bull-necked convicts with that land make free.
Loons with trumpets blowed a blare, blare, blare
On, on upward thro' the golden air!
(Are you washed in the blood of the Lamb?)

II

(*Bass drum slower and softer.*)
Booth died blind and still by faith he trod,
Eyes still dazzled by the ways of God.
Booth led boldly, and he looked the chief
Eagle countenance in sharp relief,
Beard a-flying, air of high command
Unabated in that holy land.

(*Sweet flute music.*)
Jesus came from out the court-house door,
Stretched his hands above the passing poor.
Booth saw not, but led his queer ones there
Round and round the mighty court-house square.
Then, in an instant all that blear review
Marched on spotless, clad in raiment new.
The lame were straightened, withered limbs uncurled
And blind eyes opened on a new, sweet world.

(*Bass drum louder.*)
Drabs and vixens in a flash made whole!
Gone was the weasel-head, the snout, the jowl!
Sages and sibyls now, and athletes clean,
Rulers of empires, and of forests green!

(*Grand chorus of all instruments. Tambourines to the foreground.*)

The hosts were sandalled, and their wings were fire!
(Are you washed in the blood of the Lamb?)
But their noise played havoc with the angel-choir.
(Are you washed in the blood of the Lamb?)
Oh, shout Salvation! It was good to see
Kings and Princes by the Lamb set free.
The banjos rattled and the tambourines
Jing-jing-jingled in the hands of Queens.

(Reverently sung, no instruments.)
And when Booth halted by the curb for prayer
He saw his Master thro' the flag-filled air.
Christ came gently with a robe and crown
For Booth the soldier, while the throng knelt down.
He saw King Jesus. They were face to face,
And he knelt a-weeping in that holy place.
Are you washed in the blood of the Lamb?

313   *The Eagle That Is Forgotten*

*(John P. Altgeld. Born December 30, 1847; died
March 12, 1902)*

SLEEP softly . . . eagle forgotten . . . under the stone.
Time has its way with you there, and the clay has its own.

'We have buried him now,' thought your foes, and in
    secret rejoiced.
They made a brave show of their mourning, their hatred
    unvoiced.

They had snarled at you, barked at you, foamed at you
    day after day.
Now you were ended. They praised you, . . . and laid
    you away.

The others that mourned you in silence and terror and
    truth,
The widow bereft of her crust, and the boy without youth,
The mocked and the scorned and the wounded, the lame
    and the poor
That should have remembered forever, . . . remember no
    more.

Where are those lovers of yours, on what name do they
    call
The lost, that in armies wept over your funeral pall?
They call on the names of a hundred high-valiant ones,
A hundred white eagles have risen the sons of your sons,
The zeal in their wings is a zeal that your dreaming began
The valor that wore out your soul in the service of man.

Sleep softly, . . . eagle forgotten, . . . under the stone,
Time has its way with you there and the clay has its own.
Sleep on, O brave-hearted, O wise man, that kindled the
    flame—
To live in mankind is far more than to live in a name,
To live in mankind, far, far more . . . than to live in a
    name.

314   *The Congo*

A Study of the Negro Race

*(Being a memorial to Ray Eldred, a Disciple missionary
of the Congo River)*

I. THEIR BASIC SAVAGERY

FAT black bucks in a wine-barrel room,
Barrel-house kings, with feet unstable,
Sagged and reeled and pounded on the table,   A deep rolling
Pounded on the table,   bass.
Beat an empty barrel with the handle of
        a broom,
Hard as they were able,
Boom, boom, Boom,
With a silk umbrella and the handle of a
        broom,
Boomlay, boomlay, boomlay, Boom.
THEN I had religion, THEN I had a vision.
I could not turn from their revel in derision.
THEN I SAW THE CONGO, CREEPING   More deliberate.
        THROUGH THE BLACK,   Solemnly
                                              chanted.
CUTTING THROUGH THE FOREST WITH A
        GOLDEN TRACK.
Then along that riverbank
A thousand miles
Tattooed cannibals danced in files;
Then I heard the boom of the blood-lust
        song

607

A rapidly piling climax of speed and racket.

And a thigh-bone beating on a tin-pan gong.
And 'BLOOD' screamed the whistles and the
      fifes of the warriors,
'BLOOD' screamed the skull-faced, lean witch-
      doctors,
'Whirl ye the deadly voo-doo rattle,
Harry the uplands,
Steal all the cattle,
Rattle-rattle, rattle-rattle,
Bing.
Boomlay, boomlay, boomlay, BOOM,'

With a philosophic pause.

A roaring, epic, rag-time tune
From the mouth of the Congo
To the Mountains of the Moon.
Death is an Elephant,
Torch-eyed and horrible,

Shrilly and with a heavily accented metre.

Foam-flanked and terrible.
BOOM, steal the pygmies,
BOOM, kill the Arabs,
BOOM, kill the white men,
Hoo, Hoo, Hoo.

Like the wind in the chimney.

Listen to the yell of Leopold's ghost
Burning in Hell for his hand-maimed host.
Hear how the demons chuckle and yell
Cutting his hands off, down in Hell.
Listen to the creepy proclamation,
Blown through the lairs of the forest-nation,
Blown past the white-ants' hill of clay,
Blown past the marsh where the butterflies

All the 'o' sounds very golden. Heavy accents very heavy. Light accents very light. Last line whispered.

      play:—
'Be careful what you do,
Or Mumbo-Jumbo, God of the Congo,
And all of the other

VACHEL LINDSAY

Gods of the Congo,
Mumbo-Jumbo will hoo-doo you,
Mumbo-Jumbo will hoo-doo you,
Mumbo-Jumbo will hoo-doo you.'

II. THEIR IRREPRESSIBLE HIGH SPIRITS

Wild crap-shooters with a whoop and a call   Rather shrill
and high.
Danced the juba in their gambling hall
And laughed fit to kill, and shook the town,
And guyed the policemen and laughed them
      down
With a boomlay, boomlay, boomlay, Boom.
THEN I SAW THE CONGO, CREEPING   Read exactly as
in first section.
   THROUGH THE BLACK,
CUTTING THROUGH THE FOREST WITH A
   GOLDEN TRACK.
A negro fairyland swung into view,   Lay emphasis
on the delicate
ideas. Keep as
light-footed as
possible.
A minstrel river
Where dreams come true.
The ebony palace soared on high
Through the blossoming trees to the evening
   sky.
The inlaid porches and casements shone
With gold and ivory and elephant-bone
And the black crowd laughed till their sides
   were sore
At the baboon butler in the agate door,
And the well-known tunes of the parrot band
That trilled on the bushes of that magic
   land.

With pomposity.

A troupe of skull-faced witch-men came
Through the agate doorway in suits of flame,
Yea, long-tailed coats with a gold-leaf crust
And hats that were covered with diamond-
dust.
And the crowd in the court gave a whoop
and a call
And danced the juba from wall to wall.
But the witch-men suddenly stilled the
throng

With a great deliberation and ghostliness.

With a stern cold glare, and a stern old
song:—
'Mumbo-Jumbo will hoo-doo you.' . . .

With over-whelming as-surance, good cheer, and pomp.

Just then from the doorway, as fat as shotes,
Came the cake-walk princes in their long red
coats,
Canes with a brilliant lacquer shine,
And tall silk hats that were red as wine.
And they pranced with their butterfly part-
ners there,

With growing speed and sharply marked dance-rhythm.

Coal-black maidens with pearls in their hair,
Knee-skirts trimmed with the jassamine
sweet,
And bells on their ankles and little black-
feet.
And the couples railed at the chant and the
frown
Of the witch-men lean, and laughed them
down.
(Oh, rare was the revel, and well worth
while
That made those glowering witch-men
smile.)

The cake-walk royalty then began
To walk for a cake that was tall as a man
To the tune of 'Boomlay, boomlay, BOOM,'
While the witch-men laughed, with a sinister
    air,
And sang with the scalawags prancing
    there:—

With a touch of negro dialect, and as rapidly as possible toward the end.

'Walk with care, walk with care,
Or Mumbo-Jumbo, God of the Congo,
And all of the other Gods of the Congo,
Mumbo-Jumbo will hoo-doo you.
Beware, beware, walk with care,
Boomlay, boomlay, boomlay, boom.
Boomlay, boomlay, boomlay, boom.
Boomlay, boomlay, boomlay, boom.
Boomlay, boomlay, boomlay,
BOOM.'

(Oh, rare was the revel, and well worth
    while
That made those glowering witch-men
    smile.)

Slow philosophic calm.

III. THE HOPE OF THEIR RELIGION

A good old negro in the slums of the town
Preached at a sister for her velvet gown.
Howled at a brother for his low-down ways,
His prowling, guzzling, sneak-thief days.
Beat on the Bible till he wore it out
Starting the jubilee revival shout.
And some had visions, as they stood on chairs,
And sang of Jacob, and the golden stairs,

Heavy bass. With a literal imitation of camp-meeting racket, and trance.

And they all repented, a thousand strong
From their stupor and savagery and sin and
    wrong
And slammed with their hymn books till they
    shook the room
With 'glory, glory, glory,'
And 'Boom, boom, Boom.'

Exactly as in
the first section.
Begin with
terror and
power, end with
joy.

THEN I SAW THE CONGO, CREEPING
    THROUGH THE BLACK,

CUTTING THROUGH THE JUNGLE WITH A
    GOLDEN TRACK.

And the gray sky opened like a new-rent
    veil
And showed the Apostles with their coats of
    mail.
In bright white steel they were seated round
And their fire-eyes watched where the Congo
    wound.
And the twelve Apostles, from their thrones
    on high
Thrilled all the forest with their heavenly
    cry:—

Sung to the
tune of 'Hark,
ten thousand
harps and
voices.'

'Mumbo-Jumbo will die in the jungle;
Never again will he hoo-doo you,
Never again will he hoo-doo you.'

With growing
deliberation
and joy.

Then along that river, a thousand miles
The vine-snared trees fell down in files.
Pioneer angels cleared the way
For a Congo paradise, for babes at play,
For sacred capitals, for temples clean.
Gone were the skull-faced witch-men lean.
There, where the wild ghost-gods had wailed

A million boats of the angels sailed

In a rather high key—as delicately as possible.

With oars of silver, and prows of blue
And silken pennants that the sun shone
    through.
'Twas a land transfigured, 'twas a new
    creation.
Oh, a singing wind swept the negro nation
And on through the backwoods clearing
    flew:—
'Mumbo-Jumbo is dead in the jungle.

To the tune of 'Hark, ten thousand harps and voices.'

Never again will he hoo-doo you.
Never again will he hoo-doo you.'

Redeemed were the forests, the beasts and the
    men,
And only the vulture dared again
By the far, lone mountains of the moon
To cry, in the silence, the Congo tune:—
'Mumbo-Jumbo will hoo-doo you,
Mumbo-Jumbo will hoo-doo you.

Dying down into a penetrating, terrified whisper.

Mumbo . . . Jumbo . . . will . . . hoo-doo . . .
    you.'

315 *Abraham Lincoln Walks at Midnight*

(In Springfield, Illinois)

IT is portentous, and a thing of state
That here at midnight, in our little town
A mourning figure walks, and will not rest,
Near the old court-house pacing up and down,

Or by his homestead, or in shadowed yards
He lingers where his children used to play,
Or through the market, on the well-worn stones
He stalks until the dawn-stars burn away.

A bronzed, lank man! His suit of ancient black,
A famous high top-hat and plain worn shawl
Make him the quaint great figure that men love,
The prairie-lawyer, master of us all.

He cannot sleep upon his hillside now.
He is among us:—as in times before!
And we who toss and lie awake for long
Breathe deep, and start, to see him pass the door.

His head is bowed. He thinks on men and kings.
Yea, when the sick world cries, how can he sleep?
Too many peasants fight, they know not why,
Too many homesteads in black terror weep.

The sins of all the war-lords burn his heart.
He sees the dreadnaughts scouring every main.
He carries on his shawl-wrapped shoulders now
The bitterness, the folly and the pain.

He cannot rest until a spirit-dawn
Shall come;—the shining hope of Europe free:
The league of sober folk, the Workers' Earth,
Bringing long peace to Cornland, Alp and Sea.

It breaks his heart that kings must murder still,
That all his hours of travail here for men
Seem yet in vain. And who will bring white peace
That he may sleep upon his hill again?

VACHEL LINDSAY

316   *Bryan, Bryan, Bryan, Bryan*

The Campaign of Eighteen Ninety-six,
as Viewed at the Time by a
Sixteen-Year-Old, etc.

I

IN a nation of one hundred fine, mob-hearted, lynching,
    relenting, repenting millions,
There are plenty of sweeping, swinging, stinging, gorgeous
    things to shout about,
And knock your old blue devils out.

I brag and chant of Bryan, Bryan, Bryan,
Candidate for president who sketched a silver Zion,
The one American Poet who could sing outdoors,
He brought in tides of wonder, of unprecedented splendor,
Wild roses from the plains, that made hearts tender,
All the funny circus silks
Of politics unfurled,
Bartlett pears of romance that were honey at the cores,
And torchlights down the street, to the end of the world.

There were truths eternal in the gab and tittle-tattle.
There were real heads broken in the fustian and the rattle.
There were real lines drawn.
Not the silver and the gold,
But Nebraska's cry went eastward against the dour and old,
The mean and cold.

It was eighteen ninety-six, and I was just sixteen
And Altgeld ruled in Springfield, Illinois,

When there came from the sunset Nebraska's shout of joy:
In a coat like a deacon, in a black Stetson hat
He scourged the elephant plutocrats
With barbed wire from the Platte.
The scales dropped from their mighty eyes.
They saw that summer's noon
A tribe of wonders coming
To a marching tune.

Oh, the longhorns from Texas,
The jay hawks from Kansas,
The plop-eyed bungaroo and giant giassicus,
The varmint, chipmunk, bugaboo,
The horned-toad, prairie-dog and ballyhoo,
From all the newborn states arow,
Bidding the eagles of the west fly on,
Bidding the eagles of the west fly on.
The fawn, prodactyl and thing-a-ma-jig,
The rakaboor, the hellangone,
The whangdoodle, batfowl and pig,
The coyote, wild-cat and grizzly in a glow,
In a miracle of health and speed, the whole breed abreast,
They leaped the Mississippi, blue border of the West,
From the Gulf to Canada, two thousand miles long:—
Against the towns of Tubal Cain,
Ah,—sharp was their song.
Against the ways of Tubal Cain, too cunning for the young,
The longhorn calf, the buffalo and wampus gave tongue.

These creatures were defending things Mark Hanna never
    dreamed:
The moods of airy childhood that in desert dews gleamed,
The gossamers and whimsies,

The monkeyshines and didoes
Rank and strange
Of the canyons and the range,
The ultimate fantastics
Of the far western slope,
And of prairie schooner children
Born beneath the stars,
Beneath falling snows,
Of the babies born at midnight
In the sod huts of lost hope,
With no physician there,
Except a Kansas prayer,
With the Indian raid a howling through the air

And all these in their helpless days
By the dour East oppressed,
Mean paternalism
Making their mistakes for them,
Crucifying half the West,
Till the whole Atlantic coast
Seemed a giant spiders' nest.

And these children and their sons
At last rode through the cactus,
A cliff of mighty cowboys
On the lope,
With gun and rope.
And all the way to frightened Maine the old East heard
    them call,
And saw our Bryan by a mile lead the wall
Of men and whirling flowers and beasts,
The bard and the prophet of them all.
Prairie avenger, mountain lion,

Bryan, Bryan, Bryan, Bryan,
Gigantic troubadour, speaking like a siege gun,
Smashing Plymouth Rock with his boulders from the West,
And just a hundred miles behind, tornadoes piled across the
    sky,
Blotting out sun and moon,
A sign on high.

Headlong, dazed and blinking in the weird green light,
The scalawags made moan,
Afraid to fight.

II

When Bryan came to Springfield, and Altgeld gave him
    greeting,
Rochester was deserted, Divernon was deserted,
Mechanicsburg, Riverton, Chickenbristle, Cotton Hill,
Empty: for all Sangamon drove to the meeting—
In silver-decked racing cart,
Buggy, buckboard, carryall,
Carriage, phaeton, whatever would haul,
And silver-decked farm wagons gritted, banged and rolled,
With the new tale of Bryan by the iron tires told.

The State House loomed afar,
A speck, a hive, a football,
A captive balloon!
And the town was all one spreading wing of bunting,
    plumes, and sunshine,
Every rag and flag, and Bryan picture sold,
When the rigs in many a dusty line
Jammed our streets at noon,
And joined the wild parade against the power of gold.

We roamed, we boys from High School,
With mankind,
While Springfield gleamed,
Silk-lined.
Oh, Tom Dines, and Art Fitzgerald,
And the gangs that they could get!
I can hear them yelling yet.
Helping the incantation,
Defying aristocracy,
With every bridle gone,
Ridding the world of the low down mean,
Bidding the eagles of the West fly on,
Bidding the eagles of the West fly on,
We were bully, wild and woolly,
Never yet curried below the knees.
We saw flowers in the air,
Fair as the Pleiades, bright as Orion,
—Hopes of all mankind,
Made rare, resistless, thrice refined.
Oh, we bucks from every Springfield ward!
Colts of democracy—
Yet time-winds out of Chaos from the star-fields of the
    Lord.

The long parade rolled on. I stood by my best girl.
She was a cool young citizen, with wise and laughing eyes.
With my necktie by my ear, I was stepping on my dear,
But she kept like a pattern, without a shaken curl.

She wore in her hair a brave prairie rose.
Her gold chums cut her, for that was not the pose.
No Gibson Girl would wear it in that fresh way.
But we were fairy Democrats, and this was our day.

The earth rocked like the ocean, the sidewalk was a deck.
The houses for the moment were lost in the wide wreck.
And the bands played strange and stranger music as they
    trailed along.
Against the ways of Tubal Cain,
Ah, sharp was their song!
The demons in the bricks, the demons in the grass,
The demons in the bank-vaults peered out to see us pass,
And the angels in the trees, the angels in the grass,
The angels in the flags, peered out to see us pass.
And the sidewalk was our chariot, and the flowers bloomed
    higher,
And the street turned to silver and the grass turned to fire,
And then it was but grass, and the town was there again,
A place for women and men.

III

Then we stood where we could see
Every band,
And the speaker's stand.
And Bryan took the platform.
And he was introduced.
And he lifted his hand
And cast a new spell.
Progressive silence fell
In Springfield,
In Illinois,
Around the world.
Then we heard these glacial boulders across the prairie
    rolled:
'*The people have a right to make their own mistakes. . . .*
You shall not crucify mankind
Upon a cross of gold.'

620

And everybody heard him—
In the streets and State House yard.
And everybody heard him
In Springfield,
In Illinois,
Around and around and around the world,
That danced upon its axis
And like a darling broncho whirled.

IV

July, August, suspense.
Wall Street lost to sense.
August, September, October,
More suspense,
And the whole East down like a wind-smashed fence.

Then Hanna to the rescue,
Hanna of Ohio,
Rallying the roller-tops,
Rallying the bucket-shops.
Threatening drouth and death,
Promising manna,
Rallying the trusts against the bawling flannelmouth;
Invading misers' cellars,
Tin-cans, socks,
Melting down the rocks,
Pouring out the long green to a million workers,
Spondulix by the mountain-load, to stop each new tornado.
And beat the cheapskate, blatherskite,
Populistic, anarchistic,
Deacon—desperado.

V

Election night at midnight:
Boy Bryan's defeat.
Defeat of western silver.
Defeat of the wheat.
Victory of letterfiles
And plutocrats in miles
With dollar signs upon their coats,
Diamond watchchains on their vests
And spats on their feet.
Victory of custodians,
Plymouth Rock,
And all that inbred landlord stock.
Victory of the neat.
Defeat of the aspen groves of Colorado valleys,
The blue bells of the Rockies,
And blue bonnets of old Texas,
By the Pittsburg alleys.
Defeat of alfalfa and the Mariposa lily.
Defeat of the Pacific and the long Mississippi.
Defeat of the young by the old and silly.
Defeat of tornadoes by the poison vats supreme.
Defeat of my boyhood, defeat of my dream.

VI

Where is McKinley, that respectable McKinley,
The man without an angle or a tangle,
Who soothed down the city man and soothed down the
    farmer,
The German, the Irish, the Southerner, the Northerner,
Who climbed every greasy pole, and slipped through every
    crack;

Who soothed down the gambling hall, the bar-room, the
    church,
The devil vote, the angel vote, the neutral vote,
The desperately wicked, and their victims on the rack,
The gold vote, the silver vote, the brass vote, the lead vote,
Every vote? . . .

Where is McKinley, Mark Hanna's McKinley,
His slave, his echo, his suit of clothes?
Gone to join the shadows, with the pomps of that time,
And the flame of that summer's prairie rose.

Where is Cleveland whom the Democratic platform
Read from the party in a glorious hour,
Gone to join the shadows with pitchfork Tillman,
And sledge-hammer Altgeld who wrecked his power.

Where is Hanna, bulldog Hanna,
Low-browed Hanna, who said: 'Stand pat'?
Gone to his place with old Pierpont Morgan.
Gone somewhere . . . with lean rat Platt.

Where is Roosevelt, the young dude cowboy,
Who hated Bryan, then aped his way?
Gone to join the shadows with mighty Cromwell
And tall King Saul, till the Judgment day.

Where is Altgeld, brave as the truth,
Whose name the few still say with tears?
Gone to join the ironies with Old John Brown,
Whose fame rings loud for a thousand years.

Where is that boy, that Heaven-born Bryan,
That Homer Bryan, who sang from the West?
Gone to join the shadows with Altgeld the Eagle,
Where the kings and the slaves and the troubadours rest.

317 *The Apple-Barrel of Johnny Appleseed*

ON the mountain peak, called 'Going-To-The-Sun,'
I saw gray Johnny Appleseed at prayer
Just as the sunset made the old earth fair.
Then darkness came; in an instant, like great smoke,
The sun fell down as though its great hoops broke
And dark rich apples, poured from the dim flame
Where the sun set, came rolling toward the peak,
A storm of fruit, a mighty cider-reek,
The perfume of the orchards of the world,
From apple-shadows: red and russet domes
That turned to clouds of glory and strange homes
Above the mountain tops for cloud-born souls:—
Reproofs for men who build the world like moles,
Models for men, if they would build the world
As Johnny Appleseed would have it done—
Praying, and reading the books of Swedenborg
On the mountain top called 'Going-To-The-Sun.'

WALLACE STEVENS

b. 1879

318   *The Plot Against the Giant*

FIRST GIRL

WHEN this yokel comes maundering,
Whetting his hacker,
I shall run before him,
Diffusing the civilest odors
Out of geraniums and unsmelled flowers.
It will check him.

SECOND GIRL

I shall run before him,
Arching cloths besprinkled with colors
As small as fish-eggs.
The threads
Will abash him.

THIRD GIRL

Oh, la . . . le pauvre!
I shall run before him,
With a curious puffing.
He will bend his ear then.
I shall whisper
Heavenly labials in a world of gutturals.
It will undo him.

Domination of Black

At night, by the fire,
The colors of the bushes
And of the fallen leaves,
Repeating themselves,
Turned in the room,
Like the leaves themselves
Turning in the wind.
Yes: but the color of the heavy hemlocks
Came striding.
And I remembered the cry of the peacocks.

The colors of their tails
Were like the leaves themselves
Turning in the wind,
In the twilight wind.
They swept over the room,
Just as they flew from the boughs of the hemlocks
Down to the ground.
I heard them cry—the peacocks.
Was it a cry against the twilight
Or against the leaves themselves
Turning in the wind,
Turning as the flames
Turned in the fire,
Turning as the tails of the peacocks
Turned in the loud fire,
Loud as the hemlocks
Full of the cry of the peacocks?
Or was it a cry against the hemlocks?

Out of the window,
I saw how the planets gathered
Like the leaves themselves
Turning in the wind.
I saw how the night came,
Came striding like the color of the heavy hemlocks
I felt afraid.
And I remembered the cry of the peacocks.

320 *The Ordinary Women*

THEN from their poverty they rose,
From dry catarrhs, and to guitars
They flitted
Through the palace walls.

They flung monotony behind,
Turned from their want, and, nonchalant,
They crowded
The nocturnal halls.

The lacquered loges huddled there
Mumbled zay-zay and a-zay, a-zay.
The moonlight
Fubbed the girandoles.

And the cold dresses that they wore,
In the vapid haze of the window-bays,
Were tranquil
As they leaned and looked

From the window-sills at the alphabets,
At beta b and gamma g,

627

To study
The canting curlicues

Of heaven and of the heavenly script.
And there they read of marriage-bed.
Ti-lill-o!
And they read right long.

The gaunt guitarists on the strings
Rumbled a-day and a-day, a-day.
The moonlight
Rose on the beachy floors.

How explicit the coiffures became,
The diamond point, the sapphire point,
The sequins
Of the civil fans!

Insinuations of desire,
Puissant speech, alike in each,
Cried quittance
To the wickless halls.

Then from their poverty they rose,
From dry guitars, and to catarrhs
They flitted
Through the palace walls.

321   *The Emperor of Ice-Cream*

CALL the roller of big cigars,
The muscular one, and bid him whip
In kitchen cups concupiscent curds.

Let the wenches dawdle in such dress
As they are used to wear, and let the boys
Bring flowers in last month's newspapers.
Let be be finale of seem.
The only emperor is the emperor of ice-cream.

Take from the dresser of deal,
Lacking the three glass knobs, that sheet
On which she embroidered fantails once
And spread it so as to cover her face.
If her horny feet protrude, they come
To show how cold she is, and dumb.
Let the lamp affix its beam.
The only emperor is the emperor of ice-cream.

322 *Disillusionment of Ten O'Clock*

THE houses are haunted
By white night-gowns.
None are green,
Or purple with green rings,
Or green with yellow rings,
Or yellow with blue rings.
None of them are strange,
With socks of lace
And beaded ceintures.
People are not going
To dream of baboons and periwinkles.
Only, here and there, an old sailor,
Drunk and asleep in his boots,
Catches tigers
In red weather.

323 *Bantams in Pine-Woods*

CHIEFTAIN Iffucan of Azcan in caftan
Of tan with henna hackles, halt!

Damned universal cock, as if the sun
Was blackamoor to bear your blazing tail.

Fat! Fat! Fat! Fat! I am the personal.
Your world is you. I am my world.

You ten-foot poet among inchlings. Fat!
Begone! An inchling bristles in these pines,

Bristles, and points their Appalachian tangs,
And fears not portly Azcan nor his hoos.

324 *Anecdote of the Jar*

I PLACED a jar in Tennessee,
And round it was, upon a hill.
It made the slovenly wilderness
Surround that hill.

The wilderness rose up to it,
And sprawled around, no longer wild.
The jar was round upon the ground
And tall and of a port in air.

It took dominion everywhere.
The jar was gray and bare.
It did not give of bird or bush,
Like nothing else in Tennessee.

325   *Peter Quince at the Clavier*

I

JUST as my fingers on these keys
Make music, so the selfsame sounds
On my spirit make a music, too.

Music is feeling, then, not sound;
And thus it is that what I feel,
Here in this room, desiring you,

Thinking of your blue-shadowed silk,
Is music. It is like the strain
Waked in the elders by Susanna.

Of a green evening, clear and warm,
She bathed in her still garden, while
The red-eyed elders watching, felt

The basses of their beings throb
In witching chords, and their thin blood
Pulse pizzicati of Hosanna.

II

In the green water, clear and warm,
Susanna lay.

631

She searched
The touch of springs,
And found
Concealed imaginings.
She sighed,
For so much melody.

Upon the bank, she stood
In the cool
Of spent emotions.
She felt, among the leaves,
The dew
Of old devotions.

She walked upon the grass,
Still quavering.
The winds were like her maids,
On timid feet,
Fetching her woven scarves,
Yet wavering.

A breath upon her hand
Muted the night.
She turned—
A cymbal crashed,
And roaring horns.

III

Soon, with a noise like tambourines,
Came her attendant Byzantines.

They wondered why Susanna cried
Against the elders by her side;

And as they whispered, the refrain
Was like a willow swept by rain.

Anon, their lamps' uplifted flame
Revealed Susanna and her shame.

And then, the simpering Byzantines
Fled, with a noise like tambourines.

IV

Beauty is momentary in the mind—
The fitful tracing of a portal;
But in the flesh it is immortal.

The body dies; the body's beauty lives.
So evenings die, in their green going,
A wave, interminably flowing.
So gardens die, their meek breath scenting
The cowl of winter, done repenting.
So maidens die, to the auroral
Celebration of a maiden's choral.

Susanna's music touched the bawdy strings
Of those white elders; but, escaping,
Left only Death's ironic scraping.
Now, in its immortality, it plays
On the clear viol of her memory,
And makes a constant sacrament of praise.

Sunday Morning

I

COMPLACENCIES of the peignoir, and late
Coffee and oranges in a sunny chair,
And the green freedom of a cockatoo
Upon a rug mingle to dissipate
The holy hush of ancient sacrifice.
She dreams a little, and she feels the dark
Encroachment of that old catastrophe,
As a calm darkens among water-lights.
The pungent oranges and bright, green wings
Seem things in some procession of the dead,
Winding across wide water, without sound.
The day is like wide water, without sound,
Stilled for the passing of her dreaming feet
Over the seas, to silent Palestine,
Dominion of the blood and sepulchre.

II

Why should she give her bounty to the dead?
What is divinity if it can come
Only in silent shadows and in dreams?
Shall she not find in comforts of the sun,
In pungent fruit and bright, green wings, or else
In any balm or beauty of the earth,
Things to be cherished like the thought of heaven?
Divinity must live within herself:
Passions of rain, or moods in falling snow;
Grievings in loneliness, or unsubdued
Elations when the forest blooms; gusty

Emotions on wet roads on autumn nights;
All pleasures and all pains, remembering
The bough of summer and the winter branch.
These are the measures destined for her soul.

III

Jove in the clouds had his inhuman birth.
No mother suckled him, no sweet land gave
Large-mannered motions to his mythy mind.
He moved among us, as a muttering king,
Magnificent, would move among his hinds,
Until our blood, commingling, virginal,
With heaven, brought such requital to desire
The very hinds discerned it, in a star.
Shall our blood fail? Or shall it come to be
The blood of paradise? And shall the earth
Seem all of paradise that we shall know?
The sky will be much friendlier then than now,
A part of labor and a part of pain,
And next in glory to enduring love,
Not this dividing and indifferent blue.

IV

She says, 'I am content when wakened birds,
Before they fly, test the reality
Of misty fields, by their sweet questionings;
But when the birds are gone, and their warm fields
Return no more, where, then, is paradise?'
There is not any haunt of prophecy,
Nor any old chimera of the grave,
Neither the golden underground, nor isle
Melodious, where spirits gat them home,

Nor visionary south, nor cloudy palm
Remote on heaven's hill, that has endured
As April's green endures; or will endure
Like her remembrance of awakened birds,
Or her desire for June and evening, tipped
By the consummation of the swallow's wings.

V

She says, 'But in contentment I still feel
The need of some imperishable bliss.'
Death is the mother of beauty; hence from her,
Alone, shall come fulfilment to our dreams
And our desires. Although she strews the leaves
Of sure obliteration on our paths,
The path sick sorrow took, the many paths
Where triumph rang its brassy phrase, or love
Whispered a little out of tenderness,
She makes the willow shiver in the sun
For maidens who were wont to sit and gaze
Upon the grass, relinquished to their feet.
She causes boys to pile new plums and pears
On disregarded plate. The maidens taste
And stray impassioned in the littering leaves.

VI

Is there no change of death in paradise?
Does ripe fruit never fall? Or do the boughs
Hang always heavy in that perfect sky,
Unchanging, yet so like our perishing earth,
With rivers like our own that seek for seas
They never find, the same receding shores
That never touch with inarticulate pang?
Why set the pear upon those river-banks

Or spice the shores with odors of the plum?
Alas, that they should wear our colors there,
The silken weavings of our afternoons,
And pick the strings of our insipid lutes!
Death is the mother of beauty, mystical,
Within whose burning bosom we devise
Our earthly mothers waiting, sleeplessly.

VII

Supple and turbulent, a ring of men
Shall chant in orgy on a summer morn
Their boisterous devotion to the sun,
Not as a god, but as a god might be,
Naked among them, like a savage source.
Their chant shall be a chant of paradise,
Out of their blood, returning to the sky;
And in their chant shall enter, voice by voice,
The windy lake wherein their lord delights,
The trees, like serafin, and echoing hills,
That choir among themselves long afterward.
They shall know well the heavenly fellowship
Of men that perish and of summer morn.
And whence they came and whither they shall go
The dew upon their feet shall manifest.

VIII

She hears, upon that water without sound,
A voice that cries, 'The tomb in Palestine
Is not the porch of spirits lingering.
It is the grave of Jesus, where he lay.'
We live in an old chaos of the sun,
Or old dependency of day and night,
Or island solitude, unsponsored, free,

Of that wide water, inescapable.
Deer walk upon our mountains, and the quail
Whistle about us their spontaneous cries;
Sweet berries ripen in the wilderness;
And, in the isolation of the sky,
At evening, casual flocks of pigeons make
Ambiguous undulations as they sink,
Downward to darkness, on extended wings.

327   ## The Comedian as the Letter C

I

The World without Imagination

NOTA: man is the intelligence of his soil,
The sovereign ghost. As such, the Socrates
Of snails, musician of pears, principium
And lex. Sed quæritur: is this same wig
Of things, this nincompated pedagogue,
Preceptor to the sea? Crispin at sea
Created, in his day, a touch of doubt.
An eye most apt in gelatines and jupes,
Berries of villages, a barber's eye,
An eye of land, of simple salad-beds,
Of honest quilts, the eye of Crispin, hung
On porpoises, instead of apricots,
And on silentious porpoises, whose snouts
Dibbled in waves that were mustachios,
Inscrutable hair in an inscrutable world.

WALLACE STEVENS

One eats one paté, even of salt, quotha.
It was not so much the lost terrestrial,
The snug hibernal from that sea and salt,
That century of wind in a single puff.
What counted was mythology of self,
Blotched out beyond unblotching. Crispin,
The lutanist of fleas, the knave, the thane,
The ribboned stick, the bellowing breeches, cloak
Of China, cap of Spain, imperative haw
Of hum, inquisitorial botanist,
And general lexicographer of mute
And maidenly greenhorns, now beheld himself,
A skinny sailor peering in the sea-glass.
What word split up in clickering syllables
And storming under multitudinous tones
Was name for this short-shanks in all that brunt?
Crispin was washed away by magnitude.
The whole of life that still remained in him
Dwindled to one sound strumming in his ear,
Ubiquitous concussion, slap and sigh,
Polyphony beyond his baton's thrust.

Could Crispin stem verboseness in the sea,
The old age of a watery realist,
Triton, dissolved in shifting diaphanes
Of blue and green? A wordy, watery age
That whispered to the sun's compassion, made
A convocation, nightly, of the sea-stars,
And on the clopping foot-ways of the moon
Lay grovelling. Triton incomplicate with that
Which made him Triton, nothing left of him,
Except in faint, memorial gesturings,
That were like arms and shoulders in the waves,

Here, something in the rise and fall of wind
That seemed hallucinating horn, and here,
A sunken voice, both of remembering
And of forgetfulness, in alternate strain.
Just so an ancient Crispin was dissolved.
The valet in the tempest was annulled.
Bordeaux to Yucatan, Havana next,
And then to Carolina. Simple jaunt.
Crispin, merest minuscule in the gales,
Dejected his manner to the turbulence.
The salt hung on his spirit like a frost,
The dead brine melted in him like a dew
Of winter, until nothing of himself
Remained, except some starker, barer self
In a starker, barer world, in which the sun
Was not the sun because it never shone
With bland complaisance on pale parasols,
Beetled, in chapels, on the chaste bouquets.
Against his pipping sounds a trumpet cried
Celestial sneering boisterously. Crispin
Became an introspective voyager.

Here was the veritable ding an sich, at last,
Crispin confronting it, a vocable thing,
But with a speech belched out of hoary darks
Noway resembling his, a visible thing,
And excepting negligible Triton, free
From the unavoidable shadow of himself
That lay elsewhere around him. Severance
Was clear. The last distortion of romance
Forsook the insatiable egotist. The sea
Severs not only lands but also selves.
Here was no help before reality.

Crispin beheld and Crispin was made new.
The imagination, here, could not evade,
In poems of plums, the strict austerity
Of one vast, subjugating, final tone.
The drenching of stale lives no more fell down.
What was this gaudy, gusty panoply?
Out of what swift destruction did it spring?
It was caparison of wind and cloud
And something given to make whole among
The ruses that were shattered by the large.

II

Concerning the Thunderstorms of Yucatan

In Yucatan, the Maya sonneteers
Of the Caribbean amphitheatre,
In spite of hawk and falcon, green toucan
And jay, still to the night-bird made their plea,
As if raspberry tanagers in palms,
High up in orange air, were barbarous.
But Crispin was too destitute to find
In any commonplace the sought-for aid.
He was a man made vivid by the sea,
A man come out of luminous traversing,
Much trumpeted, made desperately clear,
Fresh from discoveries of tidal skies,
To whom oracular rockings gave no rest.
Into a savage color he went on.

How greatly had he grown in his demesne,
This auditor of insects! He that saw
The stride of vanishing autumn in a park
By way of decorous melancholy; he

That wrote his couplet yearly to the spring,
As dissertation of profound delight,
Stopping, on voyage, in a land of snakes,
Found his vicissitudes had much enlarged
His apprehension, made him intricate
In moody rucks, and difficult and strange
In all desires, his destitution's mark.
He was in this as other freemen are,
Sonorous nutshells rattling inwardly.
His violence was for aggrandizement
And not for stupor, such as music makes
For sleepers halfway waking. He perceived
That coolness for his heat came suddenly,
And only, in the fables that he scrawled
With his own quill, in its indigenous dew,
Of an æsthetic tough, diverse, untamed,
Incredible to prudes, the mint of dirt,
Green barbarism turning paradigm.
Crispin foresaw a curious promenade
Or, nobler, sensed an elemental fate,
And elemental potencies and pangs,
And beautiful barenesses as yet unseen,
Making the most of savagery of palms,
Of moonlight on the thick, cadaverous bloom
That yuccas breed, and of the panther's tread.
The fabulous and its intrinsic verse
Came like two spirits parleying, adorned
In radiance from the Atlantic coign,
For Crispin and his quill to catechize.
But they came parleying of such an earth,
So thick with sides and jagged lops of green,
So intertwined with serpent-kin encoiled
Among the purple tufts, the scarlet crowns,

Scenting the jungle in their refuges,
So streaked with yellow, blue and green and red
In beak and bud and fruity gobbet-skins,
That earth was like a jostling festival
Of seeds grown fat, too juicily opulent,
Expanding in the gold's maternal warmth.

So much for that. The affectionate emigrant found
A new reality in parrot-squawks.
Yet let that trifle pass. Now, as this odd
Discoverer walked through the harbor streets
Inspecting the cabildo, the façade
Of the cathedral, making notes, he heard
A rumbling, west of Mexico, it seemed,
Approaching like a gasconade of drums.
The white cabildo darkened, the façade,
As sullen as the sky, was swallowed up
In swift, successive shadows, dolefully.
The rumbling broadened as it fell. The wind,
Tempestuous clarion, with heavy cry,
Came bluntly thundering, more terrible
Than the revenge of music on bassoons.
Gesticulating lightning, mystical,
Made pallid flitter. Crispin, here, took flight.
An annotator has his scruples, too.
He knelt in the cathedral with the rest,
This connoisseur of elemental fate,
Aware of exquisite thought. The storm was one
Of many proclamations of the kind,
Proclaiming something harsher than he learned
From hearing signboards whimper in cold nights
Or seeing the midsummer artifice
Of heat upon his pane. This was the span

Of force, the quintessential fact, the note
Of Vulcan, that a valet seeks to own,
The thing that makes him envious in phrase.

And while the torrent on the roof still droned
He felt the Andean breath. His mind was free
And more than free, elate, intent, profound
And studious of a self possessing him,
That was not in him in the crusty town
From which he sailed. Beyond him, westward, lay
The mountainous ridges, purple balustrades,
In which the thunder, lapsing in its clap,
Let down gigantic quavers of its voice,
For Crispin to vociferate again.

III

Approaching Carolina

The book of moonlight is not written yet
Nor half begun, but, when it is, leave room
For Crispin, fagot in the lunar fire,
Who, in the hubbub of his pilgrimage
Through sweating changes, never could forget
That wakefulness or meditating sleep,
In which the sulky strophes willingly
Bore up, in time, the somnolent, deep songs.
Leave room, therefore, in that unwritten book
For the legendary moonlight that once burned
In Crispin's mind above a continent.
America was always north to him,
A northern west or western north, but north,
And thereby polar, polar-purple, chilled

And lank, rising and slumping from a sea
Of hardy foam, receding flatly, spread
In endless ledges, glittering, submerged
And cold in a boreal mistiness of the moon.
The spring came there in clinking pannicles
Of half-dissolving frost, the summer came,
If ever, whisked and wet, not ripening,
Before the winter's vacancy returned.
The myrtle, if the myrtle ever bloomed,
Was like a glacial pink upon the air.
The green palmettoes in crepuscular ice
Clipped frigidly blue-black meridians,
Morose chiaroscuro, gauntly drawn.

How many poems he denied himself
In his observant progress, lesser things
Than the relentless contact he desired;
How many sea-masks he ignored; what sounds
He shut out from his tempering ear; what thoughts,
Like jades affecting the sequestered bride;
And what descants, he sent to banishment!
Perhaps the Arctic moonlight really gave
The liaison, the blissful liaison,
Between himself and his environment,
Which was, and is, chief motive, first delight,
For him, and not for him alone. It seemed
Illusive, faint, more mist than moon, perverse,
Wrong as a divagation to Peking,
To him that postulated as his theme
The vulgar, as his theme and hymn and flight,
A passionately niggling nightingale.
Moonlight was an evasion, or, if not,
A minor meeting, facile, delicate.

Thus he conceived his voyaging to be
An up and down between two elements,
A fluctuating between sun and moon,
A sally into gold and crimson forms,
As on this voyage, out of goblinry,
And then retirement like a turning back
And sinking down to the indulgences
That in the moonlight have their habitude.
But let these backward lapses, if they would,
Grind their seductions on him, Crispin knew
It was a flourishing tropic he required
For his refreshment, an abundant zone,
Prickly and obdurate, dense, harmonious,
Yet with a harmony not rarefied
Nor fined for the inhibited instruments
Of over-civil stops. And thus he tossed
Between a Carolina of old time,
A little juvenile, an ancient whim,
And the visible, circumspect presentment drawn
From what he saw across his vessel's prow.

He came. The poetic hero without palms
Or jugglery, without regalia.
And as he came he saw that it was spring,
A time abhorrent to the nihilist
Or searcher for the fecund minimum.
The moonlight fiction disappeared. The spring,
Although contending featly in its veils,
Irised in dew and early fragrancies,
Was gemmy marionette to him that sought
A sinewy nakedness. A river bore
The vessel inward. Tilting up his nose,
He inhaled the rancid rosin, burly smells

Of dampened lumber, emanations blown
From warehouse doors, the gustiness of ropes,
Decays of sacks, and all the arrant stinks
That helped him round his rude æsthetic out.
He savored rankness like a sensualist.
He marked the marshy ground around the dock,
The crawling railroad spur, the rotten fence,
Curriculum for the marvelous sophomore.
It purified. It made him see how much
Of what he saw he never saw at all.
He gripped more closely the essential prose
As being, in a world so falsified,
The one integrity for him, the one
Discovery still possible to make,
To which all poems were incident, unless
That prose should wear a poem's guise at last.

IV

The Idea of a Colony

Nota: his soil is man's intelligence.
That's better. That's worth crossing seas to find.
Crispin in one laconic phrase laid bare
His cloudy drift and planned a colony.
Exit the mental moonlight, exit lex,
Rex and principium, exit the whole
Shebang. Exeunt omnes. Here was prose
More exquisite than any tumbling verse:
A still new continent in which to dwell.
What was the purpose of his pilgrimage,
Whatever shape it took in Crispin's mind,
If not, when all is said, to drive away
The shadow of his fellows from the skies,

And, from their stale intelligence released,
To make a new intelligence prevail?
Hence the reverberations in the words
Of his first central hymns, the celebrants
Of rankest trivia, tests of the strength
Of his æsthetic, his philosophy,
The more invidious, the more desired.
The florist asking aid from cabbages,
The rich man going bare, the paladin
Afraid, the blind man as astronomer,
The appointed power unwielded from disdain.
His western voyage ended and began.
The torment of fastidious thought grew slack,
Another, still more bellicose, came on.
He, therefore, wrote his prolegomena,
And, being full of the caprice, inscribed
Commingled souvenirs and prophecies.
He made a singular collation. Thus:
The natives of the rain are rainy men.
Although they paint effulgent, azure lakes,
And April hillsides wooded white and pink,
Their azure has a cloudy edge, their white
And pink, the water bright that dogwood bears.
And in their music showering sounds intone.
On what strange froth does the gross Indian dote,
What Eden sapling gum, what honeyed gore,
What pulpy dram distilled of innocence,
That streaking gold should speak in him
Or bask within his images and words?
If these rude instances impeach themselves
By force of rudeness, let the principle
Be plain. For application Crispin strove,

Abhorring Turk as Esquimau, the lute
As the marimba, the magnolia as rose.

Upon these premises propounding, he
Projected a colony that should extend
To the dusk of a whistling south below the south,
A comprehensive island hemisphere.
The man in Georgia waking among pines
Should be pine-spokesman. The responsive man,
Planting his pristine cores in Florida,
Should prick thereof, not on the psaltery,
But on the banjo's categorical gut,
Tuck, tuck, while the flamingoes flapped his bays.
Sepulchral señors, bibbling pale mescal,
Oblivious to the Aztec almanacs,
Should make the intricate Sierra scan.
And dark Brazilians in their cafés,
Musing immaculate, pampean dits,
Should scrawl a vigilant anthology,
To be their latest, lucent paramour.
These are the broadest instances. Crispin,
Progenitor of such extensive scope,
Was not indifferent to smart detail.
The melon should have apposite ritual,
Performed in verd apparel, and the peach,
When its black branches came to bud, belle day,
Should have an incantation. And again,
When piled on salvers its aroma steeped
The summer, it should have a sacrament
And celebration. Shrewd novitiates
Should be the clerks of our experience.
These bland excursions into time to come,
Related in romance to backward flights,

However prodigal, however proud,
Contained in their afflatus the reproach
That first drove Crispin to his wandering.
He could not be content with counterfeit,
With masquerade of thought, with hapless words
That must belie the racking masquerade,
With fictive flourishes that preordained
His passion's permit, hang of coat, degree
Of buttons, measure of his salt. Such trash
Might help the blind, not him, serenely sly.
It irked beyond his patience. Hence it was,
Preferring text to gloss, he humbly served
Grotesque apprenticeship to chance event,
A clown, perhaps, but an aspiring clown.
There is a monotonous babbling in our dreams
That makes them our dependent heirs, the heirs
Of dreamers buried in our sleep, and not
The oncoming fantasies of better birth.
The apprentice knew these dreamers. If he dreamed
Their dreams, he did it in a gingerly way.
All dreams are vexing. Let them be expunged.
But let the rabbit run, the cock declaim.

Trinket pasticcio, flaunting skyey sheets,
With Crispin as the tiptoe cozener?
No, no: veracious page on page, exact.

v

A Nice Shady Home

Crispin as hermit, pure and capable,
Dwelt in the land. Perhaps if discontent

Had kept him still the pricking realist,
Choosing his element from droll confect
Of was and is and shall or ought to be,
Beyond Bordeaux, beyond Havana, far
Beyond carked Yucatan, he might have come
To colonize his polar planterdom
And jig his chits upon a cloudy knee.
But his emprize to that idea soon sped.
Crispin dwelt in the land and dwelling there
Slid from his continent by slow recess
To things within his actual eye, alert
To the difficulty of rebellious thought
When the sky is blue. The blue infected will.
It may be that the yarrow in his fields
Sealed pensive purple under its concern.
But day by day, now this thing and now that
Confined him, while it cosseted, condoned,
Little by little, as if the suzerain soil
Abashed him by carouse to humble yet
Attach. It seemed haphazard denouement.
He first, as realist, admitted that
Whoever hunts a matinal continent
May, after all, stop short before a plum
And be content and still be realist.
The words of things entangle and confuse.
The plum survives its poems. It may hang
In the sunshine placidly, colored by ground
Obliquities of those who pass beneath,
Harlequined and mazily dewed and mauved
In bloom. Yet it survives in its own form,
Beyond these changes, good, fat, guzzly fruit.
So Crispin hasped on the surviving form,
For him, of shall or ought to be in is.

Was he to bray this in profoundest brass
Arointing his dreams with fugal requiems?
Was he to company vastest things defunct
With a blubber of tom-toms harrowing the sky?
Scrawl a tragedian's testament? Prolong
His active force in an inactive dirge,
Which, let the tall musicians call and call,
Should merely call him dead? Pronounce amen
Through choirs infolded to the outmost clouds?
Because he built a cabin who once planned
Loquacious columns by the ructive sea?
Because he turned to salad-beds again?
Jovial Crispin, in calamitous crape?
Should he lay by the personal and make
Of his own fate an instance of all fate?
What is one man among so many men?
What are so many men in such a world?
Can one man think one thing and think it long?
Can one man be one thing and be it long?
The very man despising honest quilts
Lies quilted to his poll in his despite.
For realists, what is is what should be.

And so it came, his cabin shuffled up,
His trees were planted, his duenna brought
Her prismy blonde and clapped her in his hands,
The curtains flittered and the door was closed.
Crispin, magister of a single room,
Latched up the night. So deep a sound fell down
It was as if the solitude concealed
And covered him and his congenial sleep.

WALLACE STEVENS

So deep a sound fell down it grew to be
A long soothsaying silence down and down.
The crickets beat their tambours in the wind,
Marching a motionless march, custodians.

In the presto of the morning, Crispin trod,
Each day, still curious, but in a round
Less prickly and much more condign than that
He once thought necessary. Like Candide,
Yeoman and grub, but with a fig in sight,
And cream for the fig and silver for the cream,
A blonde to tip the silver and to taste
The rapey gouts. Good star, how that to be
Annealed them in their cabin ribaldries!
Yet the quotidian saps philosophers
And men like Crispin like them in intent,
If not in will, to track the knaves of thought.
But the quotidian composed as his,
Of breakfast ribands, fruits laid in their leaves,
The tomtit and the cassia and the rose,
Although the rose was not the noble thorn
Of crinoline spread, but of a pining sweet,
Composed of evenings like cracked shutters flung
Upon the rumpling bottomness, and nights
In which those trail custodians watched,
Indifferent to the tepid summer cold,
While he poured out upon the lips of her
That lay beside him, the quotidian
Like this, saps like the sun, true fortuner.
For all it takes it gives a humped return
Exchequering from piebald fiscs unkeyed.

VI

And Daughters with Curls

Portentous enunciation, syllable
To blessed syllable affined, and sound
Bubbling felicity in cantilene,
Prolific and tormenting tenderness
Of music, as it comes to unison,
Forgather and bell boldly Crispin's last
Deduction. Thrum with a proud douceur
His grand pronunciamento and devise.
The chits came for his jigging, bluet-eyed,
Hands without touch yet touching poignantly,
Leaving no room upon his cloudy knee,
Prophetic joint, for its diviner young.
The return to social nature, once begun,
Anabasis or slump, ascent or chute,
Involved him in midwifery so dense
His cabin counted as phylactery,
Then place of vexing palankeens, then haunt
Of children nibbling at the sugared void,
Infants yet eminently old, then dome
And halidom for the unbraided femes,
Green crammers of the green fruits of the world,
Bidders and biders for its ecstasies,
True daughters both of Crispin and his clay.
All this with many mulctings of the man,
Effective colonizer sharply stopped
In the door-yard by his own capacious bloom.
But that this bloom grown riper, showing nibs
Of its eventual roundness, puerile tints
Of spiced and weathery rouges, should complex

The stopper to indulgent fatalist
Was unforeseen. First Crispin smiled upon
His goldenest demoiselle, inhabitant,
She seemed, of a country of the capuchins,
So delicately blushed, so humbly eyed,
Attentive to a coronal of things
Secret and singular. Second, upon
A second similar counterpart, a maid
Most sisterly to the first, not yet awake
Excepting to the motherly footstep, but
Marvelling sometimes at the shaken sleep.
Then third, a thing still flaxen in the light,
A creeper under jaunty leaves. And fourth,
Mere blusteriness that gewgaws jollified,
All din and gobble, blasphemously pink.
A few years more and the vermeil capuchin
Gave to the cabin, lordlier than it was,
The dulcet omen fit for such a house.
The second sister dallying was shy
To fetch the one full-pinioned one himself
Out of her botches, hot embosomer.
The third one gaping at the orioles
Lettered herself demurely as became
A pearly poetess, peaked for rhapsody.
The fourth, pent now, a digit curious.
Four daughters in a world too intricate
In the beginning, four blithe instruments
Of differing struts, four voices several
In couch, four more personæ, intimate
As buffo, yet divers, four mirrors blue
That should be silver, four accustomed seeds
Hinting incredible hues, four selfsame lights

That spread chromatics in hilarious dark,
Four questioners and four sure answerers.

Crispin concocted doctrine from the rout.
The world, a turnip once so readily plucked,
Sacked up and carried overseas, daubed out
Of its ancient purple, pruned to the fertile main,
And sown again by the stiffest realist,
Came reproduced in purple, family font,
The same insoluble lump. The fatalist
Stepped in and dropped the chuckling down his craw,
Without grace or grumble. Score this anecdote
Invented for its pith, not doctrinal
In form though in design, as Crispin willed,
Disguised pronunciamento, summary,
Autumn's compendium, strident in itself
But muted, mused, and perfectly revolved
In those portentous accents, syllables,
And sounds of music coming to accord
Upon his law, like their inherent sphere,
Seraphic proclamations of the pure
Delivered with a deluging onwardness.
Or if the music sticks, if the anecdote
Is false, if Crispin is a profitless
Philosopher, beginning with green brag,
Concluding fadedly, if as a man
Prone to distemper he abates in taste,
Fickle and fumbling, variable, obscure,
Glozing his life with after-shining flicks,
Illuminating, from a fancy gorged
By apparition, plain and common things,
Sequestering the fluster from the year,
Making gulped potions from obstreperous drops,

And so distorting, proving what he proves
Is nothing, what can all this matter since
The relation comes, benignly, to its end?

So may the relation of each man be clipped.

328   *Sad Strains of a Gay Waltz*

THE truth is that there comes a time
When we can mourn no more over music
That is so much motionless sound.

There comes a time when the waltz
Is no longer a mode of desire, a mode
Of revealing desire and is empty of shadows.

Too many waltzes have ended. And then
There's that mountain-minded Hoon,
For whom desire was never that of the waltz,

Who found all form and order in solitude,
For whom the shapes were never the figures of men.
Now, for him, his forms have vanished.

There is order in neither sea nor sun.
The shapes have lost their glistening.
There are these sudden mobs of men,

These sudden clouds of faces and arms,
An immense suppression, freed,
These voices crying without knowing for what,

Except to be happy, without knowing how,
Imposing forms they cannot describe,
Requiring order beyond their speech.

Too many waltzes have ended. Yet the shapes
For which the voices cry, these, too, may be
Modes of desire, modes of revealing desire.

Too many waltzes—The epic of disbelief
Blares oftener and soon, will soon be constant.
Some harmonious skeptic soon in a skeptical music

Will unite these figures of men and their shapes
Will glisten again with motion, the music
Will be motion and full of shadows.

329 *Dance of the Macabre Mice*

IN the land of turkeys in turkey weather
At the base of the statue, we go round and round.
What a beautiful history, beautiful surprise!
Monsieur is on horseback. The horse is covered with mice.

This dance has no name. It is a hungry dance.
We dance it out to the tip of Monsieur's sword,
Reading the lordly language of the inscription,
Which is like zithers and tambourines combined:

The Founder of the State.-Whoever founded
A state that was free, in the dead of winter, from mice?
What a beautiful tableau tinted and towering,
The arm of bronze outstretched against all evil!

330 *The Idea of Order at Key West*

SHE sang beyond the genius of the sea.
The water never formed to mind or voice,
Like a body wholly body, fluttering
Its empty sleeves; and yet its mimic motion
Made constant cry, caused constantly a cry,
That was not ours although we understood,
Inhuman, of the veritable ocean.

The sea was not a mask. No more was she.
The song and water were not medleyed sound
Even if what she sang was what she heard,
Since what she sang was uttered word by word.
It may be that in all her phrases stirred
The grinding water and the gasping wind;
But it was she and not the sea we heard.

For she was the maker of the song she sang.
The ever-hooded, tragic-gestured sea
Was merely a place by which she walked to sing.
Whose spirit is this? we said, because we knew
It was the spirit that we sought and knew
That we should ask this often as she sang.

If it was only the dark voice of the sea
That rose, or even colored by many waves;
If it was only the outer voice of sky
And cloud, of the sunken coral water-walled,
However clear, it would have been deep air,
The heaving speech of air, a summer sound

Repeated in a summer without end
And sound alone. But it was more than that,
More even than her voice, and ours, among
The meaningless plungings of water and the wind,
Theatrical distances, bronze shadows heaped
On high horizons, mountainous atmospheres
Of sky and sea.

              It was her voice that made
The sky acutest at its vanishing.
She measured to the hour its solitude.
She was the single artificer of the world
In which she sang. And when she sang, the sea,
Whatever self it had, became the self
That was her song, for she was the maker. Then we,
As we beheld her striding there alone,
Knew that there never was a world for her
Except the one she sang and, singing, made.

Ramon Fernandez, tell me, if you know,
Why, when the singing ended and we turned
Toward the town, tell why the glassy lights,
The lights in the fishing boats at anchor there,
As the night descended, tilting in the air,
Mastered the night and portioned out the sea,
Fixing emblazoned zones and fiery poles,
Arranging, deepening, enchanting night.

Oh! Blessed rage for order, pale Ramon,
The maker's rage to order words of the sea,
Words of the fragrant portals, dimly-starred,
And of ourselves and of our origins,
In ghostlier demarcations, keener sounds.

331 *Poetry Is a Destructive Force*

THAT'S what misery is,
Nothing to have at heart.
It is to have or nothing.

It is a thing to have,
A lion, an ox in his breast,
To feel it breathing there.

Corazon, stout dog,
Young ox, bow-legged bear,
He tastes its blood, not spit.

He is like a man
In the body of a violent beast.
Its muscles are his own . . .

The lion sleeps in the sun.
Its nose is on its paws.
It can kill a man.

332 *The Poems of Our Climate*

I

CLEAR water in a brilliant bowl,
Pink and white carnations. The light
In the room more like a snowy air,
Reflecting snow. A newly-fallen snow
At the end of winter when afternoons return.
Pink and white carnations—one desires

So much more than that. The day itself
Is simplified: a bowl of white,
Cold, a cold porcelain, low and round,
With nothing more than the carnations there.

II

Say even that this complete simplicity
Stripped one of all one's torments, concealed
The evilly compounded, vital I
And made it fresh in a world of white,
A world of clear water, brilliant-edged,
Still one would want more, one would need more,
More than a world of white and snowy scents.

III

There would still remain the never-resting mind,
So that one would want to escape, come back
To what had been so long composed.
The imperfect is our paradise.
Note that, in this bitterness, delight,
Since the imperfect is so hot in us,
Lies in flawed words and stubborn sounds.

333   *Study of Two Pears*

I

OPUSCULUM paedagogum.
The pears are not viols,

Nudes or bottles.
They resemble nothing else.

II

They are yellow forms
Composed of curves
Bulging toward the base.
They are touched red.

III

They are not flat surfaces
Having curved outlines.
They are round
Tapering toward the top.

IV

In the way they are modelled
There are bits of blue.
A hard dry leaf hangs
From the stem.

V

The yellow glistens.
It glistens with various yellows,
Citrons, oranges and greens
Flowering over the skin.

VI

The shadows of the pears
Are blobs on the green cloth.
The pears are not seen
As the observer wills.

334   *The Glass of Water*

THAT the glass would melt in heat,
That the water would freeze in cold,
Shows that this object is merely a state,
One of many, between two poles. So,
In the metaphysical, there are these poles.

Here in the centre stands the glass. Light
Is the lion that comes down to drink. There
And in that state, the glass is a pool.
Ruddy are his eyes and ruddy are his claws
When light comes down to wet his frothy jaws

And in the water winding weeds move round.
And there and in another state—the refractions,
The *metaphysica*, the plastic parts of poems
Crash in the mind—But, fat Jocundus, worrying
About what stands here in the centre, not the glass,

But in the centre of our lives, this time, this day,
It is a state, this spring among the politicians
Playing cards. In a village of the indigenes,
One would have still to discover. Among the dogs and
      dung,
One would continue to contend with one's ideas.

335 *Dry Loaf*

IT is equal to living in a tragic land
To live in a tragic time.
Regard now the sloping, mountainous rocks
And the river that batters its way over stones,
Regard the hovels of those that live in this land.

That was what I painted behind the loaf,
The rocks not even touched by snow,
The pines along the river and the dry men blown
Brown as the bread, thinking of birds
Flying from burning countries and brown sand shores,

Birds that came like dirty water in waves
Flowing above the rocks, flowing over the sky,
As if the sky was a current that bore them along,
Spreading them as waves spread flat on the shore,
One after another washing the mountains bare.

It was the battering of drums I heard
It was hunger, it was the hungry that cried
And the waves, the waves were soldiers moving,
Marching and marching in a tragic time
Below me, on the asphalt, under the trees.

It was soldiers went marching over the rocks
And still the birds came, came in watery flocks,
Because it was spring and the birds had to come.
No doubt that soldiers had to be marching
And that drums had to be rolling, rolling, rolling.

336 *Idiom of the Hero*

I HEARD two workers say, 'This chaos
Will soon be ended.'

This chaos will not be ended,
The red and the blue house blended,

Not ended, never and never ended,
The weak man mended,

The man that is poor at night
Attended

Like the man that is rich and right.
The great men will not be blended . . .

I am the poorest of all.
I know that I cannot be mended,

Out of the clouds, pomp of the air,
By which at least I am befriended.

337 *Girl in a Nightgown*

LIGHTS out. Shades up.
A look at the weather.
There has been a booming all the spring,
A refrain from the end of the boulevards.

This is the silence of night,
This is what could not be shaken,
Full of stars and the images of stars—
And that booming wintry and dull,

Like a tottering, a falling and an end,
Again and again, always there,
Massive drums and leaden trumpets,
Perceived by feeling instead of sense,

A revolution of things colliding.
Phrases! But of fear and of fate.
The night should be warm and fluters' fortune
Should play in the trees when morning comes.

Once it was, the repose of night,
Was a place, strong place, in which to sleep.
It is shaken now. It will burst into flames,
Either now or tomorrow or the day after that.

338 *Martial Cadenza*

I

ONLY this evening I saw again low in the sky
The evening star, at the beginning of winter, the star
That in spring will crown every western horizon,
Again . . . as if it came back, as if life came back,
Not in a later son, a different daughter, another place,
But as if evening found us young, still young,
Still walking in a present of our own.

II

It was like sudden time in a world without time,
This world, this place, the street in which I was,
Without time: as that which is not has no time,
Is not, or is of what there was, is full
Of the silence before the armies, armies without
Either trumpets or drums, the commanders mute, the arms
On the ground, fixed fast in a profound defeat.

III

What had this star to do with the world it lit
With the blank skies over England, over France
And above the German camps? It looked apart.
Yet it is this that shall maintain— Itself
Is time, apart from any past, apart
From any future, the ever-living and being,
The ever-breathing and moving, the constant fire,

IV

The present close, the present realized,
Not the symbol but that for which the symbol stands,
The vivid thing in the air that never changes,
Though the air change. Only this evening I saw it again,
At the beginning of winter, and I walked and talked
Again, and lived and was again, and breathed again
And moved again and flashed again, time flashed again.

Of Modern Poetry

THE poem of the mind in the act of finding
What will suffice. It has not always had
To find: the scene was set; it repeated what
Was in the script.
　　　　　　Then the theatre was changed
To something else. Its past was a souvenir.

It has to be living, to learn the speech of the place.
It has to face the men of the time and to meet
The women of the time. It has to think about war
And it has to find what will suffice. It has
To construct a new stage. It has to be on that stage
And, like an insatiable actor, slowly　and
With meditation speak words that in the ear,
In the delicatest ear of the mind,　repeat,
Exactly, that which it wants to hear, at the sound
Of which, an invisible audience listens,
Not to the play, but to itself, expressed
In an emotion as of two people, as of two
Emotions becoming one. The actor is
A metaphysician in the dark, twanging
An instrument, twanging a wiry string that gives
Sounds passing through sudden rightnesses, wholly
Containing the mind, below which it cannot descend,
Beyond which it has no will to rise.
　　　　　　　　　It must
Be the finding of a satisfaction, and may
Be of a man skating, a woman dancing, a woman
Combing. The poem of the act of the mind.

Contrary Theses (I)

Now grapes are plush upon the vines.
A soldier walks before my door.

The hives are heavy with the combs.
Before, before, before my door.

And seraphs cluster on the domes,
And saints are brilliant in fresh cloaks.

Before, before, before my door.
The shadows lessen on the walls.

The bareness of the house returns.
An acid sunlight fills the halls.

Before, before. Blood smears the oaks.
A soldier stalks before my door.

341

No Possum, No Sop, No Taters

He is not here, the old sun,
As absent as if we were asleep.

The field is frozen. The leaves are dry.
Bad is final in this light.

In this bleak air the broken stalks
Have arms without hands. They have trunks

Without legs or, for that, without heads.
They have heads in which a captive cry

Is merely the moving of a tongue.
Snow sparkles like eyesight falling to earth,

Like seeing fallen brightly away.
The leaves hop, scraping on the ground.

It is deep January. The sky is hard.
The stalks are firmly rooted in ice.

It is in this solitude, a syllable,
Out of these gawky flitterings,

Intones its single emptiness,
The savagest hollow of winter-sound.

It is here, in this bad, that we reach
The last purity of the knowledge of good.

The crow looks rusty as he rises up.
Bright is the malice in his eye . . .

One joins him there for company,
But at a distance, in another tree.

342   *Holiday in Reality*

1

IT was something to see that their white was different,
Sharp as white paint in the January sun;

Something to feel that they needed another yellow,
Less Aix than Stockholm, hardly a yellow at all,

A vibrancy not to be taken for granted, from
A sun in an almost colorless, cold heaven.

They had known that there was not even a common
    speech,
Palabra of a common man who did not exist.

Why should they not know they had everything of their
    own
As each had a particular woman and her touch?

After all, they knew that to be real each had
To find for himself his earth, his sky, his sea.

And the words for them and the colors that they possessed.
It was impossible to breathe at Durand-Ruel's.

II

The flowering Judas grows from the belly or not at all.
The breast is covered with violets. It is a green leaf.

Spring is umbilical or else it is not spring.
Spring is the truth of spring or nothing, a waste, a fake.

These trees and their argentines, their dark-spiced branches,
Grow out of the spirit or they are fantastic dust.

The bud of the apple is desire, the down-falling gold,
The catbird's gobble in the morning half-awake—

These are real only if I make them so. Whistle
For me, grow green for me and, as you whistle and grow
    green,

Intangible arrows quiver and stick in the skin
And I taste at the root of the tongue the unreal of what is
    real.

WILLIAM CARLOS WILLIAMS

b. 1883

343   *Portrait of a Lady*

YOUR thighs are appletrees
whose blossoms touch the sky.
Which sky? The sky
where Watteau hung a lady's
slipper. Your knees
are a southern breeze—or
a gust of snow. Agh! what
sort of man was Fragonard?
—as if that answered
anything. Ah, yes—below
the knees, since the tune
drops that way, it is
one of those white summer days,
the tall grass of your ankles

flickers upon the shore—
Which shore?—
the sand clings to my lips—
Which shore?
Agh, petals maybe. How
should I know?
Which shore? Which shore?
I said petals from an appletree.

344   *Pastoral*

WHEN I was younger
it was plain to me
I must make something of myself.
Older now
I walk back streets
admiring the houses
of the very poor:
roof out of line with sides
the yards cluttered
with old chicken wire, ashes,
furniture gone wrong;
the fences and outhouses
built of barrel-staves
and parts of boxes, all,
if I am fortunate,
smeared a bluish green
that properly weathered
pleases me best
of all colors.

No one
will believe this
of vast import to the nation.

345   *Gulls*

My townspeople, beyond in the great world,
are many with whom it were far more
profitable for me to live than here with you.
These whirr about me calling, calling!
and for my own part I answer them, loud as I can,
but they, being free, pass!
I remain! Therefore, listen!
For you will not soon have another singer.

First I say this: You have seen
the strange birds, have you not, that sometimes
rest upon our river in winter?
Let them cause you to think well then of the storms
that drive many to shelter. These things
do not happen without reason.

And the next thing I say is this:
I saw an eagle once circling against the clouds
over one of our principal churches—
Easter, it was—a beautiful day!—:
three gulls came from above the river
and crossed slowly seaward!
Oh, I know you have your own hymns, I have heard
    them—

and because I knew they invoked some great protector
I could not be angry with you, no matter
how much they outraged true music—

You see, it is not necessary for us to leap at each other,
and, as I told you, in the end
the gulls moved seaward very quietly.

346   *Apology*

WHY DO I WRITE TODAY?

THE beauty of
the terrible faces
of our nonentities
stirs me to it:

colored women
day workers—
old and experienced—
returning home at dusk
in cast off clothing
faces like
old Florentine oak.

Also

the set pieces
of your faces stir me—
leading citizens—
but not
in the same way.

347 *Drink*

M Y whiskey is
a tough way of life:

The wild cherry
continually pressing back
peach orchards.

I am a penniless
rumsoak.

Where shall I have that solidity
which trees find
in the ground?

My stuff
is the feel of good legs
and a broad pelvis
under the gold hair ornaments
of skyscrapers.

348 'By the road to the contagious hospital'

B Y the road to the contagious hospital
under the surge of the blue
mottled clouds driven from the
northeast—a cold wind. Beyond, the

waste of broad, muddy fields
brown with dried weeds, standing and fallen

patches of standing water
the scattering of tall trees

All along the road the reddish
purplish, forked, upstanding, twiggy
stuff of bushes and small trees
with dead, brown leaves under them
leafless vines—

Lifeless in appearance, sluggish
dazed spring approaches—

They enter the new world naked,
cold, uncertain of all
save that they enter. All about them
the cold, familiar wind—

Now the grass, tomorrow
the stiff curl of wildcarrot leaf

One by one objects are defined—
It quickens: clarity, outline of leaf

But now the stark dignity of
entrance—Still, the profound change
has come upon them: rooted they
grip down and begin to awaken

349   '*The pure products of America*'

THE pure products of America
go crazy—
mountain folk from Kentucky

or the ribbed north end of
Jersey
with its isolate lakes and

valleys, its deaf-mutes, thieves
old names
and promiscuity between

devil-may-care men who have taken
to railroading
out of sheer lust of adventure—

and young slatterns, bathed
in filth
from Monday to Saturday

to be tricked out that night
with gauds
from imaginations which have no

peasant traditions to give them
character
but flutter and flaunt

sheer rags—succumbing without
emotion
save numbed terror

under some hedge of choke-cherry
or viburnum—
which they cannot express—

Unless it be that marriage
perhaps
with a dash of Indian blood

will throw up a girl so desolate
so hemmed round
with disease or murder

that she'll be rescued by an
agent—
reared by the state and

sent out at fifteen to work in
some hard pressed
house in the suburbs—

some doctor's family, some Elsie—
voluptuous water
expressing with broken

brain the truth about us—
her great
ungainly hips and flopping breasts

addressed to cheap
jewelry
and rich young men with fine eyes

as if the earth under our feet
were
an excrement of some sky

and we degraded prisoners
destined
to hunger until we eat filth

while the imagination strains
after deer
going by fields of goldenrod in

the stifling heat of September
Somehow
it seems to destroy us

It is only in isolate flecks that
something
is given off

No one
to witness
and adjust, no one to drive the car

350   'The crowd at the ball game'

THE crowd at the ball game
is moved uniformly

by a spirit of uselessness
which delights them—

all the exciting detail
of the chase

and the escape, the error
the flash of genius—

all to no end save beauty
the eternal—

So in detail they, the crowd,
are beautiful

for this
to be warned against

saluted and defied—
It is alive, venomous

it smiles grimly
its words cut—

The flashy female with her
mother, gets it—

The Jew gets it straight—it
is deadly, terrifying—

It is the Inquisition, the
Revolution

It is beauty itself
that lives

day by day in them
idly—

This is
the power of their faces

It is summer, it is the solstice
the crowd is

cheering, the crowd is laughing
in detail

permanently, seriously
without thought

351   *Nantucket*

F LOWERS through the window
lavender and yellow

changed by white curtains—
Smell of cleanliness—

Sunshine of late afternoon—
On the glass tray

a glass pitcher, the tumbler
turned down, by which

a key is lying—And the
immaculate white bed

Death

H E'S dead

the dog won't have to
sleep on his potatoes
any more to keep them
from freezing

he's dead
the old bastard—
He's a bastard because

there's nothing
legitimate in him any
more
   he's dead

He's sick-dead

     he's
a godforsaken curio
without
any breath in it

He's nothing at all
  he's dead

Shrunken up to skin

  Put his head on
one chair and his

feet on another and
he'll lie there
like an acrobat—

Love's beaten. He
beat it. That's why
he's insufferable—

       because
he's there needing a
shave and making love
an inside howl
of anguish and defeat—

He's come out of the man
and he's let
the man go—
                the liar

Dead
        his eyes
rolled up out of
the light—a mockery

                    which
love cannot touch—

just bury it
and hide its face—
for shame.

353   *The Yachts*

contend in a sea which the land partly encloses
shielding them from the too heavy blows
of an ungoverned ocean which when it chooses

tortures the biggest hulls, the best man knows
to pit against its beatings, and sinks them pitilessly.
Mothlike in mists, scintillant in the minute

brilliance of cloudless days, with broad bellying sails
they glide to the wind tossing green water
from their sharp prows while over them the crew crawls

ant like, solicitously grooming them, releasing,
making fast as they turn, lean far over and having
caught the wind again, side by side, head for the mark.

In a well guarded arena of open water surrounded by
lesser and greater craft which, sycophant, lumbering
and flittering follow them, they appear youthful, rare

as the light of a happy eye, live with the grace
of all that in the mind is feckless, free and
naturally to be desired. Now the sea which holds them

is moody, lapping their glossy sides, as if feeling
for some slightest flaw but fails completely.
Today no race. Then the wind comes again. The yachts

move, jockeying for a start, the signal is set and they
are off. Now the waves strike at them but they are too
well made, they slip through, though they take in canvas.

Arms with hands grasping seek to clutch at the prows.
Bodies thrown recklessly in the way are cut aside.
It is a sea of faces about them in agony, in despair

until the horror of the race dawns staggering the mind,
the whole sea become an entanglement of watery bodies
lost to the world bearing what they cannot hold. Broken,

beaten, desolate, reaching from the dead to be taken up
they cry out, failing, failing! their cries rising
in waves still as the skillful yachts pass over.

354   *The Catholic Bells*

THO' I'm no Catholic
I listen hard when the bells
in the yellow-brick tower
of their new church

ring down the leaves
ring in the frost upon them
and the death of the flowers
ring out the grackle

toward the south, the sky
darkened by them, ring in
the new baby of Mr. and Mrs.
Krantz which cannot

for the fat of its cheeks
open well its eyes, ring out

the parrot under its hood
jealous of the child

ring in Sunday morning
and old age which adds as it
takes away. Let them ring
only ring! over the oil

painting of a young priest
on the church wall advertising
last week's Novena to St.
Anthony, ring for the lame

young man in black with
gaunt cheeks and wearing a
Derby hat, who is hurrying
to 11 o'clock Mass (the

grapes still hanging to
the vines along the nearby
Concordia Halle like broken
teeth in the head of an

old man) Let them ring
for the eyes and ring for
the hands and ring for
the children of my friend

who no longer hears
them ring but with a smile
and in a low voice speaks
of the decisions of her

daughter and the proposals
and betrayals of her
husband's friends. O bells
ring for the ringing!

the beginning and the end
of the ringing! Ring ring
ring ring ring ring ring!
Catholic bells—!

355   *Fine Work with Pitch and Copper*

Now they are resting
in the fleckless light
separately in unison

like the sacks
of sifted stone stacked
regularly by twos

about the flat roof
ready after lunch
to be opened and strewn

The copper in eight
foot strips has been
beaten lengthwise

down the center at right
angles and lies ready
to edge the coping

One still chewing
picks up a copper strip
and runs his eye along it

356   *Classic Scene*

A POWER-HOUSE
in the shape of
a red brick chair
90 feet high

on the seat of which
sit the figures
of two metal
stacks—aluminum—

commanding an area
of squalid shacks
side by side—
from one of which

buff smoke
streams while under
a grey sky
the other remains

passive today—

357   *These*

are the desolate, dark weeks
when nature in its barrenness
equals the stupidity of man.

690

The year plunges into night
and the heart plunges
lower than night

to an empty, windswept place
without sun, stars or moon
but a peculiar light as of thought

that spins a dark fire—
whirling upon itself until,
in the cold, it kindles

to make a man aware of nothing
that he knows, not loneliness
itself—Not a ghost but

would be embraced—emptiness,
despair—(They
whine and whistle) among

the flashes and booms of war;
houses of whose rooms
the cold is greater than can be thought,

the people gone that we loved,
the beds lying empty, the couches
damp, the chairs unused—

Hide it away somewhere
out of the mind, let it get roots
and grow, unrelated to jealous

ears and eyes—for itself.
In this mine they come to dig—all.
Is this the counterfoil to sweetest

music? The source of poetry that
seeing the clock stopped, says,
The clock has stopped

that ticked yesterday so well?
and hears the sound of lakewater
splashing—that is now stone.

358 *Paterson: Episode 17*

B EAT hell out of it
　　Beautiful Thing
　　　spotless cap
and crossed white straps
over the dark rippled cloth—
　　Lift the stick
above that easy head
where you sit by the ivied
church, one arm
　　buttressing you
long fingers spread out
among the clear grass prongs—
　　and drive it down
　　Beautiful Thing
that your caressing body kiss
　　and kiss again
that holy lawn—

And again! obliquely—
legs curled under you as a
　　deer's leaping—

692

pose of supreme indifference
    sacrament
to a summer's day
    Beautiful Thing
in the unearned suburbs
    then pause
    the arm fallen—
what memories
of what forgotten face
brooding upon that lily stem?

    The incredible
nose straight from the brow
    the empurpled lips
and dazzled half sleepy eyes
    Beautiful Thing
of some trusting animal
    makes a temple
of its place of savage slaughter
    revealing
the damaged will incites still
    to violence
consummately beautiful Thing
and falls about your resting
    shoulders—

Gently! Gently!
as in all things an opposite
    that awakes
the fury, conceiving
    knowledge
by way of despair that has
    no place

693

to lay its glossy head—
Save only—Not alone!
        Never, if possible
alone! to escape the accepted
        chopping block
and a square hat!—

And as reverie gains and
        your joints loosen
        the trick's done!
Day is covered and we see you—
        but not alone!
drunk and bedraggled to release
the strictness of beauty
under a sky full of stars
        Beautiful Thing
and a slow moon—

                    The car
        had stopped long since
        when the others
came and dragged those out
        who had you there
        indifferent
to whatever the anesthetic
        Beautiful Thing
might slum away the bars—

Reek of it!
        What does it matter?
        could set free
only the one thing—
But you!

—in your white lace dress
    'the dying swan'
and high heeled slippers—tall
as you already were—
    till your head
through fruitful exaggeration
was reaching the sky and the
prickles of its ecstasy
    Beautiful Thing!

And the guys from Paterson
    beat up
the guys from Newark and told
them to stay the hell out
of their territory and then
socked you one
    across the nose
    Beautiful Thing
for good luck and emphasis
    cracking it
till I must believe that all
desired women have had each
    in the end
    a busted nose
and live afterward marked up
    Beautiful Thing
    for memory's sake
to be credible in their deeds

Then back to the party!
    and they maled
and femaled you jealously
    Beautiful Thing

as if to discover when and
    by what miracle
there should escape what?
still to be possessed
out of what part
    Beautiful Thing
should it look?
    or be extinguished—
Three days in the same dress
    up and down—

    It would take
a Dominie to be patient
    Beautiful Thing
with you—

The stroke begins again—
    regularly
automatic
    contrapuntal to
the flogging
like the beat of famous lines
in the few excellent poems
    woven to make you
    gracious
and on frequent occasions
    foul drunk
    Beautiful Thing
pulse of release
    to the attentive
and obedient mind.

WILLIAM CARLOS WILLIAMS

359 *The Dance*

IN Breughel's great picture, The Kermess,
the dancers go round, they go round and
around, the squeal and the blare and the
tweedle of bagpipes, a bugle and fiddles
tipping their bellies (round as the thick-
sided glasses whose wash they impound)
their hips and their bellies off balance
to turn them. Kicking and rolling about
the Fair Grounds, swinging their butts, those
shanks must be sound to bear up under such
rollicking measures, prance as they dance
in Breughel's great picture, The Kermess.

ELINOR WYLIE

1885-1928

360 *Beauty*

SAY not of Beauty she is good,
Or aught but beautiful,
Or sleek to doves' wings of the wood
Her wild wings of a gull.

Call her not wicked; that word's touch
Consumes her like a curse;

But love her not too much, too much,
For that is even worse.

O, she is neither good nor bad,
But innocent and wild!
Enshrine her and she dies, who had
The hard heart of a child.

361   *Wild Peaches*

I

WHEN the world turns completely upside down
You say we'll emigrate to the Eastern Shore
Aboard a river-boat from Baltimore;
We'll live among wild peach trees, miles from town,
You'll wear a coonskin cap, and I a gown
Homespun, dyed butternut's dark gold colour.
Lost, like your lotus-eating ancestor,
We'll swim in milk and honey till we drown.

The winter will be short, the summer long,
The autumn amber-hued, sunny and hot,
Tasting of cider and of scuppernong;
All seasons sweet, but autumn best of all.
The squirrels in their silver fur will fall
Like falling leaves, like fruit, before your shot.

2

The autumn frosts will lie upon the grass
Like bloom on grapes of purple-brown and gold.

The misted early mornings will be cold;
The little puddles will be roofed with glass.
The sun, which burns from copper into brass,
Melts these at noon, and makes the boys unfold
Their knitted mufflers; full as they can hold,
Fat pockets dribble chestnuts as they pass.

Peaches grow wild, and pigs can live in clover;
A barrel of salted herrings lasts a year;
The spring begins before the winter's over.
By February you may find the skins
Of garter snakes and water moccasins
Dwindled and harsh, dead-white and cloudy-clear.

3

When April pours the colours of a shell
Upon the hills, when every little creek
Is shot with silver from the Chesapeake
In shoals new-minted by the ocean swell,
When strawberries go begging, and the sleek
Blue plums lie open to the blackbird's beak,
We shall live well—we shall live very well.

The months between the cherries and the peaches
Are brimming cornucopias which spill
Fruits red and purple, sombre-bloomed and black;
Then, down rich fields and frosty river beaches
We'll trample bright persimmons, while you kill
Bronze partridge, speckled quail, and canvasback.

4

Down to the Puritan marrow of my bones
There's something in this richness that I hate.

I love the look, austere, immaculate,
Of landscapes drawn in pearly monotones.
There's something in my very blood that owns
Bare hills, cold silver on a sky of slate,
A thread of water, churned to milky spate
Streaming through slanted pastures fenced with stones.

I love those skies, thin blue or snowy gray,
Those fields sparse-planted, rendering meagre sheaves;
That spring, briefer than apple-blossom's breath,
Summer, so much too beautiful to stay,
Swift autumn, like a bonfire of leaves,
And sleepy winter, like the sleep of death.

362   *Let No Charitable Hope*

NOW let no charitable hope
Confuse my mind with images
Of eagle and of antelope:
I am in nature none of these.

I was, being human, born alone;
I am, being woman, hard beset;
I live by squeezing from a stone
The little nourishment I get.

In masks outrageous and austere
The years go by in single file;
But none has merited my fear,
And none has quite escaped my smile.

363 *Parting Gift*

I CANNOT give you the Metropolitan Tower;
I cannot give you heaven;
Nor the nine Visigoth crowns in the Cluny Museum;
Nor happiness, even.
But I can give you a very small purse
Made out of field-mouse skin,
With a painted picture of the universe
And seven blue tears therein.

I cannot give you the island of Capri;
I cannot give you beauty;
Nor bake you marvellous crusty cherry pies
With love and duty.
But I can give you a very little locket
Made out of wildcat hide:
Put it into your left-hand pocket
And never look inside.

364 *Innocent Landscape*

HERE is no peace, although the air has fainted,
   And footfalls die and are buried in deep grass,
And reverential trees are softly painted
   Like saints upon an oriel of glass.

The pattern of the atmosphere is spherical,
  A bubble in the silence of the sun,
Blown thinner by the very breath of miracle
  Around a core of loud confusion.

Here is no virtue; here is nothing blessed
  Save this foredoomed suspension of the end;
Faith is the blossom, but the fruit is cursèd;
  Go hence, for it is useless to pretend.

365   *Address to My Soul*

M Y soul, be not disturbed
By planetary war;
Remain securely orbed
In this contracted star.

Fear not, pathetic flame;
Your sustenance is doubt:
Glassed in translucent dream
They cannot snuff you out.

Wear water, or a mask
Of unapparent cloud;
Be brave and never ask
A more defunctive shroud.

The universal points
Are shrunk into a flower;
Between its delicate joints
Chaos keeps no power.

ELINOR WYLIE

The pure integral form,
Austere and silver-dark,
Is balanced on the storm
In its predestined arc.

Small as a sphere of rain
It slides along the groove
Whose path is furrowed plain
Among the suns that move.

The shapes of April buds
Outlive the phantom year:
Upon the void at odds
The dewdrop falls severe.

Five-petalled flame, be cold:
Be firm, dissolving star:
Accept the stricter mould
That makes you singular.

366   *Sonnets from 'One Person'*

I HEREBY swear that to uphold your house
I would lay my bones in quick destroying lime
Or turn my flesh to timber for all time;
Cut down my womanhood; lop off the boughs
Of that perpetual ecstasy that grows
From the heart's core; condemn it as a crime
If it be broader than a beam, or climb
Above the stature that your roof allows.

I am not the hearthstone nor the cornerstone
Within this noble fabric you have builded;
Not by my beauty was its cornice gilded;
Not on my courage were its arches thrown:
My lord, adjudge my strength, and set me where
I bear a little more than I can bear.

Let us leave talking of angelic hosts
Of nebulæ, and lunar hemispheres,
And what the days, and what the Uranian years
Shall offer us when you and I are ghosts;
Forget the festivals and pentecosts
Of metaphysics, and the lesser fears
Confound us, and seal up our eyes and ears
Like little rivers locked below the frosts.

And let us creep into the smallest room
That any hunted exile has desired
For him and for his love when he was tired;
And sleep oblivious of any doom
Which is beyond our reason to conceive;
And so forget to weep, forget to grieve,
And wake, and touch each other's hands, and turn
Upon a bed of juniper and fern.

EZRA POUND

367 *A Virginal*

No, no! Go from me. I have left her lately.
I will not spoil my sheath with lesser brightness,
For my surrounding air hath a new lightness;
Slight are her arms, yet they have bound me straitly
And left me cloaked as with a gauze of æther;
As with sweet leaves; as with subtle clearness.
Oh, I have picked up magic in her nearness
To sheathe me half in half the things that sheathe her.
No, no! Go from me. I have still the flavour,
Soft as spring wind that's come from birchen bowers.
Green come the shoots, aye April in the branches,
As winter's wound with her sleight hand she staunches,
Hath of the trees a likeness of the savour:
As white their bark, so white this lady's hours.

368 *The Return*

See, they return; ah, see the tentative
        Movements, and the slow feet,
        The trouble in the pace and the uncertain
        Wavering!

See, they return, one, and by one,
With fear, as half-awakened;
As if the snow should hesitate
And murmur in the wind,
                    and half turn back;
These were the 'Wing'd-with-Awe,'
                    Inviolable.

Gods of the wingèd shoe!
With them the silver hounds,
                    sniffing the trace of air!

Haie! Haie!
            These were the swift to harry;
These the keen-scented;
These were the souls of blood.

Slow on the leash,
                    pallid the leash-men!

369   *The Seafarer*
            From the Anglo-Saxon

MAY I for my own self song's truth reckon,
Journey's jargon, how I in harsh days
Hardship endured oft.
Bitter breast-cares have I abided,
Known on my keel many a care's hold,
And dire sea-surge, and there I oft spent
Narrow nightwatch nigh the ship's head

706

While she tossed close to cliffs. Coldly afflicted,
My feet were by frost benumbed.
Chill its chains are; chafing sighs
Hew my heart round and hunger begot
Mere-weary mood. Lest man know not
That he on dry land loveliest liveth,
List how I, care-wretched, on ice-cold sea,
Weathered the winter, wretched outcast
Deprived of my kinsmen;
Hung with hard ice-flakes, where hail-scur flew,
There I heard naught save the harsh sea
And ice-cold wave, at whiles the swan cries,
Did for my games the gannet's clamour,
Sea-fowls' loudness was for me laughter,
The mews' singing all my mead-drink.
Storms, on the stone-cliffs beaten, fell on the stern
In icy feathers; full oft the eagle screamed
With spray on his pinion.
                      Not any protector
May make merry man faring needy.
This he little believes, who aye in winsome life
Abides 'mid burghers some heavy business,
Wealthy and wine-flushed, how I weary oft
Must bide above brine.
Neareth nightshade, snoweth from north,
Frost froze the land, hail fell on earth then,
Corn of the coldest. Nathless there knocketh now
The heart's thought that I on high streams
The salt-wavy tumult traverse alone.
Moaneth alway my mind's lust
That I fare forth, that I afar hence
Seek out a foreign fastness.
For this there's no mood-lofty man over earth's midst,

Not though he be given his good, but will have in his
    youth greed;
Nor his deed to the daring, nor his king to the faithful
But shall have his sorrow for sea-fare
Whatever his lord will.
He hath not heart for harping, nor in ring-having
Nor winsomeness to wife, nor world's delight
Nor any whit else save the wave's slash,
Yet longing comes upon him to fare forth on the water.
Bosque taketh blossom, cometh beauty of berries,
Fields to fairness, land fares brisker,
All this admonisheth man eager of mood,
The heart turns to travel so that he then thinks
On flood-ways to be far departing.
Cuckoo calleth with gloomy crying,
He singeth summerward, bodeth sorrow,
The bitter heart's blood. Burgher knows not—
He the prosperous man—what some perform
Where wandering them widest draweth.
So that but now my heart burst from my breastlock,
My mood 'mid the mere-flood,
Over the whale's acre, would wander wide.
On earth's shelter cometh oft to me,
Eager and ready, the crying lone-flyer,
Whets for the whale-path the heart irresistibly,
O'er tracks of ocean; seeing that anyhow
My lord deems to me this dead life
On loan and on land, I believe not
That any earth-weal eternal standeth
Save there be somewhat calamitous
That, ere a man's tide go, turn it to twain.
Disease or oldness or sword-hate
Beats out the breath from doom-gripped body.

And for this, every earl whatever, for those speaking
    after—
Laud of the living, boasteth some last word,
That he will work ere he pass onward,
Frame on the fair earth 'gainst foes his malice,
Daring ado, . . .
So that all men shall honour him after
And his laud beyond them remain 'mid the English,
Aye, for ever, a lasting life's-blast,
Delight 'mid the doughty.
                     Days little durable,
And all arrogance of earthen riches,
There come now no kings nor Cæsars
Nor gold-giving lords like those gone.
Howe'er in mirth most magnified,
Whoe'er lived in life most lordliest,
Drear all this excellence, delights undurable!
Waneth the watch, but the world holdeth.
Tomb hideth trouble. The blade is layed low.
Earthly glory ageth and seareth.
No man at all going the earth's gait,
But age fares against him, his face paleth,
Grey-haired he groaneth, knows gone companions,
Lordly men, are to earth o'ergiven,
Nor may he then the flesh-cover, whose life ceaseth,
Nor eat the sweet nor feel the sorry,
Nor stir hand nor think in mid heart,
And though he strew the grave with gold,
His born brothers, their buried bodies
Be an unlikely treasure hoard.

370 *Salutation*

O GENERATION of the thoroughly smug and thor-
oughly uncomfortable,
I have seen fishermen picnicking in the sun,
I have seen them with untidy families,
I have seen their smiles full of teeth and heard ungainly
laughter.
And I am happier than you are,
And they were happier than I am;
And the fish swim in the lake and do not even own
clothing.

371 *Salutation the Second*

YOU were praised, my books,
because I had just come from the country;
I was twenty years behind the times
so you found an audience ready.
I do not disown you,
do not you disown your progeny.

Here they stand without quaint devices,
Here they are with nothing archaic about them.
Observe the irritation in general:

'Is this,' they say, 'the nonsense
that we expect of poets?'

EZRA POUND

'Where is the Picturesque?'
          'Where is the vertigo of emotion?'
'No! his first work was the best.'
          'Poor Dear! he has lost his illusions.'

Go, little naked and impudent songs,
Go with a light foot!
(Or with two light feet, if it please you!)
Go and dance shamelessly!
Go with an impertinent frolic!

Greet the grave and the stodgy,
Salute them with your thumbs at your noses.

Here are your bells and confetti.
Go! rejuvenate things!
Rejuvenate even 'The Spectator.'
          Go! and make cat calls!
Dance and make people blush,
Dance the dance of the phallus
          and tell anecdotes of Cybele!
Speak of the indecorous conduct of the Gods!
          (Tell it to Mr. Strachey)

Ruffle the skirts of prudes,
          speak of their knees and ankles.
But, above all, go to practical people—
          go! jangle their door-bells!
Say that you do no work
          and that you will live forever.

372 *A Pact*

I MAKE a pact with you, Walt Whitman—
I have detested you long enough.
I come to you as a grown child
Who has had a pig-headed father;
I am old enough now to make friends.
It was you that broke the new wood,
Now is a time for carving.
We have one sap and one root—
Let there be commerce between us.

373 *The Rest*

O HELPLESS few in my country,
O remnant enslaved!

Artists broken against her,
A-stray, lost in the villages,
Mistrusted, spoken-against,

Lovers of beauty, starved,
Thwarted with systems,
Helpless against the control;

You who can not wear yourselves out
By persisting to successes,

You who can only speak,
Who can not steel yourselves into reiteration;

You of the finer sense,
Broken against false knowledge,
You who can know at first hand,
Hated, shut in, mistrusted:

Take thought:
I have weathered the storm,
I have beaten out my exile.

374 *Epilogue*

O CHANSONS foregoing
You were a seven days' wonder.
When you came out in the magazines
You created considerable stir in Chicago,
And now you are stale and worn out,
You're a very depleted fashion,
A hoop-skirt, a calash,
An homely, transient antiquity.
Only emotion remains.
Your emotions?
    Are those of a maître-de-café.

375 *In a Station of the Metro*

THE apparition of these faces in the crowd;
Petals on a wet, black bough.

376 *L'Art,* 1910

GREEN arsenic smeared on an egg-white cloth,
Crushed strawberries! Come, let us feast our eyes.

377 *Ancient Music*

WINTER is icummen in,
Lhude sing Goddamm,
Raineth drop and staineth slop,
And how the wind doth ramm!
     Sing: Goddamm.
Skiddeth bus and sloppeth us,
An ague hath my ham.
Freezeth river, turneth liver,
     Damn you, sing: Goddamm.
Goddamm, Goddamm, 'tis why I am, Goddamm,
     So 'gainst the winter's balm.
Sing goddamm, damm, sing Goddamm,
Sing goddamm, sing goddamm, DAMM.

378 *Provincia Deserta*

AT Rochecoart,
Where the hills part
   in three ways,

And three valleys, full of winding roads,
Fork out to south and north,
There is a place of trees . . . gray with lichen.
I have walked there
          thinking of old days.
At Chalais
          is a pleached arbour;
Old pensioners and old protected women
Have the right there—
          it is charity.
I have crept over old rafters,
          peering down
Over the Dronne,
          over a stream full of lilies.
Eastward the road lies,
          Aubeterre is eastward,
With a garrulous old man at the inn.
I know the roads in that place:
Mareuil to the north-east,
          La Tour,
There are three keeps near Mareuil,
And an old woman,
          glad to hear Arnaut,
Glad to lend one dry clothing.

I have walked
          into Perigord,
I have seen the torch-flames, high-leaping,
Painting the front of that church;
Heard, under the dark, whirling laughter.
I have looked back over the stream
          and seen the high building,
Seen the long minarets, the white shafts.

715

I have gone in Ribeyrac
             and in Sarlat,
I have climbed rickety stairs, heard talk of Croy,
Walked over En Bertran's old layout,
Have seen Narbonne, and Cahors and Chalus,
Have seen Excideuil, carefully fashioned.

I have said:
             'Here such a one walked.
'Here Cœur-de-Lion was slain.
             'Here was good singing.
'Here one man hastened his step.
             'Here one lay panting.'
I have looked south from Hautefort,
             thinking of Montaignac, southward.
I have lain in Rocafixada,
             level with sunset,
Have seen the copper come down
             tingeing the mountains,
I have seen the fields, pale, clear as an emerald,
Sharp peaks, high spurs, distant castles.
I have said: 'The old roads have lain here.
'Men have gone by such and such valleys
'Where the great halls were closer together.'
I have seen Foix on its rock, seen Toulouse, and
             Arles greatly altered,
I have seen the ruined 'Dorata.'
             I have said:
'Riquier! Guido!'
             I have thought of the second Troy,
Some little prized place in Auvergnat:
Two men tossing a coin, one keeping a castle,

One set on the highway to sing.
                    He sang a woman.
Auvergne rose to the song;
                    The Dauphin backed him.
'The castle to Austors!'
                    'Pieire kept the singing—
'A fair man and a pleasant.'
                    He won the lady,
Stole her away for himself, kept her against armed
                    force:
So ends that story.
That age is gone;
Pieire de Maensac is gone.
I have walked over these roads;
I have thought of them living.

379   *The River Merchant's Wife:*
                A Letter

WHILE my hair was still cut straight across my fore-
    head
I played about the front gate, pulling flowers.
You came by on bamboo stilts, playing horse,
You walked about my seat, playing with blue plums.
And we went on living in the village of Chokan:
Two small people, without dislike or suspicion.

At fourteen I married My Lord you.
I never laughed, being bashful.
Lowering my head, I looked at the wall.
Called to, a thousand times, I never looked back.

At fifteen I stopped scowling,
I desired my dust to be mingled with yours
Forever and forever and forever.
Why should I climb the look out?

At sixteen you departed,
You went into far Ku-to-yen, by the river of swirling
      eddies,
And you have been gone five months.
The monkeys make sorrowful noise overhead.

You dragged your feet when you went out.
By the gate now, the moss is grown, the different mosses,
Too deep to clear them away!
The leaves fall early this autumn, in wind.
The paired butterflies are already yellow with August
Over the grass in the West garden;
They hurt me. I grow older.
If you are coming down through the narrows of the river
      Kiang,
Please let me know beforehand,
And I will come out to meet you
          As far as Cho-fu-Sa.

                    By Rihaku

380   *Exile's Letter*

To So-Kin of Rakuyo, ancient friend, Chancellor of
      Gen.
Now I remember that you built me a special tavern
By the south side of the bridge at Ten-Shin.

With yellow gold and white jewels, we paid for songs and
    laughter
And we were drunk for month on month, forgetting the
    kings and princes.
Intelligent men came drifting in from the sea and from
    the west border,
And with them, and with you especially
There was nothing at cross purpose,
And they made nothing of sea-crossing or of mountain-
    crossing,
If only they could be of that fellowship,
And we all spoke out our hearts and minds, and without
    regret.
And then I was sent off to South Wei,
    smothered in laurel groves,
And you to the north of Raku-hoku,
Till we had nothing but thoughts and memories in
    common.
And then, when separation had come to its worst,
We met, and travelled into Sen-Go,
Through all the thirty-six folds of the turning and twisting
    waters,
Into a valley of the thousand bright flowers,
That was the first valley;
And into ten thousand valleys full of voices and pine-
    winds.
And with silver harness and reins of gold,
Out came the East of Kan foreman and his company.
And there came also the 'True man' of Shi-yo to meet me,
Playing on a jewelled mouth-organ.
In the storied houses of San-Ko they gave us more Sennin
    music,

Many instruments, like the sound of young phœnix broods.
The foreman of Kan Chu, drunk, danced
      because his long sleeves wouldn't keep still
With that music playing,
And I, wrapped in brocade, went to sleep with my head on
    his lap,
And my spirit so high it was all over the heavens,
And before the end of the day we were scattered like
    stars, or rain.
I had to be off to So, far away over the waters,
You back to your river-bridge.

And your father, who was brave as a leopard,
Was governor in Hei Shu, and put down the barbarian
    rabble.
And one May he had you send for me,
        despite the long distance.
And what with broken wheels and so on, I won't say it
        wasn't hard going,
Over roads twisted like sheep's guts.
And I was still going, late in the year,
        in the cutting wind from the North,
And thinking how little you cared for the cost,
        and you caring enough to pay it.
And what a reception:
Red jade cups, food well set on a blue jewelled table,
And I was drunk, and had no thought of returning.
And you would walk out with me to the western corner of
    the castle,
To the dynastic temple, with water about it clear as blue
    jade,
With boats floating, and the sound of mouth-organs and
    drums,

With ripples like dragon-scales, going grass green on the
    water,
Pleasure lasting, with courtezans, going and coming without
    hindrance,
With the willow flakes falling like snow,
And the vermilioned girls getting drunk about sunset,
And the water, a hundred feet deep, reflecting green eye-
    brows
—Eyebrows painted green are a fine sight in young moon-
    light,
Gracefully painted—
And the girls singing back at each other,
Dancing in transparent brocade,
And the wind lifting the song, and interrupting it,
Tossing it up under the clouds.

                And all this comes to an end.
                And is not again to be met with.
I went up to the court for examination,
Tried Layu's luck, offered the Choyo song,
And got no promotion,
              and went back to the East Mountains
              White-headed.
And once again, later, we met at the South bridgehead.
And then the crowd broke up, you went north to San
    palace,
And if you ask how I regret that parting:
It is like the flowers falling at Spring's end
              Confused, whirled in a tangle.
What is the use of talking, and there is no end of talking,
There is no end of things in the heart.
I call in the boy,
Have him sit on his knees here

To seal this,
And send it a thousand miles, thinking.

By Rihaku

381   From *Homage to Sextus Propertius*

I

SHADES of Callimachus, Coan ghosts of Philetas
It is in your grove I would walk,
I who come first from the clear font
Bringing the Grecian orgies into Italy,
                              and the dance into Italy.
Who hath taught you so subtle a measure,
                        in what hall have you heard it;
What foot beat out your time-bar,   . .
                  what water has mellowed your whistles?

Out-weariers of Apollo will, as we know, continue their
      Martian generalities,
      We have kept our erasers in order.
A new-fangled chariot follows the flower-hung horses;
A young Muse with young loves clustered about her
                        ascends with me into the æther, . . .
And there is no high-road to the Muses.

Annalists will continue to record Roman reputations,
Celebrities from the Trans-Caucasus will belaud Roman
      celebrities
And expound the distentions of Empire,
But for something to read in normal circumstances?

For a few pages brought down from the forked hill
    unsullied?
I ask a wreath which will not crush my head.
                     And there is no hurry about it;
I shall have, doubtless, a boom after my funeral,
Seeing that long standing increases all things
                           regardless of quality.

And who would have known the towers
                     pulled down by a deal-wood horse;
Or of Achilles withstaying waters by Simois
Or of Hector spattering wheel-rims,
Or of Polydmantus, by Scamander, or Helenus and
    Deiphoibos?
Their door-yards would scarcely know them, or Paris.
Small talk O Ilion, and O Troad
                 twice taken by Oetian gods,

If Homer had not stated your case!

And I also among the later nephews of this city
                   shall have my dog's day,
With no stone upon my contemptible sepulchre;
My vote coming from the temple of Phoebus in Lycia, at
    Patara,
And in the mean time my songs will travel,
And the devirginated young ladies will enjoy them
          when they have got over the strangeness,
For Orpheus tamed the wild beasts—
               and held up the Threician river;
And Citharaon shook up the rocks by Thebes
        and danced them into a bulwark at his pleasure,
And you, O Polyphemus? Did harsh Galatea almost

Turn to your dripping horses, because of a tune, under
    Aetna?
We must look into the matter.
Bacchus and Apollo in favour of it,
There will be a crowd of young women doing homage to
    my palaver,
Though my house is not propped up by Taenarian columns
    from Laconia (associated with Neptune and Cerberus),
Though it is not stretched upon gilded beams;
My orchards do not lie level and wide
                as the forests of Phaecia,
                the luxurious and Ionian,
Nor are my caverns stuffed stiff with a Marcian vintage,
My cellar does not date from Numa Pompilius,
Nor bristle with wine jars,
Nor is it equipped with a frigidaire patent;
Yet the companions of the Muses
            will keep their collective nose in my books,
And weary with historical data, they will turn to my dance
    tune.

Happy who are mentioned in my pamphlets,
    the songs shall be a fine tomb-stone over their beauty.
        But against this?
Neither expensive pyramids scraping the stars in their route,
Nor houses modelled upon that of Jove in East Elis,
Nor the monumental effigies of Mausolus,
           are a complete elucidation of death.

Flame burns, rain sinks into the cracks
And they all go to rack ruin beneath the thud of the years.
Stands genius a deathless adornment,
        a name not to be worn out with the years.

VI

When, when, and whenever death closes our eyelids,
Moving naked over Acheron
Upon the one raft, victor and conquered together,
Marius and Jugurtha together,
                              one tangle of shadows.
Caesar plots against India,
Tigris and Euphrates shall, from now on, flow at his
    bidding,
Tibet shall be full of Roman policemen,
The Parthians shall get used to our statuary
                              and acquire a Roman religion;
One raft on the veiled flood of Acheron,
              Marius and Jugurtha together.

Nor at my funeral either will there be any long trail,
                    bearing ancestral lares and images;
No trumpets filled with my emptiness,
Nor shall it be on an Atalic bed;
              The perfumed cloths shall be absent.
A small plebeian procession.
              Enough, enough and in plenty
There will be three books at my obsequies
Which I take, my not unworthy gift, to Persephone.

You will follow the bare scarified breast
Nor will you be weary of calling my name, nor too weary
              To place the last kiss on my lips
When the Syrian onyx is broken.

              'He who is now vacant dust
              'Was once the slave of one passion:'
Give that much inscription
              'Death why tardily come?'

You, sometimes, will lament a lost friend,
       For it is a custom:
This care for past men,

Since Adonis was gored in Idalia, and the Cytharean
Ran crying with out-spread hair,
       In vain, you call back the shade,
In vain, Cynthia. Vain call to unanswering shadow,
       Small talk comes from small bones.

XII

Who, who will be the next man to entrust his girl to a
    friend?
Love interferes with fidelities;
The gods have brought shame on their relatives;
Each man wants the pomegranate for himself;
Amiable and harmonious people are pushed incontinent
    into duels,
A Trojan and adulterous person came to Menelaus under
    the rites of hospitium,
And there was a case in Colchis, Jason and that woman in
    Colchis;
And besides, Lynceus,
            you were drunk.

Could you endure such promiscuity?
           She was not renowned for fidelity;
But to jab a knife in my vitals, to have passed on a swig of
    poison,
Preferable, my dear boy, my dear Lynceus,
Comrade, comrade of my life, of my purse, of my person;
But in one bed, in one bed alone, my dear Lynceus
       I deprecate your attendance;

I would ask a like boon of Jove.
And you write of Achelöus, who contended with Hercules,
You write of Adrastus' horses and the funeral rites of
    Achenor,
And you will not leave off imitating Aeschylus.
      Though you make a hash of Antimachus,
You think you are going to do Homer.
      And still a girl scorns the gods,
Of all these young women
          not one has enquired the cause of the world,
Nor the modus of lunar eclipses
      Nor whether there be any patch left of us
After we cross the infernal ripples,
        nor if the thunder fall from predestination;
Nor anything else of importance.

Upon the Actian marshes Virgil is Phoebus' chief of police,
      He can tabulate Caesar's great ships.
He thrills to Ilian arms,
      He shakes the Trojan weapons of Aeneas,
And casts stores on Lavinian beaches.

Make way, ye Roman authors,
               clear the street, O ye Greeks,
For a much larger Iliad is in the course of construction
(and to Imperial order)
Clear the streets, O ye Greeks!

And you also follow him 'neath Phrygian pine shade:
      Thyrsis and Daphnis upon whittled reeds,
And how ten sins can corrupt young maidens;
      Kids for a bribe and pressed udders,
Happy selling poor loves for cheap apples.

Tityrus might have sung the same vixen;
             Corydon tempted Alexis,
Head farmers do likewise, and lying weary amid their oats
They get praise from tolerant Hamadryads.'
Go on, to Ascraeus' prescription, the ancient,
                     respected, Wordsworthian:
'A flat field for rushes, grapes grow on the slope.'

And behold me, small fortune left in my house.
Me, who had no general for a grandfather!
I shall triumph among young ladies of indeterminate
    character,
My talent acclaimed in their banquets,
            I shall be honoured with yesterday's wreaths.
And the god strikes to the marrow.

            Like a trained and performing tortoise,
I would make verse in your fashion, if she should com-
    mand it,
With her husband asking a remission of sentence,
            And even this infamy would not attract numer-
            ous readers
Were there an erudite or violent passion,
For the nobleness of the populace brooks nothing below its
    own altitude.
One must have resonance, resonance and sonority . . .
    like a goose.

Varro sang Jason's expedition,
                 Varro, of his great passion Leucadia,
There is song in the parchment; Catullus the highly
    indecorous,
Of Lesbia, known above Helen;

And in the dyed pages of Calvus,
      Calvus mourning Quintilia,
And but now Gallus had sung of Lycoris.
      Fair, fairest Lycoris—
The waters of Styx poured over the wound:
And now Propertius of Cynthia, taking his stand among
      these.

382   From *Hugh Selwyn Mauberley*

I

E.P. ODE POUR L'ÉLECTION DE SON SÉPULCHRE

FOR three years, out of key with his time,
He strove to resuscitate the dead art
Of poetry; to maintain 'the sublime'
In the old sense. Wrong from the start—

No hardly, but, seeing he had been born
In a half savage country, out of date;
Bent resolutely on wringing lilies from the acorn;
Capaneus; trout for factitious bait;

Ἴδμεν γάρ τοι πάνθ', ὅσ' ἐνι Τροίη
Caught in the unstopped ear;
Giving the rocks small lee-way
The chopped seas held him, therefore, that year.

His true Penelope was Flaubert,
He fished by obstinate isles;
Observed the elegance of Circe's hair
Rather than the mottoes on sun-dials.

729

Unaffected by 'the march of events,'
He passed from men's memory in *l'an trentiesme*
De son eage; the case presents
No adjunct to the Muses' diadem.

II

The age demanded an image
Of its accelerated grimace,
Something for the modern stage,
Not, at any rate, an Attic grace;

Not, not certainly, the obscure reveries
Of the inward gaze;
Better mendacities
Than the classics in paraphrase!

The 'age demanded' chiefly a mould in plaster,
Made with no loss of time,
A prose kinema, not, not assuredly, alabaster
Or the 'sculpture' of rhyme.

III

The tea-rose tea-gown, etc.
Supplants the mousseline of Cos,
The pianola 'replaces'
Sappho's barbitos.

Christ follows Dionysus,
Phallic and ambrosial
Made way for macerations;
Caliban casts out Ariel.

EZRA POUND

All things are a flowing,
Sage Heracleitus says;
But a tawdry cheapness
Shall outlast our days.

Even the Christian beauty
Defects—after Samothrace;
We see τὸ καλὸν
Decreed in the market place.

Faun's flesh is not to us,
Nor the saint's vision.
We have the press for wafer;
Franchise for circumcision.

All men, in law, are equals,
Free of Pisistratus,
We choose a knave or an eunuch
To rule over us.

O bright Apollo,
τίν' ἄνδρα, τίν' ἥρωα, τίνα θεὸν,
What god, man, or hero,
Shall I place a tin wreath upon!

IV

These fought in any case,
    and some believing,
                pro domo, in any case . . .

Some quick to arm,
some for adventure,
some from fear of weakness,

some from fear of censure,
some for love of slaughter, in imagination,
learning later . . .
some in fear, learning love of slaughter;

Died some, pro patria,
                non 'dulce' non 'et decor' . . .
walked eye-deep in hell
believing in old men's lies, then unbelieving
came home, home to a lie,
home to many deceits,
home to old lies and new infamy;
usury age-old and age-thick
and liars in public places.

Daring as never before, wastage as never before.
Young blood and high blood,
fair cheeks, and fine bodies;

fortitude as never before

frankness as never before,
disillusions as never told in the old days,
hysterias, trench confessions,
laughter out of dead bellies.

v

> There died a myriad,
> And of the best, among them,
> For an old bitch gone in the teeth,
> For a botched civilization,

Charm, smiling at the good mouth,
Quick eyes gone under earth's lid,

For two gross of broken statues,
For a few thousand battered books.

383   *Envoi*

G O, dumb-born book,
Tell her that sang me once that song of Lawes;
Hadst thou but song
As thou hast subjects known,
Then were there cause in thee that should condone
Even my faults that heavy upon me lie
And build her glories their longevity.

Tell her that sheds
Such treasure in the air,
Recking naught else but that her graces give
Life to the moment,
I would bid them live
As roses might, in magic amber laid,
Red overwrought with orange and all made
One substance and one colour
Braving time.

Tell her that goes
With song upon her lips
But sings not out the song, nor knows
The maker of it, some other mouth,
May be as fair as hers,
Might, in new ages, gain her worshippers,

When our two dusts with Waller's shall be laid,
Siftings on siftings in oblivion,
Till change hath broken down
All things save Beauty alone.

384   *Canto II*

H ANG it all, Robert Browning,
          there can be but the one 'Sordello.'
But Sordello, and my Sordello?
Lo Sordels si fo di Mantovana.
So-shu churned in the sea.
Seal sports in the spray-whited circles of cliff-wash,
Sleek head, daughter of Lir,
          eyes of Picasso
Under black fur-hood, lithe daughter of Ocean;
And the wave runs in the beach-groove:
'Eleanor, ἑλέναυς and ἑλέπτολις!'
          And poor old Homer blind, blind, as a bat,
Ear, ear for the sea-surge, murmur of old men's voices:
'Let her go back to the ships,
Back among Grecian faces, lest evil come on our own,
Evil and further evil, and a curse cursed on our children,
Moves, yes she moves like a goddess
And has the face of a god
          and the voice of Schoeney's daughters,
And doom goes with her in walking,
Let her go back to the ships,
          back among the Grecian voices.'
And by the beach-run, Tyro,
          Twisted arms of the sea-god,

EZRA POUND

Lithe sinews of water, gripping her, cross-hold,
And the blue-gray glass of the wave tents them,
Glare azure of water, cold-welter, close cover.
Quiet sun-tawny sand-stretch,
The gulls broad out their wings,
            nipping between the splay feathers;
Snipe come for their bath,
            bend out their wing-joints,
Spread wet wings to the sun-film,
And by Scios,
            to left of the Naxos passage,
Naviform rock overgrown,
            algæ cling to its edge,
There is a wine-red glow in the shallows,
            a tin flash in the sun-dazzle.

The ship landed in Scios,
            men wanting spring-water,
And by the rock-pool a young boy loggy with vine-must,
            'To Naxos? Yes, we'll take you to Naxos,
Cum' along, lad.' 'Not that way!'
'Aye, that way is Naxos.'
            And I said: 'It's a straight ship.'
And an ex-convict out of Italy
            knocked me into the fore-stays,
(He was wanted for manslaughter in Tuscany)
            And the whole twenty against me,
Mad for a little slave money.
            And they took her out of Scios
And off her course . . .
            And the boy came to, again, with the racket,
And looked out over the bows,
            and to eastward, and to the Naxos passage.

God-sleight then, god-sleight:
        Ship stock fast in sea-swirl,
Ivy upon the oars, King Pentheus,
        grapes with no seed but sea-foam,
Ivy in scupper-hole.
Aye, I, Acœtes, stood there,
        and the god stood by me,
Water cutting under the keel,
Sea-break from stern forrards,
        wake running off from the bow,
And where was gunwale, there now was vine-trunk,
And tenthril where cordage had been,
        grape-leaves on the rowlocks,
Heavy vine on the oarshafts,
And, out of nothing, a breathing,
        hot breath on my ankles,
Beasts like shadows in glass,
        a furred tail upon nothingness.
Lynx-purr, and heathery smell of beasts,
        where tar smell had been,
Sniff and pad-foot of beasts,
        eye-glitter out of black air.
The sky overshot, dry, with no tempest,
Sniff and pad-foot of beasts,
        fur brushing my knee-skin,
Rustle of airy sheaths,
        dry forms in the *æther*.
And the ship like a keel in ship-yard,
        slung like an ox in smith's sling,
Ribs stuck fast in the ways,
        grape-cluster over pin-rack,
        void air taking pelt.

Lifeless air become sinewed,
        feline leisure of panthers,
Leopards sniffing the grape shoots by scupper-hole,
Crouched panthers by fore-hatch,
And the sea blue-deep about us,
        green-ruddy in shadows,
And Lyæus: 'From now, Acœtes, my altars,
Fearing no bondage,
        fearing no cat of the wood,
Safe with my lynxes,
        feeding grapes to my leopards,
Olibanum is my incense,
        the vines grow in my homage.'

The back-swell now smooth in the rudder-chains,
Black snout of a porpoise
        where Lycabs had been,
Fish-scales on the oarsmen.
        And I worship.
I have seen what I have seen.
        When they brought the boy I said:
'He has a god in him,
        though I do not know which god.'
And they kicked me into the fore-stays.
I have seen what I have seen:
        Medon's face like the face of a dory,
Arms shrunk into fins. And you, Pentheus,
Had as well listen to Tiresias, and to Cadmus,
        or your luck will go out of you.
Fish-scales over groin muscles,
        lynx-purr amid sea . . .
And of a later year,
        pale in the wine-red algæ,

If you will lean over the rock,
   the coral face under wave-tinge,
Rose-paleness under water-shift,
   Ileuthyeria, fair Dafne of sea-bords,
The swimmer's arms turned to branches,
Who will say in what year,
   fleeing what band of tritons,
The smooth brows, seen, and half seen,
   now ivory stillness.

And So-shu churned in the sea, So-shu also,
   using the long moon for a churn-stick . . .
Lithe turning of water,
   sinews of Poseidon,
Black azure and hyaline,
   glass wave over Tyro,
Close cover, unstillness,
   bright welter of wave-cords,
Then quiet water,
   quiet in the buff sands,
Sea-fowl stretching wing-joints,
   splashing in rock-hollows and sand-hollows
In the wave-runs by the half-dune;
Glass-glint of wave in the tide-rips against sunlight,
   pallor of Hesperus,
Grey peak of the wave,
   wave, colour of grape's pulp,

Olive grey in the near,
   far, smoke grey of the rock-slide,
Salmon-pink wings of the fish-hawk
   cast grey shadows in water,
The tower like a one-eyed great goose
   cranes up out of the olive-grove,

And we have heard the fauns chiding Proteus
        in the smell of hay under the olive-trees,
And the frogs singing against the fauns
        in the half-light.
And . . .

385   From *Canto LXXXI*

WHAT thou lovest well remains,
                       the rest is dross
What thou lov'st well shall not be reft from thee
What thou lov'st well is thy true heritage
Whose world, or mine or theirs
                  or is it of none?
First came the seen, then thus the palpable
    Elysium, though it were in the halls of hell,
What thou lovest well is thy true heritage

The ant's a centaur in his dragon world.
Pull down thy vanity, it is not man
Made courage, or made order, or made grace,
    Pull down thy vanity, I say pull down.
Learn of the green world what can be thy place
In scaled invention or true artistry,
Pull down thy vanity,
                Paquin pull down!
The green casque has outdone your elegance.

'Master thyself, then others shall thee beare'
    Pull down thy vanity
Thou art a beaten dog beneath the hail,

A swollen magpie in a fitful sun,
Half black half white
Nor knowst'ou wing from tail
Pull down thy vanity
        How mean thy hates
Fostered in falsity,
        Pull down thy vanity,
Rathe˙to destroy, niggard in charity,
Pull down thy vanity,
        I say pull down.

But to have done instead of not doing
        this is not vanity
To have, with decency, knocked
That a Blunt should open
        To have gathered from the air a live tradition
or from a fine old eye the unconquered flame
This is not vanity.
    Here error is all in the not done,
all in the diffidence that faltered

H. D.

b. 1886

386   *Oread*

Whirl up, sea—
whirl your pointed pines,
splash your great pines
on our rocks,

hurl your green over us,
cover us with your pools of fir.

387 *Heat*

O WIND, rend open the heat,
cut apart the heat,
rend it to tatters.

Fruit cannot drop
through this thick air—
fruit cannot fall into heat
that presses up and blunts
the points of pears
and rounds the grapes.

Cut the heat—
plough through it,
turning it on either side
of your path.

388 *Orchard*

I SAW the first pear
as it fell—
the honey-seeking, golden-banded,
the yellow swarm
was not more fleet than I,
(spare us from loveliness)
and I fell prostrate
crying:

you have flayed us
with your blossoms,
spare us the beauty
of fruit-trees.

The honey-seeking
paused not,
the air thundered their song,
and I alone was prostrate.

O rough-hewn
god of the orchard,
I bring you an offering—
do you, alone unbeautiful,
son of the god,
spare us from loveliness:

these fallen hazel-nuts,
stripped late of their green sheaths,
grapes, red-purple,
their berries
dripping with wine,
pomegranates already broken,
and shrunken figs
and quinces untouched,
I bring you as offering.

389 *The Helmsman*

O BE swift—
we have always known you wanted us.

H. D.

We fled inland with our flocks,
we pastured them in hollows,
cut off from the wind
and the salt track of the marsh.

We worshipped inland——
we stepped past wood-flowers,
we forgot your tang,
we brushed wood-grass.

We wandered from pine-hills
through oak and scrub-oak tangles,
we broke hyssop and bramble,
we caught flower and new bramble-fruit
in our hair: we laughed
as each branch whipped back,
we tore our feet in half buried rocks
and knotted roots and acorn-cups.

We forgot——we worshipped,
we parted green from green,
we sought further thickets,
we dipped our ankles
through leaf-mould and earth,
and wood and wood-bank enchanted us——

and the feel of the clefts in the bark,
and the slope between tree and tree——
and a slender path strung field to field
and wood to wood
and hill to hill
and the forest after it.

We forgot—for a moment
tree-resin, tree-bark,
sweat of a torn branch
were sweet to the taste.

We were enchanted with the fields,
the tufts of coarse grass
in the shorter grass—
we loved all this.

But now, our boat climbs—hesitates—
    drops—
climbs—hesitates—crawls back—
climbs—hesitates—
O be swift—
we have always known you wanted us.

390   *Fragment Thirty-Six*

    I know not what to do:
     my mind is divided.
              —Sappho.

I KNOW not what to do,
my mind is reft:
is song's gift best?
is love's gift loveliest?
I know not what to do,
now sleep has pressed
weight on your eyelids.

744

H. D.

Shall I break your rest,
devouring, eager?
is love's gift best?
nay, song's the loveliest:
yet were you lost,
what rapture
could I take from song?
what song were left?

I know not what to do:
to turn and slake
the rage that burns,
with my breath burn
and trouble your cool breath?
so shall I turn and take
snow in my arms?
(is love's gift best?)
yet flake on flake
of snow were comfortless,
did you lie wondering,
wakened yet unawake.

Shall I turn and take
comfortless snow within my arms?
press lips to lips
that answer not,
press lips to flesh
that shudders not nor breaks?

Is love's gift best?
shall I turn and slake
all the wild longing?
O I am eager for you!

H. D.

as the Pleiads shake
white light in whiter water
so shall I take you?

My mind is quite divided,
my minds hesitate,
so perfect matched,
I know not what to do:
each strives with each
as two white wrestlers
standing for a match,
ready to turn and clutch
yet never shake muscle nor nerve
        nor tendon;
so my mind waits
to grapple with my mind,
yet I lie quiet,
I would seem at rest.

I know not what to do:
strain upon strain,
sound surging upon sound
makes my brain blind;
as a wave-line may wait to fall
yet (waiting for its falling)
still the wind may take
from off its crest,
white flake on flake of foam,
that rises,
seeming to dart and pulse
and rend the light,
so my mind hesitates
above the passion

quivering yet to break,
so my mind hesitates
above my mind,
listening to song's delight.

I know not what to do:
will the sound break,
rending the night
with rift on rift of rose
and scattered light?
will the sound break at last
as the wave hesitant,
or will the whole night pass
and I lie listening awake?

MARIANNE MOORE

b. 1887

391   *To a Steam Roller*

THE illustration
is nothing to you without the application.
   You lack half wit. You crush all the particles down
      into close conformity, and then walk back and forth
         on them.

Sparkling chips of rock
are crushed down to the level of the parent block.
   Were not 'impersonal judgment in aesthetic
      matters, a metaphysical impossibility,' you

might fairly achieve
it. As for butterflies, I can hardly conceive
   of one's attending upon you, but to question
      the congruence of the complement is vain, if it exists.

The Fish

      wade
      through black jade.
         Of the crow-blue mussel-shells, one keeps
         adjusting the ash-heaps;
            opening and shutting itself like

      an
      injured fan.
         The barnacles which encrust the side
         of the wave, cannot hide
            there for the submerged shafts of the

      sun,
      split like spun
         glass, move themselves with spotlight swiftness
         into the crevices—
            in and out, illuminating

      the
      turquoise sea
         of bodies. The water drives a wedge
         of iron through the iron edge
            of the cliff; whereupon the stars,

   748

pink
rice-grains, ink
  bespattered jelly-fish, crabs like green
  lilies, and submarine
    toadstools, slide each on the other.

All
external
  marks of abuse are present on this
  defiant edifice—
    all the physical features of

ac-
cident—lack
  of cornice, dynamite grooves, burns, and
  hatchet strokes, these things stand
    out on it; the chasm-side is

dead.
Repeated
  evidence has proved that it can live
  on what cannot revive
    its youth. The sea grows old in it.

393   *The Monkeys*

winked too much and were afraid of snakes. The zebras,
        supreme in
  their abnormality; the elephants with their fog-coloured
        skin

and strictly practical appendages
    were there, the small cats; and the parrakeet—
        trivial and humdrum on examination, destroying
    bark and portions of the food it could not eat.

I recall their magnificence, now not more magnificent
than it is dim. It is difficult to recall the ornament,
    speech, and precise manner of what one might
        call the minor acquaintances twenty
            years back; but I shall not forget him—that Gilga-
            mesh
            among
    the hairy carnivora—that cat with the

wedge-shaped, slate-gray marks on its forelegs and the
        resolute tail,
astringently remarking, 'They have imposed on us with
        their pale
    half-fledged protestations, trembling about
        in inarticulate frenzy, saying
            it is not for us to understand art; finding it
        all so difficult, examining the thing

as if it were inconceivably arcanic, as symmet-
rically frigid as if it had been carved out of chrysoprase
    or marble—strict with tension, malignant
        in its power over us and deeper
            than the sea when it proffers flattery in exchange
            for hemp,
    rye, flax, horses, platinum, timber, and fur.'

394   *When I Buy Pictures*

or what is closer to the truth,
when I look at that of which I may regard myself as the
     imaginary possessor,
I fix upon what would give me pleasure in my average
     moments:
the satire upon curiosity in which no more is discernible
than the intensity of the mood;
or quite the opposite—the old thing, the mediaeval dec-
     orated hat-box,
in which there are hounds with waists diminishing like the
     waist of the hour-glass,
and deer and birds and seated people;
it may be no more than a square of parquetry; the literal
     biography perhaps,
in letters standing well apart upon a parchment-like ex-
     panse;
an artichoke in six varieties of blue; the snipe-legged hiero-
     glyphic in three parts;
the silver fence protecting Adam's grave, or Michael taking
     Adam by the wrist.
Too stern an intellectual emphasis upon this quality or
     that detracts from one's enjoyment.
It must not wish to disarm anything; nor may the approved
     triumph easily be honoured—
that which is great because something else is small.
It comes to this: of whatever sort it is,
it must be 'lit with piercing glances into the life of things';
it must acknowledge the spiritual forces which have made
     it.

Poetry

I, TOO, dislike it: there are things that are important
    beyond all this fiddle.
  Reading it, however, with a perfect contempt for it, one
    discovers in
  it after all, a place for the genuine.
    Hands that can grasp, eyes
    that can dilate, hair that can rise
      if it must, these things are important not because a

high-sounding interpretation can be put upon them but be-
    cause they are
  useful. When they become so derivative as to become
    unintelligible,
  the same thing may be said for all of us, that we
    do not admire what
    we cannot understand: the bat
      holding on upside down or in quest of something
      to

eat, elephants pushing, a wild horse taking a roll, a tireless
    wolf under
  a tree, the immovable critic twitching his skin like a
    horse that feels a flea, the base-
  ball fan, the statistician—
    nor is it valid
      to discriminate against 'business documents and

school-books'; all these phenomena are important. One
    must make a distinction
  however: when dragged into prominence by half poets,
    the result is not poetry,
  nor till the poets among us can be
    'literalists of
    the imagination'—above
      insolence and triviality and can present

for inspection, imaginary gardens with real toads in them,
    shall we have
  it. In the meantime, if you demand on the one hand,
  the raw material of poetry in
    all its rawness and
    that which is on the other hand
      genuine, then you are interested in poetry.

396   *Critics and Connoisseurs*

THERE is a great amount of poetry in unconscious
fastidiousness. Certain Ming
  products, imperial floor-coverings of coach-
wheel yellow, are well enough in their way but I have
    seen something
    that I like better—a
      mere childish attempt to make an imperfectly
        ballasted animal stand up,
      similar determination to make a pup
        eat his meat from the plate.

I remember a swan under the willows in Oxford,
   with flamingo-coloured, maple-
     leaflike feet. It reconnoitred like a battle-
   ship. Disbelief and conscious fastidiousness were the
        staple
      ingredients in its
        disinclination to move. Finally its hardihood was
          not proof against its
        proclivity to more fully appraise such bits
        of food as the stream

bore counter to it; it made away with what I gave it
   to eat. I have seen this swan and
     I have seen you; I have seen ambition without
   understanding in a variety of forms. Happening to stand
     by an ant-hill, I have
        seen a fastidious ant carrying a stick north, south,
          east, west, till it turned on
        itself, struck out from the flower-bed into the
          lawn,
        and returned to the point

from which it had started. Then abandoning the stick as
   useless and overtaxing its
     jaws with a particle of whitewash—pill-like but
   heavy, it again went through the same course of
        procedure. What is
      there in being able
        to say that one has dominated the stream in an
          attitude of self-defense;
        in proving that one has had the experience
          of carrying a stick?

Peter

STRONG and slippery, built for the midnight grass-
        party confronted by four cats,
    he sleeps his time away—the detached first claw on the
        foreleg, which corresponds
    to the thumb, retracted to its tip; the small tuft of
        fronds
        or katydid legs above each eye, still numbering the
            units in each group;
            the shadbones regularly set about the mouth, to
                droop or rise

in unison like the porcupine's quills—motionless. He lets
        himself be flat-
    tened out by gravity, as it were a piece of seaweed tamed
        and weakened by
    exposure to the sun; compelled when extended, to lie
        stationary. Sleep is the result of his delusion that one
            must do as
            well as one can for oneself; sleep—epitome of
                what is to

him as to the average person, the end of life. Demonstrate
        on him how
    the lady caught the dangerous southern snake, placing a
        forked stick on either
    side of its innocuous neck; one need not try to stir
        him up; his prune-shaped head and alligator eyes are
            not a party to the
            joke. Lifted and handled, he may be dangled like
                an eel or set

up on the forearm like a mouse; his eyes bisected by pupils
of a pin's
width, are flickeringly exhibited, then covered up. May
be? I should say
might have been; when he has been got the better
of in a
dream—as in a fight with nature or with cats—we all
know it. Profound sleep is
not with him a fixed illusion. Springing about with
froglike ac-

curacy, emitting jerky cries when taken in the hand, he is
himself
again; to sit caged by the rungs of a domestic chair
would be unprofit-
able—human. What is the good of hypocrisy? It
is permissible to choose one's employment, to abandon
the wire nail, the
roly-poly, when it shows signs of being no longer
a pleas-

ure, to score the adjacent magazine with a double line of
strokes. He can
talk, but insolently says nothing. What of it? When one
is frank, one's very
presence is a compliment. It is clear that he can see
the virtue of naturalness, that he is one of those who
do not regard
the published fact as a surrender. As for the dis-
position

invariably to affront, an animal with claws wants to have to
    use
  them; that eel-like extension of trunk into tail is not an
    accident. To
 leap, to lengthen out, divide the air—to purloin, to
    pursue.
  To tell the hen: fly over the fence, go in the wrong
    way in your perturba-
      tion—this is life; to do less would be nothing but
    dishonesty.

398   The Labors of Hercules

To popularize the mule, its neat exterior
expressing the principle of accommodation reduced to a
    minimum:
to persuade one of austere taste, proud in the possession of
    home and a musician—
that the piano is a free field for etching; that his 'charm-
    ing tadpole notes'
belong to the past when one had time to play them:
to persuade those self-wrought Midases of brains
whose fourteen carat ignorance aspires to rise in value
till the sky is the limit,
that excessive conduct augurs disappointment,
that one must not borrow a long white beard and tie it on
and threaten with the scythe of time the casually curious:
to teach the bard with too elastic a selectiveness
that one detects creative power by its capacity to conquer
    one's detachment;
that while it may have more elasticity than logic,

it knows where it is going;
it flies along in a straight line like electricity,
depopulating areas that boast of their remoteness,
to prove to the high priests of caste
that snobbishness is a stupidity,
the best side out, of age-old toadyism,
kissing the feet of the man above,
kicking the face of the man below;
to teach the patron-saints-to-atheists, the Coliseum
meet-me-alone-by-moonlight maudlin troubadour
that kickups for catstrings are not life
nor yet appropriate to death—that we are sick of the earth,
sick of the pig-sty, wild geese and wild men;
to convince snake-charming controversialists
that it is one thing to change one's mind,
another to eradicate it—that one keeps on knowing
'that the Negro is not brutal,
that the Jew is not greedy,
that the Oriental is not immoral,
that the German is not a Hun'.

399   *Part of a Novel, Part of a Poem,*
          Part of a Play

THE STEEPLE-JACK

DÜRER would have seen a reason for living
    in a town like this, with eight stranded whales
to look at; with the sweet sea air coming into your house
on a fine day, from water etched
    with waves as formal as the scales
on a fish.

One by one, in two's, in three's, the seagulls keep
   flying back and forth over the town clock,
or sailing around the lighthouse without moving the
       wings —
rising steadily with a slight
   quiver of the body—or flock
mewing where

a sea the purple of the peacock's neck is
   paled to greenish azure as Dürer changed
the pine green of the Tyrol to peacock blue and guinea
grey. You can see a twenty-five-
   pound lobster; and fishnets arranged
to dry. The

whirlwind fife-and-drum of the storm bends the salt
   marsh grass, disturbs stars in the sky and the
star on the steeple; it is a privilege to see so
much confusion. Disguised by what
   might seem austerity, the sea-
side flowers and

trees are favoured by the fog so that you have
   the tropics at first hand: the trumpet-vine,
fox-glove, giant snap-dragon, a salpiglossis that has
spots and stripes; morning-glories, gourds,
   or moon-vines trained on fishing-twine
at the back

door. There are no banyans, frangipani, **nor**
   jack-fruit trees; nor an exotic serpent
life. Ring lizard and snake-skin for the foot, or crocodile;

but here they've cats, not cobras, to
   keep down the rats. The diffident
little newt

with white pin-dots on black horizontal spaced
   out bands lives here; yet there is nothing that
ambition can buy or take away. The college student
named Ambrose sits on the hill-side
   with his not-native books and hat
and sees boats

at sea progress white and rigid as if in
   a groove. Liking an elegance of which
the source is not bravado, he knows by heart the antique
sugar-bowl-shaped summer-house of
   interlacing slats, and the pitch
of the church

spire, not true, from which a man in scarlet lets
   down a rope as a spider spins a thread;
he might be part of a novel, but on the sidewalk a
sign says C. J. Poole, Steeple Jack,
   in black and white; and one in red
and white says

Danger. The church portico has four fluted
   columns, each a single piece of stone, made
modester by white-wash. This would be a fit haven for
waifs, children, animals, prisoners,
   and presidents who have repaid
sin-driven

senators by not thinking about them. There
  are a school-house, a post-office in a
store, fish-houses, hen-houses, a three-masted schooner on
the stocks. The hero, the student,
  the steeple-jack, each in his way,
is at home.

It could not be dangerous to be living
  in a town like this, of simple people,
who have a steeple-jack placing danger signs by the church
while he is gilding the solid-
  pointed star, which on a steeple
stands for hope.

THE HERO

Where there is personal liking we go.
  Where the ground is sour; where there are
  weeds of beanstalk height,
  snakes' hypodermic teeth, or
  the wind brings the 'scarebabe voice'
  from the neglected yew set with
  the semi-precious cat's eyes of the owl—
awake, asleep, 'raised ears extended to fine points', and so
on—love won't grow.

We do not like some things, and the hero
  doesn't; deviating head-stones
  and uncertainty;
  going where one does not wish
  to go; suffering and not
  saying so; standing and listening where something
  is hiding. The hero shrinks

as what it is flies out on muffled wings, with twin yellow
eyes—to and fro—

with quavering water-whistle note, low,
   high, in basso-falsetto chirps
   until the skin creeps.
   Jacob when a-dying, asked
   Joseph: Who are these? and blessed
   both sons, the younger most, vexing Joseph. And
   Joseph was vexing to some.
Cincinnatus was; Regulus; and some of our fellow
men have been, though

devout, like Pilgrim having to go slow
   to find his roll; tired but hopeful—
   hope not being hope
   until all ground for hope has
   vanished; and lenient, looking
   upon a fellow creature's error with the
   feelings of a mother—a
woman or a cat. The decorous frock-coated Negro
by the grotto

answers the fearless sightseeing hobo
   who asks the man she's with, what's this,
   what's that, where's Martha
   buried, 'Gen-ral Washington
   there; his lady, here'; speaking
   as if in a play—not seeing her; with a
   sense of human dignity
and reverence for mystery, standing like the shadow
of the willow.

Moses would not be grandson to Pharaoh.
  It is not what I eat that is
  my natural meat,
  the hero says. He's not out
  seeing a sight but the rock
  crystal thing to see—the startling El Greco
  brimming with inner light—that
covets nothing that it has let go. This then you may know
as the hero.

400   *No Swan So Fine*

N O water so still as the
  dead fountains of Versailles.' No swan,
with swart blind look askance
and gondoliering legs, so fine
  as the chintz china one with fawn-
brown eyes and toothed gold
collar on to show whose bird it was.

Lodged in the Louis Fifteenth
  candelabrum-tree of cockscomb-
tinted buttons, dahlias,
sea-urchins, and everlastings,
  it perches on the branching foam
of polished sculptured
flowers—at ease and tall. The king is dead.

401

Nine Nectarines and Other
Porcelain

ARRANGED by two's as peaches are,
at intervals that all may live—
    eight and a single one, on twigs that
    grew the year before—they look like
a derivative;
    although not uncommonly
the opposite is seen—
nine peaches on a nectarine.
    Fuzzless through slender crescent leaves
        of green or blue—or both,
        in the Chinese style—the four

    pairs' half-moon leaf-mosaic turns
out to the sun the sprinkled blush
    of puce-American-Beauty pink
    applied to beeswax gray by the
unenquiring brush
    of mercantile bookbinding.
Like the peach *Yu*, the red-
cheeked peach which cannot aid the dead,
    but eaten in time prevents death,
        the Italian peach-
        nut, Persian plum, Ispahan

    secluded wall-grown nectarine,
as wild spontaneous fruit was
    found in China first. But was it wild?
    Prudent de Candolle would not say.

MARIANNE MOORE

We cannot find flaws
  in this emblematic group
of nine, with leaf window
unquilted by curculio—
    which someone once depicted on
      this much-mended plate; or
      in the also accurate

    unantlered moose, or Iceland horse,
or ass, asleep against the old
  thick, low-leaning nectarine that is the
  colour of the shrub-tree's brownish
flower. From manifold
  small boughs, productive as the
magic willow that grew
above the mother's grave and threw
  on Cinderella what she wished,
    a bat is winging. It
    is a moonlight scene, bringing

  the animal so near, its eyes
are separate from the face—mere
  delicately drawn gray discs, out from
  itself in space. Imperial
happiness lives here
  on the peaches of long life
that make it permanent.
A fungus could have meant
  long life; a crane, a stork, a dove.
    China, with flowers and birds
    and half-beasts, became the land

  of the best china-making first.
Hunts and domestic scenes occur

in France on dinner-plates, signed on the
back with a two-finned fish; England
has an officer
in jack-boots seated in a
bosquet, the cow, the flock
of sheep, the pheasant, the peacock
sweeping near with lifted claw; the
skilled peonian rose
and the rosebud that began

with William Billingsley (once poor,
like a monkey on a dolphin, tossed
by Ocean, mighty monster) until
Josiah Spode adopted him.
Yet with the gold-glossed
serpent handles, are there green
cocks with 'brown beaks and cheeks
and dark blue combs' and mammal freaks
that, like the Chinese Certainties
and sets of Precious Things,
dare to be conspicuous?

Theirs is a race that 'understands
the spirit of the wilderness'
and the nectarine-loving kylin
of pony appearance—the long-
tailed or the tailless
small cinnamon-brown common
camel-haired unicorn
with antelope feet and no horn,
here enamelled on porcelain.
It was a Chinese who
imagined this masterpiece.

402

What Are Years?

WHAT is our innocence,
what is our guilt? All are
     naked, none is safe. And whence
is courage: the unanswered question,
the resolute doubt,—
dumbly calling, deafly listening—that
in misfortune, even death,
          encourages others
          and in its defeat, stirs

     the soul to be strong? He
sees deep and is glad, who
     accedes to mortality
and in his imprisonment, rises
upon himself as
the sea in a chasm, struggling to be
free and unable to be,
          in its surrendering
          finds its continuing.

     So he who strongly feels,
behaves. The very bird,
     grown taller as he sings, steels
his form straight up. Though he is captive,
his mighty singing
says, satisfaction is a lowly
thing, how pure a thing is joy.
          This is mortality,
          this is eternity.

Spenser's Ireland

403

has not altered;—
   the kindest place I've never been,
   the greenest place I've never seen.
Every name is a tune.
Denunciations do not affect
     the culprit;   nor blows, but it
is torture to him to not be spoken to.
They're natural,—
      the coat, like Venus'
mantle lined with stars,
buttoned close at the neck,—the
     sleeves new from disuse.

If in Ireland
   they play the harp backward at need,
   and gather at midday the seed
of the fern, eluding
their 'giants all covered with iron,' might
    there be fern   seed for unlearn-
ing obduracy and for reinstating
the enchantment?
     Hindered characters
seldom have mothers—
in Irish stories—
    but they all have grandmothers.

It was Irish;
   a match not a marriage was made
   when my great great grandmother'd said
with native genius for

disunion, 'although your suitor be
     perfection,   one objection
is enough; he is not
Irish.' Outwitting
       the fairies, befriending the furies,
whoever again
and again says, 'I'll never
      give in,' never sees

that you're not free
  until you've been made captive by
  supreme belief,—credulity
you say? When large dainty
fingers tremblingly divide the wings
    of the fly   for mid-July
with a needle and wrap it with peacock-tail,
or tie wool and
     buzzard's wing, their pride,
like the enchanter's
is in care, not madness. Con-
     curring hands divide

flax for damask
  that when bleached by Irish weather
  has the silvered chamois-leather
water-tightness of a
skin. Twisted torcs and gold new-moon-shaped
    lunulae   aren't jewelry
like the purple-coral fuchsia-tree's. If Eire—
the guillemot
     so neat and the hen
of the heath and the
linnet spinet-sweet—bespeak
     relentlessness, then

they are to me
   like enchanted Earl Gerald who
   changed himself into a stag, to
a great green-eyed cat of
the mountain. Discommodity makes
     them invis   ible; they've dis-
appeared. The Irish say your trouble is their
trouble and your
       joy their joy? I wish
I could believe it;
I am troubled; I'm dissat-
      isfied, I'm Irish.

404   *Nevertheless*

   you've seen a strawberry
      that's had a struggle; yet
      was, where the fragments met,

   a hedgehog or a star-
      fish for the multitude
      of seeds. What better food

   than apple-seeds—the fruit
      within the fruit—locked in
      like counter-curved twin

   hazel-nuts? Frost that kills
      the little rubber-plant-
      leaves of *kok-saghyz*-stalks, can't

   harm the roots; they still grow
      in frozen ground. Once where
      there was a prickly-pear-

leaf clinging to barbed wire,
    a root shot down to grow
    in earth two feet below;

as carrots form mandrakes
    or a ram's-horn root some-
    times. Victory won't come

to me unless I go
    to it; a grape-tendril
    ties a knot in knots till

knotted thirty times,—so
    the bound twig that's under-
    gone and over-gone, can't stir.

The weak overcomes its
    menace, the strong over-
    comes itself. What is there

like fortitude! What sap
    went through that little thread
    to make the cherry red!

405   *The Mind Is an Enchanting
Thing*

is an enchanted thing
    like the glaze on a
katydid-wing
        subdivided by sun
        till the nettings are legion.
Like Gieseking playing Scarlatti;

like the apteryx-awl
    as a beak, or the
kiwi's rain-shawl
        of haired feathers, the mind
        feeling its way as though blind,
walks along with its eyes on the ground.

It has memory's ear
    that can hear without
having to hear.
        Like the gyroscope's fall,
        truly unequivocal
because trued by regnant certainty,

it is a power of
    strong enchantment. It
is like the dove-
        neck animated by
        sun; it is memory's eye;
it's conscientious inconsistency.

It tears off the veil; tears
    the temptation, the
mist the heart wears,
        from its eyes,—if the heart
        has a face; it takes apart
dejection. It's fire in the dove-neck's

iridescense, in the
    inconsistencies
of Scarlatti.
        Unconfusion submits
        its confusion to proof; it's
not a Herod's oath that cannot change.

406   *In Distrust of Merits*

STRENGTHENED to live, strengthened to die for
    medals and position victories?
They're fighting, fighting, fighting the blind
    man who thinks he sees,—
who cannot see that the enslaver is
enslaved; the hater, harmed. O shining O
       firm star, O tumultuous
          ocean lashed till small things go
       as they will, the mountainous
         wave makes us who look, know

depth. Lost at sea before they fought! O
    star of David, star of Bethlehem,
O black imperial lion
    of the Lord—emblem
of a risen world—be joined at last, be
joined. There is hate's crown beneath which all is
       death; there's love's without which none
         is king; the blessed deeds bless
       the halo. As contagion
         of sickness makes sickness,

contagion of trust can make trust. They're
    fighting in deserts and caves, one by
one, in battalions and squadrons;
    they're fighting that I
may yet recover from the disease, My

Self; some have it lightly, some will die. 'Man's
        wolf to man' and we devour
                ourselves. The enemy could not
        have made a greater breach in our
                defenses. One pilot-

ing a blind man can escape him, but
        Job disheartened by false comfort knew
that nothing can be so defeating
        as a blind man who
can see. O alive who are dead, who are
proud not to see, O small dust of the earth
        that walks so arrogantly,
                trust begets power and faith is
        an affectionate thing. We
                vow, we make this promise

to the fighting—it's a promise—'We'll
        never hate black, white, red, yellow, Jew,
Gentile, Untouchable.' We are
        not competent to
make our vows. With set jaw they are fighting,
fighting, fighting,—some we love whom we know,
        some we love but know not—that
                hearts may feel and not be numb.
        It cures me; or am I what
                I can't believe in? Some

in snow, some on crags, some in quicksands,
        little by little, much by much, they
are fighting fighting fighting that where
        there was death there may
be life. 'When a man is prey to anger,

he is moved by outside things; when he holds
    his ground in patience patience
        patience, that is action or
beauty,' the soldier's defense
    and hardest armor for

the fight. The world's an orphans' home. Shall
    we never have peace without sorrow?
·without pleas of the dying for
    help that won't come? O
quiet form upon the dust, I cannot
look and yet I must. If these great patient
        dyings—all these agonies
           and woundbearings and bloodshed—
    can teach us how to live, these
        dyings were not wasted.

Hate-hardened heart, O heart of iron,
    iron is iron till it is rust.
There never was a war that was
    not inward; I must
fight till I have conquered in myself what
causes war, but I would not believe it.
        I inwardly did nothing.
           O Iscariotlike crime!
        Beauty is everlasting
           and dust is for a time.

407　　　　　*To the Stone-Cutters*

Stone-cutters fighting time with marble, you fore-
　　defeated
Challengers of oblivion
Eat cynical earnings, knowing rock splits, records fall
　　down,
The square-limbed Roman letters
Scale in the thaws, wear in the rain. The poet as well
Builds his monument mockingly;
For man will be blotted out, the blithe earth die, the brave
　　sun
Die blind and blacken to the heart:
Yet stones have stood for a thousand years, and pained
　　thoughts found
The honey of peace in old poems.

408　　　　　*Night*

The ebb slips from the rock, the sunken
Tide-rocks lift streaming shoulders
Out of the slack, the slow west
Sombering its torch; a ship's light
Shows faintly, far out,
Over the weight of the prone ocean
On the low cloud.

776

Over the dark mountain, over the dark pinewood,
Down the long dark valley along the shrunken river,
Returns the splendor without rays, the shining of shadow,
Peace-bringer, the matrix of all shining and quieter of
      shining.
Where the shore widens on the bay she opens dark wings
And the ocean accepts her glory. O soul worshipful of her
You like the ocean have grave depths where she dwells
      always,
And the film of waves above that takes the sun takes also
Her, with more love. The sun-lovers have a blond favorite,
A father of lights and noises, wars, weeping and laughter,
Hot labor, lust and delight and the other blemishes. Quiet-
      ness
Flows from her deeper fountain; and he will die; and she
      is immortal.

Far off from here the slender
Flocks of the mountain forest
Move among stems like towers
Of the old redwoods to the stream,
No twig crackling; dip shy
Wild muzzles into the mountain water
Among the dark ferns.

O passionately at peace you being secure will pardon
The blasphemies of glowworms, the lamp in my tower, the
      fretfulness
Of cities, the cressets of the planets, the pride of the stars.
This August night in a rift of cloud Antares reddens,
The great one, the ancient torch, a lord among lost
      children,

The earth's orbit doubled would not girdle his greatness,
    one fire
Globed, out of grasp of the mind enormous; but to you
    O Night
What? Not a spark? What flicker of a spark in the faint far
    glimmer
Of a lost fire dying in the desert, dim coals of a sand-pit
    the Bedouins
Wandered from at dawn . . . Ah singing prayer to what
    gulfs tempted
Suddenly are you more lost? To us the near-hand mountain
Be a measure of height, the tide-worn cliff at the sea-gate
    a measure of continuance.

The tide, moving the night's
Vastness with lonely voices,
Turns, the deep dark-shining
Pacific leans on the land,
Feeling his cold strength
To the outmost margins: you Night will resume
The stars in your time.

O passionately at peace when will that tide draw shore-
    ward?
Truly the spouting fountains of light, Antares, Arcturus,
Tire of their flow, they sing one song but they think
    silence.
The striding winter giant Orion shines, and dreams dark-
    ness.
And life, the flicker of men and moths and the wolf on the
    hill,
Though furious for continuance, passionately feeding,
    passionately

Remaking itself upon its mates, remembers deep inward
The calm mother, the quietness of the womb and the egg,
The primal and the latter silences: dear Night it is memory
Prophesies, prophecy that remembers, the charm of the
    dark.

And I and my people, we are willing to love the four-score
    years
Heartily; but as a sailor loves the sea, when the helm is for
    harbor.

Have men's minds changed,
Or the rock hidden in the deep of the waters of the soul
Broken the surface? A few centuries
Gone by, was none dared not to people
The darkness beyond the stars with harps and habitations.
But now, dear is the truth. Life is grown sweeter and
    lonelier,
And death is no evil.

409   *Boats in a Fog*

SPORTS and gallantries, the stage, the arts, the antics of
    dancers,
The exuberant voices of music,
Have charm for children but lack nobility; it is bitter
    earnestness
That makes beauty; the mind
Knows, grown adult.

                    A sudden fog-drift muffled the ocean,
A throbbing of engines moved in it,
At length, a stone's throw out, between the rocks and the
    vapor,

One by one moved shadows
Out of the mystery, shadows, fishing-boats, trailing each
    other
Following the cliff for guidance,
Holding a difficult path between the peril of the sea-fog
And the foam on the shore granite.
One by one, trailing their leader, six crept by me,
Out of the vapor and into it,
The throb of their engines subdued by the fog, patient and
    cautious,
Coasting all round the peninsula
Back to the buoys in Monterey harbor. A flight of pelicans
Is nothing lovelier to look at;
The flight of the planets is nothing nobler; all the arts lose
    virtue
Against the essential reality
Of creatures going about their business among the equally
Earnest elements of nature.

410   *Phenomena*

GREAT-ENOUGH both accepts and subdues; the
    great frame takes all creatures;
From the greatness of their element they all take beauty.
Gulls; and the dingy freightship lurching south in the eye
    of a rain-wind;
The airplane dipping over the hill; hawks hovering
The white grass of the headland; cormorants roosting upon
    the guano-
Whitened skerries; pelicans awind; sea-slime

Shining at night in the wave-stir like drowned men's
        lanterns; smugglers signaling
A cargo to land; or the old Point Pinos lighthouse
Lawfully winking over dark water; the flight of the twi-
        light herons,
Lonely wings and a cry; or with motor-vibrations
That hum in the rock like a new storm-tone of the ocean's
        to turn eyes westward
The navy's new-bought Zeppelin going by in the twilight,
Far out seaward; relative only to the evening star and the
        ocean
It slides into a cloud over Point Lobos.

411   *Haunted Country*

HERE the human past is dim and feeble and alien to us
Our ghosts draw from the crowded future.
Fixed as the past how could it fail to drop weird shadows
And make strange murmurs about twilight?
In the dawn twilight metal falcons flew over the mountain,
Multitudes, and faded in the air; at moonrise
The farmer's girl by the still river is afraid of phantoms,
Hearing the pulse of a great city
Move on the water-meadow and stream off south; the
        country's
Children for all their innocent minds
Hide dry and bitter lights in the eye, they dream without
        knowing it
The inhuman years to be accomplished,
The inhuman powers, the servile cunning under pressure,
In a land grown old, heavy and crowded.

There are happy places that fate skips; here is not one of
    them;
The tides of the brute womb, the excess
And weight of life spilled out like water, the last migra-
    tion
Gathering against this holier valley-mouth
That knows its fate beforehand, the flow of the womb,
    banked back
By the older flood of the ocean, to swallow it.

412   Shine, Perishing Republic

WHILE this America settles in the mould of its vul-
    garity, heavily thickening to empire,
And protest, only a bubble in the molten mass, pops and
    sighs out, and the mass hardens,

I sadly smiling remember that the flower fades to make
    fruit, the fruit rots to make earth.
Out of the mother; and through the spring exultances,
    ripeness and decadence; and home to the mother.

You making haste haste on decay: not blameworthy; life is
    good, be it stubbornly long or suddenly
A mortal splendor: meteors are not needed less than moun-
    tains: shine, perishing republic.

But for my children, I would have them keep their distance
    from the thickening center; corruption

Never has been compulsory, when the cities lie at the
    monster's feet there are left the mountains.

And boys, be in nothing so moderate as in love of man,
    a clever servant, insufferable master.
There is the trap that catches noblest spirits, that caught—
    they say—God, when he walked on earth.

413   *Science*

MAN, introverted man, having crossed
In passage and but a little with the nature of things this
    latter century
Has begot giants; but being taken up
Like a maniac with self-love and inward conflicts cannot
    manage his hybrids.
Being used to deal with edgeless dreams,
Now he's bred knives on nature turns them also inward:
    they have thirsty points though.
His mind forebodes his own destruction;
Actæon who saw the goddess naked among leaves and his
    hounds tore him.
A little knowledge, a pebble from the shingle,
A drop from the oceans: who would have dreamed this
    infinitely little too much?

414   *Apology for Bad Dreams*

I

IN the purple light, heavy with redwood, the slopes drop
   seaward,
Headlong convexities of forest, drawn in together to the
   steep ravine. Below, on the sea-cliff,
A lonely clearing; a little field of corn by the streamside;
   a roof under spared trees. Then the ocean
Like a great stone someone has cut to a sharp edge and
   polished to shining. Beyond it, the fountain
And furnace of incredible light flowing up from the sunk
   sun. In the little clearing a woman
Is punishing a horse; she had tied the halter to a sapling at
   the edge of the wood, but when the great whip
Clung to the flanks the creature kicked so hard she feared
   he would snap the halter; she called from the house
The young man her son; who fetched a chain tie-rope,
   they working together
Noosed the small rusty links round the horse's tongue
And tied him by the swollen tongue to the tree.
Seen from this height they are shrunk to insect size.
Out of all human relation. You cannot distinguish
The blood dripping from where the chain is fastened,
The beast shuddering; but the thrust neck and the legs
Far apart. You can see the whip fall on the flanks . . .
The gesture of the arm. You cannot see the face of the
   woman.
The enormous light beats up out of the west across the
   cloud-bars of the trade-wind. The ocean

Darkens, the high clouds brighten, the hills darken to-
    gether. Unbridled and unbelievable beauty
Covers the evening world . . . not covers, grows appar-
    ent out of it, as Venus down there grows out
From the lit sky. What said the prophet? 'I create good:
    and I create evil: I am the Lord.'

II

This coast crying out for tragedy like all beautiful places,
(The quiet ones ask for quieter suffering: but here the
    granite cliff the gaunt cypresses crown
Demands what victim? The dykes of red lava and black
    what Titan? The hills like pointed flames
Beyond Soberanes, the terrible peaks of the bare hills under
    the sun, what immolation?)
This coast crying out for tragedy like all beautiful places:
    and like the passionate spirit of humanity
Pain for its bread: God's, many victims', the painful deaths,
    the horrible transfigurements: I said in my heart,
'Better invent than suffer: imagine victims
Lest your own flesh be chosen the agonist, or you
Martyr some creature to the beauty of the place.' And I
    said,
'Burn sacrifices once a year to magic
Horror away from the house, this little house here
You have built over the ocean with your own hands
Beside the standing boulders: for what are we,
The beast that walks upright, with speaking lips
And little hair, to think we should always be fed,
Sheltered, intact, and self-controlled? We sooner more
    liable

Than the other animals. Pain and terror, the insanities of
    desire; not accidents but essential,
And crowd up from the core.' I imagined victims for those
    wolves, I made them phantoms to follow,
They have hunted the phantoms and missed the house. It is
    not good to forget over what gulfs the spirit
Of the beauty of humanity, the petal of a lost flower blown
    seaward by the night-wind, floats to its quietness.

III

Boulders blunted like an old bear's teeth break up from the
    headland; below them
All the soil is thick with shells, the tide-rock feasts of a
    dead people.
Here the granite flanks are scarred with ancient fire, the
    ghosts of the tribe
Crouch in the nights beside the ghost of a fire, they try to
    remember the sunlight,
Light has died out of their skies. These have paid some-
    thing for the future
Luck of the country, while we living keep old griefs in
    memory: though God's
Envy is not a likely fountain of ruin, to forget evils calls
    down
Sudden reminders from the cloud: remembered deaths be
    our redeemers;
Imagined victims our salvation: white as the half moon
    at midnight
Someone flamelike passed me, saying, 'I am Tamar Cauld-
    well, I have my desire,'
Then the voice of the sea returned, when she had gone by,
    the stars to their towers.

. . . Beautiful country burn again, Point Pinos down to
the Sur Rivers
Burn as before with bitter wonders, land and ocean and the
Carmel water.

IV

He brays humanity in a mortar to bring the savor
From the bruised root: a man having bad dreams, who
invents victims, is only the ape of that God.
He washes it out with tears and many waters, calcines it
with fire in the red crucible,
Deforms it, makes it horrible to itself: the spirit flies out
and stands naked, he sees the spirit,
He takes it in the naked ecstasy; it breaks in his hand, the
atom is broken, the power that massed it
Cries to the power that moves the stars, 'I have come home
to myself, behold me.
I bruised myself in the flint mortar and burnt me
In the red shell, I tortured myself, I flew forth,
Stood naked of myself and broke me in fragments,
And here am I moving the stars that are me.'
I have seen these ways of God: I know of no reason
For fire and change and torture and the old returnings.
He being sufficient might be still. I think they admit no
reason; they are the ways of my love.
Unmeasured power, incredible passion, enormous craft: no
thought apparent but burns darkly
Smothered with its own smoke in the human brain-vault:
no thought outside: a certain measure in phenomena:
The fountains of the boiling stars, the flowers on the
foreland, the ever-returning roses of dawn.

415   *Summer Holiday*

WHEN the sun shouts and people abound
One thinks there were the ages of stone and the age of
    bronze
And the iron age; iron the unstable metal;
Steel made of iron, unstable as his mother; the towered-up
    cities
Will be stains of rust on mounds of plaster.
Roots will not pierce the heaps for a time, kind rains will
    cure them,
Then nothing will remain of the iron age
And all these people but a thigh-bone or so, a poem
Stuck in the world's thought, splinters of glass
In the rubbish dumps, a concrete dam far off in the
    mountain . . .

416   *Ascent to the Sierras*

BEYOND the great valley an odd instinctive rising
Begins to possess the ground, the flatness gathers to little
    humps and barrows, low aimless ridges,
A sudden violence of rock crowns them. The crowded
    orchards end, they have come to a stone knife;
The farms are finished; the sudden foot of the sierra. Hill
    over hill, snow-ridge beyond mountain gather
The blue air of their height about them.

            Here at the foot of the pass
The fierce clans of the mountain you'd think for thousands
    of years,

Men with harsh mouths and eyes like the eagles' hunger,
Have gathered among these rocks at the dead hour
Of the morning star and the stars waning
To raid the plain and at moonrise returning driven
Their scared booty to the highlands, the tossing horns
And glazed eyes in the light of torches. The men have
    looked back
Standing above these rock-heads to bark laughter
At the burning granaries and the farms and the town
That sow the dark flat land with terrible rubies . . .
    lighting the dead . . .
        It is not true: from this land
The curse was lifted; the highlands have kept peace with
    the valleys; no blood in the sod; there is no old sword
Keeping grim rust, no primal sorrow. The people are all
    one people, their homes never knew harrying;
The tribes before them were acorn-eaters, harmless as deer.
    Oh, fortunate earth; you must find someone
To make you bitter music; how else will you take bonds
    of the future, against the wolf in men's hearts?

417   *Hurt Hawks*

I

THE broken pillar of the wing jags from the clotted
    shoulder,
The wing trails like a banner in defeat,
No more to use the sky forever but live with famine
And pain a few days: cat nor coyote
Will shorten the week of waiting for death, there is game
    without talons.

He stands under the oak-bush and waits
The lame feet of salvation; at night he remembers freedom
And flies in a dream, the dawns ruin it.
He is strong and pain is worse to the strong, incapacity is
     worse.
The curs of the day come and torment him
At distance, no one but death the redeemer will humble
    that head,
The intrepid readiness, the terrible eyes.
The wild God of the world is sometimes merciful to those
That ask mercy, not often to the arrogant.
You do not know him, you communal people, or you have
    forgotten him;
Intemperate and savage, the hawk remembers him;
Beautiful and wild, the hawks, and men that are dying,
    remember him.

II

I'd sooner, except the penalties, kill a man than a hawk;
    but the great redtail
Had nothing left but unable misery
From the bone too shattered for mending, the wing that
    trailed under his talons when he moved.
We had fed him six weeks, I gave him freedom,
He wandered over the foreland hill and returned in the
    evening, asking for death,
Not like a beggar, still eyed with the old
Implacable arrogance. I gave him the lead gift in the
    twilight. What fell was relaxed,
Owl-downy, soft feminine feathers; but what
Soared: the fierce rush: the night-herons by the flooded
    river cried fear at its rising
Before it was quite unsheathed from reality.

418   *November Surf*

SOME lucky day each November great waves awake and
    are drawn
Like smoking mountains bright from the west
And come and cover the cliff with white violent cleanness:
    then suddenly
The old granite forgets half a year's filth:
The orange-peel, eggshells, papers, pieces of clothing, the
    clots
Of dung in corners of the rock, and used
Sheaths that make light love safe in the evenings: all the
    droppings of the summer
Idlers washed off in a winter ecstasy:
I think this cumbered continent envies its cliff then. . .
    But all seasons
The earth, in her childlike prophetic sleep,
Keeps dreaming of the bath of a storm that prepares up the
    long coast
Of the future to scour more than her sea-lines:
The cities gone down, the people fewer and the hawks
    more numerous,
The rivers mouth to source pure; when the two-footed
Mammal, being someways one of the nobler animals,
    regains
The dignity of room, the value of rareness.

Rock and Hawk

Here is a symbol in which
Many high tragic thoughts
Watch their own eyes.

This gray rock, standing tall
On the headland, where the seawind
Lets no tree grow,

Earthquake-proved, and signatured
By ages of storms: on its peak
A falcon has perched.

I think, here is your emblem
To hang in the future sky;
Not the cross, not the hive,

But this; bright power, dark peace;
Fierce consciousness joined with final
Disinterestedness;

Life with calm death; the falcon's
Realist eyes and act
Married to the massive

Mysticism of stone,
Which failure cannot cast down
Nor success make proud.

420 *Rearmament*

THESE grand and fatal movements toward death: the
    grandeur of the mass
Makes pity a fool, the tearing pity
For the atoms of the mass, the persons, the victims, makes it
    seem monstrous
To admire the tragic beauty they build.
It is beautiful as a river flowing or a slowly gathering
Glacier on a high mountain rock-face,
Bound to plow down a forest, or as frost in November,
The gold and flaming death-dance for leaves,
Or a girl in the night of her spent maidenhood, bleeding
    and kissing.
I would burn my right hand in a slow fire
To change the future . . . I should do foolishly. The
    beauty of modern
Man is not in the persons but in the
Disastrous rhythm, the heavy and mobile masses, the dance
    of the
Dream-led masses down the dark mountain.

421 *Ave Caesar*

NO bitterness: our ancestors did it.
They were only ignorant and hopeful, they wanted free-
    dom but wealth too.
Their children will learn to hope for a Caesar.
Or rather—for we are not aquiline Romans but soft mixed
    colonists—

Some kindly Sicilian tyrant who'll keep
Poverty and Carthage off until the Romans arrive.
We are easy to manage, a gregarious people,
Full of sentiment, clever at mechanics, and we love our
    luxuries.

422   *The Purse-Seine*

OUR sardine fishermen work at night in the dark of the
    moon; daylight or moonlight
They could not tell where to spread the net, unable to see
    the phosphorescence of the shoals of fish.
They work northward from Monterey, coasting Santa
    Cruz; off New Year's Point or off Pigeon Point
The look-out man will see some lakes of milk-color light
    on the sea's night-purple; he points, and the helmsman
Turns the dark prow, the motorboat circles the gleaming
    shoal and drifts out her seine-net. They close the
    circle
And purse the bottom of the net, then with great labor
    haul it in.

                              I cannot tell you
How beautiful the scene is, and a little terrible, then, when
    the crowded fish
Know they are caught, and wildly beat from one wall to
    the other of their closing destiny the phosphorescent
Water to a pool of flame, each beautiful slender body
    sheeted with flame, like a live rocket
A comet's tail wake of clear yellow flame; while outside the
    narrowing

Floats and cordage of the net great sea-lions come up to
    watch, sighing in the dark; the vast walls of night
Stand erect to the stars.

            Lately I was looking from a night mountain-top
On a wide city, the colored splendor, galaxies of light:
    how could I help but recall the seine-net
Gathering the luminous fish? I cannot tell you how beau-
    tiful the city appeared, and a little terrible.
I thought, We have geared the machines and locked all
    together into interdependence; we have built the
    great cities; now
There is no escape. We have gathered vast populations
    incapable of free survival, insulated
From the strong earth, each person in himself helpless, on
    all dependent. The circle is closed, and the net
Is being hauled in. They hardly feel the cords drawing, yet
    they shine already. The inevitable mass-disasters
Will not come in our time nor in our children's, but we
    and our children
Must watch the net draw narrower, government take all
    powers—or revolution, and the new government
Take more than all, add to kept bodies kept souls—or
    anarchy, the mass-disasters.

                These things are Progress;
Do you marvel our verse in troubled or frowning while it
    keeps its reason? Or it lets go, lets the mood flow
In the manner of the recent young men into mere hysteria,
    splintered gleams, crackled laughter. But they are
    quite wrong.
There is no reason for amazement: surely one always knew
    that cultures decay, and life's end is death.

423   *Prescription of Painful Ends*

LUCRETIUS felt the change of the world in his time,
the great republic riding to the height
Whence every road leads downward; Plato in his time
watched Athens
Dance the down path. The future is a misted landscape, no
man sees clearly, but at cyclic turns
There is a change felt in the rhythm of events, as when an
exhausted horse
Falters and recovers, then the rhythm of the running
hoofbeats is changed: he will run miles yet,
But he must fall: we have felt it again in our own life
time, slip, shift and speed-up
In the gallop of the world; and now perceive that, come
peace or war, the progress of Europe and America
Becomes a long process of deterioration—starred with
famous Byzantiums and Alexandrias,
Surely—but downward. One desires at such times
To gather the insights of the age summit against future
loss, against the narrowing mind and the tyrants,
The pedants, the mystagogues, the barbarians: one builds
poems for treasuries, time-conscious poems: Lucretius
Sings his great theory of natural origins and of wise con-
duct; Plato smiling carves dreams, bright cells
Of incorruptible wax to hive the Greek honey.

                                       Our own
time, much greater and far less fortunate,
Has acids for honey, and for fine dreams

The immense vulgarities of misapplied science and decay-
    ing Christianity: therefore one christens each poem,
    in dutiful
Hope of burning off at least the top layer of the time's
    uncleanness, from the acid-bottles.

424   *The Eye*

THE Atlantic is a stormy moat; and the Mediterranean,
The blue pool in the old garden,
More than five thousand years has drunk sacrifice
Of ships and blood, and shines in the sun; but here the
    Pacific—
Our ships, planes, wars are perfectly irrelevant.
Neither our present blood-feud with the brave dwarfs
Nor any future world-quarrel of westering
And eastering man, the bloody migrations, greed of power,
    clash of faiths—
Is a speck of dust on the great scale-pan.
Here from this mountain shore, headland beyond stormy
    headland plunging like dolphins through the blue
    sea-smoke
Into pale sea—look west at the hill of water: it is half the
    planet: this dome, this half-globe, this bulging
Eyeball of water, arched over to Asia,
Australia and white Antarctica: those are the eyelids that
    never close; this is the staring unsleeping
Eye of the earth; and what it watches is not our wars.

425 *Eagle Valor, Chicken Mind*

UNHAPPY country, what wings you have! Even here,
Nothing important to protect, and ocean-far from the
    nearest enemy, what a cloud
Of bombers amazes the coast mountain, what a hornet-
    swarm of fighters,
And day and night the guns practicing.

Unhappy, eagle wings and beak, chicken brain.
Weep (it is frequent in human affairs), weep for the ter-
    rible magnificence of the means,
The ridiculous incompetence of the reasons, the bloody and
    shabby
Pathos of the result.

T. S. ELIOT

b. 1888

426 *Sweeney among the Nightingales*

ὤμοι, πέπληγμαι καιρίαν πληγὴν ἔσω.

APENECK SWEENEY spreads his knees
Letting his arms hang down to laugh,
The zebra stripes along his jaw
Swelling to maculate giraffe.

T. S. ELIOT

The circles of the stormy moon
Slide westward toward the River Plate,
Death and the Raven drift above
And Sweeney guards the hornèd gate.

Gloomy Orion and the Dog
Are veiled; and hushed the shrunken seas;
The person in the Spanish cape
Tries to sit on Sweeney's knees

Slips and pulls the table cloth
Overturns a coffee-cup,
Reorganised upon the floor
She yawns and draws a stocking up;

The silent man in mocha brown
Sprawls at the window-sill and gapes;
The waiter brings in oranges
Bananas figs and hothouse grapes;

The silent vertebrate in brown
Contracts and concentrates, withdraws;
Rachel *née* Rabinovitch
Tears at the grapes with murderous paws;

She and the lady in the cape
Are suspect, thought to be in league;
Therefore the man with heavy eyes
Declines the gambit, shows fatigue,

Leaves the room and reappears
Outside the window, leaning in,
Branches of wistaria
Circumscribe a golden grin;

The host with someone indistinct
Converses at the door apart,
The nightingales are singing near
The Convent of the Sacred Heart,

And sang within the bloody wood
When Agamemnon cried aloud,
And let their liquid siftings fall
To stain the stiff dishonoured shroud.

427 *Gerontion*

*Thou hast nor youth nor age
But as it were an after dinner sleep
Dreaming of both.*

HERE I am, an old man in a dry month,
Being read to by a boy, waiting for rain.
I was neither at the hot gates
Nor fought in the warm rain
Nor knee deep in the salt marsh, heaving a cutlass,
Bitten by flies, fought.
My house is a decayed house,
And the jew squats on the window sill, the owner,
Spawned in some estaminet of Antwerp,
Blistered in Brussels, patched and peeled in London.
The goat coughs at night in the field overhead;
Rocks, moss, stonecrop, iron, merds.
The woman keeps the kitchen, makes tea,
Sneezes at evening, poking the peevish gutter.
                         I an old man,
A dull head among windy spaces.

800

Signs are taken for wonders. 'We would see a sign!'
The word within a word, unable to speak a word,
Swaddled with darkness. In the juvescence of the year
Came Christ the tiger

In depraved May, dogwood and chestnut, flowering judas,
To be eaten, to be divided, to be drunk
Among whispers; by Mr. Silvero
With caressing hands, at Limoges
Who walked all night in the next room;

By Hakagawa, bowing among the Titians;
By Madame de Tornquist, in the dark room
Shifting the candles; Fräulein von Kulp
Who turned in the hall, one hand on the door.
    Vacant shuttles
Weave the wind. I have no ghosts,
An old man in a draughty house
Under a windy knob.

After such knowledge, what forgiveness? Think now
History has many cunning passages, contrived corridors
And issues, deceives with whispering ambitions,
Guides us by vanities. Think now
She gives when our attention is distracted
And what she gives, gives with such supple confusions
That the giving famishes the craving. Gives too late
What's not believed in, or if still believed,
In memory only, reconsidered passion. Gives too soon
Into weak hands, what's thought can be dispensed with
Till the refusal propagates a fear. Think
Neither fear nor courage saves us. Unnatural vices
Are fathered by our heroism. Virtues
Are forced upon us by our impudent crimes.
These tears are shaken from the wrath-bearing tree.

The tiger springs in the new year. Us he devours.
    Think at last
We have not reached conclusion, when I
Stiffen in a rented house. Think at last
I have not made this show purposelessly
And it is not by any concitation
Of the backward devils
I would meet you upon this honestly.
I that was near your heart was removed therefrom
To lose beauty in terror, terror in inquisition.
I have lost my passion: why should I need to keep it
Since what is kept must be adulterated?
I have lost my sight, smell, hearing, taste and touch:
How should I use them for your closer contact?

These with a thousand small deliberations
Protract the profit of their chilled delirium,
Excite the membrane, when the sense has cooled,
With pungent sauces, multiply variety
In a wilderness of mirrors. What will the spider do,
Suspend its operations, will the weevil
Delay? De Bailhache, Fresca, Mrs. Cammel, whirled
Beyond the circuit of the shuddering Bear
In fractured atoms. Gull against the wind, in the windy
    straits
Of Belle Isle, or running on the Horn,
White feathers in the snow, the Gulf claims,
And an old man driven by the Trades
To a sleepy corner.

                    Tenants of the house,
Thoughts of a dry brain in a dry season.

T. S. ELIOT

The Waste Land

'NAM Sibyllam quidem Cumis ego ipse oculis meis vidi
in ampulla pendere, et cum illi pueri dicerent: Σίβυλλα τί
θέλεις; respondebat illa: ἀποθανεῖν θέλω.'

For Ezra Pound
il miglior fabbro.

I. THE BURIAL OF THE DEAD

APRIL is the cruellest month, breeding
Lilacs out of the dead land, mixing
Memory and desire, stirring
Dull roots with spring rain.
Winter kept us warm, covering
Earth in forgetful snow, feeding
A little life with dried tubers.
Summer surprised us, coming over the Starnbergersee
With a shower of rain; we stopped in the colonnade,
And went on in sunlight, into the Hofgarten,
And drank coffee, and talked for an hour.
Bin gar keine Russin, stamm' aus Litauen, echt deutsch.
And when we were children, staying at the archduke's,
My cousin's, he took me out on a sled,
And I was frightened. He said, Marie,
Marie, hold on tight. And down we went.
In the mountains, there you feel free.
I read, much of the night, and go south in the winter.

What are the roots that clutch, what branches grow
Out of this stony rubbish? Son of man,

T. S. ELIOT

You cannot say, or guess, for you know only
A heap of broken images, where the sun beats,
And the dead tree gives no shelter, the cricket no relief,
And the dry stone no sound of water. Only
There is shadow under this red rock,
(Come in under the shadow of this red rock),
And I will show you something different from either
Your shadow at morning striding behind you
Or your shadow at evening rising to meet you;
I will show you fear in a handful of dust.

> *Frisch weht der Wind*
> *Der Heimat zu*
> *Mein Irisch Kind,*
> *Wo weilest du?*

'You gave me hyacinths first a year ago;
'They called me the hyacinth girl.'
—Yet when we came back, late, from the Hyacinth gar-
    den,
Your arms full, and your hair wet, I could not
Speak, and my eyes failed, I was neither
Living nor dead, and I knew nothing,
Looking into the heart of light, the silence.
Oed' und leer das Meer.

Madame Sosostris, famous clairvoyante,
Had a bad cold, nevertheless
Is known to be the wisest woman in Europe,
With a wicked pack of cards. Here, said she,
Is your card, the drowned Phoenician Sailor,
(Those are pearls that were his eyes. Look!)
Here is Belladonna, the Lady of the Rocks,
The lady of situations.

Here is the man with three staves, and here the Wheel,
And here is the one-eyed merchant, and this card,
Which is blank, is something he carries on his back,
Which I am forbidden to see. I do not find
The Hanged Man. Fear death by water.
I see crowds of people, walking round in a ring.
Thank you. If you see dear Mrs. Equitone,
Tell her I bring the horoscope myself:
One must be so careful these days.

Unreal City,
Under the brown fog of a winter dawn,
A crowd flowed over London Bridge, so many,
I had not thought death had undone so many.
Sighs, short and infrequent, were exhaled,
And each man fixed his eyes before his feet.
Flowed up the hill and down King William Street,
To where Saint Mary Woolnoth kept the hours
With a dead sound on the final stroke of nine.
There I saw one I knew, and stopped him, crying:
        'Stetson!
'You who were with me in the ships at Mylae!
'That corpse you planted last year in your garden,
'Has it begun to sprout? Will it bloom this year?
'Or has the sudden frost disturbed its bed?
'Oh keep the Dog far hence, that's friend to men,
'Or with his nails he'll dig it up again!
'You! hypocrite lecteur!—mon semblable,—mon frère!'

II. A Game of Chess

The Chair she sat in, like a burnished throne,
Glowed on the marble, where the glass

Held up by standards wrought with fruited vines
From which a golden Cupidon peeped out
(Another hid his eyes behind his wing)
Doubled the flames of sevenbranched candelabra
Reflecting light upon the table as
The glitter of her jewels rose to meet it,
From satin cases poured in rich profusion;
In vials of ivory and coloured glass
Unstoppered, lurked her strange synthetic perfumes,
Unguent, powdered, or liquid—troubled, confused
And drowned the sense in odours; stirred by the air
That freshened from the window, these ascended
In fattening the prolonged candle-flames,
Flung their smoke into the laquearia,
Stirring the pattern on the coffered ceiling.
Huge sea-wood fed with copper
Burned green and orange, framed by the coloured stone,
In which sad light a carvèd dolphin swam.
Above the antique mantel was displayed
As though a window gave upon the sylvan scene
The change of Philomel, by the barbarous king
So rudely forced; yet there the nightingale
Filled all the desert with inviolable voice
And still she cried, and still the world pursues,
'Jug Jug' to dirty ears.
And other withered stumps of time
Were told upon the walls; staring forms
Leaned out, leaning, hushing the room enclosed.
Footsteps shuffled on the stair.
Under the firelight, under the brush, her hair
Spread out in fiery points
Glowed into words, then would be savagely still.

'My nerves are bad to-night. Yes, bad. Stay with me.
'Speak to me. Why do you never speak. Speak.
   'What are you thinking of? What thinking? What?
'I never know what you are thinking. Think.'

I think we are in rats' alley
Where the dead men lost their bones.

'What is that noise?'
               The wind under the door.
'What is that noise now? What is the wind doing?'
               Nothing again nothing.
                       'Do
'You know nothing? Do you see nothing? Do you re-
    member
'Nothing?'

   I remember
Those are pearls that were his eyes.
'Are you alive, or not? Is there nothing in your head?'

                              But
O O O O that Shakespeherian Rag—
It's so elegant
So intelligent
'What shall I do now? What shall I do?'
'I shall rush out as I am, and walk the street
'With my hair down, so. What shall we do to-morrow?
'What shall we ever do?'
                     The hot water at ten.
And if it rains, a closed car at four.
And we shall play a game of chess,
Pressing lidless eyes and waiting for a knock upon the
    door.

When Lil's husband got demobbed, I said—
I didn't mince my words, I said to her myself,
HURRY UP PLEASE ITS TIME
Now Albert's coming back, make yourself a bit smart.
He'll want to know what you done with that money he
    gave you
To get yourself some teeth. He did, I was there.
You have them all out, Lil, and get a nice set,
He said, I swear, I can't bear to look at you.
And no more can't I, I said, and think of poor Albert,
He's been in the army four years, he wants a good time,
And if you don't give it him, there's others will, I said.
Oh is there, she said. Something o' that, I said.
Then I'll know who to thank, she said, and give me a
    straight look.
HURRY UP PLEASE ITS TIME
If you don't like it you can get on with it, I said.
Others can pick and choose if you can't.
But if Albert makes off, it won't be for lack of telling.
You ought to be ashamed, I said, to look so antique.
(And her only thirty-one.)
I can't help it, she said, pulling a long face,
It's them pills I took, to bring it off, she said.
(She's had five already, and nearly died of young George.)
The chemist said it would be all right, but I've never been
    the same.
You *are* a proper fool, I said.
Well, if Albert won't leave you alone, there it is, I said,
What you get married for if you don't want children?
HURRY UP PLEASE ITS TIME
Well, that Sunday Albert was home, they had a hot gam-
    mon,

And they asked me in to dinner, to get the beauty of it
    hot—
HURRY UP PLEASE ITS TIME
HURRY UP PLEASE ITS TIME
Goonight Bill. Goonight Lou. Goonight May. Goonight.
Ta ta. Goonight. Goonight.
Good night, ladies, good night, sweet ladies, good night,
    good night.

III. THE FIRE SERMON

The river's tent is broken: the last fingers of leaf
Clutch and sink into the wet bank. The wind
Crosses the brown land, unheard. The nymphs are
    departed.
Sweet Thames, run softly, till I end my song.
The river bears no empty bottles, sandwich papers,
Silk handkerchiefs, cardboard boxes, cigarette ends
Or other testimony of summer nights. The nymphs are
    departed.
And their friends, the loitering heirs of city directors;
Departed, have left no addresses.
By the waters of Leman I sat down and wept . . .
Sweet Thames, run softly till I end my song,
Sweet Thames, run softly, for I speak not loud or long.
But at my back in a cold blast I hear
The rattle of the bones, and chuckle spread from ear to
    ear.
A rat crept softly through the vegetation
Dragging its slimy belly on the bank
While I was fishing in the dull canal
On a winter evening round behind the gashouse
Musing upon the king my brother's wreck

And on the king my father's death before him.
White bodies naked on the low damp ground
And bones cast in a little low dry garret,
Rattled by the rat's foot only, year to year.
But at my back from time to time I hear
The sound of horns and motors, which shall bring
Sweeney to Mrs. Porter in the spring.
O the moon shone bright on Mrs. Porter
And on her daughter
They wash their feet in soda water
Et O ces voix d'enfants, chantant dans la coupole!

Twit twit twit
Jug jug jug jug jug jug
So rudely forc'd.
Tereu

Unreal City
Under the brown fog of a winter noon
Mr. Eugenides, the Smyrna merchant
Unshaven, with a pocket full of currants
C.i.f. London: documents at sight,
Asked me in demotic French
To luncheon at the Cannon Street Hotel
Followed by a weekend at the Metropole.
At the violet hour, when the eyes and back
Turn upward from the desk, when the human engine
          waits
Like a taxi throbbing waiting,
I Tiresias, though blind, throbbing between two lives,
Old man with wrinkled female breasts, can see
At the violet hour, the evening hour that strives
Homeward, and brings the sailor home from sea,

The typist home at teatime, clears her breakfast, lights
Her stove, and lays out food in tins.
Out of the window perilously spread
Her drying combinations touched by the sun's last rays,
On the divan are piled (at night her bed)
Stockings, slippers, camisoles, and stays.
I Tiresias, old man with wrinkled dugs
Perceived the scene, and foretold the rest—
I too awaited the expected guest.
He, the young man carbuncular, arrives,
A small house agent's clerk, with one bold stare,
One of the low on whom assurance sits
As a silk hat on a Bradford millionaire.
The time is now propitious, as he guesses,
The meal is ended, she is bored and tired,
Endeavours to engage her in caresses
Which still are unreproved, if undesired.
Flushed and decided, he assaults at once;
Exploring hands encounter no defence;
His vanity requires no response,
And makes a welcome of indifference.
(And I Tiresias have foresuffered all
Enacted on this same divan or bed;
I who have sat by Thebes below the wall
And walked among the lowest of the dead.)
Bestows one final patronising kiss,
And gropes his way, finding the stairs unlit . . .

She turns and looks a moment in the glass,
Hardly aware of her departed lover;
Her brain allows one half-formed thought to pass:
'Well now that's done: and I'm glad it's over.'
When lovely woman stoops to folly and

Paces about her room again, alone,
She smoothes her hair with automatic hand,
And puts a record on the gramophone.

'This music crept by me upon the waters'
And along the Strand, up Queen Victoria Street.
O City city, I can sometimes hear
Beside a public bar in Lower Thames Street,
The pleasant whining of a mandoline
And a clatter and a chatter from within
Where fishmen lounge at noon: where the walls
Of Magnus Martyr hold
Inexplicable splendour of Ionian white and gold.

> The river sweats
> Oil and tar
> The barges drift
> With the turning tide
> Red sails
> Wide
> To leeward, swing on the heavy spar.
> The barges wash
> Drifting logs
> Down Greenwich reach
> Past the Isle of Dogs.
>> Weialala leia
>> Wallala leialala

> Elizabeth and Leicester
> Beating oars
> The stern was formed
> A gilded shell
> Red and gold

The brisk swell
Rippled both shores
Southwest wind
Carried down stream
The peal of bells
White towers
        Weialala leia
        Wallala leialala

'Trams and dusty trees.
Highbury bore me. Richmond and Kew
Undid me. By Richmond I raised my knees
Supine on the floor of a narrow canoe.'

'My feet are at Moorgate, and my heart
Under my feet. After the event
He wept. He promised "a new start."
I made no comment. What should I resent?'

'On Margate Sands.
I can connect
Nothing with nothing.
The broken fingernails of dirty hands.
My people humble people who expect
Nothing.'
        la la

To Carthage then I came
Burning burning burning burning
O Lord Thou pluckest me out
O Lord Thou pluckest

burning

IV. Death by Water

Phlebas the Phoenician, a fortnight dead,
Forgot the cry of gulls, and the deep sea swell
And the profit and loss.
                              A current under sea
Picked his bones in whispers. As he rose and fell
He passed the stages of his age and youth
Entering the whirlpool.
                              Gentile or Jew
O you who turn the wheel and look to windward,
Consider Phlebas, who was once handsome and tall as you.

V. What the Thunder Said

After the torchlight red on sweaty faces
After the frosty silence in the gardens
After the agony in stony places
The shouting and the crying
Prison and palace and reverberation
Of thunder of spring over distant mountains
He who was living is now dead
We who were living are now dying
With a little patience

Here is no water but only rock
Rock and no water and the sandy road
The road winding above among the mountains
Which are mountains of rock without water
If there were water we should stop and drink
Amongst the rock one cannot stop or think
Sweat is dry and feet are in the sand
If there were only water amongst the rock

Dead mountain mouth of carious teeth that cannot spit
Here one can neither stand nor lie nor sit
There is not even silence in the mountains
But dry sterile thunder without rain
There is not even solitude in the mountains
But red sullen faces sneer and snarl
From doors of mudcracked houses

              If there were water
And no rock
If there were rock
And also water
And water
A spring
A pool among the rock
If there were the sound of water only
Not the cicada
And dry grass singing
But sound of water over a rock
Where the hermit-thrush sings in the pine trees
Drip drop drip drop drop drop drop
But there is no water

Who is the third who walks always beside you?
When I count, there are only you and I together
But when I look ahead up the white road
There is always another one walking beside you
Gliding wrapt in a brown mantle, hooded
I do not know whether a man or a woman
—But who is that on the other side of you?

What is that sound high in the air
Murmur of maternal lamentation

Who are those hooded hordes swarming
Over endless plains, stumbling in cracked earth
Ringed by the flat horizon only
What is the city over the mountains
Cracks and reforms and bursts in the violet air
Falling towers
Jerusalem Athens Alexandria
Vienna London
Unreal

A woman drew her long black hair out tight
And fiddled whisper music on those strings
And bats with baby faces in the violet light
Whistled, and beat their wings
And crawled head downward down a blackened wall
And upside down in air were towers
Tolling reminiscent bells, that kept the hours
And voices singing out of empty cisterns and exhausted
    wells.

In this decayed hole among the mountains
In the faint moonlight, the grass is singing
Over the tumbled graves, about the chapel
There is the empty chapel, only the wind's home.
It has no windows, and the door swings,
Dry bones can harm no one.
Only a cock stood on the rooftree
Co co rico co co rico
In a flash of lightning. Then a damp gust
Bringing rain

Ganga was sunken, and the limp leaves
Waited for rain, while the black clouds

Gathered far distant, over Himavant.
The jungle crouched, humped in silence.
Then spoke the thunder
DA
Datta: what have we given?
My friend, blood shaking my heart
The awful daring of a moment's surrender
Which an age of prudence can never retract
By this, and this only, we have existed
Which is not to be found in our obituaries
Or in memories draped by the beneficent spider
Or under seals broken by the lean solicitor
In our empty rooms
DA
Dayadhvam: I have heard the key
Turn in the door once and turn once only
We think of the key, each in his prison
Thinking of the key, each confirms a prison
Only at nightfall, aethereal rumours
Revive for a moment a broken Coriolanus
DA
Damyata: The boat responded
Gaily, to the hand expert with sail and oar
The sea was calm, your heart would have responded
Gaily, when invited, beating obedient
To controlling hands

                    I sat upon the shore
Fishing, with the arid plain behind me
Shall I at least set my lands in order?
London Bridge is falling down falling down falling down
Poi s'ascose nel foco che gli affina
Quando fiam uti chelidon—O swallow swallow

Le Prince d'Aquitaine à la tour abolie
These fragments I have shored against my ruins
Why then Ile fit you. Hieronymo's mad againe.
Datta. Dayadhvam. Damyata.
               Shantih   shantih   shantih

429   *Ash-Wednesday*

I

Because I do not hope to turn again
Because I do not hope
Because I do not hope to turn
Desiring this man's gift and that man's scope
I no longer strive to strive towards such things
(Why should the agèd eagle stretch its wings?)
Why should I mourn
The vanished power of the usual reign?

Because I do not hope to know again
The infirm glory of the positive hour
Because I do not think
Because I know I shall not know
The one veritable transitory power
Because I cannot drink
There, where trees flower, and springs flow, for there is
    nothing again

Because I know that time is always time
And place is always and only place
And what is actual is actual only for one time

And only for one place
I rejoice that things are as they are and
I renounce the blessèd face
And renounce the voice
Because I cannot hope to turn again
Consequently I rejoice, having to construct something
Upon which to rejoice

And pray to God to have mercy upon us
And I pray that I may forget
These matters that with myself I too much discuss
Too much explain
Because I do not hope to turn again
Let these words answer
For what is done, not to be done again
May the judgement not be too heavy upon us

Because these wings are no longer wings to fly
But merely vans to beat the air
The air which is now thoroughly small and dry
Smaller and dryer than the will
Teach us to care and not to care
Teach us to sit still.

Pray for us sinners now and at the hour of our death
Pray for us now and at the hour of our death.

II

Lady, three white leopards sat under a juniper-tree
In the cool of the day, having fed to satiety
On my legs my heart my liver and that which had been
     contained
In the hollow round of my skull. And God said

Shall these bones live? shall these
Bones live? And that which had been contained
In the bones (which were already dry) said chirping:
Because of the goodness of this Lady
And because of her loveliness, and because
She honours the Virgin in meditation,
We shine with brightness. And I who am here dissembled
Proffer my deeds to oblivion, and my love
To the posterity of the desert and the fruit of the gourd.
It is this which recovers
My guts the strings of my eyes and the indigestible por-
    tions
Which the leopards reject. The Lady is withdrawn
In a white gown, to contemplation, in a white gown.
Let the whiteness of bones atone to forgetfulness.
There is no life in them. As I am forgotten
And would be forgotten, so I would forget
Thus devoted, concentrated in purpose. And God said
Prophesy to the wind, to the wind only for only
The wind will listen. And the bones sang chirping
With the burden of the grasshopper, saying

Lady of silences
Calm and distressed
Torn and most whole
Rose of memory
Rose of forgetfulness
Exhausted and life-giving
Worried reposeful
The single Rose
Is now the Garden
Where all loves end
Terminate torment

Of love unsatisfied
The greater torment
Of love satisfied
End of the endless
Journey to no end
Conclusion of all that
Is inconclusible
Speech without word and
Word of no speech
Grace to the Mother
For the Garden
Where all love ends.

Under a juniper-tree the bones sang, scattered and shining
We are glad to be scattered, we did little good to each
        other,
Under a tree in the cool of the day, with the blessing of
        sand,
Forgetting themselves and each other, united
In the quiet of the desert. This is the land which ye
Shall divide by lot. And neither division nor unity
Matters. This is the land. We have our inheritance.

III

At the first turning of the second stair
I turned and saw below
The same shape twisted on the banister
Under the vapour in the fetid air
Struggling with the devil of the stairs who wears
The deceitful face of hope and of despair.

At the second turning of the second stair
I left them twisting, turning below;

There were no more faces and the stair was dark,
Damp, jaggèd, like an old man's mouth drivelling, be-
    yond repair,
Or the toothed gullet of an agèd shark.

At the first turning of the third stair
Was a slotted window bellied like the fig's fruit
And beyond the hawthorn blossom and a pasture scene
The broadbacked figure drest in blue and green
Enchanted the maytime with an antique flute.
Blown hair is sweet, brown hair over the mouth blown,
Lilac and brown hair;
Distraction, music of the flute, stops and steps of the mind
    over the third stair,
Fading, fading; strength beyond hope and despair
Climbing the third stair.

Lord, I am not worthy
Lord, I am not worthy

      but speak the word only.

IV

Who walked between the violet and the violet
Who walked between
The various ranks of varied green
Going in white and blue, in Mary's colour,
Talking of trivial things
In ignorance and in knowledge of eternal dolour
Who moved among the others as they walked,
Who then made strong the fountains and made fresh the
    springs

Made cool the dry rock and made firm the sand
In blue of larkspur, blue of Mary's colour,
Sovegna vos

Here are the years that walk between, bearing
Away the fiddles and the flutes, restoring
One who moves in the time between sleep and waking,
    wearing

White light folded, sheathed about her, folded.
The new years walk, restoring
Through a bright cloud of tears, the years, restoring
With a new verse the ancient rhyme. Redeem
The time. Redeem
The unread vision in the higher dream
While jewelled unicorns draw by the gilded hearse.

The silent sister veiled in white and blue
Between the yews, behind the garden god,
Whose flute is breathless, bent her head and sighed but
    spoke no word

But the fountain sprang up and the bird sang down
Redeem the time, redeem the dream
The token of the word unheard, unspoken

Till the wind shake a thousand whispers from the yew

And after this our exile

V

If the lost word is lost, if the spent word is spent
If the unheard, unspoken

Word is unspoken, unheard;
Still is the unspoken word, the Word unheard,
The Word without a word, the Word within
The world and for the world;
And the light shone in darkness and
Against the Word the unstilled world still whirled
About the centre of the silent Word.

    O my people, what have I done unto thee.

Where shall the word be found, where will the word
Resound? Not here, there is not enough silence
Not on the sea or on the islands, not
On the mainland, in the desert or the rain land,
For those who walk in darkness
Both in the day time and in the night time
The right time and the right place are not here
No place of grace for those who avoid the face
No time to rejoice for those who walk among noise and
    deny the voice

Will the veiled sister pray for
Those who walk in darkness, who chose thee and oppose
    thee,
Those who are torn on the horn between season and season,
    time and time, between
Hour and hour, word and word, power and power, those
    who wait
In darkness? Will the veiled sister pray
For children at the gate
Who will not go away and cannot pray:
Pray for those who chose and oppose

T. S. ELIOT

O my people, what have I done unto thee.

Will the veiled sister between the slender
Yew trees pray for those who offend her
And are terrified and cannot surrender
And affirm before the world and deny between the rocks
In the last desert between the last blue rocks
The desert in the garden the garden in the desert
Of drouth, spitting from the mouth the withered apple-
    seed.

O my people.

VI

Although I do not hope to turn again
Although I do not hope
Although I do not hope to turn

Wavering between the profit and the loss
In this brief transit where the dreams cross
The dreamcrossed twilight between birth and dying
(Bless me father) though I do not wish to wish these
    things
From the wide window towards the granite shore
The white sails still fly seaward, seaward flying
Unbroken wings

And the lost heart stiffens and rejoices
In the lost lilac and the lost sea voices
And the weak spirit quickens to rebel
For the bent golden-rod and the lost sea smell
Quickens to recover
The cry of quail and the whirling plover

And the blind eye creates
The empty forms between the ivory gates
And smell renews the salt savour of the sandy earth

This is the time of tension between dying and birth
The place of solitude where three dreams cross
Between blue rocks
But when the voices shaken from the yew-tree drift away
Let the other yew be shaken and reply.

Blessèd sister, holy mother, spirit of the fountain, spirit of
    the garden,
Suffer us not to mock ourselves with falsehood
Teach us to care and not to care
Teach us to sit still
Even among these rocks,
Our peace in His will
And even among these rocks
Sister, mother
And spirit of the river, spirit of the sea,
Suffer me not to be separated

And let my cry come unto Thee.

430   *The Dry Salvages*

(The Dry Salvages—presumably *les trois sauvages*—is a
small group of rocks, with a beacon, off the N.E. coast of
Cape Ann, Massachusetts. *Salvages* is pronounced to rhyme
with *assuages. Groaner:* a whistling buoy.)

T. S. ELIOT

I

I DO not know much about gods; but I think that the river
Is a strong brown god—sullen, untamed and intractable,
Patient to some degree, at first recognised as a frontier;
Useful, untrustworthy, as a conveyor of commerce;
Then only a problem confronting the builder of bridges.
The problem once solved, the brown god is almost forgotten
By the dwellers in cities—ever, however, implacable,
Keeping his seasons and rages, destroyer, reminder
Of what men choose to forget. Unhonoured, unpropitiated
By worshippers of the machine, but waiting, watching and waiting.
His rhythm was present in the nursery bedroom,
In the rank ailanthus of the April dooryard,
In the smell of grapes on the autumn table,
And the evening circle in the winter gaslight.

The river is within us, the sea is all about us;
The sea is the land's edge also, the granite
Into which it reaches, the beaches where it tosses
Its hints of earlier and other creation:
The starfish, the hermit crab, the whale's backbone;
The pools where it offers to our curiosity
The more delicate algae and the sea anemone.
It tosses up our losses, the torn seine,
The shattered lobsterpot, the broken oar
And the gear of foreign dead men. The sea has many voices,
Many gods and many voices.

                        The salt is on the briar rose,
The fog is in the fir trees.
                       The sea howl
And the sea yelp, are different voices
Often together heard; the whine in the rigging,
The menace and caress of wave that breaks on water,
The distant rote in the granite teeth,
And the wailing warning from the approaching headland
Are all sea voices, and the heaving groaner
Rounded homewards, and the seagull:
And under the oppression of the silent fog
The tolling bell
Measures time not our time, rung by the unhurried
Ground swell, a time
Older than the time of chronometers, older
Than time counted by anxious worried women
Lying awake, calculating the future,
Trying to unweave, unwind, unravel
And piece together the past and the future,
Between midnight and dawn, when the past is all decep-
    tion,
The future futureless, before the morning watch
When time stops and time is never ending;
And the ground swell, that is and was from the beginning,
Clangs
The bell.

II

Where is there an end of it, the soundless wailing,
The silent withering of autumn flowers
Dropping their petals and remaining motionless;
Where is there an end to the drifting wreckage,
The prayer of the bone on the beach, the unprayable
Prayer at the calamitous annunciation?

There is no end, but addition: the trailing
Consequence of further days and hours,
While emotion takes to itself the emotionless
Years of living among the breakage
Of what was believed in as the most reliable—
And therefore the fittest for renunciation.

There is the final addition, the failing
Pride or resentment at failing powers,
The unattached devotion which might pass for devotionless,
In a drifting boat with a slow leakage,
The silent listening to the undeniable
Clamour of the bell of the last annunciation.

Where is the end of them, the fishermen sailing
Into the wind's tail, where the fog cowers?
We cannot think of a time that is oceanless
Or of an ocean not littered with wastage
Or of a future that is not liable
Like the past, to have no destination.

We have to think of them as forever bailing,
Setting and hauling, while the North East lowers
Over shallow banks unchanging and erosionless
Or drawing their money, drying sails at dockage;
Not as making a trip that will be unpayable
For a haul that will not bear examination.

There is no end of it, the voiceless wailing,
No end to the withering of withered flowers,
To the movement of pain that is painless and motionless,
To the drift of the sea and the drifting wreckage,
The bone's prayer to Death its God. Only the hardly, barely
    prayable
Prayer of the one Annunciation.

It seems, as one becomes older,
That the past has another pattern, and ceases to be a mere
    sequence—
Or even development: the latter a partial fallacy,
Encouraged by superficial notions of evolution,
Which becomes, in the popular mind, a means of disown-
    ing the past.
The moments of happiness—not the sense of well-being,
Fruition, fulfilment, security or affection,
Or even a very good dinner, but the sudden illumination—
We had the experience but missed the meaning,
And approach to the meaning restores the experience
In a different form, beyond any meaning
We can assign to happiness. I have said before
That the past experience revived in the meaning
Is not the experience of one life only
But of many generations—not forgetting
Something that is probably quite ineffable:
The backward look behind the assurance
Of recorded history, the backward half-look
Over the shoulder, towards the primitive terror.
Now, we come to discover that the moments of agony
(Whether, or not, due to misunderstanding,
Having hoped for the wrong things or dreaded the wrong
    things,
Is not in question) are likewise permanent
With such permanence as time has. We appreciate this
    better
In the agony of others, nearly experienced,
Involving ourselves, than in our own.
For our own past is covered by the currents of action,
But the torment of others remains an experience
Unqualified, unworn by subsequent attrition.

People change, and smile: but the agony abides.
Time the destroyer is time the preserver,
Like the river with its cargo of dead Negroes, cows and
    chicken coops,
The bitter apple and the bite in the apple.
And the ragged rock in the restless waters,
Waves wash over it, fogs conceal it;
On a halcyon day it is merely a monument,
In navigable weather it is always a seamark
To lay a course by: but in the sombre season
Or the sudden fury, is what it always was.

III

I sometimes wonder if that is what Krishna meant—
Among other things—or one way of putting the same
    thing:
That the future is a faded song, a Royal Rose or a lavender
    spray
Of wistful regret for those who are not yet here to regret,
Pressed between yellow leaves of a book that has never been
    opened.
And the way up is the way down, the way forward is the
    way back.
You cannot face it steadily, but this thing is sure,
That time is no healer: the patient is no longer here
When the train starts, and the passengers are settled
To fruit, periodicals and business letters
(And those who saw them off have left the platform)
Their faces relax from grief into relief,
To the sleepy rhythm of a hundred hours.
Fare forward, travellers! not escaping from the past
Into different lives, or into any future;

T. S. ELIOT

You are not the same people who left that station
Or who will arrive at any terminus,
While the narrowing rails slide together behind you;
And on the deck of the drumming liner
Watching the furrow that widens behind you,
You shall not think 'the past is finished'
Or 'the future is before us.'
At nightfall, in the rigging and the aerial,
Is a voice descanting (though not to the ear,
The murmuring shell of time, and not in any language)
'Fare forward, you who think that you are voyaging;
You are not those who saw the harbour
Receding, or those who will disembark.
Here between the hither and the farther shore
While time is withdrawn, consider the future
And the past with an equal mind.
At the moment which is not of action or inaction
You can receive this: "on whatever sphere of being
The mind of a man may be intent
At the time of death"—that is the one action
(And the time of death is every moment)
Which shall fructify in the lives of others:
And do not think of the fruit of action.
Fare forward.
                    O voyagers, O seamen,
You who come to port, and you whose bodies
Will suffer the trial and judgement of the sea,
Or whatever event, this is your real destination.'
So Krishna, as when he admonished Arjuna
On the field of battle.
                              Not fare well,
But fare forward, voyagers.

IV

Lady, whose shrine stands on the promontory,
Pray for all those who are in ships, those
Whose business has to do with fish, and
Those concerned with every lawful traffic
And those who conduct them.

Repeat a prayer also on behalf of
Women who have seen their sons or husbands
Setting forth, and not returning:
Figlia del tuo figlio,
Queen of Heaven.

Also pray for those who were in ships, and
Ended their voyage on the sand, in the sea's lips
Or in the dark throat which will not reject them
Or wherever cannot reach them the sound of the sea bell's
Perpetual angelus.

V

To communicate with Mars, converse with spirits,
To report the behaviour of the sea monster,
Describe the horoscope, haruspicate or scry,
Observe disease in signatures, evoke
Biography from the wrinkles of the palm
And tragedy from fingers; release omens
By sortilege, or tea leaves, riddle the inevitable
With playing cards, fiddle with pentagrams
Or barbituric acids, or dissect
The recurrent image into pre-conscious terrors—
To explore the womb, or tomb, or dreams; all these are
    usual

Pastimes and drugs, and features of the press:
And always will be, some of them especially
When there is distress of nations and perplexity
Whether on the shores of Asia, or in the Edgware Road.
Men's curiosity searches past and future
And clings to that dimension. But to apprehend
The point of intersection of the timeless
With time, is an occupation for the saint—
No occupation either, but something given
And taken, in a lifetime's death in love,
Ardour and selflessness and self-surrender.
For most of us, there is only the unattended
Moment, the moment in and out of time,
The distraction fit, lost in a shaft of sunlight,
The wild thyme unseen, or the winter lightning
Or the waterfall, or music heard so deeply
That it is not heard at all, but you are the music
While the music lasts. These are only hints and guesses,
Hints followed by guesses; and the rest
Is prayer, observance, discipline, thought and action.
The hint half guessed, the gift half understood, is Incar-
     nation.
Here the impossible union
Of spheres of existence is actual,
Here the past and future
Are conquered, and reconciled,
Where action were otherwise movement
Of that which is only moved
And has in it no source of movement—
Driven by daemonic, chthonic
Powers. And right action is freedom
From past and future also.
For most of us, this is the aim

Never here to be realised;
Who are only undefeated
Because we have gone on trying;
We, content at the last
If our temporal reversion nourish
(Not too far from the yew-tree)
The life of significant soil.

JOHN CROWE RANSOM

b. 1888

431 *Agitato ma non troppo*

I HAVE a grief
(It was not stolen like a thief)
Albeit I have no bittern by the lake
To cry it up and down the brake.

None there hath been like Dante's fury
When Beatrice was given him to bury;
Except, when the young heart was hit, you know
How Percy Shelley's reed sang tremolo.

'If grief be in his mind,
Where is his fair child moaning in the wind?
Where is the white frost snowing on his head?
When did he stalk and weep and not loll in his bed?'

I will be brief,
Assuredly I have a grief,
And I am shaken; but not as a leaf.

432 *Bells for John Whiteside's Daughter*

THERE was such speed in her little body,
And such lightness in her footfall,
It is no wonder her brown study
Astonishes us all.

Her wars were bruited in our high window.
We looked among orchard trees and beyond,
Where she took arms against her shadow,
Or harried unto the pond

The lazy geese, like a snow cloud
Dripping their snow on the green grass,
Tricking and stopping, sleepy and proud,
Who cried in goose, Alas,

For the tireless heart within the little
Lady with rod that made them rise
From their noon apple-dreams and scuttle
Goose-fashion under the skies!

But now go the bells, and we are ready,
In one house we are sternly stopped
To say we are vexed at her brown study,
Lying so primly propped.

JOHN CROWE RANSOM

433   *Winter Remembered*

TWO evils, monstrous either one apart,
Possessed me, and were long and loath at going:
A cry of Absence, Absence, in the heart,
And in the wood the furious winter blowing.

Think not, when fire was bright upon my bricks,
And past the tight boards hardly a wind could enter,
I glowed like them, the simple burning sticks,
Far from my cause, my proper heat and center.

Better to walk forth in the murderous air
And wash my wound in the snows; that would be healing,
Because my heart would throb less painful there,
Being caked with cold, and past the smart of feeling.

And where I went, the hugest winter blast
Would have this body bowed, these eyeballs streaming,
And though I think this heart's blood froze not fast
It ran too small to spare one drop for dreaming.

Dear love, these fingers that had known your touch,
And tied our separate forces first together,
Were ten poor idiot fingers not worth much,
Ten frozen parsnips hanging in the weather.

434   *Vaunting Oak*

HE is a tower unleaning. But how will he not break,
If Heaven assault him with full wind and sleet,
And what uproar tall trees concumbent make!

JOHN CROWE RANSOM

More than a hundred years, more than a hundred feet
Naked he rears against the cold skies eruptive;
Only his temporal twigs are unsure of seat,

And the frail leaves of a season, which are susceptive
Of the mad humors of wind, and turn and flee
In panic round the stem on which they are captive.

Now a certain heart, too young and mortally
Linked with an unbeliever of bitter blood,
Observed, as an eminent witness of life, the tree,

And exulted, wrapped in a phantasy of good:
'Be the great oak for its long winterings
Our love's symbol, better than the summer's brood.'

Then the venerable oak, delivered of his pangs,
Put forth profuse his green banners of peace
And testified to her with innumerable tongues.

And what but she fetch me up to the steep place
Where the oak vaunted? A flat where birdsong flew
Had to be traversed; and a quick populace

Of daisies, and yellow kinds; and here she knew,
Who had been instructed of much mortality,
Better than brag in this distraught purlieu.

Above the little and their dusty tombs was he
Standing, sheer on his hill, not much soiled over
By the knobs and broken boughs of an old tree,

And she murmured, 'Established, you see him there! for-
ever.'
But, that her pitiful error be undone,
I knocked on his house loudly, a sorrowing lover,

And drew forth like a funeral a hollow tone.
'The old gentleman,' I grieved, 'holds gallantly,
But before our joy shall have lapsed, even, will be gone.'

I knocked more sternly, and his dolorous cry
Boomed till its loud reverberance outsounded
The singing of bees; or the coward birds that fly

Otherwhere with their songs when summer is sped,
And if they stayed would perish miserably;
Or the tears of a girl remembering her dread.

435 *Conrad in Twilight*

CONRAD, Conrad, aren't you old
To sit so late in your mouldy garden?
And I think Conrad knows it well,
Nursing his knees, too rheumy and cold
To warm the wraith of a Forest of Arden.

Neuralgia in the back of his neck,
His lungs filling with such miasma,
His feet dipping in leafage and muck:
Conrad! you've forgotten asthma.

Conrad's house has thick red walls
And chips on Conrad's hearth are blazing,
Slippers and pipe and tea are served,
Butter and toast, Conrad, are pleasing!
Still Conrad's back is not uncurved
And here's an autumn on him, teasing.

Autumn days in our section
Are the most used-up thing on earth
(Or in the waters under the earth)
Having no more color nor predilection
Than cornstalks too wet for the fire,
A ribbon rotting on the byre,
A man's face as weathered as straw
By the summer's flare and winter's flaw.

436   *Blackberry Winter*

IF the lady hath any loveliness, let it die.
For being drunken with the steam of Cuban cigars,
I find no pungence in the odour of stars,
And all my music goes out of me on a sigh.

But still would I sing to my maidenly apple-tree,
Before she has borne me a single apple of red;
The pictures of silver and apples of gold are dead;
But one more apple ripeneth yet maybe.

The garnished house of the Daughter of Heaven is cold.
I have seen her often, she stood all night on the hill,
Fiercely the pale youth clambered to her, till—
Hoarsely the rooster awakened him, footing the mould.

The breath of a girl is music—fall and swell—
The trumpets convolve in the warrior's chambered ear,
But I have listened, there is no one breathing here,
And all of the wars have dwindled since Troy fell.

But still I will haunt beneath my apple-tree,
Heedful again to star-looks and wind-words,
Anxious for the flash of whether eyes or swords,
And hoping a little, a little, that either may be.

437 *Old Mansion*

As an intruder I trudged with careful innocence
To mask in decency a meddlesome stare,
Passing the old house often on its eminence,
Exhaling my foreign weed on its weighted air.

Here age seemed newly imaged for the historian
After his monstrous chateaux on the Loire,
A beauty not for depicting by old vulgarian
Reiterations which gentle readers abhor.

Each time of seeing I absorbed some other feature
Of a house whose annals in no wise could be brief
Nor ignoble; for it expired as sweetly as Nature,
With her tinge of oxidation on autumn leaf.

It was a Southern manor. One need hardly imagine
Towers, white monoliths, or even ivied walls;
But sufficient state if its peacock *was* a pigeon;
Where no courts kept, but grave rites and funerals.

Indeed, not distant, possibly not external
To the property, were tombstones, where the catatalque
Had carried their dead; and projected a note too charnel
But for the honeysuckle on its intricate stalk.

Stability was the character of its rectangle
Whose line was seen in part and guessed in part
Through trees. Decay was the tone of old brick and
    shingle.
Green blinds dragging frightened the watchful heart

To assert, 'Your mansion, long and richly inhabited,
Its exits and entrances suiting the children of men,
Will not for ever be thus, O man, exhibited,
And one had best hurry to enter it if one can.'

And at last, with my happier angel's own temerity,
Did I clang their brazen knocker against the door,
To beg their dole of a look, in simple charity,
Or crumbs of legend dropping from their great store.

But it came to nothing—and may so gross denial
Which has been deplored with a beating of the breast
Never shorten the tired historian, loyal
To acknowledge defeat and discover a new quest—

The old mistress was ill, and sent my dismissal
By one even more wrappered and lean and dark
Than that warped concierge and imperturbable vassal
Who bids you begone from her master's Gothic park.

Emphatically, the old house crumbled; the ruins
Would litter, as already the leaves, this petted sward;
And no annalist went in to the lords or the peons;
The antiquary would finger the bits of shard.

But on retreating I saw myself in the token,
How loving from my foreign weed the feather curled
On the languid air; and I went with courage shaken
To dip, alas, into some unseemlier world.

438 *Philomela*

PROCNE, Philomela, and Itylus,
Your names are liquid, your improbable tale
Is recited in the classic numbers of the nightingale.
Ah, but our numbers are not felicitous,
It goes not liquidly for us.

Perched on a Roman ilex, and duly apostrophized,
The nightingale descanted unto Ovid;
She has even appeared to the Teutons, the swilled and
    gravid;
At Fontainebleau it may be the bird was gallicized;
Never was she baptized.

To England came Philomela with her pain,
Fleeing the hawk her husband; querulous ghost,
She wanders when he sits heavy on his roost,
Utters herself in the original again,
The untranslatable refrain.

Not to these shores she came! this other Thrace,
Environ barbarous to the royal Attic;
How could her delicate dirge run democratic,
Delivered in a cloudless boundless public place
To an inordinate race?

I pernoctated with the Oxford students once,
And in the quadrangles, in the cloisters, on the Cher,
Precociously knocked at antique doors ajar,
Fatuously touched the hems of the hierophants,
Sick of my dissonance.

I went out to Bagley Wood, I climbed the hill;
Even the moon had slanted off in a twinkling,
I heard the sepulchral owl and a few bells tinkling,
There was no more villainous day to unfulfil,
The diuturnity was still.

Up from the darkest wood where Philomela sat,
Her fairy numbers issued. What then ailed me?
My ears are called capacious but they failed me,
Her classics registered a little flat!
I rose, and venomously spat.

Philomela, Philomela, lover of song,
I am in despair if we may make us worthy,
A bantering breed sophistical and swarthy;
Unto more beautiful, persistently more young,
Thy fabulous provinces belong.

439   *Captain Carpenter*

CAPTAIN Carpenter rose up in his prime
Put on his pistols and went riding out
But had got wellnigh nowhere at that time
Till he fell in with ladies in a rout.

It was a pretty lady and all her train
That played with him so sweetly but before
An hour she'd taken a sword with all her main
And twined him of his nose for evermore.

Captain Carpenter mounted up one day
And rode straightway into a stranger rogue

That looked unchristian but be that as may
The Captain did not wait upon prologue.

But drew upon him out of his great heart
The other swung against him with a club
And cracked his two legs at the shinny part
And let him roll and stick like any tub.

Captain Carpenter rode many a time
From male and female took he sundry harms
He met the wife of Satan crying 'I'm
The she-wolf bids you shall bear no more arms.'

Their strokes and counters whistled in the wind
I wish he had delivered half his blows
But where she should have made off like a hind
The bitch bit off his arms at the elbows.

And Captain Carpenter parted with his ears
To a black devil that used him in this wise
O Jesus ere his threescore and ten years
Another had plucked out his sweet blue eyes.

Captain Carpenter got up on his roan
And sallied from the gate in hell's despite
I heard him asking in the grimmest tone
If any enemy yet there was to fight?

'To any adversary it is fame
If he risk to be wounded by my tongue
Or burnt in two beneath my red heart's flame
Such are the perils he is cast among.

'But if he can he has a pretty choice
From an anatomy with little to lose
Whether he cut my tongue and take my voice
Or whether it be my round red heart he choose.'

It was the neatest knave that ever was seen
Stepping in perfume from his lady's bower
Who at this word put in his merry mien
And fell on Captain Carpenter like a tower.

I would not knock old fellows in the dust
But there lay Captain Carpenter on his back
His weapons were the old heart in his bust
And a blade shook between rotten teeth alack.

The rogue in scarlet and grey soon knew his mind
He wished to get his trophy and depart
With gentle apology and touch refined
He pierced him and produced the Captain's heart.

God's mercy rest on Captain Carpenter now
I thought him Sirs an honest gentleman
Citizen husband soldier and scholar enow
Let jangling kites eat of him if they can.

But God's deep curses follow after those
That shore him of his goodly nose and ears
His legs and strong arms at the two elbows
And eyes that had not watered seventy years.

The curse of hell upon the sleek upstart
That got the Captain finally on his back
And took the red red vitals of his heart
And made the kites to whet their beaks clack clack.

JOHN CROWE RANSOM

440

Piazza Piece

—I AM a gentleman in a dustcoat trying
To make you hear. Your ears are soft and small
And listen to an old man not at all,
They want the young men's whispering and sighing.
But see the roses on your trellis dying
And hear the spectral singing of the moon;
For I must have my lovely lady soon,
I am a gentleman in a dustcoat trying.

—I am a lady young in beauty waiting
Until my truelove comes, and then we kiss.
But what grey man among the vines is this
Whose words are dry and faint as in a dream?
Back from my trellis, Sir, before I scream!
I am a lady young in beauty waiting.

441

Vision by Sweetwater

GO and ask Robin to bring the girls over
To Sweetwater, said my Aunt; and that was why
It was like a dream of ladies sweeping by
The willows, clouds, deep meadowgrass, and the river.

Robin's sisters and my Aunt's lily daughter
Laughed and talked, and tinkled light as wrens
If there were a little colony all hens
To go walking by the steep turn of Sweetwater.

Let them alone, dear Aunt, just for one minute
Till I go fishing in the dark of my mind:

Where have I seen before, against the wind,
These bright virgins, robed and bare of bonnet,

Flowing with music of their strange quick tongue
And adventuring with delicate paces by the stream,—
Myself a child, old suddenly at the scream
From one of the white throats which it hid among?

442   *Persistent Explorer*

THE noise of water teased his literal ears
Which heard the distant drumming and thus scored.
Water is falling—it fell—therefore it roared.
But he cried, That is more than water I hear.

He went yet higher, and on the dizzy brink
His eyes confirmed with vision what he had heard:
This is but tumbling water. Again he demurred:
That was not only water flashing, I think.

But listen as he might, look fast or slow,
It was water, only water, tons of it
Dropping into the gorge, and every bit
Was water—the insipid chemical H_2O.

Its thunder smote him somewhat as the loud
Words of the god that rang around a man
Walking by the Mediterranean.
Its cloud of froth was whiter than the cloud

That clothed the goddess sliding down the air
Unto a mountain shepherd; white as she
That issued from the smoke refulgently.
The cloud was, but the goddess was not there.

JOHN CROWE RANSOM

The sound was tremendous, but it was no voice
That spoke to him. The spectacle was grand
But still it spelled him nothing, nothing, and
Forbade him whether to cower or rejoice.

What would he have it spell? He scarcely knew;
Only that water and nothing but water filled
His eyes and ears, nothing but water that spilled;
And if the smoke and rattle of water drew

From the deep thickets of his mind the train,
The fierce fauns and the timid tenants there,
That burst their bonds and rushed upon the air,
Why, he must turn and beat them down again.

So be it. And no unreasonable outcry
The pilgrim made; only a rueful grin
Spread over his lips until he drew them in;
He did not sit upon a rock and die.

There were many ways of dying; witness, if he
Commit himself to the water, and descend
Wrapped in the water, turn water at the end
And flow with a great water out to sea.

But there were many ways of living too,
And let his enemies gibe, but let them say
That he would throw this continent away
And seek another country,—as he would do.

443 *Dead Boy*

THE little cousin is dead, by foul subtraction,
A green bough from Virginia's aged tree,
And none of the county kin like the transaction
Nor some of the world of outer dark, like me.

A boy not beautiful, nor good, nor clever,
A black cloud full of storms too hot for keeping,
A sword beneath his mother's heart—yet never
Woman bewept her babe as this is weeping.

A pig with a pasty face, so I had said.
Squealing for cookies, kinned by pure pretense
With a noble house. But the little man quite dead,
I can see the forebears' antique lineaments.

The elder men have strode by the box of death
To the wide flag porch, and muttering low send round
The bruit of the day. O friendly waste of breath!
Their hearts are hurt with a deep dynastic wound.

He was pale and little, the foolish neighbors say;
The first-fruits, saith the Preacher, the Lord hath taken;
But this was the old tree's late branch wrenched away,
Grieving the sapless limbs, the shorn and shaken.

444 *Parting, Without a Sequel*

SHE has finished and sealed the letter
At last, which he so richly has deserved,

With characters venomous and hatefully curved,
And nothing could be better.

But even as she gave it
Saying to the blue-capped functioner of doom,
'Into his hands,' she hoped the leering groom
Might somewhere lose and leave it.

Then all the blood
Forsook the face. She was too pale for tears,
Observing the ruin of her younger years.
She went and stood

Under her father's vaunting oak
Who kept his peace in wind and sun, and glistened
Stoical in the rain; to whom she listened
If he spoke.

And now the agitation of the rain
Rasped his sere leaves, and he talked low and gentle
Reproaching the wan daughter by the lintel;
Ceasing and beginning again.

Away went the messenger's bicycle,
His serpent's track went up the hill forever,
And all the time she stood there hot as fever
And cold as any icicle.

445   *Two in August*

T WO that could not have lived their single lives
As can some husbands and wives

Did something strange: they tensed their vocal cords
And attacked each other with silences and words
Like catapulted stones and arrowed knives.

Dawn was not yet; night is for loving or sleeping,
Sweet dreams or safekeeping;
Yet he of the wide brows that were used to laurel
And she, the famed for gentleness, must quarrel,
Furious both of them, and scared, and weeping.

How sleepers groan, twitch, wake to such a mood
Is not well understood,
Nor why two entities grown almost one
Should rend and murder trying to get undone,
With individual tigers in their blood.

She in terror fled from the marriage chamber
Circuiting the dark rooms like a string of amber
Round and round and back,
And would not light one lamp against the black,
And heard the clock that clanged: Remember, Remember.

And he must tread barefooted the dim lawn,
Soon he was up and gone;
High in the trees the night-mastered birds were crying
With fear upon their tongues, no singing nor flying
Which are their lovely attitudes by dawn.

Whether those bird-cries were of heaven or hell
There is no way to tell;
In the long ditch of darkness the man walked
Under the hackberry trees where the birds talked
With words too sad and strange to syllable.

JOHN CROWE RANSOM

446   *Antique Harvesters*

(Scene: Of the Mississippi the bank sinister, and of the Ohio the bank sinister.)

TAWNY are the leaves turned but they still hold,
And it is harvest; what shall this land produce?
A meager hill of kernels, a runnel of juice;
Declension looks from our land, it is old.
Therefore let us assemble, dry, grey, spare,
And mild as yellow air.

'I hear the croak of a raven's funeral wing.'
The young men would be joying in the song
Of passionate birds; their memories are not long.
What is it thus rehearsed in sable? 'Nothing.'
Trust not but the old endure, and shall be older
Than the scornful beholder.

We pluck the spindling ears and gather the corn.
One spot has special yield? 'On this spot stood
Heroes and drenched it with their only blood.'
And talk meets talk, as echoes from the horn
Of the hunter—echoes are the old men's arts,
Ample are the chambers of their hearts.

Here come the hunters, keepers of a rite;
The horn, the hounds, the lank mares coursing by
Straddled with archetypes of chivalry;
And the fox, lovely ritualist, in flight
Offering his unearthly ghost to quarry;
And the fields, themselves to harry.

853

Resume, harvesters. The treasure is full bronze
Which you will garner for the Lady, and the moon
Could tinge it no yellower than does this noon;
But grey will quench it shortly—the field, men, stones.
Pluck fast, dreamers; prove as you amble slowly
Not less than men, not wholly.

Bare the .arm, dainty youths, bend the knees
Under bronze burdens. And by an autumn tone
As by a grey, as by a green, you will have known
Your famous Lady's image; for so have these;
And if one say that easily will your hands
More prosper in other lands,

Angry as wasp-music be your cry then:
'Forsake the Proud Lady, of the heart of fire,
The look of snow, to the praise of a dwindled choir,
Song of degenerate specters that were men?
The sons of the fathers shall keep her, worthy of
What these have done in love.'

True, it is said of our Lady, she ageth.
But see, if you peep shrewdly, she hath not stooped;
Take no thought of her servitors that have drooped,
For we are nothing; and if one talk of death—
Why, the ribs of the earth subsist frail as a breath
If but God wearieth.

447　*Man Without Sense of Direction*

TELL this to ladies: how a hero man
Assail a thick and scandalous giant

JOHN CROWE RANSOM

Who casts true shadow in the sun,
And die, but play no truant.

This is more horrible: that the darling egg
Of the chosen people hatch a creature
Of noblest mind and powerful leg
Who cannot fathom nor perform his nature.

The larks' tongues are never stilled
Where the pale spread straw of sunlight lies.
Then what invidious gods have willed
Him to be seized so otherwise?

Birds of the field and beasts of the stable
Are swollen with rapture and make uncouth
Demonstration of joy, which is a babble
Offending the ear of the fervorless youth.

Love—is it the cause? the proud shamed spirit?
Love has slain some whom it possessed,
But his was requited beyond his merit
And won him in bridal the loveliest.

Yet scarcely he issues from the warm chamber,
Flushed with her passion, when cold as dead
Once more he walks where waves past number
Of sorrow buffet his curse-hung head.

Whether by street, or in field full of honey,
Attended by clouds of the creatures of air
Or shouldering the city's companioning many,
His doom is on him; and how can he care

JOHN CROWE RANSOM

For the shapes that would fiddle upon his senses,
Wings and faces and mists that move,
Words, sunlight, the blue air which rinses
The pure pale head which he must love?

And he writhes like an antique man of bronze
That is beaten by furies visible,
Yet he is punished not knowing his sins
And for his innocence walks in hell.

He flails his arms, he moves his lips:
'Rage have I none, cause, time, nor country—
Yet I have traveled land and ships
And knelt my seasons in the chantry.'

So he stands muttering; and rushes
Back to the tender thing in his charge
With clamoring tongue and taste of ashes
And a small passion to feign large.

But let his cold lips be her omen,
She shall not kiss that harried one
To peace, as men are served by women
Who comfort them in darkness and in sun.

448   *The Equilibrists*

FULL of her long white arms and milky skin
He had a thousand times remembered sin.
Alone in the press of people traveled he,
Minding her jacinth, and myrrh, and ivory.

JOHN CROWE RANSOM

Mouth he remembered: the quaint orifice
From which came heat that flamed upon the kiss,
Till cold words came down spiral from the head,
Grey doves from the officious tower illsped.

Body: it was a white field ready for love,
On her body's field, with the gaunt tower above,
The lilies grew, beseeching him to take,
If he would pluck and wear them, bruise and break.

Eyes talking: Never mind the cruel words,
Embrace my flowers, but not embrace the swords.
But what they said, the doves came straightway flying
And unsaid: Honor, Honor, they came crying.

Importunate her doves. Too pure, too wise,
Clambering on his shoulder, saying, Arise,
Leave me now, and never let us meet,
Eternal distance now command thy feet.

Predicament indeed, which thus discovers
Honor among thieves, Honor between lovers.
O such a little word is Honor, they feel!
But the grey word is between them cold as steel.

At length I saw these lovers fully were come
Into their torture of equilibrium;
Dreadfully had forsworn each other, and yet
They were bound each to each, and they did not forget.

And rigid as two painful stars, and twirled
About the clustered night their prison world,
They burned with fierce love always to come near,
But Honor beat them back and kept them clear.

JOHN CROWE RANSOM

Ah, the strict lovers, they are ruined now!
I cried in anger. But with puddled brow
Devising for those gibbeted and brave
Came I descanting: Man, what would you have?

For spin your period out, and draw your breath,
A kinder saeculum begins with Death.
Would you ascend to Heaven and bodiless dwell?
Or take your bodies honorless to Hell?

In Heaven you have heard no marriage is,
No white flesh tinder to your lecheries,
Your male and female tissue sweetly shaped
Sublimed away, and furious blood escaped.

Great lovers lie in Hell, the stubborn ones
Infatuate of the flesh upon the bones;
Stuprate, they rend each other when they kiss,
The pieces kiss again, no end to this.

But still I watched them spinning, orbited nice.
Their flames were not more radiant than their ice.
I dug in the quiet earth and wrought the tomb
And made these lines to memorize their doom:—

Epitaph

Equilibrists lie here; stranger, tread light;
Close, but untouching in each other's sight;
Mouldered the lips and ashy the tall skull,
Let them lie perilous and beautiful.

449   *Prelude to an Evening*

Do not enforce the tired wolf
Dragging his infected wound homeward
To sit tonight with the warm children
Naming the pretty kings of France.

The images of the invaded mind
Being as monsters in the dreams
Of your most brief enchanted headful,
Suppose a miracle of confusion:

That dreamed and undreamt become each other
And mix the night and day of your mind;
And it does not matter your twice crying
From mouth unbeautied against the pillow

To avert the gun of the swarthy soldier,
For cry, cock-crow, or the iron bell
Can crack the sleep-sense of outrage,
Annihilate phantoms who were nothing.

But now, by our perverse supposal,
There is a drift of fog on your mornings;
You in your peignoir, dainty at your orange-cup,
Feel poising round the sunny room

Invisible evil, deprived and bold.
All day the clock will metronome
Your gallant fear; the needles clicking,
The heels detonating the stair's cavern.

Freshening the water in the blue bowls
For the buckberries with not all your love,
You shall be listening for the low wind,
The warning sibilance of pines.

You like a waning moon, and I accusing
Our too banded Eumenides,
You shall make Noes but wanderingly,
Smoothing the heads of the hungry children.

450 *Painted Head*

BY dark severance the apparition head
Smiles from the air a capital on no
Column or a Platonic perhaps head
On a canvas sky depending from nothing;

Stirs up an old illusion of grandeur
By tickling the instinct of heads to be
Absolute and to try decapitation
And to play truant from the body bush;

But too happy and beautiful for those sorts
Of head (homekeeping heads are happiest)
Discovers maybe thirty unwidowed years
Of not dishonoring the faithful stem;

Is nameless and has authored for the evil
Historian headhunters neither book

JOHN CROWE RANSOM

Nor state and is therefore distinct from tart
Heads with crowns and guilty gallery heads;

So that the extravagant device of art
Unhousing by abstraction this once head
Was capital irony by a loving hand
That knew the no treason of a head like this;

Makes repentance in an unlovely head
For having vinegarly traduced the flesh
Till, the hurt flesh recusing, the hard egg
Is shrunken to its own deathlike surface;

And an image thus. The body bears the head
(So hardly one they terribly are two)
Feeds and obeys and unto please what end?
Not to the glory of tyrant head but to

The increase of body. Beauty is of body.
The flesh contouring shallowly on a head
Is a rock-garden needing body's love
And best bodiness to colorify

The big blue birds sitting and sea-shell flats
And caves, and on the iron acropolis
To spread the hyacinthine hair and rear
The olive garden for the nightingales.

451   *'Music I heard with you'*

MUSIC I heard with you was more than music,
And bread I broke with you was more than bread;
Now that I am without you, all is desolate;
All that was once so beautiful is dead.

Your hands once touched this table and this silver,
And I have seen your fingers hold this glass.
These things do not remember you, belovèd,—
And yet your touch upon them will not pass.

For it was in my heart you moved among them,
And blessed them with your hands and with your eyes;
And in my heart they will remember always,—
They knew you once, O beautiful and wise.

452   *Morning Song of Senlin*

IT is morning, Senlin says, and in the morning
When the light drips through the shutters like the dew,
I arise, I face the sunrise,
And do the things my fathers learned to do.
Stars in the purple dusk above the rooftops
Pale in a saffron mist and seem to die,
And I myself on a swiftly tilting planet
Stand before a glass and tie my tie.

CONRAD AIKEN

Vine leaves tap my window,
Dew-drops sing to the garden stones,
The robin chirps in the chinaberry tree
Repeating three clear tones.

It is morning. I stand by the mirror
And tie my tie once more.
While waves far off in a pale rose twilight
Crash on a white sand shore.
I stand by a mirror and comb my hair:
How small and white my face!—
The green earth tilts through a sphere of air
And bathes in a flame of space.

There are houses hanging above the stars
And stars hung under a sea . . .
And a sun far off in a shell of silence
Dapples my walls for me . . .

It is morning, Senlin says, and in the morning
Should I not pause in the light to remember god?
Upright and firm I stand on a star unstable,
He is immense and lonely as a cloud.
I will dedicate this moment before my mirror
To him alone, for him I will comb my hair.
Accept these humble offerings, cloud of silence!
I will think of you as I descend the stair.

Vine leaves tap my window,
The snail-track shines on the stones,
Dew-drops flash from the chinaberry tree
Repeating two clear tones.

CONRAD AIKEN

It is morning, I awake from a bed of silence,
Shining I rise from the starless waters of sleep.
The walls are about me still as in the evening,
I am the same, and the same name still I keep.

The earth revolves with me, yet makes no motion,
The stars pale silently in a coral sky.
In a whistling void I stand before my mirror,
Unconcerned, and tie my tie.

There are horses neighing on far-off hills
Tossing their long white manes,
And mountains flash in the rose-white dusk,
Their shoulders black with rains . . .
It is morning. I stand by the mirror
And surprise my soul once more;
The blue air rushes above my ceiling,
There are suns beneath my floor . . .

. . . It is morning, Senlin says, I ascend from darkness
And depart on the winds of space for I know not where,
My watch is wound, a key is in my pocket,
And the sky is darkened as I descend the stair.
There are shadows across the windows, clouds in heaven,
And a god among the stars; and I will go
Thinking of him as I might think of daybreak
And humming a tune I know . . .

Vine-leaves tap at the window,
Dew-drops sing to the garden stones,
The robin chirps in the chinaberry tree
Repeating three clear tones.

453   *'This is the shape of the leaf'*

THIS is the shape of the leaf, and this of the flower,
And this the pale bole of the tree
Which watches its bough in a pool of unwavering water
In a land we never shall see.

The thrush on the bough is silent, the dew falls softly,
In the evening is hardly a sound.
And the three beautiful pilgrims who come here together
Touch lightly the dust of the ground,

Touch it with feet that trouble the dust but as wings do,
Come shyly together, are still,
Like dancers who wait, in a pause of the music, for music
The exquisite silence to fill.

This is the thought of the first, and this of the second,
And this the grave thought of the third:
'Linger we thus for a moment, palely expectant,
And silence will end, and the bird

'Sing the pure phrase, sweet phrase, clear phrase in the
      twilight
To fill the blue bell of the world;
And we, who on music so leaflike have drifted together,
Leaflike apart shall be whirled

'Into what but the beauty of silence, silence forever?' . . .
. . . This is the shape of the tree,
And the flower, and the leaf, and the three pale beautiful
      pilgrims;
This is what you are to me.

454 *Preludes*

I

WINTER for a moment takes the mind; the snow
Falls past the arclight; icicles guard a wall;
The wind moans through a crack in the window;
A keen sparkle of frost is on the sill.
Only for a moment; as spring too might engage it,
With a single crocus in the loam, or a pair of birds;
Or summer with hot grass; or autumn with a yellow leaf.
Winter is there, outside, is here in me:
Drapes the planets with snow, deepens the ice on the moon,
Darkens the darkness that was already darkness.
The mind too has its snows, its slippery paths,
Walls bayonetted with ice, leaves ice-encased.
Here is the in-drawn room, to which you return
When the wind blows from Arcturus: here is the fire
At which you warm your hands and glaze your eyes;
The piano, on which you touch the cold treble;
Five notes like breaking icicles; and then silence.

The alarm-clock ticks, the pulse keeps time with it,
Night and the mind are full of sounds. I walk
From the fire-place, with its imaginary fire,
To the window, with its imaginary view.
Darkness, and snow ticking the window: silence,
And the knocking of chains on a motor-car, the tolling
Of a bronze bell, dedicated to Christ.
And then the uprush of angelic wings, the beating
Of wings demonic, from the abyss of the mind:
The darkness filled with a feathery whistling, wings

866

CONRAD AIKEN

Numberless as the flakes of angelic snow,
The deep void swarming with wings and sound of wings,
The winnowing of chaos, the aliveness
Of depth and depth and depth dedicated to death.

Here are the bickerings of the inconsequential,
The chatterings of the ridiculous, the iterations
Of the meaningless. Memory, like a juggler,
Tosses its colored balls into the light, and again
Receives them into darkness. Here is the absurd,
Grinning like an idiot, and the omnivorous quotidian,
Which will have its day. A handful of coins,
Tickets, items from the news, a soiled handkerchief,
A letter to be answered, notice of a telephone call,
The petal of a flower in a volume of Shakspere,
The program of a concert. The photograph, too,
Propped on the mantel, and beneath it a dry rosebud;
The laundry bill, matches, an ash-tray, Utamaro's
Pearl-fishers. And the rug, on which are still the crumbs
Of yesterday's feast. These are the void, the night,
And the angelic wings that make it sound.

What is the flower? It is not a sigh of color,
Suspiration of purple, sibilation of saffron,
Nor aureate exhalation from the tomb.
Yet it is these because you think of these,
An emanation of emanations, fragile
As light, or glisten, or gleam, or coruscation,
Creature of brightness, and as brightness brief.
What is the frost? It is not the sparkle of death,
The flash of time's wing, seeds of eternity;
Yet it is these because you think of these.
And you, because you think of these, are both

Frost and flower, the bright ambiguous syllable
Of which the meaning is both no and yes.
Here is the tragic, the distorting mirror
In which your gesture becomes grandiose;
Tears form and fall from your magnificent eyes,
The brow is noble, and the mouth is God's.
Here is the God who seeks his mother, Chaos,—
Confusion seeking solution, and life seeking death.
Here is the rose that woos the icicle; the icicle
That woos the rose. Here is the silence of silences
Which dreams of becoming a sound, and the sound
Which will perfect itself in silence. And all
These things are only the uprush from the void,
The wings angelic and demonic, the sound of the abyss
Dedicated to death. And this is you.

XIX

Watch long enough, and you will see the leaf
Fall from the bough. Without a sound it falls:
And soundless meets the grass . . . And so you have
A bare bough, and a dead leaf in dead grass.
Something has come and gone. And that is all.

But what were all the tumults in this action?
What wars of atoms in the twig, what ruins,
Fiery and disastrous, in the leaf?
Timeless the tumult was, but gave no sign.
Only, the leaf fell, and the bough is bare.

This is the world: there is no more than this.
The unseen and disastrous prelude, shaking
The trivial act from the terrific action.
Speak: and the ghosts of change, past and to come,
Throng the brief word. The maelstrom has us all.

XXVIII

The time has come, the clock says time has come.
Here in the mid-waste of my life I pause,
The hour is in my hand, and in my heart
Miscellany of shards and shreds. The clock
Ticks its iambics, and the heart its spondees,
Time has come, time has come and gone,
Winter has taken its toll, summer its harvest,
Spring has brought and taken away its illusion.

What is time, the clock says what is time,
Never the past, never the future, always the now,
What is time, the seed says it is all
Fertility turned deep by the foot of the plow.

The hour has added to the spirit's peace,
Seed has added to minute, and world to flower,
Tears have flowed to the heart till it is rotted,
Hands have worn the hand till it is hard.
Why, I have seen the all, have seen the nothing,
Have heard the monosyllable of the tomb,
Have buried stars and resurrected them,
And watched the shadow moving across a wall.

What is time, the stitch says what is time,
Always the future, never the past, never the now;
Only the seam foresees the future, but even
The longest seam will feel the foot of the plow.

Stand, take off the garments time has lent you,
The watch, the coins, the handkerchief, the shoes,
Your soul, also, and wrap it in a thought;

Display your shards and shreds on the windowsill
Among geraniums and aspidistras,
The week before, and the week before the last,
Ridiculous chronicle, taste, touch, and smell.

What is time, the heart says what is time.
The heart is ticking on the mantelpiece.
The heart says all is past and nothing future.
The heart says heart will never cease.

XXXIII

Then came I to the shoreless shore of silence,
Where never summer was nor shade of tree,
Nor sound of water, nor sweet light of sun,
But only nothing and the shore of nothing,
Above, below, around, and in my heart:

Where day was not, not night, nor space, nor time,
Where no bird sang, save him of memory,
Nor footstep marked upon the marl, to guide
My halting footstep; and I turned for terror,
Seeking in vain the Pole Star of my thought;

Where it was blown among the shapeless clouds,
And gone as soon as seen, and scarce recalled,
Its image lost and I directionless;
Alone upon the brown sad edge of chaos,
In the wan evening that was evening always;

Then closed my eyes upon the sea of nothing
While memory brought back a sea more bright,
With long, long waves of light, and the swift sun,
And the good trees that bowed upon the wind;
And stood until grown dizzy with that dream;

Seeking in all that joy of things remembered
One image, one the dearest, one most bright,
One face, one star, one daisy, one delight,
One hour with wings most heavenly and swift,
One hand the tenderest upon my heart;

But still no image came, save of that sea,
No tenderer thing than thought of tenderness,
No heart or daisy brighter than the rest;
And only sadness at the bright sea lost,
And mournfulness that all had not been praised.

O lords of chaos, atoms of desire,
Whirlwind of fruitfulness, destruction's seed,
Hear now upon the void my late delight,
The quick brief cry of memory, that knows
At the dark's edge how great the darkness is.

XLII

Keep in the heart the journal nature keeps;
Mark down the limp nasturtium leaf with frost;
See that the hawthorn bough is ice-embossed,
And that the snail, in season, has his grief;
Design the winter on the window pane;
Admit pale sun through cobwebs left from autumn;
Remember summer when the flies are stilled;
Remember spring, when the cold spider sleeps.

Such diary, too, set down as this: the heart
Beat twice or thrice this day for no good reason;
For friends and sweethearts dead before their season;
For wisdom come too late, and come to naught.

Put down 'the hand that shakes,' 'the eye that glazes';
The 'step that falters betwixt thence and hence';
Observe that hips and haws burn brightest red
When the North Pole and sun are most apart.

Note that the moon is here, as cold as ever,
With ages on her face, and ice and snow;
Such as the freezing mind alone can know,
When loves and hates are only twigs that shiver.
Add in a postscript that the rain is over,
The wind from southwest backing to the south,
Disasters all forgotten, hurts forgiven;
And that the North Star, altered, shines forever.

Then say: I was a part of nature's plan;
Knew her cold heart, for I was consciousness;
Came first to hate her, and at last to bless;
Believed in her; doubted; believed again.
My love the lichen had such roots as I,—
The snowflake was my father; I return,
After this interval of faith and question,
To nature's heart, in pain, as I began.

455   *The Nameless Ones*

PITY the nameless, and the unknown, where
bitter in heart they wait on the stonebuilt stair,
bend to a wall, forgotten, the freezing wind
no bitterer than the suburbs of the mind;

who from an iron porch lift sightless eyes,
a moment, hopeless, to inflaming skies;

shrink from the light as quickly as from pain,
twist round a corner, bend to the wall again;

are to be seen leaning against a rail
by ornamental waters where toy yachts sail;
glide down the granite steps, touch foot to float,
hate, and desire, the sunlight on the boat;

explore a sullen alley where ash-cans wait,
symbols of waste and want, at every gate;
emerge in sun to mingle with the crowd,
themselves most silent where the world most loud;

anonymous, furtive, shadows in shadow hidden;
who lurk at the garden's edge like guests unbidden;
stare through the leaves with hate, yet wait to listen
as bandstand music begins to rise and glisten;

the fierce, the solitary, divine of heart,
passionate, present, yet godlike and apart;
who, in the midst of traffic, see a vision;
and, on a park bench, come to a last decision.

456   *South End*

THE BENCHES are broken, the grassplots brown and
     bare,
the laurels dejected, in this neglected square.
Dogs couple undisturbed. The roots of trees
heave up the bricks in the sidewalk as they please.

Nobody collects the papers from the grass,
nor the dead matches, nor the broken glass.
The elms are old and shabby; the houses, around,
stare lazily through paintless shutters at forgotten ground.

Out of the dusty fountain, with the dust,
the leaves fly up like birds on a sudden gust.
The leaves fly up like birds, and the papers flap,
or round the legs of benches wrap and unwrap.

Here, for the benefit of some secret sense,
warm-autumn-afternoon finds permanence.
No one will hurry, or wait too long, or die:
all is serenity, under a serene sky.

Dignity shines in old brick and old dirt,
in elms and houses now hurt beyond all hurt.
A broken square, where little lives or moves;
these are the city's earliest and tenderest loves.

457   *Three Star Final*

WAIT here, and I'll be back, though the hours divide,
and the city streets, perplexed, perverse, delay
my hurrying footsteps, and the clocks deride
with grinning faces from the long wall of day:

wait here, beneath your narrow scrip of sky,
reading the headlines, while the snowflakes touch
on scarce-dried ink the news that thousands die,
die, and are not remembered overmuch:

yes, the unnumbered dead, whom none esteemed,
our other selves, too late or little loved;
now in the dust, proud eyes unknown, undreamed,
those who begged pity while we stood unmoved.

How can we patch our world up, now it's broken?
You, with your guilty heart, wait here and think,
while I strive back through lies and truths unspoken,
and, in the suburbs, the sunset snow turns pink:

you, in this dead-end street, which now we leave
for a more expansive, a more expensive, view;
snow falling, on a disastrous Christmas Eve,
and neon death at the end of the Avenue.

458   *Shaemus*

WE will go no more to Shaemus, at the Nip,
for sly innuendo and an Oporto Flip,
the rough but tender voice, the wide-mouthed grin,
the steady-unsteady hand that poured the gin:

memory, that flew back years to find a name,
found it, and fetched it up, still just the same;
the shaky footsteps, and then the shaky kidding:
you, the big business man, outbid, outbidding,

the mystery man, the man of deep affairs,
highbrow, and playboy, and friend of millionaires:
and you, the lovers, whose love was in your faces—
there you were, back once more—and still the traces!—

Yes, still the traces of that love he loved,
and reexamined, but as if unmoved;
the names fished up from time, or Singapore,
joined and repeated on his bar once more;

as if no let or hindrance were permitted;
as if both time and space could be outwitted;
endurance noted—in a protocol—
and then embalmed, of course, in alcohol.

And now himself, the immortal, lightly gone,
as if stepped out for a quick one—who had none.
And dead, his room inspected by his friends,
to find a will, adjust the odds and ends;

and there, the fifteen suits, the malacca cane,
the hats, and spats: in which he roved again,
far from the furnished room, the sacred bar,
immortal dandy, towards an immortal star.

459   *Nuit Blanche: North End*

RED and green neon lights, the jazz hysteria,
for all-night movie and all-night cafeteria;
you feed all night in one, and sleep in the other,
and dream that a strip-tease queen was your sweetheart's
    mother.

A nickel for a coffee-half, a dime for a seat;
the blondes and the guns are streamlined and complete;
streamlined, dreamlined, with wide open cactus spaces
between the four-foot teeth in the ten-foot faces.

CONRAD AIKEN

Hot trumpets and hot trombones for a soft-sole shuffle!
Sailors, bring in your tattoos, park your duffel!
There's a green-tailed blue-eyed mermaid stinging my
    shoulder,
and I've got to pass out before I'm a minute older.

Sawdust, spittoon, no smoking, please excuse—
afloat or ashore we mind our p's and q's.
Longhorn stand back, shorthorn stand close, is all
the circular eye makes out on the circular wall.

And still the red neon lights go round and around,
the red mouth opens and drinks with never a sound,—
red on the Square, red on the jingling Palace,
where all night long you rumbaed and drank with Alice—

red on the tattoo artist's sign, that shakes
anchors and flags together, ships and snakes,
roses, and a pink Venus, on a shell,
la la, all dancing fast in a neon hell—

while round and around the red beads wink, and faster
empty and open, pour and fill, disaster:
the red mouth opens and drinks, opens and winks,
drinks down the hotel wall, the drugstore, drinks

the Square, the statue, the bright red roofs of cabs,
and the cleaning-women, who arise with pails and swabs:
then stains the dawn, who, over the subway station,
steals in, with Sandals gray, but no elation.

460   *Speaking of Poetry*

THE ceremony must be found
that will wed Desdemona to the huge Moor.

It is not enough—
to win the approval of the Senator
or to outwit his disapproval; honest Iago
can manage that: it is not enough. For then,
though she may pant again in his black arms
(his weight resilient as a Barbary stallion's)
she will be found
when the ambassadors of the Venetian state arrive
again smothered. These things have not been changed,
not in three hundred years.

(Tupping is still tupping
though that particular word is obsolete.
Naturally, the ritual would not be in Latin.)

For though Othello had his blood from kings
his ancestry was barbarous, his ways African,
his speech uncouth. It must be remembered
that though he valued an embroidery—
three mulberries proper on a silk like silver—
it was not for the subtlety of the stitches,
but for the magic in it. Whereas, Desdemona

878

once contrived to imitate in needlework
her father's shield, and plucked it out
three times, to begin again, each time
with diminished colors. This is a small point
but indicative.

Desdemona was small and fair,
delicate as a grasshopper
at the tag-end of summer: a Venetian
to her noble finger tips.

O, it is not enough
that they should meet, naked, at dead of night
in a small inn on a dark canal. Procurers
less expert than Iago can arrange as much.

The ceremony must be found

Traditional, with all its symbols
ancient as the metaphors in dreams;
strange, with never before heard music; continuous
until the torches deaden at the bedroom door.

461   *The Return*

(*After a phrase by Giorgio de Chirico*)

NIGHT and we heard heavy and cadenced hoofbeats
Of troops departing: the last cohorts left
By the North Gate. That night some listened late
Leaning their eyelids toward Septentrion.

JOHN PEALE BISHOP

Morning flared and the young tore down the trophies
And warring ornaments: arches were strong
And in the sun but stone; no longer conquests
Circled our columns; all our state was down

In fragments. In the dust, old men with tufted
Eyebrows whiter than sunbaked faces gulped
As it fell. But they no more than we remembered
The old sea-fights, the soldiers' names and sculptors'.

We did not know the end was coming: nor why
It came; only that long before the end
Were many wanted to die. Then vultures starved
And sailed more slowly in the sky.

We still had taxes. Salt was high. The soldiers
Gone. Now there was much drinking and lewd
Houses all night loud with riot. But only
For a time. Soon the taverns had no roofs.

Strangely it was the young the almost boys
Who first abandoned hope; the old still lived
A little, at last a little lived in eyes.
It was the young whose child did not survive.

Some slept beneath the simulacra, until
The gods' faces froze. Then was fear.
Some had response in dreams, but morning restored
Interrogation. Then O then, O ruins!

Temples of Neptune invaded by the sea
And dolphins streaked like streams sportive
As sunlight rode and over the rushing floors
The sea unfurled and what was blue raced silver.

JOHN PEALE BISHOP

The Hours

In the real dark night of the soul it is always three o'clock in the morning.—F. SCOTT FITZGERALD

I

ALL day, knowing you dead,
I have sat in this long-windowed room,
Looking upon the sea and, dismayed
By mortal sadness, though without thought to resume
Those hours which you and I have known—
Hours when youth like an insurgent sun
Showered ambition on an aimless air,
Hours foreboding disillusion,
Hours which now there is none to share.
Since you are dead, I leave them all alone.

II

A day like any day. Though any day now
We expect death. The sky is overcast,
And shuddering cold as snow the shoreward blast.
And in the marsh, like a sea astray, now
Waters brim. This is the moment when the sea
Being most full of motion seems motionless.
Land and sea are merged. The marsh is gone.
And my distress
Is at the flood. All but the dunes are drowned.
And brimming with memory I have found
All hours we ever knew, but have not found
The key. I cannot find the lost key
To the silver closet you as a wild child hid.

JOHN PEALE BISHOP

III

I think of all you did
And all you might have done, before undone
By death, but for the undoing of despair.
No promise such as yours when like the spring
You came, colors of jonquils in your hair,
Inspired as the wind, when the woods are bare
And every silence is about to sing.

None had such promise then, and none
Your scapegrace wit or your disarming grace;
For you were bold as was Danaë's son,
Conceived like Perseus in a dream of gold.
And there was none when you were young, not one,
So prompt in the reflecting shield to trace
The glittering aspect of a Gorgon age.

Despair no love, no fortune could assuage . . .
Was it a fault in your disastrous blood
That beat from no fortunate god,
The failure of all passion in mid-course?
You shrank from nothing as from solitude,
Lacking the still assurance, and pursued
Beyond the sad excitement by remorse.

Was it that having shaped your stare upon
The severed head of time, upheld and blind,
Upheld by the stained hair,
And seen the blood upon that sightless stare,
You looked and were made one
With the strained horror of those sightless eyes?
You looked, and were not turned to stone.

JOHN PEALE BISHOP

IV

You have outlasted the nocturnal terror,
The head hanging in the hanging mirror,
The hour haunted by a harrowing face.
Now you are drunk at last. And that disgrace
You sought in oblivious dives you have
At last, in the dissolution of the grave.

V

I have lived with you the hour of your humiliation.
I have seen you turn upon the others in the night
And of sad self-loathing
Concealing nothing
Heard you cry: *I am lost. But you are lower!*
And you had that right.
The damned do not so own their damnation.

I have lived with you some hours of the night,
The late hour
When the lights lower,
The later hour
When the lights go out,

When the dissipation of the night is past,
Hour of the outcast and the outworn whore,
That is past three and not yet four—
When the old blackmailer waits beyond the door
And from the gutter with unpitying hands
Demands the same sad guiltiness as before,
The hour of utter destitution
When the soul knows the horror of its loss
And knows the world too poor

For restitution,
        Past three o'clock
And not yet four—
        When not pity, pride,
Or being brave,
Fortune, friendship, forgetfulness of drudgery
Or of drug avails, for all has been tried,
And nothing avails to save
The soul from recognition of its night.

The hour of death is always four o'clock.
It is always four o'clock in the grave.

VI

Having heard the bare word that you had died,
All day I have lingered in this lofty room,
Locked in the light of sea and cloud,
And thought, at cost of sea-hours, to illume
The hours that you and I have known,
Hours death does not condemn, nor love condone.

And I have seen the sea-light set the tide
In salt succession toward the sullen shore
And while the waves lost on the losing sand
Seen shores receding and the sands succumb.

The waste retreats; glimmering shores retrieve
Unproportioned plunges; the dunes restore
Drowned confines to the disputed kingdom—
Desolate mastery, since the dark has come.

The dark has come. I cannot pluck you bays,
Though here the bay grows wild. For fugitive

As surpassed fame the leaves this sea-wind frays.
Why should I promise what I cannot give?

I cannot animate with breath
Syllables in the open mouth of death.
Dark, dark. The shore here has a habit of light.
O dark! I leave you to oblivious night!

EDNA ST. VINCENT MILLAY

b. 1892

463   *Afternoon on a Hill*

I WILL be the gladdest thing
    Under the sun!
I will touch a hundred flowers
    And not pick one.

I will look at cliffs and clouds
    With quiet eyes,
Watch the wind bow down the grass,
    And the grass rise.

And when lights begin to show
    Up from the town,
I will mark which must be mine,
    And then start down!

464   *Passer Mortuus Est*

DEATH devours all lovely things:
  Lesbia with her sparrow
Shares the darkness,—presently
  Every bed is narrow.

Unremembered as old rain
  Dries the sheer libation;
And the little petulant hand
  Is an annotation.

After all, my erstwhile dear,
  My no longer cherished,
Need we say it was not love,
  Just because it perished?

465   *Song of a Second April*

APRIL this year, not otherwise
  Than April of a year ago,
Is full of whispers, full of sighs,
  Of dazzling mud and dingy snow;
  Hepaticas that pleased you so
Are here again, and butterflies.

There rings a hammering all day,
  And shingles lie about the doors;

In orchards near and far away
   The grey wood-pecker taps and bores;
   And men are merry at their chores,
And children earnest at their play.

The larger streams run still and deep,
   Noisy and swift the small brooks run;
Among the mullein stalks the sheep
   Go up the hillside in the sun,
   Pensively,—only you are gone,
You that alone I cared to keep.

466   *Memorial to D.C.*
          (Vassar College, 1918)

O*, LOVELIEST throat of all sweet throats,*
   Where now no more the music is,
With hands that wrote you little notes
   I write you little elegies!

ELEGY

   Let them bury your big eyes
   In the secret earth securely,
   Your thin fingers, and your fair,
   Soft, indefinite-coloured hair,—
   All of these in some way, surely,
   From the secret earth shall rise;
   Not for these I sit and stare,
   Broken and bereft completely:
   Your young flesh that sat so neatly

On your little bones will sweetly
Blossom in the air.

But your voice . . . never the rushing
Of a river underground,
Not the rising of the wind
In the trees before the rain,
Not the woodcock's watery call,
Not the note the white-throat utters,
Not the feet of children pushing
Yellow leaves along the gutters
In the blue and bitter fall,
Shall content my musing mind
For the beauty of that sound
That in no new way at all
Ever will be heard again.

Sweetly through the sappy stalk
Of the vigourous weed,
Holding all it held before,
Cherished by the faithful sun,
On and on eternally
Shall your altered fluid run,
Bud and bloom and go to seed:
But your singing days are done;
But the music of your talk
Never shall the chemistry
Of the secret earth restore.
All your lovely words are spoken.
Once the ivory box is broken,
Beats the golden bird no more.

467 *Recuerdo*

WE were very tired, we were very merry—
We had gone back and forth all night on the ferry.
It was bare and bright, and smelled like a stable—
But we looked into a fire, we leaned across a table,
We lay on a hill-top underneath the moon;
And the whistles kept blowing, and the dawn came soon.

We were very tired, we were very merry—
We had gone back and forth all night on the ferry;
And you ate an apple, and I ate a pear,
From a dozen of each we had bought somewhere;
And the sky went wan, and the wind came cold,
And the sun rose dripping, a bucketful of gold.

We were very tired, we were very merry,
We had gone back and forth all night on the ferry.
We hailed, 'Good-morrow, mother!' to a shawl-covered
     head,
And bought a morning paper, which neither of us read;
And she wept, 'God bless you!' for the apples and the
     pears,
And we gave her all our money but our subway fares.

468 *'Pity me not because the light of day'*

PITY me not because the light of day
At close of day no longer walks the sky;

Pity me not for beauties passed away
From field and thicket as the year goes by;
Pity me not the waning of the moon,
Nor that the ebbing tide goes out to sea,
Nor that a man's desire is hushed so soon,
And you no longer look with love on me.
This have I known always: Love is no more
Than the wide blossom which the wind assails,
Than the great tide that treads the shifting shore,
Strewing fresh wreckage gathered in the gales:
Pity me that the heart is slow to learn
What the swift mind beholds at every turn.

469   *'Love is not all: it is not
meat nor drink'*

LOVE is not all: it is not meat nor drink
Nor slumber nor a roof against the rain;
Nor yet a floating spar to men that sink
And rise and sink and rise and sink again;
Love can not fill the thickened lung with breath,
Nor clean the blood, nor set the fractured bone;
Yet many a man is making friends with death
Even as I speak, for lack of love alone.
It well may be that in a difficult hour,
Pinned down by pain and moaning for release,
Or nagged by want past resolution's power,
I might be driven to sell your love for peace,
Or trade the memory of this night for food.
It well may be. I do not think I would.

470 *The Return*

Earth does not understand her child,
   Who from the loud gregarious town
Returns, depleted and defiled,
   To the still woods, to fling him down.

Earth can not count the sons she bore:
   The wounded lynx, the wounded man
Come trailing blood unto her door;
   She shelters both as best she can.

But she is early up and out,
   To trim the year or strip its bones;
She has no time to stand about
   Talking of him in undertones

Who has no aim but to forget,
   Be left in peace, be lying thus
For days, for years, for centuries yet,
   Unshaven and anonymous;

Who, marked for failure, dulled by grief,
   Has traded in his wife and friend
For this warm ledge, this alder leaf:
   Comfort that does not comprehend.

ARCHIBALD MACLEISH

471 *The Too-Late Born*

WE too, we too, descending once again
The hills of our own land, we too have heard
Far off—Ah, que ce cor a longue haleine—
The horn of Roland in the passages of Spain,
The first, the second blast, the failing third,
And with the third turned back and climbed once more
The steep road southward, and heard faint the sound
Of swords, of horses, the disastrous war,
And crossed the dark defile at last, and found
At Roncevaux upon the darkening plain
The dead against the dead and on the silent ground
The silent slain—

472 *The End of the World*

QUITE unexpectedly as Vasserot
The armless ambidextrian was lighting
A match between his great and second toe
And Ralph the lion was engaged in biting
The neck of Madame Sossman while the drum
Pointed, and Teeny was about to cough
In waltz-time swinging Jocko by the thumb—
Quite unexpectedly the top blew off:

And there, there overhead, there, there, hung over
Those thousands of white faces, those dazed eyes,
There in the starless dark the poise, the hover,
There with vast wings across the canceled skies,
There in the sudden blackness the black pall
Of nothing, nothing, nothing—nothing at all.

473   *Ars Poetica*

A POEM should be palpable and mute
As a globed fruit

Dumb
As old medallions to the thumb

Silent as the sleeve-worn stone
Of casement ledges where the moss has grown—

A poem should be wordless
As the flight of birds

A poem should be motionless in time
As the moon climbs

Leaving, as the moon releases
Twig by twig the night-entangled trees,

Leaving, as the moon behind the winter leaves,
Memory by memory the mind—

A poem should be motionless in time
As the moon climbs

A poem should be equal to:
Not true

For all the history of grief
An empty doorway and a maple leaf

For love
The leaning grasses and two lights above the sea—

A poem should not mean
But be

474 *You, Andrew Marvell*

And here face down beneath the sun
And here upon earth's noonward height
To feel the always coming on
The always rising of the night

To feel creep up the curving east
The earthy chill of dusk and slow
Upon those under lands the vast
And ever climbing shadow grow

And strange at Ecbatan the trees
Take leaf by leaf the evening strange
The flooding dark about their knees
The mountains over Persia change

And now at Kermanshah the gate
Dark empty and the withered grass
And through the twilight now the late
Few travelers in the westward pass

ARCHIBALD MACLEISH

And Baghdad darken and the bridge
Across the silent river gone
And through Arabia the edge
Of evening widen and steal on

And deepen on Palmyra's street
The wheel rut in the ruined stone
And Lebanon fade out and Crete
High through the clouds and overblown

And over Sicily the air
Still flashing with the landward gulls
And loom and slowly disappear
The sails above the shadowy hulls

And Spain go under and the shore
Of Africa the gilded sand
And evening vanish and no more
The low pale light across that land

Nor now the long light on the sea

And here face downward in the sun
To feel how swift how secretly
The shadow of the night comes on . . .

475   *American Letter*
          for Gerald Murphy

THE WIND is east but the hot weather continues,
Blue and no clouds, the sound of the leaves thin,

Dry like the rustling of paper, scored across
With the slate-shrill screech of the locusts.

                          The tossing of
Pines is the low sound. In the wind's running
The wild carrots smell of the burning sun.
Why should I think of the dolphins at Capo di Mele?
Why should I see in my mind the taut sail
And the hill over St.-Tropez and your hand on the tiller?
Why should my heart be troubled with palms still?
I am neither a sold boy nor a Chinese official
Sent to sicken in Pa for some Lo-Yang dish.
This is my own land, my sky, my mountain:
This—not the humming pines and the surf and the sound
At the Ferme Blanche, nor Port Cros in the dusk and the
      harbor
Floating the motionless ship and the sea-drowned star.
I am neither Po Chü-i nor another after
Far from home, in a strange land, daft
For the talk of his own sort and the taste of his lettuces.
This land is my native land. And yet
I am sick for home for the red roofs and the olives,
And the foreign words and the smell of the sea fall.
How can a wise man have two countries?
How can a man have the earth and the wind and want
A land far off, alien, smelling of palm-trees
And the yellow gorse at noon in the long calms?

It is a strange thing—to be an American.
Neither an old house it is with the air
Tasting of hung herbs and the sun returning
Year after year to the same door and the churn
Making the same sound in the cool of the kitchen
Mother to son's wife, and the place to sit

ARCHIBALD MACLEISH

Marked in the dusk by the worn stone at the wellhead—
That—nor the eyes like each other's eyes and the skull
Shaped to the same fault and the hands' sameness.
Neither a place it is nor a blood name.
America is West and the wind blowing
America is a great word and the snow,
A way, a white bird, the rain falling,
A shining thing in the mind and the gulls' call.
America is neither a land nor a people,
A word's shape it is, a wind's sweep—
America is alone: many together,
Many of one mouth, of one breath,
Dressed as one—and none brothers among them:
Only the taught speech and the aped tongue.
America is alone and the gulls calling.
It is a strange thing to be an American.
It is strange to live on the high world in the stare
Of the naked sun and the stars as our bones live.
Men in the old lands housed by their rivers.
They built their towns in the vales in the earth's shelter.
We first inhabit the world. We dwell
On the half earth, on the open curve of a continent.
Sea is divided from sea by the day-fall. The dawn
Rides the low east with us many hours;
First are the capes, then are the shorelands, now
The blue Appalachians faint at the day rise;
The willows shudder with light on the long Ohio:
The Lakes scatter the low sun: the prairies
Slide out of dark: in the eddy of clean air
The smoke goes up from the high plains of Wyoming:
The steep Sierras arise: the struck foam
Flames at the wind's heel on the far Pacific.

Already the noon leans to the eastern cliff: ·
The elms darken the door and the dust-heavy lilacs.

It is strange to sleep in the bare stars and to die
On an open land where few bury before us:
(From the new earth the dead return no more.)
It is strange to be born of no race and no people.
In the old lands they are many together. They keep
The wise past and the words spoken in common.
They remember the dead with their hands, their mouths
    dumb.
They answer each other with two words in their meeting.
They live together in small things. They eat
The same dish, their drink is the same and their proverbs.
Their youth is like. They are like in their ways of love.
They are many men. There are always others beside them.
Here it is one man and another and wide
On the darkening hills the faint smoke of the houses.
Here it is one man and the wind in the boughs.

Therefore our hearts are sick for the south water.
The smell of the gorse comes back to our night thought.
We are sick at heart for the red roofs and the olives;
We are sick at heart for the voice and the foot fall . . .

Therefore we will not go though the sea call us.

This, this is our land, this is our people,
This that is neither a land nor a race. We must reap
The wind here in the grass for our soul's harvest:
Here we must eat our salt or our bones starve.
Here we must live or live only as shadows.
This is our race, we that have none, that have had

Neither the old walls nor the voices around us,
This is our land, this is our ancient ground—
The raw earth, the mixed bloods and the strangers,
The different eyes, the wind, and the heart's change.
These we will not leave though the old call us.
This is our country-earth, our blood, our kind.
Here we will live our years till the earth blind us—
The wind blows from the east. The leaves fall.
Far off in the pines a jay rises.
The wind smells of haze and the wild ripe apples.

I think of the masts at Cette and the sweet rain.

476   *Empire Builders*

The Museum Attendant:

This is *The Making of America in Five Panels:*

This is Mister Harriman making America:
Mister-Harriman-is-buying-the-Union-Pacific-at-
     Seventy:
The Sante Fe is shining on his hair:

This is Commodore Vanderbilt making America:
Mister-Vanderbilt-is-eliminating-the-short-interest-in-
     Hudson:
Observe the carving on the rocking chair:

This is J. P. Morgan making America:
(The Tennessee Coal is behind to the left of the Steel
     Company:)
Those in mauve are braces he is wearing:

This is Mister Mellon making America:
Mister-Mellon-is-represented-as-a-symbolical-figure-in-
    aluminum-
Strewing-bank-stocks-on-a-burnished-stair:

This is the Bruce is the Barton making America:
Mister-Barton-is-selling-us-Doctor's-Deliciousest-
    Dentifrice:
This is he in beige with the canary:

You have just beheld the Makers making America:
This is *The Making of America in Five Panels:*
America lies to the west-southwest of the Switch-Tower:
There is nothing to see of America but land:

The Original Document
under the Panel Paint:
    'To Thos. Jefferson Esq. his obd't serv't
    M. Lewis: captain: detached:
                    Sir:

Having in mind your repeated commands in this matter:
And the worst half of it done and the streams mapped:

And we here on the back of this beach beholding the
Other ocean—two years gone and the cold

Breaking with rain for the third spring since St. Louis:
The crows at the fishbones on the frozen dunes:

The first cranes going over from south north:
And the river down by a mark of the pole since the
    morning:

And time near to return, and a ship (Spanish)
Lying in for the salmon: and fearing chance or the

Drought or the Sioux should deprive you of these dis-
  coveries—
Therefore we send by sea in this writing:

                                        Above the
Platte there were long plains and a clay country:
Rim of the sky far off: grass under it:

Dung for the cook fires by the sulphur licks:
After that there were low hills and the sycamores:

And we poled up by the Great Bend in the skiffs:
The honey bees left us after the Osage River:

The wind was west in the evenings and no dew and the
Morning Star larger and whiter than usual—

The winter rattling in the brittle haws:
The second year there was sage and the quail calling:

All that valley is good land by the river:
Three thousand miles and the clay cliffs and

Rue and beargrass by the water banks
And many birds and the brant going over and tracks of

Bear elk wolves marten: the buffalo
Numberless so that the cloud of their dust covers them:

The antelope fording the fall creeks: and the mountains
    and
Grazing lands and the meadow lands and the ground

Sweet and open and well-drained:
                                    We advise you to
Settle troops at the forks and to issue licenses:

Many men will have living on these lands:
There is wealth in the earth for them all and the wood
    standing

And wild birds on the water where they sleep:
There is stone in the hills for the towns of a great
    people . . .'

You have just beheld the Makers making America:

They screwed her scrawny and gaunt with their seven-
    year panics:
They bought her back on their mortgages old-whore-
    cheap:
They fattened their bonds at her breasts till the thin
    blood ran from them:

Men have forgotten how full clear and deep
The Yellowstone moved on the gravel and grass grew
When the land lay waiting for her westward people!

477 *Pole star for this year*

WHERE the wheel of light is turned:
Where the axle of the night is
Turned: is motionless: where holds
And has held ancient sureness always:

Where of faring men the eyes
At oar bench at the rising bow
Have seen—torn shrouds between—the Wain
And that star's changelessness: not changing:

There upon that intent star:
Trust of wandering men: of truth
The most reminding witness: we
Fix our eyes also: waylost: the wanderers:

We too turn now to that star:
We too in whose trustless hearts
All truth alters and the lights
Of earth are out now turn to that star.

Liberty of man and mind
That once was mind's necessity
And made the West blaze up has burned
To bloody embers and the lamp's out:

Hope that was a noble flame
Has fanned to violence and feeds
On cities and the flesh of men
And chokes where unclean smoke defiles it:

903

Even the small spark of pride
That taught the tyrant once is dark
Where gunfire rules the starving street
And justice cheats the dead of honor:

Liberty and pride and hope
And every guide-mark of the mind
That led our blindness once has vanished.
This star will not. Love's star will not.

Love that has beheld the face
A man has with a man's eyes in it
Bloody from the slugger's blows
Or heard the cold child cry for hunger—

Love that listens where the good:
The virtuous: the men of faith:
Proclaim the paradise on earth
And murder starve and burn to make it—

Love that cannot either sleep
Or keep rich music in the ear
Or lose itself for the wild beat
The anger in the blood makes raging—

Love that hardens into hate—
Love like hatred and as bright—
Love is that one waking light
That leads now when all others darken.

ARCHIBALD MACLEISH

478   *Speech to those who say Comrade*

THE BROTHERHOOD is not by the blood certainly:
But neither are men brothers by speech—by saying so:
Men are brothers by life lived and are hurt for it:

Hunger and hurt are the great begetters of brotherhood:
Humiliation has gotten much love:
Danger I say is the nobler father and mother:

Those are as brothers whose bodies have shared fear
Or shared harm or shared hurt or indignity.
Why are the old soldiers brothers and nearest?

For this: with their minds they go over the sea a little
And find themselves in their youth again as they were in
Soissons and Meaux and at Ypres and those cities:

A French loaf and the girls with their eyelids painted
Bring back to aging and lonely men
Their twentieth year and the metal odor of danger:

It is this in life which of all things is tenderest—
To remember together with unknown men the days
Common also to them and perils ended:

It is this which makes of many a generation—
A wave of men who having the same years
Have in common the same dead and the changes.

The solitary and unshared experience
Dies of itself like the violations of love
Or lives on as the dead live eerily:

The unshared and single man must cover his
Loneliness as a girl her shame for the way of
Life is neither by one man nor by suffering.

Who are the born brothers in truth? The puddlers
Scorched by the same flame in the same foundries:
Those who have spit on the same boards with the blood
     in it:

Ridden the same rivers with green logs:
Fought the police in the parks of the same cities:
Grinned for the same blows: the same flogging:

Veterans out of the same ships—factories—
Expeditions for fame: the founders of continents:
Those that hid in Geneva a time back:

Those that have hidden and hunted and all such—
Fought together: labored together: they carry the
Common look like a card and they pass touching.

Brotherhood! No word said can make you brothers!
Brotherhood only the brave earn and by danger or
Harm or by bearing hurt and by no other.

Brotherhood here in the strange world is the rich and
Rarest giving of life and the most valued:
Not to be had for a word or a week's wishing.

479 *Brave New World*

Bᴜᴛ you, Thomas Jefferson,
You could not lie so still,
You could not bear the weight of stone
On the quiet hill,

You could not keep your green grown peace
Nor hold your folded hand
If you could see your new world now,
Your new sweet land.

There was a time, Tom Jefferson,
When freedom made free men.
The new found earth and the new freed mind
Were brothers then.

There was a time when tyrants feared
The new world of the free.
Now freedom is afraid and shrieks
At tyranny.

Words have not changed their sense so soon
Nor tyranny grown new.
The truths you held, Tom Jefferson,
Will still hold true.

What's changed is freedom in this age.
What great men dared to choose
Small men now dare neither win
Nor lose.

Freedom, when men fear freedom's use
But love its useful name,
Has cause and cause enough for fear
And cause for shame.

We fought a war in freedom's name
And won it in our own.
We fought to free a world and raised
A wall of stone.

Your countrymen who could have built
The hill fires of the free
To set the dry world all ablaze
With liberty—

To burn the brutal thorn in Spain
Of bigotry and hate
And the dead lie and the brittle weed
Beyond the Plate:

Who could have heaped the bloody straw,
The dung of time, to light
The Danube in a sudden flame
Of hope by night—

Your countrymen who could have hurled
Their freedom like a brand
Have cupped it to a candle spark
In a frightened hand.

Freedom that was a thing to use
They've made a thing to save
And staked it in and fenced it round
Like a dead man's grave.

You, Thomas Jefferson,
You could not lie so still,
You could not bear the weight of stone
On your green hill,

You could not hold your angry tongue
If you could see how bold
The old stale bitter world plays new—
And the new world old.

PHELPS PUTNAM

1894-1948

480   *Hasbrouck and the Rose*

HASBROUCK was there and so were Bill
And Smollet Smith the poet, and Ames was there.
After his thirteenth drink, the burning Smith,
Raising his fourteenth trembling in the air,
Said, 'Drink with me, Bill, drink up to the Rose.'
But Hasbrouck laughed like old men in a myth,
Inquiring, 'Smollet, are you drunk? What rose?'
And Smollet said, 'I drunk? It may be so;
Which comes from brooding on the flower, the flower
I mean toward which mad hour by hour
I travel brokenly; and I shall know,
With Hermes and the alchemists—but, hell,
What use is it talking that way to you?
Hard-boiled, unbroken egg, what can you care
For the enfolded passion of the Rose?'
Then Hasbrouck's voice rang like an icy bell:

'Arcane romantic flower, meaning what?
Do you know what it meant? Do I?
We do not know.
Unfolding pungent Rose, the glowing bath
Of ecstasy and clear forgetfulness;
Closing and secret bud one might achieve
By long debauchery—
Except that I have eaten it, and so
There is no call for further lunacy.
In Springfield, Massachusetts, I devoured
The mystic, the improbable, the Rose.
For two nights and a day, rose and rosette
And petal after petal and the heart,
I had my banquet by the beams
Of four electric stars which shone
Weakly into my room, for there,
Drowning their light and gleaming at my side,
Was the incarnate star
Whose body bore the stigma of the Rose.
And that is all I know about the flower;
I have eaten it—it has disappeared.
There is no Rose.'

Young Smollet Smith let fall his glass; he said,
'O Jesus, Hasbrouck, am I drunk or dead?'

481   *Ballad of a Strange Thing*

HIS name was Chance, Jack Chance, he said,
And that his family was dead.

PHELPS PUTNAM

He was a lucid fool, his eyes
Were cool and he beyond surprise.
Into the township Pollard Mill
He came in autumn alone one day,
Loafing along those roads which still,
Though dying in the grass, report
That lumber-sledges went that way.
He came idly and in our town
He raised a flight of birds, a brown
And silver flock, and underneath
Their wings were tinged with gold; his breath
Blew and the birds dipped and rose
As if they surely lived which were
But lies of the calm sorcerer.

Autumn came bringing free
Melancholy, but to me
Brought Jack, when I was sitting there
In the open barn door-way where
The sun moved in and I could get,
Drifting by, the sound and smell
Of late bees and of mignonette
From the dying garden by the wall,
And hear the thin defeated bell
Of distant time, and see the tall
Elms beyond the orchard slopes
Rising improbably, like hopes
Swaying above the mind, and I
Was sitting there and he came by.
Under his hat I saw his eyes
Measuring without disguise
The ripeness of my house,
And measuring myself, and he

Turned in and approached and spoke to me.
He had decided undismayed
This was the place for Chance, and I
The boy for him; and so he stayed.

And then the days moved gravely by,
Time drowned in fluent clarity
Flowing between him and me,
Who only lay along the walls
Unshamed of indolence, and heard
The dusty harvesters' harsh calls
To sweating teams, loading the sheaves
On the steep withered fields—their care
Was none of ours; or reasoned there
Where the mill-pond burned with leaves
And rustled at the dam, on those
Stark thoughts that rose
Out of cool spoken words, or we
Loafing in the arbor ate
Slowly the warm grapes, the rusty
Creaking swallows skimmed
The long ridgepoles, the day grew late
Easily, and dimmed.

At night we made a fire to mark
A spot of mirth against the dark,
There in a pasture which lay high
On the nearness of the sky.
Other countrymen would come,
Young farmers, farmers' men and sons,
One after one they learned to come
And laugh with Chance and tap the old
Keg of cider, acrid gold,

Which we had borne carefully
Out of the cellar where it lay,
Drowsing wickedly it lay
Waiting for us to set free
Its vigor and its treachery.
Then Jack would sing his bawdy songs:
That old ballad which belongs
To timelessness, *The Bastard King*,
Or *Doctor Tanner*, or *Mademoiselle*,
Or *Lil* who died of letchering.
She died with her boots on, as they tell,
With a champion lad between her knees.
Or he would sometimes please,
If drinking brought delusion near,
To tell corrosive tales, the mere
Garments of lies, the cunning kind
Which echo somewhat in the mind,
And then they go, and you are more
Dull and baffled than before.

There went by then, in such a way,
Serene October; the last day
Came and the night was newly cold,
But the fire was high and the old
Cider burned within and we,
A dozen foolish farmers, kept
Alive the late hilarity
Of autumn, and the township slept.
Then Chance arose from where he sat
Against the keg and cocked his hat
Sideways and walking slow around
The fire, said—'I have always found

Nothing new among much change;
But this I tell you now is strange:

It was at noon, the hour of sleep
For those who use their nights
In the deluding piracy
Of shadowy delights.

And so I slept, above the bank
Above the River Still,
Under an oak, the least of two
That rose under the hill.

But a sound crept through my nerves
And I woke and I could hear
Feet running fast and close,
Down the hill and near,

Then stop; and heard a noise like sobs
And stood up quietly
And peering saw that a breathless girl
Was clutching the other tree.

And then a man came following,
Loping leisurely,
And when he stood beside her said,
"I knew you would wait for me."

And then she turned at bay; she was
Astonishingly rare,
A young ascetic fury she
Was something almost strange to me
With her honey fallen hair.

PHELPS PUTNAM

"Yes—and have waited even too long,
Before now, to be glad,
Watching your insolence too long—
Oh, you were the gorgeous lad
With your dark lovely face and all
The women you have had.

I have seen the rabbits follow you
Unasked and eagerly;
O ladies, you should see him now,
Begging a kiss of me."

She ceased, and we all three were still
While he admired her,
And I kept hidden watching them,
For I have that character.

He did not mock her when he spoke,
"Where do they get these dull
Flash melodramas in their skulls?
And such a dainty skull.

Listen, I keep no list of names
For vanity; and I
Dislike the names and the odors and ways
Of women; I am shy
Of their domestic wills; and I
Am tired of the melting lie.

But there you are—and sometimes love
Is more than remembered skill."
"Love," she said, "is the rust which ate
The clean rancor of my will."

He raised his quiet hand to touch
Her hair, but she
Turned sharply down the bank and he
Now followed instantly.

And there below the godly stream
Was whispering in its beard,
And she cried, "Save me, River Still!"
Then stepped and disappeared.

Well—so far nothing strange;
But after that the queer
Began, and I have seen these things,
And I, the bastard son of change,
Would dare to call them queer.

I saw the girl had gone entirely,
And in her place a dry
Shivering graceful sheaf of reeds
Sprang up, suddenly high;

And that he, following so close
That her hair was in his face,
Clutched and had no girl but had
Sharp reeds in his embrace.

He stepped back, looking at his hands
All laced with blood; a spike
Broke short and stood between his ribs
Most murderous like.

This feller was not eager now,
But only dazed,

And pulled the wet spike from his side,
Fumbling and amazed.

He stooped slowly to bathe his hands,
Then from his pocket drew
A folded knife and cut one reed,
Murmuring, "This will do.

Sometimes there's music in these girls,
Sometimes," and sitting then
He made a whistle which he tried
And changed and tried again.

He blew five even notes and stopped,
But the sound rippled away
Slowly, as if a sweet clang came
From the leaves and hummed away.

And then there came along the bank
A black majestic goat
With yellow eyes and gilded horns
And a white beard at its throat.

The goat lay down before his feet
Respectfully, dipping its head,
And the man laughed and, "Can this be
A messenger?" he said.

And played again and now more wild
And cloudily intricate,
And the goat arose and danced like one
Hieratic and sedate.

917

And that is all,' said Chance, and then
He said, 'So long,' and walked away
Casually, as if the night were day.
And we jumped up calling, and then
Stood silent for over us coldly fell
Five piercing notes, each like a spark;
We stood there stiffly and immersed,
Hearing laughter in the dark,
Until I spoke, being the first,
'We had better go home now to bed;
We have drunk too much,' I said.

Thereafter the rains beat down
The autumn, the drenched leaves came down
From the black trees, choking the ditches,
And over the sea came sons-of-bitches
With a hollow quarrel, the talking rats
Of England and of Europe slithered
Down the hawsers, doffed their hats
And squealed; and the plague spread and came,
Taking the cleanly name
Of honor for its strange device,
Even to our town; the conscript lice
Played soldiers over Pollard Mill
And pitched their camp on the River Still;
But no more Jack, and we were more
Dull and baffled than before.

E. E. CUMMINGS

b. 894

482   *'it is at moments after*
         i have dreamed'

it is at moments after i have dreamed
of the rare entertainment of your eyes,
when (being fool to fancy) i have deemed

with your peculiar mouth my heart made wise;
at moments when the glassy darkness holds

the genuine apparition of your smile
(it was through tears always) and silence moulds
such strangeness as was mine a little while;

moments when my once more illustrious arms
are filled with fascination, when my breast
wears the intolerant brightness of your charms:

one pierced moment whiter than the rest

—turning from the tremendous lie of sleep
i watch the roses of the day grow deep.

483   *'all in green went my love riding'*

all in green went my love riding
on a great horse of gold
into the silver dawn.

four lean hounds crouched low and smiling
the merry deer ran before.

Fleeter be they than dappled dreams
the swift sweet deer
the red rare deer.

Four red roebuck at a white water
the cruel bugle sang before.

Horn at hip went my love riding
riding the echo down
into the silver dawn.

four lean hounds crouched low and smiling
the level meadows ran before.

Softer be they than slippered sleep
the lean lithe deer
the fleet flown deer.

Four fleet does at a gold valley
the famished arrow sang before.

Bow at belt went my love riding
riding the mountain down
into the silver dawn.

four lean hounds crouched low and smiling
the sheer peaks ran before.

Paler be they than daunting death
the sleek slim deer
the tall tense deer.

Four tall stags at a green mountain
the lucky hunter sang before.

All in green went my love riding
on a great horse of gold
into the silver dawn.

four lean hounds crouched low and smiling
my heart fell dead before.

484   *'the hours rise up'*

the hours rise up putting off stars and it is
dawn
into the street of the sky light walks scattering poems

on earth a candle is
extinguished   the city
wakes
with a song upon her
mouth having death in her eyes

and it is dawn
the world
goes forth to murder dreams . . .

i see in the street where strong
men are digging bread
and i see the brutal faces of
people contented hideous hopeless cruel happy

and it is day,

in the mirror
i see a frail
man
dreaming
dreams
dreams in the mirror

and it
is dusk   on earth

a candle is lighted
and it is dark.
the people are in their houses
the frail man is in his bed
the city

sleeps with death upon her mouth having a song in her eyes
the hours descend,
putting on stars . . .

in the street of the sky night walks scattering poems

485   *'o sweet spontaneous earth'*

o sweet spontaneous
earth how often have
the
doting

          fingers of
prurient philosophers pinched
and
poked

thee
, has the naughty thumb
of science prodded
thy

     beauty   how
often have religions taken
thee upon their scraggy knees
squeezing and

buffeting thee that thou mightest conceive
gods
          (but
true

to the incomparable
couch of death thy

rhythmic
lover

thou answerest

them only with

spring)

486   *'spring omnipotent goddess'*

spring omnipotent goddess thou dost
inveigle into crossing sidewalks the
unwary june-bug and the frivolous angleworm
thou dost persuade to serenade his
lady the musical tom-cat, thou stuffest
the parks with overgrown pimply
cavaliers and gumchewing giggly
girls and not content
Spring, with this
thou hangest canary-birds in parlor windows

spring slattern of seasons you
have dirty legs and a muddy
petticoat, drowsy is your
mouth your eyes are sticky
with dreams and you have
a sloppy body
from being brought to bed of crocuses

E. E. CUMMINGS

When you sing in your whiskey-voice

                the grass

rises on the head of the earth
and all the trees are put on edge

spring,
of the jostle of
thy breasts and the slobber
of your thighs
i am so very

           glad that the soul inside me Hollers
for thou comest and your hands
are the snow

and thy fingers are the rain,
and i hear
the screech of dissonant
flowers, and most of all

i hear your stepping
               freakish feet
               feet incorrigible
ragging the world,

487   *'the Cambridge ladies'*

the Cambridge ladies who live in furnished souls
are unbeautiful and have comfortable minds
(also, with the church's protestant blessings
daughters, unscented shapeless spirited)
they believe in Christ and Longfellow, both dead,
are invariably interested in so many things—

at the present writing one still finds
delighted fingers knitting for the is it Poles?
perhaps. While permanent faces coyly bandy
scandal of Mrs. N and Professor D
. . . . the Cambridge ladies do not care, above
Cambridge if sometimes in its box of
sky lavender and cornerless, the
moon rattles like a fragment of angry candy

488   Poem, or Beauty Hurts Mr. Vinal

take it from me kiddo
believe me
my country, 'tis of

you, land of the Cluett
Shirt Boston Garter and Spearmint
Girl With The Wrigley Eyes(of you
land of the Arrow Ide
and Earl &
Wilson
Collars)of you i
sing: land of Abraham Lincoln and Lydia E. Pinkham,
land above all of Just Add Hot Water And Serve—
from every B. V. D.

let freedom ring

amen. i do however protest, anent the un
-spontaneous and otherwise scented merde which
greets one(Everywhere Why)as divine poesy per
that and this radically defunct periodical. i would

suggest that certain ideas gestures
rhymes, like Gillette Razor Blades
having been used and reused
to the mystical moment of dullness emphatically are
Not To Be Resharpened. (Case in point

if we are to believe these gently O sweetly
melancholy trillers amid the thrillers
these crepuscular violinists among my and your
skyscrapers—Helen & Cleopatra were Just Too Lovely,
The Snail's On The Thorn enter Morn and God's
In His andsoforth

do you get me?)according
to such supposedly indigenous
throstles Art is O World O Life
a formula: example, Turn Your Shirttails Into
Drawers and If It Isn't An Eastman It Isn't A
Kodak therefore my friends let
us now sing each and all fortissimo A-
mer
i

ca, I
love,
You. And there're a
hun-dred-mil-lion-oth-ers, like
all of you successfully if
delicately gelded(or spaded)
gentlemen(and ladies)—pretty

littleliverpill-
hearted-Nujolneeding-There's-A-Reason

americans(who tensetendoned and with
upward vacant eyes, painfully
perpetually crouched, quivering, upon the
sternly allotted sandpile
—how silently
emit a tiny violetflavoured nuisance:Odor?

ono.
comes out like a ribbon lies flat on the brush

489   *'she being Brand'*

she being Brand

-new;and you
know consequently a
little stiff i was
careful of her and(having

thoroughly oiled the universal
joint tested my gas felt of
her radiator made sure her springs were O.

K.)i went right to it flooded-the-carburetor cranked her

up,slipped the
clutch(and then somehow got into reverse she
kicked what
the hell)next
minute i was back in neutral tried and

again slo-wly;bare,ly nudg.   ing(my

E. E. CUMMINGS

lev-er Right-
oh and her gears being in
A I shape passed
from low through
second-in-to-high like
greased lightning just as we turned the corner of Divinity

avenue i touched the accelerator and give

her the juice,good

was the first ride and believe i we was
happy to see how nice she acted right up to
the last minute coming back down by the Public
Gardens i slammed on
the

internalexpanding
&
externalcontracting
brakes Bothatonce and

brought allofher tremB
-ling
to a:dead.

stand-
;Still)

490　　　*'a man who had fallen
among thieves'*

a man who had fallen among thieves
lay by the roadside on his back
dressed in fifteenthrate ideas
wearing a round jeer for a hat

fate per a somewhat more than less
emancipated evening
had in return for consciousness
endowed him with a changeless grin

whereon a dozen staunch and leal
citizens did graze at pause
then fired by hypercivic zeal
sought newer pastures or because

swaddled with a frozen brook
of pinkest vomit out of eyes
which noticed nobody he looked
as if he did not care to rise

one hand did nothing on the vest
its wideflung friend clenched weakly dirt
while the mute trouserfly confessed
a button solemnly inert.

Brushing from whom the stiffened puke
i put him all into my arms
and staggered banged with terror through
a million billion trillion stars

E. E. CUMMINGS

491   *'next to of course god'*

'next to of course god america i
love you land of the pilgrims' and so forth oh
say can you see by the dawn's early my
country 'tis of centuries come and go
and are no more what of it we should worry
in every language even deafanddumb
thy sons acclaim your glorious name by gorry
by jingo by gee by gosh by gum
why talk of beauty what could be more beaut-
iful than these heroic happy dead
who rushed like lions to the roaring slaughter
they did not stop to think they died instead
then shall the voice of liberty be mute?'

He spoke. And drank rapidly a glass of water

492   *'my sweet old etcetera'*

my sweet old etcetera
aunt lucy during the recent

war could and what
is more did tell you just
what everybody was fighting

for,
my sister

isabel created hundreds
(and
hundreds)of socks not to
mention shirts fleaproof earwarmers

etcetera wristers etcetera, my
mother hoped that

i would die etcetera
bravely of course my father used
to become hoarse talking about how it was
a privilege and if only he
could meanwhile my

self etcetera lay quietly
in the deep mud et

cetera
(dreaming,
et
    cetera, of
Your smile
eyes knees and of your Etcetera)

493

'*come, gaze with me upon*
this dome'

come, gaze with me upon this dome
of many coloured glass, and see
his mother's pride, his father's joy,
unto whom duty whispers low

'thou must!' and who replies 'I can!'
—yon clean upstanding well dressed boy
that with his peers full oft hath quaffed
the wine of life and found it sweet—

a tear within his stern blae eye,
upon his firm white lips a smile,
one thought alone: to do or die
for God for country and for Yale

above his blond determined head
the sacred flag of truth unfurled,
in the bright heyday of his youth
the upper class American

unsullied stands, before the world:
with manly heart and conscience free,
upon the front steps of her home
by the high minded pure young girl

much kissed, by loving relatives
well fed, and fully photographed
the son of man goes forth to war
with trumpets clap and syphilis

494   *'you shall above all things be
glad and young'*

you shall above all things be glad and young.
For if you're young,whatever life you wear

it will become you;and if you are glad
whatever's living will yourself become.
Girlboys may nothing more than boygirls need:
i can entirely her only love

whose any mystery makes every man's
flesh put space on;and his mind take off time

that you should ever think,may god forbid
and(in his mercy)your true lover spare:
for that way knowledge lies,the foetal grave
called progress,and negation's dead undoom.

I'd rather learn from one bird how to sing
than teach ten thousand stars how not to dance

495   *'the way to hump a cow'*

the way to hump a cow is not
to get yourself a stool
but draw a line around the spot
and call it beautifool

to multiply because and why
dividing thens by nows
and adding and(i understand)
is hows to hump a cows

the way to hump a cow is not
to elevate your tool
but drop a penny in the slot
and bellow like a bool

to lay a wreath from ancient greath
on insulated brows
(while tossing boms at uncle toms)
is hows to hump a cows

E. E. CUMMINGS

the way to hump a cow is not
to push and then to pull
but practicing the art of swot
to preach the golden rull

to vote for me(all decent mem
and wonens will allows
which if they don't to hell with them)
is hows to hump a cows

496   *'as freedom is a breakfastfood'*

as freedom is a breakfastfood
or truth can live with right and wrong
or molehills are from mountains made
—long enough and just so long
will being pay the rent of seem
and genius please the talentgang
and water most encourage flame

as hatracks into peachtrees grow
or hopes dance best on bald men's hair
and every finger is a toe
and any courage is a fear
—long enough and just so long
will the impure think all things pure
and hornets wail by children stung

or as the seeing are the blind
and robins never welcome spring
nor flatfolk prove their world is round

nor dingsters die at break of dong
and common's rare and millstones float
—long enough and just so long
tomorrow will not be too late

worms are the words but joy's the voice
down shall go which and up come who
breasts will be breasts thighs will be thighs
deeds cannot dream what dreams can do
—time is a tree(this life one leaf)
but love is the sky and i am for you
just so long and long enough

497 *'buy me an ounce and i'll sell*
you a pound'

buy me an ounce and i'll sell you a pound.
Turn
gert
    (spin!
helen)the
slimmer the finger the thicker the thumb(it's
whirl,
girls)
round and round

early to better is wiser for worse.
Give
liz
    (take!
tommy)we
order a steak and they send us a pie(it's

try,
boys)
mine is yours

ask me the name of the moon in the man.
Up
sam
  (down!
alice)a
hole in the ocean will never be missed(it's
in,
girls)
yours is mine

either was deafer than neither was dumb.
Skip
fred
   (jump!
neddy)but
under the wonder is over the why(it's
now,
boys)
here we come

498   *'my father moved through dooms*
of love'

my father moved through dooms of love
through sames of am through haves of give,
singing each morning out of each night
my father moved through depths of height

937

this motionless forgetful where
turned at his glance to shining here;
that if(so timid air is firm)
under his eyes would stir and squirm

newly as from unburied which
floats the first who,his april touch
drove sleeping selves to swarm their fates
woke dreamers to their ghostly roots

and should some why completely weep
my father's fingers brought her sleep:
vainly no smallest voice might cry
for he could feel the mountains grow.

Lifting the valleys of the sea
my father moved through griefs of joy;
praising a forehead called the moon
singing desire into begin

joy was his song and joy so pure
a heart of star by him could steer
and pure so now and now so yes
the wrists of twilight would rejoice

keen as midsummer's keen beyond
conceiving mind of sun will stand,
so strictly(over utmost him
so hugely)stood my father's dream

his flesh was flesh his blood was blood:
no hungry man but wished him food;
no cripple wouldn't creep one mile
uphill to only see him smile.

E. E. CUMMINGS

Scorning the pomp of must and shall
my father moved through dooms of feel;
his anger was as right as rain
his pity was as green as grain

septembering arms of year extend
less humbly wealth to foe and friend
than he to foolish and to wise
offered immeasurable is

proudly and(by octobering fiame
beckoned)as earth will downward climb,
so naked for immortal work
his shoulders marched against the dark

his sorrow was as true as bread:
no liar looked him in the head;
if every friend became his foe
he'd laugh and build a world with snow.

My father moved through theys of we,
singing each new leaf out of each tree
(and every child was sure that spring
danced when she heard my father sing)

then let men kill which cannot share,
let blood and flesh be mud and mire,
scheming imagine,passion willed,
freedom a drug that's bought and sold

giving to steal and cruel kind,
a heart to fear,to doubt a mind,
to differ a disease of same,
conform the pinnacle of am

though dull were all we taste as bright,
bitter all utterly things sweet,
maggoty minus and dumb death
all we inherit,all bequeath

and nothing quite so least as truth
—i say though hate were why men breathe—
because my father lived his soul
love is the whole and more than all

499   *'it's over a(see just'*

it's over a(see just
over this)wall
the apples are(yes
they're gravensteins)all
as red as to lose
and as round as to find.

Each why of a leaf says
(floating each how)
you're which as to die
(each green of a new)
you're who as to grow
but you're he as to do

what must(whispers)be **must**
be(the wise fool)
if living's to give
so breathing's to steal—
five wishes are five
and one hand is a **mind**

940

then over our thief goes
(you go and i)
has pulled(for he's we)
such fruit from what bough
that someone called they
made him pay with his now.

But over a(see just
over this)wall
the red and the round
(they're gravensteins)fall
with kind of a blind
big sound on the ground

500   *'a salesman is an it that stinks Excuse'*

a salesman is an it that stinks Excuse

Me whether it's president of the you were say
or a jennelman name misder finger isn't
important whether it's millions of other punks
or just a handful absolutely doesn't
matter and whether it's in lonjewray

or shrouds is immaterial it stinks

a salesman is an it that stinks to please

but whether to please itself or someone else
makes no more difference than if it sells
hate condoms education snakeoil vac
uumcleaners terror strawberries democ
ra(caveat emptor)cy superfluous hair

or Think We've Met subhuman rights Before

501   *'plato told'*

plato told

him:he couldn't
believe it(jesus

told him;he
wouldn't believe
it)lao

tsze
certainly told
him,and general
(yes

mam)
sherman;
and even
(believe it
or

not)you
told him:i told
him;we told him
(he didn't believe it,no

sir)it took
a nipponized bit of
the old sixth

avenue
el;in the top of his head:to tell

him

E. E. CUMMINGS

502 *'pity this busy monster, manunkind'*

pity this busy monster,manunkind,

not. Progress is a comfortable disease:
your victim(death and life safely beyond)

plays with the bigness of his littleness
—electrons deify one razorblade
into a mountainrange;lenses extend

unwish through curving wherewhen till unwish
returns on its unself.
                              A world of made
is not a world of born—pity poor flesh

and trees,poor stars and stones,but never this
fine specimen of hypermagical

ultraomnipotence. We doctors know

a hopeless case if—listen:there's a hell
of a good universe next door;let's go

503   *'what if a much of a which
                of a wind'*

what if a much of a which of a wind
gives the truth to summer's lie;
bloodies with dizzying leaves the sun
and yanks immortal stars awry?

Blow king to beggar and queen to seem
(blow friend to fiend:blow space to time)
—when skies are hanged and oceans drowned,
the single secret will still be man

what if a keen of a lean wind flays
screaming hills with sleet and snow:
strangles valleys by ropes of thing
and stifles forests in white ago?
Blow hope to terror;blow seeing to blind
(blow pity to envy and soul to mind)
—whose hearts are mountains,roots are trees,
it's they shall cry hello to the spring

what if a dawn of a doom of a dream
bites this universe in two,
peels forever out of his grave
and sprinkles nowhere with me and you?
Blow soon to never and never to twice
(blow life to isn't:blow death to was)
—all nothing's only our hugest home;
the most who die, the more we live

504   *all ignorance toboggans into know*

all ignorance toboggans into know
and trudges up to ignorance again:
but winter's not forever,even snow
melts;and if spring should spoil the game, what then?

all history's a winter sport or three:
but were it five,i'd still insist that all

history is too small for even me;
for me and you,exceedingly too small.

Swoop(shrill collective myth)into thy grave
merely to toil the scale to shrillerness
per every madge and mabel dick and dave
—tomorrow is our permanent address

,and there they'll scarcely find us(if they do,
we'll move away still further:into now

505 *'darling! because my blood can sing'*

darling! because my blood can sing
and dance(and does with each your least
your any most very amazing now
or here)let pitiless fear play host
to every isn't that's under the spring
—but if a look should april me,
down isn't's own isn't go ghostly they

doubting can turn men's see to stare
their faith to how their joy to why
their stride and breathing to limp and prove
—but if a look should april me,
some thousand million hundred more
bright worlds than merely by doubting have
darkly themselves unmade makes love

armies(than hate itself and no
meanness unsmaller)armies can

E. E. CUMMINGS

immensely meet for centuries
and(except nothing)nothing's won
—but if a look should april me
for half a when,whatever is less
alive than never begins to yes

but if a look should april me
(though such as perfect hope can feel
only despair completely strikes
forests of mind,mountains of soul)
quite at the hugest which of his who
death is killed dead. Hills jump with brooks.
trees tumble out of twigs and sticks;

506   *'o by the by'*

o by the by
has anybody seen
little you-i
who stood on a green
hill and threw
his wish at blue

with a swoop and a dart
out flew his wish
(it dived like a fish
but it climbed like a dream)
throbbing like a heart
singing like a flame

E. E. CUMMINGS

blue took it my
far beyond far
and high beyond high
bluer took it your
but bluest took it our
away beyond where

what a wonderful thing
is the end of a string
(murmurs little you-i
as the hill becomes nil)
and will somebody tell
me why people let go

STEPHEN VINCENT BENÉT

1898-1943

507   *For All Blasphemers*

Adam was my grandfather,
A tall, spoiled child,
A red, clay tower
In Eden, green and mild.
He ripped the Sinful Pippin
From its sanctimonious limb.
Adam was my grandfather—
And I take after him.

Noah was my uncle
And he got dead drunk.
There were planets in his liquor-can
And lizards in his bunk.
He fell into the Bottomless
Past Hell's most shrinking star.
Old Aunt Fate has often said
How much alike we are.

Lilith, she's my sweetheart
Till my heartstrings break,
Most of her is honey-pale
And all of her is snake.
Sweet as secret thievery,
I kiss her all I can,
While Somebody Above remarks
'That's not a nice young man!'

Bacchus was my brother,
Nimrod is my friend.
All of them have talked to me
On how such courses end.
But when His Worship takes me up
How can I fare but well?
For who in gaudy Hell will care?
—And I shall be in Hell.

508   *American Names*

I HAVE fallen in love with American names,
The sharp names that never get fat,

STEPHEN VINCENT BENÉT

The snakeskin-titles of mining-claims,
The plumed war-bonnet of Medicine Hat,
Tucson and Deadwood and Lost Mule Flat.

Seine and Piave are silver spoons,
But the spoonbowl-metal is thin and worn,
There are English counties like hunting-tunes
Played on the keys of a postboy's horn,
But I will remember where I was born.

I will remember Carquinez Straits,
Little French Lick and Lundy's Lane,
The Yankee ships and the Yankee dates
And the bullet-towns of Calamity Jane.
I will remember Skunktown Plain.

I will fall in love with a Salem tree
And a rawhide quirt from Santa Cruz,
I will get me a bottle of Boston sea
And a blue-gum nigger to sing me blues.
I am tired of loving a foreign muse.

Rue des Martyrs and Bleeding-Heart-Yard,
Senlis, Pisa, and Blindman's Oast,
It is a magic ghost you guard
But I am sick for a newer ghost,
Harrisburg, Spartanburg, Painted Post.

Henry and John were never so
And Henry and John were always right?
Granted, but when it was time to go
And the tea and the laurels had stood all night,
Did they never watch for Nantucket Light?

I shall not rest quiet in Montparnasse.
I shall not lie easy at Winchelsea.
You may bury my body in Sussex grass,
You may bury my tongue at Champmédy.
I shall not be there. I shall rise and pass.
Bury my heart at Wounded Knee.

509   *Litany for Dictatorships*

FOR all those beaten, for the broken heads,
The fosterless, the simple, the oppressed,
The ghosts in the burning city of our time . . .

For those taken in rapid cars to the house and beaten
By the skilful boys, the boys with the rubber fists,
—Held down and beaten, the table cutting their loins,
Or kicked in the groin and left, with the muscles jerking
Like a headless hen's on the floor of the slaughter-house
While they brought the next man in with his white eyes
        staring.
For those who still said 'Red Front' or 'God Save the
        Crown!'
And for those who were not courageous
But were beaten nevertheless.
For those who spit out the bloody stumps of their teeth
Quietly in the hall,
Sleep well on stone or iron, watch for the time
And kill the guard in the privy before they die,
Those with the deep-socketed eyes and the lamp burning.

For those who carry the scars, who walk lame—for those
Whose nameless graves are made in the prison-yard
And the earth smoothed back before morning and the lime
    scattered.

For those slain at once. For those living through months
    and years
Enduring, watching, hoping, going each day
To the work or the queue for meat or the secret club,
Living meanwhile, begetting children, smuggling guns,
And found and killed at the end like rats in a drain.

For those escaping
Incredibly into exile and wandering there.
For those who live in the small rooms of foreign cities
And who yet think of the country, the long green grass,
The childhood voices, the language, the way wind smelt
    then,
The shape of rooms, the coffee drunk at the table,
The talk with friends, the loved city, the waiter's face,
The gravestones, with the name, where they will not lie
Nor in any of that earth. Their children are strangers.

For those who planned and were leaders and were beaten
And for those, humble and stupid, who had no plan
But were denounced, but grew angry, but told a joke,
But could not explain, but were sent away to the camp,
But had their bodies shipped back in the sealed coffins,
'Died of pneumonia.' 'Died trying to escape.'

For those growers of wheat who were shot by their own
    wheatstacks,

For those growers of bread who were sent to the ice-locked
    wastes,
And their flesh remembers their fields.

For those denounced by their smug, horrible children
For a peppermint-star and the praise of the Perfect State,
For all those strangled or gelded or merely starved
To make perfect states; for the priest hanged in his
    cassock,
The Jew with his chest crushed in and his eyes dying,
The revolutionist lynched by the private guards
To make perfect states, in the names of the perfect states.

For those betrayed by the neighbors they shook hands with
And for the traitors, sitting in the hard chair
With the loose sweat crawling their hair and their fingers
    restless
As they tell the street and the house and the man's name.

And for those sitting at table in the house
With the lamp lit and the plates and the smell of food,
Talking so quietly; when they hear the cars
And the knock at the door, and they look at each other
    quickly
And the woman goes to the door with a stiff face,
Smoothing her dress.

     'We are all good citizens here.
We believe in the Perfect State.'

        And that was the last
Time Tony or Karl or Shorty came to the house
And the family was liquidated later.
It was the last time.

STEPHEN VINCENT BENÉT

We heard the shots in the night
But nobody knew next day what the trouble was
And a man must go to his work. So I didn't see him
For three days, then, and me near out of my mind
And all the patrols on the streets with their dirty guns
And when he came back, he looked drunk, and the blood
    was on him.

For the women who mourn their dead in the secret night,
For the children taught to keep quiet, the old children,
The children spat-on at school.
                            For the wrecked laboratory,
The gutted house, the dunged picture, the pissed-in well,
The naked corpse of Knowledge flung in the square
And no man lifting a hand and no man speaking.

For the cold of the pistol-butt and the bullet's heat,
For the rope that chokes, the manacles that bind,
The huge voice, metal, that lies from a thousand tubes
And the stuttering machine-gun that answers all.

For the man crucified on the crossed machine-guns
Without name, without resurrection, without stars,
His dark head heavy with death and his flesh long sour
With the smell of his many prisons—John Smith, John
    Doe,
John Nobody—oh, crack your mind for his name!
Faceless as water, naked as the dust,
Dishonored as the earth the gas-shells poison
And barbarous with portent.
                            This is he.
This is the man they ate at the green table
Putting their gloves on ere they touched the meat.

This is the fruit of war, the fruit of peace,
The ripeness of invention, the new lamb,
The answer to the wisdom of the wise.
And still he hangs, and still he will not die,
And still, on the steel city of our years
The light fails and the terrible blood streams down.

We thought we were done with these things but we were
     wrong.
We thought, because we had power, we had wisdom.
We thought the long train would run to the end of Time.
We thought the light would increase.
Now the long train stands derailed and the bandits loot it.
Now the boar and the asp have power in our time.
Now the night rolls back on the West and the night is solid.
Our fathers and ourselves sowed dragon's teeth.
Our children know and suffer the armed men.

510   *Nightmare at Noon*

THERE are no trenches dug in the park, not yet.
There are no soldiers falling out of the sky.
It's a fine, clear day, in the park. It is bright and hot.
The trees are in full, green, summer-heavy leaf.
An airplane drones overhead but no one's afraid.
There's no reason to be afraid, in a fine, big city
That was not built for a war. There is time and time.

There was time in Norway and time, and the thing fell.
When they woke, they saw the planes with the black crosses.
When they woke, they heard the guns rolling in the street.
They could not believe, at first. It was hard to believe.

954

STEPHEN VINCENT BENÉT

They had been friendly and thriving and inventive.
They had had good arts, decent living, peace for years.
Those were not enough, it seems.
There were people there who wrote books and painted
  pictures,
Worked, came home tired, liked to be let alone.
They made fun of the strut and the stamp and the strained
  salute,
They made fun of the would-be Caesars who howl and
  foam.
That was not enough, it seems. It was not enough.
When they woke, they saw the planes with the black crosses.

There is grass in the park. There are children on the long
  meadow
Watched by some hot, peaceful nuns. Where the ducks are
  fed
There are black children and white and the anxious
  teachers
Who keep counting them like chickens. It's quite a job
To take so many school-kids out to the park,
But when they've eaten their picnic, they'll go home.
(And they could have better homes, in a rich city.)
But they won't be sent to Kansas or Michigan
At twenty-four hours' notice,
Dazed, bewildered, clutching their broken toys,
Hundreds on hundreds filling the blacked-out trains.
Just to keep them safe, just so they may live not die.
Just so there's one chance that they may not die but live.
That does not enter our thoughts. There is plenty of time.

In Holland, one hears, some children were less lucky.
It was hard to send them anywhere in Holland.

It is a small country, you see. The thing happened quickly.
The bombs from the sky are quite indifferent to children.
The machine-gunners do not distinguish. In Rotterdam
One quarter of the city was blown to bits.
That included, naturally, ordinary buildings
With the usual furnishings, such as cats and children.
It was an old, peaceful city, Rotterdam,
Clean, tidy, full of flowers.
But that was not enough, it seems.
It was not enough to keep all the children safe.
It was ended in a week, and the freedom ended.

There is no air-raid siren yet, in the park.
All the glass still stands, in the windows around the park.
The man on the bench is reading a Yiddish paper.
He will not be shot because of that, oddly enough.
He will not even be beaten or imprisoned.
Not yet, not yet.
You can be a Finn or a Dane and an American.
You can be German or French and an American,
Jew, Bohunk, Nigger, Mick—all the dirty names
We call each other—and yet American.
We've stuck to that quite a while.
Go into Joe's Diner and try to tell the truckers
You belong to a Master Race and you'll get a laugh.
What's that, brother? Double-talk?
I'm a stranger here myself but it's a free country.
It's a free country . . .
Oh yes, I know the faults and the other side,
The lyncher's rope, the bought justice, the wasted land,
The scale on the leaf, the borers in the corn,
The finks with their clubs, the grey sky of relief,
All the long shame of our hearts and the long disunion.

STEPHEN VINCENT BENÉT

I am merely remarking—as a country, we try.
As a country, I think we try.

They tried in Spain but the tanks and the planes won out.
They fought very well and long.
They fought to be free but it seems that was not enough.
They did not have the equipment. So they lost.
They tried in Finland. The resistance was shrewd,
Skilful, intelligent, waged by a free folk.
They tried in Greece, and they threw them back for a
        while
By the soul and spirit and passion of common men.
Call the roll of fourteen nations. Call the roll
Of the blacked-out lands, the lands that used to be free.

But do not call it loud. There is plenty of time.
There is plenty of time, while the bombs on London fall
And turn the world to wind and water and fire.
There is time to sleep while the fire-bombs fall on London.
They are stubborn people in London.

We are slow to wake, good-natured as a country.
(It is our fault, and our virtue.) We like to raise
A man to the highest power and then throw bricks at him.
We don't like war and we like to speak our minds.
We're used to speaking our minds.
                              There are certain words,
Our own and others', we're used to—words we've used,
Heard, had to recite, forgotten,
Rubbed shiny in the pocket, left home for keepsakes,
Inherited, stuck away in the back-drawer,
In the locked trunk, at the back of the quiet mind.

Liberty, equality, fraternity.
To none will we sell, refuse or deny, right or justice.
We hold these truths to be self-evident.

I am merely saying—what if these words pass?
What if they pass and are gone and are no more,
Eviscerated, blotted out of the world?
We're used to them, so used that we half-forget,
The way you forget the looks of your own house
And yet you can walk around it, in the darkness.
You can't put a price on sunlight or the air,
You can't put a price on these, so they must be easy
They were bought with belief and passion, at great cost.
They were brought with the bitter and anonymous blood
Of farmers, teachers, shoemakers and fools
Who broke the old rule and the pride of kings.
And some never saw the end and many were weary,
Some doubtful, many confused.
They were bought by the ragged boys at Valmy mill,
The yokels at Lexington with the long light guns
And the dry, New England faces,
The iron barons, writing a charter out
For their own iron advantage, not the people,
And yet the people got it into their hands
And marked it with their own sweat.
It took long to buy these words.
It took a long time to buy them and much pain.

Thenceforward and forever free.
Thenceforward and forever free.
No man may be bound or fined or slain till he has been
      judged by his peers.
To form a more perfect Union.

The others have their words too, and strong words,
Strong as the tanks, explosive as the bombs.

The State is all, worship the State!
The Leader is all, worship the Leader!
Strength is all, worship strength!
Worship, bow down or die!

I shall go back through the park to my safe house,
This is not London or Paris.
This is the high, bright city, the lucky place,
The place that always had time.
The boys in their shirtsleeves here, the big, flowering girls,
The bicycle-riders, the kids with the model planes,
The lovers who lie on the grass, uncaring of eyes,
As if they lay on an island out of time,
The tough kids, squirting the water at the fountain,
Whistled at by the cop.
The dopes who write 'Jimmy's a dope' on the tunnel walls.
These are all quite safe and nothing will happen to them.
Nothing will happen, of course.
Go tell Frank the Yanks aren't coming, in Union Square.
Go tell the new brokers' story about the President.
Whatever it is. That's going to help a lot.
There's time to drink your highball—plenty of time.
Go tell fire it only burns in another country,
Go tell the bombers this is the wrong address,
The hurricane to pass on the other side.
Go tell the earthquake it must not shake the ground.

The bell has rung in the night and the air quakes with it.

I shall not sleep tonight when I hear the plane.

HART CRANE

1899-1932

511 *Legend*

As silent as a mirror is believed
Realities plunge in silence by . . .

I am not ready for repentance;
Nor to match regrets. For the moth
Bends no more than the still
Imploring flame. And tremorous
In the white falling flakes
Kisses are,—
The only worth all granting.

It is to be learned—
This cleaving and this burning,
But only by the one who
Spends out himself again.

Twice and twice
(Again the smoking souvenir,
Bleeding eidolon!) and yet again.
Until the bright logic is won
Unwhispering as a mirror
Is believed.

Then, drop by caustic drop, a perfect cry
Shall string some constant harmony,—
Relentless caper for all those who step
The legend of their youth into the noon.

512   *Black Tambourine*

THE interests of a black man in a cellar
Mark tardy judgment on the world's closed door.
Gnats toss in the shadow of a bottle,
And a roach spans a crevice in the floor.

Æsop, driven to pondering, found
Heaven with the tortoise and the hare;
Fox brush and sow ear top his grave
And mingling incantations on the air.

The black man, forlorn in the cellar,
Wanders in some mid-kingdom, dark, that lies,
Between his tambourine, stuck on the wall,
And, in Africa, a carcass quick with flies.

513   *Praise for an Urn*

In Memoriam: Ernest Nelson

IT was a kind and northern face
That mingled in such exile guise
The everlasting eyes of Pierrot
And, of Gargantua, the laughter.

His thoughts, delivered to me
From the white coverlet and pillow,
I see now, were inheritances—
Delicate riders of the storm.

The slant moon on the slanting hill
Once moved us toward presentiments
Of what the dead keep, living still,
And such assessments of the soul

As, perched in the crematory lobby,
The insistent clock commented on,
Touching as well upon our praise
Of glories proper to the time.

Still, having in mind gold hair,
I cannot see that broken brow
And miss the dry sound of bees
Stretching across a lucid space.

Scatter these well-meant idioms
Into the smoky spring that fills
The suburbs, where they will be lost.
They are no trophies of the sun.

5I4   *Chaplinesque*

WE make our meek adjustments,
Contented with such random consolations
As the wind deposits
In slithered and too ample pockets.

For we can still love the world, who find
A famished kitten on the step, and know
Recesses for it from the fury of the street,
Or warm torn elbow coverts.

We will sidestep, and to the final smirk
Dally the doom of that inevitable thumb
That slowly chafes its puckered index toward us,
Facing the dull squint with what innocence
And what surprise!

And yet these fine collapses are not lies
More than the pirouettes of any pliant cane;
Our obsequies are, in a way, no enterprise.
We can evade you, and all else but the heart:
What blame to us if the heart live on.

The game enforces smirks; but we have seen
The moon in lonely alleys make
A grail of laughter of an empty ash can,
And through all sound of gaiety and quest
Have heard a kitten in the wilderness.

515   *Repose of Rivers*

THE willows carried a slow sound,
A sarabande the wind mowed on the mead.
I could never remember
That seething, steady leveling of the marshes
Till age had brought me to the sea.

Flags, weeds. And remembrance of steep alcoves
Where cypresses shared the noon's
Tyranny; they drew me into hades almost.
And mammoth turtles climbing sulphur dreams
Yielded, while sun-silt rippled them
Asunder . . .

How much I would have bartered! the black gorge
And all the singular nestings in the hills
Where beavers learn stitch and tooth.
The pond I entered once and quickly fled—
I remember now its singing willow rim.

And finally, in that memory all things nurse;
After the city that I finally passed
With scalding unguents spread and smoking darts
The monsoon cut across the delta
At gulf gates . . . There, beyond the dykes

I heard wind flaking sapphire, like this summer,
And willows could not hold more steady sound.

516   *The Wine Menagerie*

INVARIABLY when wine redeems the sight,
Narrowing the mustard scansions of the eyes,
A leopard ranging always in the brow
Asserts a vision in the slumbering gaze.

Then glozening decanters that reflect the street
Wear me in crescents on their bellies. Slow
Applause flows into liquid cynosures:
—I am conscripted to their shadows' glow.

Against the imitation onyx wainscoting
(Painted emulsion of snow, eggs, yarn, coal, manure)
Regard the forceps of the smile that takes her.
Percussive sweat is spreading to his hair. Mallets,
Her eyes, unmake an instant of the world . . .

HART CRANE

What is it in this heap the serpent pries—
Whose skin, facsimile of time, unskeins
Octagon, sapphire transepts round the eyes;
—From whom some whispered carillon assures
Speed to the arrow into feathered skies?

Sharp to the window-pane guile drags a face,
And as the alcove of her jealousy recedes
An urchin who has left the snow
Nudges a cannister across the bar
While August meadows somewhere clasp his brow.

Each chamber, transept, coins some squint,
Remorseless line, minting their separate wills—
Poor streaked bodies wreathing up and out,
Unwitting the stigma that each turn repeals:
Between black tusks the roses shine!

New thresholds, new anatomies! Wine talons
Build freedom up about me and distill
This competence—to travel in a tear
Sparkling alone, within another's will.

Until my blood dreams a receptive smile
Wherein new purities are snared; where chimes
Before some flame of gaunt repose a shell
Tolled once, perhaps, by every tongue in hell.
—Anguished, the wit that cries out of me:

'Alas,—these frozen billows of your skill!
Invent new dominoes of love and bile . . .
Ruddy, the tooth implicit of the world
Has followed you. Though in the end you know

And count some dim inheritance of sand,
How much yet meets the treason of the snow.

'Rise from the dates and crumbs. And walk away,
Stepping over Holofernes' shins—
Beyond the wall, whose severed head floats by
With Baptist John's. Their whispering begins.

'—And fold your exile on your back again;
Petrushka's valentine pivots on its pin.'

517   *Voyages*

I

ABOVE the fresh ruffles of the surf
Bright striped urchins flay each other with sand.
They have contrived a conquest for shell shucks,
And their fingers crumble fragments of baked weed
Gaily digging and scattering.

And in answer to their treble interjections
The sun beats lightning on the waves,
The waves fold thunder on the sand;
And could they hear me I would tell them:

O brilliant kids, frisk with your dog,
Fondle your shells and sticks, bleached
By time and the elements; but there is a line
You must not cross nor ever trust beyond it
Spry cordage of your bodies to caresses
Too lichen-faithful from too wide a breast.
The bottom of the sea is cruel.

HART CRANE

II

And yet this great wink of eternity,
Of rimless floods, unfettered leewardings,
Samite sheeted and processioned where
Her undinal vast belly moonward bends,
Laughing the wrapt inflections of our love;

Take this Sea, whose diapason knells
On scrolls of silver snowy sentences,
The sceptred terror of whose sessions rends
As her demeanors motion well or ill,
All but the pieties of lovers' hands.

And onward, as bells off San Salvador
Salute the crocus lustres of the stars,
In these poinsettia meadows of her tides,—
Adagios of islands, O my Prodigal,
Complete the dark confessions her veins spell.

Mark how her turning shoulders wind the hours,
And hasten while her penniless rich palms
Pass superscription of bent foam and wave,—
Hasten, while they are true,—sleep, death, desire,
Close round one instant in one floating flower.

Bind us in time, O Seasons clear, and awe.
O minstrel galleons of Carib fire,
Bequeath us to no earthly shore until
Is answered in the vortex of our grave
The seal's wide spindrift gaze toward paradise.

III

Infinite consanguinity it bears—
This tendered theme of you that light
Retrieves from sea plains where the sky
Resigns a breast that every wave enthrones;
While ribboned water lanes I wind
Are laved and scattered with no stroke
Wide from your side, whereto this hour
The sea lifts, also, reliquary hands.

And so, admitted through black swollen gates
That must arrest all distance otherwise,—
Past whirling pillars and lithe pediments,
Light wrestling there incessantly with light,
Star kissing star through wave on wave unto
Your body rocking!
              and where death, if shed,
Presumes no carnage, but this single change,—
Upon the steep floor flung from dawn to dawn
The silken skilled transmemberment of song;

Permit me voyage, love, into your hands . . .

518   *To Brooklyn Bridge*

H OW many dawns, chill from his rippling rest
The seagull's wings shall dip and pivot him,
Shedding white rings of tumult, building high
Over the chained bay waters Liberty—

Then, with inviolate curve, forsake our eyes
As apparitional as sails that cross
Some page of figures to be filed away;
—Till elevators drop us from our day . . .

I think of cinemas, panoramic sleights
With multitudes bent toward some flashing scene
Never disclosed, but hastened to again,
Foretold to other eyes on the same screen;

And Thee, across the harbor, silver-paced
As though the sun took step of thee, yet left
Some motion ever unspent in thy stride,—
Implicitly thy freedom staying thee!

Out of some subway scuttle, cell or loft
A bedlamite speeds to thy parapets,
Tilting there momently, shrill shirt ballooning,
A jest falls from the speechless caravan.

Down Wall, from girder into street noon leaks,
A rip-tooth of the sky's acetylene;
All afternoon the cloud-flown derricks turn . . .
Thy cables breathe the North Atlantic still.

And obscure as that heaven of the Jews,
Thy guerdon . . . Accolade thou dost bestow
Of anonymity time cannot raise:
Vibrant reprieve and pardon thou dost show.

O harp and altar, of the fury fused,
(How could mere toil align thy choiring strings!)
Terrific threshold of the prophet's pledge,
Prayer of pariah, and the lover's cry,—

Again the traffic lights that skim thy swift
Unfractioned idiom, immaculate sigh of stars,
Beading thy path—condense eternity:
And we have seen night lifted in thine arms.

Under thy shadow by the piers I waited;
Only in darknesss is thy shadow clear.
The City's fiery parcels all undone,
Already snow submerges an iron year . . .

O Sleepless as the river under thee,
Vaulting the sea, the prairies' dreaming sod,
Unto us lowliest sometime sweep, descend
And of the curveship lend a myth to God.

The Harbor Dawn

519

INSISTENTLY through sleep—a tide of
    voices—
They meet you listening midway in your
    dream,
The long, tired sounds, fog-insulated noises:
Gongs in white surplices, beshrouded wails,
Far strum of fog horns . . . signals dis-
    persed in veils.

400 years and
more . . . or is
it from the
soundless
shore of sleep
that time

And then a truck will lumber past the
    wharves
As winch engines begin throbbing on some
    deck;

970

Or a drunken stevedore's howl and thud
    below
Comes echoing alley-upward through dim
    snow.

And if they take your sleep away sometimes
They give it back again. Soft sleeves of
    sound
Attend the darkling harbor, the pillowed
    bay;
Somewhere out there in blankness steam

Spills into steam, and wanders, washed
    away
—Flurried by keen fifings, eddied
Among distant chiming buoys—adrift. The
    sky,
Cool feathery fold, suspends, distills
This wavering slumber. . . Slowly—
Immemorially the window, the half-cov-
    ered chair,
Ask nothing but this sheath of pallid air.

And you beside me, blessèd now while
    sirens
Sing to us, stealthily weave us into day—
Serenely now, before day claims our eyes
Your cool arms murmurously about me lay.

    recalls you
    to your love,
    there in a
    waking
    dream to
    merge your
    seed

While myriad snowy hands are clustering at
    the panes—

your hands within my hands are deeds;
my tongue upon your throat—singing
arms close; eyes wide, undoubtful
                    dark

                        drink the dawn—
a forest shudders in your hair!

—with
whom?

The window goes blond slowly. Frostily
        clears.
From Cyclopean towers across Manhattan
        waters
—Two—three bright window-eyes aglitter,
        disk
The sun, released—aloft with cold gulls
        hither.

Who is the
woman with
us in the
dawn? . . .
whose is the
flesh our feet
have moved
upon?

The fog leans one last moment on the sill.
Under the mistletoe of dreams, a star—
As though to join us at some distant hill—
Turns in the waking west and goes to sleep.

520

The River

STICK your patent name on a signboard
brother—all over—going west—young man
Tintex—Japalac—Certain-teed Overalls ads
and lands sakes! under the new playbill
        ripped
in the guaranteed corner—see Bert Wil-
        liams what?
Minstrels when you steal a chicken just

. . . and past
the din and
slogans of
the year—

972

save me the wing for if it isn't
Erie it ain't for miles around a
Mazda—and the telegraphic night coming
    on Thomas

a Ediford—and whistling down the tracks
a headlight rushing with the sound—can
    you
imagine—while an EXPRESS makes time like
SCIENCE—COMMERCE and the HOLYGHOST
RADIO ROARS IN EVERY HOME WE HAVE THE
    NORTHPOLE
WALLSTREET AND VIRGINBIRTH WITHOUT
    STONES OR
WIRES OR EVEN RUNning brooks connecting
    ears
and no more sermons windows flashing roar
Breathtaking—as you like it . . . eh?

           So the 20th Century—so
whizzed the Limited—roared by and left
three men, still hungry on the tracks, plod-
    dingly
watching the tail lights wizen and converge,
    slip-
ping gimleted and neatly out of sight.

          *

The last bear, shot drinking in the Dakotas
Loped under wires that span the mountain
    stream.
Keen instruments, strung to a vast precision

to those
whose
addresses are
never near

Bind town to town and dream to ticking
dream.
But some men take their liquor slow—and
count
—Though they'll confess no rosary nor
clue—
The river's minute by the far brook's year.
Under a world of whistles, wires and steam
Caboose-like they go ruminating through
Ohio, Indiana—blind baggage—
To Cheyenne tagging . . . Maybe Kala-
mazoo.

Time's rendings, time's blendings they con-
strue
As final reckonings of fire and snow;
Strange bird-wit, like the elemental gist
Of unwalled winds they offer, singing low
My Old Kentucky Home and *Casey Jones*,
Some Sunny Day. I heard a road-gang
chanting so.
And afterwards, who had a colt's eyes—one
said,
'Jesus! Oh I remember watermelon days!'
And sped
High in a cloud of merriment, recalled
'—And when my Aunt Sally Simpson
smiled,' he drawled—
'It was almost Louisiana, long ago.'

'There's no place like Booneville though,
Buddy,'
One said, excising a last burr from his vest,

'—For early trouting.' Then peering in the
　　can,
'—But I kept on the tracks.' Possessed,
　　resigned,
He trod the fire down pensively and
　　grinned,
Spreading dry shingles of a beard . . .

　　　　　　　　　　　　　　　　Behind
My father's cannery works I used to see
Rail-squatters ranged in nomad raillery,
The ancient men—wifeless or runaway
Hobo-trekkers that forever search
An empire wilderness of freight and rails.
Each seemed a child, like me, on a loose
　　perch,
Holding to childhood like some termless
　　play.
John, Jake or Charley, hopping the slow
　　freight
—Memphis to Tallahassee—riding the
　　rods,
Blind fists of nothing, humpty-dumpty
　　clods.

Yet they touch something like a key per-
　　haps.
From pole to pole across the hills, the
　　states
—They know a body under the wide rain; *but who have*
Youngsters with eyes like fjords, old repro- *touched her,*
　　bates *knowing her*
　　　　　　　　　　　　　　　　　　without name

With racetrack jargon,—dotting immensity
They lurk across her, knowing her yonder
    breast
Snow-silvered, sumac-stained or smoky
    blue—
Is past the valley-sleepers, south or west.
—As I have trod the rumorous midnights,
    too,

And past the circuit of the lamp's thin flame
(O Nights that brought me to her body
    bare!)
Have dreamed beyond the print that bound
    her name.
Trains sounding the long blizzards out—I
    heard
Wail into distances I knew were hers.
Papooses crying on the wind's long mane
Screamed redskin dynasties that fled the
    brain,
—Dead echoes! But I knew her body there,
Time like a serpent down her shoulder,
    dark,
And space, an eaglet's wing, laid on her
    hair.

Under the Ozarks, domed by Iron Moun-
    tain,
The old gods of the rain lie wrapped in
    pools
Where eyeless fish curvet a sunken fountain
And re-descend with corn from querulous
    crows.

nor the
myths of her
fathers . . .

976

Such pilferings make up their timeless eat-
age,
Propitiate them for their timber torn
By iron, iron—always the iron dealt cleav-
age!
They doze now, below axe and powder
horn.

And Pullman breakfasters glide glistening
steel
From tunnel into field—iron strides the
dew—
Straddles the hill, a dance of wheel on
wheel.
You have a half-hour's wait at Siskiyou,
Or stay the night and take the next train
through.
Southward, near Cairo passing, you can see
The Ohio merging,—borne down Tennes-
see;
And if it's summer and the sun's in dusk
Maybe the breeze will lift the River's musk
—As though the waters breathed that you
might know
*Memphis Johnny, Steamboat Bill, Missouri
Joe.*
Oh, lean from the window, if the train
slows down,
As though you touched hands with some
ancient clown,
—A little while gaze absently below
And hum *Deep River* with them while they
go.

Yes, turn again and sniff once more—look
see,
O Sheriff, Brakeman and Authority—
Hitch up your pants and crunch another
quid,
For you, too, feed the River timelessly.
And few evade full measure of their fate;
Always they smile out eerily what they
seem.
I could believe he joked at heaven's gate—
Dan Midland—jolted from the cold brake-
beam.

Down, down—born pioneers in time's des-
pite,
Grimed tributaries to an ancient flow—
They win no frontier by their wayward
plight,
But drift in stillness, as from Jordan's brow.

You will not hear it as the sea; even stone
Is not more hushed by gravity . . . But slow,
As loth to take more tribute—sliding prone
Like one whose eyes were buried long ago

The River, spreading, flows—and spends
your dream.
What are you, lost within this tideless spell?
You are your father's father, and the
stream—
A liquid theme that floating niggers swell.

Damp tonnage and alluvial march of days—

HART CRANE

Nights turbid, vascular with silted shale
And roots surrendered down of moraine
    clays:
The Mississippi drinks the farthest dale.

O quarrying passion, undertowed sunlight!
The basalt surface drags a jungle grace
Ochreous and lynx-barred in lengthening
    might;
Patience! and you shall reach the biding
    place!

Over De Soto's bones the freighted floors
Throb past the City storied of three
    thrones.
Down two more turns the Mississippi pours
(Anon tall ironsides up from salt lagoons)

And flows within itself, heaps itself free.
All fades but one thin skyline 'round . . .
    Ahead
No embrace opens but the stinging sea;
The River lifts itself from its long bed,

Poised wholly on its dream, a mustard glow
Tortured with history, its one will—flow!
—The Passion spreads in wide tongues,
    choked and slow,
Meeting the Gulf, hosannas silently below.

HART CRANE

521

The Dance

Then you
shall see her
truly—your
blood
remembering
its first
invasion of
her secrecy,
its first
encounters
with her kin,
her chieftain
lover . . . his
shade that
haunts the
lakes and
hills

THE swift red flesh, a winter king—
Who squired the glacier woman down the
sky?
She ran the neighing canyons all the spring;
She spouted arms; she rose with maize—to
die.

And in the autumn drouth, whose burnished
hands
With mineral wariness found out the stone
Where prayers, forgotten, streamed the
mesa sands?
He holds the twilight's dim, perpetual
throne.

Mythical brows we saw retiring—loth,
Disturbed and destined, into denser green.
Greeting they sped us, on the arrow's oath:
Now lie incorrigibly what years between . . .

There was a bed of leaves, and broken play;
There was a veil upon you, Pocahontas,
bride—
O Princess whose brown lap was virgin
May;
And bridal flanks and eyes hid tawny pride.

I left the village for dogwood. By the canoe
Tugging below the mill-race, I could see

Your hair's keen crescent running, and the
    blue
First moth of evening take wing stealthily.

What laughing chains the water wove and
    threw!
I learned to catch the trout's moon whisper;
    I
Drifted how many hours I never knew,
But, watching, saw that fleet young crescent
    die,—

And one star, swinging, take its place, alone,
Cupped in the larches of the mountain
    pass—
Until, immortally, it bled into the dawn.
I left my sleek boat nibbling margin
    grass . . .

I took the portage climb, then chose
A further valley-shed; I could not stop.
Feet nozzled wat'ry webs of upper flows;
One white veil gusted from the very top.

O Appalachian Spring! I gained the ledge;
Steep, inaccessible smile that eastward bends
And northward reaches in that violet wedge
Of Adirondacks!—wisped of azure wands,

Over how many bluffs, tarns, streams I
    sped!

—And knew myself within some boding
    shade:—
Grey tepees tufting the blue knolls ahead,
Smoke swirling through the yellow chestnut
    glade . . .

A distant cloud, a thunder-bud—it grew,
That blanket of the skies: the padded foot
Within,—I heard it; 'til its rhythm drew,
—Siphoned the black pool from the heart's
    hot root!

A cyclone threshes in the turbine crest,
Swooping in eagle feathers down your back;
Know, Maquokeeta, greeting; know death's
    best;
—Fall, Sachem, strictly as the tamarack!

A birch kneels. All her whistling fingers fly.
The oak grove circles in a crash of leaves;
The long moan of a dance is in the sky.
Dance, Maquokeeta: Pocahontas grieves . . .

And every tendon scurries toward the
    twangs
Of lightning deltaed down your saber hair.
Now snaps the flint in every tooth; red
    fangs
And splay tongues thinly busy the blue
    air . . .

Dance, Maquokeeta! snake that lives before,
That casts his pelt, and lives beyond!
    Sprout, horn!

Spark, tooth! Medicine-man, relent,
    restore—
Lie to us,—dance us back the tribal morn!

Spears and assemblies: black drums thrusting
    on—
O yelling battlements,—I, too, was liege
To rainbows currying each pulsant bone:
Surpassed the circumstance, danced out the
    siege!

And buzzard-circleted, screamed from the
    stake;
I could not pick the arrows from my side.
Wrapped in that fire, I saw more escorts
    wake—
Flickering, sprint up the hill groins like a
    tide.

I heard the hush of lava wrestling your
    arms,
And stag teeth foam about the raven throat;
Flame cataracts of heaven in seething
    swarms
Fed down your anklets to the sunset's moat.

O, like the lizard in the furious noon,
That drops his legs and colors in the sun,
—And laughs, pure serpent, Time itself,
    and moon
Of his own fate, I saw thy change begun!

And saw thee dive to kiss that destiny

Like one white meteor, sacrosanct and blent
At last with all that's consummate and free
There, where the first and last gods keep
    thy tent.

*

Thewed of the levin, thunder-shod and
    lean,
Lo, through what infinite seasons dost thou
    gaze—
Across what bivouacs of thin angered slain,
And see'st thy bride immortal in the maize!

Totem and fire-gall, slumbering pyramid—
Though other calendars now stack the sky,
Thy freedom is her largesse, Prince, and
    hid
On paths thou knewest best to claim her by.

High unto Labrador the sun strikes free
Her speechless dream of snow, and stirred
    again,
She is the torrent and the singing tree;
And she is virgin to the last of men . . .

West, west and south! winds over Cumber-
    land
And winds across the llano grass resume
Her hair's warm sibilance. Her breasts are
    fanned
O stream by slope and vineyard—into
    bloom!

And when the caribou slant down for salt
Do arrows thirst and leap? Do antlers shine
Alert, star-triggered in the listening vault
Of dusk?—And are her perfect brows to
    thine?

We danced, O Brave, we danced beyond
    their farms,
In cobalt desert closures made our vows . . .
Now is the strong prayer folded in thine
    arms,
The serpent with the eagle in the boughs.

522   *National Winter Garden*

OUTSPOKEN buttocks in pink beads
Invite the necessary cloudy clinch
Of bandy eyes. . . . No extra mufflings here:
The world's one flagrant, sweating cinch.

And while legs waken salads in the brain
You pick your blonde out neatly through the smoke.
Always you wait for someone else though, always—
(Then rush the nearest exit through the smoke).

Always and last, before the final ring
When all the fireworks blare, begins
A tom-tom scrimmage with a somewhere violin,
Some cheapest echo of them all—begins.

And shall we call her whiter than the snow?
Sprayed first with ruby, then with emerald sheen—
Least tearful and least glad (who knows her smile?)
A caught slide shows her sandstone grey between.

Her eyes exist in swivellings of her teats,
Pearls whip her hips, a drench of whirling strands.
Her silly snake rings begin to mount, surmount
Each other—turquoise fakes on tinselled hands.

We wait that writhing pool, her pearls collapsed,
—All but her belly buried in the floor;
And the lewd trounce of a final muted beat!
We flee her spasm through a fleshless door. . . .

Yet, to the empty trapeze of your flesh,
O Magdalene, each comes back to die alone.
Then you, the burlesque of our lust—and faith,
Lug us back lifeward—bone by infant bone.

523 *The Tunnel*

> To Find the Western path
> Right thro' the Gates of Wrath.
> —*Blake*

PERFORMANCES, assortments, résumés—
Up Times Square to Columbus Circle lights
Channel the congresses, nightly sessions,
Refractions of the thousand theatres, faces—
Mysterious kitchens . . . You shall search them all.

Some day by heart you'll learn each famous sight
And watch the curtain lift in hell's despite;
You'll find the garden in the third act dead,
Finger your knees—and wish yourself in bed
With tabloid crime-sheets perched in easy sight.

Then let you reach your hat
and go.
As usual, let you—also
walking down—-exclaim
to twelve upward leaving
a subscription praise
for what time slays.

Or can't you quite make up your mind to ride;
A walk is better underneath the L a brisk
Ten blocks or so before? But you find yourself
Preparing penguin flexions of the arms,—
As usual you will meet the scuttle yawn:
The subway yawns the quickest promise home.

Be minimum, then, to swim the hiving swarms
Out of the Square, the Circle burning bright—
Avoid the glass doors gyring at your right,
Where boxed alone a second, eyes take fright
—Quite unprepared rush naked back to light:
And down beside the turnstile press the coin
Into the slot. The gongs already rattle.

And so
of cities you bespeak
subways, rivered under streets
and rivers . . . In the car

the overtone of motion
underground, the monotone
of motion is the sound
of other faces, also underground—

'Let's have a pencil Jimmy—living now
at Floral Park
Flatbush—on the Fourth of July—
like a pigeon's muddy dream—potatoes
to dig in the field—travlin the town—too—
night after night—the Culver line—the
girls all shaping up—it used to be—'

Our tongues recant like beaten weather vanes.
This answer lives like verdigris, like hair
Beyond extinction, surcease of the bone;
And repetition freezes—'What

'what do you want? getting weak on the links?
fandaddle daddy don't ask for change—is THIS
FOURTEENTH? it's half past six she said—if
you don't like my gate why did you
swing on it, why *didja*
swing on it
anyhow—'

And somehow anyhow swing—

The phonographs of hades in the brain
Are tunnels that re-wind themselves, and love
A burnt match skating in a urinal—
Somewhere above Fourteenth TAKE THE EXPRESS
To brush some new presentiment of pain—

988

HART CRANE

'But I want service in this office SERVICE
I said—after
the show she cried a little afterwards but—'

Whose head is swinging from the swollen strap?
Whose body smokes along the bitten rails,
Bursts from a smoldering bundle far behind
In back forks of the chasms of the brain,—
Puffs from a riven stump far out behind
In interborough fissures of the mind . . . ?
And why do I often meet your visage here,
Your eyes like agate lanterns—on and on
Below the toothpaste and the dandruff ads?
—And did their riding eyes right through your side,
And did their eyes like unwashed platters ride?
And Death, aloft,—gigantically down
Probing through you—toward me, O evermore!
And when they dragged your retching flesh,
Your trembling hands that night through Baltimore—
That last night on the ballot rounds, did you
Shaking, did you deny the ticket, Poe?

For Gravesend Manor change at Chambers Street.
The platform hurries along to a dead stop.

The intent escalator lifts a serenade
Stilly
Of shoes, umbrellas, each eye attending its shoe, then
Bolting outright somewhere above where streets
Burst suddenly in rain . . . The gongs recur:
Elbows and levers, guard and hissing door.
Thunder is galvothermic here below . . . The car
Wheels off. The train rounds, bending to a scream,

Taking the final level for the dive
Under the river—
And somewhat emptier than before,
Demented, for a hitching second, humps; then
Lets go . . . Toward corners of the floor
Newspapers wing, revolve and wing.
Blank windows gargle signals through the roar.
And does the Dæmon take you home, also,
Wop washerwoman, with the bandaged hair?
After the corridors are swept, the cuspidors—
The gaunt sky-barracks cleanly now, and bare,
O Genoese, do you bring mother eyes and hands
Back home to children and to golden hair?

Dæmon, demurring and eventful yawn!
Whose hideous laughter is a bellows mirth
—Or the muffled slaughter of a day in birth—
O cruelly to inoculate the brinking dawn
With antennæ toward worlds that glow and sink;—
To spoon us out more liquid than the dim
Locution of the eldest star, and pack
The conscience navelled in the plunging wind,
Umbilical to call—and straightway die!

O caught like pennies beneath soot and steam,
Kiss of our agony thou gatherest;
Condensed, thou takest all—shrill ganglia
Impassioned with some song we fail to keep.
And yet, like Lazarus, to feel the slope,
The sod and billow breaking,—lifting ground,
—A sound of waters bending astride the sky
Unceasing with some Word that will not die . . .!

*

A tugboat, wheezing wreaths of steam,
Lunged past, with one galvanic blare stove up the
    River.
I counted the echoes assembling, one after one,
Searching, thumbing the midnight on the piers.
Lights, coasting, left the oily tympanum of waters;
The blackness somewhere gouged glass on a sky.
And this thy harbor, O my City, I have driven under,
Tossed from the coil of ticking towers . . . Tomorrow,
And to be . . . Here by the River that is East—
Here at the waters' edge the hands drop memory;
Shadowless in that abyss they unaccounting lie.
How far away the star has pooled the sea—
Or shall the hands be drawn away, to die?

Kiss of our agony Thou gatherest,
                    O Hand of Fire
                            gatherest—

524   *Imperator Victus*

BIG guns again
No speakee well
But plain.

Again, again—
And they shall tell
The Spanish Main

The Dollar from the Cross.

Big guns again.
But peace to thee,
Andean brain.

That defunct boss.

Big guns again,
Atahualpa,
Imperator Inca—

Slain.

525   *The Hurricane*

Lo, Lord, Thou ridest!
Lord, Lord, Thy swifting heart

Naught stayeth, naught now bideth
But's smithereened apart!

Ay! Scripture flee'th stone!
Milk-bright, Thy chisel wind

Rescindeth flesh from bone
To quivering whittlings thinned—

Swept—whistling straw! Battered,
Lord, e'en boulders now out-leap

Rock sockets, levin-lathered!
Nor, Lord, may worm out-deep

Thy drum's gambade, its plunge abscond!
Lord God, while summits crashing

Whip sea-kelp screaming on blond
Sky-seethe, high heaven dashing—

Thou ridest to the door, Lord!
Thou bidest wall nor floor, Lord!

526 *The Broken Tower*

THE bell-rope that gathers God at dawn
Dispatches me as though I dropped down the knell
Of a spent day—to wander the cathedral lawn
From pit to crucifix, feet chill on steps from hell.

Have you not heard, have you not seen that corps
Of shadows in the tower, whose shoulders sway
Antiphonal carillons launched before
The stars are caught and hived in the sun's ray?

The bells, I say, the bells break down their tower;
And swing I know not where. Their tongues engrave
Membrane through marrow, my long-scattered score
Of broken intervals . . . And I, their sexton slave!

Oval encyclicals in canyons heaping
The impasse high with choir. Banked voices slain!
Pagodas, campaniles with reveilles outleaping—
O terraced echoes prostrate on the plain! . . .

And so it was I entered the broken world
To trace the visionary company of love, its voice
An instant in the wind (I know not whither hurled)
But not for long to hold each desperate choice.

My word I poured. But was it cognate, scored
Of that tribunal monarch of the air
Whose thigh embronzes earth, strikes crystal Word
In wounds pledged once to hope—cleft to despair?

The steep encroachments of my blood left me
No answer (could blood hold such a lofty tower
As flings the question true?)—or is it she
Whose sweet mortality stirs latent power?—

And through whose pulse I hear, counting the strokes
My veins recall and add, revived and sure
The angelus of wars my chest evokes:
What I hold healed, original now, and pure . . .

And builds, within, a tower that is not stone
(Not stone can jacket heaven)—but slip
Of pebbles—visible wings of silence sown
In azure circles, widening as they dip

The matrix of the heart, lift down the eye
That shrines the quiet lake and swells a tower . . .
The commodious, tall decorum of that sky
Unseals her earth, and lifts love in its shower.

ALLEN TATE

b. 1899

527   *Ode to the Confederate Dead*

ROW after row with strict impunity
The headstones yield their names to the element,
The wind whirrs without recollection;
In the riven troughs the splayed leaves
Pile up, of nature the casual sacrament
To the seasonal eternity of death;
Then driven by the fierce scrutiny
Of heaven to their election in the vast breath,
They sough the rumour of mortality.

Autumn is desolation in the plot
Of a thousand acres where these memories grow
From the inexhaustible bodies that are not
Dead, but feed the grass row after rich row.
Think of the autumns that have come and gone!—
Ambitious November with the humors of the year,
With a particular zeal for every slab,
Staining the uncomfortable angels that rot
On the slabs, a wing chipped here, an arm there:
The brute curiosity of an angel's stare
Turns you, like them, to stone,
Transforms the heaving air
Till plunged to a heavier world below
You shift your sea-space blindly
Heaving, turning like the blind crab.

Dazed by the wind, only the wind
The leaves flying, plunge

You know who have waited by the wall
The twilight certainty of an animal,
Those midnight restitutions of the blood
You know—the immitigable pines, the smoky frieze
Of the sky, the sudden call: you know the rage,
The cold pool left by the mounting flood,
Of muted Zeno and Parmenides.
You who have waited for the angry resolution
Of those desires that should be yours tomorrow,
You know the unimportant shrift of death
And praise the vision
And praise the arrogant circumstance
Of those who fall
Rank upon rank, hurried beyond decision—
Here by the sagging gate, stopped by the wall.

Seeing, seeing only the leaves
Flying, plunge and expire

Turn your eyes to the immoderate past,
Turn to the inscrutable infantry rising
Demons out of the earth—they will not last.
Stonewall, Stonewall, and the sunken fields of hemp,
Shiloh, Antietam, Malvern Hill, Bull Run.
Lost in that orient of the thick-and-fast
You will curse the setting sun.

Cursing only the leaves crying
Like an old man in a storm

You hear the shout, the crazy hemlocks point
With troubled fingers to the silence which
Smothers you, a mummy, in time.

                                    The hound bitch
Toothless and dying, in a musty cellar
Hears the wind only.

                            Now that the salt of their blood
Stiffens the saltier oblivion of the sea,
Seals the malignant purity of the flood,
What shall we who count our days and bow
Our heads with a commemorial woe
In the ribboned coats of grim felicity,
What shall we say of the bones, unclean,
Whose verdurous anonymity will grow?
The ragged arms, the ragged heads and eyes
Lost in these acres of the insane green?
The gray lean spiders come, they come and go;
In a tangle of willows without light
The singular screech-owl's tight
Invisible lyric seeds the mind
With the furious murmur of their chivalry.

   We shall say only the leaves
   Flying, plunge and expire

We shall say only the leaves whispering
In the improbable mist of nightfall
That flies on multiple wing;
Night is the beginning and the end
And in between the ends of distraction
Waits mute speculation, the patient curse

That stones the eyes, or like the jaguar leaps
For his own image in a jungle pool, his victim.
What shall we say who have knowledge
Carried to the heart? Shall we take the act
To the grave? Shall we, more hopeful, set up the
    grave
In the house? The ravenous grave?

                                            Leave now

The shut gate and the decomposing wall:
The gentle serpent, green in the mulberry bush,
Riots with his tongue through the hush—
Sentinel of the grave who counts us all!

528   *Last Days of Alice*

ALICE grown lazy, mammoth but not fat,
Declines upon her lost and twilight age;
Above in the dozing leaves the grinning cat
Quivers forever with his abstract rage:

Whatever light swayed on the perilous gate
Forever sways, nor will the arching grass,
Caught when the world clattered, undulate
In the deep suspension of the looking-glass.

Bright Alice! always pondering to gloze
The spoiled cruelty she had meant to say
Gazes learnedly down her airy nose
At nothing, nothing thinking all the day.

998

ALLEN TATE

Turned absent-minded by infinity
She cannot move unless her double move,
The All-Alice of the world's entity
Smashed in the anger of her hopeless love,

Love for herself who, as an earthly twain,
Pouted to join her two in a sweet one;
No more the second lips to kiss in vain
The first she broke, plunged through the glass alone—

Alone to the weight of impassivity,
Incest of spirit, theorem of desire,
Without will as chalky cliffs by the sea,
Empty as the bodiless flesh of fire:

All space, that heaven is a dayless night,
A nightless day driven by perfect lust
For vacancy, in which her bored eyesight
Stares at the drowsy cubes of human dust.

—We too back to the world shall never pass
Through the shattered door, a dumb shade-harried crowd
Being all infinite, function depth and mass
Without figure, a mathematical shroud

Hurled at the air—bless éd without sin!
O God of our flesh, return us to Your wrath,
Let us be evil could we enter in
Your grace, and falter on the stony path!

529 *The Oath*

IT was near evening, the room was cold
Half dark; Uncle Ben's brass bullet-mould
And powder-horn and Major Bogan's face
Above the fire in the half-light plainly said:
There's naught to kill but the animated dead.
Horn nor mould nor major follows the chase.
Being cold I urged Lytle to the fire
In the blank twilight with not much left untold
By two old friends when neither's a great liar.
We sat down evenly in the smoky chill.
There's precious little to say between day and dark,
Perhaps a few words on the implacable will
Of time sailing like a magic barque
Or something as fine for the amenities,
Till dusk seals the window, the fire grows bright,
And the wind saws the hill with a swarm of bees.
Now meditating a little on the firelight
We heard the darkness grapple with the night
And give an old man's valedictory wheeze
From his westward breast between his polar jaws;
Then Lytle asked: Who are the dead?
Who are the living and the dead?
And nothing more was said.
So I, leaving Lytle to that dream,
Decided what it is in time that gnaws
The ageing fury of a mountain stream
When suddenly as an ignorant mind will do
I thought I heard the dark pounding its head
On a rock, crying: *Who are the dead?*
Then Lytle turned with an oath—By God it's true!

The Wolves

THERE are wolves in the next room waiting
With heads bent low, thrust out, breathing
At nothing in the dark; between them and me
A white door patched with light from the hall
Where it seems never (so still is the house)
A man has walked from the front door to the stair.
It has all been forever. Beasts claw the floor.
I have brooded on angels and archfiends
But no man has ever sat where the next room's
Crowded with wolves, and for the honor of man
I affirm that never have I before. Now while
I have looked for the evening star at a cold window
And whistled when Arcturus spilt his light,
I've heard the wolves scuffle, and said: So this
Is man; so—what better conclusion is there—
The day will not follow night, and the heart
Of man has a little dignity, but less patience
Than a wolf's, and a duller sense that cannot
Smell its own mortality. (This and other
Meditations will be suited to other times
After dog silence howls his epitaph.)
Now remember courage, go to the door,
Open it and see whether coiled on the bed
Or cringing by the wall, a savage beast
Maybe with golden hair, with deep eyes
Like a bearded spider on a sunlit floor
Will snarl—and man can never be alone.

531 *The Cross*

THERE is a place that some men know,
I cannot see the whole of it
Nor how I came there. Long ago
Flame burst out of a secret pit
Crushing the world with such a light
The day-sky fell to moonless black,
The kingly sun to hateful night
For those, once seeing, turning back:
For love so hates mortality
Which is the providence of life
She will not let it blessèd be
But curses it with mortal strife,
Until beside the blinding rood
Within that world-destroying pit
—Like young wolves that have tasted blood,
Of death, men taste no more of it.
So blind, in so severe a place
(All life before in the black grave)
The last alternatives they face
Of life, without the life to save,
Being from all salvation weaned—
A stag charged both at heel and head:
Who would come back is turned a fiend
Instructed by the fiery dead.

ALLEN TATE

Sonnets at Christmas

I

THIS is the day His hour of life draws near,
Let me get ready from head to foot for it
Most handily with eyes to pick the year
For small feed to reward a feathered wit.
Some men would see it an epiphany
At ease, at food and drink, others at chase
Yet I, stung lassitude, with ecstasy
Unspent argue the season's difficult case
So: Man, dull critter of enormous head,
What would he look at in the coiling sky?
But I must kneel again unto the Dead
While Christmas bells of paper white and red,
Figured with boys and girls spilt from a sled,
Ring out the silence I am nourished by.

II

Ah, Christ, I love you rings to the wild sky
And I must think a little of the past:
When I was ten I told a stinking lie
That got a black boy whipped; but now at last
The going years, caught in an accurate glow,
Reverse like balls englished upon green baize—
Let them return, let the round trumpets blow
The ancient crackle of the Christ's deep gaze.
Deafened and blind, with senses yet unfound,
Am I, untutored to the after-wit

Of knowledge, knowing a nightmare has no sound;
Therefore with idle hands and head I sit
In late December before the fire's daze
Punished by crimes of which I would be quit.

533   *Aeneas at Washington*

I MYSELF saw furious with blood
Neoptolemus, at his side the black Atridae,
Hecuba and the hundred daughters, Priam
Cut down, his filth drenching the holy fires.
In that extremity I bore me well,
A true gentleman, valorous in arms,
Disinterested and honourable. Then fled:
That was a time when civilization
Run by the few fell to the many, and
Crashed to the shout of men, the clang of arms:
Cold victualing I seized, I hoisted up
The old man my father upon my back,
In the smoke made by sea for a new world
Saving little—a mind imperishable
If time is, a love of past things tenuous
As the hesitation of receding love.

(To the reduction of uncitied littorals
We brought chiefly the vigor of prophecy,
Our hunger breeding calculation
And fixed triumphs)

                              I saw the thirsty dove
In the glowing fields of Troy, hemp ripening
And tawny corn, the thickening Blue Grass

All lying rich forever in the green sun.
I see all things apart, the towers that men
Contrive I too contrived long, long ago.
Now I demand little. The singular passion
Abides its object and consumes desire
In the circling shadow of its appetite.
There was a time when the young eyes were slow,
Their flame steady beyond the firstling fire,
I stood in the rain, far from home at nightfall
By the Potomac, the great Dome lit the water,
The city my blood had built I knew no more
While the screech-owl whistled his new delight
Consecutively dark.

                           Stuck in the wet mire
Four thousand leagues from the ninth buried city
I thought of Troy, what we had built her for.

534   *Winter Mask*

To the memory of W. B. Yeats

I

TOWARDS nightfall when the wind
Tries the eaves and casements
(A winter wind of the mind
Long gathering its will)
I lay the mind's contents
Bare, as upon a table,

And ask, in a time of war,
Whether there is still
To a mind frivolously dull
Anything worth living for.

II

.If I am meek and dull
And a poor sacrifice
Of perverse will to cull
The act from the attempt,
Just look into damned eyes
And give the returning glare;
For the damned like it, the more
Damnation is exempt
From what would save its heir
With a thing worth living for.

III

The poisoned rat in the wall
Cuts through the wall like a knife,
Then blind, drying, and small
And driven to cold water,
Dies of the water of life:
Both damned in eternal ice,
The traitor become the boor
Who had led his friend to slaughter,
Now bites his head—not nice,
The food that he lives for.

IV

I supposed two scenes of hell,
Two human bestiaries,

Might uncommonly well
Convey the doom I thought;
But lest the horror freeze
The gentler estimation
I go to the sylvan door
Where nature has been bought
In rational proration
As a thing worth living for.

v

Should the buyer have been beware?
It is an uneven trade
For man has wet his hair
Under the winter weather
With only fog for shade:
His mouth a bracketed hole
Picked by the crows that bore
Nature to their hanged brother,
Who rattles against the bole
The thing that he lived for.

vi

I asked the master Yeats
Whose great style could not tell
Why it is man hates
His own salvatiòn,
Prefers the way to hell,
And finds his last safety
In the self-made curse that bore
Him towards damnatiòn:
The drowned undrowned by the sea,
The sea worth living for.

535 *Seasons of the Soul*

To the memory of John Peale Bishop, 1892–1944

> *Allor porsi la mano un poco avante,*
> *e colsi un ramicel da un gran pruno;*
> *e il tronco suo gridò: Perchè mi schiante?*

I. SUMMER

SUMMER, this is our flesh,
The body you let mature;
If now while the body is fresh
You take it, shall we give
The heart, lest heart endure
The mind's tattering
Blow of greedy claws?
Shall mind itself still live
If like a hunting king
It falls to the lion's jaws?

Under the summer's blast
The soul cannot endure
Unless by sleight or fast
It seize or deny its day
To make the eye secure.
Brothers-in-arms, remember
The hot wind dries and draws
With circular delay
The flesh, ash from the ember,
Into the summer's jaws.

ALLEN TATE

It was a gentle sun
When, at the June solstice
Green France was overrun
With caterpillar feet.
No head knows where its rest is
Or may lie down with reason
When war's usurping claws
Shall take the heart escheat—
Green field in burning season
To stain the weevil's jaws.

The southern summer dies
Evenly in the fall:
We raise our tired eyes
Into a sky of glass,
Blue, empty, and tall
Without tail or head
Where burn the equal laws
For Balaam and his ass
Above the invalid dead,
Who cannot lift their jaws.

When was it that the summer
(Daylong a liquid light)
And a child, the new-comer,
Bathed in the same green spray,
Could neither guess the night?
The summer had no reason;
Then, like a primal cause
It had its timeless day
Before it kept the season
Of time's engaging jaws.

Two men of our summer world
Descended winding hell
And when their shadows curled
They fearfully confounded
The vast concluding shell:
Stopping, they saw in the narrow
Light a centaur pause
And gaze, then his astounded
Beard, with a notched arrow,
Part back upon his jaws.

II. AUTUMN

It had an autumn smell
And that was how I knew
That I was down a well:
I was no longer young;
My lips were numb and blue,
The air was like fine sand
In a butcher's stall
Or pumice to the tongue:
And when I raised my hand
I stood in the empty hall.

The round ceiling was high
And the gray light like shale
Thin, crumbling and dry:
No rug on the bare floor
Nor any carved detail
To which the eye could glide;
I counted along the wall
Door after closed door
Through which a shade might slide
To the cold and empty hall.

ALLEN TATE

I will leave this house, I said,
There is the autumn weather—
Here, nor living nor dead;
The lights burn in the town
Where men fear together.
Then on the bare floor,
But tiptoe lest I fall,
I walked years down
Towards the front door
At the end of the empty hall.

The door was false—no key
Or lock, and I was caught
In the house; yet I could see
I had been born to it
For miles of running brought
Me back where I began.
I saw now in the wall
A door open a slit
And a fat grizzled man
Come out into the hall:

As in a moonlit street
Men meeting are too shy
To check their hurried feet
But raise their eyes and squint
As through a needle's eye
Into the faceless gloom,—
My father in a gray shawl
Gave me an unseeing glint
And entered another room!
I stood in the empty hall

And watched them come and go
From one room to another,
Old men, old women—slow,
Familiar; girls, boys;
I saw my downcast mother
Clad in her street-clothes,
Her blue eyes long and small,
Who had no look or voice
For him whose vision froze
Him in the empty hall.

III. WINTER

Goddess sea-born and bright,
Return into the sea
Where eddying twilight
Gathers upon your people—
Cold goddess, hear our plea!
Leave the burnt earth, Venus,
For the drying God above,
Hanged in his windy steeple,
No longer bears for us
The living wound of love.

All the sea-gods are dead.
You, Venus, come home
To your salt maidenhead,
The tossed anonymous sea
Under shuddering foam—
Shade for lovers, where
A shark swift as your dove
Shall pace our company
All night to nudge and tear
The livid wound of love.

ALLEN TATE

And now the winter sea:
Within her hollow rind
What sleek facility
Of sea-conceited scop
To plumb the nether mind!
Eternal winters blow
Shivering flakes, and shove
Bodies that wheel and drop—
Cold soot upon the snow
Their livid wound of love.

Beyond the undertow
The gray sea-foliage
Transpires a phosphor glow
Into the circular miles:
In the centre of his cage
The pacing animal
Surveys the jungle cove
And slicks his slithering wiles
To turn the venereal awl
In the livid wound of love.

Beyond the undertow
The rigid madrepore
Resists the winter's flow—
Headless, unageing oak
That gives the leaf no more.
Wilfully as I stood
Within the thickest grove
I seized a branch, which broke;
I heard the speaking blood
(From the livid wound of love)

Drip down upon my toe:
'We are the men who died
Of self-inflicted woe,
Lovers whose stratagem
Led to their suicide.'
I touched my sanguine hair
And felt it drip above
Their brother who, like them,
Was maimed and did not bear
The living wound of love.

IV. SPRING

Irritable spring, infuse
Into the burning breast
Your combustible juice
That as a liquid soul
Shall be the body's guest
Who lights, but cannot stay
To comfort this unease
Which, like a dying coal,
Hastens the cooler day
Of the mother of silences.

Back in my native prime
I saw the orient corn
All space but no time,
Reaching for the sun
Of the land where I was born:
It was a pleasant land
Where even death could please
Us with an ancient pun—
All dying for the hand
Of the mother of silences.

ALLEN TATE

In time of bloody war
Who will know the time?
Is it a new spring star
Within the timing chill,
Talking, or just a mime,
That rises in the blood—
Thin Jack-and-Jilling seas
Without the human will?
Its light is at the flood,
Mother of silences!

It burns us each alone
Whose burning arrogance
Burns up the rolling stone,
This earth—Platonic cave
Of vertiginous chance!
Come, tired Sisyphus,
Cover the cave's egress
Where light reveals the slave,
Who rests when sleeps with us
The mother of silences.

Come, old woman, save
Your sons who have gone down
Into the burning cave:
Come, mother, and lean
At the window with your son
And gaze through its light frame
These fifteen centuries
Upon the shirking scene
Where men, blind, go lame:
Then, mother of silences,

Speak, that we may hear;
Listen, while we confess
That we conceal our fear;
Regard us, while the eye
Discerns by sight or guess
Whether, as sheep foregather
Upon their crooked knees,
We have begun to die;
Whether your kindness, mother,
Is mother of silences.

HOWARD BAKER

b. 1905

536   *Ode to the Sea*

O FIRST created and creating source,
Beloved rib of elemental force;
  Being, in whose deep thighs
  Nascence remotely lies,
Whose golden arms still dripping of the stream
And liquid eyes inform my deepest dream—
  Spotless daughter of Time,
  Teach me his paradigm!
Patient and perfect literate, say how
I may conciliate the Then and Now!

What is the Now? Is it my present glance
Drifting upon this shaken blue expanse?

The showering sun upon my face,
My breath inhaling salty space?

Time seems to focus on this lonely beach;
It crowds my taste and sight, and pours the speech
  Of living Sea into my ear
  So that naught is, but what I hear:

Behind me but a silent mesa land
Recessive from this fragrant step of sand,
  Only the shelving gulf before,
  Lifting a low deep-structured roar.

Yet listen, for that crumbling sound is one
With the long roll of winds behind the sun;
  And vision, freed, may mark
  This glow-worm Earth in dark
Lowlands of space, or moving closer see
Our globe beclouded like an April tree
  With green beneath the spray:
  There, on the green and gray
Danubian plains, our race made dusky stage;
There sleeps pale Crete, there northern forges rage.

The present time is not so small nor dense
That it lies here encompassed by my sense;
  And past and future times are naught
  But modes of individual thought.

Pondering this, I watch the balanced sea—
How from the surf the smooth blue arches flee
  Out, out upon the globe's cold side
  Where purest magnitudes abide,

Where time, eventless, melts away, and then
Grows absolute, devoid of deeds of men!
 Devoid of pride, of shame and crime,
 And time itself devoid of time!

Deep hollow Sea, I am but human kind!
Your sloping azure dales dismay my mind;
 I see your mantle swirled
 Along an empty world
Beckoning where I cannot come, and live.
And live! Ask, Sea, no more than I can give!
 Love with the lover dies;
 With drowned and bleaching thighs,
Clutching your gift of seaweed in my hand,
I should return still undissolved to land!

Man lives with shadeless meadows at his side;
He reckons that his earthly deeds provide
 Fruits for a shading temporal vine,
 Gourds for the well, cool, green, and fine;

The shaggy vine in multiplicity
Matches the pale perfections of the sea,
 But the clear modes of Sea prevail
 Over the vine's complex detail:

Up from the bright sea-coasts our history twines
Sensitive, frail,—uncared for, it declines.
 We know the grip of long sea-hours,
 But count our days by drouths and showers.

In modes of specious presentness, what store,
O Sea, of past events, endows this shore?

What was the quick gaunt ring
  Of voices by the spring?
And what the silent gazing wonderment
Of eyes on nameless tree and creature bent?
  Where wept the old grandee
  Recurrent harms of Sea?
And where emerged from waves upon these sands
That priest who carried God in drenchèd hands?

Fragments!—From fragments history here descends
Upon a bare mud house where seaward bends
  A river-bed. The folk are poor,
  The moon silent as the spoor

Of the coyote. Mongrels hold the wall
For shade, and roam by night. Prayers recall
  Stanchioning names to tongues inside—
  Names like the ruined spars the tide

Casts up, the craft's homeport and tons unknown.
Sometimes the folk, when dry east winds have blown,
  Stooping for shells along the beach,
  With sea-roar blend a bird-like speech.

Evenings with desert glooms enclose their days.
Westward each night the sea's low radiance strays
  Into a brilliant sky.
  So institutions die.
Conserving Sea! To what auroral plains
Have you consigned the meaning of the names
  Augustine, Abelard,
  Aquinas, Bede, Bernard?
Permanent, lossless, undiminished Sea,
Change is the law of your stability!

Swift from the sea comes change; and Christendom—
Like childhood gardens echoing the hum
    Of words from the parental lip—
    Vanishes with the rising ship.

The liner slanting southward changes place
Mysteriously, as if both sea and space,
    Under compulsions of its will,
    Retreat from it while it stands still:

It rends perspectives, it commands the Now!
I with the sea's low eyes inspect its bow,
    Its funnels, inset decks and bridge,
    Steadily from my splashëd ridge.

How well I know the structures of my age!
This long, compact, careering ship is gauge
    And archetype of them all:
    Here man's import is small
Beside the turbine, his rewards are slight;
And yet for some the engines spin delight.
    The ship has rich cuisine,
    Damasks of frosty sheen,
Flowers and wine, with music brass and bold;
And tools, to flay the heathen, in the hold.

Wreathed with horizons momentarily green,
Drunk as a caesar who has lately seen
    Auspice in birds' fastidious flight,
    The ship assails the casual night.

Think that this Leviathan of Ocean,
This dense projection of incarnate motion,

Moves only under someone's hand,
Labors, and answers his command;

Whatever weaker nations it offends,
However it disrupts their codes for ends
   Potentially both good and ill,
   It shapes the world to someone's will.

Men and not monsters warp the bounds of Sea.
Yet may not thoughtless men still monsters be?
   Not fate but men unlock
   The energies of rock,
And to what ends? O guileful Sea, they ask
Only in your false presentness to bask,
   And recklessly to throw
   Their navies on those slow
Confounding graveyards, where dank weeds enchain
The junks of China and the fleets of Spain!

Nations, as thoughtless as Narcissus, drown
Amidst their shattered triumph, and go down
   Gasping a pledge still to restore
   What time has riven from their shore!

I, on my coppery beach, regret the falls,
Not of their banners, but their sober halls.
   —And suddenly there blows on me
   The sterner discipline of Sea:

History is long. Nor men nor nations bear
Lasting degrees of value. They who stare
   Backwards see but themselves impure.
   Man is collective. Change is sure.

The surf is brushing at my steps; I seek
An aged cliff that stands among the sleek
 Young chargers of the sea.
 Bounds of anemone
And areas by sea-urchins held, devise
The narrow range in which the tides will rise
 And fall, though cliffs themselves
 And all the earth's vast shelves
Crumble. And there the mode of permanence
Is fram'd in the sea-tide's changeful cadence.

Sibilant, whispering Sea, beyond the steep
And thorny reach of doubt, your peace hangs deep;
 In its abundant room
 One views the ways of doom
And, viewing, may withhold the part of fear.
O steady in your variance, appear
 Unceasing in my eye,
 And let me now descry
My course, for I return to inland ground
Burdened, yet to the nascent future bound!

ROBERT PENN WARREN

b. 1905

537 *The Ballad of Billie Potts*

(When I was a child I heard this story from an old lady who was a relative of mine. The scene, according to her version, was in the section of Western Kentucky known

ROBERT PENN WARREN

as 'Between the Rivers,' the region between the Cum-
berland and the Tennessee. Years later, I came across
another version in a book on the history of the outlaws
of the Cave Inn Rock, or the Cave-In-Rock. The name
of Bardstown in the present account refers to Bards-
town, Kentucky, where the first race track west of the
mountains was laid out late in the Eighteenth Century.)

Big Billie Potts was big and stout
In the land between the rivers.
His shoulders were wide and his gut stuck out
Like a croker of nubbins and his holler and shout
Made the bob-cat shiver and the black-jack leaves shake
In the section between the rivers.
He would slap you on your back and laugh.

Big Billie had a wife, she was dark and little
In the land between the rivers,
And clever with her wheel and clever with her kettle,
But she never said a word and when she sat
By the fire her eyes worked slow and narrow like a cat
In the land between the rivers.
Nobody knew what was in her head.

They had a big boy with fuzz on his chin
So tall he ducked the door when he came in,
A clabber-headed bastard with snot in his nose
And big red wrists hanging out of his clothes
And a whicker when he laughed where his father had a
    beller
In the section between the rivers.
They called him Little Billie.
He was their darling.

1023

(It is not hard to see the land, what it was.
Low hills and oak. The fetid bottoms where
The slough uncoiled and in the tangled cane,
Where no sun comes, the muskrat's astute face
Was lifted to the yammering jay; then dropped.
Some cabin where the shag-bark stood and the
Magnificent tulip-tree; both now are gone.
But the land is there, and as you top a rise,
Beyond you all the landscape steams and simmers
—The hills, now gutted, red, cane-brake and black-jack
    yet.
The oak leaf steams under the powerful sun.
'Mister, is this the right road to Paducah?'
The red face, seamed and gutted like the hill,
Slow under time, and with the innocent savagery
Of Time, the bleared eyes rolling, answers from
Your dream: 'They names hit so, but I ain't bin.')

Big Billie was the kind who laughed but could spy
The place for a ferry where folks would come by.
He built an inn and folks bound West
Hitched their horses there to take their rest
And grease the gall and grease the belly
And jaw and spit under the trees
In the section between the rivers.
Big Billie said: 'Git down, friend, and take yore ease!'
He would slap you on your back and set you at his table.

(Leaning and slow, you see them move
In massive passion colder than any love:
Their lips move but you do not hear the words
Nor trodden twig nor fluted irony of birds
Nor hear the rustle of the heart

That, heave and settle, gasp and start,
Heaves like a fish in the ribs' dark basket borne
West from the great water's depth whence it was torn.
Their names are like the leaves, but are forgot
—The slush and swill of the world's great pot
That foamed at the range's lip, and spilled
Like quicksilver across green baize, the unfulfilled
Disparate glitter, gleam, wild symptom, seed
Flung in the long wind: silent, proceed
Past meadow, salt-lick, and the lyric swale;
Enter the arbor, shadow of trees, fade, fail.)

Big Billie was sharp at swap and trade
And could smell the nest where the egg was laid,
He could read and cipher and they called him squire
In the land between the rivers.
And he added up his money while he sat by the fire
And sat in the shade while folks sweated and strove,
For he was the one who fatted and throve
In the section between the rivers.
'Thank you kindly, sir,' Big Billie would say
When the man in the black coat paid him at streak of day
And swung to the saddle and was ready to go
And rode away and didn't know
That he was already as good as dead,
For at midnight the message had been sent ahead:
'Man in black coat, riding bay mare with star.'

(There was a beginning but you cannot see it.
There will be an end but you cannot see it.
They will not turn their faces to you though you call,
Who pace a logic merciless as light,

Whose law is their long shadow on the grass,
Sun at the back; pace, pass,
And passing nod in that glacial delirium
While the tight sky shudders like a drum
And speculation rasps its idiot nails
Across the dry slate where you did the sum.

The answer is in the back of the book but the page is gone.
And grandma told you to tell the truth but she is dead.
And heedless, their hairy faces fixed
Beyond your call or question now, they move
Under the infatuate weight of their wisdom,
Precious but for the preciousness of their burden,
Sainted and sad and sage as the hairy ass, who bear
History like bound faggots, with stiff knees;
And breathe the immaculate climate where
The lucent leaf is lifted, lank beard fingered, by no breeze,
Rapt in the fabulous complacency of fresco, vase, or frieze:

And the testicles of the fathers hang down like old lace.)

Little Billie was full of piss and vinegar
And full of sap as a maple tree
And full of tricks as a lop-eared pup,
So one night when the runner didn't show up,
Big Billie called Little and said, 'Saddle up,'
And nodded toward the man was taking his sup
With his belt unlatched and his feet to the fire.
Big Billie said, 'Give Amos a try,
Fer this feller takes the South Fork and Amos'll be nigher
Than Baldy or Buster, and Amos is sly
And slick as a varmint, and I don't deny
I lak bizness with Amos fer he's one you kin trust

In the section between the rivers,
And hit looks lak they's mighty few.
Amos will split up fair and square.'

Little Billie had something in his clabber-head
In addition to snot, and he reckoned he knew
How to skin a cat or add two and two.
So long before the sky got red
Over the land between the rivers,
He hobbled his horse back in the swamp
And squatted on his hams in the morning dew and damp
And scratched his stomach and grinned to think
How his Pap would be proud and his Mammy glad
To know what a thriving boy they had
In the section between the rivers.
He always was a good boy to his darling Mammy.

(Think of yourself riding away from the dawn,
Think of yourself and the unnamed ones who had gone
Before, riding, who rode away from *goodbye, goodbye,*
And toward *hello,* toward Time's unwinking eye;
And like the cicada had left, at cross-roads or square,
The old shell of self, thin, ghostly, translucent, light as
    air;
At dawn riding into the curtain of unwhispering green,
Away from the vigils and voices into the green
World, land of the innocent bough, land of the leaf.
Think of your face green in the submarine light of the
    leaf.

Or think of yourself crouched at the swamp-edge,
Dawn-silence past last owl-hoot and not yet at day-verge
First bird-stir, titmouse or drowsy warbler not yet.

You touch the grass in the dark and your hand is wet.
Then light: and you wait for the stranger's hoofs on the
    soft trace,
And under the green leaf's translucence the light bathes
    your face.

Think of yourself at dawn: Which are you? What?)

Little Billie heard hoofs on the soft grass,
But he squatted and let the rider pass,
For he didn't want to waste good lead and powder
Just to make the slough-fish and swamp-buzzards prouder
In the land between the rivers.
But he saw the feller's face and thanked his luck
It was the one Pap said was fit to pluck.
So he got on his horse and cantered up the trace.
Called, 'Hi thar!' and the stranger watched him coming,
And sat his mare with a smile on his face,
Just watching Little Billie and smiling and humming
In the section between the rivers.
Little Billie rode up and the stranger said,
'Why, bless my heart, if it ain't Little Billie!'

'Good mornen,' said Billie, and said, 'My Pap
Found somethen you left and knowed you'd be missen,
And he ain't wanten nuthen not proper his'n.'
But the stranger didn't do a thing but smile and listen
Polite as could be to what Billie said.
But he must have had eyes in the side of his head
As they rode along beside the slough
In the land between the rivers,
Or known what Billie was out to do,
For when Billie said, 'Mister, I've brung hit to you,'

And reached his hand for it down in his britches,
The stranger just reached his own hand, too.

'Boom!' Billie's gun said, and the derringer, 'Bang!'
'Oh, I'm shot!' Billie howled and grabbed his shoulder.
'Not bad,' said the stranger, 'for you're born to hang,
But I'll save some rope 'fore you're a minute older
If you don't high-tail to your honest Pap
In the section between the rivers.'
Oh, Billie didn't tarry and Billie didn't linger,
For Billie didn't trust the stranger's finger
And didn't admire the stranger's face
And didn't like the climate of the place,
So he turned and high-tailed up the trace,
With blood on his shirt and snot in his nose
And pee in his pants for he'd wet his clothes,
And the stranger just sits and admires how he goes,
And says, 'Why, that boy would do right well back on the
    Bardstown track!'

'You fool!' said his Pap, but his Mammy cried
To see the place where the gore-blood dried
Round the little hole in her darling's hide.
She wiped his nose and patted his head,
But Pappy barred the door and Pappy said,
'That bastard has maybe got some friends
In the section between the rivers,
And you can't say how sich bizness ends
And a man ain't sure he kin trust his neighbors,
Fer thar's mortal spite fer him sweats and labors
Even here between the rivers.'
He didn't ask Little how he felt,
But said, 'Two hundred in gold's in my money belt,

And take the roan and the brand-new saddle
And stop yore blubberen and skeedaddle,
And the next time you try and pull a trick
Fer God's sake don't talk but do hit quick.'
So Little Billie took his leave
And left his Mammy there to grieve
And left his Pappy in Old Kaintuck
And headed West to try his luck
And left the land between the rivers,
For it was Roll, Missouri,
It was Roll, roll, Missouri.
And he was gone nigh ten long year
And never sent word to give his Pappy cheer
Nor wet pen in ink for his Mammy dear.
For Little Billie never was much of a hand with a pen-
    staff.

(There is always another country and always another place.
There is always another name and another face.
And the name and the face are you, and you
The name and the face, and the stream you gaze into
Will show the adoring face, show the lips that lift to you
As you lean with the implacable thirst of self,
As you lean to the image which is yourself,
To set the lip to lip, fix eye on bulging eye,
To drink not of the stream but of your deep identity,
But water is water and it flows,
Under the image on the water the water coils and goes
And its own beginning and its end only the water knows.

There are many countries and the rivers in them
—Cumberland, Tennessee, Ohio, Colorado, Pecos, Little
    Big Horn,

And Roll, Missouri, roll.
But there is only water in them.

And in the new country and in the new place
The eyes of the new friend will reflect the new face
And his mouth will speak to frame
The syllables of the new name
And the name is you and is the agitation of the air
And is the wind and the wind runs and the wind is every-
    where.

The name and the face are you.
The name and the face are always new
And they are you.
Are new.

For they have been dipped in the healing flood.
For they have been dipped in the redeeming blood.
For they have been dipped in Time
And Time is only beginnings
Time is only and always beginnings
And is the redemption of our crime
And is our Saviour's priceless blood.

For Time is always the new place,
And no-place.
For Time is always the new name and the new face,
And no-name and no-face.

For Time is motion
For Time is innocence
For Time is West.)

Oh, who is coming along the trace,
Whistling along in the late sunshine,
With a big black hat above his big red face
And a long black coat that swings so fine?
Oh, who is riding along the trace
Back to the land between the rivers,
With a big black beard growing down to his guts
And silver mountings on his pistol-butts
And a belt as broad as a saddle-girth
And a look in his eyes like he owned the earth?
And meets a man riding up the trace
And looks right sharp and scans his face
And says, 'Durn if'n hit ain't Joe Drew!'
'I reckin hit's me,' says Joe and gives a spit,
'But whupped if'n I figger how you knows hit,
Fer if'n I'm Joe, then who air you?'
And the man with the black beard says: 'Why, I'm Little
    Billie!'
And Joe Drew says: 'Wal, I'll be whupped.'

'Be whupped,' Joe said, 'and whar you goen?'
'Oh, I'm just visiten back whar I done my growen
In the section between the rivers,
Fer I bin out West and taken my share
And I reckin my luck helt out fer fair,
So I done come home,' Little Billie said,
'To see my folks if'n they ain't dead.'
'Ain't dead,' Joe answered, and shook his head,
'But that's the best a man kin say,
Fer hit looked lak when you went away
You taken West yore Pappy's luck
And maybe now you kin bring hit back
To the section between the rivers.'

Little Billie laughed and jingled his pockets and said:
    'Ain't nuthen wrong with my luck.'

And said: 'Wal, I'll be gitten on home,
But after yore supper why don't you come
And we'll open a jug and you tell me the news
In the section between the rivers.
But not too early fer hit's my aim
To git me some fun 'fore they know my name,
And tease 'em and fun 'em, fer you never guessed
I was Little Billie what went out West.'
And Joe Drew said: 'Durn if'n you always wuzn't a hand
    to git yore fun.'

(Over the plain, over mountain and river, drawn,
Wanderer with slit-eyes adjusted to distance,
Drawn out of distance, drawn from the great plateau
Where the sky heeled in the unsagging wind and the cheek
    burned,
Who stood beneath the white peak that glimmered like a
    dream,
And spat, and it was morning and it was morning.
You lay among the wild plums and the kildees cried.
You lay in the thicket under the new leaves and the kildees
    cried,
For you all luck, for all the astuteness of your heart,
And would not stop and would not stop
And the clock ticked all night long in the furnished room
And would not stop
And the *El*-train passed on the quarters with a whish like a
    terrible broom
And would not stop

And there is always the sound of breathing in the next
     room
And it will not stop
And the waitress says, 'Will that be all, sir, will that be all?'
And will not stop
And the valet says, 'Will that be all, sir, will that be all?'
And will not stop
For nothing is ever all and nothing is ever all,
For all your experience and your expertness of human vices
     and of valor
At the hour when the ways are darkened.

Though your luck held and the market was always satis-
     factory,
Though the letter always came and your lovers were always
     true,
Though you always received the respect due to your
     position,
Though your hand never failed of its cunning and your
     glands always thoroughly knew their business,
Though your conscience was easy and you were assured of
     your innocence,
You became gradually aware that something was missing
     from the picture,
And upon closer inspection exclaimed: 'Why, I'm not in it
     at all!'
Which was perfectly true.

Therefore you tried to remember when you had last had
     whatever it was you had lost,
But it was a long time back.
And you decided to retrace your steps from that point,
But it was a long way back.

It was, nevertheless, absolutely essential to make the effort,
And since you had never been a man to be deterred by
　　difficult circumstances,
You came back.
For there is no place like home.)

He joked them and he teased them and he had his fun
And they never guessed that he was the one
Had been Mammy's darling and Pappy's joy
When he was a great big whickering boy
In the land between the rivers,
And he jingled his pockets and he took his sop
And patted his belly which was full nigh to pop
And wiped the buttermilk out of his beard
And took his belch and up and reared
Back from the table and cocked his chair
And said, 'Old man, ain't you got any fresh drinken water,
　　this here ain't fresher'n a hoss puddle?'
And the old woman said: 'Pappy, why don't you take the
　　young gentleman down to the spring so he kin git hit
　　good and fresh?'
And the old woman gave the old man a straight look.
She gave him the bucket but it was not empty but it was
　　not water.

Oh, the stars are shining and the meadow is bright
But under the trees is dark and night
In the land between the rivers.
Oh, on the trace the fireflies spark
But under the trees is night and dark,
And way off yonder is the whippoorwill
And the owl off yonder hoots on the hill
But under the trees is dark and still

In the section between the rivers.
And the leaves hang down in the dark of the trees
And there is the spring in the dark of the trees
And there is the spring as black as ink
And one star in it caught through a chink
Of the leaves that hang down in the dark of the trees,
And the star is there but it does not wink.
And Little Billie gets down on his knees
And props his hands in the same old place
To sup the water at his ease;
And the star is gone but there is his face.
'Just help yoreself,' Big Billie said;
Then set the hatchet in his head.
They went through his pockets and they buried him in the
    dark of the trees.
'I figgered he was a ripe 'un,' the old man said.
'Yeah, but you wouldn't done nuthen hadn't bin fer me,'
    the old woman said.

(The reflection is shadowy and the form not clear,
For the hour is late, is late, and scarcely a glimmer comes
    here
Under the leaf, the bough, in its innocence dark;
And under your straining face you can scarcely mark
The darkling gleam of your face little less than the water
    dark.

But perhaps what you lost was lost in the pool long ago
When childlike you lost it and then in your innocence rose
    to go
After kneeling, as now, with your thirst beneath the leaves:
And years it lies here and dreams in the depth and grieves,
More faithful than mother or father in the light or dark
    of the leaves.

But after, after the irrefutable modes and marches,
After waters that never quench the thirst in the throat that
    parches,
After the sleep that sieves the long day's dubieties
And the cricket's corrosive wisdom under the trees,
After the rumor of wind and the bright anonymities,

You come, weary of greetings and the new friend's smile,
Weary in art of the stranger, worn with your wanderer's
    wile,
Weary of innocence and the husks of Time,
Prodigal, back to the homeland of no-Time,
To ask forgiveness and the patrimony of your crime;

And kneel in the untutored night as to demand
What gift—oh, father, father—from that dissevering
    hand?)

'And whar's Little Billie?' Joe Drew said.
'Air you crazy,' said Big, 'and plum outa yore head,
Fer you knows he went West nigh ten long year?'
'Went West,' Joe said, 'but I seen him here
In the section between the rivers,
Riden up the trace as big as you please
With a long black coat comen down to his knees
And a big black beard comen down to his guts
And silver mountens on his pistol-butts
And he said out West how he done struck
It rich and wuz bringen you back yore luck.'
'I shore-God could use some luck,' Big Billie said,
But his woman wet her lips and craned her head
And said: 'Come riden with a big black beard, you say?'
And Joe: 'Oh, hit wuz Billie as big as day.'

And the old man's eyes bugged out of a sudden and he
    croaked like a sick bull-frog and said: 'Come riden
    with a long black coat?'

Oh, the night is still and the grease-lamp low
And the old man's breath comes wheeze and slow.
Oh, the blue flame sucks on the old rag wick
And the old woman's breath comes sharp and quick,
And there isn't a sound under the roof
But her breath's hiss and his breath's puff,
And there isn't a sound outside the door
As they hearken but cannot hear any more
The creak of the saddle or the plop of the hoof,
For a long time now Joe Drew's been gone
And left them sitting there alone
While the dark outside gets big and still,
For the owl doesn't hoot off there on the hill
Any more and is quiet, and the whippoorwill
Is quiet in the dark of the trees and still
In the land between the rivers.
And so they sit and breathe and wait
And breathe while the night gets big and late,
And neither of them gives move or stir
And she won't look at him and he won't look at her.
He doesn't look at her but he says: 'Git me the spade.'

She grabbled with her hands and he dug with the spade
Where the leaves let down the dark and shade
In the land between the rivers.
She grabbled like a dog in the hole they made,
But stopped of a sudden and then she said,
'I kin put my hand on his face.'
They light up a pine-knot and lean at the place

Where the man in the black coat slumbers and lies
With trash in his beard and dirt on his face;
And the torch-flame shines in his wide-open eyes.
Down the old man leans with the flickering flame
And moves his lips, says: 'Tell me his name.'
'Ain't Billie, ain't Billie,' the old woman cries,
'Oh, hit ain't my Billie, fer he wuz little
And helt to my skirt while I stirred the kittle
And called me Mammy and hugged me tight
And come in the house when hit fell night.'
But the old man leans down with the flickering flame
And croaks: 'But tell me his name.'
'Oh, he ain't got none, fer he just come riden
From some fer place whar he'd bin biden,
And ain't got a name and never had none,
But Billie, my Billie, he had one.
And hit wuz Billie, hit wuz his name.'
But the old man croaked: 'Tell me his name.'
'Oh, he ain't got none and hit's all the same,
But Billie had one, and he wuz little
And offen his chin I would wipe the spittle
And wiped the drool and kissed him thar
And counted his toes and kissed him whar
The little black mark wuz under his tit,
Shaped lak a clover under his left tit,
With a shape fer luck and I'd kiss hit—'
And the old man blinks in the pine-knot flare
And his mouth comes open like a fish for air,
Then he says right low, 'I had nigh fergot.'
'Oh, I kissed him on his little luck-spot
And I kissed and he'd laff as lak as not—'
The old man said: 'Git his shirt open.'

The old woman opened the shirt and there was the birth-
mark under the left tit.
It was shaped for luck.

(The bee knows, and the eel's cold ganglia burn,
And the sad head lifting to the long return,
Through brumal deeps, in the great unsolsticed coil,
Carries its knowledge, navigator without star,
And under the stars, pure in its clamorous toil,
The goose hoots north where the starlit marshes are.
The salmon heaves at the fall, and, wanderer, you
Heave at the great fall of Time, and gorgeous, gleam
In the powerful arc, and anger and outrage like dew,
In your plunge, fling, and plunge to the thunderous stream:
Back to the silence, back to the pool, back
To the high pool, motionless, and the unmurmuring dream.
And you, wanderer, back,
Brother to pinion and the pious fin that cleave
Their innocence of air and the disinfectant flood
And wing and welter and weave
The long compulsion and the circuit hope
Back,
And bear through that limitless and devouring fluidity
The itch and humble promise which is home.
And you, wanderer, back,
For the beginning is death and the end may be life,
For the beginning was definition and the end may be
definition,
And our innocence needs, perhaps, new definition,
And the wick needs the flame
But the flame needs the wick.
And the father waits for the son.
The hour is late,

ROBERT PENN WARREN

The scene familiar even in shadow,
The transaction brief,
And you, wanderer, back,
After the striving and the wind's word,
To kneel
Here in the evening empty of wind or bird,
To kneel in the sacramental silence of evening
At the feet of the old man
Who is evil and ignorant and old,
To kneel
With the little black mark under your heart,
Which is your name,
Which is shaped for luck,
Which is your luck.)

W. H. AUDEN

b. 1907

538   *Another Time*

For us like any other fugitive,
Like the numberless flowers that cannot number
And all the beasts that need not remember,
It is today in which we live.

So many try to say Not Now,
So many have forgotten how
To say I Am, and would be
Lost, if they could, in history.

Bowing, for instance, with such old-world grace
To a proper flag in a proper place,
Muttering like ancients as they stump upstairs
Of Mine and His or Ours and Theirs.

Just as if time were what they used to will
When it was gifted with possession still,
Just as if they were wrong
In no more wishing to belong.

No wonder then so many die of grief,
So many are so lonely as they die;
No one has yet believed or liked a lie,
Another time has other lives to live.

539   *Herman Melville*

(For Lincoln Kirstein)

TOWARDS the end he sailed into an extraordinary
    mildness,
And anchored in his home and reached his wife
And rode within the harbour of her hand,
And went across each morning to an office
As though his occupation were another island.

Goodness existed: that was the new knowledge
His terror had to blow itself quite out
To let him see it; but it was the gale had blown him
Past the Cape Horn of sensible success
Which cries: 'This rock is Eden. Shipwreck here.'

But deafened him with thunder and confused with
    lightning:
—The maniac hero hunting like a jewel
The rare ambiguous monster that had maimed his sex,
Hatred for hatred ending in a scream,
The unexplained survivor breaking off the nightmare—
All that was intricate and false; the truth was simple.

Evil is unspectacular and always human,
And shares our bed and eats at our own table,
And we are introduced to Goodness every day,
Even in drawing-rooms among a crowd of faults;
He has a name like Billy and is almost perfect
But wears a stammer like a decoration:
And every time they meet the same thing has to happen;
It is the Evil that is helpless like a lover
And has to pick a quarrel and succeeds,
And both are openly destroyed before our eyes.

For now he was awake and knew
No one is ever spared except in dreams;
But there was something else the nightmare had distorted—
Even the punishment was human and a form of love:
The howling storm had been his father's presence
And all the time he had been carried on his father's breast.

Who now had set him gently down and left him.
He stood upon the narrow balcony and listened:
And all the stars above him sang as in his childhood
'All, all is vanity,' but it was not the same;
For now the words descended like the calm of mountains—
—Nathaniel had been shy because his love was selfish—

But now he cried in exultation and surrender
'The Godhead is broken like bread. We are the pieces.'

And sat down at his desk and wrote a story.

540   *September 1, 1939*

I SIT in one of the dives
On Fifty-second Street
Uncertain and afraid
As the clever hopes expire
Of a low dishonest decade:
Waves of anger and fear
Circulate over the bright
And darkened lands of the earth,
Obsessing our private lives;
The unmentionable odour of death
Offends the September night.

Accurate scholarship can
Unearth the whole offence
From Luther until now
That has driven a culture mad,
Find what occurred at Linz,
What huge imago made
A psychopathic god:
I and the public know
What all schoolchildren learn,
Those to whom evil is done
Do evil in return.

W. H. AUDEN

Exiled Thucydides knew
All that a speech can say
About Democracy,
And what dictators do,
The elderly rubbish they talk
To an apathetic grave;
Analysed all in his book,
The enlightenment driven away,
The habit-forming pain,
Mismanagement and grief:
We must suffer them all again.

Into this neutral air
Where blind skyscrapers use
Their full height to proclaim
The strength of Collective Man,
Each language pours its vain
Competitive excuse:
But who can live for long
In an euphoric dream;
Out of the mirror they stare,
Imperialism's face
And the international wrong.

Faces along the bar
Cling to their average day:
The lights must never go out,
The music must always play,
All the conventions conspire
To make this fort assume
The furniture of home;
Lest we should see where we are,
Lost in a haunted wood,

Children afraid of the night
Who have never been happy or good.

The windiest militant trash
Important Persons shout
Is not so crude as our wish:
What mad Nijinsky wrote
About Diaghilev
Is true of the normal heart;
For the error bred in the bone
Of each woman and each man
Craves what it cannot have,
Not universal love
But to be loved alone.

From the conservative dark
Into the ethical life
The dense commuters come,
Repeating their morning vow;
'I *will* be true to the wife,
I'll concentrate more on my work,'
And helpless governors wake
To resume their compulsory game:
Who can release them now,
Who can reach the deaf,
Who can speak for the dumb?

Defenceless under the night
Our world in stupor lies;
Yet, dotted everywhere,
Ironic points of light
Flash out wherever the Just
Exchange their messages:

May I, composed like them
Of Eros and of dust,
Beleaguered by the same
Negation and despair,
Show an affirming flame.

541   *In Memory of Sigmund Freud*
              (d. Sept. 1939)

WHEN there are so many we shall have to mourn,
When grief has been made so public, and exposed
              To the critique of a whole epoch
              The frailty of our conscience and anguish,

Of whom shall we speak? For every day they die
Among us, those who were doing us some good,
              And knew it was never enongh but
              Hoped to improve a little by living.

Such was this doctor: still at eighty he wished
To think of our life, from whose unruliness
              So many plausible young futures
              With threats or flattery ask obedience.

But his wish was denied him; he closed his eyes
Upon that last picture common to us all,
              Of problems like relatives standing
              Puzzled and jealous about our dying.

For about him at the very end were still
Those he had studied, the nervous and the nights,

And shades that still waited to enter
The bright circle of his recognition

Turned elsewhere with their disappointment as he
Was taken away from his old interest
　　　　To go back to the earth in London,
　　　　An important Jew who died in exile.

Only Hate was happy, hoping to augment
His practice now, and his shabby clientèle
　　　　Who think they can be cured by killing
　　　　And covering the gardens with ashes.

They are still alive but in a world he changed
Simply by looking back with no false regrets;
　　　　All that he did was to remember
　　　　Like the old and be honest like children.

He wasn't clever at all: **he** merely told
The unhappy Present to recite the Past
　　　　Like a poetry lesson till sooner
　　　　Or later it faltered at the line where

Long ago the accusations had begun,
And suddenly knew by whom it had been judged,
　　　　How rich life had been and how silly,
　　　　And was life-forgiven and more humble.

Able to approach the Future as a friend
Without a wardrobe of excuses, without
　　　　A set mask of rectitude or an
　　　　Embarrassing over-familiar gesture.

No wonder the ancient cultures of conceit
In his technique of unsettlement foresaw
        The fall of princes, the collapse of
        Their lucrative patterns of frustration.

If he succeeded, why, the Generalised Life
Would become impossible, the monolith
        Of State be broken and prevented
        The co-operation of avengers.

Of course they called on God: but he went his way,
Down among the Lost People like Dante, down
        To the stinking fosse where the injured
        Lead the ugly life of the rejected.

And showed us what evil is: not as we thought
Deeds that must be punished, but our lack of faith,
        Our dishonest mood of denial,
        The concupiscence of the oppressor.

And if something of the autocratic pose,
The paternal strictness he distrusted, still
        Clung to his utterance and features,
        It was a protective imitation

For one who lived among enemies so long;
If often he was wrong and at times absurd,
        To us he is no more a person
        Now but a whole climate of opinion.

Under whom we conduct our differing lives:
Like weather he can only hinder or help,
        The proud can still be proud but find it
        A little harder, and the tyrant tries

To make him do but doesn't care for him much.
He quietly surrounds all our habits of growth;
   He extends, till the tired in even
   The remotest most miserable duchy

Have felt the change in their bones and are cheered,
And the child unlucky in his little State,
   Some hearth where freedom is excluded,
   A hive whose honey is fear and worry,

Feels calmer now and somehow assured of escape;
While as they lie in the grass of our neglect,
   So many long-forgotten objects
   Revealed by his undiscouraged shining

Are returned to us and made precious again;
Games we had thought we must drop as we grew up,
   Little noises we dared not laugh at,
   Faces we made when no one was looking.

But he wishes us more than this: to be free
Is often to be lonely; he would unite
   The unequal moieties fractured
   By our own well-meaning sense of justice.

Would restore to the larger the wit and will
The smaller possesses but can only use
   For arid disputes, would give back to
   The son the mother's richness of feeling.

But he would have us remember most of all
To be enthusiastic over the night
   Not only for the sense of wonder
   It alone has to offer, but also

Because it needs our love: for with sad eyes
Its delectable creatures look up and beg
           Us dumbly to ask them to follow;
           They are exiles who long for the future

That lies in our power. They too would rejoice
If allowed to serve enlightenment like him,
           Even to bear our cry of 'Judas,'
           As he did and all must bear who serve it.

One rational voice is dumb: over a grave
The household of Impulse mourns one dearly loved.
           Sad is Eros, builder of cities,
           And weeping anarchic Aphrodite.

542   *The Flight into Egypt*

I

JOSEPH

MIRROR, let us through the glass
No authority can pass.

MARY

Echo, if the strong should come,
Tell a white lie or be dumb.

VOICES OF THE DESERT

It was visitors' day at the vinegar works
In Tenderloin Town when I tore my time;

A sorrowful snapshot was my sinful wage:
Was that why you left me, elusive bones?
  Come to our bracing desert
  Where eternity is eventful,
    For the weather-glass
    Is set at Alas,
  The thermometer at Resentful.

MARY

The Kingdom of the Robbers lies
Between Time and our memories;

JOSEPH

Fugitives from Space must cross
The waste of the Anonymous.

VOICES OF THE DESERT

How should he figure my fear of the dark?
The moment he can he'll remember me,
The silly, he locked in the cellar for fun,
And his dear little doggie shall die in his arms.
  Come to our old-world desert
  Where everyone goes to pieces;
    You can pick up tears
    For souvenirs
  Or genuine diseases.

JOSEPH

Geysers and volcanoes give
Sudden comical relief;

W. H. AUDEN

MARY

And the vulture is a boon
On a dull hot afternoon.

VOICES OF THE DESERT

All Father's nightingales knew their place,
The gardens were loyal: look at them now.
The roads are so careless, the rivers so rude,
My studs have been stolen; I must speak to the sea.
  Come to our well-run desert
  Where anguish arrives by cable,
    And the deadly sins
    May be bought in tins
  With instructions on the label.

MARY

Skulls recurring every mile
Direct the thirsty to the Nile;

JOSEPH

And the jackal's eye at night
Forces Error to keep right.

VOICES OF THE DESERT

In a land of lilies I lost my wits,
Nude as a number all night I ran
With a ghost for a guest along green canals;
By the waters of waking I wept for the weeds.

W. H. AUDEN

Come to our jolly desert
Where even the dolls go whoring;
*   Where cigarette-ends*
*   Become intimate friends,*
And it's always three in the morning.

JOSEPH AND MARY

Safe in Egypt we shall sigh
For lost insecurity;
Only when her terrors come
Does our flesh feel quite at home.

II

RECITATIVE

Fly, Holy Family, from our immediate rage,
That our future may be freed from our past; retrace
    The footsteps of law-giving
  Moses, back through the sterile waste,

Down to the rotten kingdom of Egypt, the damp
Tired delta where in her season of glory our
    Forefathers sighed in bondage;
  Abscond with the Child to the place

That their children dare not revisit, to the time
They do not care to remember; hide from our pride
    In our humiliation;
  Fly from our death with our new life.

III

NARRATOR

Well, so that is that. Now we must dismantle the tree,
Putting the decorations back into their cardboard boxes—
Some have got broken—and carrying them up to the attic.
The holly and the mistletoe must be taken down and burnt,
And the children got ready for school. There are enough
Left-overs to do, warmed-up, for the rest of the week—
Not that we have much appetite, having drunk such a lot,
Stayed up so late, attempted—quite unsuccessfully—
To love all of our relatives, and in general
Grossly overestimated our powers. Once again
As in previous years we have seen the actual Vision and
    failed
To do more than entertain it as an agreeable
Possibility, once again we have sent Him away,
Begging though to remain His disobedient servant,
The promising child who cannot keep His word for long.
The Christmas Feast is already a fading memory,
And already the mind begins to be vaguely aware
Of an unpleasant whiff of apprehension at the thought
Of Lent and Good Friday which cannot, after all, now
Be very far off. But, for the time being, here we all are,
Back in the moderate Aristotelian city
Of darning and the Eight-Fifteen, where Euclid's
    geometry
And Newton's mechanics would account for our experience,
And the kitchen table exists because I scrub it.
It seems to have shrunk during the holidays. The streets
Are much narrower than we remembered; we had
    forgotten
The office was as depressing as this. To those who have seen

The Child, however dimly, however incredulously,
The Time Being is, in a sense, the most trying time of all.
For the innocent children who whispered so excitedly
Outside the locked door where they knew the presents to be
Grew up when it opened. Now, recollecting that moment
We can repress the joy, but the guilt remains conscious;
Remembering the stable where for once in our lives
Everything became a You and nothing was an It.
And craving the sensation but ignoring the cause,
We look round for something, no matter what, to inhibit
Our self-reflection, and the obvious thing for that purpose
Would be some great suffering. So, once we have met the
    Son,
We are tempted ever after to pray to the Father;
'Lead us into temptation and evil for our sake.'
They will come, all right, don't worry; probably in a form
That we do not expect, and certainly with a force
More dreadful than we can imagine. In the meantime
There are bills to be paid, machines to keep in repair,
Irregular verbs to learn, the Time Being to redeem
From insignificance. The happy morning is over,
The night of agony still to come; the time is noon:
When the Spirit must practise his scales of rejoicing
Without even a hostile audience, and the Soul endure
A silence that is neither for nor against her faith
That God's Will will be done, that, in spite of her prayers,
God will cheat no one, not even the world of its triumph.

IV

CHORUS

He is the Way.
Follow Him through the Land of Unlikeness;
You will see rare beasts, and have unique adventures.

W. H. AUDEN

He is the Truth.
Seek Him in the Kingdom of Anxiety;
You will come to a great city that has expected your return
    for years.

He is the Life.
Love Him in the World of the Flesh;
And at your marriage all its occasions shall dance for joy.

DELMORE SCHWARTZ

b. 1913

543   *The Ballet of the Fifth Year*

WHERE the sea gulls sleep or indeed where they fly
Is a place of different traffic. Although I
Consider the fishing bay (where I see them dip and curve
And purely glide) a place that weakens the nerve
Of will, and closes my eyes, as they should not be
(They should burn like the street-light all night quietly,
So that whatever is present will be known to me),
Nevertheless the gulls and the imagination
Of where they sleep, which comes to creation
In strict shape and color, from their dallying
Their wings slowly, and suddenly rallying
Over, up, down the arabesque of descent,
Is an old act enacted, my fabulous intent
When I skated, afraid of policemen, five years old,
In the winter sunset, sorrowful and cold,
Hardly attained to thought, but old enough to know
Such grace, so self-contained, was the best escape to know.

544   *'All of us always turning away*
for solace'

ALL of us always turning away for solace

From the lonely room where the self must be honest,
All of us turning from being alone (at best
Boring) because what we want most is to be
Interested,
        play billiards, poking a ball
On the table, play baseball, batting a ball
On the diamond, play football, kicking a ball
On the gridiron,
        70,000 applauding.

This amuses, this indeed is our solace:
Follow the bouncing ball! O, fellow, follow,
See what is here and clear, one thing repeated,
Bounding, evasive, caught and uncaught, fumbled,
—Follow the bouncing ball; and thus you follow,
Fingering closely your breast on the left side,

The bouncing ball you turned from for solace.

545   *'All clowns are masked'*

ALL clowns are masked and all *personae*
Flow from choices; sad and gay, wise,

1058

DELMORE SCHWARTZ

Moody and humorous are chosen faces,
And yet not so! For all are circumstances,
Given, like a tendency
To colds or like blond hair and wealth,
Or war and peace or gifts for mathematics,
Fall from the sky, rise from the ground, stick to us
In time, surround us: Socrates is mortal.

Gifts and choices! All men are masked,
And we are clowns who think to choose our faces
And we are taught in time of circumstances
And we have colds, blond hair and mathematics,
For we have gifts which interrupt our choices,
And all our choices grasp in Blind Man's Buff:
'My wife was very different, after marriage,'
'I practise law, but botany's my pleasure,'
Save postage stamps or photographs,
But save your soul! Only the past is immortal.

Decide to take a trip, read books of travel,
Go quickly! Even Socrates is mortal,
Mention the name of happiness: it is
Atlantis, Ultima Thule, or the limelight,
Cathay or Heaven. But go quickly
And remember: there are circumstances,
And he who chooses chooses what is given,
He who chooses is ignorant of Choice,
—Choose love, for love is full of children,
Full of choices, children choosing
Botany, mathematics, law and love,
So full of choices! So full of children!
And the past is immortal, the future is inexhaustible!

546   *for Rhoda*

CALMLY we walk through this April's day,
Metropolitan poetry here and there,
In the park sit pauper and *rentier*,
The screaming children, the motor car
Fugitive about us, running away,
Between the worker and the millionaire
Number provides all distances,
It is Nineteen Thirty-Seven now,
Many great dears are taken away,
What will become of you and me
(This is the school in which we learn . . .)
Besides the photo and the memory?
(. . . that time is the fire in which we burn.)

(This is the school in which we learn . . .)
What is the self amid this blaze?
What am I now that I was then
Which I shall suffer and act again,
The theodicy I wrote in my high school days
Restored all life from infancy,
The children shouting are bright as they run
(This is the school in which they learn . . .)
Ravished entirely in their passing play!
(. . . that time is the fire in which they burn.)

Avid its rush, that reeling blaze!
Where is my father and Eleanor?
Not whete are they now, dead seven years,
But what they were then?

No more? No more?
From Nineteen-Fourteen to the present day,
Bert Spira and Rhoda consume, consume
Not where they are now (where are they now?)
But what they were then, both beautiful;
Each minute bursts in the burning room,
The great globe reels in the solar fire,
Spinning the trivial and unique away.
(How all things flash! How all things flare!)
What am I now that I was then?
May memory restore again and again
The smallest color of the smallest day:
Time is the school in which we learn,
Time is the fire in which we burn.

547   *Prothalamion*

'little soul, little flirting,
  little perverse one
    where are you off to now?
little wan one, firm one
  little exposed one . . .
    and never make fun of me again.'

Now I must betray myself.
The feast of bondage and unity is near,
And none engaged in that great piety
When each bows to the other, kneels, and takes
Hand and hand, glance and glance, care and care,
None may wear masks or enigmatic clothes,

For weakness blinds the wounded face enough.
In this sense, see my shocking nakedness.

I gave a girl an apple when five years old,
Saying, Will you be sorry when I am gone?
Ravenous for such courtesies, my name
Is fed like a raving fire, insatiate still.
But do not be afraid.
For I forget myself. I do indeed
Before each genuine beauty, and I will
Forget myself before your unknown heart.

I will forget the speech my mother made
In a restaurant, trapping my father there
At dinner with his whore. Her spoken rage
Struck down the child of seven years
With shame for all three, with pity for
The helpless harried waiter, with anger for
The diners gazing, avid, and contempt,
And great disgust for every human being.
I will remember this. My mother's rhetoric
Has charmed my various tongue, but now I know
Love's metric seeks a rhyme more pure and sure.

For thus it is that I betray myself,
Passing the terror of childhood at second hand
Through nervous, learnéd fingertips.
At thirteen when a little girl died,
I walked for three weeks neither alive nor dead,
And could not understand and still cannot
The adult blind to the nearness of the dead,
Or carefully ignorant of their own death.
—This sense could shadow all time's curving fruits,

But we will taste of them the whole night long,
Forgetting no twelfth night, no fête of June,
But in the daylight knowing our nothingness.

Let Freud and Marx be wedding guests indeed!
Let them mark out the masks that face us there,
For of all anguish, weakness, loss and failure,
No form is cruel as self-deception, none
Shows day-by-day a bad dream long lived
And unbroken like the lies
We tell each other because we 'are rich or poor.
Though from the general guilt not free
We can keep honor by being poor.

The waste, the evil, the abomination
Is interrupted. The perfect stars persist
Small in the guilty night,
                          and Mozart shows
The irreducible incorruptible good
Risen past birth and death, though he is dead.
Hope, like a face reflected on the windowpane,
Remote and dim, fosters a myth or dream,
And in that dream, I speak, I summon all
Who are our friends somehow and thus I say:

'Bid the jewellers come with monocles,
Exclaiming, Pure! Intrinsic! Final!
Summon the children eating ice cream
To speak the chill thrill of immediacy.
Call for the acrobats who tumble
The ecstasy of the somersault.
Bid the self-sufficient stars be piercing
In the sublime and inexhaustible blue.

'Bring a mathematician, there is much to count,
The unending continuum of my attention:
Infinity will hurry his multiplied voice!
Bring the poised impeccable diver,
Summon the skater, precise in figure,
He knows the peril of circumstance,
The risk of movement and the hard ground.
Summon the florist! And the tobacconist!
All who have known a plant-like beauty:
Summon the charming bird for ignorant song.

'You, Athena, with your tired beauty,
Will you give me away? For you must come
In a bathing suit with that white owl
Whom, as I walk, I will hold in my hand.
You too, Crusoe, to utter the emotion
Of finding Friday, no longer alone;
You too, Chaplin, muse of the curbstone,
Mummer of hope, you understand!'

But this is fantastic and pitiful,
And no one comes, none will, we are alone,
And what is possible is my own voice,
Speaking its wish, despite its lasting fear;
Speaking its hope, its promise and its fear
The voice drunk with itself and rapt in fear,
Exaggeration, braggadocio,
Rhetoric and hope, and always fear:

'For fifty-six or for a thousand years,
I will live with you and be your friend,
And what your body and what your spirit bears
I will like my own body cure and tend.

DELMORE SCHWARTZ

But you are heavy and my body's weight
Is great and heavy: when I carry you
I lift upon my back time like a fate
Near as my heart, dark when I marry you.

'The voice's promise is easy, and hope
Is drunk, and wanton, and unwilled;
In time's quicksilver, where our desires grope,
The dream is warped or monstrously fulfilled.
In this sense, listen, listen, and draw near:
Love is inexhaustible and full of fear.'

This life is endless and my eyes are tired,
So that, again and again, I touch a chair,
Or go to the window, press my face
Against it, hoping with substantial touch,
Colorful sight, or turning things to gain once more
The look of actuality, the certainty
Of those who run down stairs and drive a car.
Then let us be each other's truth, let us
Affirm the other's self, and be
The other's audience, the other's state,
Each to the other his sonorous fame.

Now you will be afraid, when, waking up,
Before familiar morning, by my mute side
Wan and abandoned then, when, waking up,
You see the lion or lamb upon my face
Or see the daemon breathing heavily
His sense of ignorance, his wish to die,
For I am nothing because my circus self
Divides its love a million times.

I am the octopus in love with God,
For thus is my desire inconclusible,
Until my mind, deranged in swimming tubes,
Issues its own darkness, clutching seas,
—O God of my perfect ignorance,
Bring the New Year to my only sister soon,
Take from me strength and power to bless her head,
Give her the magnitude of secular trust,
Until she turns to me in her troubled sleep,
Seeing me in my wish, free from self-wrongs.

KARL SHAPIRO

b. 1913

548   *The Dome of Sunday*

WITH focus sharp as Flemish-painted face
In film of varnish brightly fixed
And through a polished hand-lens deeply seen,
Sunday at noon through hyaline thin air
Sees down the street,
And in the camera of my eye depicts
Row-houses and row-lives:
Glass after glass, door after door the same,
Face after face the same, the same,
The brutal visibility the same;

As if one life emerging from one house
Would pause, a single image caught between
Two facing mirrors where vision multiplies
Beyond perspective,

1066

KARL SHAPIRO

A silent clatter in the high-speed eye
Spinning out photo-circulars of sight.

I see slip to the curb the long machines
Out of whose warm and windowed rooms pirouette
Shellacked with silk and light
The hard legs of our women.
Our women are one woman, dressed in black.
The carmine printed mouth
And cheeks as soft as muslin-glass belong
Outright to one dark dressy man,
Merely a swagger at her curvy side.

This is their visit to themselves:
All day from porch to porch they weave
A nonsense pattern through the even glare,
Stealing in surfaces
Cold vulgar glances at themselves.

And high up in the heated room all day
I wait behind the plate glass pane for one,
Hot as a voyeur for a glimpse of one,
The vision to blot out this woman's sheen;
All day my sight records expensively
Row-houses and row-lives.

But nothing happens; no diagonal
With melting shadow falls across the curb:
Neither the blinded negress lurching through fatigue,
Nor exiles bleeding from their pores,
Nor that bright bomb slipped lightly from its rack
To splinter every silvered glass and crystal prism,
Witch-bowl and perfume bottle

And billion candle-power dressing-bulb,
No direct hit to smash the shatter-proof
And lodge at last the quivering needle
Clean in the eye of one who stands transfixed
In fascination of her brightness.

549   *University*

To hurt the Negro and avoid the Jew
Is the curriculum. In mid-September
The entering boys, identified by hats,
Wander in a maze of mannered brick
  Where boxwood and magnolia brood
  And columns with imperious stance
  Like rows of ante-bellum girls
   Eye them, outlanders.

In whited cells, on lawns equipped for peace,
Under the arch, and lofty banister,
Equals shake hands, unequals blankly pass;
The exemplary weather whispers, 'Quiet, quiet'
  And visitors on tiptoe leave
  For the raw North, the unfinished West,
  As the young, detecting an advantage,
   Practice a face.

Where, on their separate hill, the colleges,
Like manor houses of an older law,
Gaze down embankments on a land in fee,
The Deans, dry spinsters over family plate,

Ring out the English name like coin,
Humor the snob and lure the lout.
Within the precincts of this world
    Poise is a club.

But on the neighboring range, misty and high,
The past is absolute: some luckless race
Dull with inbreeding and conformity
Wears out its heart, and comes barefoot and bad
    For charity or jail. The scholar
    Sanctions their obsolete disease;
    The gentleman revolts with shame
        At his ancestor.

And the true nobleman, once a democrat,
Sleeps on his private mountain. He was one
Whose thought was shapely and whose dream was broad;
This school he held his art and epitaph.
    But now it takes from him his name,
    Falls open like a dishonest look,
    And shows us, rotted and endowed,
        Its senile pleasure.

550   *Midnight Show*

THE year is done, the last act of the vaudeville,
The last top hat and patent leather tappity-tap
Enclosed in darkness. Pat. Blackout. Only the organ
Groans, groans, its thousand golden throats in love;
While blue lowlight suffuses mysteries of sleep
Through racks of heads, and smoothly parts the gauzy veil
That slips, the last pretense of peace, into the wings.

With raucous crash the music rises to its feet,
And pouring from the hidden eye like God the Light
The light white-molten cold fills out the vacant field
With shattered cities, striped ships, and maps with lines
That crawl—symbols of horror, symbols of obscenity;
A girl astride a giant cannon, holding a flag;
Removal of stone and stained glass saints from a known
      cathedral.

And the Voice, the loving and faithful pointer, trots beside
Reel after reel, taking death in its well-trained stride.
The Voice, the polite, the auctioneer, places his hints
Like easy bids. The lab assistant, the Voice, dips
Their pity like litmus papers into His rancid heart.—
Dream to be surfeited, nerves clogged up with messages,
And, backed up at the ganglion, the news refused.

Dream to be out in snow where every corner Santa,
Heart of one generation's dreams, tinkles a bell.
We know him too. He is the Unemployed, but clowns
As the Giver, receiving pennies in a cast-iron pot.
Dream to be cold with Byrd at the world's bottom. Dream
To be warm in the Vatican, photographing a manuscript.
Dream to be there, a cell in Europe's poisoned blood.

Revulsion cannot rouse our heads for pride or protest.
The eye sees as the camera, a clean moronic gaze,
And to go is not impossible but merely careless.
O wife, what shall we tell the children that we saw?
O son, what shall we tell our father? And O my friend,
What shall we tell our senses when the lights go up
And noiselessly the golden curtains crash together!

Hollywood

FARTHEST from any war, unique in time
Like Athens or Baghdad, this city lies
Between dry purple mountains and the sea.
The air is clear and famous, every day
Bright as a postcard, bringing bungalows
    And sights. The broad nights advertise
For love and music and astronomy.

Heart of a continent, the hearts converge
On open boulevards where palms are nursed
With flare-pots like a grove, on villa roads
Where castles cultivated like a style
Breed fabulous metaphors in foreign stone,
    And on enormous movie lots
Where history repeats its vivid blunders.

Alice and Cinderella are most real.
Here may the tourist, quite sincere at last,
Rest from his dream of travels. All is new,
No ruins claim his awe, and permanence,
Despised like customs, fails at every turn.
    Here where the eccentric thrives,
Laughter and love are leading industries.

Luck is another. Here the body-guard,
The parasite, the scholar are well paid,
The quack erects his alabaster office,
The moron and the genius are enshrined,
And the mystic makes a fortune quietly;

Here all superlatives come true
And beauty is marketed like a basic food.

O can we understand it? Is it ours,
A crude whim of a beginning people,
A private orgy in a secluded spot?
Or alien like the word *harem*, or true
Like hideous Pittsburgh or depraved Atlanta?
    Is adolescence just as vile
As this its architecture and its talk?

Or are they parvenus, like boys and girls?
Or ours and happy, cleverest of all?
Yes. Yes. Though glamorous to the ignorant
This is the simplest city, a new school.
What is more nearly ours? If soul can mean
    The civilization of the brain,
This is a soul, a possibly proud Florence.

552   *Drug Store*

I do remember an apothecary,
And hereabouts 'a dwells

I T baffles the foreigner like an idiom,
And he is right to adopt it as a form
Less serious than the living-room or bar;
    For it disestablishes the cafe,
Is a collective, and on basic country.

Not that it praises hygiene and corrupts
The ice-cream parlor and the tobacconist's

Is it a center; but that the attractive symbols
     Watch over puberty and leer
Like rubber bottles waiting for sick-use.

Youth comes to jingle nickels and crack wise;
The baseball scores are his, the magazines,
Devoted to lust, the jazz, the coca-cola,
     The lending-library of love's latest.
He is the customer; he is heroized.

And every nook and cranny of the flesh
Is spoken to by packages with wiles.
'Buy me, buy me,' they whimper and cajole;
     The hectic range of lipsticks pouts,
Revealing the wicked and the simple mouth.

With scarcely any evasion in their eye
They smoke, undress their girls, exact a stance;
But only for a moment. The clock goes round;
     Crude fellowships are made and lost;
They slump in booths like rags, not even drunk.

553   *Troop Train*

IT stops the town we come through. Workers raise
Their oily arms in good salute and grin.
Kids scream as at a circus. Business men
Glance hopefully and go their measured way.
And women standing at their dumbstruck door
More slowly wave and seem to warn us back,

As if a tear blinding the course of war
Might once dissolve our iron in their sweet wish.

Fruit of the world, O clustered on ourselves
We hang as from a cornucopia
In total friendliness, with faces bunched
To spray the streets with catcalls and with leers.
A bottle smashes on the moving ties
And eyes fixed on a lady smiling pink
Stretch like a rubber-band and snap and sting
The mouth that wants the drink-of-water kiss.

And on through crummy continents and days,
Deliberate, grimy, slightly drunk we crawl,
The good-bad boys of circumstance and chance,
Whose bucket-helmets bang the empty wall
Where twist the murdered bodies of our packs
Next to the guns that only seem themselves.
And distance like a strap adjusted shrinks,
Tightens across the shoulder and holds firm.

Here is a deck of cards; out of this hand
Dealer, deal me my luck, a pair of bulls,
The right draw to a flush, the one-eyed jack.
Diamonds and hearts are red but spades are black,
And spades are spades and clubs are clovers—black.
But deal me winners, souvenirs of peace.
This stands to reason and arithmetic,
Luck also travels and not all come back.

Trains lead to ships and ships to death or trains,
And trains to death or trucks, and trucks to death,
Or trucks lead to the march, the march to death,
Or that survival which is all our hope;

And death leads back to trucks and trains and ships.
But life leads to the march, O flag! at last
The place of life found after trains and death
—Nightfall of nations brilliant after war.

554   *Nigger*

A ND did ever a man go black with sun in a Belgian
       swamp,
On a feathery African plain where the sunburnt lioness lies,
And a cocoanut monkey grove where the cockatoos scratch
       the skies,
And the zebras striped with moonlight grasses gaze and
       stomp?

With a swatch of the baboon's crimson bottom cut for a lip,
And a brace of elephant ivories hung for a tusky smile,
With the muscles as level and lazy and long as the lifting
       Nile,
And a penis as loaded and supple and limp as the slaver's
       whip?

Are you beautiful still when you walk downtown in a
       knife-cut coat
And your yellow shoes dance at the corner curb like a brand
       new car,
And the buck with the arching pick looks over the new-laid
       tar
As you cock your eye like a cuckoo bird on a two-o'clock
       note?

When you got so little in steel-rim specs, when you taught
    that French,
When you wrote that book and you made that speech in the
    bottom south,
When you beat that fiddle and sang that role for Othello's
    mouth,
When you blew that horn for the shirt-sleeve mob and the
    snaky wench?

When you boxed that hun, when you raped that trash that
    you didn't rape,
When you caught that slug with a belly of fire and a face
    of gray,
When you felt that loop and you took that boot from a
    KKK,
And your hands hung down and your face went out in a
    blast of grape?

Did the Lord say yes, did the Lord say no, did you ask the
    Lord
When the jaw came down, when the cotton blossomed out
    of your bones?
Are you coming to peace, O Booker T. Lincoln Roosevelt
    Jones,
And is Jesus riding to raise your wage and to cut that cord?

555   *The Geographers*

> *Do, child, go to it grandam, child,*
> *Give grandam kingdom, and it grandam will*
> *Give it a plum, a cherry, and a fig:*
> *There's a good grandam.*—KING JOHN.

1076

WHOSE is the river, Excellency, whose the fish,
Whose locks, whose docks, whose dykes, whose toadstools,
    Baron;
Whose duchies, Duke; whose mandates, Metternich;
Whose visas; women in whose rowboats, Charon?

And these are your instructions. To look far,
Be protocol, correct before your Maker,
Stand on the logic of the things that are,
The solid citizen of His little acre.

New colors for new states, new drawing pens,
Inkpots for fleshpots, new Aladdin lamps,
New cameras for new moons through a new lens,
New numbered money, bright new postage stamps.

Whose mobs, whose ballots, and whose bottled beers,
Whose battleships, whose gold eggs from whose goose,
Whose turf, whose surf, whose polo ponies, Peers,
Whose sky-sedans, whose clouds, whose air, Clare Luce?

I have had, I had, I had had, and I hold;
The line protrudes, folds over, now indents;
Yet seen from Jupiter things are as of old;
Wars cannot change the shapes of continents.

556   *Elegy for a Dead Soldier*

I

A WHITE sheet on the tail-gate of a truck
Becomes an altar; two small candlesticks
Sputter at each side of the crucifix

Laid round with flowers brighter than the blood,
Red as the red of our apocalypse,
Hibiscus that a marching man will pluck
To stick into his rifle or his hat,
And great blue morning-glories pale as lips
That shall no longer taste or kiss or swear.
The wind begins a low magnificat,
The chaplain chats, the palmtrees swirl their hair,
The columns come together through the mud.

II

We too are ashes as we watch and hear
The psalm, the sorrow, and the simple praise
Of one whose promised thoughts of other days
Were such as ours, but now wholly destroyed,
The service record of his youth wiped out,
His dream dispersed by shot, must disappear.
What can we feel but wonder at a loss
That seems to point at nothing but the doubt
Which flirts our sense of luck into the ditch?
Reader of Paul who prays beside this fosse,
Shall we believe our eyes or legends rich
With glory and rebirth beyond the void?

III

For this comrade is dead, dead in the war,
A young man out of millions yet to live,
One cut away from all that war can give,
Freedom of self and peace to wander free.
Who mourns in all this sober multitude
Who did not feel the bite of it before
The bullet found its aim? This worthy flesh,
This boy laid in a coffin and reviewed—

Who has not wrapped himself in this same flag,
Heard the light fall of dirt, his wound still fresh,
Felt his eyes closed, and heard the distant brag
Of the last volley of humanity?

IV

By chance I saw him die, stretched on the ground,
A tattooed arm lifted to take the blood
Of someone else sealed in a tin. I stood
During the last delirium that stays
The intelligence a tiny moment more,
And then the strangulation, the last sound.
The end was sudden, like a foolish play,
A stupid fool slamming a foolish door,
The absurd catastrophe, half-prearranged,
And all the decisive things still left to say.
So we disbanded, angrier and unchanged,
Sick with the utter silence of dispraise.

V

We ask for no statistics of the killed,
For nothing political impinges on
This single casualty, or all those gone,
Missing or healing, sinking or dispersed,
Hundreds of thousands counted, millions lost.
More than an accident and less than willed
Is every fall, and this one like the rest.
However others calculate the cost,
To us the final aggregate is *one*,
One with a name, one transferred to the blest;
And though another stoops and takes the gun,
We cannot add the second to the first.

VI

I would not speak for him who could not speak
Unless my fear were true: he was not wronged,
He knew to which decision he belonged
But let it choose itself. Ripe in instinct,
Neither the victim nor the volunteer,
He followed, and the leaders could not seek
Beyond the followers. Much of this he knew;
The journey was a detour that would steer
Into the Lincoln Highway of a land
Remorselessly improved, excited, new,
And that was what he wanted. He had planned
To earn and drive. He and the world had winked.

VII

No history deceived him, for he knew
Little of times and armies not his own;
He never felt that peace was but a loan,
Had never questioned the idea of gain.
Beyond the headlines once or twice he saw
The gathering of a power by the few
But could not tell their names; he cast his vote,
Distrusting all the elected but not the law.
He laughed at socialism; *on mourrait
Pour les industriels?* He shed his coat
And not for brotherhood, but for his pay.
To him the red flag marked the sewer main.

VIII

Above all else he loathed the homily,
The slogan and the ad. He paid his bill
But not for Congressmen at Bunker Hill.

Ideals were few and those there were not made
For conversation. He belonged to church
But never spoke of God. The Christmas tree,
The Easter egg, baptism, he observed,
Never denied the preacher on his perch,
And would not sign Resolved That or Whereas.
Softness he had and hours and nights reserved
For thinking, dressing, dancing to the jazz.
His laugh was real, his manners were home made.

IX

Of all men poverty pursued him least;
He was ashamed of all the down and out,
Spurned the panhandler like an uneasy doubt,
And saw the unemployed as a vague mass
Incapable of hunger or revolt.
He hated other races, south or east,
And shoved them to the margin of his mind.
He could recall the justice of the Colt,
Take interest in a gang-war like a game.
His ancestry was somewhere far behind
And left him only his peculiar name.
Doors opened, and he recognized no class.

X

His children would have known a heritage,
Just or unjust, the richest in the world,
The quantum of all art and science curled
In the horn of plenty, bursting from the horn,
A people bathed in honey, Paris come,
Vienna transferred with the highest wage,
A World's Fair spread to Phoenix, Jacksonville,
Earth's capitol, the new Byzantium,

Kingdom of man—who knows? Hollow or firm,
No man can ever prophesy until
Out of our death some undiscovered germ,
Whole toleration or pure peace is born.

XI

The time to mourn is short that best becomes
The military dead. We lift and fold the flag,
Lay bare the coffin with its written tag,
And march away. Behind, four others wait
To lift the box, the heaviest of loads.
The anesthetic afternoon benumbs,
Sickens our senses, forces back our talk.
We know that others on tomorrow's roads
Will fall, ourselves perhaps, the man beside,
Over the world the threatened, all who walk:
And could we mark the grave of him who died
We would write this beneath his name and date:

EPITAPH

Underneath this wooden cross there lies
A Christian killed in battle. You who read,
Remember that this stranger died in pain;
And passing here, if you can lift your eyes
Upon a peace kept by a human creed,
Know that one soldier has not died in vain.

557   *The Conscientious Objector*

THE gates clanged and they walked you into jail
More tense than felons but relieved to find

KARL SHAPIRO

The hostile world shut out, the flags that dripped
From every mother's windowpane, obscene
The bloodlust sweating from the public heart,
The dog authority slavering at your throat.
A sense of quiet, of pulling down the blind
Possessed you. Punishment you felt was clean.

The decks, the catwalks, and the narrow light
Composed a ship. This was a mutinous crew
Troubling the captains for plain decencies,
A *Mayflower* brim with pilgrims headed out
To establish new theocracies to west,
A Noah's ark coasting the topmost seas
Ten miles above the sodomites and fish.
These inmates loved the only living doves.

Like all men hunted from the world you made
A good community, voyaging the storm
To no safe Plymouth or green Ararat;
Trouble or calm, the men with Bibles prayed,
The gaunt politicals construed our hate.
The opposite of all armies, you were best
Opposing uniformity and yourselves;
Prison and personality were your fate.

You suffered not so physically but knew
Maltreatment, hunger, ennui of the mind.
Well might the soldier kissing the hot beach
Erupting in his face damn all your kind.
Yet you who saved neither yourselves nor us
Are equally with those who shed the blood
The heroes of our cause. Your conscience is
What we come back to in the armistice.

RANDALL JARRELL

b. 1914

558　　　　　　*For an Emigrant*

I

IN that bad year and city of your birth
They traded bread for bank-notes weight for weight,
And nothing but the statues kept the smile
The waltzers wore once: excluding, innocent,
The face of old and comfortable injustice.
And if you wept,
Dropped red into a city where the husbandless
And fatherless were crying too, who cared
For one more cry or one more child? You grew;

Time put words into your mouth, and you put sugar
Upon your window-sill and waited for a brother—
The stork was greedy, ate, brought nothing in return.
And life was thinking of you, took you back to Prague;
At school there, timid, boisterous, you spoke
The unaccustomed Czech—
The children laughed at you. But you were learning
New words and a new life, the old
City and its new country too were learning
Man's strength: to be just; yes, to be free.

'I saw summer in my time.' Summer is ending.
The storms plunge from the tree of winter, death
Moves like an impulse over Europe. Child,

What man is just or free?—but fortunate,
Warm in time's hand, turning and trusting to his face;
And that face changes.
Time is a man for men, and He is willing
For many a new life, for others death. Already
He buys His trench-coat, falls, writes His big book;

Points here, points here: to Jews, the wicked friends—
His words are the moments of a man's life.
And now the men march. One morning you awoke
And found Vienna gone, your father said:
'Us next!' And you were next.
Us next!
Cried map and mouth, oppressors and oppressed,
The appeasers as they gave your life—but you were gone.
'I had a tongue, a city.' *What is your name?*
'My name is what my name was.' *You have no name.*

So the dream spoke to you: in Zurich, Paris,
In London on a lawn; the unbefriending sea
Cried to you, 'Stranger!'—superb, inhospitable,
The towers of the island turned their gaze
Past the girl who stared up to the great statue:
So green, so gay . . .
That is how you came. Your face shows white
Against the dark time, your words are indistinct,
One cry among so many, lost in the great sound

Of degradation and agony, the peoples dying.
The net was laid for you; and you are free.
Free—to be homeless, to be friendless, to be nameless,
To stammer the hard words in the foreign night.

To remember; and free also, child,
To love and to be loved,
To see in one face the land, the tongue, the time—
Blind with your joy, to whisper: Happiness
Is possible and difficult: to learn at last
New words and a new country, a new love.

II

(In augmentation)

If I could only stop there—stop telling there,
Stop time there; fix those eyes upon their life,
The answerers and answered; fix in their light dream
The lips parting for their laugh, the grateful and faultless
And stupid laughter of the child, the joy of ignorance;
But you must wake, poor Beauty.
And here where Locke's page sparkled white as dew
The woman's face must come, to choose and suffer
And lose its beauty and at last find beautiful

Its death. . . You escaped from nothing; the westering
      soul
Finds Europe waiting for it over every sea.
The statue in the harbor stretched its hand
Above you in His gesture, He is here
To turn on you in love or in denunciation
The eyes that are your own.
If they are evil, they are evil really,
As a child's are evil: blind in the unbearable
Magnificence of bronze; so absolute in their assurance
Of power and of innocence: the statue's eyes.

And what looks timidly from their clear depths
Is the child's loneliness, his passionate rejection
Of his own helplessness and pain, the man's
Denial of the knowledge he cannot endure.
The mouth says: 'I made me, I shall last, be sure.
Time is my will.
Surely the tears are iron within my eyes.
Look, and find life here about my lips—
Who has not loved me? I shall never die.'

And not those lips alone. O what mouth will not shape,
Blood wash and spittle moisten, tongue caress
That lie and all man's versions of that lie?
—The facets of the look the lives are mirroring,
The maze where all of us are wandering: that History
Where nothing is not repeated.
Where mistress and Mother fuse at last into a face,
And Time and my father and the terrible finger
Of all I cannot face and must adore—

The Accuser, the Appeaser, the inhuman Judge—
Are Hitler: a separate peace: the real history
Where there is nothing that can cause except my lies,
Where there is nothing that can last except my life,
Where there is nothing. . . *That* is the world
You must escape from: the America where each
Can think still, 'I am innocent.'
But there is guilt enough for all: existence is guilt enough.
Because of us, because of what we did or did not do,
See, the men die. 'And they are the innocent?'

Irremediably. They? Those innocents whom we forgive
Because their failure is intolerable, the final guilt

Only forgiving hides from us? Forgive today
And next day fail, and die, and be forgiven?
Forgive, forgive? Forgive no one.
Understand and blame.
'But I am all of them. That face, that world is mine.'
Change, then. Learn what you can, love what you can:
    when they kill you,
Let them look at your face and remember your life
And cry—'You stranger, you damned stranger!'

559 *The Soldier Walks Under the Trees of the University*

THE walls have been shaded for so many years
By the green magnificence of these great lives
Their bricks are darkened till the end of time.
(Small touching whites in the perpetual
Darkness that saturates the unwalled world;
Saved from the sky by leaves, and from the earth by stone)
The pupils trust like flowers to the shades
And interminable twilight of these latitudes.

In our zone innocence is born in banks
And cultured in colonies the rich have sown:
The one is spared here what the many share
To write the histories that others are.
The oak escapes the storm that broke the reeds,
They read here; they read, too, of reeds,
Of storms; and are, almost, sublime
In their read ignorance of everything.

The poor are always—somewhere, but not here;
We learn of them where they and Guilt subsist
With Death and Evil: in books, in books, in books.
Ah, sweet to contemplate the causes, not the things!
The soul learns fortitude in libraries,
Enduring patience in another's pain,
And pity for the lives we do not change:
All that the world would be, if it were real.

When will the boughs break blazing from these trees,
The darkened walls float heavenward like soot?
The days when men say: 'Where we look is fire—
The iron branches flower in my veins?'
In that night even to be rich is difficult,
The world is something even books believe,
The bombs fall all year long among the states,
And the blood is black upon the unturned leaves.

560   *The Sick Nought*

DO the wife and baby travelling to see
Your grey pajamas and sick worried face
Remind you of something, soldier? I remember
You convalescing washing plates, or mopping
The endless corridors your shoes had scuffed;
And in the crowded room you rubbed your cheek
Against your wife's thin elbow like a pony.
But you are something there are millions of.
How can I care about you much, or pick you out
From all the others other people loved
And sent away to die for them? You are a ticket

Someone bought and lost on, a stray animal:
You have lost even the right to be condemned.
I see you looking helplessly around, in histories,
Bewildered with your terrible companions, Pain
And Death and Empire: what have you understood, to die?
Were you worth, soldiers, all that people said
To be spent so willingly? Surely your one theory, to live,
Is nonsense to the practice of the centuries.
What is demanded in the trade of states
But lives, but lives?—the one commodity.
To sell the lives we were too poor to use,
To lose the lives we were too weak to keep—
This was our peace, this was our war.

561   *Prisoners*

WITHIN the wires of the post, unloading the cans of
    garbage,
The three in soiled blue denim (the white ball on their
    backs
Sending its chilly *North* six yards to the turning blackened
Sights of the cradled rifle, to the eyes of the yawning
    guard)
Go on all day being punished, go on all month, all year
Loading, unloading; give their child's, beast's sigh—of
    despair,
Of endurance and of existence, look unexpectingly
At the big guard, dark in his khaki, at the dust of the
    blazing plain,
At the running or crawling soldiers in their soiled and
    shapeless green.

1090

The prisoners, the guard, the soldiers—they are all, in their
    way, being trained.
From these moments, repeated forever, our own new world
    will be made.

562   *The Death of the Ball Turret*
               Gunner

FROM my mother's sleep I fell into the State,
And I hunched in its belly till my wet fur froze.
Six miles from earth, loosed from its dream of life,
I woke to black flak and the nightmare fighters.
When I died they washed me out of the turret with a hose.

563   *Losses*

IT was not dying: everybody died.
It was not dying: we had died before
In the routine crashes—and our fields
Called up the papers, wrote home to our folks,
And the rates rose, all because of us.
We died on the wrong page of the almanac,
Scattered on mountains fifty miles away;
Diving on haystacks, fighting with a friend,
We blazed up on the lines we never saw.
We died like ants or pets or foreigners.
(When we left high school nothing else had died
For us to figure we had died like.)

In our new planes, with our new crews, we bombed
The ranges by the desert or the shore,
Fired at towed targets, waited for our scores—
And turned into replacements and woke up
One morning, over England, operational.
It wasn't different: but if we died
It was not an accident but a mistake
(But an easy one for anyone to make).
We read our mail and counted up our missions—
In bombers named for girls, we burned
The cities we had learned about in school—
Till our lives wore out; our bodies lay among
The people we had killed and never seen.
When we lasted long enough they gave us medals;
When we died they said, 'Our casualties were low.'
They said, 'Here are the maps'; we burned the cities.

It was not dying—no, not ever dying;
But the night I died I dreamed that I was dead,
And the cities said to me: 'Why are you dying?
We are satisfied, if you are; but why did I die?'

ROBERT LOWELL

b. 1917

564   *Children of Light*

OUR fathers wrung their bread from stocks and stones
And fenced their gardens with the Redmen's bones;
Embarking from the Nether Land of Holland,
Pilgrims unhoused by Geneva's night,

They planted here the Serpent's seeds of light;
And here the pivoting searchlights probe to shock
The riotous glass houses built on rock,
And candles gutter by an empty altar,
And light is where the landless blood of Cain
Is burning, burning the unburied grain.

565 *Christmas Eve Under Hooker's Statue*

TONIGHT a blackout. Twenty years ago
I hung my stocking on the tree, and hell's
Serpent entwined the apple in the toe
To sting the child with knowledge. Hooker's heels
Kicking at nothing in the shifting snow,
A cannon and a cairn of cannon balls
Rusting before the blackened Statehouse, know
How the long horn of plenty broke like glass
In Hooker's gauntlets. Once I came from Mass;

Now storm-clouds shelter Christmas, once again
Mars meets his fruitless star with open arms,
His heavy saber flashes with the rime,
The war-god's bronzed and empty forehead forms
Anonymous machinery from raw men;
The cannon on the Common cannot stun
The blundering butcher as he rides on Time—
The barrel clinks with holly. I am cold:
I ask for bread, my father gives me mould;

His stocking is full of stones. Santa in red
Is crowned with wizened berries. Man of war,

Where is the summer's garden? In its bed
The ancient speckled serpent will appear,
And black-eyed susan with her frizzled head.
When Chancellorsville mowed down the volunteer,
'All wars are boyish,' Herman Melville said;
But we are old, our fields are running wild:
Till Christ again turn wanderer and child.

566   *As a Plane Tree by the Water*

DARKNESS has called to darkness, and disgrace
Elbows about our windows in this planned
Babel of Boston where our money talks
And multiplies the darkness of a land
Of preparation where the Virgin walks
And roses spiral her enamelled face
Or fall to splinters on unwatered streets.
Our Lady of Babylon, go by, go by,
I was once the apple of your eye;
Flies, flies are on the plane tree, on the streets.

The flies, the flies, the flies of Babylon
Buzz in my ear-drums while the devil's long
Dirge of the people detonates the hour
For floating cities where his golden tongue
Enchants the masons of the Babel Tower
To raise tomorrow's city to the sun
That never sets upon these hell-fire streets
Of Boston, where the sunlight is a sword
Striking at the withholder of the Lord:
Flies, flies are on the plane tree, on the streets.

Flies strike the miraculous waters of the iced
Atlantic and the eyes of Bernadette
Who saw Our Lady standing in the cave
At Massabielle, saw her so squarely that
Her vision put out reason's eyes. The grave
Is open-mouthed and swallowed up in Christ.
O walls of Jericho! And all the streets
To our Atlantic wall are singing: 'Sing,
Sing for the resurrection of the King.'
Flies, flies are on the plane tree, on the streets.

567   *The Exile's Return*

THERE mounts in squalls a sort of rusty mire,
Not ice, not snow, to leaguer the Hôtel
De Ville, where braced pig-iron dragons grip
The blizzard to their rigor mortis. A bell
Grumbles when the reverberations strip
The thatching from its spire,
The search-guns click and spit and split up timber
And nick the slate roofs on the Holstenwall
Where torn-up tilestones crown the victor. Fall
And winter, spring and summer, guns unlimber
And lumber down the narrow gabled street
Past your gray, sorry and ancestral house
Where the dynamited walnut tree
Shadows a squat, old, wind-torn gate and cows
The bristling podestà. You will not see
Strutting children or meet
The peg-leg and reproachful chancellor
With a forget-me-not in his button-hole

When the unseasoned liberators roll
Into the Market Square, ground arms before
The Rathaus; but already lily-stands
Burgeon the risen Rhineland, and a rough
Cathedral lifts its eye. Pleasant enough,
Voi ch'entrate, and your life is in your hands.

568 *The Dead in Europe*

AFTER the planes unloaded, we fell down
Buried together, unmarried men and women;
Not crown of thorns, not iron, not Lombard crown,
Not grilled and spindle spires pointing to heaven
Could save us. Raise us, Mother, we fell down
Here hugger-mugger in the jellied fire:
Our sacred earth in our day was our curse.

Our Mother, shall we rise on Mary's day
In Maryland, wherever corpses married
Under the rubble, bundled together? Pray
For us whom the blockbusters marred and buried;
When Satan scatters us on Rising-day,
O Mother, snatch our bodies from the fire:
Our sacred earth in our day was our curse.

Mother, my bones are trembling and I hear
The earth's reverberations and the trumpet
Bleating into my shambles. Shall I bear,
(O Mary!) unmarried man and powder-puppet,
Witness to the Devil? Mary, hear,
O Mary, marry earth, sea, air and fire;
Our sacred earth in our day is our curse.

569 *The Drunken Fisherman*

Wallowing in this bloody sty,
I cast for fish that pleased my eye
(Truly Jehovah's bow suspends
No pots of gold to weight its ends);
Only the blood-mouthed rainbow trout
Rose to my bait. They flopped about
My canvas creel until the moth
Corrupted its unstable cloth.

A calendar to tell the day;
A handkerchief to wave away
The gnats; a couch unstuffed with storm
Pouching a bottle in one arm;
A whiskey bottle full of worms;
And bedroom slacks: are these fit terms
To mete the worm whose molten rage
Boils in the belly of old age?

Once fishing was a rabbit's foot—
O wind blow cold, O wind blow hot,
Let suns stay in or suns step out:
Life danced a jig on the sperm-whale's spout—
The fisher's fluent and obscene
Catches kept his conscience clean.
Children, the raging memory drools
Over the glory of past pools.

Now the hot river, ebbing, hauls
Its bloody waters into holes;

A grain of sand inside my shoe
Mimics the moon that might undo
Man and Creation too; remorse,
Stinking, has puddled up its source;
Here tantrums thrash to a whale's rage.
This is the pot-hole of old age.

Is there no way to cast my hook
Out of this dynamited brook?
The Fisher's sons must cast about
When shallow waters peter out.
I will catch Christ with a greased worm,
And when the Prince of Darkness stalks
My bloodstream to its Stygian term . . .
On water the Man-Fisher walks.

570 *The Quaker Graveyard in Nantucket*

(For Warren Winslow, Dead at Sea)

*Let man have dominion over the fishes of the sea and
the fowls of the air and the beasts and the whole
earth, and every creeping creature that moveth upon the
earth.*

I

A BRACKISH reach of shoal off Madaket,—
The sea was still breaking violently and night
Had steamed into our North Atlantic Fleet,
When the drowned sailor clutched the drag-net. Light
Flashed from his matted head and marble feet,
He grappled at the net

With the coiled, hurdling muscles of his thighs:
The corpse was bloodless, a botch of reds and whites,
Its open, staring eyes
Were lustreless dead-lights
Or cabin-windows on a stranded hulk
Heavy with sand. We weight the body, close
Its eyes and heave it seaward whence it came,
Where the heel-headed dogfish barks its nose
On Ahab's void and forehead; and the name
Is blocked in yellow chalk.
Sailors, who pitch this portent at the sea
Where dreadnaughts shall confess
Its hell-bent deity,
When you are powerless
To sand-bag this Atlantic bulwark, faced
By the earth-shaker, green, unwearied, chaste
In his steel scales: ask for no Orphean lute
To pluck life back. The guns of the steeled fleet
Recoil and then repeat
The hoarse salute.

II

Whenever winds are moving and their breath
Heaves at the roped-in bulwarks of this pier,
The terns and sea-gulls tremble at your death
In these home waters. Sailor, can you hear
The Pequod's sea wings, beating landward, fall
Headlong and break on our Atlantic wall
Off 'Sconset, where the yawing S-boats splash
The bellbuoy, with ballooning spinnakers,
As the entangled, screeching mainsheet clears
The blocks: off Madaket, where lubbers lash

The heavy surf and throw their long lead squids
For blue-fish? Sea-gulls blink their heavy lids
Seaward. The winds' wings beat upon the stones,
Cousin, and scream for you and the claws rush
At the sea's throat and wring it in the slush
Of this old Quaker graveyard where the bones
Cry out in the long night for the hurt beast
Bobbing by Ahab's whaleboats in the East.

III

All you recovered from Poseidon died
With you, my cousin, and the harrowed brine
Is fruitless on the blue beard of the god,
Stretching beyond us to the castles in Spain,
Nantucket's westward haven. To Cape Cod
Guns, cradled on the tide,
Blast the eelgrass about a waterclock
Of bilge and backwash, roil the salt and sand
Lashing earth's scaffold, rock
Our warships in the hand
Of the great God, where time's contrition blues
Whatever it was these Quaker sailors lost
In the mad scramble of their lives. They died
When time was open-eyed,
Wooden and childish; only bones abide
There, in the nowhere, where their boats were tossed
Sky-high, where mariners had fabled news
Of Is, the swashing castle. What it cost
Them is their secret. In the monster's slick
I see the Quakers drown and hear their cry:
'If God himself had not been on our side,
If God himself had not been on our side,

When the Atlantic rose against us, why,
Then it had swallowed us up quick.'

IV

This is the end of the whaleroad and the whale
Who spewed Nantucket bones on the thrashed swell
And stirred the troubled waters to whirlpools
To send the Pequod packing off to hell:
This is the end of them, three-quarters fools,
Snatching at straws to sail
Seaward and seaward on the turntail whale,
Spouting out blood and water as it rolls,
Sick as a dog to these Atlantic shoals:
Clamavimus, O depths. Let the sea-gulls wail

For water, for the deep where the high tide
Mutters to its hurt self, mutters and ebbs.
Waves wallow in their wash, go out and out,
Leave only the death-rattle of the crabs,
The beach increasing, its enormous snout
Sucking the ocean's side.
This is the end of running on the waves;
We are poured out like water. Who will dance
The mast-lashed master of Leviathans
Up from this field of Quakers in their unstoned graves?

V

When the whale's viscera go and the roll
Of its corruption overruns this world
Beyond tree-swept Nantucket and Wood's Hole
And Martha's Vineyard, Sailor, will your sword
Whistle and fall and sink into the fat?
In the great ash-pit of Jehoshaphat

The bones cry for the blood of the white whale,
The fat flukes arch and whack about its ears,
The death-lance churns into the sanctuary, tears
The gun-blue swingle, heaving like a flail,
And hacks the coiling life out: it works and drags
And rips the sperm-whale's midriff into rags,
Gobbets of blubber spill to wind and weather,
Sailor, and gulls go round the stoven timbers
Where the morning stars sing out together
And thunder shakes the white surf and dismembers
The red flag hammered in the mast-head. Hide,
Our steel, Jonas Messias, in Thy side.

VI

OUR LADY OF WALSINGHAM

There once the penitents took off their shoes
And then walked barefoot the remaining mile;
And the small trees, a stream and hedgerows file
Slowly along the munching English lane,
Like cows to the old shrine, until you lose
Track of your dragging pain.
The stream flows down under the druid tree,
Shiloah's whirlpools gurgle and make glad
The castle of God. Sailor, you were glad
And whistled Sion by that stream. But see:

Our Lady, too small for her canopy,
Sits near the altar. There's no comeliness
At all or charm in that expressionless
Face with its heavy eyelids. As before,
This face, for centuries a memory,
Non est species, neque decor,

Expressionless, expresses God: it goes
Past castled Sion. She knows what God knows,
Not Calvary's Cross nor crib at Bethlehem
Now, and the world shall come to Walsingham.

VII

The empty winds are creaking and the oak
Splatters and splatters on the cenotaph,
The boughs are trembling and a gaff
Bobs on the untimely stroke
Of the greased wash exploding on a shoal-bell
In the old mouth of the Atlantic. It's well;
Atlantic, you are fouled with the blue sailors,
Sea-monsters, upward angel, downward fish:
Unmarried and corroding, spare of flesh
Mart once of supercilious, wing'd clippers,
Atlantic, where your bell-trap guts its spoil
You could cut the brackish winds with a knife
Here in Nantucket, and cast up the time
When the Lord God formed man from the sea's slime
And breathed into his face the breath of life,
And blue-lung'd combers lumbered to the kill.
The Lord survives the rainbow of His will.

571 *Falling Asleep over the Aeneid*

*An old man in Concord forgets to go to Morning
Service. He falls asleep, while reading Virgil, and
dreams that he is Aeneas at the funeral of Pallas, an
Italian prince.*

ROBERT LOWELL

The sun is blue and scarlet on my page,
And *yuck-a, yuck-a, yuck-a, yuck-a,* rage
The yellowhammers mating. Yellow fire
Blankets the captives dancing on their pyre,
And the scorched lictor screams and drops his rod.
Trojans are singing to their drunken God,
Ares. Their helmets catch on fire. Their files
Clank by the body of my comrade—miles
Of filings! Now the scythe-wheeled chariot rolls
Before their lances long as vaulting poles,
And I stand up and heil the thousand men,
Who carry Pallas to the bird-priest. Then
The bird-priest groans, and as his birds foretold,
I greet the body, lip to lip. I hold
The sword that Dido used. It tries to speak,
A bird with Dido's sworded breast. Its beak
Clangs and ejaculates the Punic word
I hear the bird-priest chirping like a bird.
I groan a little. 'Who am I, and why?'
It asks, a boy's face, though its arrow-eye
Is working from its socket. 'Brother, try,
O Child of Aphrodite, try to die:
To die is life.' His harlots hang his bed
With feathers of his long-tailed birds. His head
Is yawning like a person. The plumes blow;
The beard and eyebrows ruffle. Face of snow,
You are the flower that country girls have caught,
A wild bee-pillaged honeysuckle brought
To the returning bridegroom—the design
Has not yet left it, and the petals shine;
The earth, its mother, has, at last, no help:
It is itself. The broken-winded yelp

Of my Phoenician hounds, that fills the brush
With snapping twigs and flying, cannot flush
The ghost of Pallas. But I take his pall,
Stiff with its gold and purple, and recall
How Dido hugged it to her, while she toiled,
Laughing—her golden threads, a serpent coiled
In cypress. Now I lay it like a sheet;
It clinks and settles down upon his feet,
The careless golden hair that seemed to burn
Beforehand. Left foot, right foot—as they turn,
More pyres are rising: armored horses, bronze,
And gagged Italians, who must pass by ones
Across the bitter river, when my thumb
Tightens into their wind-pipes. The beaks drum;
Their headman's cow-horned death's head bites its tongue,
And stiffens, as it eyes the hero slung
Inside his feathered hammock on the crossed
Staves of the eagles that we winged. Our cost
Is nothing to the lovers, whoring Mars
And Venus, father's lover. Now the car's
Plumage is ready, and my marshals fetch
His squire, Acoetes, white with age, to hitch
Aethon, the hero's charger, and its ears
Prick, and it steps and steps, and stately tears
Lather its teeth; and then the harlots bring
The hero's charms and baton—but the King,
Vain-glorious Turnus, carried off the rest.
'I was myself, but Ares thought it best
The way it happened.' At the end of time,
He sets his spear, as my descendants climb
The knees of Father Time, his beard of scalps,
His scythe, the arc of steel that crowns the Alps.

The elephants of Carthage hold those snows,
Terms of Numidian horse unsling their bows,
The flaming turkey-feathered arrows swarm
Beyond the Alps. 'Pallas,' I raise my arm
And shout, 'Brother, eternal health. Farewell
Forever.' Church is over, and its bell
Frightens the yellowhammers, as I wake,
And watch the whitecaps wrinkle up the lake.
Mother's great aunt, who died when I was eight,
Stands by the parlor sabre. 'Boy, it's late.
Virgil must keep the Sabbath.' Forty years!
It all comes back. My Uncle Charles appears,
Blue-capped and bird-like. Phillips Brooks and Grant
Are frowning at his coffin, and my aunt,
Hearing his colored volunteers parade
Through Concord, laughs, and tells her English maid
To clip his yellow nostril hairs, and fold
His colors on him. It is I. I hold
His sword to keep from falling, for the dust
On the stuffed birds is breathless, for the bust
Of young Augustus weighs on Virgil's shelf:
It scowls into my glasses at itself.

BIBLIOGRAPHICAL NOTE

The general reader of poetry should not be encumbered with dates or with bibliography. But one of the pleasures in reading a poet is to follow his development, and I have consequently arranged all my selections in order of their composition, so far as that was known. In the case of both Anne Bradstreet and Edward Taylor I have preserved the seventeenth-century spelling for the reason that many of Taylor's homely words and phrases have passed out of usage and could not otherwise be reproduced.

The following notes indicate, in the briefest possible fashion, the first appearance of the poems in volume form. Figures in parentheses refer to poem numbers in this book.

Anne Bradstreet (*c.* 1612-72). (1) served as a prologue to Mrs. Bradstreet's long poems in the manner of Du Bartas, first published as *The Tenth Muse, Lately Sprung up in America* (1650). (2-5) were added in a second edition published after her death, under the title *Several Poems Compiled with Great Variety of Wit and Learning* (1678). (6) did not appear in print until *Works* (1867).

Edward Taylor (*c.* 1645-1729). Written mainly between 1680 and 1725, none of Taylor's poems were printed until his *Poetical Works* were issued in 1939. Those included here seem to range in date from the early 1680's to 1703. 'Meditations' *X* and *XL* have been printed only in *The New England Quarterly* (1943).

Philip Freneau (1752-1832). (14-18) appeared between 1782 and 1788 and were collected in *Poems* (1795).

Joel Barlow (1754-1812). (19), *The Hasty Pudding: A Poem in Three Cantos* (1796); (20), written just before Barlow died after pursuing Napoleon into Poland on a diplomatic mission, was not printed until long after the poet's death, and not in its full text until 1938 (in *The Huntington Library Quarterly*).

William Cullen Bryant (1794-1878). (21-25), *Poems* (1821); (26), *Poems* (1834).

Ralph Waldo Emerson (1803-82). (27-33), written during the 1830's, and (34-44), written after 1840, were collected in *Poems* (1847). (45-48), written between 1851 and 1857, were collected in *May Day* (1867). (50) was written just before that book was published. (49) and Emerson's other quatrains were collected after his death.

Henry Wadsworth Longfellow (1807-82). (51), *Voices of the Night* (1839); (52), *The Waif* (1845); (53-54), *The Belfry of Bruges* (1846); (55), *The Seaside and the Fireside* (1850); (56-57), *The Courtship of Miles Standish* (1858); (58), *Tales of a Wayside Inn* (1863); (59) served as preface to Longfellow's translation of *The Divine Comedy* (1867-70); (60), *Aftermath* (1874); (61), *The Masque of Pandora* (1875); (62), *Ultima Thule* (1880); (63), written in 1879, was not printed until after his death; (64), his last poem, completed only a few days before he died, *In the Harbor* (1882).

John Greenleaf Whittier (1807-92). (65), written in 1847, was subsequently placed at the beginning of Whittier's *Collected Poems;* (66-67), *Songs of Labor* (1850); (68), *The Panorama* (1856); (69), *Home Ballads and Poems* (1860); (70), *Snow-Bound* (1866); (71), *Among the Hills* (1869).

Oliver Wendell Holmes (1809-94). Both (72) and (73)

were included in *The Autocrat of the Breakfast Table* (1858).

Edgar Allan Poe (1809-49). (74-76), *Tamerlane and Other Poems* (1827); (77-79), *Al Aaraaf* (1829); (80-83), *Poems* (1831); (84), written in 1834, (85), written in 1839, (86) and (87), written in 1844 and 1845, all included in *The Raven and Other Poems* (1845); (88), written in 1847, and (89-92), all written in 1849, *Collected Poems* (1850).

Jones Very (1813-80). (93-99) appeared in *Essays and Poems* (1839); (100-103) were collected in 1883 and 1886, after Very's death.

Henry David Thoreau (1817-62). (104-109) were written, like most of Thoreau's poetry, in the early 1840's. Scattered through *A Week on the Concord and Merrimack Rivers* (1849) and *Walden* (1854), they were not included in a single volume until *Collected Poems* (1943).

James Russell Lowell (1819-91). (110-111), *A Fable for Critics* and *The Biglow Papers*, both appeared in 1848.

Walt Whitman (1819-92) called his book *Leaves of Grass* in all its editions. He divided it into sections in his various revisions, and finally arranged the poems in a thematic order. (112-114), *Inscriptions* (1865-7); (115-116), first issue of *Leaves of Grass* (1855); (117-121), *Children of Adam* (1856-65); (122-126), *Calamus* (1860); (127), *Sea-Drift* (1859); (128-130), *By the Roadside* (1860-65); (131-139), *Drum Taps* (1865); (140), *Memories of President Lincoln* (1865); (141-142), *Sea-Drift* (1867, 1871); (143-144), *Whispers of Heavenly Death* (1871); (145-146), *Sands at Seventy* (1888).

BIBLIOGRAPHICAL NOTE

Herman Melville (1819-91). (147-149), *Battle Pieces* (1866); (150), *Clarel* (1876); (151), *John Marr and Other Sailors* (1888).

Henry Timrod (1828-67). (152-154), written between 1861 and 1867, were not collected until after Timrod's death, in *Poems* (1873).

Emily·Dickinson (1830-86). (155, 157-169, 171-183, 185-186, 188-198, 202) appeared in the three series of *Poems* issued between 1890 and 1896 by Miss Dickinson's friends Mabel Loomis Todd and Thomas Wentworth Higginson. Although several additional volumes of poems by Miss Dickinson have been published, these first collections contained the bulk of her best work. (199-201) were included in *The Single Hound* (1914), (156) in *Further Poems* (1929), (170) in *Unpublished Poems* (1937), (184, 187) in *Bolts of Melody* (1945). Since no attempt has been made to date Miss Dickinson's poems in any of the volumes issued so far, I have followed the thematic arrangement adopted by her first editors.

Miss Dickinson's poems require a peculiar additional note. Since her manuscripts have not even yet been made available for systematic collation, we are far from possessing an accurate edition. How wide the discrepancy may still be between some of her poems and their printed form may be judged by comparing (198), which follows the text finally given by Millicent Todd Bingham in 1945, and its earlier version. In their effort to improve Miss Dickinson's rhymes, the first editors had thus altered the opening stanzas:

> I heard a fly buzz when I died;
> The stillness round my form
> Was like the stillness in the air
> Between the heaves of storm.

> The eyes beside had wrung them dry
> And breaths were gathering sure
> For that last onset, when the king
> Be witnessed in his power.

> I willed my keepsakes, signed away
> What portion of me I
> Could make assignable,—and then
> There interposed a fly,

Sidney Lanier (1842-81). (203), written in 1868, and (204-207), written between 1877 and 1880, were collected in *Poems* (1884).

William Vaughn Moody (1869-1910). (208-209), *Poems* (1901).

Edwin Arlington Robinson (1869-1935). (210-218), *The Children of the Night* (1897); (219), *Captain Craig* (1902); (220-222), *The Town Down the River* (1910); (223-227), *The Man Against the Sky* (1916); (228-229), *Avon's Harvest* (1921); (230-231), *Dionysus in Doubt* (1925).

Edgar Lee Masters (1869-1950). (232-247), *Spoon River Anthology* (1915).

Trumbull Stickney (1874-1904). (248-249), *Dramatic Verses* (1902); (250-253), *Poems* (1905).

Amy Lowell (1874-1925). (254), *Men, Women and Ghosts* (1916); (255-256), *What's O'Clock* (1925).

Robert Frost (b. 1875). (257), placed by Frost at the front of his *Collected Poems*; (258-266), *A Boy's Will* (1913); (267-269), *North of Boston* (1914); (270-277), *Mountain Interval* (1916); (278-286), *New Hampshire* (1923); (287-292), *West-Running Brook* (1928); (293-

294), *A Further Range* (1936); (295-296), *A Witness Tree* (1942).

Carl Sandburg (b. 1878). (297-303), *Chicago Poems* (1916); (304-305), *Cornhuskers* (1918); (306-308), *Smoke and Steel* (1920); (309-311), *The People, Yes* (1936).

Vachel Lindsay (1879-1931). (312-313), *General William Booth Enters into Heaven* (1913); (314-315), *The Congo* (1914); (316), *The Golden Whales of California* (1920); (317), *Going-to-the-Sun* (1923).

Wallace Stevens (b. 1879). (318-327), *Harmonium* (1923); (328-330), *Ideas of Order* (1935); (331-340), *Parts of a World* (1942); (341-342), *Transport to Summer* (1947).

William Carlos Williams (b. 1883) has indicated the dates of his poems as follows: (343), *Transitional* (1913); (344-347), *Al Que Quiere* (1917); (348-350), *Spring and All* (1923); (351-352), *Collected Poems* (1934); (353-354), *An Early Martyr* (1935); (355), *Adam & Eve and the City* (1936); (356-358), *Collected Poems* (1938); (359), *The Wedge* (1944).

Elinor Wylie (1885-1928). (360-361), *Nets to Catch the Wind* (1921); (362-363), *Black Armour* (1923); (364-365), *Trivial Breath* (1928); (366), *Angels and Earthly Creatures* (1929).

Ezra Pound (b. 1885). (367-369), *Ripostes* (1912); (370-378), *Lustra* (1912, 1915); (379-380), *Cathay* (1915); (381), *Homage to Sextus Propertius* (1917); (382-383), *Hugh Selwyn Mauberley* (1920); (384), *XVI Cantos* (1925); (385), *Pisan Cantos* (1948).

BIBLIOGRAPHICAL NOTE

H.D. (*Hilda Doolittle*, b. 1886). (386-389), *Sea Garden* (1916); (390), *Heliodora* (1924).

Marianne Moore (b. 1887). (391-395), *Poems* (1921); (396-398), *Observations* (1925); (399-401), *Selected Poems* (1935); (402-403), *What Are Years* (1941); (404-406), *Nevertheless* (1944).

Robinson Jeffers (b. 1887). (407), *Tamar* (1924); (408-415), *Roan Stallion* (1925); (416-417), *Cawdor* (1928); (418), *Thurso's Landing* (1932); (419-421), *Solstice* (1935); (422), *Such Counsels You Gave to Me* (1937); (423), *Be Angry at the Sun* (1941); (424-425), *The Double Axe* (1948).

T. S. Eliot (b. 1888). (426-427), *Poems* (1920); (428), *The Waste Land* (1922); (429), *Ash Wednesday* (1930); (430), *Four Quartets* (1943). In the case only of Eliot was I unable to get permission for as many poems as I would have liked. Faced with a limit of a thousand lines, I chose outstanding poems from each of the successive stages of his development. But I regret the necessary omission of 'The Love Song of J. Alfred Prufrock,' 'Whispers of Immortality,' 'The Hollow Men,' 'Animula,' and 'Marina.'

John Crowe Ransom (b. 1888). (431-440), *Chills and Fever* (1924); (441-448), *Two Gentlemen in Bonds* (1927); (449-450), *Selected Poems* (1945).

Conrad Aiken (b. 1889). (451), *Turns and Movies* (1916); (452), *The Charnel Rose* (1918); (453), *Priapus and the Pool* (1922); (454), *Preludes for Memnon* (1931); (455-459), *Brownstone Eclogues* (1942).

John Peale Bishop (1892-1944). (460-461), *Now With His Love* (1933); (462), written in 1941, did not appear in volume form until *Collected Poems* (1948).

BIBLIOGRAPHICAL NOTE

Edna St. Vincent Millay (b. 1892). (463), *Renascence* (1917); (464-466), *Second April* (1921); (467), *Some Figs from Thistles* (1922); (468), *The Harp-Weaver* (1923); (469), *Fatal Interview* (1931); (470), *Wine from these Grapes* (1934).

Archibald MacLeish (b. 1892). (471-473), *Streets in the Moon* (1926); (474-475), *New Found Land* (1930); (476), *Frescoes for Mr. Rockefeller's City* (1933); (477-478), *Public Speech* (1936); (479), *Actfive* (1948).

Phelps Putnam (1894-1948). (480-481), *Trinc* (1927).

E. E. Cummings (b. 1894). (482-487), *Tulips and Chimneys* (1923); (488-493), *Is 5* (1926); (494), *Collected Poems* (1938); (495-498), *Fifty Poems* (1940); (499-506), *1×1* (1944).

Stephen Vincent Benét (1898-1943). (507), *Tiger Joy* (1925); (508), *Ballads and Poems* (1931); (509), *Burning City* (1936); (510), *Nightmare at Noon* (1940).

Hart Crane (1899-1932). (511-517), *White Buildings* (1926); (518-523), *The Bridge* (1930); (524-526), *Collected Poems* (1933).

Allen Tate (b. 1899). (527), *Mr. Pope and Other Poems* (1928); (528-531), *Poems* (1932); (532-533), *The Mediterranean* (1936); (534-535), *The Winter Sea* (1944).

Howard Baker (b. 1905). (536), *A Letter from the Country* (1941).

Robert Penn Warren (b. 1905). (537), *Selected Poems, 1923-1943* (1944).

W. H. Auden (b. 1907). (538-541), *Another Time* (1940); (542), *For the Time Being* (1944).

BIBLIOGRAPHICAL NOTE

Delmore Schwartz (b. 1913). (543-547), *In Dreams Begin Responsibilities* (1938).

Karl Shapiro (b. 1913). (548-552), *Person, Place, and Thing* (1942); (553-556), *V-Letter* (1944); (557), *Trial of a Poet* (1947).

Randall Jarrell (b. 1914). (558), *Blood for a Stranger* (1942); (559-563), *Little Friend, Little Friend* (1945).

Robert Lowell (b. 1917). (564-570), *Lord Weary's Castle* (1946); (571), *The Kenyon Review* (1948).

INDEX OF AUTHORS

The references are to the numbers of the poems.

INDEX OF FIRST LINES

INDEX OF FIRST LINES

INDEX OF FIRST LINES

INDEX OF FIRST LINES

INDEX OF FIRST LINES

INDEX OF FIRST LINES

INDEX OF FIRST LINES

INDEX OF FIRST LINES

INDEX OF FIRST LINES

INDEX OF FIRST LINES

INDEX OF FIRST LINES

INDEX OF FIRST LINES

INDEX OF FIRST LINES

INDEX OF FIRST LINES